PSYCHOLOGY

PSYCHOLOGY
An Introduction

FOURTH EDITION

Charles G. Morris
University of Michigan

with the editorial staff of Prentice-Hall

PRENTICE-HALL, INC.
Englewood Cliffs, New Jersey

Library of Congress Cataloging in Publication Data

Morris, Charles G.
   Psychology: an introduction.

   Bibliography: pp. 561–582
   Includes indexes.
   1. Psychology. I. Title.
BF121.M598 1982   150   81-15764
ISBN 0-13-734293-4   AACR2

Printed in the United States of America

10 9 8 7 6 5 4 3 2 1

PRENTICE-HALL INTERNATIONAL, INC. *London*
PRENTICE-HALL OF AUSTRALIA, PTY. LIMITED, *Sydney*
PRENTICE-HALL OF CANADA, LTD., *Toronto*
PRENTICE-HALL OF INDIA PRIVATE LIMITED. *New Delhi*
PRENTICE-HALL OF JAPAN, INC., *Tokyo*
PRENTICE-HALL OF SOUTHEAST ASIA PTE. LTD., *Singapore*
WHITEHALL BOOKS LIMITED, *Wellington, New Zealand*

Credits: Art Director: Florence Dara Silverman; Production Editor: Madalyn Stone; Book Designer: Andy Zutis; Page Layout: Joan Greenfield; Cover Designer: Joan Greenfield; Cover Art: (copyright) Joan Greenfield; Line Art: Danmark and Michaels, Inc.; Photo Researchers: Anita Duncan and Ilene Churna; Manufacturing Buyer: Ray Keating.

Text acknowledgments: Grateful acknowledgment is made to the following sources for permission to reprint: Box, p. 138: Excerpt abridged from pp. 20–23 in *Brave New World* by Aldous Huxley. Copyright 1932, 1960, by Aldous Huxley. Reprinted by permission of Harper & Row, Publishers, Inc. Box, p. 394: H. P. Laughlin, *The Ego and Its Defenses*. New York: Appleton-Century-Crofts, 1970, p. 227. Courtesy of Appleton-Century-Crofts, Publishing Division of Prentice-Hall, Inc. Box, p. 443: L. Hersher, Ed., *Four Psychotherapies*. New York: Appleton-Century-Crofts, 1970, pp. 29–32. Courtesy of Appleton-Century-Crofts, Publishing Division of Prentice-Hall, Inc. Box, p. 445: Excerpts abridged from p. 514 of *Introduction to Psychology*, 6th Edition, by E. R. Hilgard et al. New York: Harcourt Brace Jovanovich, 1971, and from p. 282 of *Psychiatry*, *41*, 1978, "Thoughts on Computerized Psychotherapy," by Spero. Box, p. 452: John B. P. Shaffer, *Humanistic Psychology*, © 1978, pp. 92–93. Reprinted by permission of Prentice-Hall, Inc. **Credits for chapter opening photos:** p. xviii—Photo Researchers; p. 24—Lester V. Bergman & Associates; p. 68—P. W. Grace, Photo Researchers; p. 106—Jean B. Hollyman, Photo Researchers; p. 134—Susan McCartney, Photo Researchers; p. 168—Roy W. Hankey, Photo Researchers; p. 204—Alexander Lowry, Photo Researchers; p. 240—Larry B. Nicholson, Jr., Photo Researchers; p. 278—Southwick, Stock, Boston; p. 310—George Bellerose, Stock, Boston; p. 344—George Holton, Photo Researchers; p. 374—Warren Uzzle, Photo Researchers; p. 404—Norman Thompson, Taurus Photos; p. 438—Waitriss-Baldwin, Woodfin Camp & Associates; p. 470—Mimi Forsyth, Monkmeyer; p. 508—UPI.

ISBN 0-13-734293-4

Contents

1

The Science of Psychology

1

2

Biology and Behavior

25

Childhood
69

**Adolescence
and Adulthood**
107

Learning
135

**Information
Processing
and Memory**
169

**Cognition and
Altered States**
205

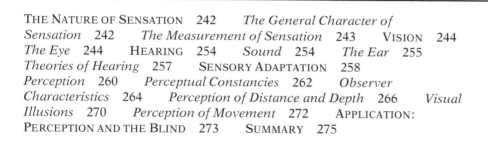

**Sensation
and Perception**
241

**Motivation
and Emotion**
279

10 Measuring Intelligence and Creativity 311

11 Personality 345

12 Adjustment 375

13 Abnormal Behavior 405

14

**Therapies
439**

15

**Social
Psychology
471**

16

**Issues in
Social Psychology
509**

Preface

Although psychology is a relatively new science, it has developed a standard body of knowledge that all students need to master. However, the basic content of psychology is also constantly changing and growing, as our knowledge of human behavior becomes more profound. The fourth edition of *Psychology: An Introduction* has been carefully written to meet the challenge of blending what is new in the science of psychology with what has traditionally been taught to students taking their first psychology course. As in the previous three editions, I have tried to write a text that is useful to teachers and easily accessible to students.

Students who use this book will be introduced to the basic perspectives, concepts, and findings of psychology, to its vocabulary, and to how psychologists work and do research. I hope, also, that the book will excite students about the science of psychology and encourage them to pursue the subject, either on their own or in advanced courses. To this end, I have tried to convey the excitement and thrill of discovery felt by the men and women who have shaped this science, from the earliest theoreticians to present-day researchers.

This is an introductory book, and it includes a wide range of theoretical viewpoints. I have avoided portraying psychology as a monolithic science whose rules and principles are static and unchangeable. On the contrary, the student is made aware of the controversies, conflicting theories, and loose ends that abound in a science that seeks to understand why individual human beings behave the way they do. I believe this avoidance of any rigid theoretical posture is a major strength of this text because it encourages students to think, discover, and to ask questions for themselves.

There are many ways to write an introductory textbook, and the approach I have chosen is perhaps best described as "uncluttered." A conscious decision was made to keep interruptions in the text and diversions on the page to a minimum. I am convinced that there is no adequate substitute for an interesting, clear, well-written text. The reception given to the previous editions by teachers and students has strengthened this conviction.

In preparing this fourth edition, I have been keenly aware of the problem that exists in attempting to give the ever-broadening field of psychology adequate coverage within the time constraints of the introductory course. I have tried to strike a balance between including new material and revising material already in the text. New topics and research have been incorporated throughout the book, and much of what remains from the third edition has been painstakingly reviewed and rewritten.

Plan of the Fourth Edition

The fourth edition has been reorganized to be more adaptable to the many different approaches to teaching introductory psychology. As part of this new flexibility, the former division of the chapters into parts has been dropped, and many of the chapters themselves have been rearranged. The order of the chapters reflects what I consider to be the most logical presentation of introductory psychology, but the chapters have been written to be independent of each other, and the extensive cross-referencing enables the instructor to teach them as he or she thinks best.

Thus, most of the physiology of psychology, which was formerly divided among several chapters, is now concentrated in Chapter 2, "Biology and Behavior." This chapter, which now includes sections on the minor senses and the biology of motivation, can be treated as a unit or taught in conjunction with other chapters, depending on the nature of the course and the needs of the students. Three other chapters have also been extensively reorganized, so that closely related topics are now discussed within the framework of a single chapter. Chapter 6 now combines information processing with memory. Chapter 8 discusses both sensation and perception. And Chapter 9 covers emotion and motivation.

This edition also features a revised and expanded coverage of social psychology, which is now presented in two chapters. Chapter 15, "Social Psychology," has been updated and completely rewritten. A new Chapter 16, "Issues in Social Psychology," gives extensive treatment to topics like prejudice, the environment, aggression, and violence that were either omitted or only touched upon in previous editions.

Other highlights include a new treatment of adult development in Chapter 6, which is now organized around developmental issues like friendship, marriage, and work. Chapter 10 has a greatly expanded discussion of the current debate on intelligence testing. Chapter 13, "Abnormal Behavior," has been entirely revised to reflect the changes in classification and terminology introduced by _DSM III_.

Finally, a major new feature entitled "Application" has been added to the end of each chapter. Each application is an essay of two to four pages that discusses how a topic from the chapter applies to real-life situations. Topics of the applications range from careers in psychology to the feminist critique of Freud and the validity of the plea of insanity as a defense in criminal trials.

READABILITY

As were previous editions, this text has been written in a way that will keep the reader reading. Each chapter is introduced with relevant anecdotes, provocative questions, or clear explanations. The introductions are meant to ease students carefully into the subject matter, to show them where the chapter is going, and to stimulate their curiosity.

Throughout, the text illustrates concepts with meaningful examples before it teaches "the facts." In this way, the reader is already aware, in a broad and practical sense, of the important issues when the substantive material is presented.

The language of the text has been kept clear and concise, and it should make for pleasant reading. Psychological terms are introduced gradually, allowing the reader to become comfortable with them before they are integrated into the language of the book.

IN-TEXT LEARNING AIDS

A number of aids are included in this text, all aimed at making psychology easier to understand. Each chapter begins with a chapter outline and ends with a comprehensive, numbered summary. Boxed inserts appear in every chapter. These inserts range from in-depth treatments of issues raised in the text, to recent research, theories, and controversies, and to clinical case histories. Drawings, charts, and graphs are keyed to many discussions and provide visual clarification of many of the concepts, experimental designs, and data presented. The photographs that appear throughout the book, many in color, are directly linked to the text and are meant to inform as well as to illustrate. Psychological terms appear in boldface type and are defined as they are introduced; italics have been used for emphasis and for secondary terms.

GLOSSARY. An extensive glossary at the end of the book will enable readers to find definitions quickly and efficiently.

Supplements

This fourth edition brings with it a full list of supplementary publications designed to aid both student and teacher. A new *Instructor's Manual* has been written that provides lecture, discussion, and demonstration ideas; suggestions for term papers and projects; and annotated film lists. The revised and expanded *Test Item File* contains multiple-choice questions for each chapter. Two versions of the student workbook are available: the *Study Guide and Workbook*, which has been prepared to make the text easier for the reader to use, and a new *PSI/Unit Mastery Workbook* that divides the text into small, digestable units. Teachers who choose the PSI format for their students are provided with a volume of *PSI/Unit Mastery Tests* containing several separate tests for each unit.

Acknowledgments

The publication of a textbook is a difficult, time-consuming project to which many people must contribute. With the publication of the fourth edition, I must restate the debt of gratitude I owe to all the people associated with the first three editions. I was fortunate then, as now, in being aided by interested professionals who gave freely of their time and expertise.

This edition has benefited from extensive critical reviews by the following professors: Ellen Banks, Daemen College; Francisco X. Barrios, University of Northern Iowa; Kent Bath, State University College at Buffalo; Robert Bauer, Fairmont State College; Robert Beck, Wake Forest University; Lucy Butler Bell, Daytona Beach Community College; Thomas E. Billimek, San Antonio College; David Brodzinsky, Douglass College-Rutgers University; Patrick J. Capretta, Miami University; James Coyne, University of California, Berkeley; Glenn S. Davidson, Ball State University; Stephen F. Davis, Emporia State University; Kay Deaux, Purdue University; John Dill, Lorain County Community College; Kathleen M. Dillon, Western New England College; Karen Duffy, State University of New York at Geneseo; Donald Elman, Kent State University; Randall Engle, University of South Carolina; Irene Hanson Frieze, University of Pittsburgh; Solomon M. Fulero, Sinclair Community College; Bernard S. Gorman, Nassau Community College; Michael J. Green, North Harris County College; Pryor Hale, Piedmont Virginia Community College; Leonard W. Hamilton, Rutgers University; Constance Hammen, University of California, Los Angeles; Joanne Higgins, Black Hawk College; William R. Jenson, The University of Wisconsin-Platteville; V. Sue Jones, North Lake College; James W. Kalat, North Carolina State University; Paul Kaplan, Suffolk County Community College; John T. Kenny, Shelby State Community College; Thomas H. Leahey, Virginia Commonwealth University; Charles F. Levinthal, Hofstra University; Howard B. Lyman, University of Cincinnati; Richard McCarbery, Lorain County Community College; Merlin Madsen, Ricks College; Colin Martindale, University of Main at Orono; Lawrence E. Melamed, Kent State University; Alan Monat, California State University, Hayward; Ken Murdoff, Lane Community College; Daniel Perlman, The University of Manitoba; Ronald H. Peters, Iowa State University; John B. Pittenger, University of Arkansas at Little Rock; Howard R. Pollio, The University of Tennessee; Thomas K. Srull, University of Illinois; Vivian K. Travis, Winthrop College; Mildred Treumann, Moorhead State University; James S. Uleman, New York University; Diana S. Woodruff, Temple University.

I would also like to thank Thomas H. Leahey of Virginia Commonwealth University, and Mark Azzato, Moshe Benjamin, Tom Ward, Oliver Hill, Mike Lerner, Mike Flannagan, Karen Mulvany, Anne Thompson, David Reuman, and Liz Perl for their valuable research.

The talented Prentice-Hall staff deserves special mention. Art Director Florence Silverman, Manufacturing Buyer Ray Keating, and Marketing Manager Bill Webber made contributions far beyond the call of duty.

I especially want to thank Madalyn Stone, who oversaw production of the text, for her diligence, expertise, and perseverance.

Additional acknowledgment must be made to photo researchers Anita Duncan and Ilene Churna, and to Dave Crook, Judy Gies, Kevin Mulligan, and Steve Polikoff whose writing skills helped make the book what it is.

I wish to extend my warmest thanks to my editor, Gerald Lombardi, for his hard work and commitment to the book.

PSYCHOLOGY

Outline

Chapter 1

The Science of Psychology

What makes you hungry? Why do you love one person and dislike another? How do you see colors? Can you be sure that you are more intelligent than your friends? And, will your intelligence decline as you grow older? How does a child learn to speak a language? Is our society too violent? Why do people handle stress differently? Why do people behave the way they do? When is their behavior abnormal? And, how can they be helped?

The questions that psychologists ask are endless and varied. As psychology students, you will learn to look deeply into human behavior and to ask complex and precise questions. Can a newborn baby see colors? What is the relation between the nervous system and hormones? How do these relations change under the influence of drugs? Are humans instinctively aggressive? What is personality and how is it formed?

Not all psychologists are concerned with asking theoretical questions about behavior. For example, if someone is often afraid of meeting new people, or if a person becomes so obsessed with neatness that he or she cannot function properly, they may turn to a psychologist for help. Other psychologists may put their knowledge to use in industry, schools, or, in fact, any place where groups of people must live or work together.

As we will see, psychology is a relatively young field and it is changing year by year as thousands of studies are added to its literature. What distinguishes psychology from other studies of individual human behavior, however, is that it is based on the scientific method. Above all, psychology is a science that seeks to understand behavior and what is involved in creating and influencing it.

The Goals of Psychology

Like other sciences, psychology seeks to *explain, predict,* and *control* what it studies. Take, for example, sex differences. Some people believe that women are naturally caring and unaggressive. Others argue that this is just a **stereotype.** Psychologists try to determine how the sexes differ in their behavior. They try to *explain* these differences on the basis of anatomy, body chemistry, early experiences, **learning,** and social interactions.

Suppose that a team of researchers believes that women are unaggressive only when they are around men (because men expect them to be passive). The first step in research might be to test the idea to see if it enables them to *predict* female behavior. An ad might be placed in the paper offering a fee to women to join in an **experiment.** Half the women might be sent to a male interviewer and half to a female. Both would give the women a hard time, insulting them in subtle and less subtle ways. If more women argue with the female interviewer than with the male, the researchers might conclude that their premise was right.

Control in psychology is generally directed toward therapeutic ends. A therapist might help an unhappy woman to overcome her feeling that it is wrong for her to compete in business by giving support or encouraging her ambitions. Here, a psychologist is trying to change or control behavior and feelings.

Psychology is not alone in trying to explain, predict, and control behavior. The behavioral sciences—anthropology, sociology, political science, and psychology—are so closely related that it is often hard to tell where one ends and the next begins. For example, all of them would regard a campus protest as a good subject for study. But how would their approaches differ?

An anthropologist would see the day's activities in terms of cultural patterns and rituals. He or she would note that making speeches from a soapbox is a long and honored American tradition; that linking arms to form a human barricade resembles the snake dance of Japanese protesters; that in political movements, as in primitive societies, people often call others, who are not related to them, "brother" and "sister."

A sociologist would be most interested in the interactions of the groups that were formed and in the bonds formed between people. Crowds, the sociologist would note, behave differently from individuals and from small groups. The crowd develops an organizational structure and a status system. It makes and enforces its own codes of correct and incorrect behavior.

A political scientist would focus on the distribution of power and authority among leaders and groups. An economist, being concerned mainly with the distribution of goods, would note that the students have a different attitude toward property than do most Americans. An historian would try to compare this event to others in the past and would seek its causes.

A psychologist surveying the same situation would be most interested in how each person in the crowd behaved. The psychologist would wonder

why some apparently conservative students had been attracted to the scene. Listening to the speeches, he or she would hear words and phrases that might be clues about the kind of people the leaders were and about their **motives**. The psychologist might follow up with interviews and case studies.

So although psychology has much in common with other behavioral sciences, it is unique because it stresses the individual. We turn now to a brief history of this relatively young science.

The Growth of Psychology

WUNDT AND TITCHENER: STRUCTURALISM

In 1879 Wilhelm Wundt, physiologist and philosopher, opened the first psychological laboratory in Europe at the University of Leipzig in Germany. Wundt had stated his intentions quite plainly 5 years before in *Principles of Physiological Psychology*. The mind, he argued, must be studied objectively and scientifically. Apparently no one at Leipzig took him seriously at the time, and only four students attended Wundt's first lecture.

This was a surprise. People had always regarded their mental processes—their thoughts and dreams—with awe. In ancient Greece, Plato had divided the world into two realms, one pure and abstract, the other physical and mundane. Even in the 18th century, the glorification of Reason and discoveries in the natural sciences did not dispel the idea that mind and matter, spirit and body, are separate.

Wundt refused to see the mind in mystical terms. Thinking, he argued, is a natural event like wind in a storm or the beating of the heart. Why did this radical view go unchallenged? First, British philosophers, including Hobbes and Locke, had asserted that physical sensations are the basis of thought. Second, by 1879 the scientific method commanded great respect in the academic community. Perhaps most important, the traditionalists of the time had their hands full with Charles Darwin. Compared to evolution, scientific psychology seemed tame.

By the mid-1880s Wundt's new psychological lab had many students. Wundt's main concern at this point was with techniques for uncovering the natural laws of the human mind. To find the basic units of thought, he began by looking at **perception**. When we look at an object like a banana, for example, we immediately think, here is a fruit, something to peel and eat. But these are associations. All we *see* is a long yellow object.

Wundt and his co-workers wanted to strip perception of its associations, to find the very *atoms* of thought. To do this, they trained themselves in the art of objective introspection, observing and recording their perceptions and feelings. Some days, for example, were spent listening to the ticking of a metronome. Which rhythms are most pleasant? Does a fast tempo excite, a slow beat relax? They recorded their reactions in minute detail, including measures of their heartbeat and respiration. However crude and irrelevant

Wilhelm Wundt
(The Bettmann Archive)

Edward Bradford Titchener
(The Granger Collection)

all this may seem to us, it did introduce measurement and experiment into psychology, which until this time had been a branch of philosophy.

Perhaps the most important product of the Leipzig lab was its students; they took the new science to universities around the world. Among them was Edward Bradford Titchener. British by birth but German in training and temperament, Titchener became the leader of American psychology soon after he became professor of psychology at Cornell University, a post he held until his death in 1927.

Psychology, Titchener wrote, is the science of consciousness—physics with the observer kept in. In physics an hour or a mile is an exact measure. To the observer, however, an hour may seem to pass in seconds, a mile may seem endless. Psychology studies this phenomenon; it is the study of experience. Titchener broke experience down into three basic elements: physical sensations (including sights and sounds); affections or feelings (which are like sensations, but less clear); and **images** (such as memories and dreams). When we recognize a banana, according to Titchener's scheme, we combine a physical sensation (what we see) with feelings (liking or disliking bananas) and with images (memories of other bananas). Even the most complex thoughts and feelings, Titchener argued, can be reduced to these simple elements. Psychology's role is to identify the elements and show how they are combined. Because it stresses the basic units of experience and the combinations in which they occur, this school of psychology is called **structuralism**.

SIR FRANCIS GALTON: INDIVIDUAL DIFFERENCES

Sir Francis Galton
(The Bettmann Archive)

Meanwhile, Francis Galton, Darwin's half-cousin, was dabbling in medicine,* experimenting with electricity, exploring the Sudan and Southwest Africa, charting weather, and poring over the biographies of famous people. Born into a rich and famous family, Galton never had to work for a living. Throughout his life, he remained an intellectual adventurer—to the great gain of psychology. Galton was a pioneer in the development of mental tests and the study of **individual differences.** He was impressed by the number of exceptional people in his own family and studied the histories of other families. His research suggested that genius might be hereditary. Intrigued, Galton invented tests to measure individual capacities and worked out ways of comparing scores. He found a wide range of abilities and complex relations between one ability and another. Later he became interested in mental imagery and word associations. With himself as subject, he wrote down the first 2 things called to mind by each of 75 words. He then tried to explain his reactions in terms of his past experiences. Madness also fascinated Galton. He decided the best way to study madness was to become mad himself. He thus began to pretend that everyone he saw on his walks through the park was out to get him—including the dogs.

*Galton and the faculty at Trinity College did not agree on how to study medicine. Galton thought his idea of sampling each potion in the pharmacy, starting with the *A*'s, was quite ingenious. The faculty did not!

WILLIAM JAMES: FUNCTIONALISM

William James, the first American-born psychologist, was as versatile and innovative as Galton. In his youth, he studied chemistry, physiology, anatomy, biology, and medicine. Then, in 1872, he accepted an offer to teach physiology at Harvard. There, James read philosophy in his free time and saw a link between it and physiology. The two seemed to converge in psychology.

In 1875 James began a class in psychology (commenting that the first lecture he ever heard on the subject was his own). He set aside part of his laboratory for psychological experiments. He also began work on a text, *The Principles of Psychology,* which was published in 1890.

William James
(The Bettman Archive)

In preparing his lectures and his textbook, James studied structuralist writings thoroughly and decided that something in Wundt's and Titchener's approach was wrong. He concluded that the atoms of experience—pure sensations without associations—simply did not exist. Our minds are constantly weaving associations, revising experience, starting, stopping, jumping back and forth in time. Consciousness, James argued, is a continuous flow, not an assemblage of bits of sensation and pieces of imagery. Perceptions and associations, sensations and emotions, cannot be separated. We see a banana, not a long yellow object.

Still focusing on everyday experience, James turned to the study of habit. Much of what we do is automatic. We do not have to think about how to get dressed, open a door, or walk down the street. James suggested that when we repeat something several times, our nervous systems are changed so that each time we open a door, it is easier to open than the last time.

This was the clue he needed. The biologist in him firmly believed that all activity—from the beating of the heart to the perception of a banana—is functional. If we could not recognize a banana, we would have to figure out what it was each time we saw one. Thus, mental associations allow us to benefit from previous experience. Once we have solved a problem, the solution becomes automatic. This, James argued, is the essence of adaptation.

With *The Principles of Psychology* James thus forged a new link between psychology and natural science. Applying biological principles to the mind, he arrived at a **functionalist** theory of mental life and behavior. Functionalist theory is concerned, for example, not just with learning or sensation or perception, but rather with how an organism uses its learning or sensory and perceptual abilities to function in its environment. James also argued for the value of subjective (untrained) introspection and insisted that psychology focus on everyday, true-to-life experiences.

In 1894 one of James's students, James R. Angell, became the head of the new Department of Psychology at the University of Chicago. John Dewey, who had studied structuralist psychology at Johns Hopkins, became professor of philosophy at Chicago that same year. Together, they made Chicago the center of the functionalist school of psychology. Building on James's work, they began to look for parallels between animal and human behavior; they also began to look for ways of applying psychological knowledge in education.

JOHN B. WATSON: BEHAVIORISM

John B. Watson
(The Bettmann Archive)

John B. Watson was the first student to receive a doctorate in psychology from the University of Chicago. Watson's dissertation was on learning in rats. One of the department's requirements was that he speculate on the kind of consciousness that produced the behavior he observed in his experiments. Watson found this absurd. He doubted that rats had any consciousness at all. Nevertheless, he complied with the regulations, received his degree, and returned to his laboratory to think about consciousness.

Ten years and many experiments later, Watson was ready to confront both the structuralist and functionalist schools. In "Psychology As the Behaviorist Views It" (1913), he argued that the whole idea of consciousness, of mental life, is superstition, a relic from the Middle Ages. You cannot define consciousness any more than you can define a soul, Watson argued. You cannot locate it or measure it. He felt that to base a science on something that vague was ridiculous. For Watson, psychology was the study of observable, measurable behavior—and nothing more.

Watson's position was based largely on Ivan Pavlov's famous experiments. Some years before, this Russian scientist had noticed that the dogs in his laboratory began to drool as soon as they heard their feeder coming—even before they could see their dinner. Pavlov had always thought that salivation was a natural response to food, and he found the dogs' anticipation odd. He decided to see if he could teach them to drool at the sound of a tuning fork, even when no food was in the room. He explained this as follows: All behavior is a response to some stimulus in the environment. In ordinary life, food (the **stimulus**) makes dogs salivate (the **response**). All Pavlov did was to train his animals to expect food when they heard a certain sound. He called this training **conditioning**.

In a famous experiment with an 11-month-old child, Watson showed that people can also be conditioned. Little Albert was a secure, happy baby who had no reason to fear soft, furry, white rats. Watson gave him one. Each time Albert reached out to pet the rat, Watson hit a metal bar with a hammer. Soon Albert was afraid not only of white rats but also of white rabbits, white dogs, white fur coats—and even of a Santa Claus mask (Watson & Rayner, 1920). Thus, conditioning changed the child's behavior radically.*

Watson saw no reason to refer to consciousness or mental life to explain this change. Little Albert simply responded to the environment—in this case the coincidence of the loud noises and white, furry things. Watson felt the same was true for adults. Words, he argued are simply a verbal response; when we think, we are really talking to ourselves; emotions are a glandular response, and all behavior can be explained with the stimulus–response formula. Psychology, he felt, must be purged of "mentalism."

In the 1920s, when Watson's behaviorist theory was first published, American psychologists had all but exhausted the structuralist approach. Wundtian experiments had lost their novelty and attraction. So, Watson's

---

*Watson had planned to work further with Albert—to take away the fears he had caused the boy to develop—but, unfortunately, Albert's mother took the boy away before Watson had the chance (Watson & Rayner, 1920).

orthodox scientific approach (if you cannot see it and measure it, forget it) found a warm audience. Moreover, Watson suggested two new fields of study: learning and child development.

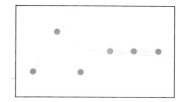

Figure 1–1

GESTALT PSYCHOLOGY

Meanwhile, in Germany, a group of psychologists was attacking structuralism from another angle. Wertheimer, Köhler, and Koffka were all interested in perception, particularly in certain tricks that the mind plays on itself. Why, they asked, when we are shown a series of still pictures flashed at a constant rate (movies or "moving" neon signs), do they seem to move? The eye sees only a series of still pictures. What makes us perceive motion?

The structuralists, as you will recall, wanted to strip perception to its elements. A trained Wundtian introspectionist, for example, would see nothing but six dots in Figure 1-1. This is unreal, Wertheimer and his colleagues argued. Anyone else looking at this would see a triangle and a line formed by the dots.

Phenomena like these were the force behind a new school of thought, **Gestalt psychology.** Roughly translated from German, gestalt means "whole" or "form." When applied to perception, it refers to our tendency to see patterns, to distinguish an object from its background, to complete pictures from a few cues. Like James, the Gestalt psychologists thought that the attempt to break perception and thought down into their elements was misguided. When we look at a tree we see just that, a tree.

In the 1930s the Gestalt school broke up, primarily because Nazism was on the rise. Wertheimer, Köhler, and Koffka all eventually settled in America.

B. F. SKINNER: S-R PSYCHOLOGY

Behaviorism was thriving when the Gestalt psychologists reached America. B. F. Skinner was one of the leaders of behaviorism. Like Watson, Skinner believed that psychology should only study observable and measurable behavior. Also like Watson, Skinner explained behavior in terms of the stimulus–response formula.* He too was primarily interested in changing behavior through conditioning—and discovering natural laws of behavior in the process. But his approach was subtly different from that of his predecessor.

Watson had changed Little Albert's behavior by changing the stimulus. As far as Albert knew, white rats made loud, scary noises. For Albert to learn this, Watson had had to repeat the experience over and over, making a loud noise every time Albert saw a rat. Skinner added a new element— **reinforcement.** He rewarded his subjects for behaving the way he wanted them to behave. For example, an animal (rats and pigeons are Skinner's

B. F. Skinner
(Ken Heyman)

*In their writings, psychologists usually abbreviate the terms "stimulus" and "response" as S and R, respectively. This shorthand, appropriately, gave this school of psychology its name.

Sigmund Freud
(The Bettmann Archive)

favorite subjects) is put in a special cage (called a **Skinner box**) and allowed to explore. Eventually the animal will reach up and press a lever or peck at a disk on the wall. A food pellet drops into the box. Gradually the animal learns that pressing the bar or pecking at the disk always brings food. Why does the animal learn this? Because it has been reinforced, or rewarded. Skinner thus made the animal an active agent in its own conditioning.

SIGMUND FREUD: PSYCHOANALYTIC PSYCHOLOGY

Psychoanalysis was the dark horse of psychology. Sigmund Freud was largely unknown in the United States until the late 1920s. By then he had worked his clinical discoveries into a comprehensive theory of mental life that differed radically from those of his American colleagues.

Freud believed the following: Much of our behavior is governed by hidden motives and unconscious wishes. It is as if a part of each of us never grows up. The adult in us struggles to control the infant, but with only partial success. Childish desires and wishes surface in mistakes called "Freudian slips" as well as in our dreams. We feel that many of our impulses are forbidden or sinful. Therefore, we do not want to admit them to our consciousness. Often this conflict leads to vague feelings of anxiety and sometimes to exaggerated fears.

Freud not only found that adult problems could be traced back to childhood experiences, but he also maintained that unconscious feelings were always sexual. A little boy, he argued, desires his mother and wants to destroy his rival—her husband and his father. Of all Freud's concepts, this—the idea of **infant sexuality**—was the most shocking. Many of Freud's own colleagues rejected his emphasis on sex. Alfred Adler, for example, felt the child's sense of inferiority in relation to "big people" was central to personality. Carl Jung emphasized self-realization in the context of the racial history and religious impulse of the human species.

Nonetheless, Freudian theory had a huge impact on academic psychology (particularly on the study of personality), and it is still controversial. Some psychologists accept the theories of the unconscious, infantile sexuality, and dream interpretation; others find them ridiculous. But few ignore Freud. Freud the doctor also founded **psychotherapy,** with his famous "talking cure," psychoanalysis.

SOME NEW SCHOOLS

In the past 40 years these different views of psychology have been challenged and revised, as discoveries in one area have suggested new possibilities in another. Nowhere is this more evident than in cognitive psychology.

Cognitive psychology is the study of thought processes in the broadest sense. Many psychologists, among them E. C. Tolman, concluded that once we learn that a particular response to a situation or stimulus works, we begin to see the stimulus in a new way. They suggested that there was more to learning than just single responses to stimuli. Cognitive psychology

Jean Piaget
(Yves, DeBraine, Black Star)

studies all the ways in which people perceive, interpret, store, and use information. For example, when you read a story, how much of it do you remember? What parts do you remember? How do you reorganize what you remember, so that when you are asked about it you can reproduce what you have read?

One of the leading members of the cognitive school of psychology was Jean Piaget. An avid child-watcher, Piaget became particularly interested in children's adaptation to their environments. Through his research he discerned a series of stages through which all children pass. As children gather experience in the world, they not only develop more complex ideas about the nature of their environment but also become able to deal with these ideas in more abstract, symbolic ways.

Cognitive psychology is rapidly expanding and now affects almost every area of psychology. Further discussion of cognition will be found throughout this text.

Existential psychology, as the name suggests, draws on the existential philosophy made famous in the 1940s by Jean-Paul Sartre and others. Psychoanalyst Rollo May argues that modern Americans are lost souls—a people without myths and heroes. Patriotism, hard work, and freedom have lost their magical appeal. A sense of meaninglessness and alienation, existential psychologists believe, results in apathy and psychological problems, in alcoholism and drug addiction. R. D. Laing, another existential psychologist, feels that we must reevaluate our attitude toward psychotic behavior. For Laing, such behavior is not abnormal. It is a reasonable response to an abnormal world. Existential psychology seeks to help people find an inner sense of identity, so that they can care, commit themselves, and love.

Humanistic psychology and existential psychology are closely related. Both argue that people must learn how to realize their potential. But where existential psychology emphasizes an inner sense of identity and willpower, humanistic psychology focuses on nonverbal experience, the unity of mind and body, communication through touch, altered states of consciousness, and letting go. Only by opening ourselves to sensations—touching others and listening to our own bodies—can we reach **self-actualization** and joy in others, said psychologist Abraham Maslow.

Rollo May
(Photograph © 1981 by Jill Krementz)

Methods of Psychology

As we noted earlier, all of us know something about human behavior. We observe ourselves and others. We exchange experiences, philosophies, and gossip with friends. We speculate on why people act as they do. How does the psychologist's knowledge differ from common sense?

Psychologists are scientists, and like all scientists they are skeptics. If you met your friends on your way across campus and told them that you were depressed because you had an exam, they would probably believe you. But you may be always depressed. You may feel bad because you were up all night studying or because you skipped breakfast. Before psychologists

When people are unaware that they are being watched, they act more naturally. A one-way mirror makes such observations possible.
(Bohdan Hrynewyck, Stock, Boston)

would accept your simple statement, "I am depressed because I have an exam," they would have to rule out all other possible explanations. This is the essence of the **scientific method.**

Obviously psychologists cannot put your depression under a microscope or dissect your anxiety. But they can study you scientifically in other ways. Any of the specialists we discussed earlier may use any or all of the following methods.

THE NATURALISTIC-OBSERVATION METHOD

We have all heard about the virtue of "telling it like it is." Psychologists use this method to study animal or human behavior in its natural context instead of in the laboratory under imposed conditions. Most of us use this method in everyday life without realizing it. When you watch dogs play in the park, or observe how your professors conduct their classes, you are using a form of **naturalistic observation.** A psychologist with this real-life orientation might observe behavior in a school or a factory. Another might actually join a family to study the behavior of its members. Still another might observe animals in nature, not in cages. The primary advantage of this method is that the observed behavior will be more natural, spontaneous, and varied than in a laboratory.

For example, W. H. Whyte (1956) wanted to see how people living in a suburban community chose their friends. He kept tabs on his subjects by reading the local newspaper. The social column told him when parties were given and who was invited. After collecting such data for some time, Whyte noticed that there were definite friendship patterns in the community. *Proximity*—people's nearness to each other—was the critical factor in determining which people became friends. Whyte concluded that all things being equal, people are more apt to make friends with those who live nearby. He might have been able to learn this by asking people, but he could not have found it out in a laboratory.

Whyte restricted his observations to one specific behavior—going to parties. It is not always possible, however, to make such restrictions. Because naturalistic observation does not interfere with people's behavior in any way, the psychologist using it has to take people's behavior as it comes. A naturalistic observer cannot suddenly yell "Freeze!" when he or she wants to study what is going on in more detail. Nor can he or she tell people to stop what they are doing because it is not what the psychologist wants to study.

There are both advantages and disadvantages to naturalistic observation. One of the central problems is observer bias. Any police officer will tell you how unreliable eyewitnesses can be. Even psychologists who are trained observers may subtly distort what they see to conform to what they hope to see. Also, in their detailed notes of the observation, psychologists may not record behavior that they think is not relevant. When using this method, it may be desirable to rely on a team of trained observers who pool their notes. This often results in a more complete picture than one observer could draw alone.

Another problem is that the behavior observed depends on the particular

10

time, place, and group of people involved. Unlike laboratory experiments that can be repeated again and again, each natural situation is a one-time-only occurrence. Because of this, scientific psychologists do not like to make general statements based on information from naturalistic studies. They will first test the information under controlled conditions in the laboratory before they apply it to situations other than the original.

Despite these disadvantages, naturalistic observation is a valuable tool for psychologists. After all, real-life behavior is what psychology is about. Although the complexity of behavior may present problems, naturalistic observation is a boon to experimental psychologists. It gives them new ideas and suggestions for research. Experimental researchers can then study these ideas more systematically and in more detail in their laboratories than can researchers in the field. It also helps researchers to keep their perspective by reminding them of the larger world outside the lab.

THE EXPERIMENTAL METHOD

Psychologists want to get at the root causes of phenomena. Perhaps a psychologist has noticed that most students in her Monday morning class are unusually quiet and do not respond to her questions. She suspects this is because they stay up late on Sunday nights. Thus, the psychologist begins with a hunch or **hypothesis.** Students who do not get enough sleep find it difficult to remember facts and ideas. But this commonsense explanation is not enough. The psychologist wants proof—facts that are unbiased. She wants to know that all other possible explanations have been ruled out. To test her hypothesis, she decides to conduct an experiment on the relationship between sleep and learning.

Her first step is to pick **subjects,** people she can observe, to see whether her hypothesis is right. She decides to use student volunteers. To keep her results from being influenced by sex differences or intelligence levels, she chooses a group made up of equal numbers of men and women who scored between 520 and 550 on their College Boards.

Next she designs a learning task. She needs something that none of her subjects will know in advance. If she chooses a chapter in a history book, for example, she runs the risk that some of her subjects may be history buffs. Considering various possibilities, the psychologist decides to print a page of geometric forms, each labeled with a nonsense word. Circles are "glucks," triangles "pogs," and so on. She will give the students one-half hour to learn the names, then take away the study sheets and ask them to label a new page of geometric forms.

Now the psychologist is ready to consider procedures. Asking people if they have slept well is not a reliable measure. Some may say no to have an excuse for doing poorly in the test. Others will say yes because they do not want a psychologist to think they are unstable and cannot sleep. Two people who both say they slept well may not mean the same thing. So the researcher decides to intervene—to control the situation a little more closely. Everyone in the experiment, she decides, will spend the night in the same dormitory. They will be kept awake until 4:00 A.M., and then they will be awakened at 7:00 A.M. sharp. She and her colleagues will patrol the halls

(Sybil Shelton, Monkmeyer)

to make sure that no one falls asleep ahead of schedule. They will check to see who is sleeping soundly between 4:00 and 7:00. By determining the amount of sleep the subjects get, the psychologist is introducing and controlling an essential element of the experimental method—an **independent variable.** The psychologist believes that the students' ability to learn her labels for geometric forms will depend on their having had a good night's sleep. Performance on the learning task (number of correct answers) thus becomes the **dependent variable.** If the independent variable (the amount of sleep) is changed, the dependent variable (performance on the learning task) should also be changed, according to the hypothesis.

At this point the experimenter begins looking for loopholes. Maybe sleeping in a strange room and knowing that they are participating in an experiment—not lack of sleep—will affect students' performance on the learning task. To be sure that her experiment measures only the effects of inadequate sleep she divides the subjects into two groups. The two groups contain equal numbers of males and females of the same ages and with the same College Board scores. One of the groups, the **experimental group,** will be kept awake until 4:00 in the morning. The other, the **control group,** will be allowed to go to sleep whenever they please. Because the only consistent difference between the two groups is the amount of sleep they get, the difference in how the two groups perform in the morning will allow the experimenter to learn if sleep affects their ability to learn.

Finally, the psychologist questions her own objectivity. She is inclined to think that lack of sleep inhibits students' learning, but she does not want to prejudice the results. That is, she wants to avoid **experimenter bias.** She decides to ask a third person, someone who does not know which subject did or did not sleep all night, to score the tests.

The psychologist will interpret even the most definitive findings with some caution. Only after other researchers in other laboratories with other subjects have repeated an experiment and found the same results does the psychologist really consider the original conclusion reliable. (Psychology, like all science, is a communal enterprise.)

For some studies, a laboratory may be less suitable than a naturalistic setting. Ellsworth (1977) has noted that the laboratory is not the best setting for testing variables such as fear, conflict, grief, or love. It may be hard for subjects to express these feelings beyond limited levels in the laboratory. The strange and unfamiliar environment of the laboratory may also affect these feelings and reactions. For example, behavior patterns between parents and children are very different in the laboratory than in the home. In the laboratory, young children are more anxious and parents behave more positively toward their children than at home (Bronfenbrenner, 1977). Finally, in the laboratory, the subjects *know* that they are being observed by psychologists. They may try to appear healthy, normal, tolerant, and intelligent (Ellsworth, 1977). This increases the problem of testing, in the laboratory, people's true responses to situations.

But is the naturalistic versus experimental approach always an either–or proposition? Bronfenbrenner (1977) thinks not. He points out that, too often, problems arise not from the choice of approach but from defects in the research design. This is usually caused, he contends, by not considering factors in the *environment* in which the research takes place. He applies this critique equally to the experimental environment of the laboratory and to the naturalistic environment of the home. For example, laboratory experimenters must remember that their studies are done in environments that are unfamiliar, artificial, and temporary for the subjects. Naturalistic researchers also tend to ignore environmental influences in their efforts to keep the conditions unstructured and unguided.

Bronfenbrenner suggests that all scientific investigations start with experiments designed not to test hypotheses but to examine and determine the relations between the subject and the environment in which the research is to be conducted. This principle would apply for both experimental and naturalistic approaches.

Both environments contain people; therefore, Bronfenbrenner maintains, research takes place within a social system. Psychologists must be aware that this system exists and that it influences both the course of and the results of the research. The experimenters must allow for how the subject may interact with people within the social environment. This includes the experimenters themselves. Only by allowing for such influences and designing their experiments accordingly can researchers hope to evolve methods leading to more accurate and meaningful results.

THE CORRELATIONAL METHOD

An experiment is one of the most reliable ways to investigate behavior, but it is not always the most practical way. Suppose a psychologist wants to find out what makes a good pilot. Perhaps the Air Force has asked him to study this question because it costs thousands of dollars to train a single pilot, and each year many trainees quit. The psychologist could conduct an experiment—he might raise 10 children in playrooms filled with toy planes, cars, baseballs, and stuffed animals. This method, which studies the same group of subjects over time, is called the *longitudinal method*. It would probably tell the psychologist what he wanted to know, but both he and the Air Force would have to wait years for the result.

The *correlational method* provides a shortcut. The psychologist would begin by choosing 100 proven pilots and 100 unsuccessful ones. To gather information, he could give his pilots a variety of aptitude and personality tests. Suppose he found that all the successful pilots score higher than the unsuccessful pilots on mechanical aptitude tests, and that all the successful pilots are cautious people who do not like to take chances. There seems to be some **correlation** between these traits and success as a pilot. He could then recommend that the Air Force use certain tests to choose the next group of trainees. Suppose he also found that all the pilots played golf, came from large cities, and liked pecan pie. There is no logical reason why these facts should go with piloting a plane; they just do. Puzzled, the psychologist might test another group of pilots for these characteristics. If he found that these pilots, too, played golf, came from large cities, and liked pecan pie, he could conclude that a correlation existed, even though he could not explain it.

Through correlational studies psychologists can thus identify relations between two or more variables without needing to explain why these

There are several kinds of tests used to measure intelligence. Here, an educational psychologist monitors the speed and accuracy of this woman placing forms in their appropriate position.
(Photo Researchers, Inc.)

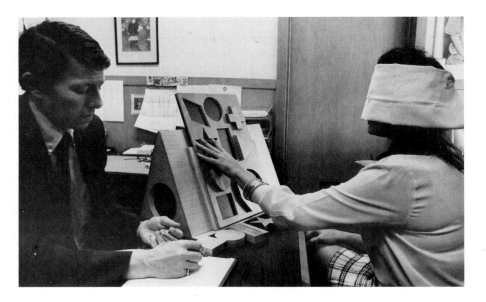

relations exist. This method has been extremely useful in making standardized tests. Intelligence tests, College Boards, tests for clerical and mechanical aptitude—all are based on extensive correlational studies. A person's performance on a test of clerical aptitude, for example, may be compared to success or failure in an office job.

Most psychologists use several methods to study a single problem. For example, a researcher interested in **creativity** might begin by giving a group of college students a creativity test that she invented. She compares people's scores with their scores on intelligence tests and with their grades to see if there is a correlation between them. Then she spends several weeks observing a college class and interviewing teachers, students, and parents to correlate classroom behavior and the adults' evaluations with the students' scores on the creativity test. She decides to test some of her ideas with an experiment and uses a group of the students as subjects. Her findings might cause her to revise the test, or they might give the teachers and parents new insight about a particular student.

ETHICS IN RESEARCH

It is likely that you will have the chance to be a subject in an experiment in your psychology department. You will probably be offered a small sum of money or class credit to participate. But it is possible that your participation may puzzle you and that you will learn the true purpose of the experiment only after it is over. Is this deception necessary to psychology experiments? And what if the experiment should cause you discomfort?

Most psychologists agree that these questions raise ethical issues. And so, more than 25 years ago the American Psychological Association (APA) drew up a code for treating experimental subjects (American Psychological Association, 1953). But in 1963, the issue of ethics was raised again when Stanley Milgram published the results of several experiments.

Milgram hired people to help him with a learning experiment and told them that they were to teach other people, the "learners," by giving them electric shocks when they gave wrong answers. The shocks could be given in various intensities from "slight shock" to "severe shock." The people were told to increase the intensity of the shock each time the learner made a mistake. As the shocks increased in intensity, the learners began to protest that they were being hurt. They cried out in pain and became increasingly upset as the shocking continued. The people giving the shocks often became concerned and frightened and asked if they could stop. But the experimenter politely but firmly pointed out that they were expected to continue.

Stanley Milgram

This was the crux of the experiment. Milgram was investigating obedience, not learning. He wanted to find out whether anyone in the situation just described would actually go all the way and give the highest level of shock. Would they follow their consciences, or would they obey the experimenter? Incredibly, 65 percent of Milgram's subjects did go all the way, even though the learner stopped answering toward the end, and many subjects worried that the shocks might have done serious damage.

So Milgram found out what he wanted to know. But to do it, he had to deceive his subjects. The stated purpose of the experiment, to test learning, was a lie. The shock machines were fake. The learners received no shocks at all. And the learners themselves were Milgram's accomplices who had been trained to act as though they were being hurt (Milgram, 1963).

Although the design of this experiment is not typical of the vast majority of psychological experiments, it caused such a public uproar that the profession began to reevaluate its ethical health. In the wake of the controversy, a new code of ethics on psychological experimentation was approved.

Controversy has continued on this issue. Those favoring strict ethical controls still feel that the rights of the subject are of prime importance. They believe that procedures should never be emotionally or physically distressing, and that the experimenter should first tell the potential subject what can be expected to happen. Some psychologists have described deliberately misleading experiments as "confidence games" (Forward, Canter, & Kirsch, 1976). They suggest, instead, the use of role-playing methods, in which subjects are asked to act "as if" they were engaged in particular behaviors for the purpose of the experiment.

Despite these criticisms, many psychologists insist that strict ethical rules could damage the scientific validity of an experiment and could cripple future research. "Absolute moral values corrupt absolutely" (Gergen, 1973, p. 908). These psychologists also point out that few subjects—by their own admission—have been appreciably harmed. Even in Milgram's manipulative experiment, only 1.3 percent of the subjects reported negative feelings about their experience (Milgram, 1964).

Cooper (1976) has argued that, under some conditions, deception may be good scientific and moral judgment. In discussing Milgram's experiment, he notes that "few of us would have considered the study to be ethical if Milgram had been nondeceptive, that is, if the shock machine were real and the learner actually received 450 volts" (p. 607).

Between these two positions are those who feel that research should be done to disclose exactly what effects experimental procedures have on subjects. They say that if psychology is really the science it claims to be, it should prove, and not just assert, the need for a strict experimental code.

Holmes (1976*b*) noted that the experimental code adopted by the American Psychological Association advocated clarifying the nature of the study to participants once the experiment was over. This could eliminate misconceptions and harmful aftereffects. Holmes, however, goes on to say that little or no evidence existed at the time to show that the procedure would work. No reference was made to the lack of evidence, and no attempt was made to encourage further research on the subject. Experimentation by Holmes (1976*a*, 1976*b*) after the code's adoption has shown that debriefing could, in fact, work.

Often the debate on ethical issues in psychological experiments has focused on laboratory methods. But questions have also been raised about the ethics of conducting naturalistic research studies. Is it ethical to study and collect data on people who are parking their cars or shopping in a store without first telling them that they are subjects of research? One study found that many people would indeed feel harassed, or that their privacy had been invaded, if they were unknowingly observed and studied (Wilson & Donnerstein, 1976). In fact, 38 percent of the people questioned stated that the public should protest against such methods of research.

In the long run, psychology can only benefit from the ethical-standards controversy. Although unanimous acceptance of a formal code of ethics is a long way off, very few experiments raise serious ethical questions. If a serious breach in ethics is suspected, it is investigated, and the offenders are asked to change their research methods.

The Social Relevance of Psychology

According to this psychologist, the best way to decide what toys will sell is to ask the people who play with them—children.
(UPI)

PURE VERSUS APPLIED PSYCHOLOGY

All of us, psychologists included, are curious about what makes people tick. In the sciences, two basic approaches are used to satisfy those curiosities. The first is **pure research**—that is, research for its own sake. Usually pure research is carried out because of a theory or because of other research. It is only rarely a response to a pressing practical problem. If pure research findings are then used in concrete, practical ways, it is then known as **applied psychology.** This is the second basic approach to psychological research. Pure research may not have immediate practical application to social problems. Applied psychology, however, is the direct study of the problems of the teacher, the worker, the spouse, or perhaps of the wider social effects of racism or militarism. But no one can tell in advance if a study will have social relevance or whether a piece of applied research will turn out to have major theoretical importance.

This distinction between scholarly theory and practical use is an old one. Psychologists, themselves, have mixed views about it. In a survey of some 2,500 graduate students and faculty in the psychology departments of over

100 American universities, nearly half of those polled chose social relevance as "the most important issue confronting contemporary psychology" (Lipsey, 1974, p. 542). When asked where they would like to work, however, many of the respondents rated institutions stressing "help with social problems" as their least favorite choice. Most preferred scholarly, pure-research-oriented universities (Lipsey, 1974).

This contradiction reminds us that the harmony between pure and applied psychology is not yet perfect. Theory without testing and application, however, tends to become sterile. As one psychologist put it, "Theory for theory's sake is scientism, not science" (Bass, 1974, p. 871). The reverse is also true. Practice without theory to support it tends to become mere technology.

(Photo Researchers, Inc.)

USING ANIMALS IN PSYCHOLOGICAL RESEARCH

The breach between pure and applied science has raised questions about the use of animal subjects in research designed to help us learn more about human behavior. Some psychologists believe that, since psychology is the science of behavior, animal behavior is just as interesting as human behavior. But however interesting animal behavior may be, what possible relevance does the behavior of a 7-inch-long laboratory rat have to everyday human problems? Immediately, none perhaps. But many experiments—systematic brain surgery, for example—simply cannot be performed on human beings and so must be done with animals if anything at all is to be learned. Psychologists also use animal subjects because their behavior is simpler than human behavior and their genetic histories and immediate environments can be controlled more easily. The short life spans of some animals also make it possible to study behavior over many generations, which would be highly impractical or even impossible with humans. Moreover, with animals there are no "social" complications between experimenter and subject.

The trained psychologist must reflect carefully on the limitations in comparing animal and human behavior. Without analysis, there is a danger that animal studies may lead to grandiose and faulty conclusions about human social behavior (Mason & Lott, 1976). Certainly, "mental illness" in a rat is different from that in a human. If we are careful not to equate animal behavior with human behavior, research using animals can, in fact, add much to our understanding of behavior, including human behavior.

Application

CAREERS IN PSYCHOLOGY

Within the past 15 years, psychology has become one of the most popular majors in the college curriculum. In 1970–1971, 37,000 stu-

17

dents were awarded BAs in psychology. By 1980–1981, that figure had doubled. What happens to these people? Do they all go on to careers in psychology as clinicians, psychiatric social workers, researchers, or the like? What kinds of jobs do they look for and what kinds of jobs do they find once they are equipped with their hard-earned degrees?

Surveys show that between one-third and two-thirds of those with bachelor's degrees in psychology do not go on to graduate school. Many use their study of psychology as a general preparation for life—an informative and worthwhile course of study that indirectly relates to and prepares them for careers in other fields, such as law and medicine. For those who do pursue advanced degrees, the opportunities for a career in psychology are widespread and varied.

Colleges and universities employ about 50 percent of the people who hold advanced degrees in psychology. For many of them, teaching is a secondary activity; they devote most of their time to counseling or research. Outside of the universities, holders of advanced degrees work in many places: in the public schools, in prisons, in hospitals and mental health clinics, in government agencies, in the military, and in business. Only a small number of psychologists are in private practice, though that number is increasing.

Recently, the American Psychological Association (APA) developed standards that were later written into many state licensing laws. These standards require people in psychological settings and in private practice to be supervised by a doctoral-level psychologist. Such regulations limit the opportunities for those people with master's degrees to move into higher positions. Although there are jobs available to those with master's degrees, most of them are in non-urban areas and in community psychology, clinical psychology, counseling, or in school, industrial, or organizational psychology.

In discussing careers in psychology, it is important to distinguish among psychiatrists, psychoanalysts, and psychologists. Although they may provide overlapping services, their main functions differ. A *psychiatrist* is a medical doctor who has completed 3 years of residency training in psychiatry. He or she specializes in the diagnosis and treatment of abnormal behavior. Besides giving psychotherapy, the psychiatrist also takes medical responsibility for the patient. As a physician, he or she may prescribe drugs and use other medical procedures to help a patient. A *psychoanalyst* is a psychiatrist who has received additional specialized training in psychoanalytic theory and practice.

Most, but not all, *psychologists* hold PhD degrees in psychology—the result of 4 to 6 years of study in a graduate program in psychology. The PhD program for psychologists includes broad exposure to the theories and findings of psychology, a special focus on a subdiscipline—such as experimental or social psychology—and extensive training in research methods. Certain subdisciplines, such as clinical and counseling psychology, require additional training in diagnosis and psychotherapy; requirements also include 1 year of training in

Marriage counseling is an aspect of counseling psychology. With the help of the psychologist, the husband and wife work to resolve their problems.
(Bohdan Hrynewyck, Stock, Boston)

psychotherapy in an internship program that is accredited by the APA.

Years ago, when competition for jobs was less intense than it is today, graduate students in psychology specialized in a single area, or subdiscipline, such as clinical, developmental, or educational psychology. Current employment conditions, however, require students to branch out. Psychology students on the graduate level now often specialize in two fields, such as a major in experimental psychology and a minor in industrial, or school/clinical psychology, or developmental/aging, and so on. Such training may provide breadth in a traditional area and depth in an applied specialty. The major areas of specialization are described below.

Clinical Psychology. Most psychologists specialize in clinical psychology, and learn to diagnose and treat problems of adjustment. They are the people we often hear referred to as "shrinks." Clinical psychologists treat groups as well as individuals and may be in private practice or may work for public agencies. Clinical psychologists often work in community health centers, out-patient programs, clinics, day-care centers, schools, and so on. Nearly 50 percent of the clinicians with PhDs work in educational institutions. Increasingly, all clinical psychologists are expected to get their PhDs. Thus, many people with master's degrees are now enrolling in PhD programs to remain certified clinicians. Psychiatric social workers receive two years of postgraduate training in social work. They are specially trained to deal with psychological problems that are related to family and social situations. Because of their training, they are often called upon to collect information about a patient's home and to interview relatives. The social worker also participates in therapy with patients.

Counseling Psychology. Counseling psychologists are concerned with "normal" problems of adjustment that most of us face sooner or later, such as choosing a career or coping with marital problems. Most have PhD degrees. Although most counseling psychologists work in academic settings, there are also jobs available in hospitals and in community mental health centers (Fretz & Stang, 1980).

In evaluating children's psychological personalities, the clinical psychologist uses pictures, games, and other techniques.
(Carol Wolinsky, Stock, Boston)

Developmental Psychology. The developmental psychologist studies mental and physical growth in humans from the prenatal period through childhood, adolescence, adulthood, and old age. The "child psychologist" is a developmental psychologist who specializes in the study of children. Most developmental psychologists have a PhD degree. More than 70 percent of all developmental psychologists work in universities, where they research such areas as aging, cognition, socialization, and sex roles (Fretz & Stang, 1980).

Educational Psychology. Educational psychologists study human learning processes in the educational setting. They are especially interested in testing, intelligence and creativity, genius and retardation, and related topics. Most have a PhD degree and work in educational settings, though some also work in the military, in business, and in industry.

Environmental Psychology. Environmental psychology is a combination of several different fields of study, all addressing themselves to the interaction of people and their environment. How does the layout of a park relate to its frequency of use? What are the psychological effects of traffic noise? How do physical surroundings mold personality and attitudes? These are the kinds of questions that are studied by environmental psychologists.

Experimental Psychology. Experimental psychologists investigate such basic processes as learning, memory, sensation, perception, cognition, motivation, and emotion. Most experimental psychologists work in universities, and a PhD is almost always required.

Industrial/Organizational Psychology. Industrial and organizational psychologists address themselves to the problems of training personnel, improving working conditions, and studying the effects of automation on humans. Many organizational and industrial psychologists have a master's degree, although the PhD is increasingly expected for the most responsible positions (Fretz & Stang, 1980).

Personality Psychology. Personality psychologists study the differences in traits among people, such as anxiety, sociability, self-esteem, the need for achievement, and aggressiveness. Most personality psychologists teach and do research in academic institutions, and most have the PhD degree.

Personnel Psychology. Personnel psychologists, unlike industrial psychologists, focus on the hiring, assignment, and promotion of employees to enhance their job satisfaction and productivity. These psychologists work in the personnel departments of businesses and rely heavily on interview and test data to make their assessments. Although a master's degree is usually required for this position, jobs as test administrators and interviewers are available for those with bachelor's degrees.

Psychobiology. Physiological psychologists investigate the extent to which behavior is caused by physical changes in the body. They particularly concentrate on the brain, nervous system, and the body's biochemistry. Over 70 percent of all biopsychologists teach and do research in educational institutions; the remainder work in hospitals or drug companies. Most have a PhD (Fretz & Stang, 1980).

School Psychology. School psychologists specialize in learning problems. They work with children who need special help, administer various tests, and also work with teachers and administrators to solve and prevent problems. Most school psychologists hold master's degrees.

Social Psychology. Social psychologists investigate the influence of people on one another. How are people influenced by those around them? Why do we like some people and dislike others? Do opposites really attract? Do people behave differently in groups than they do when they are alone? Most social psychologists work in academic settings and have the PhD degree.

Although most of the specializations discussed so far require graduate degrees in psychology, there are several opportunities for those who do not want to study beyond the college level. One possibility is teaching psychology at the high school level. Nearly one million students are currently enrolled in high school psychology courses across the nation. Although full-time high school psychology teachers are rare—many double as teachers of other subjects or as counselors—opportunities do exist. Most high schools require a bachelor's degree and teacher certification, although a master's degree is preferable; in some states, the MA is specifically required after a certain number of years.

Recently, several community colleges have started offering associate degree programs in psychology. These training programs produce a large supply of people who are well qualified for paraprofessional jobs in state hospitals, mental health centers, and other human service settings. Job responsibilities may include the screening and evaluation of new patients, record keeping, other direct patient-contact activities, and assistance in community consultation.

Summary

1. Psychology is the science that studies behavior and the unseen processes that shape behavior. Psychologists seek to *explain, predict,* and *control* behavior. Psychology is one of the behavioral sciences, but it is unique in its emphasis on the individual.

2. Wilhelm Wundt established Europe's first psychological laboratory at the University of Leipzig in 1879, where he intended to study the mind in an objective and scientific manner. He introduced measurement and experiment into psychology, which until then had been a branch of philosophy.

3. One of Wundt's students, Edward Bradford Titchener, became professor of psychology at Cornell University and the leader of American psychology. Wundt and Titchener both believed that psychology's role is to identify the basic elements of experience and to show how they are combined. This school of psychology is known as *structuralism*.

4. Sir Francis Galton pioneered the study of individual differences and the development of mental tests.

5. William James, the first native American psychologist, believed that sensations cannot be separated from associations. Mental associations, he claimed, allow us to benefit from previous experience. James firmly believed that all activity is functional, and by applying biological principles to the mind, he arrived at the *functionalist theory* of mental life and behavior.

6. John B. Watson confronted both the structuralist and functionalist schools, stating that we can no more define "consciousness" than we can define the "soul." Psychology, he maintained, should only concern itself with observable, measurable behavior. Watson's theory is part of the *behaviorist school* of psychology. Watson based much of his work on Pavlov's conditioning experiments and thought that all behavior could be explained by stimulus and response.

7. While Watson was working in America, a new school of thought, *Gestalt psychology*, was being developed in Germany. Roughly translated, *gestalt* means "whole" or "form." Gestalt psychologists suggested that learning depends on insight and on the perception of relationships. They concentrated on our tendency to see patterns, to distinguish an object from its background, to complete pictures from a few cues.

8. Behaviorism was thriving in America when B. F. Skinner replaced Watson as its leader. Skinner's beliefs were similar to Watson's but he made the animal an active agent in the conditioning process by adding reinforcement, or reward, to stimulate learning. Skinner's work led to a school of psychology known as *S-R psychology*.

9. *Psychoanalysis* was not seen as a part of psychology until the late 1920s, after Freud had worked out his theories on the conflict between unconscious desires and the demands of society. This conflict, he felt, often leads to anxiety or exaggerated fears. His theories remain controversial today. Freud also founded psychotherapy with his famous "talking cure."

10. *Cognitive psychology* is the study of thought processes in the broadest sense. It is concerned with how people perceive, interpret, store, and use information.

11. *Existential psychology* views the alienation and meaninglessness of contemporary life as contributing to apathy and psychological problems. Existential psychology seeks to lead people to an inner sense of identity so that they can care, commit themselves, and love.

12. *Humanistic psychology* emphasizes communication through the senses in order to achieve self-actualization and joy through other people.

13. Psychologists use scientific methods to study behavior. The *naturalistic-observation method* is used to study animal and human behavior in natural settings, instead of in the laboratory.

14. The *experimental method* begins with an idea or hypothesis about the relationship between two or more variables. To find if they are related, the experimenter manipulates the *independent variable* to see how it affects the *dependent variable*. The experimenter uses precautionary *controls* to help ensure that he or she is observing only the effects of the one independent variable.

15. The *correlational method* is a means of investigating the relationships between certain characteristics and behavior variables without necessarily manipulating or controlling those variables. As a result, it is often difficult to explain why the correlation exists.

16. More than 25 years ago the American Psychological Association drew up a code of ethics on how to treat subjects in psychological experiments. Although not all psychologists believe that such a code is needed, very few do work that raises serious ethical questions.

17. Psychologists have two basic approaches to satisfying their curiosity. *Pure research* is done for its own sake rather than to solve a specific problem. In *applied research*, the psychologist directly studies real social problems. Most psychologists draw from both approaches in their attempts to understand behavior.

18. Psychologists use animals in research because some types of experiments cannot be done on humans. Animals also have shorter life spans, which lets a researcher study behavior over several generations, and animals' genetic history and immediate environment can be better controlled. Psychologists are careful about generalizing from animal to human behavior. They do find, however, that animal research makes a large contribution to their knowledge of behavior.

Outline

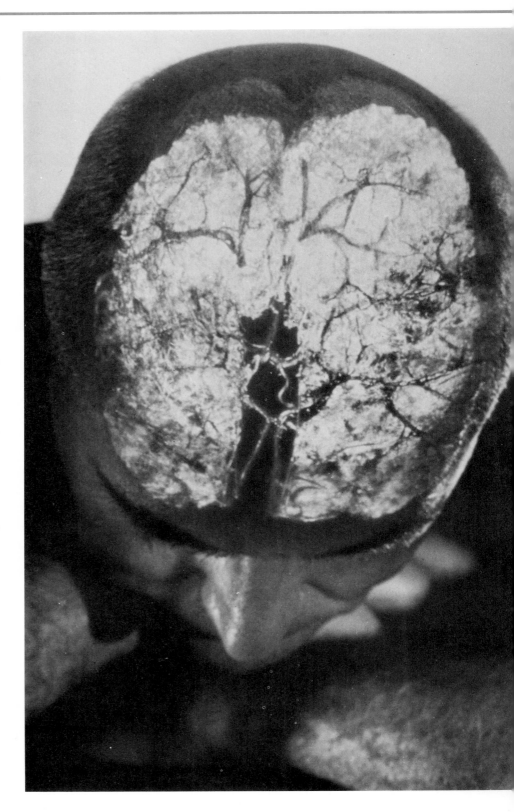

Chapter 2

Biology
and Behavior

The radio says it is 9:00 A.M. but your new watch reads 9:05, so you set it back 5 minutes. Later in the day, you look at your watch and see that it says 3:15 P.M., but according to the clock in the library it is only 3:00. A little annoyed, you go to a watchmaker and explain your problem. He opens the watch case and examines the maze of tiny gears and levers inside. He discovers the difficulty, replaces the mainspring, and you are back on time.

In this chapter we are going to take our cue from the watchmaker. Psychology is the study of behavior. But often we cannot understand behavior unless we know a little about what goes on inside the human body, what makes us tick. Most of the time—when the watch is running perfectly or when the body is functioning normally—we tend to forget about the very complex activities that are constantly going on. But nonetheless they continue: the cells keep functioning and reproducing themselves; the organs and glands keep regulating such diverse activities as digestion and growth; and the nervous system keeps receiving, interpreting, and sending messages. And it is with the nervous system that this chapter begins.

The **nervous system** is one of the body's two major coordinating and integrating mechanisms. The more we learn about the nervous system, the more certain we become that all of its parts work together, all the time, to integrate the body's extraordinarily complex activities.

To understand how intricate these activities are, consider the processes involved in what seems to be even the simplest occurrence. At one time or another, most of us have burned our fingers on a match. What happens next? "It's simple," you might say, "I automatically snatch my hand away from the heat."

But, in fact, your body's response to a burn is not simple at all. Instead, it involves a highly complex set of activities. Special sensory neurons pick up the message that your fingers are burned. They pass this information along to the spinal cord, which triggers a quick withdrawal of your hand. This withdrawal is an involuntary, automatic response to the burn. But the message also goes to a vast network of neurons that transmit the message throughout the central nervous system. The sympathetic nervous system goes on "emergency alert." You breathe faster. Your heart pounds. Your entire body mobilizes itself against the wound. Meanwhile, your brain interprets the messages being sent to it, registers the pain, and relays messages back through the network of neurons, which cause you to turn your hand over, examine the burn, and perhaps walk over to the sink and run cold water over it. So what seems like a "simple reflex" is actually the result of an incredibly complex information processing system: the body's nervous system.

The Nervous System

The nervous system has many parts that all work together. Since these parts are various, complex, and to a large extent, still a mystery, it is best to approach the nervous system by looking first at each part by itself. We will start with the smallest part, the individual **neuron.** This cell underlies the activity of the entire nervous system.

THE NEURON

There are an estimated one hundred billion nerve cells, or neurons, in the nervous system. Although neurons vary in shape and size, they all are specialized to receive and to transmit information.

Like all other cells, a neuron has a nucleus—a cell body where **metabolism** and respiration take place—and a cell membrane that encloses the whole cell. Unlike other cells, however, neurons have tiny fibers that extend out from the cell body (see Figure 2–1). These extensions enable the neuron to perform its special job—to receive messages from surrounding cells, carry them a certain distance, and then pass them on to other cells. The short fibers branching out around the cell body are called **dendrites.** The dendrites pick up messages coming in from their surroundings and carry them to the cell body. The single long fiber extending from the cell body is called an **axon.** The axon fiber is very thin and usually much longer than the dendrites. In adults the axons that run from the brain to the base of the spinal cord may be as long as 3 feet, but most axons are only 1 or 2 inches. The axon carries outgoing messages either by relaying them to the next neuron in the series or by directing a muscle or gland to take action. When we talk about a **nerve,** we mean not a single fiber but a group of axons bundled together like parallel wires in an electrical cable.

The axon shown in Figure 2–1 is surrounded by a fatty covering called a **myelin sheath.** The myelin sheath seems to speed up the transmission of **neural impulses.** The sheath is pinched at intervals, which makes the axon

"I realize that those of you who are planning to go into psychiatry may find this dull."
(Drawing by Ed Fisher; © 1962 The *New Yorker Magazine, Inc.*)

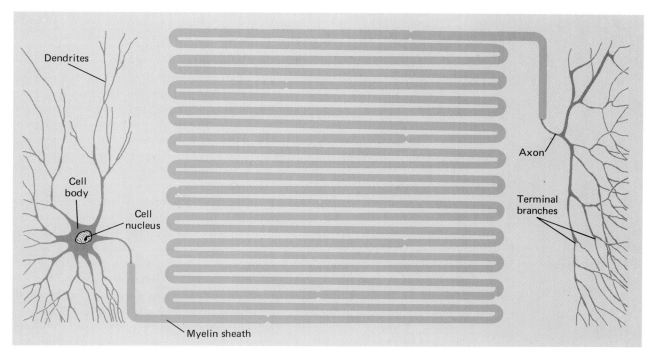

Dendrites

Cell body

Cell nucleus

Axon

Terminal branches

Myelin sheath

Figure 2–1
A typical neuron.

resemble a string of microscopic sausages. Not all axons are covered by myelin sheaths, but myelinated axons are found throughout the body.

Although all neurons relay messages, the kind of information they collect and the places to which they carry it help to distinguish between types of neurons. For example, neurons that collect messages from inside and outside the body and carry those messages to the spinal cord or to the brain are called **sensory** (or afferent) **neurons.** Neurons that carry messages from the spinal cord or the brain to the muscles and to the glands are called **motor** (or efferent) **neurons.** Neurons that carry messages from one neuron to another are called **interneurons** (association neurons). These inter-neurons make up a "great intermediate net" that performs by far the bulk of the work of the nervous system. Indeed, interneurons account for 99.98 percent of all the neurons in the central nervous system (Nauta & Fairtag, 1979). This vast web of connected interneurons is charged with a tremendous amount of information from all directions. How these neurons respond to all this information determines our thoughts, memories, and perceptions—all the things that make human beings human (Hubel, 1979).

THE NEURAL IMPULSE

What messages do the neurons carry? And what code do they use to help the parts of the body communicate with each other? The nervous system speaks a language that all the body's cells can understand: simple yes–or–no, on–or–off electrochemical impulses called *action potentials* (Hodgkin & Huxley, 1952).

When a neuron is resting, its cell membrane forms a barrier between two semiliquid solutions. One of these solutions is inside the neuron, the other is outside of it. Both solutions contain electrically charged particles, or ions. The particles outside the neuron are mostly sodium and chloride ions. Potassium and organic ions are mostly inside the neuron. Since more negative ions are inside the neuron than outside of it, the electrical charge inside the neuron is negative relative to the outside. Positive and negative ions, like the positive and negative poles of a magnet, are attracted to each other. Without the cell membrane to separate them, the positively charged ions outside the neuron and the negatively charged ions inside the neuron would flow together and neutralize one another. The membrane separates them and keeps the neuron in a state of **polarization**—a sort of electrical equilibrium.

But the cell membrane is a very selective gatekeeper. While the neuron is in a resting state, the membrane lets many substances pass freely. It refuses, however, to allow sodium ions to slip into the neuron from the outside. When the neuron receives a message—that is, when a point on the cell membrane is adequately stimulated—it suddenly opens and allows the sodium ions to rush in. When enough sodium has entered the neuron to make the inside positively charged in relation to the outside, the cell membrane closes and does not allow any more sodium to enter.

The breakdown of the cell membrane does not occur at only one point. In fact, as soon as the cell membrane allows sodium to enter the neuron at one point, the next point on the membrane opens. More sodium ions flow into the neuron at this next point and depolarize this part of the neuron. The process is repeated along the length of the neuron. When this happens we say the neuron has fired.

After firing, the neuron, for a period of about one-thousandth of a second (the **absolute refractory period**), will not fire no matter how strong the incoming messages may be. This is not surprising if we remember that the neuron has stopped letting sodium in. But then the cell begins to pump potassium ions out until the inside of the neuron returns to a negative charge relative to the outside (see Figure 2–2). This is called the **relative refractory period.** During this phase, which lasts for only a few thousandths of a second, the neuron will fire, but only if the incoming message is considerably stronger than is normally necessary to make it fire.

This whole process occurs very quickly, but there is a wide range in the speed with which individual neurons conduct electrochemical impulses. In some of the largest myelinated axons, the fastest impulses may travel at speeds of nearly 400 feet per second. Axons with myelinated sheaths can conduct impulses very rapidly because the impulses can leapfrog along the string of gaps, or *nodes,* that lie along the myelin sheaths (Stevens, 1979). Neurons without such sheaths tend to be slower. Their impulses are conducted in a steady flow, much as the fuse on a firecracker burns down until it sets off an explosion. The slowest of these unmyelinated neurons—those with small axons—poke along at little more than 3 feet per second.

The neuron does not fire in response to every impulse that it receives. If the incoming message is not strong enough to make the neuron fire, it may simply cause a *graded potential* in a tiny area of the neuron—no more than a millimeter long (see Figure 2–2). This potential simply fades away, leaving the neuron in its normal polarized state. In other words, the incoming

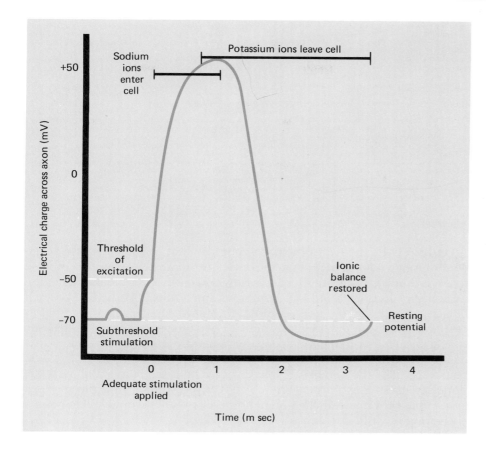

Figure 2–2
The flow of ions in and out of the cell during the firing of a neuron.
(Adapted from Neil R. Carlson, *Physiology of Behavior*. Boston: Allyn and Bacon, 1977.)

message must be above a certain **threshold** of intensity to cause a nervous impulse, just as you must pull the trigger hard enough to fire a gun.

Pulling even harder on the trigger of a gun will not cause the bullet to travel any faster or any farther. It either fires because you pulled hard enough, or it does not fire because you did not pull hard enough. But if you pull it again and again, and if other people around you are firing *their* guns at the same time, there will be a volley of shots. This will convey very different information than a single shot to someone who hears it.

Likewise, although a neuron either fires or does not, it can also convey a lot of information by firing quickly or slowly. Even though each neuron is limited to simple on–or–off messages, the number of neurons firing at a given moment and the number of times they fire allow a very complex message to be communicated.

THE SYNAPSE

We have been discussing the operation of a single neuron. But the billions of neurons in the nervous system work together to coordinate the body's activities. How do they interact? How does a message get from one neuron to another?

Figure 2–3
A highly simplified drawing of the synapse, showing the synaptic vesicles and the tiny space that separates most neurons from one another.

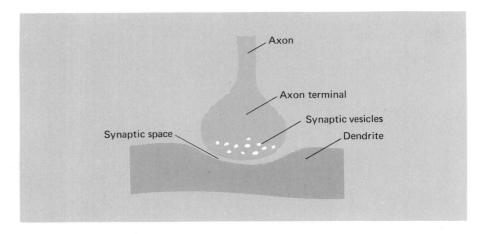

Let us retrace the path of a neural impulse that starts when one of the dendrites of a neuron picks up a message. The dendrite carries the impulse to the cell body, and from there it travels down the axon. Near its end, the axon begins to branch out into numerous small fibers. At the end of each fiber is a tiny knob, or **axon terminal.** A minute gap separates the end of each terminal from the dendrites or cell body of another neuron. This tiny space is called a **synaptic space** (or synaptic cleft). The entire area composed of the axon terminal, synaptic space, and dendrite of the next neuron is called the **synapse.** For the average neuron, there are about 1,000 synapses. Even if we accept the conservative estimate that the nervous system has only about 100 billion neurons, our bodies would still contain a staggering 100 trillion synapses!

If the neural impulse is to travel on to the next neuron, it must somehow travel across the synaptic space. Traditionally, there has been a lively controversy about what actually happened at the synaptic space. The electrical impulse, some said, simply jumps across the gap. No, argued others, the transfer is chemical. We now know that the chemical-transfer notion is correct. What happens is this: Most axon terminals contain a number of tiny oval sacs called **synaptic vesicles** (see Figure 2–3). When the neural impulse reaches the end of the axon, it causes these vesicles to release a chemical. This chemical transmitter is what actually travels across the gap between the two neurons and affects the next neuron.

One major question still not answered is exactly how many kinds of **chemical-transmitter substances** exist. About 30 are known or suspected. It is certain that 2 of them are **acetylcholine** and **norepinephrine.** Other probable transmitter substances are **epinephrine** (also called adrenaline), **serotonin,** and **dopamine** (Axelrod, 1974). Some chemicals that are released, however, do not cause the next neuron to fire. Some vesicles release **inhibitory chemicals** that counteract the effects of the excitatory chemicals. When an inhibitory chemical is present, more of the excitatory chemical is needed to cause the next neuron to fire. The inhibitory chemicals act as filters, letting through only the strongest neural impulses.

Another major question to be answered is what happens to the chemical transmitter substance after the "receiving" neuron has fired. If it remained loose in the synaptic gap, the neuron would continue to fire every time it

SYNAPSES AND DRUGS

The effects of many drugs can be understood by their effects on synapses. While studying the role of these chemical-transmitter substances, scientists have learned a lot about how people react to psychoactive drugs. Some drugs stimulate the release of a particular chemical from an axon terminal; others inhibit the normal release of a certain substance. Amphetamines, for example, both release norepinephrine and block its breakdown. They also cause postsynaptic firing. All of this depletes the synaptic supply of norepinephrine so that more has to be created. This, in turn, excites the central nervous system and the sympathetic nervous system, leading to a state of alertness or arousal—a "high." But to the extent that the amphetamine produces norepinephrine, the body stops producing it. In other words, the body now depends on the drug to produce and release enough norepinephrine. When the amphetamine wears off, however, there is a rebound effect: Because of its dependence on the drug, the body is no longer producing enough norepinephrine on its own. Thus, as the drug wears off, there is a shortage of norepinephrine, which causes feelings of lassitude and extreme apathy—a "crash." This feeling lasts until the body can again produce enough norepinephrine on its own. As a result, people who are addicted to amphetamines may suffer from disruption of thought processes, hallucinations, and feelings of persecution. These symptoms are shared by some kinds of schizophrenics, and this along with other evidence has led some scientists to believe that schizophrenia and manic depression may also result from imbalances in similar chemical-transmitter substances.

Many psychoactive drugs act by imitating the behavior of natural transmitter substances. Mescaline, for instance, is structurally similar to norepinephrine. LSD and psilocybin are similar to serotonin. In a sense, these drugs "fool" the next axon terminal, neuron, or dendrite into letting them in. The result is that they cause perceptual problems and hallucinations.

Some antidepressants, such as norepinephrine and serotonin, work by enhancing the effects of natural transmitters in the brain. These drugs prevent the transmitter substances from being reabsorbed into the synaptic vesicles. As a result, the neurons keep firing, causing a state of high arousal in the nervous system. Cocaine, a stimulant, appears to work in this way. Even the caffeine found in coffee, tea, and artificially colored drinks affects the nervous system by acting on the synapses of the brain (Iversen, 1979, pp. 144–145).

completed its refractory period. One of the chemicals, acetylcholine, seems to be destroyed by other chemicals that are found in the fluids around the synapse. Norepinephrine and dopamine, however, are recycled—they are taken back into the vesicles to be used again.

The situation we have been describing so far is highly simplified. If one neuron were connected to only two other neurons—one at each end—the nervous system could not perform all its interlocking functions. What actually happens is much more complicated. The axon terminals of a single neuron can reach the dendrites of many other neurons; the dendrites and cell bodies have synapses to the axons of other neurons over their entire surface. Thus, each neuron practically can affect and be affected by the activity of thousands of other neurons. Each neuron is thus indirectly linked to every other neuron in the nervous system.

DIVISIONS OF THE NERVOUS SYSTEM

Try to imagine all the billions of cells in the human nervous system, all communicating with one another in the same code, at the same time, and at tremendous speeds; all are connected through an incredibly complex

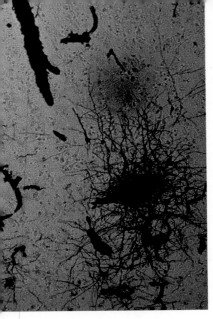

Human brain cells magnified
14,800 times.
(Russ Kinne, Photo Researchers)

series of interlocking circuits; all are carrying a multitude of messages at the same time. Then add all the cells that are directly exposed to external conditions—all the sense receptors that respond to heat and cold, light and dark, sound and silence, and so on—and then send the messages along the neural pathways. The complexity is staggering. By contrast, managing an airport seems like child's play!

How does the nervous system keep all its messages straight? One reason the communication lines do not get jammed is that each type of receptor cell communicates to the higher nerve centers through its own private set of neural pathways. These separate routes provide us with one way of dividing up the nervous system for study.

When the nervous system is being described in a structural way—that is, where its parts are—it is seen as having two divisions: the **central nervous system** and the **peripheral nervous system.** The central nervous system consists of the brain and the spinal cord. The peripheral nervous system consists of all the other nerves that connect the brain and the spinal cord to the **receptors** (cells in the sense organs) and the **effectors** (cells in the muscles and glands). An important part of the peripheral nervous system is the **autonomic nervous system,** which serves the muscles and glands in the body.

THE AUTONOMIC NERVOUS SYSTEM

To understand the autonomic nervous system we must make one more distinction. The autonomic nervous system consists of two branches: the **sympathetic** and **parasympathetic divisions.** These two divisions act in almost total opposition to each other, but both are directly involved in controlling and integrating the actions of the glands and the blood vessels within the body.

THE SYMPATHETIC DIVISION. The nerve fibers of the pathways of the sympathetic division are busiest when you are frightened or angry. They carry messages that tell the body to prepare for an emergency and to get ready to act quickly or strenuously. In response to messages from the sympathetic division, your heart pounds, you breathe faster, your pupils enlarge, digestion stops. The sympathetic nervous system also tells the adrenal glands to start producing epinephrine, which is pumped into the bloodstream and further strengthens these reactions. Sympathetic nerve fibers connect to every internal organ in the body; this explains why the body's reaction to sudden stress is so widespread, although the sympathetic system can also act selectively on a single organ.

THE PARASYMPATHETIC DIVISION. Parasympathetic nerve fibers connect to the same organs as the sympathetic nerve fibers, but the messages they carry tell the organs to do just the opposite of what the sympathetic division has directed. By transmitting the chemical substance acetylcholine, the parasympathetic division says, in effect, "Okay, the heat's off, back to normal." The heart then goes back to beating at its normal rate, the stomach muscles relax, digestion starts again, breathing slows down, and

32

the pupils of the eyes get smaller. Thus, the parasympathetic division compensates for the sympathetic division and lets the body rest after stress.

Usually these two systems work together: After the sympathetic division has aroused the body, the parasympathetic division follows with messages to relax. In most people, however, one division or the other tends to dominate. In ulcer patients, for example, the parasympathetic division tends to dominate: they salivate heavily, their hearts beat rather slowly, and their digestive systems are often overactive. People whose sympathetic division dominates show the opposite symptoms: their mouths are dry, their palms are moist, and their hearts beat quickly even when they are resting.

The autonomic nervous system traditionally has been regarded as the "automatic" part of the body's response mechanism. No one, it was believed, could tell their own autonomic nervous system when to speed up or slow down the heart's beating or when to stop or start the digestive processes. These things were thought to run as automatically as the way a thermostat controls the temperature of a room. The latest evidence, however, suggests that we have more control over the autonomic nervous system than we may realize. Several studies (reported in Chapter 5) seem to show that people (and animals) can indeed manipulate this so-called automatic part of the nervous system.

THE CENTRAL NERVOUS SYSTEM

The central nervous system, as we said earlier, is composed of the brain and the spinal cord. The brain is surely the most fascinating part of the whole nervous system. Containing more than 90 percent of the system's neurons, it is the seat of awareness and reason, the place where learning, memory, hate, love, and fear are centered. It is the part of us that decides what to do, and, later, whether that decision was right or wrong, and it imagines how things might have turned out if we had acted differently. The spinal cord tends to be less fully appreciated than the brain, but without it a person could not function.

THE SPINAL CORD. The complex cable of nerves that connects the brain to most of the rest of the body is known as the **spinal cord.** The spinal cord is made up of bundles of long, nearly round nerve fibers. The inside of the spinal cord is a grayish color, while outside the coverings of myelin sheaths give it a whitish appearance. The spinal cord has two basic functions: The first is to carry messages to and from the brain; the second is to cause **reflex movements.** For example, when you touch a lighted match, as we mentioned at the start of the chapter, a message signaling pain comes into your spinal cord from the sense receptors of your hand. The message is processed in the spinal cord, and an impulse is sent out causing the almost instantaneous response of pulling your hand away (see Figure 2–4). Because of how the neural circuits are arranged, the same incoming message produces the same response every time. The message also travels to the brain, but by the time it gets there you have probably already reacted. Most of these spinal reflexes are protective; they enable the body to avoid

Figure 2–4
Simple reflexes are controlled by the spinal cord. The message travels from the sense receptors near the skin through the afferent nerve fibers to the spinal cord. In the gray matter of the spinal cord, the messages are relayed through association neurons to the efferent nerve fibers, which carry them to the muscle cells that cause the reflex movement.

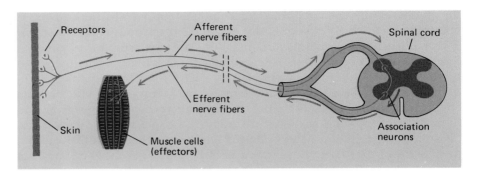

damage and maintain muscle tone and position. Some other reflexes, which are not protective, do pass through circuits in the brain before action is taken. One reflex that involves the brain is a sneeze. You generally know when you are about to sneeze and sometimes you can control it.

We talk of the brain and the spinal cord as two distinct structures, but there is no real boundary between them. At its upper end, the spinal cord enlarges and merges into the lower part of the brain, called the **brainstem.***
In an evolutionary sense, the brainstem contains many of the brain's oldest structures. In humans the brainstem is rather like a stalk that supports the other parts of the brain.

THE BRAIN. The nervous system develops quite early in the human embryo. As soon as the brain begins to take shape, we can detect three distinct cores: the **hindbrain,** the **midbrain,** and the **forebrain** (see Figure 2–5). In the fully developed adult brain, they are not so easily distinguished from one another, but we can still use these three basic divisions to describe the parts of the brain, what they do, and how they interact to influence our behavior.

Since it is found in even the most primitive vertebrates, the hindbrain is believed to have been the earliest part of the brain to evolve. The part of the hindbrain nearest to the spinal cord is the **medulla,** a narrow structure about 1.5 inches long. The medulla controls breathing and many important reflexes, such as those that help us stand upright. The medulla is also the point at which many of the nerves from the higher parts of the brain cross; the nerves from the left part of the brain cross to the right side of the body, and vice versa.

Above the medulla lies the **pons,** a structure slightly wider than the medulla, which connects the **cerebral cortex** at the top of the brain to the topmost section of the hindbrain, the **cerebellum.** The cerebellum is composed of two hemispheres. It performs a wide range of functions. It handles certain reflexes, especially those that have to do with balance and breathing, and it coordinates the body's actions to ensure that movements go together in efficient sequences. The cerebellum also has an important role in organizing eye movements. It allows you to keep your eyes fixed on a particular point while your head and body are moving, and it controls the eye movements that are used to follow an object in motion (Llinas, 1975).

*The brainstem includes all of the brain's parts except the cerebrum and the cerebellum. Many of these parts are treated separately in the following discussion.

Above the pons and cerebellum the brainstem widens even more to form the midbrain. The midbrain is in the middle, as the name implies, between the hindbrain at the base and the forebrain at the top. The midbrain is especially important to hearing and sight. It is also one of several places in the brain where pain is registered. Supported by the brainstem, budding out above it, and drooping over somewhat to fit into the skull, is the forebrain. Some of the forebrain's most influential areas are the **thalamus,** the **hypothalamus,** and the cerebral cortex.

Inside the two cerebral hemispheres, in the central core of the forebrain and more or less directly over the brainstem, are the two egg-shaped structures that make up the thalamus. Except for the sense of smell, the thalamus relays and translates incoming messages from sense receptors throughout the body. Many of the messages that travel from one part of the cerebral cortex to another also pass through the thalamus. Some of the neurons in the thalamus seem to be important in regulating the electrical activity of the cerebral cortex; other neurons in the thalamus control the activities of the autonomic nervous system.

Below the thalamus is a smaller structure called the hypothalamus. This part of the forebrain exerts an enormous influence on many kinds of motivation. Centers in the hypothalamus govern eating, drinking, sexual behavior, sleeping, and temperature control. The hypothalamus is also directly involved in emotional behavior. Centers in the hypothalamus direct the body to produce the organized and integrated patterns of behavior that we recognize as rage, terror, and pleasure. In times of stress, the hypothalamus appears to perform a crucial integrating function. It acts

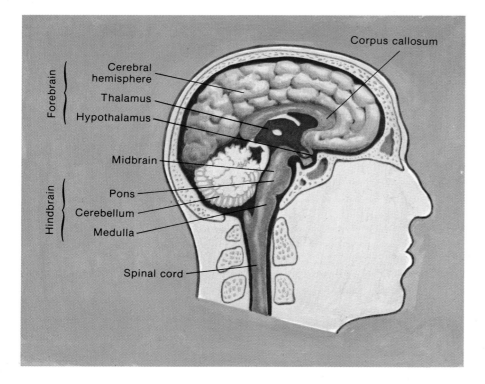

Figure 2–5

A cross section of the midline structures of the brain, showing the cerebral cortex and subcortical areas.

directly on both the sympathetic and parasympathetic divisions by determining which messages are sent out over the autonomic nervous system. It also acts indirectly by controlling the activities of the anterior pituitary, which is located just below it, and by stimulating several other endocrine glands as well.

Ballooning out over the brainstem are the two hemispheres that form the cerebral cortex. They fold down over the brainstem and hide most of it. A great mass of white matter (myelinated axon fibers), called the **corpus callosum,** connects the two hemispheres to each other and to the other parts of the nervous system. The cerebral cortex itself is made of gray matter, of unmyelinated axons and cell bodies. The cerebral cortex is the most recent part of the nervous system to evolve and is more highly developed in humans than in any other animal. It accounts for about 80 percent of the human brain's weight and contains 70 percent of the neurons in the central nervous system. If it were spread out, it would cover about 1.5 square feet, so in order to fit inside the skull, the cerebral cortex has developed an intricate pattern of folds—hills and valleys called convolutions. These convolutions form a pattern in every brain that is as unique as a fingerprint.

The two hemispheres of the cerebral cortex are responsible for different functions. The sensory messages from the right side of the body generally travel to the left hemisphere of the cerebral cortex, crossing in the medulla. Those from the left side of the body travel to the right hemisphere. Likewise, the motor messages that control the muscles and glands on the right side of the body originate in the left hemisphere, and vice versa. For this reason, damage to the left side of the brain affects the right side of the body, and vice versa.

But the two hemispheres are not equal partners. In each person, one hemisphere dominates. The most obvious effect of this domination is whether you are right- or left-handed. In general, if you are right-handed, your left cerebral cortex is dominant. If the hemispheres only controlled physical dexterity, the domination of one side of the brain over the other would not matter much. Most of us probably do not care with which hand we do things. But each hemisphere also controls our uniquely human faculties, and each is responsible for different abilities. For example, the left hemisphere does our analytical thinking and talks for us. The right side is relatively illiterate, artistic, and silent.

The neural organization of the two hemispheres seems to be different. Each one employs different mechanisms to understand the outside world, and each has special abilities (Levy, 1979). Recently, scientists have found that the right side of the brain is not *completely* illiterate, as they once thought. It can decipher written or spoken language and can come up with meaning, but it cannot turn meaning into words (Levy, 1979). On the other hand, the right hemisphere is superior to the left in spatial abilities and the rather specific capacities to remember faces, melodies, and abstract visual patterns.

Since information travels from one hemisphere to the other by way of the corpus callosum, the different abilities of the hemispheres do not usually affect us very much. The two halves work together. In fact, laboratory

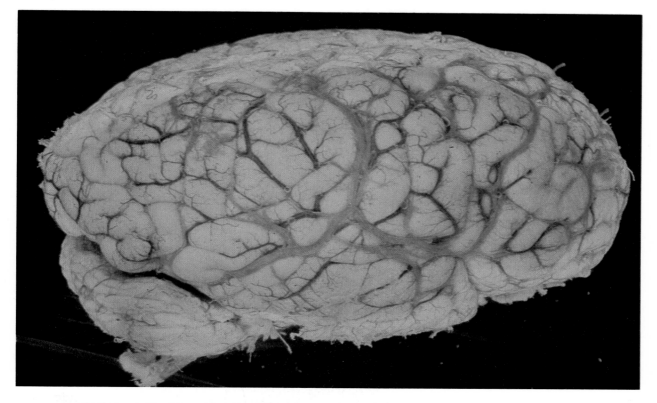

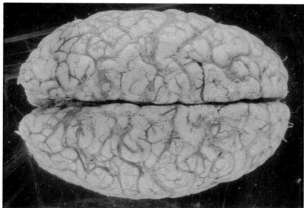

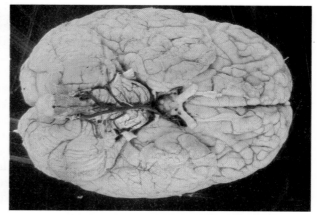

experiments have shown that this cooperation is essential in many tasks. For example, a test was given to a person whose cerebral hemispheres had been surgically separated. The subject was asked to reproduce a simple pattern with each hand by assembling colored blocks. Frequent errors were made with each hand, but the errors were of different sorts. The test showed that each side of the brain is responsible for different skills. It also showed that neither hemisphere *alone* is able to analyze patterns correctly. Apparently, the two hemispheres must work together (Geschwind, 1979).

Shown in the top photo and in the one bottom left are the top and bottom of the human brain. The photo at bottom right is of the blood vessels found in the brain.

(© Lester V. Bergman & Associates)

Figure 2–6
A side view of the human cerebral cortex and cerebellum.

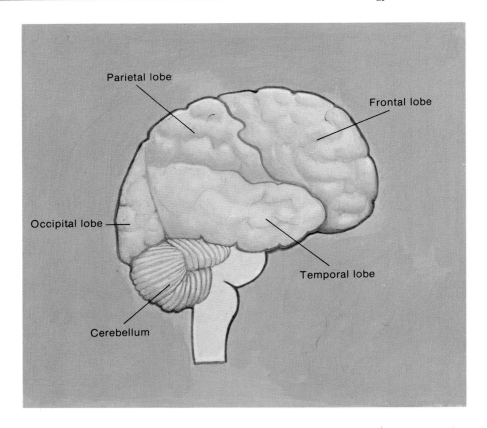

The areas of the cerebral cortex where messages from the sense receptors register are called **sensory projection areas.** The areas of the cerebral cortex where response messages start their trip down the brainstem to tell the muscles and glands what to do are called **motor projection areas.** There are also large areas throughout the cerebral cortex that are neither completely sensory nor completely motor. These are called **association areas;** they make up over 75 percent of the area of the cerebral cortex. It is in the association areas that messages coming in from separate senses are combined into meaningful impressions, and where motor messages going out are integrated so the body can make coordinated movements. The association areas are involved in all of the activities we commonly attribute to the brain: learning, thinking, remembering, talking. The largest of the association areas is located in the **frontal lobe** of the brain, just under the forehead. The frontal lobe appears to be the location of the higher mental processes—of abstract thinking and problem solving. The activities of the association areas are very highly integrated. The various association areas seem to work together to a large extent, which becomes most obvious when a person suffers damage to one of them. The association areas seem to be able to take over for one another, unlike the projection areas, where brain damage to a particular area usually results in loss of all or part of the specific or motor capability localized in that area. The amount and kind of malfunction seem to depend not only on where the association areas are damaged, but also on the extent of the injury, how long it lasts, where the damage occurs, and on such personal characteristics as age, sex, and education.

THE RETICULAR ACTIVATING SYSTEM. We have divided the brain into three separate sections to simplify our discussion. But the brain itself often ignores the distinctions made in textbooks and sets up systems that jump across the boundaries, using parts of the hindbrain, midbrain, and forebrain together to perform certain functions. One such circuit is the reticular activating system (see Figure 2–7).

The **reticular activating system,** or RAS, is made up of a netlike bundle of neurons running through the hindbrain, the midbrain, and a part of the forebrain called the hypothalamus. Its main job seems to be to send "Wake up!" signals to the higher parts of the brain when an incoming message is important. When two or more messages come in at the same time, which happens all the time, the RAS apparently decides which one is most urgent. Some messages seem to be toned down by the RAS; others never reach the higher centers at all. Because the RAS is selective, we may concentrate our attention on one message and ignore distracting messages from the sense receptors; we may read an interesting book, for example, while the TV is blaring, telephones are ringing, and people are talking in other parts of the room.

THE LIMBIC SYSTEM. Another example of the interconnected operations of the central nervous system is provided by the **limbic system,** a ring of structures around the thalamus in the center of each cerebral hemisphere (see Figure 2–8). The limbic system includes the hypothalamus, part of the

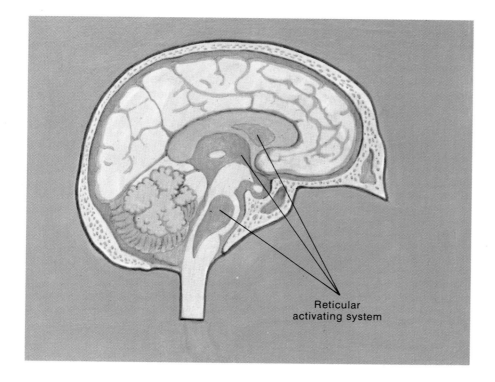

Reticular
activating system

Figure 2–7
A cross section similar to that in Figure 2–5, showing the location of the reticular activating system.

Figure 2–8
A stylized picture of how different areas of the limbic system interact during emotional stress.
(From C. Levinthal, *The Physiological Approach in Psychology*. Englewood Cliffs, N.J.: Prentice-Hall, 1979.)

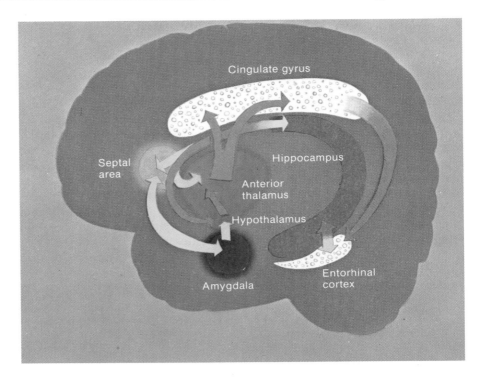

thalamus, and several other forebrain structures that lie inside the cortex. It also contains nerve fibers that connect it to the cerebral cortex and to the brainstem.

Although much of how it functions remains a mystery, the limbic system is believed to affect or control learning, emotional behavior, and many autonomic responses, such as breathing, heart rate, and intestinal activity, which are important parts of emotional activity. For example, one of its parts, the **hippocampus,** plays an important role in memory. Patients with a damaged hippocampus cannot form new memories. They can remember things that happened years ago but may forget the recent death of a near relative.

PSYCHOSURGERY AND ELECTRICAL STIMULATION

Psychosurgery and **electrical stimulation of the brain** presume that our varied behaviors originate in precise locations in the brain. Psychosurgery involves operating on the brain to change a person's behavior. An early and crude operation was the **prefrontal lobotomy.** This was done to calm psychotic patients. It did subdue them, but it also left them listless and impaired their creativity and intelligence. And once the operation was performed, the results could not be undone.

Today psychosurgeons can use brain "atlases" and electrodes to perform more precise surgery and with less destruction of brain tissue. Also, new areas of the brain, mainly in the limbic system, are being discussed and studied as better targets for psychosurgery. Since the functions of the brain are extremely well integrated, and since knowledge of the mechanisms of that integration is still so basic, some researchers are skeptical about the use of even limited psychosurgery (Chorover, 1974). Because of these concerns, psychosurgery is used today only as a last resort.*

Electrical stimulation of the brain, or ESB, is a nondestructive means of tapping the brain to see how it controls—or impairs—actions and emotions. Stimulating part of the brain with electrical current produces a "counterfeit" nerve impulse. The brain is fooled into thinking that it has received a real impulse from one of its sensory receptors. It thinks something is really going on "out there" and behaves, and makes a subject behave, accordingly.

For example, in a much-publicized demonstration, José Delgado (1969) implanted a radio-controlled electrode in the brain of a bull bred especially for bullfighting, one that will charge any human being. He went into the arena with the bull, carrying only a radio transmitter. When the bull charged him, Delgado pressed a button on the transmitter, sending an impulse to the electrode in the bull's brain, and the bull stopped in his tracks. The experiment suggests that the stimulation had a direct effect on the bull's aggressive tendencies, or, according to Delgado, "the result seemed to be a combination of motor effect . . . plus behavioral inhibition of the aggressive drive." The social implications for the future are provocative: Should we be concerned with such "behavioral inhibition" for humans?

Although intracerebral electrodes are now being used for therapeutic purposes in many parts of the world, visions of a Big Brother controlling our behavior seem to be premature. According to neuropsychologist Elliot Valenstein (1973), we are a long way from practical manipulation of human behavior through brain control. For example, did Delgado really find the precise location in the bull's brain that controls aggression? Valenstein contends that the electric shock to the bull's brain was like hitting it on the side of the head, and, as the bull turned its head away from the "blow," its body followed. Valenstein suggests that rather than being pacified after repeated shocks, as Delgado claimed, the bull was simply confused and frustrated and just gave up (Valenstein, 1973).

This raises an important point. No single area of the brain is likely to be the sole source of any given emotion or behavior. As Valenstein (1973) states: "Unfortunately, the nervous system is not organized in a way that makes it possible to separate functions in terms of their social implications" (p. 352).

Recent experiments by Valenstein and others have shown that electrical brain stimulation in animals does not produce a consistent motivational state or behavior (Valenstein, 1977). Environmental changes, for example, often produce different responses to the same stimulation in the same subjects. Not surprisingly, tests with human subjects show an even wider difference in their responses. The same patient exhibits different behav-

*The therapeutic uses of psychosurgery are discussed more fully in Chapter 14.

ioral responses to identical brain stimulation given at different times.

The social implications of psychosurgery and ESB research must be carefully considered. There are obvious dangers in seeing such options as neat solutions to social problems, in confusing patient "management" with patient betterment, or in equating pleasure with happiness. Social solutions must still be sought for social problems. Despite some successes in ESB inhibition of aggression, such psychotechnology has yet to make significant contributions to behavioral therapy.

The Minor Senses

The workings of the nervous system can be illustrated by the senses. Vision and hearing will be treated in Chapter 7, but much can be learned from the so-called "minor senses": smell, taste, touch, and so on. In general, sensation occurs when a receptor cell in one of the sense organs, the nose or tongue, for example, is stimulated by energy from within or without the body. In a process called **transduction,** this energy is coded and changed into an electrochemical impulse. This impulse is then conveyed by the nervous system to the brain. Along the way, the nervous system further codes the message so that the brain receives precise and detailed data.

SMELL

Our sense of smell is activated by chemical substances that are carried by airborne molecules that enter the nose. The receptors for this sense are located high in each nasal cavity, in a patch of tissue called the **olfactory epithelium** (see Figure 2–9). The olfactory epithelium is only about one-

Figure 2–9
The location of the olfactory epithelium.

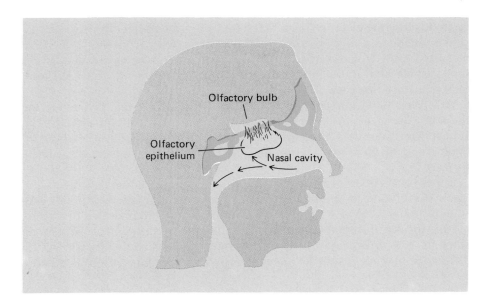

half the size of a postage stamp, but it is packed with millions of receptor cells. As we breathe, airborne molecules are carried into the nasal cavities, and they activate the receptors in the epithelium, which are specialized neurons.

We know very little about what kinds of molecules carry what kinds of odors. One of the most promising explanations is the stereochemical theory of odors proposed by John E. Amoore and his colleagues (1964). According to this theory, there are seven primary categories of odors. In five of these categories the molecules have a distinctive shape or size and fit into a corresponding "hole" in the olfactory epithelium, much as a key fits into a lock. The other two basic odors seem to depend on their electrical charge rather than on their molecular shape or size.

Unfortunately, this theory does not explain how fitting a molecule into a particular receptor cell triggers a nerve impulse. But the axons of the receptors carry the messages directly to the **olfactory bulbs** in the brain. Since these fibers do not pass through the thalamus, as other sensory fibers do, the sense of smell's route to the cerebral cortex is the most direct. And unlike the other sense sources, the fibers from the nose travel only to the olfactory bulb on the same side, without crossing over. The olfactory bulbs can communicate "across the hall" to each other and "upstairs" to the olfactory projection areas in the cerebral cortex. The connections from the olfactory bulb to the cerebral cortex are extremely intricate: For every one thousand nerve fibers that enter the olfactory bulb, only one fiber leaves the bulb headed for the cortex.

(George E. Jones III, Photo Researchers)

TASTE

To understand taste, we must first distinguish it from *flavor*. The flavor of food is a complex combination of taste and smell. If you hold your nose when you eat, most of the food's flavor is eliminated, although you will still be able to experience sensations of *bitterness*, *saltiness*, *sourness*, or *sweetness*. In other words, you will get the taste, but not the flavor.

The receptor cells for the sense of taste lie inside the **taste buds,** most of which are found on the tip, sides, and back of the tongue. An adult has about 10,000 taste buds. The number of taste buds decreases with age, which may explain why older people lose their interest in food—they simply cannot taste it as well as they used to.

The taste buds are contained in the tongue's **papillae,** small bumps you can see if you look at your tongue in the mirror. Each taste bud contains a cluster of taste receptors, or hair cells (see Figure 2–10). About every 7 days these hair cells die and are replaced. The chemical substances in the foods we eat are dissolved in saliva and are carried down into the crevices between the papillae of the tongue, where they come into contact with the hairs of the taste receptors. The chemical interaction between these food substances and the taste cells depolarizes adjacent neurons, sending a nerve impulse to the brain. The same nerves that carry messages about taste also conduct information about chewing, swallowing, and the temperature and texture of food.

We experience only four primary taste qualities: sweet, sour, salt, and

(Steven Green-Armytage, Photo Researchers)

Figure 2–10
A diagram of a single taste bud.

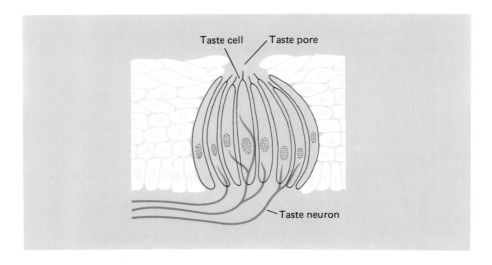

Figure 2–11
A schematic map of the tongue, showing the locations most sensitive to the four basic taste qualities.

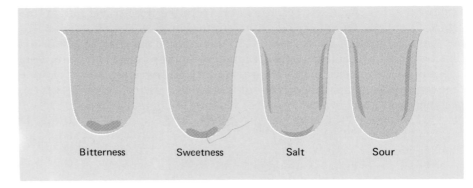

bitter. All other tastes result from combinations of these four. The tip of the tongue is most sensitive to sweetness, the front to bitterness, and the sides to sourness. The tip and sides together are most sensitive to saltiness (see Figure 2–11). But each area can distinguish all of the four qualities to some degree (Collings, 1974; McBurney & Collings, 1977). The middle of the tongue does not respond to taste at all.

Once experimenters realized that there were four primary tastes, they tried to isolate four kinds of taste receptors to match each taste. They have not succeeded. Taste seems to be coded by the overall pattern of neural firing, rather than by separate receptors for each taste. Further processing for taste may occur as the nerve impulse travels to the brain, but exactly where or how this occurs is unknown.

THE VESTIBULAR SENSE

The **vestibular sense** is the sense of equilibrium that governs the awareness of body position and movement. Birds and fish rely on it to tell them which way is up and in which direction they are headed when they cannot see well.

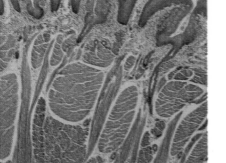

Photomicrograph of the human tongue.
(Walker, Photo Researchers)

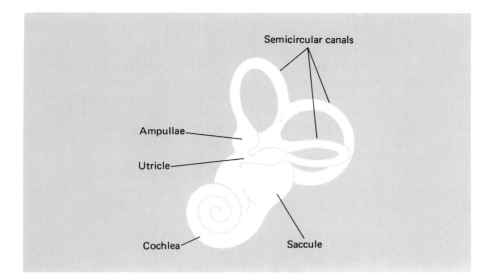

Figure 2–12
The vestibular organ.

The receptors for the vestibular sense lie in the inner ear. This sense has two subsystems—both contained in the **vestibular organ** (see Figure 2–12). The first subsystem includes three **semicircular canals,** each with an **ampulla.** Each canal is filled with fluid that shifts when the head is moved in any direction. The movement of the fluid stimulates the receptors in the ampullae—tiny hairlike projections that are pushed and pulled by the moving fluids. The hair cells stimulate the nerve cells around them to fire, sending messages about the speed and direction of bodily rotation.

The second subsystem includes the two **vestibular sacs** that lie just below the ampullae: the **utricle** and the **saccule.** Both sacs are filled with a jellylike fluid that contains tiny crystals, called **otoliths.** When the head is tipped backward or forward, or toward one side or the other, the otoliths brush against the hairs of the receptor cells. This causes the nerve cells at the base of the receptor cells to fire, sending messages about the position of the head.

The nerve impulses from both of these subsystems travel to the brain on the auditory nerve, but their ultimate destinations in the brain are not fully known. Some messages from the vestibular system go to the cerebellum, which controls many of the reflexes involved in coordinated movement. Others go to the areas of the brain that control eye movements. Still others go to the areas that send messages to the internal body organs, and some go to the cerebral cortex for analysis and response.

Occasionally, the vestibular sense is overwhelmed by the visual sense. This is what happens when we watch an automobile chase scene that is filmed from inside a moving car. We feel a sensation of movement, because our eyes are telling our brain that we are moving, even though the organs in our inner ear insist that we are sitting still.

In higher vertebrates and in humans, the vestibular system seems not to be essential for survival. People who have had one or even both vestibular organs removed seem to function normally, as long as they have visual cues and the feedback from body movements and positions on which to rely.

The vestibular sense is adapted to respond to quick and sudden movement changes—as those found on a rollercoaster ride. Why is the ride different when you close your eyes?
(R. V. Fuschetto, Photo Researchers)

PRESSURE AND TEMPERATURE

What we normally think of as the sense of touch is really several sensations: *pressure, warmth, cold,* and *pain.* All other tactile sensations result from some combination of these four. Usually messages from all these senses are combined, but it is possible to separate them and to map the areas of the skin that respond most strongly to each sense. In general, the most numerous areas are the skin areas that respond to pain, followed by those that record pressure. The least numerous are the areas that are sensitive to cold and to warmth.

Some parts of the body are more sensitive than others to all of these sensations. For example, the hands, feet, and the face (especially the lips and tongue) are much more sensitive than the back, the upper arms, or the calves of the legs. The most sensitive areas are represented in the cerebral cortex by the most fiber endings; they also seem to contain more cell bodies and nerve endings.

Many kinds of receptors have been located in the skin. At one time, physiologists confidently pointed to one receptor or another as the specific receptor for each of the four skin sensations. Studies have not revealed, however, a consistent set of relations between the various types of receptors and the separate sensations. Skin sensations may not be caused by separate receptors for each kind of stimulus, but by the rate at which these receptors fire. In other words, it may be that the way these messages are *coded* determines the sensation we feel (McBurney & Collings, 1977).

The receptors in the skin fall into three general categories: free nerve endings, basket nerve endings, and encapsulated end organs (see Figure 2–13). **Free nerve endings,** which cover most of the skin area, are found just below the surface of the skin. Free nerve endings are usually thought to be involved with the sensation of pain, but they are also probably sensitive to warmth and cold, and may even send messages about pressure.

Basket nerve endings are nerve fibers that are wrapped around the base of hairs. They are distributed over about 90 percent of the body's surface. They respond to touch or light pressure; when the hair they are entwined around is moved, they fire off a message about the intensity and direction of the touch. But also recall that some of the most sensitive areas of the body—such as the lips and the fingertips—have no hair at all, and thus no basket nerve endings.

The third general class of receptors in the skin, **encapsulated end organs,** vary in location, size, and structure. They all share one feature: a nerve fiber ending inside of some sort of capsule or shell. Most of these receptors are found quite near the surface of the skin and are responsive to pressure; some are also sensitive to temperature.

The nerve fibers from all of these receptors travel to the brain through the spinal cord. Before they reach the top of the spinal cord and enter the brain, all the nerve fibers have crossed over: Messages from the left side of the body reach the projection areas in the right cerebral hemisphere; messages from the right side of the body go to the left hemisphere.

The sense of temperature appears to depend on at least 2 kinds of receptors: those that respond to temperatures at least 1 to 2 degrees centigrade (3 to 6 degrees Farenheit) warmer than body temperature, and

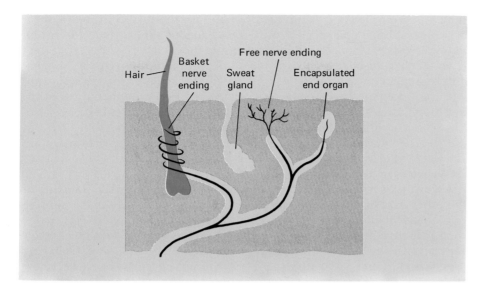

Figure 2–13
The three types of sensory receptors in the skin.

Hair
Basket nerve ending
Sweat gland
Free nerve ending
Encapsulated end organ

those that respond only to temperatures of at least 1 to 2 degrees centigrade colder than body temperature. When one set of receptors sends in messages, the brain reads them as "warm." When the other set signals, the brain reads "cold." If both sets are activated at once, the brain reads their combined pattern of firing as "hot." Thus, you might sometimes think you are touching something hot when you are really touching something warm and something cool at the same time. This phenomenon is known as **paradoxical heat.** It is easier to study cold receptors because cold receptors are easier to find. They fire constantly at about 5 to 15 impulses per second. This rate increases to over 100 impulses per second when there is a sudden drop in temperature.

PAIN

Pain differs from the other senses of touch in the extent to which people react to it. To return to our earlier example, most of us react to the pain caused by a burn by pulling our hands away. But one person may calmly run some cold water over the burn, while another may scream with pain. In other words, people *perceive* and respond to pain differently. This is the psychological component of pain. People also have differing physiological reactions to pain. For example, there is the case of a Canadian girl who felt nothing when she inadvertently bit off part of her tongue and who got third-degree burns on her knee from kneeling on a hot radiator (Baxter & Olszewski, 1960; McMurray, 1950). In contrast, some people feel extreme "spontaneous pain" when there is no apparent reason for it (see Chapter 7).

How do we explain the differences in how people respond to painful stimuli? There are three main approaches. The first stresses the actions of a specific set of nerve fibers that are responsible for conducting pain impulses. The primary pain receptors, as we mentioned above, are the networks of free nerve endings that overlap and penetrate many layers of skin. According to this approach, a painful stimulus activates several networks at once and sends several simultaneous messages to the brain. Psychologists have not found pain receptors for each type of pain, but they have recently discovered two kinds of nerve fibers that appear to carry different pain messages. One kind of fiber carries "fast, sharp, well-localized" pain messages, while another kind carries "slow, aching or burning, long-duration, and poorly localized pain" (Liebeskind & Paul, 1977).

A second approach is the pattern theory of pain. According to this theory, pain does not have its own set of special receptors. Instead, pain perception is based on the intensity of the stimulus and how the nervous system codes it (Weisenberg, 1977).

A third theory, known as the **gate-control theory,** contains elements of the other two approaches to the study of pain. It also tries to explain the psychological differences of how people experience pain. According to this theory, there is a neural "gate" mechanism in the spinal cord that controls the transmission of nerve impulses to the brain (Mulzack & Wall, 1965). The theory states that large fibers exist in the sensory nerves that can be stimulated to "close the gate" on pain by preventing the impulses from reaching the brain. There are also small fibers that react with interneurons in the spinal cord to let the pain through, or to "open the gate." Certain areas of the brainstem can also send out signals to fibers connected to the spinal cord, which can effectively block pain. Gate-control theory offers the hope that manual or electronic stimulation of the large fibers can be used to help diminish pain.

The gate-control theory also explains how pain messages can be modified considerably on their trip to the brain. Messages from the other senses can inhibit or enhance the nerve impulses from the pain receptors. Interference in the higher brain centers can also reduce, or even block, sensations of pain. For example, people under hypnosis can be made to feel no pain (Hilgard, 1969). The same principles may be important in the dramatic success of acupuncture in China (see box on p. 49).

The details of gate-control theory have been challenged by other findings, but research has also supported the idea that pain messages can be blocked by intense stimulation and that the brain can send pain-blocking signals to fibers in the spinal cord. Some of the most intriguing support comes from recent experiments on powerful painkilling drugs such as morphine and other members of the opiate family. There is evidence that these drugs do not dull the brain as you might expect; rather they stimulate parts of the brain that in turn inhibit transmission of pain impulses in the spinal cord (Levinthal, 1979).

Recent research also suggests that the brain may produce its own painkilling substances known as *enkephalins* (from the Greek for "in the head"). Enkephalins appear to reduce pain by inhibiting the neurons that transmit pain messages in the brain. Other natural painkillers are called endorphins. These are chains of amino acids that act like neurotransmitters. One endorphin was found to be 48 times more potent than morphine when injected directly into the brain, and 3 times more powerful when injected into the bloodstream (Snyder, 1977).

The discovery of natural painkilling substances raised the hope that

ACUPUNCTURE—SHUTTING THE GATE ON PAIN

Acupuncture, as most of us know, is an analgesic (or painkilling) technique. Special needles are inserted at specific sites in the body. These needles may be rotated rapidly or used to conduct mild electric currents. Although the needles are inserted in areas that are far from the area of pain, they have been shown to be effective in relieving that pain. In one documented thyroid operation, pain was relieved by inserting one needle into a site on each forearm of the patient. In another case, during an operation to remove a patient's stomach, four needles were inserted into the patient's external ears (Dimond, 1971). Unlike patients who are anesthetized during surgery, these patients are conscious and alert throughout their operations. Postsurgical pain seems to be decreased, as the pain-relieving effects last for several hours after the needles have been removed. There is also some evidence that healing after surgery is accelerated. According to Chinese tradition, acupuncture brings the yin (spirits) and the yang (blood) forces back into harmony. But why does it work?

It now seems likely that the stimulation of the nervous system that is involved in acupuncture produces a greater amount of the body's natural painkillers (enkephalins and endorphins). How do we know this? Scientists reached this conclusion when they electrically stimulated areas of the brain and found that this increased the body's production of enkephalins and endorphins and blocked the sensation of pain. By contrast drugs which inhibited the production of the body's internal painkillers also blocked the effects of acupuncture. Thus it appears that the mysterious painkilling effects of acupuncture may be understandable in terms of the release of the body's own painkilling substances (Olson et al., 1979, p. 289).

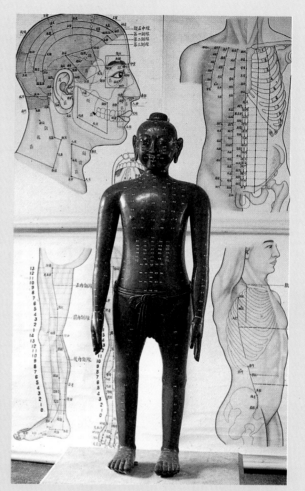

(Brian Brake, Photo Researchers)

scientists had found painkillers that would not be as addictive as the opiates. Unfortunately, this does not seem to be true. Repeated administration of these substances has produced tolerance and dependence, symptoms similar to those of drug addiction (Olson et al., 1979). The reason seems to be that while endorphins normally may inhibit pain transmission messages, the administration of artificial substances (including drugs such as morphine) causes the body to stop producing its own painkillers. As production of enkephalins and endorphins decreases, more of the outside drug is needed to replace them. When the artificial drug is cut off, the body is temporarily left with little or no natural pain-inhibiting mechanisms at all, and the drug user suffers withdrawal symptoms (Hughes et al., 1975).

The Endocrine System

The nervous system is not the only mechanism that helps to regulate the functioning of our bodies. To return to our earlier example, when we burn a hand, we quickly withdraw it from the heat. We do this by reflex because of how messages are processed by the nervous system. But our response to the burn does not end there. Instead, a complex pattern of hormonal secretions is triggered. These secretions are released automatically through internal organs called **endocrine glands.** Some of the endocrine glands are controlled by the nervous system; others respond directly to conditions inside the body. The glands that make up the **endocrine system** are the source of the chemical substances called **hormones.** Hormones, acting either singly or together, are responsible for differences in vitality among people; for the readiness of nerves and muscles to react; for the rates of metabolism, growth, and sexual development; for the body's preparations for pregnancy and childbirth; and for emotional balance in general. The endocrine glands release hormones directly into the bloodstream, which then carries them to whatever body tissues they act upon—their "target" tissues. Some hormones affect organs directly. Others act on other hormones, either increasing or canceling out their effects. Some hormones regulate the activity of many organs; others affect only one.

The endocrine system, like the nervous system, has its own specific tasks, but the two systems also work together. Their close relationship helps to maintain **homeostasis,** that is, they keep conditions inside the body

Figure 2–14
The glands of the endocrine system.

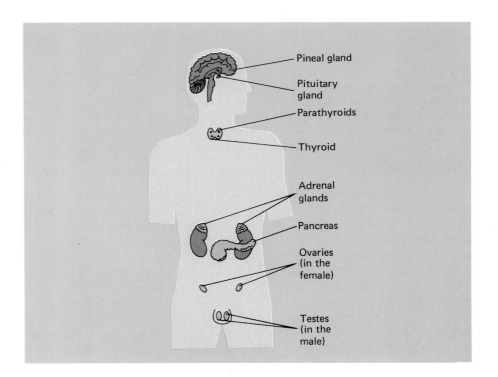

in balance so that the specialized cells can continue to function correctly.

There are many endocrine glands located throughout the body. The operations of these glands are extremely complex. Rather than discuss each gland individually, we shall focus on how the endocrine and nervous systems interact to affect hunger, thirst, and sex.

HUNGER

Laboratory experiments demonstrate that, in part, **hunger** is set in motion by a chemical imbalance in the blood. A simple sugar called **glucose** can be stored in the liver only in small quantities and for a short time. When the amount of glucose in the blood (the blood-sugar level) falls below a certain point, receptors in the nervous system are activated, signaling that you should eat and replenish your glucose supply. After eating, when the blood-sugar level has risen, the nervous system seems to "turn off" hunger. A second, long-term regulator controls the body's weight by monitoring fat stores in the body and by regulating the intake of food to provide just enough energy to maintain normal activities, without storing up excessive fat deposits (Kennedy, 1953).

For years, researchers believed that two areas of the hypothalamus worked together to monitor the blood-sugar level and the amount of body fat. Recent studies, however, have cast doubt on these beliefs, and it is no longer clear exactly where in the nervous system the monitoring occurs. But this is less important for our purposes than the fact that the endocrine system works closely with the nervous system in controlling hunger.

The amount of blood sugar is greatly affected by two hormones—insulin and glucagon—that are secreted by the pancreas, a large endocrine gland located near the stomach. When the pancreas releases insulin into the bloodstream, the blood-sugar level drops, stomach contractions start, and hunger increases. Conversely, when the pancreas releases the hormone glucagon into the bloodstream, the blood-sugar level rises, stomach contractions decrease, and hunger drops. The pancreas itself is greatly affected by the sympathetic nervous system. And two other hormones—one from the pituitary gland, the other from the adrenal gland—also affect the blood-sugar level, and are themselves affected by the nervous system and other endocrine glands.

The picture then is one of constant interaction between the nervous system, the endocrine glands, and back again to the nervous system in an intricately complex pattern that ultimately controls hunger. Of course, what people eat, and how much, is also affected by learning, by cultural influences, and by individual factors. We will look at these aspects of hunger in Chapter 9.

THIRST

The physiology of **thirst** is a little better understood than that of hunger. Thirst is controlled by two delicate balances within the body: the level of fluids outside the body's cells and the level of fluids inside the body's cells.

(Dennis Purse, Photo Researchers)

(Bruce Roberts, Photo Researchers)

Salt causes water to leave the body's cells; therefore, a high level of salt in the body causes the cells to become dehydrated. This triggers the hypothalamus, which releases antidiuretic hormone (ADH) to the pituitary or "master endocrine gland." This results in both drinking and in increased retention of the water that is already in the body.

A second thirst regulator depends on the amount of fluid *outside* the body's cells: specifically, blood flow to the kidneys and to the heart. Dehydration causes the levels of extracellular fluids to drop, and less blood flows to the kidneys and through the heart. The kidneys react by emitting the hormone renin that in turn increases the amount of another chemical, angiotensin, in the bloodstream. The bloodstream carries angiotensin to the brain, which results in our becoming thirsty. It also causes the adrenal glands (endocrine glands) to secrete the hormone aldosterone, which causes the body to retain salt.

To some extent, the two thirst controls are independent—one can be damaged without affecting the other—though normally the two regulators appear to interact and to strengthen one another. But gross interference with the hypothalamus will inactivate both mechanisms.

As with hunger, the mechanisms governing thirst are even more complex than the previous description suggests. Recent studies indicate that other chemicals besides sodium chloride are monitored by the hypothalamus. And, it appears that other parts of the brain—particularly the limbic system—are involved. Moreover, the central nervous system gets much of its information from structures controlled by the endocrine system. And of course, learned, individual, and cultural factors can also affect how we respond to thirst. We will discuss these aspects of thirst in Chapter 9.

SEX

When we look at sexual behavior, we see the clearest example of the interconnections between the nervous and endocrine systems. In animals, **sex hormones**—chiefly **testosterone** for males and **estrogen** for females—are essential to sexual behavior. Both of these hormones are present in the male and the female body, but in very different amounts. These hormones are produced by endocrine glands called **gonads**—the male **testis** and the female **ovary.** The testes also produce sperm, and the ovaries also produce the eggs necessary for sexual reproduction. Hormones are also responsible for the development of secondary sexual characteristics at adolescence, such as the deepening of the male voice, the growth of body hair, and the distribution of fat. In most species, the female is receptive to sex only at certain times—when she is *in heat,* or, in more technical language, in **estrus.** At this time, her ovaries secrete more estrogen into her bloodstream, and she is receptive to the advances of the male. Only during estrus can she become pregnant.

As we move up the evolutionary scale, hormones become less important in determining sexual behavior. While lower mammals depend more heavily on the hormonal system than on neural mechanisms, in human beings it works the other way around. The central nervous system—particularly the hypothalamus—is crucial in determining sexual behavior for both men and women, and the brain appears to regulate the interaction between hormones and neurons (Levinthal, 1979). This helps to explain why human females can be receptive to sexual arousal during the whole hormonal cycle, not just when reproduction is possible. Hormones affect women's fertility as they affect the fertility of lower animals, but the sex drive itself operates more or less independently of the hormonal fertility cycle—though women seem to be somewhat more receptive during the first half of the menstrual cycle (Rogel, 1978).

As the cerebral cortex becomes more involved in sexuality, experience and learning become more instrumental in sexual arousal and behavior. This explains not only why the human sex drive is not cyclical, but also why the stimuli that activate the sex drive are almost infinite—the phrase "soft lights and sweet music" comes to mind. The stimulus need not be the sexual partner—it can be a visual, auditory, or tactile sensation, a picture, or a fantasy. Human sexual behavior is also affected by a wide range of variables: social and sexual experience, poor nutrition, emotions (particularly one's feelings about one's sex partner), and age. We shall look more closely at these factors in Chapter 7.

We have discussed some of the components of the endocrine system that affect basic motives. There are two other important glands in this system that we should also mention. One is the **thyroid,** located just below the larynx, which produces **thyroxin,** a substance that regulates the body's metabolism rate (how fast food becomes energy). The second are the **adrenal glands,** which secrete epinephrine and norepinephrine, the transmitter substances released during stress, that we discussed earlier in this chapter.

(Edward Lettau, Photo Researchers)

Genetics

Genetics is the study of how plants, animals, and people pass traits from one generation to the next. In this context, a trait is the characteristic that is being expressed: curly hair, a crooked little finger, the inability of the blood to clot, or an allergy to poison ivy.

Gregor Mendel (1822–1884), a Moravian abbot, gave modern genetics its beginning in 1867 when he reported the results of his research on many years of systematically breeding peas. Mendel believed that every trait was controlled by elements that were transmitted from one generation to the next. He called these elements **genes.**

CELL MECHANISMS IN HEREDITY

Much more is known today about the mechanism of **heredity.** We know, for example, that within a cell nucleus genes are lined up on tiny threadlike bodies called **chromosomes,** which can be seen under a microscope. The chromosomes are arranged in pairs, and each species has its own number of pairs. Mice have 20 pairs, monkeys have 27, peas have 7. Human beings have 23 pairs of chromosomes in every normal body cell (see Figure 2–15).

When one of these normal human cells divides, each of the 46 chromosomes in the cell nucleus splits in 2. The cell matter that surrounds the nucleus also separates and the 2 new cells are exact copies of the parent cell. Each new cell contains a full set of 46 chromosomes, or 23 pairs.

When sex cells, called **gametes,** are formed, however, the chromosomes do not pair. Only one member of each pair of chromosomes goes into each gamete. Gametes thus have only 23 chromosomes, not 46. Moreover, each gamete formed has received a different and random collection of its 23 chromosomes from the original 46. When a female sex cell, an **ovum,** is fertilized by a male sex cell, a **sperm,** they form a one-celled **zygote.** Thus the zygote has 46 chromosomes: the 23 chromosomes from the mother's ovum plus the 23 chromosomes from the father's sperm.

Each set of chromosomes carries a complete set of genes. Any given gene may exist in two or more alternate forms. We can think of a gene for eye color, for example, as having one form, _B_, which will result in brown eyes and another form, _b_, which will result in blue eyes. If a boy receives _B_ genes from both parents, his eyes will be brown. If he receives _b_ genes from both parents, his eyes will be blue. But if he inherits a _B_ gene from one parent and a _b_ gene from the other, his eyes will be brown (see Figure 2–16). The _B_ form is thus said to be a **dominant gene,** and the _b_ form is called **recessive.** Although the boy with one _B_ gene and one _b_ gene has brown eyes, the recessive _b_ gene is still present and can be passed on to an offspring, who will have blue eyes if he or she also receives a _b_ gene from the other parent.

Figure 2–15
The 46 human chromosomes, separated into 23 pairs. In Down's Syndrome, or Mongolism, there are three number-21 chromosomes, as in the inset at right.

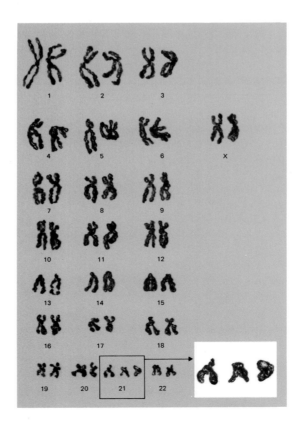

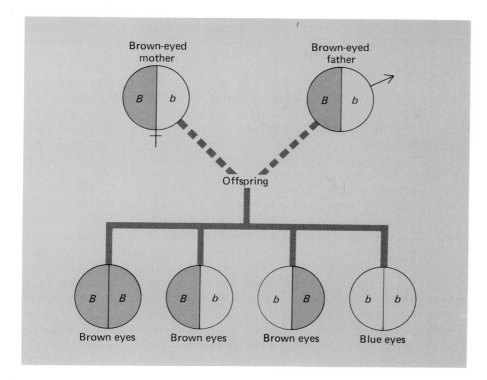

Figure 2–16
Transmission of eye color by dominant (B) and recessive (b) genes. This figure represents the four possible mixtures of eye-color genes in these parents' offspring. Since three out of the four combinations lead to brown-eyed children, the chance that any child will have brown eyes is 75 percent.

The existence of dominant and recessive genes helps to explain why a characteristic that can be seen or measured, called the **phenotype** (brown eyes, for example), may not exactly reflect a person's genetic makeup, called the **genotype**. A brown-eyed person might have *BB* or *Bb* (or *bB*) genes.

BIOCHEMICAL GENETICS

In the last 25 years our understanding of how genetic information is transmitted has greatly advanced. It is now understood that the biochemical basis for the gene is **deoxyribonucleic acid (DNA)**. The nucleus of every cell contains DNA with enough genetic coding to direct the development of one single cell into a fully grown adult with billions of cells. It is, in fact, DNA that enables a cell to reproduce exact copies of itself.

DNA also supervises the production of proteins by the cell. These proteins are the fundamental elements of all bodily substances and are the chemical middlemen that control all the basic life processes. DNA controls their manufacture by sending out molecules of **ribonucleic acid (RNA)** that carry the appropriate instructions to other parts of the cell where the proteins are produced. RNA also ensures that the necessary ingredients are available to manufacture proteins.

The discoveries of DNA and RNA help to provide a picture of how the genetic processes operate, but there is still much to be learned. Often, we do not even know which genes and chromosomes govern certain characteristics that are clearly inherited. In some situations, however, we do have specific knowledge about the effects of individual genes and chromosomes.

Behavior Genetics

While Mendel was studying plants and formulating his genetic laws, Charles Darwin (1809–1882) was collecting his world-shaking evidence on the evolution of animal species. Darwin gradually came to recognize the importance of biological inheritance in behavioral traits such as basic intelligence and athletic skills. It was his half-cousin, Francis Galton (1822–1911), however, who first attempted to explain the transmission of behavioral traits and who devised tests to measure these traits. Galton's work laid the foundations of what is known today as **behavior genetics.**

The central concern of behavior genetics is to determine the influence of heredity on behavior. How much influence heredity has on behavior forms the basis of the long-standing argument called the "nature–nurture controversy." In other words, are you the way you are because of your genes or because of your environment? Using animals other than humans, researchers have detected hereditary influences on such characteristics as general activity, willingness to explore strange environments, aggressiveness, eating habits, and territoriality.

In human behavior, psychologists have related genetics to intelligence and to disorders like **schizophrenia.** (See Chapter 13.) But we still know relatively little about the mechanisms of genetic inheritance in human beings, and here the goals of the behavior geneticists are more ambitious. They seek not only to measure heredity's effects on behavior but also to analyze chromosomes biochemically to discover how the so-called "good traits" (notably, intelligence) are determined genetically.

GENETICS AND DEVELOPMENT

One of the clearest examples of genetic determination is whether a person is male or female. In human cells, 22 of the 23 pairs of chromosomes are structurally similar and contain equal amounts of genetic information. The members of the 23rd pair, the **sex chromosomes,** are not at all similar (look again at Figure 2–15). Females have 2 equivalent **X chromosomes,** so named because they look like the letter X. Males, however, have 1 X chromosome and 1 smaller **Y chromosome,** which is named for its resemblance to the letter Y.

The genetic makeup of the father's sperm determines the sex of the offspring. The mother has only X chromosomes, but the father has Ys as well as Xs (see Figure 2–17). If the father contributes an X chromosome, the child will be a girl. If the father contributes a Y chromosome, the child will be a boy. The Y chromosome appears to contain some kind of genetic information that directs certain cells in the unborn child to become testes. The hormones produced by the testes then take over and cause the other male characteristics to develop.

The Y chromosome, however, is smaller than the X chromosome and thus cannot carry as much information. Also, it pairs with an X chromosome when the zygote is formed. This explains why several inherited conditions occur far more frequently in males than in females (where the Xs are paired). Inherited conditions that can be traced to the sex chromosomes are called **sex-linked characteristics.** Among others, they include the disease **hemophilia,** red–green color blindness, and some forms of muscular dystrophy.

This does not mean that the effects of heredity are always immediately apparent. In some cases, they become evident only as a person develops. An example is adult sexual characteristics that develop in adolescence. In these cases, we say that the genetic trait is latent; that is, having the proper genes provides a person with the potential for a trait, but that trait may not necessarily show up unless the environment cooperates. Thus, in many cases, both "nature" and "nurture" influence the realization of genetic potential. For example, a white Himalayan rabbit has genetic potential for black paws, but they will become black only if the rabbit is raised in a cold environment. Raising the rabbit in a warm environment keeps its paws white (Sinnott, Dunn, & Dobzhansky, 1958).

We have been talking about some characteristics that are caused by specific genes carried on the X or the Y chromosome. But most of our characteristics—unlike hemophilia or color blindness—cannot be traced this easily. With other traits—intelligence and height, for instance—most of us fall somewhere in the middle of a continuum. Most traits, in other words, are not characteristics that can be traced back to a single gene.

To understand the genetic transmission of most human traits, we must introduce the concept of **polygenic inheritance.** Most human traits are determined by the interaction of several separate genes. The reverse is also

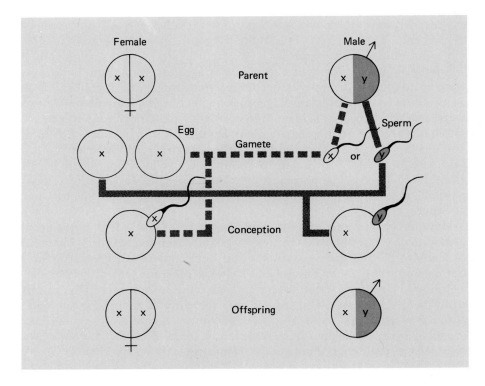

Figure 2–17
Sex is determined by the X and Y chromosomes. Females inherit two X chromosomes; males inherit one X and one Y.

(Van Bucher, Photo Researchers)

true—one gene can sometimes affect many traits. The genes that contribute to a particular polygenic trait may all be located on the same chromosome, or they may be spread over several chromosomes. Each gene in a polygenic system appears to act independently, as do the genes that "single-handedly" control a specific trait. But instead of having an all-or-none effect, each of the genes in a polygenic system makes a small contribution to the trait in question. Like the instruments in a symphony orchestra, each contributing a separate note to the sound that reaches the audience, the genes in a polygenic system have a cumulative effect.

It is thus more difficult to study polygenic inheritance than it is to trace the origins of traits that are determined by single genes. Complicated statistical techniques have been developed to analyze the effects of large numbers of genes acting together in a polygenic system. But we also have to account for the effects of the environment on how a trait develops.

How can psychologists decide whether heredity is a major determinant of some trait? One way to approach the problem of the **heritability** of a trait in humans is through the study of twins. All **identical twins,** so-called because they develop from the division of a single fertilized ovum, are identical in genetic makeup. Any differences between them should, therefore, be due to environmental differences. **Fraternal twins,** however, develop from two separate fertilized egg cells and have no more in common genetically than other brothers and sisters. The differences between fraternal twins are thus due both to genetics and environment.

The most significant studies involving comparisons of twins have concerned the heritability of schizophrenia. As we mentioned earlier, schizophrenia seems to be strongly influenced by genetic factors. In a classic American study of 1,000 pairs of twins (Kallman, 1953), it was found that where one fraternal twin was schizophrenic, the other was schizophrenic in 69 percent of the cases. Thus, there is good reason to conclude that schizophrenia is highly heritable.

Another way to study trait heritability is to study whole family groups. Here again there is strong evidence for a genetic basis for schizophrenia. In cases where both parents are schizophrenic, between 45 and 68 percent of their children are also schizophrenic. Where neither parent is schizophrenic, only 5 to 10 percent of their children have the disorder. Such findings (as opposed to those involving identical twins) do not rule out the role of environment. Growing up in a household in which a parent and both grandparents are schizophrenic might cause a child to become schizophrenic, even if the child does not have the genetic potential for that disorder.

How can we more clearly isolate the influence of household atmosphere in studies of schizophrenia? One way is to study adopted children. If a child of a schizophrenic parent is adopted at birth and raised thereafter in a normal home, is that child more or less likely to become schizophrenic than an adopted child whose natural parents are not schizophrenic? One recent study located 47 people who had schizophrenic mothers but who had been adopted at birth. Of these 47, 5 had become schizophrenic. In another group of people who had been adopted at birth, but who did not have schizophrenic parents, there was no schizophrenia at all (Heston, 1966). Thus, although schizophrenia is highly heritable, both heredity and environment determine whether this trait will be displayed. Studies of biological and adoptive families have also suggested that chronic alcoholism and suicide—two phenomena that would at first appear to be tightly linked to environmental influences—seem to have a strong genetic factor. This might help to explain why everyone who drinks does not become an alcoholic, and why only a few people turn to suicide when they despair (Kety, 1979).

GENETIC ABNORMALITIES

Since the sequence of events that governs genetic transmission is very complex, it is amazing that there are not more mistakes. A few do occur. Sometimes when a gamete is formed—long before fertilization may occur—one or more of the chromosome pairs fails to separate normally. One of the ovum or sperm cells might get both members of the chromosome pair, while the other new gamete gets neither. Or a chromosome may break as it is splitting. The part that is broken off may migrate mistakenly to one of the new cells, where it will become extra genetic material. The other cell formed at the same time will lack this crucial piece of chromosomal material. If one of these abnormal gametes is later involved in fertilization, the resulting organism will be defective, if it survives at all. Such genetic abnormalities, when they survive, disrupt the biochemical processes in the organism; this, in turn, affects the organism's behavior.

(Harvey Stein).

One such abnormality is called **Down's syndrome,** or mongolism. People with this condition are severely retarded; intelligence quotients (IQs) usually range from 20 to 60.* Distinctive physical features—slanted eyes and flattened facial contours—are the reason for the term mongolism. The condition has been traced to the chromosome pair that is usually numbered 21. Those born with Down's syndrome have inherited more than the 2 normal members of this chromosome pair—sometimes a complete 3rd chromosome (as in Figure 2–15), sometimes just an extra fragment of chromosome–21 material.

Sex chromosomes can also be inherited abnormally. One example is the male genetic makeup XYY, where an extra male chromosome is carried. For a time, some researchers believed that this might cause the inheritance of criminal tendencies, since studies among prison inmates turned up many XYYs. Many psychologists question the link between the XYY genetic makeup and antisocial behavior, mainly because of the small number of nonprisoners that have been studied so far. The social consequences are such that these psychologists want to wait for more research before they conclude anything about the effects that an XYY genetic makeup may have on behavior.

SOCIAL IMPLICATIONS OF BEHAVIOR GENETICS

Science is not simply a process that takes place in a lab; instead, it has widespread effects on society at large. The implications of research in

*The average IQ for normal people is around 100. For more details about IQ, see Chapter 10.

(Timothy Eagan, Woodfin Camp & Associates)

behavior genetics are particularly important, because the findings may affect our evolution as a species. If we know that certain mental or physical deficiencies are largely hereditary, should society take steps to avert "more of the same"? If scientists could demonstrate a genetic influence for genius, should society try to breed only geniuses?

Eugenics is the science of improving a species through restrictive or selective breeding. This is a common practice among animal breeders all over the world. Eugenic measures relating to human breeding have long been practiced in the United States. The first law for the sterilization of the feebleminded was passed in Indiana in 1907. When this law was first applied, Judge Oliver Wendell Holmes defended it, saying that such sterilization would make it possible for society to "prevent those who are manifestly unfit from continuing their kind" (Buck vs. Bell, 274 U.S. 200, p. 207, cited in McClearn & DeFries, 1973, pp. 267–268). But who decides which traits make a person "manifestly unfit"? The moral dilemma that results and examples such as the *genocide* practiced by Nazi Germany have combined to make "eugenics" a dirty word for most people. Some scientists also feel that there are dangers involved in manipulating basic evolutionary processes. An international conference of biologists recently advised restrictions on some kinds of genetic research (McElheny, 1975).

There are however, positive aspects to eugenics, or *genetic engineering*. In only the past decade, progress in biochemistry and medicine—in birth control, artificial insemination, organ transplants, prenatal sex determination—has been breathtaking. By informing parents of possible risks, genetic counselors can help couples who are concerned about passing on problem traits to their children.

Certainly, any scientific research may be abused. But the issues of behavior genetics are being brought to the attention of the government and the general public at a time when most research is still at the one-celled-animal level. The issues raised by behavior genetics are moral, legal, and political, as well as scientific. And if these issues receive attention at the same time that scientific research is progressing, the chances are great that we will use the knowledge wisely and effectively.

Application

CLONING

In Woody Allen's movie *Sleeper*, doctors look on as a nervous Woody Allen and an equally nervous Diane Keaton pretend they are about to perform a delicate operation. The year is 2073. The leader of a frightening, totalitarian society has been killed in an explosion, but his faithful followers have managed to salvage his nose. The nose now lies on the operating table, ready to be cloned. This involves removing a cell from the nose, and letting it divide and grow until it produces an

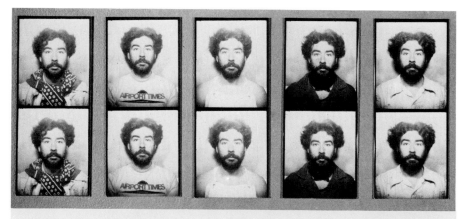

(Credit: Herman Costa)

exact copy of the dead leader. Fortunately for Allen and Keaton, the nose is destroyed before this can be accomplished.

Science fiction? Yes . . . and no. Cloning, which comes from the Greek word for *twig*, is performed by removing a cell or cell nucleus from one organism and activating this cell so that it grows into a duplicate of the organism from which it was taken. When you take a cutting from a plant and root it in water, you are actually cloning a new plant. But cloning animals is another story. Early experiments succeeded in cloning frogs, but scientists only recently succeeded in cloning the first mammals—three mice. Dr. Karl Illmensee and Dr. Peter C. Hoppe performed the experiment at the University of Geneva. They took the nuclei from embryonic mouse cells and implanted them in recently fertilized mouse eggs from which the original nuclei had been removed. The embryos had developed in eggs taken from black mice, but the donor embryos were from two different strains of mice—gray and agouti, the color of wild mice. The newly doctored cells were then cultured for several days until they began to divide. Then 16 of these newly divided cells, along with 44 white mouse embryos that had not received nuclear transplants, were implanted in 5 female white mice. These white mouse embryos were included so that the size of the litter would be normal. The foster mothers gave birth to a total of 35 mice. Of these, 32 were white. Of the other 3, 2 were gray, and 1 was agouti.

Revolutionary as this experiment was, technically it was not cloning. In true cloning, two or more identical animals must be produced. But the distinction is very fine, and it is possible that by the time you read this, "true clones" will have been produced in mice.

To all intents and purposes, however, the experiment was a success, and it has given rise to worldwide concern and controversy. If frogs and mice can be cloned, are human beings next? The prospect of human cloning raises a host of political and ethical issues. Who would be selected, and why? What would we do about the threat of misuse—governments could clone masses of obedient workers, those with enough money could clone themselves, and sinister plots to reproduce a line of tyrants like Hitler could endanger the entire world.

And there would be other problems. What about the "right to life" of transplants that did not turn out to be normal? Perhaps most importantly, however, cloning challenges our most cherished beliefs about the family and the individual. Would clones be treated "like everyone else," or would they be considered freaks and curiosities? And what would happen to the nuclear family when parents could produce children without sex or pregnancy?

One scientist, Kafatos, has already called for a ban on further experiments. Like other observers, he believes that the time to examine the social, political, and ethical issues raised by the possibility of cloning is *before* we start such experiments with human beings (Marx, 1981). But many scientists believe that it is too soon to raise these issues. Human cloning, they believe, is highly unlikely, primarily because of the way the genetic information in our cells is coded. At first, this material is undifferentiated. In a sense, we are all clones during the first stages of our development. But as the cells continue to divide and develop into an embryo, they begin to specialize. Only the part of the genetic code that is needed to produce each part of the body remains active. One group of cells begins to form an elbow, another forms a liver, and still another forms the big toe. The rest of the genetic material in the nucleus of each of the millions of cells is "switched off."

To clone a human being, scientists would have to get hold of a cell that has not yet "switched off" the genetic instructions that make it possible to duplicate an entire human being. But most experts agree that by the time we are adults—or perhaps even a long time before birth—the genetic information is already irreversibly committed to specialization. Scientists have found that frogs may be cloned fairly successfully when the nucleus is taken from a very young embryo. But by the next embryonic stage, there is only a 15 to 20 percent chance of success. And no one has successfully cloned any adult animal by transplanting a nucleus taken from another adult.

Cell specialization is not the only obstacle to human cloning. Since we know that environment plays a very important role in personality development, we would have to duplicate not only a person's genetic makeup, but also his or her *environment*—an impossible feat. For example, Dr. Lewis Thomas asks us to imagine that we want to clone a prominent diplomat to oversee future problems in the Middle East (Thomas, 1979). To duplicate his environment, we would have to clone his parents; in fact, we would somehow have to step back in time and clone his parents as they were when he was a small child. We would also have to clone his brothers and sisters, teachers and playmates, and all his acquaintances. And then, to make sure that they were exactly as they had been when they influenced the personality of our diplomat, we would have to clone everyone who was important in *their* environment. In short, says Thomas, we would have to clone the whole world.

In other words, the possibility that noses will be used to duplicate dictators is very remote. Instead, Thomas advises us to take a different tack altogether. "Look for ways to get mutations more quickly, new variety, different songs. Fiddle around, if you must fiddle, but never with ways to keep things the same, no matter who, not even yourself. Heaven, somewhere ahead, has got to be a change" (Thomas, p. 56).

Summary

1. The body's two major coordinating mechanisms are the *nervous system,* which uses electrical messages, and the *endocrine system,* which uses chemical messages.

2. The nervous system is made up of *neurons* that are specialized to receive and transmit information. Neurons have tiny fibers called *dendrites* and a single long fiber called an *axon* extending out from the cell body. A *nerve* is a group of axons bundled together.

3. *Sensory* (or afferent) neurons carry information to the spinal cord or to the brain. *Motor* (or efferent) neurons carry messages from the spinal cord or the brain to the muscles and glands. *Interneurons* (association neurons) make the connection between incoming and outgoing messages. Interneurons account for 99.98 percent of all the neurons in the central nervous system.

4. Neurons conduct electrochemical impulses called *action potentials.* When a neuron is resting, its cell membrane keeps it in a state of *polarization,* with positive ions on the outside and negative ions on the inside. When sodium ions flow into the neuron and depolarize the whole length of the neuron, the process will cause the neuron to fire. The incoming message must be above a certain *threshold* to cause a nerve impulse. Otherwise, the *graded potential* will fade away, leaving the neuron in its normal polarized state. The number of neurons firing at any given moment and the number of times they fire affect the complexity of the message.

5. Axons with myelinated sheaths conduct impulses more rapidly than those without myelin sheaths.

6. Near its end, the axon branches out into numerous fibers, each of which has a tiny *axon terminal* at its end. A minute gap, called a *synaptic space* or *synaptic cleft,* separates the end of each terminal from the next neuron. A synapse is made up of the axon terminal, synaptic cleft, and dendrite of the next neuron. For the average neuron, there are about 1,000 synapses. When the neural impulse reaches the end of an axon, it causes tiny sacs called synaptic vesicles to release a chemical substance, which then travels across the gap and causes the next neuron to fire.

7. The *peripheral nervous system* consists of nerves that connect the brain and spinal cord to *receptors* (cells in the sense organs) and *effectors* (cells in the muscles and glands).

8. The *autonomic nervous system* (a division of the peripheral nervous system) is composed of the *sympathetic* and *parasympathetic* divisions. The sympathetic division directs the body to respond to stress. The parasympathetic division directs the body to settle down after a period of stress.

9. The *central nervous system* is made up of the brain and spinal cord. The spinal cord is a complex cable of nerves that connects the brain to most of the rest of the body. It carries messages to and from the brain and controls certain reflex movements.

10. At its upper end the spinal cord enlarges and merges into the *brainstem,* which supports the other parts of the brain above it.

11. The *hindbrain* consists of the *medulla,* which controls breathing and many other reflexes, and which is the place where many of the nerves from the higher parts of the brain cross; the *pons* is a pathway for those nerves that connect the cerebral cortex at the top of the brain to the *cerebellum,* which handles certain reflexes and coordinates the body's movements.

12. The *midbrain* is especially important to hearing and sight. The midbrain is also one of several places in the brain where pain is registered.

13. The *forebrain* is composed of the *thalamus,* which acts as a relay station for messages from the sense receptors and for messages from one part of the cerebral cortex to another, controlling the activities of the autonomic nervous system; the *hypothalamus,* which influences many kinds of motivation and emotional behavior; and the *cerebral cortex.*

14. The two *hemispheres* of the cerebral cortex are responsible for different functions. The left hemisphere controls the right side of the body, the right hemisphere controls the left. Each controls different skills as well. The left hemisphere is verbal and analytical. The right hemisphere is artistic and good in spatial abilities.

15. The various functions of the cerebral cortex are performed in the *sensory projection areas,* where messages from the sense receptors are registered; in the *motor projection areas,* where messages to the muscles and glands originate; and in the *association areas,* which are involved in the higher mental processes like thinking, learning, remembering, and talking.

16. The *reticular activating system* is made up of a netlike bundle of neurons that runs through the hindbrain, midbrain, and part of the forebrain. Its primary function is to filter incoming messages and alert higher parts of the brain if a message is important.

17. The *limbic system,* a ring of structures in the center of each cerebral hemisphere, plays an important role in learning, memory, and emotional behavior.

18. *Psychosurgery* and *electrical stimulation of the brain (ESB)* at-

tempt to change behavior through direct physical manipulation of the brain.

19. Receptor cells for the sense of smell are located in the *olfactory epithelium*, high in the nasal cavity. Airborne molecules activate these specialized neurons, which then carry the messages directly to the brain.

20. The receptor cells for the sense of taste lie in the taste buds on the tongue. Each taste bud contains a cluster of taste receptors, or hair cells, that cause their adjacent neurons to fire when they become activated by the chemical substances in food. We experience only four primary taste qualities—sweet, sour, salt, and bitter—and these combine to form all other tastes.

21. The *vestibular sense* tells us what position we are in with respect to gravity. The receptors for this sense are located in the vestibular organ in the inner ear.

22. The receptors in the skin fall into three general categories. *Free nerve endings* are found just below the surface of the skin and are traditionally thought to be involved in the sensation of pain, but may also play a role in sensations of warmth and cold and, perhaps, even pressure. The *basket nerve ending* wraps around the base of a hair and responds to touch or light pressure. In *encapsulated end organs* a nerve fiber ends inside some sort of capsule or shell. The nerve fibers from all these different receptors travel to the brain through the spinal cord, crossing at various points so that messages from the left side of the body reach the right cerebral hemisphere, and vice versa.

23. The sense of temperature depends on two sets of receptors: one set for warmth and one for cold. If both sets are activated at the same time, the brain reads their combined pattern of firing as hot. This is known as *paradoxical heat*.

24. Pain is subject to more individual interpretation than the other senses. There are three approaches to the theory of pain. One approach maintains that the primary pain receptors are the free nerve endings, which act in networks to send messages to the brain. The second approach is the pattern theory, which maintains that pain perception is based on the intensity of the stimulus and the way the nervous system codes it.

25. A third approach to pain, which has elements of the other two theories, is called *gate-control theory*. According to this theory, our pain-signaling system contains a gatelike mechanism which, depending on the level of activity in large fibers, may be open, partially open, or closed. If the gate is closed, no pain message will get through to the brain and there will be no sensation of pain. The exact mechanism proposed by gate-control theory appears to have been disproved, but its basic principles have been successfully applied in the area of pain research.

26. *Enkephalins* and *endorphins* reduce pain by inhibiting the firing of neural pain impulses to the brain. Acupuncture therapy seems to

work by chemically stimulating the release of these substances, which then block pain impulses.

27. The *endocrine system* is made up of internal organs called glands, which secrete chemical substances called hormones directly into the bloodstream. Along with the nervous system, the endocrine system contributes to *homeostasis*, the keeping in balance of conditions inside the body so that other cells can continue to function correctly.

28. *Physiological motives*, also called *primary drives*, are activated by certain physiological states, such as the need for food, water, and sex.

29. Hunger is the result of a complex interaction between the nervous system and the endocrine glands.

30. Thirst is controlled by the level of fluids outside and inside of the body's cells. Thirst results from the interaction of the endocrine glands, the kidneys, and the nervous system.

31. *Sexual motivation* is first and foremost a physiological drive. The role of hormones in the human sex drive, however, is minimal compared with the importance of learning and experience. Learning and experience influence both the stimuli that elicit the drive and the behavior that results.

32. *Genetics* is the study of how traits are passed on from one generation to the next. *Genes* are the basic elements of heredity. They exist in the nucleus of every living cell and are lined up on tiny threadlike bodies called *chromosomes*, which are arranged in pairs.

33. Each gene may exist in two or more alternate forms and may be *dominant* or *recessive*. Because of dominant and recessive genes, a person's *genotype*, his or her underlying genetic makeup, can differ from his or her *phenotype*, the characteristics that can be seen or measured.

34. *Deoxyribonucleic acid—DNA—*forms the biochemical base of the gene. DNA controls the cell's production of proteins by manufacturing molecules of *ribonucleic acid—RNA—*that carry the DNA's instructions to other parts of the cell, where proteins are manufactured.

35. *Behavior genetics* explores the relationships between heredity and behavior. Some issues examined by behavior geneticists are the inheritance of sex characteristics, intelligence, and schizophrenia.

36. Sex is determined by the X and Y chromosomes. A female receives an X chromosome from each parent; a male receives one X (from his mother) and one Y (from his father). *Sex-linked characteristics*, such as hemophilia, a red–green color blindness, and certain forms of muscular dystrophy occur far more frequently in males than in females. This is because the smaller Y chromosome does not contain the dominant gene needed to cancel out the X chromosome's recessive gene for that characteristic.

37. Most traits, like intelligence and height, are transmitted by *polygenic inheritance*. Several genes interact to produce the trait, each one making a small contribution. Thus most traits are seen to be part of a continuum.

38. *Genetic abnormalities*, such as Down's syndrome, occur when one or more of the chromosomes fail to separate normally.

39. *Eugenics*, the science of improving a species through selective breeding, raises important social issues. Although animals have been bred eugenically for centuries, there is no systematic eugenics program applied to humans because of the racial and political overtones involved, and because of the moral dilemma involved by who decides which traits are good and which are bad.

Outline

Chapter 3

Childhood

An old king, realizing that his end was near, summoned his three sons to his bedside. "My sons," said the dying monarch, "I must decide which among you is to inherit my kingdom. I will ask each of you one question, and this is it: If you could spend your childhood over again, how would you spend it?"

The first son sprang forward. "I would spend it with reckless abandon!" he said. "Childhood is the only time we are not held accountable for the consequences of our actions."

The second son regarded his brother reproachfully. "I would not spend it at all," he said. "I would save it carefully until I grew old enough to appreciate it fully."

"And you, my son?" said the aged ruler to his third son. "If you could spend your childhood over again, how would you spend it?"

"I would neither spend it foolishly nor hoard it selfishly," said the third son. "I would invest it in the pursuit of love, knowledge, and experience so that my later years might reap the dividends."

"Truly, such a wise answer should not go unrewarded," said the king. "The kingdom shall be yours."

If each of us were asked to answer the old king's question, our responses would be varied and would reflect our individual experiences from our earliest moments of life to the present day. We may remember our childhood with fondness or with regret—or we may hardly remember it at all. Yet none of us can deny the importance and the seeming miracle of childhood: When it ends, a helpless infant should have acquired most of the capabilities of an adult.

Developmental psychology is the study of that miracle and more: It is the study of human growth and experience, from the time we were carried in our mothers' wombs to our deaths. In this chapter, we discuss what psychologists have learned about human development in childhood. In Chapter 4, we examine **adolescence** and **adulthood**.

Methods and Issues in Developmental Psychology

In Chapter 1, we discussed the three basic methods used to study human behavior: the naturalistic-observation method, the correlational method, and the experimental method. When psychologists study how people develop, they may use any or all of these methods.

Suppose, for example, that a psychologist was investigating how children's home environments influence their intelligence. Using the first method, a psychologist might go to children's homes and observe how the children and their parents interact. To do a correlational study, a psychologist might simply have the parents answer a questionnaire about home environment, about how they behave with their children, and so on. The psychologist could then correlate these responses with the children's IQ scores. In the experimental method, a psychologist might split a group of children into two groups. Let us say that for a year one group would be placed during the day in a special, enriched environment, designed to promote high IQ scores. The other group would receive no special treatment at all. At the end of the year a psychologist would then test both groups' IQ scores and compare the results.

The results of these methods by themselves might not satisfy a developmental psychologist. Although they might show how different kinds of experiences may relate to IQ scores, much of developmental psychology is concerned with how people change as they age. To study such changes, psychologists use two methods. In the first method, the longitudinal method, the researcher studies a fixed group of people through a period of time. The same people are observed, interviewed, or tested at several ages. In our example, this might mean studying IQ scores of the same people at ages 4, 12, 20, and 60. In the second method, the cross-sectional method, a sample of people of different ages is selected and studied at one point in time. Then comparisons are made between the different age groups. Again, in our hypothetical study, this might mean comparing IQ scores of 4-year-olds with 12-year-olds, and so on.

Each of these methods is useful for studying developmental issues; hence, psychologists often use data gathered from all of them. These *converging data* can then be combined to provide a much fuller picture than any one method could give (Liebert, 1974).

Besides using various methods to study human **development,** psychologists often approach their studies from varying points of view. For example, some developmental psychologists are interested in the ages at which stages of development occur. Others are more concerned with why or how development takes place. The first group would be interested in *when* children begin to speak. The second group would be more interested in *how* children learn to speak. Some psychologists emphasize the importance of heredity, while others stress experience or environmental influences. Some see change as abrupt and discontinuous; others view development as a gradual, continuous process. In this chapter and in the next, we shall see how these differing viewpoints come into play as we discuss various aspects of human development from infancy through adulthood.

(Bruce Roberts, Photo Researchers)

Prenatal Development

During the earliest period of prenatal (before birth) development, survival is the most important issue. Immediately after conception, the fertilized egg divides many times, beginning the process that will change it from a one-celled organism into a highly complex human being. The cell ball implants itself in the uterus. Around it grows a placenta, which carries food to it and waste products from it as the organism grows. In time, the major organ systems and physical features develop. If all goes well, by the end of this stage of development the organism is recognizably human and is now called a fetus. The fetal period begins in the 8th week after conception and lasts until birth. (It is usually early in this period that a woman discovers that she is pregnant.) The important role of this period is the preparation of the fetus for independent life.

THE PRENATAL ENVIRONMENT

At one time, scientists thought that the development of the child before birth was limited to the processes of growth and heredity. They thought that it was only at birth that experience and learning began to influence development. Today, we know that prenatal development is a complex process and that the unborn baby is profoundly affected by its environment. Developmental psychologists are now studying development before birth very closely.

From the 2nd week after conception until birth, the baby is linked to its mother, and thus to the outside world, through the placenta. Many changes in the mother's body chemistry, whether as a result of nutrition, drugs, disease, or prolonged stress or excitement, affect the fetus directly through the placenta. A selective biological barrier does keep certain substances in the mother's body from reaching the fetus, but it does not provide as much protection as the fetus really needs.

Good nutrition is at least as important for the fetus as it is for us, yet malnutrition is a worldwide problem. Although malnutrition is especially widespread in the developing countries, even in the United States the diets of expectant mothers are often inadequate. In the prenatal period, the physical effects of malnutrition can have profound psychological effects on the fetus. Seriously deprived babies may be born with smaller brains and bodies than the well-nourished. If infants have been malnourished both before and after birth, their brains may be 60 percent smaller than normal (Wyden, 1971). This, in turn, can extensively affect many psychological processes. Children who are deprived of protein during the fetal period often score lower on IQ tests than children whose mothers supplied them with an adequate diet. These lower scores indicate impaired intellectual functioning, damage that is usually difficult or impossible to repair.

Besides malnutrition, drugs pose a particular threat to the unborn child. If the mother is a heavy drinker, her baby may be born mentally retarded, be unusually small and slow to develop, and may suffer from other serious

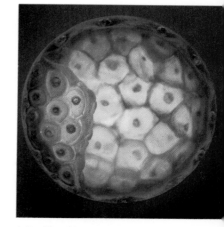

A fertilized human egg, shortly after conception when it has divided many times.
(Russ Kinne, Photo Researchers)

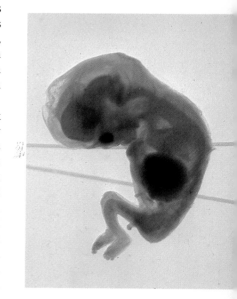

This 2-month-old human fetus can be affected by changes in its mother's body.
(Tom McHugh, Photo Researchers)

PARENTS AND PREGNANCY

(Edward Lettan, Photo Researchers)

It is not only the unborn child who changes during its 9 months in the womb. Parents, too, are affected by the experience of expecting a child. The most obvious effects are on the mother. Besides the physiological changes of pregnancy, women must cope with emotional and social changes. The pregnant woman looks different and feels different—and people often treat her differently, too. She may suddenly be treated as if she were fragile or "special." Some women must adjust their careers to fit the new reality, and they may be anxious about the other life changes that having a child will entail: in their marriages, financial status, and personal freedom. If this emotional stress is unusually heavy or prolonged, it can make pregnancy a difficult time for the mother.

For fathers, too, pregnancy is a time of emotional change. Some men feel "shut out" by their wives' new preoccupation. And men, too, worry about financial burdens, whether they will be good parents, and whether their children will be healthy and strong.

How great a problem pregnancy is, of course, varies from one set of parents to another. Some people seem to be able to cope with it much better than others. This may be the result of class and social norms as much as individual differences in personality and character. In the Victorian era, for example, pregnancy was one of the great social taboos. Pregnant women were not expected to be seen in public once their condition became obvious. The use of the word "pregnant" was itself frowned upon. Polite persons spoke of a woman's "delicate condition" or said that she was *enceinte* (the French word for pregnant; one wonders what word polite Frenchmen used).

Yet this behavior was limited to the middle and upper classes. Working-class women were expected to take pregnancy in their stride, to work right up to the birth of their child, and to be up and about very soon afterward. Economic necessity demanded it. Of course, these rigid social norms ignored the fact that there were many robust "ladies" and fragile laundresses. But society expected different behaviors from each class, and people usually struggled to conform to them. Today, we recognize to some degree that pregnancy *is* a delicate time for all parents with varying, but significant effects.

abnormalities (Segal, 1973; Warner & Rossett, 1975). If the mother is a heavy user of narcotics, her baby may be born addicted to them and may experience withdrawal symptoms right after birth. If she smokes heavily, the baby may be underdeveloped and may be born prematurely.

Certain diseases can also injure the fetus, particularly early in pregnancy. German measles (rubella) is especially dangerous. It can lead to eye damage, heart malformations, deafness, and mental retardation. Other diseases, such as syphilis and diabetes, can also produce serious defects in the fetus. To bear a healthy child, a prospective mother must maintain a balanced diet high in protein, avoid the use of any drugs (including prescription drugs) without a doctor's supervision, and shun exposure to communicable diseases.

Moreover, as we mentioned earlier, prolonged stress or excitement on the part of the mother can directly affect the health of the fetus. Maternal stress and its effects on the fetus were studied during World War II. Sontag (1944) found that pregnant women who were afraid, anxious, or angry had babies with higher heart rates and digestive problems, including an intolerance for certain foods. Moreover, many of these babies weighed less at birth and were hyperactive for weeks or months.

The protection given the fetus by the placenta helps to ensure that most babies will survive the prenatal period without serious problems. In most cases, the protective systems do work, and a healthy baby is born.

CHILDBIRTH

The view that the real business of development begins only after a baby is born overlooked not only the effects of prenatal environment but also the effects of childbirth itself. Modern Western medicine has done much to decrease the risks of childbirth for both mother and baby, but some people feel that the usual hospital procedure is an impersonal and even harsh atmosphere—for the mother *and* for the child.

According to the French obstetrician Frederick Leboyer, birth is traumatic for the infant: the glaring lights, the sudden harsh voices, the swift cutting of the umbilical cord, the doctor's traditional slap on the baby's bottom. In *Birth Without Violence* (1975), Leboyer proposed that the delivery room be dimly lit and that everyone keep silent to avoid shocking the baby, who has been accustomed only to the quiet dark of the womb. After birth, the baby should be placed on the mother's stomach and gently massaged (by mother and doctor) for 4 or 5 minutes; only then should the umbilical cord be severed. The child is then bathed in a basin of warm water where, Leboyer says, he is "free as in the distant good old days of pregnancy when he could play, move around in a boundless ocean. What might have remained of fear, stiffness, tension now melts away like snow in the sunshine" (p. 113).

These few minutes after delivery are all that distinguishes Leboyer's method from standard obstetrical practice. All the resources of modern medicine are available should an emergency arise, and the mother's care during pregnancy and after delivery follows conventional guidelines.

Despite this, the French medical community has been unsympathetic to his method, and American doctors seem to be equally skeptical. Some obstetricians have charged Leboyer with unmedical foolishness, even with quackery. Others claim his ideas are medically dangerous. Undue delay in cutting the umbilical cord could invite infection, and a "good hearty scream" helps to assure proper breathing. But other doctors, like Fernand Lamaze (1970) and Grantly Dick-Read (1953), have also been concerned about providing the baby with a gentle welcome, though their methods are not as extreme as Leboyer's. They advocate *natural childbirth.* In this method, the mother (and often the father) prepare for the delivery, as little medication as possible is used, and the mother participates in the birth.

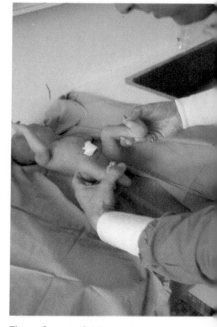

The reflexes of this newborn baby are being tested. Some psychologists believe that the traditional delivery and the hospital environment are traumatic for the newborn.
(Richard Frieman, Photo Researchers)

(Catherine Ursillo, Photo Researchers)

Since the mother is trained to use breathing and muscular control to help during labor, the baby is often born more quickly and more safely than if drugs were used and the mother anesthetized and unable to help during delivery.

Unlike Leboyer's method, natural childbirth lets the father be part of the process by attending preparation classes with his wife; by learning about what is happening to her; and, often, by being present during the delivery itself. Many couples report that the experience is emotionally fulfilling and rewarding.

No matter which method of childbirth is used, from the moment a baby is born an attachment forms between the mother and the child. Studies have suggested that the more physical contact a mother has with her baby during the hours and days after birth, the closer the attachment will be (Kennell et al., 1975; Ringler et al., 1978). Since both the Leboyer method and natural childbirth help increase contact between mother and child, it is likely that these methods serve to strengthen this vital attachment.

Our childhood is longer than that of any other species, mainly because we are less well-equipped for life than animals are when we are born. For many animals, development occurs mainly in the womb, and the young are able to become self-sufficient in a short time. In contrast, the bulk of human development occurs after we are born.

For the first few weeks, newborn babies sleep as much as 20 hours a day, waking only when they are hungry, uncomfortable, or startled. Their bodies even give signs of dreaming: rapid eye movements, tremors, and sudden jerks. Within a few days, they begin to follow moving objects with their eyes and even seem to prefer brightly colored and patterned objects.

Although they are relatively insensitive to external pain, such as the prick of a diaper pin, newborn babies are acutely aware of internal discomfort, such as hunger. They react negatively to strong smells, but do not seem to find some odors pleasant and others disgusting, as adults do.

The only emotion newborns express directly is general excitement, usually shown by tearless crying and thrashing about. Hunger, pain, and fear all bring on the same response. Infant crying varies in intensity, but not in content or style. When warm and full, newborn babies smile with pleasure. They may also smile because of gas pains. But they do not smile in a social way, in response to other people, for a while. Newborn babies recognize neither their mothers, nor their fathers, nor even their own feet. They are completely at the mercy of their own bodies and of those who care for them.

Left lying in their cribs, newborns are helpless. They can neither lift their heads nor turn over by themselves, and they show no interest in reaching out for pretty things dangling nearby. When someone picks up a newborn, however, the baby begins searching for a nipple, grasping the adult with surprising strength. **Rooting behavior,** as this is called, is a reflex that directs babies toward the food they need.

Another reflex that is crucial for the infant's survival is **sucking.** Shortly after birth, newborns will suck on anything that touches their faces: a bottle, a pacifier, a finger. Within a few days, they seem to adjust to their mothers' feeding styles and begin to suck rhythmically. At first they shut their eyes and concentrate fiercely. Later they begin to look around while

NONMATERNAL CAREGIVERS

Many people assume that the average child is brought up in a conventional nuclear family: Father is the breadwinner; mother stays home and takes care of the children. But in fact, the nuclear family is more and more becoming a myth. In 1978, less than 50 percent of all American families conformed to this pattern (Craig, 1980). The divorce rate is skyrocketing, and many children are being raised by single parents. Although the vast majority of these single parents are women, there is a small but significant number of single fathers. And as traditional sex roles are questioned, increasing numbers of parents have chosen to reverse family **roles:** Father stays at home with the children while mother goes to work. Even without complete role reversals, more married women are working. In 1976, over 50 percent of all married women with school-aged children worked outside the home (Craig, 1980).

When mothers—with or without partners—go to work, who takes care of the children? A survey conducted as early as 1968 showed that nearly 50 percent of the preschoolers with working mothers were cared for at home by relatives or nonrelatives. About 33 percent were looked after in someone else's home or in a family day-care situation: 50 percent of them by relatives, the other 50 percent by nonrelatives. Of the remaining 16 percent, 50 percent of them were enrolled in group-care centers, while the other 50 percent were cared for by their mothers as they worked (Low & Spindar, 1968). Since that study was conducted, the number of children with working mothers has increased, and day-care facilities are more numerous.

How does day care affect children? The answer depends on a variety of factors, among them: parental attachment, the quality of the care, the age of the child, and the personal and socioeconomic characteristics of the child and the family. Most studies show that nonmaternal care starting before the age of 2 years does not impair the child's attachment to the mother. These "early starters" also tend to interact more with other children, both in positive and negative ways. Children raised in day-care centers interact more with unfamiliar adults and less with their mothers (or principal caregivers) than children raised at home. The overall social and emotional adjustment of children who have spent time in day-care centers seems to be as good as that of children cared for at home (Etaugh, 1980). But it is important to remember that most studies of day-care facilities take place in univer-

(**Will McIntyre, Photo Researchers**)

sity-sponsored centers. The quality of the care in these centers is generally higher than in most other facilities, and it may not reflect the general effects of day care on children.

In general, then, good quality nonmaternal care does not appear to have bad effects on the intellectual and cognitive functioning of middle-class children. And as we will see in Chapter 10, for some children good quality day care may even contribute to higher levels of intellectual performance (Etaugh, 1980).

We have been using the term "nonmaternal care" to mean day care. But what about children who are raised by fathers rather than mothers? Unfortunately, there is still little reliable research on this question. When two parents choose to "reverse roles," Lamb (1979) believes that there is not necessarily any adverse effect on the child, provided that the father has a secure sense of his own masculinity and communicates this to the child. Lamb is less hopeful about the prospects for children of single parents of *either* sex. Single parents, unless they have strong support from friends and community (such as day-care facilities and financial security), are in a difficult position to raise children in a happy, healthy atmosphere. But Lamb does believe that single fathers have a better chance than single mothers of raising well-adjusted children. Why? Because our society still tends to award child custody to mothers rather than to fathers. The men who do get custody tend to be people who very much *want* to raise their children.

nursing and will stop when anything catches their attention. Apparently infants are not able to do more than one thing at a time.

Nevertheless, Jerome Bruner and his colleagues have shown that babies can and do control their sucking. In one experiment, these researchers put infants in "front-row seats" in a laboratory movie theater and gave them pacifiers that were connected to the projector. If the babies sucked hard enough, the picture would come into focus. Surprisingly, even 3-week-old babies were able to focus the picture. They sucked extra hard, looked up quickly when the picture faded, and then began sucking again. This was surprising not only because the infants were able to coordinate sucking and looking, but also because they were smart enough to realize that they could control the movie—and were interested enough to do it (Pines, 1970).

The Newborn Baby

Figure 3–1
Individual differences between babies show up very soon after birth. Such differences are caused by genetic factors, prenatal environment, and the circumstances at birth.
(Both, Russ Kinne, Photo Researchers)

INDIVIDUAL DIFFERENCES

We have been talking about newborns as if they were all the same, but from birth infants show individual differences. One baby curls quietly in an adult's arms; another squirms and kicks with great energy. One sleeps through a rock concert in the next room; another wails when a dog barks two houses away. One baby feels almost limp when picked up; another is always tense and rigid. What do these differences mean? Some researchers have suggested that these individual characteristics express the child's inborn temperament. For example, Brazelton (1969) distinguishes three general temperamental types: the quiet baby, the active baby, and the average baby. In another study based on 14 years of research, Thomas, Chess, and Birch (1970) concluded that most children retain the same general temperament from birth to adolescence. They described babies as "easy," "difficult," or "slow-to-warm-up." They defined "easy" children as those who are relaxed and adaptable from birth. In later life such children find school quite agreeable and learn rather easily how to make friends and how to play by the rules. "Difficult" children, on the other hand, are moody and intense. They react violently to new people and new situations, sometimes withdrawing from them, at other times protesting until the well-meaning adult gives up. "Slow-to-warm-up" children are relatively inactive, withdrawn, and slow to react. Unlike the tantrum-prone, "difficult" babies, these children seem reluctant to express themselves. In later life they often have difficulty in competitive and social situations.

Many psychologists are cautious about categorizing babies as "quiet" or "active," "easy" or "difficult." These psychologists point out that the same baby may go through all these states in a single day. While one style or another will usually dominate, it should not be thought of as unchanging. Moreover, about one-third of the children in the study we have described did not fit any of the three categories.

Other psychologists flatly reject the belief that temperament is inborn, or predetermined. True, some children who were grumpy at birth are nasty at age 8 and impossible at age 12, but it is not necessarily because they were "born that way." Rather, these psychologists suggest that infants behave the way they do because they are part of a social system in which various people—the infant, the mother, the father, siblings, and so on—influence each other's behavior and temperament (Bronfenbrenner, 1977). Suppose, for example, that an infant has digestive troubles and cries constantly. An inexperienced mother or father might consider such a child difficult and hard to please. Yet another set of parents might react quite calmly to the same situation. Such parents would treat their children differently, and as a result their children would probably have other temperaments. While the debate continues about the causes of individual differences, no one denies that infants do differ from one another from the moment they are born. Therefore, we must remember that there are individual exceptions to almost all the general principles that we will explore in this chapter.

The newborn baby, as we have seen, is physiologically advanced in some ways. But the simple act of picking up a toy, for example, requires the following abilities that the baby lacks: judging how far away the toy is, crawling or walking to it, and coordinating an arm and hand to pick it up. Most babies need almost a year before they can cross a room and grab something they want. Much of this chapter concerns how babies develop these abilities.

Physical and Motor Development

The physical development of an infant is guided by **maturation,** a more or less automatic unfolding of development that begins with conception. It is as if the body had certain goals—say, a height of 6 feet. Poor nutrition may hinder growth somewhat, but only a very bad diet will prevent the body from approaching its genetically determined height. Maturation does not affect only size—it leads to dramatic changes in the physical traits of the body. Most obviously, proportions change (see Figure 3–2). Puberty causes

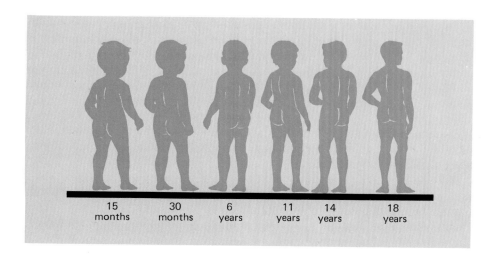

| 15 months | 30 months | 6 years | 11 years | 14 years | 18 years |

Figure 3–2
Body proportions at various ages. As the child ages, the head becomes relatively smaller and the legs longer in proportion to the rest of the body.
(From Nancy Bayley, "Individual Patterns of Development." *Child Development*, 1956, 27, 45–74. Reprinted with the permission of the Society for Research in Child Development, Inc.)

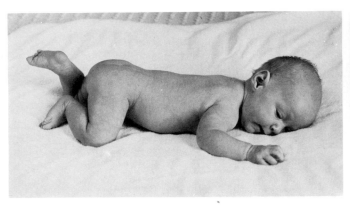

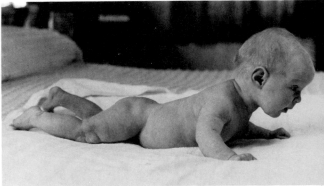

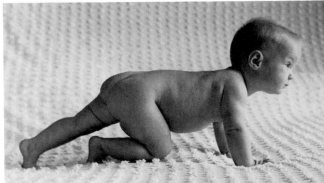

Figure 3–3
The normal sequence of motor development. Newborns are only capable of simple reflexes. At about 1 month they begin to lift their shoulders; they start to crawl at about 4 to 6 months. By 9 months they can sit up by themselves. They can stand upright at about 10 months. At about 13 months they begin to walk alone.
(All, Suzanne Szasz)

(K. Lehner, The Image Bank)

distinct changes in body chemistry that have definite effects on appearance and behavior. These and other changes are genetically "preprogrammed."

Maturation also makes new behavior possible. Within a year, most babies are sitting up, crawling around, and beginning to walk with a little help. As soon as they can walk, they try to jump and climb. At each stage their view of the world changes markedly. By age 7 months they are curious about everything they see; by age 10 months they can act on their curiosity, crawl through open doors, and push books off tables. Along the way, they work out a number of techniques, like crawling, that will be abandoned later.

In describing infants' motor development, psychologists focus on walking and grasping. Both appear as reflexes in newborns, although neither is of much use to them at that point. Held up, with their bodies dangling, infants pump their legs up and down like runners. This reflex seems to disappear after 7 to 9 weeks. When they begin practice walking again at 6 to 11 months, the picture is quite different, for by then they can pull themselves up (see Figure 3–3). Gradually, their attempts become more deliberate, and with only a little support they begin to walk forward. They soon learn heel-to-toe coordination, and after practice (and many falls), they straighten up and walk.

What happens if parents do not encourage the baby to walk even when he or she is ready? Hopi Indian babies who have been strapped to stiff, confining cradleboards from birth learn to walk just as easily as Hopi babies who have been allowed to scramble around as they liked (Dennis & Dennis, 1940). There seem to be critical periods when a child is most able to

start certain activities. Children who are bedridden from the age of 13 to 18 months (the average "walking readiness" period) find learning to walk after this period much more difficult.

Does encouragement or training help a child to walk sooner? A recent experiment indicated that early encouragement does, indeed, have results. A group of 1-week-old babies was trained by their mothers in walking and "foot-placing" exercises each day for a 7-week period, while a second group of babies was not. The babies who had been helped through the motions of walking were significantly more active and walked sooner than the others. Thus, this first 8-week period of life, before the newborn's walking reflex disappears, seems critical for developing walking ability (Zelazo et al., 1972).

Grasping also changes as the baby develops. Newborn infants have a very firm grip. From birth to 24 weeks, many babies can hang by their hands like monkeys, and most can support 90 percent of their weight. Like the walking of newborns, grasping also appears to be a reflex action. At about 6 months, this grasping reflex disappears, but by this time infants can control their thumbs (see Figure 3–3).* Most infants use both hands at first. At about 2 years, as their skills increase, they begin to show a preference for one hand or the other.

---

*This last step is particularly important. The fact that a human being's thumb is independent of the other fingers enables a person to make and handle tools: to push a plow, swing a hammer, or control a pen.

DEVELOPMENTAL NORMS FOR CHILDREN

Physical and motor development seem to follow a fairly predictable timetable until the body's goals are realized. This fact enables psychologists to establish **developmental norms.** Norms have several uses. Although they do not predict the day on which a child will walk, norms do alert parents and doctors to extremes. For example, brain damage may not be discovered until a parent notices that a baby has not tried to lift his or her head by age 4 months. At the opposite extreme, the child who walks at 11 months, starts talking at 14 months, and is throwing a ball at 3 years may be happier starting school a year early. The child who develops more slowly than the norm will not, however, always lag behind. Einstein, the story goes, did not begin to talk until he was 3 years old—1½ years late, according to most norms!

Norms also suggest patterns of child development. During the 1st month, infants' heads must be supported when they are lifted. By the 5th week, however, infants can lift their own heads, and in another month, their chests. They do not begin to sit up alone for 3 to 5 months after that, and only start to reach for things at age 6 months. Learning to walk takes even longer: The average baby cannot stand up alone until the age of 10½ months.

Researchers have also discovered variations in the rate different parts of the body mature. The brain and the rest of the nervous system develop rapidly, reaching nearly adult proportions at 6 or 7 years. The body grows quickly (though not as quickly as the nervous system) for the first 6 years, and then slows down until adolescence.

We have described physical and motor development as gradual, steady processes. That is, as children get older and bigger, most seem to become more proficient at any kind of perceptual, intellectual, or motor task. But this assumption has been questioned by Bower (1976), who describes development as a somewhat irregular process. According to Bower, infants

Figure 3–4
Patterns of growth of various parts of the body. The nervous system develops relatively early; sexual characteristics do not appear until puberty (see Chapter 4).
(Adapted from C. W. Jackson, "Some Aspects of Form and Growth." In W. J. Robbins et al., *Growth.* New Haven, Conn.: Yale University Press, 1928)

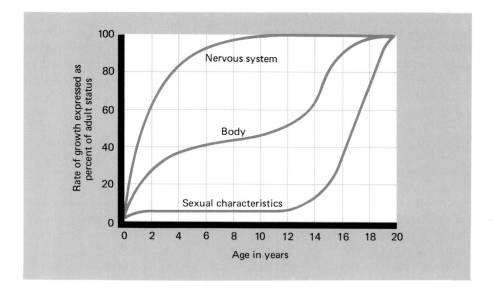

seem to acquire a particular ability, lose it for a while, and then regain the skill later in their development. For example, newborn infants show a striking aptitude for imitation—a talent that requires a high degree of coordination between the baby's senses and muscles. Newborns can mimic adults who stick out their tongues, open their mouths, or widen their eyes. Yet as the infant develops, this remarkable ability seems to disappear quickly and does not return until the end of the child's 1st year. Also, as we saw earlier, infants show the reflex of "walking" in their first 2 months. The reflex then disappears until real walking begins near the end of the 1st year. If Bower's observations on development are confirmed, we may have to modify our ideas about the simplicity and steadiness of physical and motor development.

Perceptual Development

What does the world look like to infants? Infants, of course, cannot *tell* the researcher anything, but their bodies do send signals. Researchers can tell what babies are looking at by watching reflections from their eyes. After they are 6 months old, infants' hearts beat faster when they are afraid just as adults' hearts do. Infants can even be taught to perform some action that lets the researcher know when they have seen a stimulus. These methods have enabled psychologists to study whether infants see only a meaningless swirl of images or whether they are born knowing, in some primitive way, the concepts of distance, color, and so on. As a first step toward answering this question, researchers had to determine whether young infants can tell one thing from another. Perhaps, as William James suggested, an infant's world is all "blooming, buzzing confusion."

VISUAL DISCRIMINATION

One way that infants sort out what they see is by separating what moves from what does not. Even newborns will give more **attention** to a moving object than to a stationary one (Gregg et al., 1976). Older infants show the same interest in motion (Bergman et al., 1971; Carpenter, 1974). But most of the things infants are exposed to—cribs, walls, ceilings—do not move. What do infants make of these?

Some of the most important "visual discrimination" experiments were devised by Robert Fantz. His method was simple: He showed infants a variety of pictures and patterned cards to see which they liked best. Preference was measured by how long the infant looked at a card. In one experiment Fantz showed 1- to 15-week-old babies one card with a black-and-white pattern and one card that was plain gray. All the infants spent more time looking at the patterned card (Fantz, 1961). Similar techniques show that infants prefer faces to other stimuli and bright colors to pastels.

Fantz's study suggests that babies recognize a pattern. It also suggests that they can recognize the human face at an early age. But what about

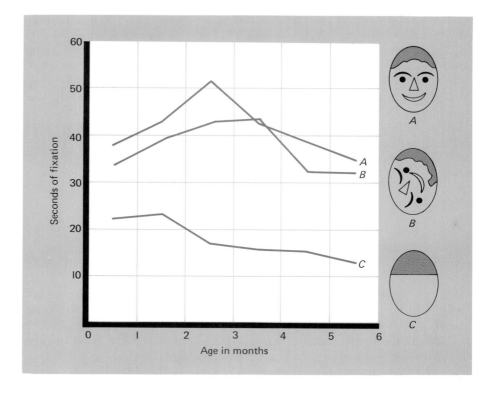

dimensions? Before babies begin to crawl and learn from experience that it takes effort to go from the crib to the door, do they realize that the door is far away? Before they have dropped a rattle from their crib a hundred times, do they perceive depth?

DEPTH PERCEPTION

Psychologists use an ingenious device—the visual cliff—for experiments on depth perception (see Figure 3–6). A table is divided into three parts. The center is a solid board. On one side, the table surface is dropped 1 inch or so; on the other side (the visual cliff), the drop is about 40 inches. The side of the visual cliff is covered with glass at the level of the centerboard so that infants who cross over will not fall. The three parts are covered with a checkerboard pattern to make it easier to tell where one part ends and the next begins. An infant is placed on the centerboard, and his or her mother stands on one side or the other, encouraging the infant to crawl toward her.

All of the 6- to 14-month-old infants tested by Walk and Gibson (1961) refused to crawl over the deep side to their mothers. Some peered down over the cliff, others cried, and still others patted the glass with their hands. When their mothers stood on the shallow side, however, the babies crawled to them. Obviously, then, 6-month-olds perceive depth. What about the younger babies? Because infants younger than 6 months cannot crawl, they were placed on one side or the other and their pulse rates measured (Campos, Langer, & Krowitz, 1970). When they were placed on the deep

side of the cliff, the infants' hearts slowed down—a reaction typical of infants and adults who stop to orient themselves in new situations. Thus, babies younger than 6 months seemed to know that something was different on the deep side, but did not know how to react.

Figure 3–6
The visual cliff. The child pats the glass on the deep side, but is reluctant to crawl across it to his mother.
(Both, William Vandivert)

OBJECT PERCEPTION

Adults take it for granted that people and objects are solid. At the movies, we know that if we reach out to touch the actors all we will feel is the screen. But does an infant understand this?

To see if infants know that objects are solid, T. G. R. Bower (1971) projected an optical illusion of a hanging ball. All the 16- to 24-week-old infants tested were surprised when they reached for the illusion and found that it had no substance.

Adults also take *object permanence* for granted. We assume that a box locked in the closet will still be there when we come back. But does an infant realize that a ball that rolls under a chair does not disappear?

Experiments done by Bower (1971) suggest that infants develop a sense of object permanence when they are about 18 weeks old. In his experiments, Bower used a toy train that went behind a screen. When 16-week-old and 22-week-old infants watched the toy train disappear behind the left side of a screen, they looked to the right, expecting it to reappear. If the researcher took the train off the table and lifted the screen, all the babies seemed surprised not to see the train. This seems to show that all the babies

Figure 3–7

One of the ambiguous drawings used by Reese to test perceptual set in children. The figure can be seen either as a rat or as a man's face.

(From Hayne W. Reese, "'Perceptual Set' in Young Children." _Child Development_, 1963, _34_, 151–159. Reprinted with the permission of the Society for Research in Child Development, Inc.)

had a sense of object permanence. But the second part of the experiment showed that this was not really the case. The researcher substituted a ball for the train when the train went behind the screen. The 22-week-old babies seemed puzzled and looked back to the left side for the original object. But the 16-week-old infants did not seem to notice the switch (Bower, 1971). Thus, the 16-week-old babies seemed to have a sense of "something permanence," while the 22-week-old babies had a sense of object permanence based on a specific object.

Bower also tested the concept of _person permanence._ Using mirrors, he showed infants multiple images of their mothers. Bower found that infants less than 20 weeks old were generally pleased with the multiple images. However, older infants were disturbed; they seemed aware that there should be only one mother (Bower, 1971).

PERCEPTUAL SET

If you show children something that can be seen in many ways, what will they say they see? H. W. Reese (1963) created a number of ambiguous drawings, such as the one shown in Figure 3–7. Depending on how you look at it, the figure could be either a man's face or a rat. Reese paired the ambiguous drawings with sets of nonambiguous drawings that suggested only one way of looking at them (the rat-man, for example, was paired with pictures that clearly showed human faces). First Reese showed the children the nonambiguous drawings; then he asked them to sort the ambiguous figures into piles of human, animal, or inanimate figures. Preschool children were not influenced by the nonambiguous pictures. School-age children, however, almost always followed the suggestions, putting the rat-man in the human pile if they had seen drawings that were clearly human first. This suggests that when older children are given an idea, they limit their perception along the lines imposed by the idea: They accept a **perceptual set.** Younger children do not.

THE ROLE OF EXPERIENCE

What can we conclude from these experiments? Does perception develop naturally with the growth of the child, as these studies suggest? Is it a process of maturation and therefore relatively independent of experience? Many psychologists do not think so.

Animals have been studied to determine how experience relates to the development of perception. In one of the earliest studies, Riesen (1947) tested if chimpanzees who had been raised in darkness for 16 months could perform visually oriented tasks when exposed to light. He found that the chimpanzees' visual responsiveness had been severely inhibited. Objects with which they were familiar through touch—their feeding bottle, for example—were not visually recognized for a long time. "Visual learning," Riesen explained, "so characteristic of the normal adult primate, is thus not an innate capacity independent of visual experience, but requires a long apprenticeship in the use of the eyes" (p. 108).

Studies with young kittens have shown that the *kind* of visual stimulation that infants receive may also affect visual functioning. Blakemore and Cooper (1970) placed one group of 2-week-old kittens in cages covered with black-and-white vertical stripes. They placed another group in similar cages covered with horizontal stripes. After 5 months, both groups of kittens showed permanent visual defects, including clumsy movements and the inability to perceive objects properly. Moreover, kittens raised in a horizontally striped cage ignored vertically oriented objects, and those raised in a vertically striped cage ignored horizontally oriented objects. The researchers concluded that the brain's visual center may adjust permanently to the kind of visual stimulation it receives during maturation.

Other factors besides the quantity and quality of visual stimulation may also affect visual functioning. Studies have shown that feedback from movements that are self-produced may also influence the development of perception. Held and Hein (1963) placed two young kittens in a special apparatus that allowed one kitten to move relatively freely as it pulled the other kitten, whose movements were restrained. Although both kittens received the same visual stimulation, the passive, restrained kitten failed in a number of visual tests. It had not received the sensory-motor feedback needed to develop normal visual functioning.

Do the effects of visual deprivation from an early age also apply to humans? Research on this question has, of course, been limited. Evidence suggests that those people who had been blind from birth and whose sight had been restored through surgery often have permanent visual defects that may stem from a lack of early visual stimulation (Riesen, 1950). Thus, there is good evidence to suggest that stimulation, experience, and learning all contribute to perceptual development. Depth and object perception may be inborn, but without experience they will not mature properly.

Memory Development

We have already talked about Robert Fantz's experiments on infant perception. He also discovered that babies prefer to look at new and interesting things when they can choose between something familiar and something new. Fantz (1965) showed infants a display screen. On one side of the screen he displayed the same pattern, over and over; on the other side he used a new pattern each time. The infants looked longer at the new pattern.

What does this tell us? For one thing, it tells us that babies, too, can be bored. But more importantly the experiment implies that the babies could *remember* the old pattern. Otherwise, they would not prefer the new one. In one study, 18-, 24-, and 30-week-old babies were shown photographs of a familiar female face looking in various directions, and of another female face that they had never seen before. The younger babies reacted only to the changes in direction. They did not show that they understood either that it was the same face seen from different angles or that there were two different faces. But the 30-week-old babies appeared to recognize both

The memories of infants can be tested with a machine—shown here—that was first developed by Robert Frantz. (Photo by David Linton, from *Scientific American*)

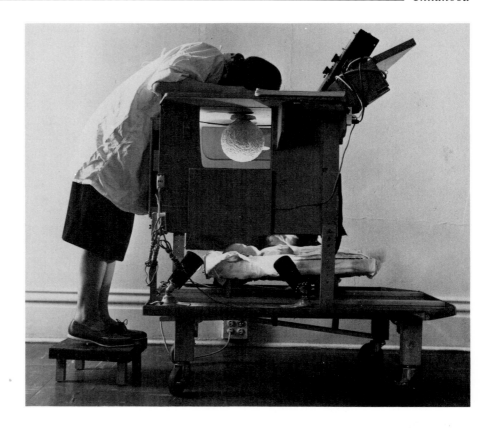

concepts (Cohen, 1979). In another experiment, 5-month-old infants who were only given 2 minutes to become familiar with a face still remembered something about that face 2 weeks later (Fagan, 1973).

Around 18 to 30 weeks then, babies develop some kind of memory, which seems to expand as they grow older. But why does memory emerge at this age? Psychologists like Jean Piaget believe that recall depends on some form of *symbolism*. Our most basic symbols—words and language—do not emerge fully until 18 or 24 months. As far as we know, children cannot remember the bird they saw yesterday unless they have a concept of "bird." Children may have some kind of mental symbols or images that enable them to recall something before they know the word for it, but since they cannot communicate this to us verbally, it is hard for us to know.

As children grow older, their capacity to remember continues to grow. This partly reflects their growing knowledge about the world in general. And in part it reflects their increasing skill at judging what they can and cannot remember and at learning strategies to help them remember—like making lists, for example (Flavell, 1977). In part it also reflects that as children grow older they become better at "shutting out" what is unimportant in order to remember what is important. These changes, then, obviously affect more than memory. They also affect children's ability to learn—that is, their cognitive abilities. We will come to cognition later in this chapter, but first let us discuss language, which is clearly important to memory.

Language Development

No change is more dramatic for a child than the acquisition of language. Like motor abilities and perception, language depends on both physical maturation—control of the muscles that move the mouth and tongue—and experience.

A BRIEF CHRONOLOGY

At about 2 months of age the infant begins to coo—a rather nondescript word for rather nondescript sounds. In another 1 or 2 months the infant enters the "babbling" stage and starts to repeat sounds. Gradually the infant's babbling starts to resemble the rhythms of adult speech. Between 8 and 10 months, infants seem to take special pleasure in "talking" aloud to themselves as they work at grabbing hold of things and at crawling. At this age vocalizing is still primarily nonsocial. Soon, however, infants start to imitate sounds and use their voices to get attention. By 10 or 11 months, they show signs of understanding things said to them.

By about 12 months of age infants utter their first word, usually "Dada." During the next 6 to 8 months they build a vocabulary of one-word sentences: [Pick me] "Up!"; [I want to go] "Out!"; [Tickle me] "Again!" They may also use compound words, such as "Awgone" [all gone]. To these they add words that they use to address people—"Bye-bye" being a

(Hella Hammid, Rapho/Photo Researchers)

favorite—and a few exclamations such as "Ouch!" Most small children are also interested in possessives: [The shoes are] "Daddy's." But perhaps the overwhelming passion of 2-year-olds is naming. For example, at play the child will say the word "block" over and over, looking at a parent for approval each time.

Soon the child begins to form two- and three-word sentences of nouns and attributes. A typical beginner's sentences are "Baby crying," "My ball," "Dog barking." A number of psychologists have recorded mother–child dialogues at this age to see just what children pick up and what they omit. Children at this age most noticeably omit auxiliary verbs—[Can] "I have that?" "I [am] eating it"—and prepositions and articles—"It [is] time [for] Sarah [to] take [a] nap." Apparently children seize the most important words, probably those their parents stress.

During the next few months (age 3 to 4) children begin to fill in their sentences: "Billy school" becomes "Billy goes to school." They start to use the past tense as well as the present. They ask more questions and learn to use "Why?" effectively—and sometimes monotonously. By age 5 or 6 years, a child probably has a vocabulary of over 2,500 words and can make sentences of 6 or 8 words.

THEORIES OF LANGUAGE DEVELOPMENT

We have seen that language helps to develop memory. But how do we learn language? Most children seem to enjoy making sounds and words, and seem quite easily to pick up the rules for putting them together. But what prompts children to learn to talk in the first place?

Language is so crucial to human behavior that various psychologists have developed special theories to explain how children learn to communicate. B. F. Skinner (1957) believed that parents and other people around the infant listen to the cooing and babbling and *reinforce* or reward the child for making the sounds that most resemble adult speech. If a child says something that sounds like "Mama," his mother gives him a hug. As the child gets older, he or she is only reinforced for sounding more and more like an adult and for using the words correctly. If the child calls an aunt "Mama," there is less likely to be a rewarding hug. In other words, by this time children are only reinforced when they call the right person "Mama." In this way, Skinner maintained, children learn to master language and grammatical construction.

Other psychologists reject the theory of reinforcement, but maintain that children *imitate* adult language. Some researchers feel that when children start making two- and three-word sentences, they have already developed simple rules for word order. These simple rules have been made, apparently, by parroting adult sentences, but in abbreviated form. Although children omit many words, they nearly always put the main words in the right order. This is particularly remarkable because most parents seem to pay more attention to content than to word order when they correct their children's speech (Brown, 1973a).

Most psychologists and linguistic specialists believe that neither simple reinforcement nor imitation alone can explain the impressive speed, accuracy, and originality with which children learn to use language. They believe that children develop a complex concept of linguistic rules that enables them to build sentences. Noam Chomsky (1965) rejects the notion that children must be *taught* language. Instead, he feels that children are born with an *internal* device for processing the adult speech they hear around them. This mechanism enables children to understand the basic rules of grammar, to make sense of what they hear, and to form their own sentences.

Most psychologists now believe that children are born with a biological capacity for language, which is stimulated by their environment—the speech they hear from the day they are born. For example, a child points to a pair of shoes, and the mother says, "Those shoes are Daddy's." We know that without a social environment—people to talk with—children are slow to pick up words and rules that enable them to communicate and learn. Institutionalized children, who cannot expect an adult's smile to reward their efforts, and deaf children, who lack the self-satisfaction of hearing themselves make noises, babble like other children. The institutionalized child, however, takes much longer to start talking than the child who is raised in a family, and the deaf child requires special training. Clearly, "feedback," in the form of listening to oneself and to others, influences language development.

When the child first uses actual words, the process is very concrete, that is, the child identifies words with situations and functions. Stone and Church (1968) described a child who called all red cars "engines"—for fire engines—long before he used the word "red' or had grasped the more abstract concept of colors. On word-association tests in which people are asked to listen to a word and then say the first word that comes into their minds, adults associate the cue word "table" with "chair." Given the same cue, children associate "table" with "eat." At this stage, then, children are more aware of what things do or are used for than of similarities between them (Brown & Berko, 1960).

Later, children begin forming sentences, at first by joining two words together. One key element in this learning process seems to be *practice*. One mother put a tape recorder in her little boy's bedroom and recorded his talk after he had been left alone for the night. When she played it back, she heard "what color . . . what color blanket . . . what color mop . . . what color glass . . . what color TV . . . red ant . . . fire . . . like lipstick . . . blanket . . . now the blue blanket." The child was playing with words and phrases, trying them on for size (Moskowitz, 1978).

At age $2\frac{1}{2}$ to 3, children commonly make certain mistakes that indicate they are beginning to learn more sophisticated grammatical rules. Often the child will proudly announce, "I saw some sheeps" or "I digged a hole." Obviously, the words "sheeps" or "digged" were not learned by imitating adults. Rather, the child applied the logical rules for making plurals and past tenses, unaware that some words are irregular. In other words, children seem to know what they *want* to say before they can say it correctly by adult standards. In another case, a child was talking about a "fis" (Moskowitz, 1978). The adult repeated "fis" and the child became indignant. "Fis!" the child said impatiently. Eventually, the adult tried "fish" and the child, satisfied at last, said, "Yes, fis."

Cognitive Development

The process of acquiring, storing, retrieving, and revising knowledge is called **cognition.** The field of cognitive development focuses on the growth of intellectual activities such as using and understanding language, remembering, thinking, and perceiving. In this section we look at cognitive development, beginning with the theories of Jean Piaget.

PIAGET'S APPROACH

Jean Piaget (1896–1980) entered the study of cognitive development through a back door: He was trained as a zoologist, a perspective that shows in his work. For example, Piaget saw all behavior in terms of a person's adaptation to the environment. Unlike animals, people have few reflexes and must learn how to deal with their environment.

Piaget first became interested in human adaptation while watching his own children at play. Observing them with the trained eyes of a scientist, he began to see their games as confrontations with their surroundings. In other words, through play they were learning to adapt.

As Piaget's children grew, he noticed that their approach to environmental problems changed dramatically at different ages. Was it simply that their coordination improved, or do older children think differently than their younger brothers and sisters? Piaget became an avid child-watcher: He played with them, asked about their activities, and devised games that would show how they were thinking.* Gradually, he discerned a pattern, a series of stages through which, in Piaget's view, all children pass.

SENSORY-MOTOR STAGE *(birth–2 years).* As Piaget saw it, the baby's first step is to apply the skills that he or she has at birth—sucking and grasping—to a broad range of activities. Small babies delight in putting things into their mouths: their own hands, their toys, and so on. Gradually, they divide the world into what they can suck and what they cannot. Similarly, young babies will grasp a rattle instinctively. Then, at some point, they realize that the noise being produced comes from the rattle. They begin to shake everything they get hold of, trying to reproduce the sound, and eventually start to distinguish between things that make noise and things that do not. In this way infants start to organize their experiences, fitting them into **categories. Schemata,** as Piaget called these simple frameworks, are the first step toward intentional behavior and adaptive problem solving. Unusual things that are not part of their schemata, such as a strange adult or a moving mechanical dog, are apt to disturb children at this stage (Kagan, 1976).

By the end of the sensory-motor stage, children have developed a sense

---

*Piaget's approach is unusual. In developing theories, most researchers test as many children as they can to arrive at solid generalizations. Piaget chose instead to study a small number of children intensively as they went about their daily lives. This is a form of naturalistic-observation, which is discussed in Chapter 1.

Piaget viewed play as an important part of children's adapting to their surroundings.
(Wayne Behling, *The Ipsilanti Press*)

of object permanence (which we discussed earlier). When a baby begins to look for a ball that has rolled under a chair, we know that he or she realizes that the ball still exists. Also, by the end of this stage, children have a sense of self-recognition—the ability to name themselves correctly in a mirror (Berntenthal & Fischer, 1976). Object permanence is crucial to cognitive development, for it enables the child to begin to see how things happen.

PREOPERATIONAL THOUGHT *(2–7 years)*. Children are action oriented when they enter the preoperational stage. Their thought is tightly bound to physical and perceptual experiences. But as their ability to remember and anticipate grows, children begin to use symbols to represent the external world. The most obvious example of representation is language, and it is in this stage that children begin to use words to stand for objects.

Piaget suggested a number of ways in which preoperational thinking differs from the thinking of older children and adults. Small children, he said, are extremely egocentric: They cannot distinguish between themselves and the outside world. They assume that objects have feelings, just as they do; they consider their own psychological processes—for example, dreams—to be real, concrete events. According to Piaget, children in the preoperational stage cannot put themselves in someone else's place.

Although they may be self-centered most of the time, under certain conditions even 4-year-olds seem to take into account the perspectives of other people (M. L. Hoffman, 1977). Hoffman cites several studies that support this idea. In one study, 4-year-olds chose birthday presents that were appropriate for their mothers. If the children had been entirely self-centered, they probably would have picked toys they liked as gifts for their mothers (Marvin, 1975). In other studies, 4-year-olds were found to use simple forms of speech when talking to 2-year-olds (Gelman, 1979), and

Figure 3–8
In this experiment, Piaget pours the beads from one of the short, wide containers into the tall, narrow one. Children in the preoperational stage will usually say that the tall container has more beads in it.

they gave very detailed directions to people whom they thought could not see (Maratsos, 1973).

Piaget also suggested that children in the preoperational stage tend to focus on the one aspect of a display or event that attracts their attention and to ignore all the others. In a famous experiment, Piaget asked preoperational children to fill two identical short, wide containers with beads (Figure 3–8). When they had finished, he poured the beads from one container into a tall, narrow container and asked the children whether it had more beads in it than the other. The children always said yes, the tall one had more, even though Piaget had not added or taken away any beads. In a more recent experiment, Gelman (1979) found that very young children (aged $2\frac{1}{2}$ to 4 years) could identify changes in the number of objects that occurred solely from adding or subtracting—even if the children did not see the changes occur. If the color or shape of the objects also changed, however, then the children became confused and could not perceive any change in the number of the objects. These results indicate that very young children can only concentrate on one aspect of a thing at a time: height, width, number, color. The dominant feature of what a child sees becomes the center of his or her attention.

The children were also confused in these experiments because young children cannot mentally retrace their steps to reach a conclusion: "If we poured the beads back into the original container, it would look the same as before. The number of beads must be the same." Both self-centeredness and irreversibility are shown in an example cited by Phillips (1969). A 4-year-old boy was asked if he had a brother, and he replied, "Yes." The child was then asked the brother's name: "Jim." "Does Jim have a brother?" "No." The child could not think of himself as somebody else's brother, nor could he work backwards.

CONCRETE OPERATIONS *(7–11 years).* During this stage children become more flexible than they were in the preoperational stage. They learn to retrace their thoughts, correct themselves, and start over if necessary. They learn to consider more than one dimension at a time, and to look at a single object or problem in different ways.

Another bead game illustrates all these abilities and shows how children between the ages of 7 and 11 have grown intellectually. Piaget gave children of different ages a box of 20 wooden beads: 2 were white, the rest brown. He asked them whether the wooden beads or the brown beads would make the longest necklace. Children under 7 decided that there were more brown beads, ignoring the fact that *all* the beads were wooden. Children 7 and older laughed at the question: They knew that all the beads were wooden (Piaget & Szeminska, 1952).

In this stage, by about age 10, children also become more able to infer what another person knows or may be thinking (Shantz, 1975). At about the same time, children become aware that the other person may be equally capable of inferring their thoughts.

Although quite logical in their approach to problems, children in the concrete operations stage can only think in terms of concrete things that they can handle or imagine handling. In contrast, adults can think in abstract terms, can formulate hypotheses and accept or reject them without first testing them. This ability develops in the next stage.

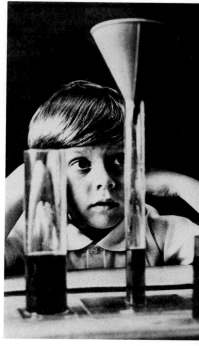

(Sam Falk, *New York Times*)

FORMAL OPERATIONS *(11–15 years).* To test the development of abstract thinking, children in the concrete and the formal operations stages were given a variety of objects and asked to separate them into two piles: things that would float and things that would not (Inhelder & Piaget, 1958). The objects included cubes of different weights, matches, sheets of paper, a lid, pebbles, and so on. Piaget then let the children test their selections in a pail of water, asking them to explain why some things floated while others sank.

The younger children were not very good at classifying the objects. When questioned they gave *individual* reasons for each one: The nail sank because it was too heavy, the lid floated because it had edges, and so on. The older children seemed to know what would float. When asked to explain their choices, they began to make comparisons and cross-comparisons, gradually concluding that neither weight nor size alone determined if an object would float: It was the relation between these two dimensions that was important. Thus, they approximated Archimedes' law: objects float if their density is less than that of water.

Younger children solve complex problems by testing their ideas in the real world; their explanations are concrete and specific. Adolescents can think in abstract terms and can test their ideas internally, with logic. As a result, they can go beyond the here and now to understand things in terms of cause and effect, to consider the *possibilities* as well as the realities, and to develop **concepts.** We will explore in greater detail the kinds of cognitive changes that occur during adolescence in Chapter 4.

CRITICISMS OF STAGE THEORY

The work of Piaget has led to a good deal of research. Developmental psychologists have focused on two of Piaget's assumptions: that there are distinct stages in cognitive development, and that a person must go through each stage to reach the next.

T. G. R. Bower (1976) has argued that development does not always

IMPRINTING

In nature, young animals of many species follow their mothers around. Why? Because they have *imprinted* on their mothers. A young animal often becomes attached to (and may follow) the first object that produces a social response, even though this object may not be the animal's mother. In some experiments, young ducks and geese have imprinted on decoys, balls, and even the experimenter (Hoffman & DePaulo, 1977; Lorenz, 1935).

Several traditional assumptions about imprinting have been questioned by recent research (Hoffman & DePaulo, 1977). For example, imprinting was thought to differ from other types of learning because the animal always seemed to follow the first object presented to it regardless of how many other objects it was shown later. But in fact, imprinting on one object does not appear to prevent imprinting on a second object; it may actually make it easier.

Many species show imprinting behavior, though species differ in the tendency to imprint. What makes an object attractive for imprinting also is species spe-cific: Young ducks, for example, are likely to be attracted to anything that moves, while baby monkeys give their hearts to soft things they can cling to.

Human beings may not imprint exactly as animals do, but at least one investigator thinks that human babies go through critical periods for social attachments. Stendler (1952) suggested that the ages between 8 to 9 months and 2 to 3 years may be such critical periods. For example, children who are deprived of their usual caregivers during those times appear most likely to show overdependency. An interesting aspect of research on imprinting in human beings involves the adoption of children. Many prospective parents prefer to adopt young children, apparently in the belief that infants have few memories to interfere with forming a bond with their new parents. If, as Hoffman and DePaulo (1977) claim, previous experience with imprinting makes animals more likely to form a second bond, then older children may become just as attached to adoptive parents as infants do.

progress in this smooth way. For example, he found that during the first 11 or 12 years, children appear to master and then to lose the concept of conservation of weight; for example, they do not realize that a pound of feathers weighs the same as a pound of lead, even though the feathers make a bigger pile. Children finally reach a stable understanding of this concept when they are about 13 years old. There also appear to be "fits and starts" in children's memory development that do not follow Piaget's outline (Liben, 1974; Samuels, 1974).

Horn (1976) feels that much of the evidence that seems to support the idea of developmental stages has been misinterpreted. For example, simple observation tells us that an average child can do things at the age of 4 that he or she could not do at the age of 2. But that does not necessarily mean that something happens to a child of 2 that prepares him or her to have the skills of a 4-year-old. Horn suggests that a child can reach a later developmental stage (and perform the tasks associated with it) without having gone through the earlier stages, just as some children can walk without ever having crawled.

Perhaps it would be better to see Piaget's model as an ideal, not as a real picture of cognitive development. The interests and abilities of the particular child and the demands of the environment may influence the development of cognitive abilities in ways not accounted for by Piaget (Kagan, 1976). Thus, cognitive development might be best viewed as an ongoing, continuous process, rather than as separate stages with "breaks" between them.

Personality Development

Newborn babies are completely helpless; they are also completely sel-fish. This condition of complete dependency and selfishness is only the first in a series of conflicts that children must resolve. In doing so, each child establishes the unique but fairly consistent pattern of behavior that we call *personality*.

ATTACHMENT AND AUTONOMY

Nature supplies the infant with a mother to care for him or her. *Attachment theory* suggests that the newborn's few activities—sucking, clinging, crying—serve to *attach* the baby to the mother, and the mother to her baby. For a long time, child psychologists emphasized the feeding of the infant as the primary source of **attachment.** Feeding, they hypothesized, was the infant's first and most important experience of the world. Because the mother satisfies her baby's need for food, the infant begins to see her in a positive way, which causes the baby's first social attachment to form. Researchers no longer think, however, that oral gratification is so over-whelmingly important. Parents and caregivers also provide warmth and "contact comfort": They talk to, hold, and smile at the baby. Clearly, all these actions help to develop attachment, although psychologists disagree about which is most important.

Most infants raised in a family become very attached to their mothers. For example, most infants go through a period when they are terrified if their mother leaves the room. This attachment seems strongest between the ages of 6 months and 1 year, when most infants are very frightened of strangers.

As soon as they can crawl, all infants begin to leave their mothers—if only briefly. Exploration and separation are essential to children's development. If they were constantly at their mothers' sides, infants would never learn to

A baby's first social attach-ment is to his or her mother.
(Erika Stone, Photo Researchers)

(Drawing by Kraus; © 1960 *The New Yorker Magazine*, Inc.)

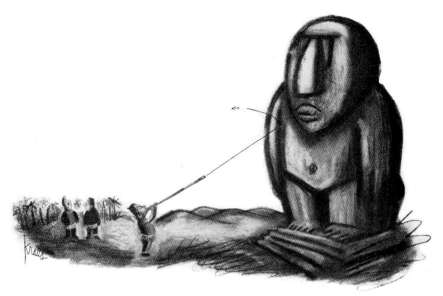

"Pointless rebellion against authority, if you ask me."

do anything for themselves and would never develop a sense of **autonomy.**

At first glance, autonomy and attachment may seem to be polar opposites, but in fact they are simply different sides of the same coin. Recent research indicates that the stronger the attachment between mother—or principal caregiver—and child, the more autonomous the child is likely to be. This may seem paradoxical, but it makes more sense if we reflect that a strong mother-child attachment provides a sense of *security*.

Studies of children with varying degrees of attachment to their mothers have shown that, in new situations, children who feel they have a secure "home base"—a secure relationship with their mothers—are more likely to venture out from that base to explore these new situations. These children apparently know that when they finish exploring, they can return to the haven of maternal protection (Ainsworth et al., 1979). Studies of children from the age of 1 through 6 years have shown that babies who are securely attached to their mothers at the age of 1 are later more at ease with other children, more interested in exploring new play situations, and more enthusiastic and persistent when presented with new tasks (Main, 1973; Matas, Arend, & Sroufe, 1978; Waters, Wittman, & Sroufe, 1979). Therefore, mother—child attachments, far from being a sign of excessive dependency, actually seem to strengthen the child's growing desire for autonomy.

At about 2 years old, children begin to test their strength by refusing everything: "No, I won't get dressed." "I won't go to sleep." The child's first efforts to be independent, however, may not be entirely welcome to the parents. The parents' attachment to the child, the mischief children get into as they begin to explore, and the extra demands on the parents' time and energy may explain this, although research on these questions is far from conclusive (Haith & Campos, 1977). The usual outcome of these first moves toward independence is that the parents begin to discipline the child. Children are expected to eat at a particular time, not to pull the cat's tail or to kick their sisters, and to respect other people's rights. The constant push-and-pull between such restraints and the need for independence often causes difficulties for both parents and children. But it is an essential step in developing a balance between dependence and autonomy.

IMITATION AND IDENTIFICATION

As children are exposed to discipline, their own needs conflict with their parents' desires. One of the ways that children resolve such **conflicts** is by imitating adults and identifying with those they know. Parents, other adults, older siblings—even television—all provide **models** of behavior for children to imitate. For example, a child may want to strike out when frustrated or hurt, but often a parent will inhibit such violent reactions. How does a child learn to accept these feelings and behave in acceptable ways? In large part, a child learns through **imitation,** the conscious copying of other people's behavior.

Identification is the unconscious copying of another person's characteristics. For example, children may adopt their parents' values because they want love and approval, or because they fear punishment and rejection. Identification may also help children overcome fear and frustration. Children are always being told that there are some things they may not do because they are "too young." A child can evade these prohibitions in play and fantasy by unconsciously identifying with "big people" and mentally living through them.

Unfortunately, the effects of imitation and identification can also be negative and destructive. Perhaps today's most controversial example is the impact on children's behavior of the violence presented on television. One study found that on Saturday morning cartoon shows there was an average of one violent act every 2 minutes (Gerbner, 1972). A later study calculated an average of 21.5 violent acts per hour of cartoons (Slaby, Quarfoth, & McConnachie, 1976).

Does all this violence actually affect children's behavior? One famous

Television provides role models for children to imitate that may not always be positive.
(Alice Kandell, Photo Researchers)

experiment on the effects of violence on television was conducted by Bandura, Ross, and Ross (1963). Four groups of children were taken to a room, one group at a time, and asked to perform a simple task. The first group was allowed to work in peace; the other groups were exposed to various forms of **aggression** while they worked. While the second group of children worked, an adult came into the room and began beating up a large doll—yelling at it, throwing it into the air, sitting on its head. The third group of children was just shown a film of this on TV. The fourth group saw a similar film, but the characters were costumed like cartoon characters.

The children were then taken into a waiting room and told they could play with the toys there. But as soon as they had started to play, the experimenter said, "No, these are my favorite toys. I'm saving them for the other children. You go into the other room." The other room contained the doll that the adult had abused in the first part of the experiment. The children in the second, third, and fourth groups tended to take out their frustrations on the doll, more or less imitating the adult's behavior. The children who had seen the film on TV of the adult's tantrum were the most aggressive. Two later studies indicated that after seeing films in which an adult attacked a human victim, young children were moved to imitate the adult and physically assault another person (Hanratty, 1969; Hanratty et al., 1969).

Several later studies have confirmed that viewing violence on TV can lead to aggressive behavior (Liebert & Baron, 1972; Stein & Friedrich, 1972). Moreover, a preference for violent TV programs in childhood has been related to aggressive and antisocial behavior in adolescence (Lefkowitz et al., 1972). A recent review of the effects of violence on TV indicates that many popular television programs not only teach children to value aggression but also show them new and exciting ways to express it (Liebert & Schwartzberg, 1977).

Some observers may rationalize the violence of television programming, asking, "Isn't it better that children learn about violence safely, by watching TV, rather than by actually being exposed to it?" But remember what Bandura and his colleagues found: The children who had seen the TV film of an adult's tantrum behaved more aggressively than the children who had seen the actual tantrum. This may be because filmed violence is not threatening; it does not have the emotional impact of real-life violence. Children who watch violence on TV at home feel safe and relaxed. These factors may help to reduce children's **inhibitions** about displaying the aggressive behavior they have learned from watching television. Thus, the main problem with violence on TV may be not its quantity, but rather its unrealistic setting. (See Chapter 16.)

PEER GROUPS

In our society, children generally have few important social relations outside their family for the first 4 or 5 years. They may play with other children, but usually their mother or caregiver is near. Going to school changes this. The child's world suddenly fills with "significant others"— peers and teachers. The number of models for the child to imitate and to

ANDROGYNY

"Shakespeare was androgynous," Virginia Woolf observed 50 years ago. In a speech on "Women and Fiction," she concluded that the most powerful writers are those who have found a way to fuse the male and female sides of their natures. "It is when this fusion takes place that the mind is fully fertilized and uses all its faculties" (Woolf, 1957).

The concept of **androgyny** (from the Greek "andro," meaning male, and "gyne," meaning female) is popular today largely because the women's movement has focused attention on what it means to be a woman—and thus also a man—in our society. As women begin to press for equal pay and equal job opportunities, they also call for a reevaluation of sex roles, and raise some fundamental questions: What does it mean to be a woman or a man? What does it mean to be "feminine" or "masculine"?

The traditional female role of wife and mother requires nurturant qualities: patience, warmth, and expressiveness. But feminists argue that these qualities are often used to keep women from achieving other goals. Patience and warmth are fine in the nursery, but not much good in the corporate boardroom. Men, however, are expected to be strong, aggressive, and competitive—qualities more advantageous in business than in personal relations. Like most societies, ours has assigned men and women rigid sex roles, but are not people capable of more flexible behavior? We know that women can be tough and aggressive, and that men can be gentle and nurturing. As sex roles are studied, many men and women are feeling that rigid ideas of sex-appropriate behavior limit their capacity to lead full, expressive lives. The answer, some have concluded, is androgyny, in which both masculine and feminine sides of our natures may be expressed.

Psychologists, too, have become interested in androgyny. One of them, Sandra Lipsitz Bem, did an experiment to find out whether androgynous people are really more adaptable (Bem, 1974, 1977). To measure how masculine, feminine, or androgynous a person is, she designed the Bem Sex Role Inventory (BSRI), which was made up of a list of 60 personality characteristics. It included 20 traits that our society considers "masculine"—ambition, self-reliance, assertiveness—20 traits that are considered "feminine"—affection, gentleness, understanding—and 20 traits that are neutral—honesty, friendliness, and amiability. Bem arrived at this list after studying how a group of undergraduates rated the desirability of various traits for each sex. On the test, people used these traits to describe themselves, on a scale of 1—never or almost never true—to 7—always or almost always true. The difference between the total points assigned to masculine and feminine adjectives tells us how sex-typed a person is. If a person has approximately equal masculine and feminine scores, he or she is considered androgynous.

Bem and her colleagues tested more than 1,500 undergraduates and found that 50 percent of the students stuck with the "appropriate" sex role, 15 percent identified with the opposite sex, and about 30 percent were androgynous. They then went on to see whether androgynous people are actually more adaptable, testing students for independence—a typically "masculine" trait—or conformity—a typically "feminine" trait. Students came to a lab for what they thought was an experiment on humor. Each person sat in a booth equipped with earphones and a microphone and watched cartoons that had already been rated according to how funny they were. As each cartoon appeared on the screen, students heard the experimenter ask each student in turn to rate the film. Actually, what the students were hearing was a preprogrammed tape on which people claimed that funny cartoons were not funny, and vice versa. "Feminine" women found it much harder to be assertive and to resist conforming to these opinions than "masculine" men or androgynous students. In another test, masculine men were found to be much less playful than androgynous women, and to behave much less warmly around babies than androgynous men did.

To find out whether sex-typed people actually avoid behavior traditionally appropriate only for the opposite sex, Bem and her colleagues asked students to perform certain tasks in exchange for payment. Students were given 30 pairs of activities, one masculine—oiling a hinge—and one feminine—preparing baby bottles—as well as some choices that were neutral—peeling an orange, for example. Masculine men and feminine women consistently avoided the activity that was not appropriate for their sex, even though these activities always paid more! Sex-typed students were especially anxious about behaving appropriately when the experimenter was a member of the opposite sex. From these experiments and others, Bem concluded that rigid sex roles do restrict behavior. By contrast, androgynous men and women tended to be more flexible—independent and assertive in one situation, warm and sympathetic in another.

Peer group influences begin at a very early age, usually when the child first leaves home for school.
(Hella Hammid, Rapho/Photo Researchers)

identify with increases. Gradually, children transfer some of their feelings of attachment to their teachers and peer group.

Leaving the protection of home and family for the new world of school can be quite an adjustment for many children. Children's early attachments to peers often occur when they find friends with whom to explore their new environment (Mueller & Lucas, 1975). Play is another way that children develop the skills needed to interact with people outside their family (Bruner, 1973).

Peers have an important influence on a child's personality development. To refer back to our discussion of violence on TV, one study found that young boys were more likely to imitate televised aggression if an aggressive peer was present (O'Carroll et al., 1976). But, peers can also stimulate a child to play more creatively (Rubenstein & Howes, 1976). Thus, the peer group can provide both positive and negative models for behavior and development.

Application

SEX TYPING AND SEX ROLES

In Chapter 2 we learned how genes determine the sex of a child. But how does **sex-typed behavior** (or gender-related behavior) develop?

Until recently, most people assumed that men and women differ emotionally and psychologically because they have different anatomies. All societies presume that this is true and assign distinctive roles to each sex. In the United States, for example, men are supposed to support their families, enjoy watching sports, and never cry. Women are expected to take care of children and the house, cater to their husbands, and weep at the drop of a hanky. Our standard sex roles limit both sexes: Ambitious women are portrayed as ruthless

100

and sexually unprincipled, while sensitive, gentle men have their masculinity questioned.

How valid is the notion of inborn sex differences? Not very valid, according to psychologists. But there *are* some differences. From very early childhood, boys tend to be more aggressive than girls. In early childhood, girls tend to excel in **verbal ability.** From the preschool years to early adolescence, the verbal abilities of both sexes tend to become equal. But girls then spurt ahead again and continue to excel verbally, at least through the high school years. Boys, however, begin in high school to excel in their ability to perceive figures in space and to understand the relations between these figures. This visual–spatial superiority continues into adulthood (Maccoby & Jacklin, 1974).

Are these differences the result of biology or culture? At first, boys may be more aggressive because they have higher levels than do girls of the hormone testosterone, which is thought to be related to aggressive behavior. But aggression is also an area where parents seem to have very different expectations for boys than for girls (Sears et al., 1957). As a result, any inborn sex differences are quickly affected by learning and parents' teaching. As for the discrepancy between the sexes in verbal, mathematical, and visual–spatial abilities, there is evidence that these differences can be modified greatly by training (Craig, 1980).

In fact, most of the differences assumed to distinguish women from men now appear to be primarily, if not entirely, the result of culture rather than biology. Newborn baby girls behave like baby boys do, and 2-year-old girls and boys are about equal in cognitive development and social skills. A 2-year-old boy is just as likely to be fearful, dependent, and interested in caring for others as girls have been thought to be (Williams, 1977). As children get older, however, their behavior conforms more and more to our culture's version of how men and women should act.

How are children socialized into these stereotyped sex roles? Children first learn about sex-appropriate behavior from their parents, and the parents' attitudes have a great influence on the child's feelings about being a boy or a girl. In one study, parents were asked to describe their newborn children (Rubin, Provenzano, & Luria, 1974). The parents were much more likely to describe their newborn daughters as delicate, beautiful, and weak. Newborn sons, on the other hand, were seen as strong, well-coordinated, and robust. As all the babies were the same height and weight, these descriptions appeared to reflect the parents' expectations rather than actual physical characteristics.

It is also possible that infants *themselves* notice differences between their father's and mother's behavior toward them. From the start, mothers are more apt to assume caregiving tasks, while fathers interact with their children through vigorous play. This continues for some months. The fact that mothers and fathers represent very different experiences for babies may affect children's ideas

This girl obviously prefers (at this moment) to play with a hammer and nails rather than with a doll. But what Mom and Dad have to say about her choice of toys may strongly influence her future actions.
(Susanne Szasz, Photo Researchers)

about what it means to be male or female (Lamb, 1979).

As children grow up, parents seem to increase their emphasis on sex-appropriate behavior (Block, 1975). Girls are more likely to be coddled, while boys are encouraged to be adventuresome and independent. Boys are more likely than girls to be discouraged from showing their emotions. A boy who bursts into tears may be told that "only sissies cry." Girls are trained to be mothers, boys to be breadwinners. Thus, boys play doctor and cops-and-robbers, while girls play nurse and mother their dolls. Parents dress children in sex-typed clothing and encourage them to act like an adult male or female.

As more women work outside the home, fathers will become more active in child rearing (Hoffman, 1977). This trend pleases many observers. They believe that if both mother and father share in child care and work outside the home, children will have a family model that avoids rigid sex roles. The working mother provides a self-sufficient model for her children, especially if the father takes on some of the household chores. Children who see their parents sharing domestic duties learn that there is not "men's work" and "women's work"—there is just work.

In several studies, however, fathers have been found to treat sons and daughters more differently than mothers do. Fathers are much more likely to prefer male children to female children (Coombs, 1975), and to describe infants in sex-typed language (Fagot, 1974; Rubin, 1974). Fathers are more concerned with their sons' rather than with their daughters' cognitive development; their daughters are more encouraged to develop social skills (Block et al., 1974). Fathers also tend to encourage their daughters to "daydream" or to wonder about life. They are more willing to comfort them, and they generally have warmer relations with their daughters than with their sons (Block, 1975).

These studies suggest that as fathers become more directly involved in child care, there could be more sex-role differentiation and a resulting decrease in the options made available to young girls. Perhaps, however, as men become more aware of the rewards of nurturance and more flexible in their own parental roles, they will encourage their children to be equally "liberated" from traditional sexual stereotypes.

Moreover, **socialization** only begins in the home. Schools and the mass media express cultural values and are apt to be slow to reflect changes in people's attitudes. Textbooks often portray women and girls in subordinate roles. Girls are steered toward classes in cooking and sewing, while boys are expected to learn such skills as woodworking and auto repair. Girls' interest in such traditionally female careers as nursing or teaching is encouraged, while boys have a freer choice.

The mass media—particularly television—also portray sexual stereotypes. The harried housewife in commercials, the macho cops and private eyes, and the bikini-clad females who sell cars all teach children certain values about being men and women. Even *Sesame Street* has come under fire for rigid sexual stereotyping and negative female role models (Bergman, 1974).

Thus, most children are subtly bombarded with pressures to conform to sexual stereotypes. Many girls still assume that they can only be happy as wives and mothers, that they should be beautiful, and that they must find a man to whom to attach themselves. Boys learn that they are expected to be domineering and that it is normal to be aggressive. Parents who do not accept such stereotypes can provide their children with more alternatives, but they also have to be aware that socialization continues outside the home.

Summary

1. *Developmental psychology* is the study of the stages of life from the fetal stage through birth, childhood, adolescence, adulthood, aging, and death.
2. Developmental psychologists may use either the experimental, the correlational, or the naturalistic-observation method, or some combination of these methods, to study developmental issues.
3. Some developmental psychologists emphasize heredity; others stress the influence of environment. Some see change as abrupt and discontinuous; others view development as gradual and on-going.
4. At one time, scientists thought that the unborn child was only affected by the processes of growth and heredity. Today they know that the *prenatal environment* also has important effects on development.
5. Fetal development can be harmed by the mother's diet, by any drugs she may take, by diseases she may contract during pregnancy, or by psychological stress.
6. Some doctors believe that the typical hospital experience of childbirth provides a harsh atmosphere for both mother and child. Frederick Leboyer proposes a method of delivery in which the atmosphere is more gentle, and the child is not "shocked" by bright lights, noises, the quick cutting of the umbilical cord, or a slap on the bottom. *Natural childbirth* prepares mothers (and often, fathers) for the birth experience by training the mother to use breathing and muscular control. No matter what method of childbirth is used, the mother–child attachment begins to form immediately after birth.
7. The newborn baby's body structures are all present and many are fully functioning at birth. The newborn is completely helpless

when lying down, but when picked up, the newborn immediately begins grasping quite hard and searching for a nipple. This reflex is known as *rooting behavior*. Another important reflex is *sucking*, which appears shortly after birth.

8. Newborn infants show *individual differences* in both physical and emotional behavior.

9. *Maturation*, the process by which the body fulfills its genetically determined potential, involves growth and changes in the physical character of the body, which make new behavior possible.

10. Some changes, such as walking and the development of secondary sex characteristics, occur spontaneously; others, such as talking, depend more on learning.

11. *Motor abilities*, like walking and grasping, develop in sequence. Walking progresses from lifting up the head, sitting up, crawling around, and walking with help, to walking unsupported. Mature grasping takes longer to develop and proceeds from the refined use of fingers, thumbs, and fingertips to holding and manipulating objects.

12. Psychologists have established *developmental norms*, which show approximately when certain behaviors should appear. The norms may be useful for indicating either retarded or advanced development.

13. *Perceptual development* refers to how the baby sees the world and how the baby's view changes. Depth perception, object perception, and visual discrimination seem to be inborn, but experience and physical maturation are necessary for them to develop and mature.

14. Very young infants can recognize things, but it is probably not until later that they can recall them. This is because they lack words (*symbols*). As memory develops, it also becomes cognition. The fact that children remember something means that they *know* what it is.

15. B. F. Skinner believes that children develop language skills through *reinforcement*. Other theorists stress *imitation*. Noam Chomsky believes that children have an innate ability to understand language—they somehow *process* what they hear and then are able to use correct grammar to express themselves. It now appears that language is part of the complex cognitive processes monitored by the brain.

16. The field of *cognitive development* focuses on the growth of intellectual activities such as using and understanding language, remembering, thinking, and perceiving.

17. Jean Piaget's theory of cognitive development described a series of stages through which all children must pass. In the *sensory-motor stage* (from birth to 2 years), children respond with the reflexes of sucking and grasping, gradually begin to explore and experiment, and organize their experiences into categories.

18. During the *preoperational stage* (from 2 to 7 years), the child acquires systematic methods for representing the external world internally. According to Piaget, during this stage the child is egocentric and centers on only one aspect of an event. The child is mentally unable to reverse a situation.

19. During the *concrete operations stage* (from 7 to 11 years), the child learns to retrace his or her thoughts, to consider more than one dimension at a time, and to look at a single object or problem in several ways.

20. The *formal operations stage* (from 11 to 15 years) marks the development of abstract thinking and the ability to formulate concepts.

21. Piaget assumes that there are distinct *stages* of cognitive development. Other psychologists question this assumption and suggest that cognitive development is not this clear-cut.

22. In attempting to resolve problems such as their dependency versus their selfishness, children begin to develop a *personality*.

23. The *attachment* between a mother or caregiver and an infant is the beginning of the child's social development. The mother or caregiver satisfies the need for food and gives warmth, contact, and auditory and visual stimulation.

24. As soon as most babies can crawl, they begin to explore and to separate themselves from their mothers. They begin to develop a sense of *autonomy*. Autonomy is fostered by a strong mother–child attachment.

25. One of the ways children solve conflicts is by *imitating* and *identifying* with parents, other adults, older brothers and sisters, and TV—all of which provide *models* for behavior.

26. When children go to school, the *peer group* becomes more important. It can provide positive or negative models for a child's development.

27. Despite common assumptions about the "natural" and "biological" differences between the sexes, most research on the subject does not support the notion of profound sexual differences. Males, however, do tend to be more aggressive than females. This difference may be hormonal at first, but socialization probably accounts for the discrepancy later. Females tend to excel in verbal abilities, while males excel in visual–spatial ones. But these differences apparently can be modified through training.

28. All societies presume the existence of significant sex differences, and assign distinctive (and often opposite) roles to each sex. In the United States, females have been expected to be unaggressive, nurturing, and caring; males have been expected to be assertive, competent, and emotionally tough. Children are socialized into stereotyped sex roles through pressure at home (such as the use of sex-typed toys and clothing), and through sex stereotyping in the schools and through the mass media.

Outline

Chapter 4

Adolescence and Adulthood

William Shakespeare wrote: "All the world's a stage . . . and one man in his time plays many parts." Starting out as a "mewling and puking" infant, he moves on to become a schoolboy "creeping unwillingly to school," a lover "sighing like a furnace," a soldier "seeking the bubble reputation," a justice "full of wise saws," a pantaloon "with spectacles on nose and pouch on side," and finally, in second childhood, "mere oblivion, sans teeth, sans eyes, sans taste, sans everything."*

Not surprisingly, much of what Shakespeare wrote about the various ages of man is still valid. Babies still cry; people still fall in love; our bodies still age and decline. But there is more to it than that. In the 400 years or so since Shakespeare's time, social scientists have added many insights to the mystery we call aging. At one time, childhood was seen as the source of almost all the important characteristics in human development. It was generally believed that once a person passed from childhood to adolescence and adulthood, significant psychological development stopped. This is no longer accepted. Recent research has concluded, as Shakespeare did long ago, that development continues after childhood through several important developmental stages. Although these stages differ somewhat from those described by the poet, they are no less distinct.

The first stage beyond childhood is adolescence. No longer considered just a continuation of childhood, adolescence is now recognized as a distinct stage of life that adds unique contributions to a person's growth. Following adolescence are the stages of young, middle, and late adulthood. Until recently, these three stages were lumped together and simply termed adulthood. Just as infancy, however, differs from childhood, and childhood differs from adolescence, so too do the three stages of adulthood differ

*William Shakespeare, *As You Like It*, act 2, scene 7, line 139.

from one another. Adulthood is no longer considered a period in which people simply play out their lives according to the patterns they developed in their youth. Adulthood is now known to be a time of continuous growth, during which people's attitudes, emotions, physical condition, cognitive abilities, and personalities change dramatically. In this chapter, we explore the various aspects of aging at each step in the life cycle from adolescence to adulthood.

Adolescence

Adolescence begins when a child's body shows signs of becoming an adult's body. Our discussion of adolescence begins with the nature of these physiological changes.

PHYSICAL DEVELOPMENT

Adolescence begins at about age 11 or 12 and continues, roughly, until age 17. This stage of development begins with the physical changes that mark puberty—when sexual reproduction becomes possible—and ends with maturity. These years bring the most dramatic physiological changes in humans since the first 2 years of life. The rapid growth that characterizes adolescence affects almost every part of the body.

Each sex undergoes its own sequence of development. The average girl has a 2-year head start on the average boy. But the rate of growth during adolescence varies considerably with each person. For most girls, the first visible evidence of puberty—usually development of the breasts—appears between the ages of 8 and 13. Rapid growth in height begins about 18 months later, and by age 15 or 16 the average girl has reached 98 percent of her adult height. The appearance of pubic hair usually accompanies the growth spurt. Menarche, or the onset of *menstruation*, usually occurs somewhere between the ages of 10 and 17.

For most boys, the first evidence of puberty—growth of the testes and scrotum—occurs between the ages of 10 and 15. Penis growth begins about a year later. The male growth spurt usually begins between the ages of 10 and 16 and ends between the ages of 13 and 19. The average boy reaches 98 percent of his adult height by the age of 17 or 18. Pubic hair first appears between the ages of 10 and 14 and is fully grown by the age of 15 to 18. A beard generally begins to grow about 2 years after pubic hair appears.

The development of **secondary sex characteristics**—beards, chest and pubic hair in boys; breasts, wider hips, and pubic hair in girls—reflects the development of **primary sex characteristics:** the ability to reproduce as shown by menstruation, sperm production, and the hormonal changes that create sexual desire. Together, these signs of sexual maturity are probably the most difficult changes the adolescent must deal with. Adolescents need to know that what they are changing into is as acceptable as what they were. They are especially sensitive to being treated differently than they

A GROWING TREND

Researchers have learned that in the last 100 years, children in the United States and many European nations have become increasingly taller than children of earlier times (Tanner, 1966). Since the beginning of the 20th century, in each decade the average heights of American and European children at ages 5 to 7 have increased roughly 1 to 2 centimeters (.39 to .79 inches), and the average heights of adolescents have increased about 2 to 3 centimeters (.79 to 1.18 inches) (Tanner, 1970).

This trend primarily represents earlier maturation among children. For example, since 1850 there have been consistent reductions in the average age of the onset of menarche in females in Western Europe (Tanner, 1970). The causes of this trend remain unclear. Tanner (1970) suggests that improved nutrition and reductions in disease occurrence have helped growth.

were before, because although their bodies are changing, inside they are still, at least in early adolescence, essentially children. The reactions of other people become especially important to an adolescent. Parents who are anxious and uncertain about their children's emerging sexuality may find it difficult to help their children through the transition. As we noted in Chapter 3, however, one's peers also influence this stage of development. The reactions of peers to a person's problems are of particular importance.

Although adolescence happens to everyone, it does not happen to everyone in the same way or at the same time. There is much competition among adolescents because of this wide variation in development. Adolescents compare themselves with one another to see how they rate.

In general, people who mature earlier do seem to have an easier time than those who mature later. This is particularly true for boys. Boys who mature earlier do better in sports and social activities, which earns them the respect of other boys (Conger, 1977). Boys who mature later are much more likely to feel inadequate and anxious (Jones, 1958; Jones & Bayley, 1950; Mussen & Jones, 1957, 1958). For girls, however, early maturation appears to be a mixed blessing. A girl who develops earlier may be admired by other girls, but she is also likely to be taunted or treated as a sex object by boys (Clausen, 1975).

Adolescents' competition is particularly unfortunate because they need the support of their peers. It is important for them to share common fears and anxieties, to help each other become more independent, and to cope with the changes that occur at this stage. We will come back to the topic of family and friends, but first let us look at some other aspects of change in adolescence.

The adolescent years—those between the ages of 11 and 17—are a time of discovery and experimentation.
(Suzanne Szasz, Photo Researchers)

COGNITIVE DEVELOPMENT

Just as the body takes on adult forms and functions during adolescence, a person also thinks more and more like an adult and less like a child. Adolescents not only know more than younger children do, but they can use that knowledge in new ways. There are changes in both how adolescents think and in what they know.

During adolescence, young people begin to think like adults, that is, they can manipulate knowledge, think abstractly, and can even form general rules about their world.

(Christa Armstrong, Photo Researchers)

In Chapter 3, we discussed an experiment in which children were asked to sort objects into things that would float and things that would not float. The children were also asked to explain *why* particular objects floated or sank (Inhelder & Piaget, 1958). Children from 7 to 11 years of age showed little skill in classifying the objects. They also gave *individual* reasons for each decision. But, adolescents—who fall into Piaget's stage of formal operations—not only knew what would float, but also could make a general rule for predicting if an object would float.

It is particularly significant that adolescents searched for a general rule. Younger children can think logically, but only in terms of concrete things. Adolescents can manipulate and understand abstract concepts (Piaget, 1969). With this ability, adolescents can formulate general rules about the world and then test them against the facts. In other words, adolescents can deal with ideas systematically and scientifically, rather than in the haphazard way that younger children do.

As these cognitive changes occur, adolescents become more interested in the structures and ideas of society. And, in turn, they become increasingly sensitive to the wide gap between how things are and how they think they could or should be. This may dissatisfy and depress them and, often, may lead to a period of rebellion, which, in turn, may give way to an idealistic sense of purpose and responsibility (Elkind, 1968).

The development of formal-operational thought also leads to greater introspection and self-analysis among adolescents (Elkind, 1968). Adolescents can distinguish between their own thoughts and those of others, and

The cognitive changes that occur during adolescence make young people more aware of their surroundings, and probably more aware of the gap between what, ideally, should be, and what really is. This realization may lead to a personal goal—a commitment to closing the gap; it may also lead to depression and rebellion.

(© 1976 by Joel Gordon)

can reflect in a more complex way on their feelings, attitudes, and actions. Unfortunately, at first this introspection may lead them into a kind of egocentrism (Elkind, 1969). Because they are painfully preoccupied with themselves, adolescents come to feel that they are "on stage," that their peers are always judging their appearance and behavior. This makes them continually play to their imaginary audience by dressing in a particular fashion, cultivating a distinctive image, and so on.

Just as adolescents often misinterpret others' feelings, they also tend to overvalue their own. Adolescents believe that their feelings are unique in content and intensity. This sense of self-importance is what Elkind (1969) has called a "personal fable." The adolescent feels that no one else can reach the same heights of ecstasy or descend to the same depths of misery. This fable may lead the adolescent to write anguished poetry or to talk to a personal god.

It is not until about the age of 15 or 16 that the egocentrism of early adolescence gives way to more mature thought. As adolescents begin to distinguish the true thoughts of others, the real audience replaces the imaginary one. As they begin to reach out to others and to form more mature relationships, they also judge themselves more realistically (Elkind, 1969).

MORAL DEVELOPMENT AND THE GROWTH OF CONSCIENCE

Psychologists, as well as philosophers and theologians, have long been fascinated by how children develop morality. How do they come to know right from wrong? How does a child develop a conscience?

According to Freud, the conscience develops as the child identifies with the parents and takes on their standards. Other psychologists have emphasized how parents enforce discipline and how this affects the child's moral development. For example, Sears, Maccoby, and Levin (1957) found that children were more likely to tell their mothers, on their own, that they did something wrong, if previously their mothers had withdrawn love as the usual method of discipline, not inflicted physical punishment.

Some psychologists describe moral development in terms of stages, which are thought to be fairly consistent from child to child. Piaget (1932) has identified various stages in children's awareness and their use of moral rules. These stages correspond closely to Piaget's stages of cognitive development. At first, children think of rules as specific examples. Then, in the stage Piaget calls "moral realism," they rigidly view rules as "sacred" dictates handed down by adults. Finally, in the stage of "autonomous morality," children learn that rules are not hard–and–fast; rather they are arbitrary guidelines made up as people go about learning to live and to get along with one another.

A similar theory is proposed by Kohlberg (1963, 1967, 1968). He argues that as children grow older, they go through three distinct levels of moral development. Each level requires a more advanced level of cognitive development than the one before it (Kohlberg & Gilligan, 1971). The first level is the *preconventional* level, which occurs during Piaget's stage of

(Alice Kandell, Photo Researchers)

concrete operations. At this level, very young children interpret behavior in light of its physical consequences—whether they are rewarded or punished for it. At this level, older children define "right" behavior as that which satisfies needs, particularly their own. In adolescence, the shift to formal-operational thought allows the progression to Kohlberg's second, or _conventional_, level of moral development. At this level, the adolescent first defines right behavior as that which pleases or helps others and is approved of by them. This leads to an emphasis on conformity and on "being nice" to gain approval (Mischel, 1976). But this phase soon gives way to concern over maintaining and conforming to the social order—which may include the family, the peer group, and society. The third, or _postconventional_, level requires advanced formal-operational thought. This level is marked by an emphasis on abstract principles quite apart from the concern with the power of those who enforce them, or from their effect on particular groups or societies. At first these principles are apt to be those decided upon by society; later this gives way to ethical principles that are universal.

Any person may show one predominant type of moral reasoning, but at times that person's moral judgments will fit into a lower level and at times they will fit into a higher level. Although cognitive development is needed for principled moral reasoning, it is no guarantee of advanced moral development (Kohlberg & Gilligan, 1971). It is more useful to view moral development as an interaction between people's cognitive abilities and their experiences in society (Aronfreed, 1976). Moral values are, after all, part of one's culture. Hindu children, for example, learn to value life in all its forms, while Americans are taught that only human life is really important. It is in adolescence that people come to see, probably for the first time, how the accident of having been born into a particular culture has influenced their values, their opportunities, and their personalities.

PERSONALITY AND SOCIAL DEVELOPMENT

In adolescence, people start seriously thinking about assuming adult responsibilities: They plan what to do with the rest of their lives. They delve into themselves, see who they are, and find out where they fit into society. In simpler times, this was an easier task. Career, life-style, and personal philosophies were largely determined by family background. But as our society grows more complex and as wider opportunities develop, choices get more difficult. We place great emphasis on individual freedom and responsibility, and we provide few guidelines to help young people ease smoothly into adulthood.

Before adolescents decide what they want to be, they must first find out who they are. According to Erik Erikson (1968), this quest for identity is the main task of adolescence. The young child has many fragmented "selves"—son or daughter, brother or sister, friend, student, and so forth. An adolescent must integrate these many roles—and new ones such as being a member of a peer, racial, or ethnic group—into a unified **identity.** According to Erikson, if a person fails to do this, he or she will suffer **role confusion** and may try in vain to be all things to all people.

The influence of the parents is perhaps the most important factor affecting the adolescent's ability to establish a clear and independent sense of identity. Adolescents who have rewarding relationships with *both* parents have a better chance to develop a strong identity (Conger, 1977). One study found that children of parents who stressed "democratic" child-rearing practices—such as open discussion of issues concerning behavior and discipline—were the most likely to develop confidence and independence (Elder, 1963). Parents can also effectively demonstrate independence to their children. For example, educated professional women are more likely to have had mothers who worked outside the home (Hoffman & Nye, 1974). The working mother seems to provide a more independent role model for her children than the nonworking mother (L. W. Hoffman, 1977). Erikson (1963) also observed that a background of love and trust is essential for an adolescent to achieve a positive self-image and identity.

The peer group is also important in the adolescent's quest for identity. At a time when the adolescent must choose among a confusing number of occupations, life-styles, ideologies, and sex-role models—and is caught in a twilight zone between childhood and adulthood—the understanding and support of peers can be essential (Conger, 1977). Peers are all the more important at this time because the adolescent is trying to become more independent of parents and older siblings and thus may cling to friends instead.

(Christa Armstrong, Photo Researchers)

Unfortunately, as we saw earlier, an adolescent's peers are not always a source of support and encouragement. Peer pressures often encourage the adolescent to conform to group norms, rather than to be more independent. What appears at first as rebellion against parental values may actually be a desperate need to follow the rules of the peer group and maintain peer popularity and approval. Coleman (1974) has called the high school "a cruel jungle of dating and rating" (p. 51), a place where only the fittest survive socially. Those who do not measure up find themselves left out. Pressure to be "in" and the fear of being "out" can cause far more emotional strain than academic pressures.

Even socially successful adolescents may not be completely comfortable with their peers. Adolescents have their own subcultures, with values that are often quite different from those of their family. Attitudes toward sex, drugs, alcohol, and grades are among the many possible sources of conflict. The adolescent must somehow reconcile the worlds of family and peers to develop a sense of identity and an independent course of action.

Clearly, adolescence is a time of turmoil and conflict for many young people. They must adjust to physiological changes, cognitive maturity, and a growing need for identity and independence. The peers to whom they turn for understanding are grappling with the same issues and problems and so may provide little guidance.

Moreover, the youth's parents may also be having their own "identity crisis" (Chilman, 1968). The mother may have sacrificed her career to raise children and may wonder what her life will be like when her youngest child leaves home. The father may feel that his hopes of success are fading and may regret his past career decisions (Conger, 1977). Thus, both the adolescent and his or her parents may be going through difficult developmental periods at the same time. This can make life even more confusing and rough for all concerned.

113

The Transition to Adulthood

In our culture, adult status is not bestowed on a person automatically after adolescence: It must be _earned_. Yet there is no clear-cut line to cross; we have no formal rites of passage. An adolescent can reach the age at which he or she is legally an adult without necessarily assuming adult responsibilities. Thus, there is usually a transition period between adolescence and adulthood—termed "young adulthood"—which prepares a person for adulthood (Eisenstadt, 1961).

This transition period results, in part, from our emphasis on higher education. College and postgraduate studies are needed for many of the more interesting and challenging careers. Most young people are encouraged to continue their education beyond high school if at all possible. This prolongs their years of financial dependence. Because they are not financially independent, most young people cannot fully enter into adult roles.

One particularly difficult aspect of this transition period is sexuality. Until recently, our society has assumed that the years between puberty and marriage will be ones of sexual abstinence. In theory, this prevents sexual expression among both adolescents and unmarried young adults. Surveys indicate that in recent years, however, sexual activity has increased significantly in both groups. As Kimmel (1974) observes, the young adult now faces more freedom of choice in sexual relations. While this freedom may be welcomed by some, it may also add one more difficult task to this developmental period: that of developing one's personal values about sexual intimacy in an era of rapidly changing—and competing—sexual mores and ideologies. As with other decisions, young adults must sort out their options as society becomes increasingly complex and diversified.

(Roy Eni, Photo Researchers)

Young adulthood has been described in somewhat differing ways by various psychologists. To Erik Erikson (1968), young adulthood is a crucial turning point with the choice of *intimacy* on the one hand or *isolation* on the other. He believes that the principal task of this stage is to form true relationships: that is, to recognize and to value others as unique persons, rather than to use them to define one's own identity. If a person fails to establish intimacy, however, he or she "may settle for highly stereotyped relationships and come to retain a deep sense of isolation" (p. 136).

Robert White (1966) identifies many interrelated "growth trends" that seem to be typical of young adulthood. One must bring one's sense of self into focus and eliminate inconsistencies; narrow the range and deepen the quality of relationships; become more selective about and more deeply involved with work and hobbies; relate abstract moral philosophies to human life and thus build a highly personal system of values; and apply one's values to create a real concern for others' feelings.

Adulthood

Since World War II, the U.S. population has become composed of many more adults than ever before, and they are living longer. For example, in 1980 about 1 out of every 10 Americans was 65 years old, or older. By the year 2000, our government estimates that 1 out of every 8 Americans will be in this age group. Partly as a result of these figures, the study of adulthood, once relatively neglected, is now an exciting area of research. In their efforts to understand the physical, cognitive, and personality changes that occur during adulthood, psychologists use the same two methods of research that we discussed in Chapter 3: cross-sectional and longitudinal studies. Of the two, cross-sectional studies are by far the more popular with researchers on adulthood, because a longitudinal study of the same people would take 50 years or more to complete! Cross-sectional studies, however, cannot separate the relative importance of age differences and genera-

115

tional differences. For example, a woman who was 60 years old in 1981 lived through the Great Depression as a teen-ager and may have been greatly affected by that experience. By contrast, her son, who was only 35 years old in 1981, matured during the relatively prosperous 1950s and 1960s. Thus, it is hard to know if differences between them reflect their different ages, or their belonging to different generations, or both. It is tempting to try to discover "pure" age differences, but Baltes and Labouvie (1973) note that generational factors may be just as crucial in shaping an adult's development as is aging. If this is true, the psychology of adulthood may require continual revisions to include the effects not only of age, but also of each generation's life experiences.

The three stages of adulthood—young, middle, and late—are as different from one another as adolescence is from childhood. Young adults need to form close personal relationships and to avoid isolation. For people in their 20s, deciding on a life's work is also a central concern. This is even more true for those whose identity, time, and energy will be closely tied to a career outside the home. It is also in their 20s that many people decide about marriage. Once married, people must continue to adopt new roles and accept new senses of permanence and responsibility. The birth of the first child demands still more adjustments. For the woman, especially, parenthood can become a real crisis.

In their 30s, people tend to settle down. They usually come to accept themselves, both their good and bad qualities. Many men in their early 30s have a crisis in which they feel dissatisfied with the shape of their lives, but for most men this passes quickly.

At the start of middle adulthood, many people start to realize that time

Each stage of adulthood has its own concerns. Young people in their 20s and 30s are concerned with careers, finding a marriage partner, and starting a family. In middle adulthood, people become aware that the time in which to achieve their career goals is growing short. Late adulthood brings a renewed appreciation of the importance of family relationships.

(Left to right: Ray Ellis, Rapho/Photo Researchers; Chester Higgins, Jr., Rapho/Photo Researchers; Ray Ellis, Photo Researchers; Horst Ebersberg, Photo Researchers; Nancy J. Pierce, Photo Researchers)

  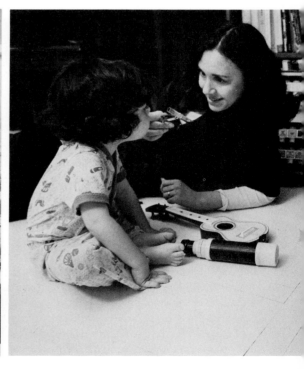

is getting short. The pressure to achieve life goals becomes acute. Some people may start a new career because they want a new challenge or a second chance to reach their goals. While men often become more sensitive and vulnerable in their 40s, women may become more assertive. By this time, most children have "left the nest," which rejuvenates many women. Both men and women become aware of the physical aspects of aging during this period. Menopause is an obvious turning point for women, but men also become more concerned about their health.

Later in middle adulthood, the awareness that one's time is limited may cause many people to turn inward and become somewhat reflective. Personal needs often become important. People become more "private." A mark of adjustment during this period is the discovery of new interests to fill the gaps left by the end of work and the decrease in family demands

In late adulthood, retirement may leave a person with little sense of identity or purpose, with more "free" time, but with not much to do. Family relationships—important throughout the life cycle—often become more important during this period. The physical realities of aging are unavoidable as people face illnesses and death. Perhaps one of the greatest challenges of late adulthood is our society's attitudes toward old age. Contrary to popular belief, many of the pleasures associated with youth persist into old age. People in their 70s and 80s have both the need and the capacity for sex and physical affection. Intelligence does not necessarily decline with age, although some motor functions weaken as the body ages. To assume that **senility** is the same as old age is wrong. Very few people become senile, and many people whose behavior is called "senile" merely act that way because they feel that is what society expects.

"O.K., so you're forty, you've lived half your life. Look at the bright side. If you were a horse, you'd already be dead fifteen years."

(Drawing by Mulligan; © 1961 *The New Yorker Magazine*, Inc.)

PHYSIOLOGICAL CHANGES

Aging means that each person undergoes **senescence,** a gradual and inevitable decline in life processes (Hendricks & Hendricks, 1977). Through this decline, a person's vulnerability to stress—such as a fatal disease—increases. Work performance may also be affected. A person may have less energy and may find some tasks harder.

There are several theories about why we age. The most obvious is that our bodies simply wear out or wear down. But aging is not simply a matter of bodily wear-and-tear; that can often be counteracted by rest and treatment. The body's self-regulating mechanisms also begin to break down, which causes problems with control of body temperature, hormonal secretions, blood-sugar level, and kidney function. There are cumulative effects of stress due to chronic illness, radiation, smoking, overeating, and lack of exercise. There is a decline in the number of cells, a stiffening of the proteins called collagen and elastin, a limit to the number of times cells can reproduce, and an increase in cellular mutation. One theory even suggests that death benefits the species. Once people pass the reproductive stage, their tissues are programmed to die on schedule.

What physiological changes normally come with aging? Baldness and gray hair, some loss of hearing ability and vision, and a slowing of the nervous system may occur. The skin becomes wrinkled and dry. Blood vessels become frail and break more easily. Muscles shrink and posture gets poorer. The bone mass decreases, and bones become hollow and weak. Vertebral discs become thinner and the vertebrae collapse, which may result in loss of stature. The number and diameter of muscle fibers decrease. Muscles need more time to relax and contract. Total and vital lung capacity decrease. The muscles that line the rib cage weaken. There is more threat of kidney failure. Strokes may cause cognitive and motor impairment. Sleep patterns change.

Sometimes, however, conditions blamed on the aging process may be caused by disease. Since illness is common among the aged, it is often hard to distinguish its effects from those of age itself. Recent studies have shown that, up to a certain age, the effects of aging are relatively insignificant if a person is not ill (Kimmel, 1974). Unfortunately, few older people are perfectly healthy. Eighty-five percent of all people over age 65, and nearly two-thirds of the population over age 75, report at least one chronic illness: arthritis, rheumatism, heart disease, and hypertension being the most common.

Perhaps even more important than the physical effects of aging, however, are the psychological results of those changes. In a society oriented toward youth and beauty, even the young and attractive feel insecure about their appearance. This problem becomes more serious as a person ages. In some cases, this severely affects one's self-image. For example, a 40-year-old woman or man who needs to wear glasses for the first time may find this physical change quite threatening—even though the actual loss of vision may be slight.

Many people also mistakenly assume that an inevitable stage of senescence is senility, a state marked by lapses of memory, haziness of thought, and other signs of mental and physical decay (Kimble, 1977). In fact, as we

(Betty Lane, Photo Researchers)

noted earlier, very few people become senile. Many old people *act* senile, not because they are, but because that is how society expects them to behave. Just as little girls were once supposed to be silly and little boys were supposed to be tough, society expects the aged to be confused and forgetful—and people tend to do what is expected of them. As long as society expects its old people to be eccentric, most of them will appear to be just that.

COGNITIVE CHANGES

The kinds of qualitative changes in cognition that Piaget proposed generally end in adolescence or young adulthood. During adulthood itself, a person continues to use the formal-operational thinking processes that emerged earlier. Although there are some researchers (e.g., Riegel, 1973*b*) who believe that there might be more stages of adult cognition, there is little evidence of what those stages are. Therefore, in this section our primary emphasis is on measurable gains or losses in abilities that are present at the start of adulthood.

In many societies, age is equated with wisdom. Our society, however, seems to believe that to be old is to be feebleminded. Until recently, it was accepted as fact that from around age 30 intelligence began to decline. Today, however, many psychologists question whether intelligence declines with age at all (Baltes & Schaie, 1976; Horn & Donaldson, 1976). Some research shows that the more biologically based intellectual abilities—such as memory span—do decline after adolescence, whereas abilities that reflect experience increase through most of adulthood. Tests have shown, however, that even differences between the basic abilities of the young and the middle-aged are not great (Stevens-Long, 1979).

Some longitudinal studies of people up to the age of 50 suggest that intelligence continues to grow—in ever smaller amounts—during early adulthood. Other studies suggest that intellect can grow past the age of 70 (Baltes & Schaie, 1974). Conger (1977) believes that many cognitive abilities hold up quite well for most people until age 60, and until much later for those who are healthy and intellectually active.

(Peter Miller, Photo Researchers)

This view of continuous cognitive growth has been questioned by other researchers who insist that there is a cognitive decline related to aging, at least for some important abilities. For example, Horn (1976) argues that, starting in early adulthood, certain cognitive capacities—among them inductive reasoning and spatial orientation—do indeed decline. Horn's theory is strengthened by Redeck and Taube, who, in a study of the Wechsler Adult Intelligence Scale (see Chapter 10), found that while there was no decline in such things as information, comprehension, attention, and rote memory, other tests of alertness, speed of learning, and ability to perceive and analyze problems dropped sharply (Shaie, 1974).

One of the problems in studying cognitive changes in adulthood is that different techniques—such as cross-sectional and longitudinal studies—often produce conflicting or inconsistent findings when applied to different cognitive abilities. Moreover, environmental factors may affect how adults score on intelligence tests (Baltes & Labouvie, 1973). And IQ tests may seem more relevant to young people than to older adults, which may explain why young people do better on them. It is also possible that higher education itself promotes better performance on tests. This would introduce a generational difference, since before World War II not many people went to college (Kimmel, 1974). Furthermore, the social structure of our culture often forces the elderly to be relatively inactive. Both physical and mental idleness may add to cognitive decline during old age (Neugarten, 1976). All these factors make it difficult to draw firm conclusions about the relationship between physical aging and general intelligence.

What about memory? Do older people have trouble remembering? Research suggests that age does affect both learning and memory. Old people do not use the same memory devices that young people do, which makes them appear not to learn as well. Also, older people have trouble processing new data, which causes serious problems with long-term memory (Stevens-Long, 1979).

A significant memory loss or a decline of learning ability would seem to contribute to a decline in other intellectual abilities. Most people, however, develop ways of making up for the slight impairment of these functions, so that their day-to-day performance does not change much. For example, Schaie (1976) found that most people suffered no decline in their ability to solve problems before their 50s, and only a slight decline in their 60s and mid-70s. Only in the 80s was significant decline the rule.

Does creativity decline with age? A study by Harvey Lehman (1953) found that most of a person's high-quality creative work is done in early adulthood and declines thereafter. By the age of 50, people have made 80 percent of their best contributions. Botwinick (1967) also pinpoints the age of peak production of high quality work in the arts, sciences, and humanities as between the ages of 30 and 39. Wayne Dennis (1966) found evidence, however, that creativity continues well past middle age, especially in fields where much of the routine work can be done by younger people. Moreover, Dennis cites several people in history who have done significant creative work at an advanced age. Among these are Benjamin Franklin, who invented the bifocal lens at the age of 78; Mahatma Gandhi, who, at the age of 72, won India's independence; Claude Monet, who began his water-lily series at the age of 73; and the architect Frank Lloyd Wright, who designed the Guggenheim Museum when he was 91 years of age.

Finally, whether reduced creativity is a result of aging or of cultural expectation is not clear. As Stevens-Long (1979) states: "There are compelling arguments in support of the notion that the present experiential and environmental conditions of older people stultify creativity in old age. Poverty, illness, malnutrition, lack of education, racism, sexism, and the negative view our society has of the aging personality all contribute to declining creativity" (pp. 361–362).

CHANGES IN SOCIAL RELATIONSHIPS

FRIENDSHIP. The importance of friends fluctuates over a person's life span. During young adulthood, when people are most inclined to form deep personal attachments, most people come to appreciate the support and affection of old friends. This has an important effect on the development of identity, on feelings of continuity, and on the perception of time. But Haan and Day (1974) report that by the end of young adulthood, most people have as many close friends as they want, usually three or four. Friendships formed by adults are often quite strong, and they last as one grows older (Hess, 1971). In fact, Bischoff (1976) found that friends are often more influential to a middle-aged man than is his wife.

Friendships formed by adults are usually quite strong and last over the years. However, unlike friendships formed in earlier years, middle-aged friendships stress the quality rather than the frequency of the interaction.
(Bruce Roberts, Rapho/Photo Researchers)

Friendship in later life may be more complex than it is for the young. This is particularly true for older people living in age-segregated communities where peer relations are important for adjustment and morale. In such settings, the residents look out for one another, come into frequent contact, and make and keep new friendships.

For most people, however, the frequency, if not the intensity, of contact with friends declines over the life span. Newlyweds and young students enjoy daily contact with their friends. Adults in late middle age may contact their friends once a month or less. People in middle and late adulthood are more concerned with the quality of their friendships than with their frequency of interaction. To older people, shared experience and the emotional and personal aspects of friendship—neither of which is dimmed by separation—are more important than they are to the young, who base intimacy on sharing current experiences (Lowenthal et al., 1975; Troll, 1975).

MARRIAGE AND SEXUALITY. More than 90 percent of Americans between the ages of 25 and 34 are married (Stevens-Long, 1979). Marital satisfaction, however, varies during the marriage and affects men and women in different ways. Husbands report most dissatisfaction during the years before retirement. Wives report most dissatisfaction with marriage during the parental years (Rollins & Feldman, 1970).

Children complicate all marriages. Parents of adolescent children find themselves under special strains as they try to juggle many roles: parents, workers, homemakers, citizens, friends, members of civic and other groups, as well as being husbands and wives. Once children leave the home, many parents find renewed marital satisfaction. In fact, married couples with "empty nests" are often among the happiest (Campbell, 1975; Miller,

According to one poll—and to this contented couple— marriage seems to improve with age.

(Arthur Glauberman, Photo Researchers)

1976; Rollins & Feldman, 1970). For the first time in years, they can be together and enjoy one another's company (Stinnett et al., 1972).

In a study of older couples, Stinnett et al. (1972) found that 90 percent saw their relationship as either "happy" or "very happy." More than 50 percent said that their marriage had improved with time; and most of those polled felt that the later years of their marriage were the best. Among the pleasures of marriage cited by older couples were companionship, shared feelings and common interests, and being taken care of. Throughout the three stages of adulthood, mutuality and intimacy are important. They may even become more important as one gets older. Then, a person leaves behind one set of roles—such as worker and parent—so that other roles— such as spouse and companion—assume more importance.

Most of the sexual experiences between men and women in America occur in marriage (Simon & Gagnon, 1970). The frequency of physical affection, however, from kissing to sexual intercourse, tends to decline over the years. Masters and Johnson (1970) claim that with age there is a general slowing of sexual response and intensity.

Contrary to popular belief, however, the physiological effects of menopause have no direct effect on a woman's sexual interest levels (Comfort, 1976). In fact, except for fertility, sexual effectiveness persists longer in women than in men. The most common reasons for sexual inactivity in older women are social convention, lack of a partner, or role-playing (Comfort, 1976).

FAMILY. Establishing a family seems to be the major turning point in most adults' lives (Lowenthal & Chiriboga, 1972). With the birth of the first child, many adjustments have to be made in a marriage. "Husband" and "wife" become "father" and "mother." "Couple" becomes "family." This can be a real crisis for the woman especially. If she has been involved in a career, she may suddenly have conflicting values. She may feel frustrated if she abandons her career and anxious or guilty if she continues to work. Inexperienced parents may be terrified of responsibility, plagued by inadequacy, and stricken by guilt over mixed emotions about the baby. The husband may feel "left out." The wife may resent her husband's freedom from child-raising.

For women in middle adulthood, dealing with adolescent children can also be very difficult. Most women cite this as the most unsatisfactory phase of their marriage. But men in middle adulthood often express increased interest in marriage and in family life. When the first-born grows up and leaves home, the worst stage of family life for the woman seems to be over. Most women look forward to their children's leaving home and find renewed enjoyment in their marriages; they often feel rejuvenated by the freedom from responsibility. Often the sadder figure may be the father who decides to get to know his children just when they have left home or are struggling to define themselves as young adults outside of the family.

At the same time that middle-aged parents are launching their children, they are also faced with increasing responsibilities to their own, now aging parents. The role reversal that occurs at this stage can sometimes be difficult and can be filled with anxiety and resentment. Studies have shown, however, that most relationships between middle-aged children and their parents are quite good (Hill et al., 1970). This is at least partly due to time and maturity. The middle-aged child may at last be able to see a parent as a person, and the aging parents can step back from their parental role and let the child run his or her own life without interference.

Throughout their lives, Americans tend to turn first to their families in times of need or when there is a conflict between the demands of friends or kin. As people age, family relationships become more, not less, important. For most elderly people, families are the main source of intimacy and emotional support, a fact not fully reflected in age-segregated retirement communities.

DIVORCE AND THE DEATH OF A SPOUSE. One-third of all first marriages now end in divorce. Yet, within 3 years of a divorce, 75 percent of both males and females remarry (Stevens-Long, 1979). As more women work and become more emotionally independent, they have fewer reasons to stay in unsatisfactory marriages—particularly since the religious, economic, social, and legal obstacles to divorce have weakened in the past 20 years.

Divorce and separation affect people in different ways. Women are often more distressed before a separation; men have more problems after it. Older people are apt to be more unhappy after a separation than younger people (Chiriboga, 1978).

By contrast, the death of a spouse seems to be more difficult for the young of both sexes. Although the grief experienced by widowed people of all ages is related to the importance of the spouse, young adults are more apt to feel guilt or self-reproach about the events surrounding their spouses' deaths (Glick et al., 1974). Their grief may be so intense and prolonged that it may impair their work and social lives.

Recovery from the death of a spouse is related to one's options, or resources—i.e., money, education, contacts outside the home, and so on (Lopata, 1973). When a woman's husband dies, she not only loses a friend, a companion, an escort, and a sexual partner, she often also loses a primary source of financial support. Twenty-six percent of all widows have never worked; 40 percent have not worked while they were married. As a result, many widows cannot support themselves and both their social and financial standing plummets, causing them to become withdrawn and isolated.

Men have somewhat different problems. In studies involving widows and widowers of the same age, Atchley (1975) found that widows had more anxiety but that widowers seemed to feel more aimless. For many men, their wives are their only friends, and men are often not prepared to live alone. Although men of all ages find it easier to form new sexual relationships than women do—marriage between an older man and a younger woman is still socially more acceptable than marriage between an older woman and a younger man—women have social skills that they use to make friends with other women and that help assuage their grief. This is even more true for older women, who often have a more extensive social network than have older men.

WORK. Young adulthood is consumed by the need for economic security and success. Deciding on a life's work is a central concern of most people in their 20s. Although some men wander from job to job, most men select, through education or experience, a career path by their mid-20s. Much of their identity and most of their time and energy are tied to that career. More women are making similar career choices in their 20s, but often they still pick a "job" rather than a "career." At this point in their lives, they may choose work that will not tie them down in one place, that will not stop them from getting home on time at night, or that will not interfere with child care. For better or for worse, most women do not start a professional career until after their 20s, if they have one at all.

In their early 30s, many men go through a crisis in which they become dissatisfied with the shape of their lives and feel that it is their last chance to set things right (Levinson, 1978). Just how difficult this time of life is for men is debatable. Some researchers see mid-life as a time of tremendous turmoil, and there is some evidence to support this view. At mid-life, marriage is often least satisfying (Pineo, 1961), and neurotic disorders most frequent (Weintraub & Aronson, 1968). The rates for first-admission alcoholism are highest for people in middle adulthood. The number of suicides, especially among men, also increases at this time. Infidelity and desertion become major problems. And peptic ulcers, hypertension, and heart disease flare up (Rosenberg & Farrell, 1976).

Other researchers, however, find less evidence that a severe mid-life crisis occurs. Some studies show that most people in middle adulthood believe themselves to be happy, satisfied, confident, and in control. They rarely, if ever, describe life as a crisis.

However traumatic mid-life may be, many middle-aged men and women turn to second careers at this point to find new rewards and challenges. With the current stress on personal growth and values, however, many middle-aged men are no longer willing to risk their health, family, friends, and their free time just for job promotions. It should not be surprising, then, that mid-life often involves not only changes in careers, but also renewed interest in families, friends, and hobbies.

LEISURE. It can be hard, however, to balance work and leisure. Although most Americans spend about as much time away from work as they do on the job, many middle-aged people in the United States and in other Western nations believe in the work ethic and are uneasy about free time. Although this attitude may be changing, especially among the young, for many middle-aged people leisure is not a legitimate concept. They seem to feel that the right to enjoy one's self depends on first having worked long and hard. In other words, a person has to earn it (Parker, 1975; Pfeiffer & Davis, 1974). Too much leisure is thought to lead to decadence, decline, and social instability.

Educators have tried to change people's attitudes about free time to help them to get more pleasure and satisfaction from leisure activities. Teaching people how to do various activities, however—such as games and crafts—is one thing; but teaching them to enjoy them and to value doing them is something else. Perhaps leisure will only be accepted as worthwhile and honorable when people feel as positive about it as they do about work.

A study at Duke University found that Americans spend most of their leisure time watching TV. Only 50 percent of the Duke sample spent any

People's attitudes toward—and participation in—leisure activities depend on, among other things, their feelings about the work ethic and how much money they make.
(Margaret Durrance, Photo Researchers)

time participating in a sport or a hobby. Few were even spectators in any outdoor activities. And even fewer used their leisure time to do volunteer work. Gordon, Gaitz, and Scott (1977) found that, in general, doing something active with one's free time decreases with age. As one would expect, this is even more true for those activities that involve exertion and excitement. Activity that requires very intense personal involvement—such as highly competitive sports—declines sharply after about age 44. With age, however, more time is spent in activities that offer relaxation and solitude, such as reading, fishing, or painting.

Another important factor in people's attitudes toward leisure is money. Cottrell and Atchley (1969) found that adults with higher incomes seemed to be more leisure-oriented than other adults. Perhaps, as part of the work ethic, Americans believe that one's ability to pay for leisure makes it more legitimate.

(Richard B. Klein, Nancy Palmer Photo Agency)

DEALING WITH RETIREMENT. The first Social Security legislation in the United States was enacted in 1935, thereby granting official status to "retirement." Since then, retirement has become a normal and important part of life, instead of being merely a preparation for death.

Although retirement has become an accepted phase of life, the role of the retiree is, at best, ambiguous. Retired people are supposed to live their own lives, to pay their own way, to have reasonable self-respect, and to be socially responsible (Atchley, 1977; Donahue, Orbach, & Pollack, 1960). But exactly what does that entail on a day-to-day basis? Unlike other roles in life, such as student, worker, child, or spouse, the duties of retirees are unclear. Are retirees supposed to sit on the porch and watch life go by, or should they join civic groups, play golf, and be foster grandparents? Those who have trouble filling their days find it hard to adjust to retirement. Most of the men in the previously mentioned Duke sample (1977) felt that they had too much free time.

As with leisure, money influences people's attitudes toward retirement. Shanas (1972) found that what Americans miss most about their work is not the responsibility, usefulness, power, fulfillment, or the sense of a job well done, but the money. If retirement means a major loss of financial freedom, a person is less eager to forego his or her salary and to retire.

But more than money is involved. In a general sense, people's attitudes toward retirement are tied to their attitudes toward work. People who were fulfilled by their jobs were often less interested in retiring than those whose jobs were unrewarding (Atchley, 1976). Blue-collar workers, for example, often look forward to retirement; professionals more often do not. Other factors, such as education and age, are also important. Highly educated men are less interested in retiring than uneducated ones, although well-educated women tend to leave the work force earlier than their less well-educated counterparts. Younger workers, to whom work is less crucial, favor retirement. Older people who are closer to actual retirement are less disposed to leave work.

For those, then, whose job fulfills goals that other activities or roles do not, and for those to whom work goals stay important, retirement demands major adjustment and reorganization. The **activity substitution theory** asserts that successful adjustment to retirement depends on a new activity

125

being substituted for the lost job. The new activity then provides the satisfaction previously given by the old job (Friedman & Havighurst, 1954; Shanas, 1972). This is supported by evidence that people who work past normal retirement age have higher morale than those who do not (Carp, 1968). Many other people who cannot stay at their jobs after age 65 seek a second career as a substitute for the first.

For many people, then, retirement can cause problems. Is it also a time of crisis? Retirement has often been thought to lead to physical illness and disability, psychological problems, social disturbances, and cognitive decline. Streib and Schneider (1971), however, found that this was not true. On the contrary, their research suggests that health improves slightly after retirement, and that most retired people are satisfied and well-adjusted.

Streib and Schneider see retirement as a form of disengagement: People disengage themselves from the role of worker and move into another and equally satisfying role in life. Their theory, called *differential disengagement*, asserts that disengagement occurs at different rates and degrees according to the roles a person plays during his or her lifetime. New roles and new activities develop as a person withdraws from one role to another. Retirement, thus, is a crisis only for those who have not achieved, or who have not at least begun to achieve, the transition from an active (worker) role to a passive (retiree) role during middle age.

This same **theory of disengagement** also applies to a person's adjustment to old age. Cumming and Henry (1961) state that old age is marked by a lessened involvement with society. In other words, the elderly have spent a long time fulfilling their social obligations and, as a reward, are allowed by society to withdraw, to rest, to relax, and to be free. When this disengagement from society is mutual, all is well. If people are forced to disengage before they are ready, however, then their adjustment problems will be greater.

Some psychologists do not accept disengagement theory as it pertains to adjustment to aging. For example, Maddox (1970) argues that the more active and productive a person is, the more satisfied he or she will be at any stage of life. According to Maddox, old people want to continue to be active and productive. They disengage not because they want to, but because our society provides no outlet for their energies.

Recent research contradicts both the substitution and disengagement theories. Neither withdrawal nor continued engagement necessarily insures that a person will remain happy and satisfied with life. Like young adults and those in middle age, older people get satisfaction from various life-styles. Problems with adjustment to old age occur when people cannot live lives that fulfill their own needs and desires. Active, highly involved, and satisfied people can be happy and satisfied throughout their lives if they are given opportunities for continued involvement. People who choose to be less involved when they are young can also enjoy old age, if they are allowed to avoid the responsibilities and activities that they never wanted to begin with. Neugarten and Hagestad (1977) believe that one's earlier personality predicts how well a person will adjust to the aging process. People with well-integrated personalities tend to adjust well to old age. Those who are less satisfied with their lives continue to have difficulty in old age.

Death and Dying

Death is seldom central to a person's final years. In fact, it may loom larger in middle age when the first awareness of mortality coincides with a greater interest in living (Kimmel, 1974). A study undertaken to compare attitudes toward death and dying among young adults and people over age 65 found that 19 percent of the young were afraid of death, compared to only 1.7 percent of the elderly (Rogers, 1980). When asked to describe the worst aspect of death, 36 percent of the young adults mentioned "an end to experience," while only 9 percent of the elderly felt that way.

According to Simone de Beauvoir (1972), the elderly person, while aware of the imminence of death, may be more concerned with taking stock of past accomplishments. If people have been successful in the main tasks of life, they will have a sense of integrity. If people cannot accept the events of their lives, however, the result will be despair, for it is now too late to change things (Erikson, 1968).

Robert Butler (1963) asserts that this kind of life review is universal among those near to death. This does not mean, however, that old people brood about the past. For example, Paul Cameron (1972) found that most people, including the elderly, concentrate on the present.

Recent research shows that nearness to death—apart from age or illness—may itself cause psychological changes. Lieberman (1965) tells of a nurse who could predict the death of her patients because they "just seemed to act differently." Several researchers have been startled to find an accurate sign of impending death, which they call the "terminal drop." The terminal drop is a noticeable decline in assertiveness, cognitive organiza-

THE LIVING WILL

Death was traditionally defined as a stoppage of the heartbeat and a cessation of breathing. Today, however, sophisticated machines can keep the vital organs functioning—or even replace them—long after a patient has gone into a terminal coma or all hope of recovery is lost. Patients can linger between life and death for weeks, unconscious, kept alive only by their connection to a machine. Many people consider this "life" worse than death. As a result, three new definitions of death have been proposed: (1) irreversible brain damage with no chance for a return to consciousness; (2) no possibility of getting the heart to beat on its own again; (3) total brain death (Mant, 1968).

None of these definitions has been accepted, however, by the medical or legal professions, and the controversy over what constitutes legal death goes on. Some families urge doctors to "pull the plug" on patients who are being kept alive only by machines with no hope of regaining consciousness. Doctors argue with clergymen and legal authorities over the same issue.

Without official criteria, people are deciding the issue for themselves. The Euthanasia Education Council publishes a document called "The Living Will" that lets people name the conditions under which they wish to be considered legally dead. Addressed to "any individual who may become responsible for my health, welfare or affairs," the document states: "If the situation should arise in which there is no reasonable expectation of my recovery from physical or mental disability, I request that I be allowed to die and not be kept alive by artificial means or 'heroic measures'" (Stevens-Long, 1979).

tion, and IQ as measured by psychological tests. As a person nears death, there is a sharp decline in these functions (Kleemeier, 1962; Lieberman & Coplay, 1969; Riegel & Meyer, 1967).

Psychiatrist Elizabeth Kübler-Ross (1969) interviewed more than 200 dying people of all ages to try to understand the different aspects of the dying process. From these interviews she isolated five sequential stages through which people pass as they react to their own impending death.

The first stage is *denial*. The person refuses to accept the prognosis, insists it is a mistake, and consults other doctors. In the second stage, the person recognizes the verdict and feels intense *anger* and resentment. These emotions are directed at nurses, doctors, family—anyone with whom the dying person comes into contact. The patience and understanding of others is very important at this time. The third stage is marked by *bargaining*—with the doctor, with the illness, or with God—in a desperate attempt to buy time. The bargaining seems to be a healthy attempt to cope with the awareness of death. In the fourth stage, the person accepts that death is coming, and the result is *depression*. Finally, the dying person moves from depression to full *acceptance*. This stage is characterized by "quiet expectation." The person is typically tired, weak, and unemotional.

According to Kübler-Ross (1969), the central problem that Americans have in coping with death is that we fear and deny it. Because we do not believe we could possibly die of natural causes, we associate death with "a bad act, a frightening happening" (p. 2). She observes that while some other cultures are *death affirming*, American culture is *death denying*. "We are reluctant to reveal our age; we spend fortunes to hide our wrinkles; we prefer to send our old people to nursing homes" (Kübler-Ross, 1975, p. 28). We also shelter children from death and dying. By trying to "protect" children from unpleasant realities, we may actually make them very afraid of death (Kübler-Ross, 1975).

Kübler-Ross believes that we depersonalize dying people at a time when they badly need comfort and compassion. In part, this may be because relating to dying people can be very painful for family and friends—and for nurses, doctors, and mental health professionals (Pattison, 1977). Often dying people are separated from everyone and everything that is familiar and meaningful to them and are "segregated" with other sick and dying people in a hospital or nursing home. It is even more difficult to cope with fears about dying when a person feels alone and perhaps discarded (Kübler-Ross, 1975).

Kübler-Ross's work has increased our understanding of the emotional needs of the dying person (Kastenbaum & Costa, 1977). In the last decade, medical and other professional schools have begun to teach that death is a natural event and that families should be helped to accept it.

There is, however, some doubt about the accuracy of Kübler-Ross's five-stage model of dying. Shibles (1974) suggests that the stages are too narrow and fixed. Kastenbaum (1977) has argued that there is no evidence that every person moves through all five stages. Pattison (1977) believes that a dying person, like someone who is not dying, has a continual ebb and flow of emotions.

Even more seriously, some health-care professionals apply the Kübler-Ross model in a rigid and destructive manner. Clinical personnel may patronize the dying person before he or she "is in the anger stage" (Kastenbaum & Costa, 1977, p. 242). Or *they* may become angry if a person does not move neatly into the "next" stage. In extreme cases, professionals actually demand that individuals "die in the right way" (Pattison, 1977, p. 304). Pattison points out that Kübler-Ross cited many examples of people who did not precisely follow the five-stage model. He adds: "From my own personal contacts with Dr. Kübler-Ross, I believe she would be dismayed at the manner in which her stages of dying have been misused to force artificial patterns of dying upon the dying person" (p. 304).

Application

HOSPICE CARE FOR THE DYING

In the Middle Ages, a "hospice" was a way station and a refuge where pilgrims and travelers could find food, rest, and comfort on their journey. Today's **hospice** is a center for the dying that seeks to minister to their medical, psychological, and social needs.

"I am less afraid of death than I am of dying," is a remark often heard by doctors and counselors from dying patients. And, in truth, the pain and loneliness of the dying are often fearsome—and to a certain extent, inescapable. Yet, the American way of dying may have made things worse. In the past, most people who had a terminal disease suffered and died at home and were consoled somewhat by familiar faces and surroundings. Today, the terminally ill are more apt to spend their last days, or even months, in a hospital or a nursing home. Seventy percent of all Americans now live part of their last year in one of these facilities (Wellborn, 1978). We have come to take this situation for granted. But its effect on both the dying and their families has often been to make the process of dying even more painful and frightening than it has to be.

There is now a new health-care facility for the terminally ill: the hospice. With in-patient facilities and home-care services, the hospice helps a dying patient and his or her family live with as little pain and as much comfort as possible until the patient's death.

The key features that distinguish a hospice from a hospital or nursing home are the treatment of people who cannot be cured and the attention given to their families. Hospitals seek to help the patient recover from disease. Nursing and convalescent homes exist to provide long-term care for the elderly or the handicapped. Neither are equipped to deal with those patients suffering from an incurable disease—especially cancer—who may expect to live for less than a year. Moreover, hospitals and nursing homes have only minimal resources for helping these patients' families deal with the emotional trauma of watching a loved one die. By contrast, hospices exist solely to deal with the dying and their survivors, not with the ill or the elderly.

The first goal of hospice care is to control pain, not to try to cure its causes. For example, Hospice, Inc., in New Haven, Connecticut, uses a mixture of morphine and water for pain relief while still allowing the patient to be active and alert. But the hospice also recognizes that pain control succeeds best when it is related to the patient's mental and emotional well-being. Hospice treatment, therefore, includes a constant program of comfort, counseling, and care designed to help patients cope with the situation. Allaying patient fears is a major part of this program. At Hospice, Inc., Dr. Sylvia Lack, the head physician, tries to prepare dying patients for the inevitable. She explains that 50 percent of terminal patients do not experience pain; that pain, if it comes, does not have to be endured; and that pain control should start when pain is still mild—patients should not feel guilty for asking for relief even in the earliest stages (Duboise, 1981).

Hospice patients spend their last days either in the hospice itself or, in most cases, at home. Hospice, Inc. requires that a "primary caregiver"—a relative, spouse, or friend—live with the patient. The hospice staff teaches these primary caregivers how to attend to the patient and that care must be available at all times. Volunteers help provide companionship, transportation, shopping assistance, or bedside sitting.

Hospices also recognize the need to comfort the family and friends of the dying patient throughout the whole period of grief, which means after death as well as before it. Dr. Elizabeth Kübler-Ross found that it was often harder for the family to accept death than it was for the dying patient. Officials at Hospice, Inc. write: "The bereaved are more vulnerable to physical and psychological disease; care for the survivors . . . is needed until [they] can cope for themselves, or until other resources such as mental health services, family physician, extended family, or minister are found to provide the help needed" (Duboise, 1981). Outside professionals can advise the bereaved on insurance policies, bills, lawyers, and funeral preparations. A grieving person can return to the hospice staff for help at any time.

Besides the psychological and spiritual uplift provided by hospices, there are also noteworthy dollar savings. Professional planners of the hospice movement report that "61 percent of one hospice's patients die at home (compared with the 2 percent of all American deaths which occur at home)" (Duboise, 1981). According to the American Hospital Association, in 1978 the average cost of a day's hospital care was $151.79. Hospice, Inc. placed the cost of its Home Care Service at approximately $750 per patient over a 3-month period (Wellborn, 1978).

All of the benefits of hospices, however, depend on how well they can overcome the negative American attitudes toward death and

This is Hospice, Inc., of New Haven, Conn.
(Nikki Lindberg)

dying and toward institutions associated with them. People who lived near Hospice, Inc., for example, feared that a "death house" was coming to their neighborhood. As a means of dispelling this image, the hospice was designed to appear as pleasant as possible. With a glass-walled, staff dining room and a day-care center playground facing the street, the facility resembles a suburban school. Passers-by see children playing and people moving about busily.

The "death house" fear reveals our "death-denying culture." America emphasizes youth and physical beauty and has traditionally devoted its energies to growth and to problems that can be solved. Death is not a form of growth. It is not a "problem" that can be solved by science, technology, or money. It is, instead, a natural event, the last stage of living, and one that all human beings have to undergo— and watch others undergo. It is in accepting death, as part of the life process, that the hospice movement renders perhaps its greatest service to the dying and their families. Hospices can encourage people to share their needs and fears and thus help them overcome their dread of what they may not want to accept—but cannot avoid.

Summary

1. Each person experiences significant—and interrelated—physical, cognitive, and personality changes throughout all stages of the life cycle.

2. The period known as *adolescence* begins at approximately 11 or 12 years of age and continues roughly until the age of 17. These years are marked by the most dramatic physiological changes since the first 2 years of life.

3. During adolescence, people develop primary and secondary sex characteristics and experience increased sexual drives.

4. The young child can only think in concrete terms. The adolescent, who is capable of formal-operational thought, can manipulate abstract concepts.

5. Piaget has identified various stages in children's awareness and use of moral rules. Kohlberg has argued that as children grow older, they go through three distinct levels of moral development: the preconventional level, the conventional level, and the post-conventional level.

6. According to Erik Erikson, the quest for *identity* is the principal task of adolescence. The adolescent must integrate many "selves" into a coherent, consistent, and unified whole. The adolescent's peers play an important role in this quest and in many other aspects of his or her life.

7. In our culture, adult status must be earned. There is a transition period between adolescence and adulthood, known as "young adulthood," in which the individual is being "prepared," or is actively preparing for adulthood.

8. Erik Erikson and Robert White are among the psychologists who have offered views on young adulthood. Erikson views young adulthood as a crucial turning point involving the move either toward _intimacy_ or _isolation_. White describes many interrelated growth trends: bringing one's sense of self into focus; narrowing and deepening the quality of personal relationships; increasing selectivity in one's interests; relating moral philosophies to life; and creating empathy with and concern for others.

9. Both _longitudinal_ and _cross-sectional_ studies of adulthood and aging pose certain methodological problems. Longitudinal studies are expensive and may outlive their originators. Cross-sectional studies cannot easily sort out the relative effects of age and generational experience.

10. Family and work cycles present various demands on people during adulthood, but these demands are only loosely related to specific ages. Nonetheless, certain developmental tasks are more likely to arise at some ages than at others.

11. From their 20s to their 60s and beyond, adults go through personality and social changes that correspond to the pressures of deciding on a career, adjusting to marriage and parenthood, reevaluating the course of one's life, and coping with retirement and the limitations of old age.

12. The three stages of adulthood—young, middle, and late—are as different from one another as childhood is from adolescence. Adulthood is a time of continuous growth in which people's attitudes, emotions, physical condition, cognitive ability, and personalities undergo dramatic change.

13. The importance of friends fluctuates throughout the life span. Friendship in later life is more complex and persistent than it is for the young.

14. Establishing a family seems to be the major turning point in the lives of most adults. When the first-born child grows up and leaves home, the most difficult stage of family life appears to be over.

15. Reactions to divorce and widowhood vary. Men are more apt to remarry and find it easier to form new sexual relationships, but women have more social skills and a wider network of friends to console them.

16. Researchers disagree about the intensity of a midlife crisis, but people's attitude toward work often changes in middle adulthood. Many people switch careers, become more security conscious about having a job, or devote more time to interests outside of work.

17. The work ethic tends to make many Americans uneasy with leisure time. Age and income strongly affect what people do with

their free time. Participation in strenuous activities declines after one's 40s. Being able to pay for it seems to make people more comfortable with leisure activity.

18. Aging means that each person undergoes a gradual and inevitable decrease in physiological efficiency, known as senescence. Some researchers believe that this is a result of simple wear-and-tear on the body. Others attribute senescence to an increasing breakdown of the body's self-regulating mechanisms. In many instances, conditions traditionally attributed to the aging process may actually be the result of disease.

19. Many people mistakenly assume that senility is an inevitable stage of senescence, a state that is marked by lapses of memory, haziness of thought, and other signs of mental and physical deterioration. In fact, very few people become senile, and researchers have found no age-related increases in the frequency of such syndromes.

20. There is conflicting evidence about whether the cognitive abilities of adults suffer a general decline due to aging. Some researchers believe that skills and capacities decline over time. Others feel that intelligence continues to grow.

21. Income, educational level, occupational status, and age are the most important factors influencing attitudes toward retirement. Although researchers used to think that people missed the sense of accomplishment and self-worth they derived from their work before retirement, what Americans miss most about their work is the money.

22. The activity substitution theory asserts that successful adjustment to retirement depends on replacing the lost job with a new activity. The theory of disengagement holds that old age is marked by a lessened involvement with society. It may be, however, that a person adjusts best to aging by living as he or she chooses.

23. Death may not be a central concern for the aged. Elderly people may be more concerned with taking stock of past accomplishments.

24. Elizabeth Kübler-Ross has described five sequential stages through which people pass as they react to their own diagnosed death: denial, anger, bargaining, depression, and acceptance. Her work has done much to promote greater understanding of the emotional needs of the dying. Some evidence exists, however, that not all dying people go through the experience in the way Kübler-Ross describes.

Outline

Chapter 5

Learning

Many of us think of learning as the process of acquiring facts or knowledge, and as something that takes place primarily in school. But there are many kinds of learning that are going on at all times. Most of what we do and what we do not do, most of what we are and what we are not result from learning. There are many activities that are obvious illustrations of learning: talking, writing, reading, operating a typewriter, memorizing a poem. We learn not to touch a hot stove or where to buy our favorite pastry. We learn to understand the meaning of foreign policy or why our friends act as they do. Learning enables us to satisfy our basic needs and pursue our special interests. Most of our likes and dislikes, preferences and prejudices, attitudes, beliefs, and superstitions are learned. In essence, life is a continuous learning experience; we learn to be human, we learn to be individuals.

Some of the simplest, most basic learning is called conditioning. Conditioning is a general term—used for animals as well as for human beings. It refers to the acquiring of fairly specific patterns of behaviors in the presence of well-defined stimuli. We will see that there are two main types of conditioning: **classical conditioning** and **operant conditioning**.

Our discussion begins with the first of these processes—classical conditioning. This simple kind of learning provides a convenient starting point for examining the learning process—what it is and how we can observe it.

Classical conditioning was discovered almost by accident by Ivan Pavlov (1849–1936), a Russian physiologist who was studying the digestive processes. Since animals salivate when food is placed in their mouths, Pavlov inserted tubes into the salivary glands of dogs to measure how much saliva they produced when they were given food. Pavlov noticed, however, that the dogs salivated before the food was in their mouths: The mere sight of food made them drool. In fact, they even drooled at the sound of the experimenter's footsteps. This aroused Pavlov's curiosity. What was making the dogs salivate even before they had the food in their mouths?

Classical Conditioning

The Russian physiologist
Ivan Pavlov.
(The Bettmann Archive)

PAVLOV'S CONDITIONING EXPERIMENTS

Pavlov's dogs always salivated when food was placed in their mouths. They did not have to learn to do this; their mouths watered naturally. Pavlov, however, wanted to teach the dogs to salivate when food was not present. He devised an experiment in which he sounded a bell just before the food was brought into the room. A ringing bell does not usually make a dog's mouth water. But after hearing the bell many times just before getting fed, Pavlov's dogs began to salivate as soon as the bell rang. They had learned that the bell signaled the appearance of food, and their mouths watered on cue, even if no food followed. The dogs had been conditioned to respond to a new stimulus, the bell, which would not normally have caused salivation (Pavlov, 1927).

Pavlov's experiment illustrates the four essential elements of classical conditioning. The first is an **unconditioned stimulus** (US), like food, which invariably causes a certain reaction—salivation, in this case. That reaction—the **unconditioned response** (UR)—is the second factor and always results from the unconditioned stimulus. Whenever the dog is given food (US), its mouth waters (UR). The third element is the neutral stimulus—in this case, the ringing of the bell—which is called the **conditioned stimulus** (CS). At first, the conditioned stimulus does not bring about the desired response. Dogs do not normally salivate at the sound of a bell—unless they have been conditioned to react in this way. Such a reaction is the fourth element in the classical conditioning process: the **conditioned response** (CR). The conditioned response is the behavior the animal has learned to produce in response to the conditioned stimulus. Usually,

Figure 5–1
Pavlov's apparatus for classical conditioning of a dog's salivation. The experimenter sits behind a two-way mirror and controls the presentation of the conditioned stimulus (bell) and the unconditioned stimulus (food). A tube runs from the dog's salivary glands to a vial, where the drops of saliva are collected as a way of measuring the strength of the dog's response.

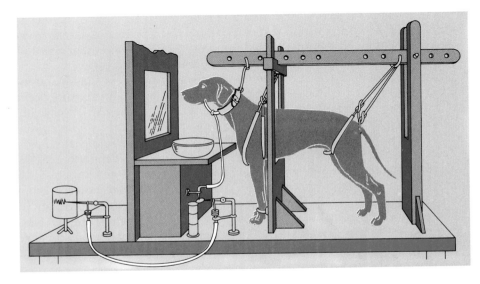

the unconditioned response and the conditioned response—salivation, in our example—are basically the same.

CLASSICAL CONDITIONING IN HUMAN BEINGS

We begin to learn even before we are born (see Chapter 3). Babies who are only 5 to 10 days old can learn to blink their eyes when they hear a tone (Lipsitt, 1971). Babies blink naturally when a puff of air is blown in their eyes. The puff of air is an unconditioned stimulus. Blinking—the babies' natural reaction—is an unconditioned response. If a tone—a conditioned stimulus—is sounded just before the puff of air is blown into their eyes, the babies soon begin to blink their eyes whenever they hear the tone. By blinking as soon as they hear the tone, the babies are producing a conditioned response.

Adults can also learn by classical conditioning. One group of experimenters conditioned a group of asthma sufferers to react to substances that had previously not affected them. First they exposed the asthmatics to something they were allergic to, like dust or pollen (an unconditioned stimulus). Of course, the dust or pollen caused an attack of asthma (an unconditioned response). Then the experimenters presented a neutral substance (a conditioned stimulus). Initially, the asthmatics had no reaction to this neutral substance. But when the neutral substance was repeatedly followed by dust or pollen, the asthma sufferers began to wheeze and sniffle as soon as the neutral substance was presented. These attacks were conditioned responses: The people had to learn to react in this way. In some cases, even a picture of the conditioned stimulus triggered an attack of asthma (Dekker, Pelzer, & Groen, 1957). This study and others like it help to explain why asthma attacks are sometimes brought on by such seemingly neutral events as hearing the national anthem, seeing a waterfall, or listening to a political speech.

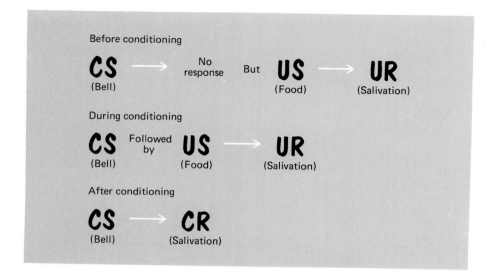

Before conditioning

CS (Bell) → No response   But   US (Food) → UR (Salivation)

During conditioning

CS (Bell) Followed by US (Food) → UR (Salivation)

After conditioning

CS (Bell) → CR (Salivation)

Figure 5–2
A paradigm of the classical conditioning process.

NECESSARY FACTORS IN CLASSICAL CONDITIONING

Conditioning is not automatic. Learning does not occur unless certain requirements are met. For example, the conditioned stimulus must be strong and distinctive enough for the subject to perceive it easily. Another factor that significantly affects the success of the learning process is the order in which the conditioned stimulus and the unconditioned stimulus are presented. The most effective method is the one used in all of the experiments we have described: presenting the conditioned stimulus just before the unconditioned stimulus. Remember that Pavlov rang his bell before he gave the dogs their food. Presenting the conditioned stimulus and the unconditioned stimulus together is less effective. If the bell had rung at the same time that the dogs had gotten their food, they probably would not have salivated later at the bell alone. Backward conditioning—presenting the unconditioned stimulus before the conditioned stimulus—seldom results in effective learning. It would have been very difficult for Pavlov's dogs to learn to salivate when they heard a bell if they had already received their food before the bell rang.

The amount of time between the occurrence of the conditioned stimulus and the unconditioned stimulus is also critical to the success of learning. If this time lapse—called the interstimulus interval—is either too short or too long, it will impair learning. The most effective **interstimulus interval**

BRAVE NEW WORLD

In Aldous Huxley's *Brave New World,* science rules and humanity is its servant. Babies are bred in test tubes and ''parent'' is a dirty word. The novel has a fictional account of the use of classical conditioning to prepare children for their future roles as workers. Early in the book, the Director of Hatcheries and Conditioning demonstrates how 8-month-old infants are conditioned to fear flowers and books:

Infant Nurseries. Neo-Pavlovian Conditioning Rooms, announced the notice board. . . . Between the rose bowls the books were duly set out—a row of nursery quartos opened invitingly each at some gaily coloured image of beast or fish or bird. . . . The babies . . . began to crawl toward those clusters of sleek colours, those shapes so gay and brilliant on the white pages. . . . Small hands reached out uncertainly, touched, grasped, unpetalling the transfigured roses, crumpling the illuminated pages of the books. The Director waited until all were happily busy. Then, ''Watch carefully,'' he said. And, lifting his hand, he gave the signal.

The Head Nurse, who was standing by a switchboard at the other end of the room, pressed down a little lever.

There was a violent explosion. Shriller and ever shriller, a siren shrieked. Alarm bells maddeningly sounded.

The children started, screamed; their faces were distorted with terror.

He waved his hand again, and the Head Nurse pressed a second lever. The screaming of the babies suddenly changed its tone. There was something desperate, almost insane, about the sharp spasmodic yelps to which they now gave utterance. Their little bodies twitched and stiffened; their limbs moved jerkily as if to the tug of unseen wires.

''We can electrify that whole strip of floor,'' bawled the Director in explanation. ''But that's enough,'' he signaled to the nurse.

The explosions ceased, the bells stopped ringing, the shriek of the siren died down from tone to tone into silence. The stiffly twitching bodies relaxed, and what had become the sob and yelp of infant maniacs broadened out once more into a normal howl of ordinary terror.

''Offer them the flowers and the books again.''

The nurses obeyed; but at the approach of the roses, at the mere sight of those gaily coloured images of pussy and cock-a-doodle-do and baa-baa black sheep, the infants shrank away in horror; the volume of their howling suddenly increased.

''Observe,'' said the Director triumphantly, ''observe.''

Books and loud noises, flowers and electric shocks—already in the infant mind these couples were uncompromisingly linked; and after two hundred repetitions of the same or a similar lesson would be wedded indissolubly (Huxley, 1939).

LEARNING CURVES

Learning can be measured in many ways. In classical conditioning, we can look for an increase in the strength of the conditioned response, or more often we look for an increase in the likelihood of getting the conditioned response when the conditioned stimulus is presented. When we plot any of these measures on a graph, over trials or blocks of trials, we have a **learning curve.**

The shape of the learning curve will vary, depending on what we are measuring. If we are measuring the strength of the conditioned response or the numbers of trials on which we get the conditioned response, the curve will be low on the left and move upward to the right.

In most cases, whether we are drawing a graph of strength of response or of percentage of trials showing the conditioned response, the steepest part of the curve will be at the left. This is because most improvement comes early in the learning process. Then, as the increase in learning on each trial becomes smaller, the curve will gradually level off.

A typical learning curve based on strength of response.

is usually somewhere between a fraction of a second and a few seconds, depending on which animal is being conditioned and what it is supposed to learn. Pavlov found that if he waited too long after sounding the bell before he gave the dogs their food, the dogs would not learn.

An interesting exception to the short interstimulus interval is food aversion. If an animal eats something and later—up to 12 hours later among rats—becomes violently ill, it may still show a learned aversion for that type of food, despite the long interval between eating and becoming ill (Schwartz, 1980). Another feature of food aversion is that the animal learns to dislike a specific food, but makes no connection between its aversion for the food and all the other stimuli that were present when it ate the food. The way the food looks and the characteristics of the room in which it is eaten play no part in the conditioning process (Dickinson & Mackintosh, 1978). Moreover, an animal that becomes ill after eating some new food will usually show a learned aversion for that new food, but not for its normal food. Many of us have had the same experience. If we become ill several hours after trying a new dressing on our regular salad, we are apt to suspect the dressing—rightly or wrongly—and not the salad. Indeed, we may develop a strong aversion for that dressing no matter how much we first enjoyed it.

This experience illustrates another unique characteristic of food aversion: One trial is usually enough for considerable learning to occur. Most classical conditioning requires repeated trials to build up the learned association between the conditioned stimulus, like Pavlov's bell, and the unconditioned stimulus, like food. Pavlov had to pair the bell with the food several times before the bell alone would cause a dog's mouth to water.

Conditioning is usually cumulative. Each trial builds on the learner's previous experience. But this does not mean that learning will increase indefinitely or by an equal amount on each successive trial. At first, the strength of the conditioned response—one way of measuring the effectiveness of classical conditioning—increases greatly each time the conditioned stimulus and the unconditioned stimulus are paired. Learning eventually reaches a point of diminishing returns: The amount of each increase gradually becomes smaller and smaller. Finally, the rate of learning levels off and continues at the same strength on subsequent trials.

The spacing of learning trials is as important as the number of trials conducted. Learning is more effective if the pairing of the conditioned stimulus and unconditioned stimulus is experienced at evenly spaced intervals, neither too far apart nor too close together. If trials follow each other very quickly or are too far apart, more trials are needed before learning will occur.

What if, on some of the trials, either the conditioned stimulus or the unconditioned stimulus is missing? This is called **intermittent pairing.** It reduces both the rate of learning and the final level of learning, though learning does still occur. The more carefully all these factors are controlled, the more likely it is that learning will occur. But this does not necessarily mean that the learned response will continue indefinitely, as we shall see next.

EXTINCTION AND SPONTANEOUS RECOVERY

Going back to Pavlov's dogs, what happens when the dog has learned to salivate upon hearing a bell, but after hearing the bell then repeatedly fails to get food? The dog's response to the bell—the amount of salivation—will gradually decrease until eventually the dog will no longer salivate when it hears the bell. This process is known as **extinction.** If the conditioned stimulus (the bell) appears alone so often that the learner no longer associates it with the unconditioned stimulus (the food), and stops making the conditioned response (salivation), extinction has taken place.

Once a response has been extinguished, is the learning gone forever? Pavlov trained his dogs to salivate when they heard a bell, then caused the learning to extinguish. A few days later, the same dogs were again taken to the laboratory. As soon as they heard the bell, their mouths began to water. The response that had been learned and then extinguished reappeared on its own, with no retraining. This phenomenon is known as **spontaneous recovery.** The response was only about half as strong as it had been before extinction, but spontaneous recovery does indicate that learning is not permanently lost.

To understand spontaneous recovery, we have to take a closer look at what happens during extinction. Let us begin with a dog that has learned a particular response, like salivating when it hears a bell. If the bell is rung over and over again but is not followed by the appearance of food, the conditioned response becomes extinguished. The animal's mouth no longer waters when it hears the bell. The animal has learned to suppress or inhibit the learned response. We are not, however, simply teaching this

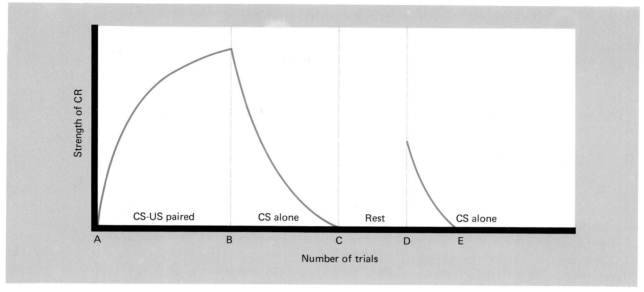

Figure 5–3
From point *A* to point *B* the conditioned stimulus and the unconditioned stimulus were paired and learning continued to increase. From *B* to *C*, however, the conditioned stimulus was presented alone. By point *C* the response had been extinguished. After a rest period from *C* to *D*, spontaneous recovery occurred—the learned response reappeared at about half the strength it had at point *B*. When the conditioned stimulus was again presented alone, the response extinguished rapidly (point *E*).

learned behavior and then erasing it. Inhibition is the result of new learning that works in the opposite direction to the original learning. When inhibition becomes as strong as the original learning, the animal will no longer produce the conditioned response. Extinction has occurred.

We have been talking about inhibition as something that temporarily blocks a learned response. A sudden change in the learner's surroundings or routine can also block a conditioned response. When Pavlov's assistants would ask him to come and look over their projects to see how well the dogs were doing, the animals sometimes failed to perform. Pavlov realized that his presence had disrupted the dogs' usual routine and interfered with their performance. He called this effect **external inhibition.** Something in the dogs' surroundings—the presence of a strange person in the room—made it seem that extinction had occurred.

GENERALIZATION

Certain situations or objects may resemble one another enough so that the learner will react to one as he or she has learned to react to the other. Pavlov noticed that after his dogs had been conditioned to salivate when they heard a bell, their mouths would often water when they heard a buzzer or the ticking of a metronome. Their conditioned response had been generalized to other noises that sounded like the bell. Reacting to a stimulus that is similar to the one you have learned to react to is called **stimulus generalization.**

The well-known case of Little Albert provides a clear example of stimulus generalization (Watson & Rayner, 1920). The experimenters started by showing a white rat to Albert, an 11-month-old boy. At first the child showed no fear. He crawled toward the rat and wanted to play with it. But every time he approached the rat, the experimenters made a loud noise

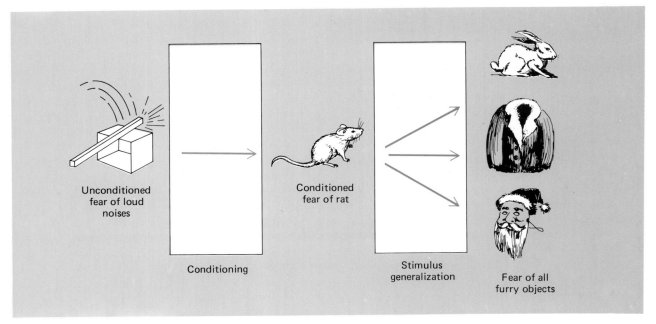

Figure 5–4
Diagram of Little Albert's laboratory experience. He started with an unconditioned fear of loud noises, then learned to fear a white rat. Finally his fear generalized to all furry objects.

by striking a steel bar. Since nearly all children are afraid of loud noises, Albert's natural reaction was fear. After just a few times, he began to cry and crawl away whenever he saw the rat. So far we have a simple case of classical conditioning. An unconditioned stimulus—the loud noise—caused the unconditioned response of fear. Next, Albert learned to associate the loud noise with the rat, so that the rat (conditioned stimulus) then caused him to be afraid (conditioned response). The experimenters next showed Albert a white rabbit. He cried and tried to crawl away. He had generalized from the white rat to the similar stimulus of the white rabbit. In fact, his fear generalized to a number of white furry objects—a fur coat, for example, and even a Santa Claus mask.

DISCRIMINATION

It is also possible to train animals and people not to generalize, but to react only to a single, specific object or event. This process is called **discrimination,** and in effect it is the reverse of generalization. The subject learns to respond to only one stimulus and to inhibit the response in the presence of all other stimuli.

Pavlov's method for training an animal to discriminate was to present two similar sounds but to follow only one of them with an unconditioned stimulus. The dog learned to salivate only when it heard the sound that was followed by the unconditioned stimulus (food), but not when it heard the other sound. It had learned to discriminate.

Learning to discriminate is very important in everyday life. As we noted earlier, most children fear all loud noises. Since thunder cannot harm a child, however, it would be helpful if children learned not to be afraid every time they heard it. Not all mushrooms are good to eat, and not all

(R. F. Head, Photo Researchers)

strangers are unfriendly. Thus, discrimination is one of the most important parts of learning.

HIGHER-ORDER CONDITIONING

After Pavlov's dogs had learned to salivate when they heard a bell, he decided to teach them to salivate when they saw a black square. But this time, instead of showing them the square and following it with food, he showed them the square and followed it with the bell. The dogs eventually learned to salivate when they saw the square. The bell was used as an unconditioned stimulus and the black square was used as a conditioned stimulus. This procedure is known as **higher-order conditioning**, not because it is more complex or because it involves any new principles, but simply because it is learning based on previous learning.

Higher-order conditioning is more difficult to learn because it races against extinction. The dogs that learn to respond to a square are no longer getting any food. In fact, the square is a signal that the bell will follow and that the bell will *not* be followed by food. Without the food, the dogs will soon stop salivating when they hear the bell. If this happens, they cannot learn to salivate when they see the square. To avoid this problem, food must be given to the dogs once in a while, so that their mouths will continue to water when they hear the bell.

Psychologists are still divided on the importance of classical conditioning in complex human learning. Could the conditioned response be the fundamental unit in all changes in behavior? Or, as many researchers believe, is classical conditioning too simple to have much bearing on the more complex types of learning that humans can do? Regardless of the outcome of this debate, we are exposed to simple classical conditioning every day in education, advertising, and politics. And, because it is simple, classical conditioning is an important laboratory tool in the effort to isolate the factors involved in learning in general (Peterson, 1975).

EXPERIMENTAL NEUROSIS

When an animal is taught to discriminate between two similar stimuli—two sounds or two shapes projected on a screen—it learns to respond to one but not to the other. In one experiment a dog learned to salivate when it saw a circle, but not when it saw an ellipse (Pavlov, 1927). The shape of the ellipse was gradually changed, making it more and more circular. When the distinction between the circle and the ellipse was too fine for the dog to detect, discrimination broke down. The animal was not only unable to discriminate between the two shapes that were now very similar, but also lost the ability to discriminate between the original circle and the ellipse.

At this point an interesting side effect showed up: The dog became agitated and upset. It began to bark, tried to attack the conditioning apparatus, and acted fearful. Drawing an analogy to human neurotic behavior, we say that the dog was suffering from **experimental neurosis.** The prolonged stress of being unable to decide which shape to respond to had caused a breakdown and led to the animal's abnormal behavior. Experimental neuroses in both animals and humans can persist for long periods. In some cases, symptoms have lasted for 13 years (Liddell, 1956).

Operant Conditioning

(Syd Greenberg, Photo Researchers)

As it has traditionally been viewed, classical conditioning is concerned with behavior that invariably follows a particular event: the salivation that automatically occurs when food is placed in the mouth; the blink of the eye that always results when a puff of air strikes the eye. In classical conditioning, we usually learn to tranfer this reaction to another stimulus that would not normally produce it: salivating at the sound of a bell, blinking to a tone. In a sense classical conditioning is passive. The behavior is initially *elicited* by the unconditioned stimulus.

Most behavior, however, initially seems to be *emitted* rather than elicited, that is, most behavior is usually voluntary rather than inevitably triggered by outside events. You wave your hand to hail a taxi. A dog begs at the dinner table for food. A child stops crying to avoid further scolding. These and similar actions are sometimes called **operant behavior.** They are designed to operate on the environment in a way that will gain something desired or avoid something unpleasant.

To explain how operant behavior is learned, we turn to a second major kind of learning: **instrumental,** or **operant conditioning.** This kind of learning also occurs both in animals and in people.

Anyone who has ever trained a dog to do tricks, such as sitting up, fetching, or rolling over knows that the best method of training is to reward the dog with a bit of food each time it gives the desired response. This is operant conditioning. You use the food to *reinforce* the correct behavior. Incorrect behavior may be either ignored (no reward) or punished (by a swat with a rolled-up newspaper, for example). This is the essence of operant conditioning. Correct responses are reinforced; incorrect responses are either ignored or punished.

One of the many kinds of equipment used in laboratory experiments on operant conditioning is the **Skinner box,** named after B. F. Skinner, the American psychologist who developed many of the techniques of operant conditioning. A Skinner box for rats is small and bare except for a bar with a cup underneath it. The rat must learn to press the bar, which releases food pellets into the cup.

In Skinner's original conditioning experiment (1932), a hungry rat was put into the box. The animal began to explore until it happened to press the bar, and a pellet of food dropped into the cup. The rat ate the pellet and continued to explore until it hit the bar again. After two or three times, the rat learned that it could get food by pressing the bar. The food reinforced the bar-pressing response, and the rat pressed the bar again and again.

The Skinner box. Except for its subject, the rat, the box is rather bare: This one's only features are a bar—which the rat has discovered—and a food cup.
(Will Rapport, courtesy of B. F. Skinner)

ACQUISITION OF THE RESPONSE

We have said that classical conditioning deals with behavior that is initially a natural, automatic response. This implies that it is relatively easy to produce the desired responses. All Pavlov had to do when he wanted his dogs to salivate was to put food in their mouths. But operant behavior does not automatically follow from a stimulus. A rat has a set of natural responses to hunger, but the operant behavior of pressing a bar in a cage is not one of them. Until it learns to press the bar, the rat will go hungry. Thus, the first problem in operant conditioning is to make the desired response occur so that it can then be reinforced and learned. This problem is common to scientists in the laboratory, to teachers in the classroom, to parents, and, in fact, to all of us in everyday life. Many of the means of evoking operant behavior are a matter of common sense. We use them even without thinking about them.

"Boy, do we have this guy conditioned. Every time I press the bar down, he drops a pellet in."

One of the most common ways of getting the desired behavior is simply to wait for the subject to hit upon the correct response. The first time babies say "Mama" is by accident. But if their mothers smile and hug them, they will learn to repeat the sound. If this were the only method, learning would be slow indeed. One way to speed up the process and maximize the likelihood that the correct response will be discovered is to increase motivation. A hungry rat is more active and therefore more likely to press the food bar than is a well-fed rat. Another means of effecting the desired response is to narrow down a large number of potential responses, thereby improving the chances that the correct response will occur. This can be done by restricting the environment and then allowing the subjects to respond freely in it. In the simple environment of a Skinner box, a rat quickly discovers bar-pressing, since there are relatively few other possible responses.

Outside of the laboratory, it is rarely possible to arrange the environment so conveniently. But the experimenter can aid learning by guiding or "forcing" the learner through the correct movements. Many mothers help their babies to wave "bye-bye" by guiding their hands through the motion so that they will know how to do it in the future. Explaining and demonstrating what is to be done are also important ways of helping a person produce the desired response. Instructions may be as simple as a mother's command to "Say please," or as complicated as a videotaped golf swing in slow motion. When the Federal Communications Commission (FCC) banned cigarette commercials on TV, they showed their belief that modeling a response—lighting up a cigarette—would encourage people to imitate it. They removed the model to discourage the habit. Verbal instruction and modeling are often presented together. For example, an adult teaches a child how to tie a shoe by demonstrating and describing the procedure step by step. The importance of models in learning will be discussed later in this chapter.

A very effective procedure for acquiring a new response is to start by reinforcing partial responses—the small bits of behavior that make up the whole. Little by little, the complete response is shaped. This approach, called shaping, was used to get a boy who suffered from cataracts to wear glasses. Although he was in danger of going blind, the boy refused to wear the glasses and threw terrible tantrums at the mere mention of them. The glasses were left in his room and the child was given candy if he touched them. Soon he began to carry them around, and eventually he started to wear them. He was rewarded each step of the way, until he learned to wear the glasses (Wolf, Mees, & Risley, 1964).

People can acquire responses through modeling behavior, which is often accompanied by verbal instruction.

(Suzanne Szasz, Photo Researchers)

A pigeon in a Skinner box. Skinner found that the bird would repeat whatever action it had been doing just before food was dropped into the box, even though this coincidence—i.e., the pigeon's behavior and the subsequent reinforcement of food pellets—was accidental.
(Will Rapport, courtesy of B. F. Skinner)

REINFORCEMENT

Once the desired response has been produced, how do we ensure that it will be repeated? We do just what the animal trainer does—we reward the correct response. Psychologists call this reward a reinforcement, since it strengthens the desired response and increases the likelihood that it will be repeated.

Whenever something we do is followed closely by a reinforcement, we will tend to repeat the action—even if the reinforcement is not produced directly by what we have done. In one of Skinner's experiments (1948) a pigeon was placed in a Skinner box that contained only a food hopper. There was nothing the bird could do to get the food—no disk to peck or bar to press—but at random intervals Skinner dropped a few grains of food into the hopper. He found that the pigeon began to repeat whatever it had been doing just before it was given food: standing on one foot, hopping around, or strutting around with its neck stretched out. None of these actions had had anything to do with getting the food. It was pure coincidence that the food appeared when the bird was standing on one foot, for example. But that action would usually be repeated. Skinner said that the bird's behavior was "superstitious," because of its similarity to how people sometimes behave when they learn to be afraid of a black cat or the number *13*.

Following an action or response with something pleasant is called **positive reinforcement.** Most of our examples have involved positive reinforcement: giving a dog a treat when it performs a trick or giving a rat food when it presses a bar. Following a response by removing something unpleasant is called **negative reinforcement.** In the laboratory, a rat can learn to press a bar to turn off an electric shock (negative reinforcement), and it can learn to press a bar to get food (positive reinforcement). Negative reinforcement should not be confused with punishment, which will be discussed later in this section. Punishment uses an unpleasant condition to eliminate undesirable behavior. In negative reinforcement the easing of an unpleasant situation is used to strengthen a desired response.

Both positive and negative reinforcement result in learning. A child might learn to play the piano in order to receive praise (positive reinforcement) or to avoid a scolding for not practicing (negative reinforcement). A dog that learns to open the back door with its paws may be doing so either for the positive reinforcement of getting outside to play or for the negative reinforcement of avoiding a bath.

In **escape training,** a person learns how to end an unpleasant condition—to take aspirin for a headache, for example. An end to the headache, or even a lessening of the pain, is a negative reinforcement. Nothing can be done to prevent the unpleasant event from starting; only after it starts can anything be done to stop it. Escape learning is not just fleeing from a situation. It entails learning how to end an unpleasant situation, like the rat that learns to press a bar to turn off an electric shock.

Avoidance training also uses negative reinforcement to promote learning. Unlike escape training, in avoidance training the unpleasant condition can be prevented from ever occurring. Avoidance training with animals usually

BEHAVIORISTICALLY, THE METHOD IS NOT MADNESS

Stimuli, responses, and reinforcers are the stock in trade not only of learning theorists but of actors as well—at least of so-called method actors at the famed Actors Studio in New York, whose graduates include Marlon Brando, Jane Fonda, Dustin Hoffman, Sidney Poitier, and Al Pacino. The method is taught by Lee Strasberg and his staff. Here pupils learn how to produce in themselves the feelings that make performances believable and compelling. It is not a coincidence that Stanislavski, the Russian who first worked out the principles of responsive or method acting, knew Ivan Pavlov, the man who experimented with the dogs.

Stanislavski's two basic ideas are that acting is not simply imitation and that inspiration can be controlled through both internal and external stimuli. The internal stimuli can be imagined from memory, in which case the actor attempts to recapture relevant emotions by remembering moments from his or her own personal experience.

For example, to play a bereaved widow, an actress may recall memories of the death of her own father. To effectively play Lady Macbeth's "Out, damned spot!" scene, she might imagine that she had a large spider on each hand. To communicate insanity, Strasberg told one performer trying to portray Salome to imagine that John the Baptist's head was "the cutest puppy you have ever seen."

Such "internal work" causes actual physiological changes, and it has been experimentally shown that method actors have better GSR (galvanic skin response) control than other actors (Stern & Lewis, 1968).

Method actors also learn and practice self-observation to help them bring their real-life responses to the stage, and their teachers shape and reward them to increase this realism, gradually increasing the price of praise.

includes some sort of warning device, like a light or a buzzer. An animal is placed in the box. The experimenter first sounds a buzzer, then a few seconds later turns on the shock. After the first few times, the animal will discover that the buzzer warns it of the shock to come. If the rat presses a bar after hearing the buzzer, no shock will be administered. Pressing the bar after the shock has already started will have no effect. In avoidance training, the animal must learn to press the bar after hearing the buzzer, but before the shock starts, in order to prevent the shock from occurring. At first this usually happens accidentally. But once the rat has learned that pressing the bar prevents the shock, it will run to the bar whenever it hears the buzzer and will avoid the shock altogether. Avoidance responses can be helpful, as when we learn to carry an umbrella when it looks like rain or not to drink from bottles labeled "Poison." Sometimes avoidance learning persists even when it is no longer effective. A child who learns not to go into deep water may build up a fear that remains even after he or she has learned to swim. In other cases, avoidance behavior may persist even when the fear has been removed. It seems that the fear that was essential for learning the avoidance response is not necessary in the long run for sustaining the learned response.

PUNISHMENT

From the time when we are very young, we learn to expect **punishment**, either physical or verbal, from parents, teachers, peer groups, or society at large if we violate certain codes of behavior. Reinforcement will cause

(Christa Armstrong, Photo Researchers)

To inhibit a certain response, punishment should be applied right after the misbehavior occurred. Ideally, a better or more correct way of behaving should be pointed out at the same time the punishment is being applied.
(Christy Park, Monkmeyer Press)

a response to become stronger. Will punishment cause a response to disappear?

Obviously, punishment does not always work. Children often continue to misbehave even after they have been repeatedly punished. Many criminals come out of prison only to return within a short time. The effectiveness of punishment depends entirely on how and when it is used. Punishment should follow as soon as possible after the undesirable behavior has occurred. Children who misbehave should be punished right away so that they know that what they have done was wrong. If punishment comes too late, the children may not know why they are being punished. It is also important to avoid inadequate punishment. If a parent merely warns a child not to misbehave again, the effect may be less than if the warning is accompanied by a slap on the hand. The parent should also try to apply punishment consistently—to punish the child every time he or she misbehaves. If punishment is not applied consistently, the misbehavior may persist. Rewards that follow right after a punishment, such as hugging a child right after a spanking, should be avoided. This can confuse the child since the punishment and the reward are being received at the same time.

One of the problems with using punishment is that is can often disrupt the learning process. When children are learning to read and the teacher scolds them every time they mispronounce a word, they may only become frightened. As they become more frightened and confused, they mispronounce more words and get scolded more. In time they may become so scared that they will not want to read at all.

By itself, punishment simply inhibits responses. Ideally, punishment should be paired with reinforcement of the desired behavior. This is a more productive approach, since it teaches an alternative behavior to replace what is being punished. Children who mispronounce words while reading might learn faster if the teacher, besides scolding them, also praises them for pronouncing other words correctly. The praise acts as a positive reinforcement for learning to pronounce words correctly. It also makes the children less fearful about learning in general.

PRIMARY AND SECONDARY REINFORCERS

A **primary reinforcer** is one that is rewarding in and of itself, without any association with other reinforcers. Food, water, sex, and ending pain are primary reinforcers. A **secondary reinforcer** is one whose value has to be learned through association with other reinforcers. It is referred to as secondary not because it is less important, but because it is learned. A rat learns to get food by pressing a bar; then a buzzer is sounded every time the rat presses the bar and gets food. Even if the rat stops getting the food, it will continue to press the bar just to hear the buzzer. Although the buzzer has no value by itself to the rat, it has become a secondary reinforcer.

Money is a secondary reinforcer. Although money is just paper or metal, through its association with food, clothing, and other primary reinforcers it becomes a powerful reward. Children come to value money only after they learn that it will buy such things as candy (primary reinforcer). Then the money becomes a secondary reinforcer. Chimpanzees have learned to work for poker chips, which they insert into a vending machine to get the primary reinforcer, raisins. The poker chips have become secondary reinforcers for the chimps.

Although some reinforcers are quite separate from the desired behavior— for example, praise from another person when you do well on an exam— other reinforcers are closely tied to the behavior. For example, the stalking and sexual behaviors of animals have been shown to be intrinsically reinforcing, that is, reinforcing all by themselves. In other words, as soon as the behavior occurs, the animal is rewarded by the behavior itself. As you might expect, such behaviors are very hard to extinguish.

SCHEDULES OF REINFORCEMENT

Seldom, either in life or the laboratory, are we rewarded every time we do something. And this is just as well, for *partial reinforcement,* where rewards are given for some correct responses but not for every one, results in a behavior that will persist longer than one learned by *continuous reinforcement.* It takes longer to learn in the first place with only partial reinforcement. The program for choosing which responses to reinforce is called the **schedule of reinforcement.** Schedules can be either fixed or varied and can be based on either the number of responses or on the elapsed time between responses. The most common reinforcement schedules are the **fixed interval** and the **variable interval,** which are based on time, and the **fixed ratio** and the **variable ratio,** which are based on the number of correct responses.

On a fixed-interval schedule, subjects are reinforced for the first correct response after a certain time has passed: They learn to wait for a set period before responding. On a fixed-interval schedule, subjects begin making responses shortly before the set amount of time has gone by, in anticipation of the reinforcement that is to come. For example, although a cake recipe

(Yerkes Regional Primate Research Center, Emory University, Atlanta, Georgia)

Figure 5–5
(Left) The typical pattern of responses on a fixed-interval schedule of reinforcement. The small markings along the colored line indicate points at which reinforcement is given. As the time for reinforcement approaches, the number of responses increases and the slope becomes steeper. The rate of responding is low immediately after reinforcement, so the curve is nearly flat at that point. (Right) On a variable-interval schedule of reinforcement, the rate of responding is relatively constant.

(After B. F. Skinner, "Teaching Machines." Copyright © 1961 by *Scientific American,* Inc. All rights reserved.)

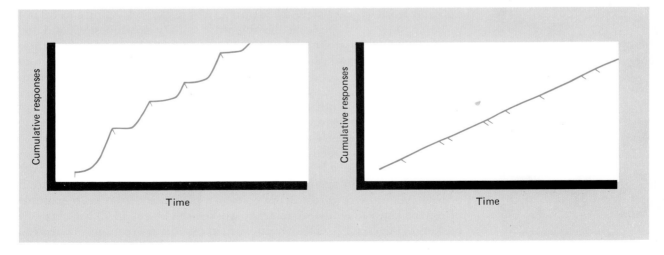

These office workers are clocking into their jobs. Since they make this same response at set intervals, i.e., at the same time every day, they may be said to be operating on a fixed-interval schedule.
(Michael Uffer, Photo Researchers)

may say, "Bake for 45 minutes," you will probably start checking to see if the cake is done shortly before the time is up. Performance also tends to fall off immediately after the reinforcement, and tends to pick up again as the time for the next reinforcement draws near. A rat learns to press a bar to get food, but it gets food only for the first response in any 5-minute period. The rat will stop pressing the bar right after it gets its food, but will begin pressing it more frequently as the next time for getting the food approaches.

A variable-interval schedule reinforces correct responses after varying lengths of time. One reinforcement might be given after 6 minutes, the next after 4 minutes, the next after 5 minutes, the next after 3 minutes. Subjects learn to give a slow, steady pattern of responses, being careful not to be so slow as to miss all the rewards. If they are too slow and fail to respond at the appointed time for reinforcement, they will not get their reward. When exams are given at fixed intervals—like midterms and finals—students will tend to increase their studying just before an exam; studying will then decrease sharply right after the exam until shortly before the next one. On the other hand, if several exams are given during a semester at unpredictable intervals, students have to keep studying at a steady rate all the time, because on any given day there might be an exam.

On a fixed-ratio schedule, a certain number of responses must occur before reinforcement is presented. This results in a high response rate because it is advantageous to make many responses in a short time in order to get more rewards. Being paid on a piecework basis is an example of a fixed-ratio schedule. A migrant worker might get $3.00 for every 10 baskets of cherries he picks. The more he picks, the more money he makes.

(Ray Ellis, Rapho/Photo Researchers)

A fixed-ratio schedule results in a pause after reinforcement is received, then a rapid and steady response rate until the next reinforcement.

On a variable-ratio schedule, the number of responses necessary to gain reinforcement is not constant. The slot machine is a good example of a variable-ratio schedule. It may pay off, but you have no idea when. Since there is always a chance of hitting the jackpot, the temptation to keep playing is great. Subjects on a variable-ratio schedule tend not to pause after reinforcement and have a high rate of response over a long period of time. Since they never know when reinforcement may come, they keep on trying.

DELAY OF CONSEQUENCES

It is generally accepted that a delay between the behavior and its results will weaken or even eliminate the effectiveness of the reinforcement or punishment. One unusual situation mentioned in our discussion of classical conditioning is food aversion, where relatively long intervals between eating and becoming ill do not reduce learning. But even with food aversion, the longer the delay the greater is the reduction in learning.

The effect of delaying reinforcement may actually be due to other events interfering with the learning process (Wickelgren, 1977). By minimizing the distraction the learner is subjected to between the behavior and the reinforcement, it is possible to delay reinforcement or punishment without decreasing learning too much. The same effect may be achieved by repeatedly reminding the learner that the reinforcement or punishment is coming. This forms a link between the learner's response and the delayed reinforcement or punishment that follows.

Figure 5–6

(Left) A high rate of responding and a moderate pause after each reinforcement are characteristic of the fixed-ratio schedule of reinforcement. (Right) The variable-ratio schedule of reinforcement leads to a high rate of responding, with a slight pause after each reinforcement. Sometimes an animal will even forgo eating the food that it has earned, preferring to get on with the business of earning the next reinforcement.

(After B. F. Skinner, "Teaching Machines." Copyright © 1961 by *Scientific American,* Inc. All rights reserved.)

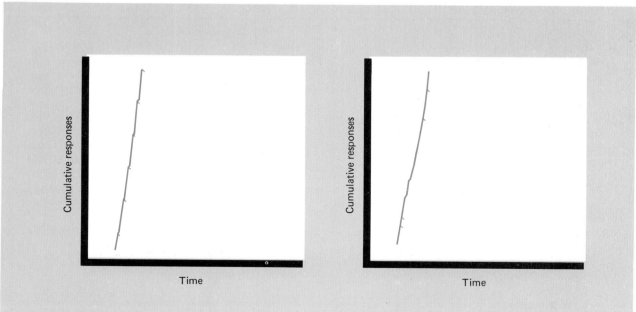

Time   Time

GENERALIZATION

As we saw in classical conditioning, a response can generalize from one stimulus to a similar one. Conversely, the same stimulus will sometimes bring about different, but similar, responses. Generalization also occurs in operant conditioning.

An example of stimulus generalization in operant conditioning is a baby who is hugged and kissed for saying "Mama" when he or she sees the mother, and begins to call everyone "Mama"—including the mailman. Although the person the baby sees—the stimulus—changes, the baby responds with the same word. In the same way, the skills you learn when playing tennis may be generalized to badminton, Ping-Pong, and squash.

Response generalization occurs when the same stimulus leads to different, but similar, responses. The baby who calls everyone "Mama" may also call the mother "Dada" or "gaga"—other sounds that have been learned—until it is learned that only "Mama" is correct. In response generalization, the response changes, but the stimulus remains constant.

DISCRIMINATION

The ability to tell the difference or discriminate between similar stimuli— or even to determine if the right stimulus is present—is as essential in operant conditioning as it is in classical conditioning. Knowing what to do has little value if the learner does not know when to do it.

Discrimination is taught by reinforcing a response only in the presence of certain stimuli. In this way, pigeons have been trained to peck at a red disk, but not at a green one. First the pigeon is taught to peck

QUALITY CONTROL THROUGH OPERANT CONDITIONING

The scene is a drug factory. A conveyor belt carries the tiny gelatin capsules that will soon be filled with one of our modern wonder drugs. A quality-control inspector stands by the moving belt and scrutinizes each capsule as it passes by. If a capsule is bumpy or dented, if its color is not quite right, the inspector pushes a button and the defective capsule is removed from the belt. There is nothing unusual about this— except that the inspector is a pigeon.

So far, no human quality-control inspector need worry about being replaced by a bird. But psychopharmacologist Thom Verhave has successfully conditioned pigeons to perform the exact discrimination task outlined above—to look at drug capsules as they move by on a belt and whenever an imperfect capsule appears, to signal by pecking at a disk (Verhave, 1966).

Verhave's conditioning procedure was very simple: He placed the bird in a cage that contained a small window, a lighted disk, and an automatic food hopper. When the bird correctly identified a defective capsule by pecking twice on the disk, it was rewarded with food. Eventually the bird learned to perform the whole inspection process. It would peck at the disk once to turn on a light behind the window so it could see the capsule. If the capsule was acceptable, the pigeon then pecked one more time at the disk, which turned off the light and moved the next capsule up. One out of every ten capsules was misshapen or off-color, and when the bird saw one of these, it pecked twice at the disk and was rewarded with food. Within a week, Verhave's pigeons were signaling defective capsules with 99 percent accuracy, no small achievement for any inspector—human or pigeon.

at a disk. Then it is presented with two disks, one red and one green. The bird gets food when it pecks at the red one, but not when it pecks at the green one. Eventually it learns to discriminate between the two and will only peck at the red disk. Babies who call everyone "Mama" learn to discriminate between their own mothers and other people and to use "Mama" only for their own mothers. Of course, this could be done by punishing the children for calling other people "Mama." But more commonly we teach children to discriminate by reinforcing them for using "Mama" correctly and not reinforcing them when they use the term for other people.

EXTINCTION AND SPONTANEOUS RECOVERY

Extinction was discussed earlier in connection with classical conditioning. In operant conditioning, extinction is the result of withholding reinforcement. Withholding reinforcement does not usually produce an immediate decrease in the frequency of the response. When reinforcement is first discontinued, there is often a brief increase in responding before it declines. The behavior itself also changes at the start of extinction. It becomes more variable and often more forceful. For instance, if you try to open a door by turning the knob and pushing the door, but find that it will not open, you may continue to try. You may turn the knob more violently and you may even kick or pound on the door. But if the door still will not budge, your attempts will decrease, and you will finally stop trying to get the door open altogether.

Several factors affect how easy or how hard it is to extinguish learned actions. The stronger the original learning, the harder it is to stop the action from being performed. The greater the variety of settings in which learning takes place, the harder it is to extinguish it. Rats trained to run in a single straight alley for food will stop running sooner than rats trained in several different alleys that vary in width, brightness, floor texture, and other features. Complex behavior is also much more difficult to

If the expected reinforcement for an action does not occur—as the woman shown here expects to receive food for the money she put in the machine—the behavior of the subject often becomes more intense (here the woman kicks the machine) before it disappears altogether (extinction).
(All by Irene Springer)

The behavior chain of Barnabus the rat.
(Wide World Photos)

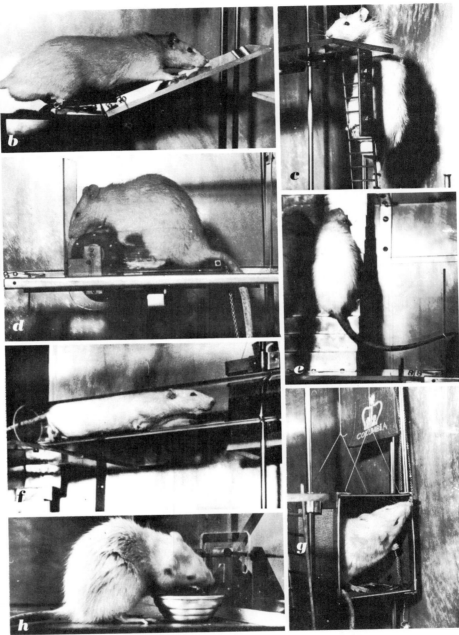

extinguish than simple behavior. Since complex behavior consists of many actions, each single action that makes up the total behavior must be extinguished.

The schedule of reinforcement used during conditioning has a major effect on the extinction process. Partial reinforcement creates stronger learning than continuous reinforcement. This is because the subject does not expect reinforcement for each response and has learned to continue responding in anticipation of eventual reinforcement. During extinction it

BEHAVIOR CHAINS

Operant behavior is not usually a matter of isolated acts. Rather, most operant behavior is a chain, or series of events. One event acts as a cue for the next, which in turn stimulates the next link in the chain. **Behavior chains** that are taught by means of operant conditioning must be learned one link at a time. The case of Barnabus, a laboratory rat at Columbia University, suggests just how long these chains can be, even among nonhumans.

At the signal of a flashing light, Barnabus would dash up a circular path to a landing. Here he would cross a moat and climb a ladder to a second landing. He then got into a wagon and pedaled to the bottom of a stairway, which he climbed to a third platform. There he squeezed through a tube and entered an elevator. As the elevator descended, he pulled a chain, which raised the university flag. When he finally reached the floor of his cage, Barnabus pressed a bar and was rewarded with food (Pierrel & Sherman, 1963). Every step of this complicated behavior chain was taught by **shaping.** Each reaction was rewarded, and each reward triggered the next link in the chain.

Behavior chains are most readily learned if they are taught backward, with the last part of the chain learned first. The best way to teach someone to hit a baseball is to tie the ball to a string that is suspended from a tree, so that the learner can first try hitting the ball when it is not moving. After this has been learned, the person can then go backward in the chain and learn to hit a ball thrown by a pitcher—how to judge its speed and direction, when to swing and when to wait.

will take the subject longer to learn that no reinforcement will be presented and to stop responding.

Avoidance training is especially hard to extinguish, because it is based on fear of an unpleasant or painful situation. But if the unpleasant situation no longer exists, then continued response to the warning is pointless and may even be harmful. The usual method of extinction—withholding reinforcement—will not work. Responding to the warning is reinforced because the unpleasant event does not happen. This reinforcement obviously cannot be withheld by the event's ceasing to exist, because the subject has no way of finding that out as long as he or she continues to respond to the warning. For this reason, standard conditioning procedures are generally ineffective and special means must be used to extinguish avoidance responses.

Extinction will be easier if the nonreinforced experiences occur in rapid succession. This is just the opposite of learning, which occurs in fewer trials if the trials are distributed over time. Extinction can also be speeded up if the learner is put in a situation that is different from the one in which the response was learned. The response is weaker in a new situation, and it will disappear much more rapidly.

Removing the reinforcement will eventually cause a response to be extinguished, but punishment can be used to eliminate the response even faster. Punishing a response adds another deterrent. If the punishment is used correctly and consistently, the response will be eliminated quickly.

Spontaneous recovery, the reappearance of the original learning after it has been extinguished, also occurs in operant conditioning. Rats that have their bar-pressing behavior extinguished will sometimes start pressing the bar spontaneously when they are placed in the Skinner box again after a lapse of time.

Contemporary Views of Conditioning

Early research on conditioning produced several concepts that seemed to make complex behavior more understandable. But the life span of concepts, especially scientific ones, is becoming shorter as the pace of research speeds up. The work of Pavlov, Skinner, and others has generated a huge amount of interest and investigation. Today, neither the basic distinction between classical and operant conditioning nor even the body of assumptions central to conditioning itself remains unquestioned.

WHO'S AFRAID OF THE BIG BAD WOLF?

One interesting aspect of human learning is the formation of phobias. Phobias are irrational fears of things like high places, cats, spiders, snakes, and the dark. Sigmund Freud explained phobias in terms of unresolved inner conflicts. A different explanation has been suggested by Wolpe and Rachman (1960), who see phobias simply as a case of classical conditioning: An object comes to be feared after being linked with a frightening stimulus. Although phobias can be classically conditioned in this way, in other respects they do not follow most rules of classical conditioning.

In the first place, phobias are not affected by standard extinction procedures. For example, a woman has developed a fear of dogs because of one frightening experience in the past. According to traditional learning theory, each time she sees a dog and nothing frightening happens, her fear of dogs should decrease. But this does not happen. Her fear may become stronger each time she sees a dog or even thinks about dogs.

Furthermore, phobias, as with food aversions, can sometimes be learned in one trial, which is not the case with typical laboratory fear conditioning. Moreover, the range of stimulus objects that result in phobic fear is limited. Classical conditioning theory would lead us to expect that any object could become a source of a phobia if it were paired with a stimulus that arouses fear and anxiety. But this is not true for most phobias. "Only rarely, if ever, do we have pajama phobias, grass phobias, electric-outlet phobias, hammer phobias, even though these things are likely to be associated with trauma in our world" (Seligman, 1972, p. 455).

Seligman suggests that all these nonconformities can be explained by the concept of preparedness.

(Howard Earl Uible, Photo Researchers)

All the common objects of phobia—heights, snakes, cats, the dark, and so on—represent "events related to the survival of the human species through the long course of evolution" (p. 455). Thus humans may be prepared to develop phobias about these things, just as a pigeon is prepared to develop a pecking response.

CLASSICAL CONDITIONING
VERSUS OPERANT CONDITIONING

Traditionally, classical and operant conditioning have been regarded as very different learning processes. Work done in the last 10 years, however, has suggested that beyond the different procedures used, the two kinds of learning may not really be that different. In fact, they may be the same kind of learning simply brought about in two different ways. At least four differences originally thought to distinguish classical from operant conditioning have been questioned in recent years (Hearst, 1975).

1. Psychologists tend to assume that classical conditioning is associated with involuntary behavior such as salivation and fear, while operant conditioning is associated with voluntary actions. Research suggests, however, that classical conditioning can also be used to shape voluntary movements (Brown & Jenkins, 1968). Moreover, operant conditioning of involuntary processes has occurred in **"autonomic conditioning"** studies in which both humans and animals have been taught to control certain biological functions such as blood pressure, heart rate, and skin temperature.

2. It has been assumed that in classical conditioning the unconditioned response and the conditioned response are similar, if not identical. For example, Pavlov's dogs salivated in response to both the food and the bell. Research suggests that in classical conditioning the conditioned response and the unlearned response may be quite different. In operant conditioning, the subject supposedly learns a response that is very unlike the normal, unconditioned response to the same stimulus. For example, a rat may be taught to open a door when a light goes on. Whatever the rat's normal response to the light, it has little or nothing to do with opening a door. But in operant conditioning there seem to be limits on how far a learned response can diverge from the normal response to the stimulus. Keller and Marian Breland, besides being psychologists, trained animals to perform in shows. Their experiences provide delightful examples of how hard it is to ignore an animal's innate responses in operant conditioning (Breland & Breland, 1972). For example, a bantam chicken that they tried to condition to stand on a platform for 12 to 15 seconds scratched so much that they finally gave up and billed it instead as a "dancing chicken." A raccoon that had been trained to insert a coin into a container for food suddenly became a miser. It reverted to its natural "washing" response, rubbing the coins together and refusing to drop them in the slot.

3. In our initial discussion, we said that in classical conditioning the unconditioned stimulus draws out the desired response from the subject. In operant conditioning, the subjects spontaneously come up with the response, which is then reinforced. The behavior to be learned is elicited in one case and emitted in the other. But, in operant conditioning, once the operant response becomes linked to a stimulus, the operant response looks and acts very much like an unconditioned response. If a rat is trained to open a door when a light goes on, the light elicits the door-opening behavior just like an unconditioned stimulus in classical conditioning.

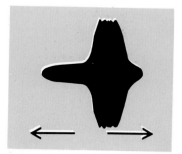

A model like this was used by Tinbergen (1948) to study prepared fear responses in certain birds. When the model moved to the left (looking like a goose), the birds ignored it. When it moved to the right (looking like a hawk), the birds would give warning cries and would try to escape, even when they had never seen the model before.

(Frank Lotz Miller, *Black Star*)

(Owen Franken, Stock, Boston)

4. Finally, if the two forms of learning are truly different, they should also differ in such things as extinction, generalization, or discrimination. In fact, as we have seen, there are very few differences between the two kinds of learning in any of these processes.

All of this evidence suggests that classical and operant conditioning may simply be two different procedures for achieving the same end. If so, psychologists may have been overstressing the differences and paying too little attention to the similarities between the two. Learning occurs in both cases, and the nature of learning itself remains open to new theories. In the next section we shall discuss several theories that also challenge traditional views of conditioning.

COGNITIVE LEARNING

Traditional theories of learning give only "objective" definitions of the learning process and have little use of "inner causes," such as individual cognition: "If you cannot measure it, forget it." Some psychologists, however, are no longer content with this description of what goes on in learning. They argue that strict stimulus–response formulas leave many questions about learning unclear or unanswered. Why does a change in behavior become "relatively permanent"? We can agree something was learned, but how exactly did it happen? Is it more than a connection between an external stimulus and a visible response? Should we distinguish between learning—what goes on inside a person—and performance—what a person does that tells you learning has taken place?

Recently, many psychologists have begun to reassess classical and operant conditioning from the viewpoint of *cognitive* or internal factors that may be involved in learning. For example, lower species may learn only simple stimulus–response associations, but higher forms of cognitive mediation, such as the learning of expectations, may apply for birds and mammals, including, of course, human beings.

Cognitive theorists have by no means abandoned the classic notions of stimulus–response conditioning; but they maintain that cognitive processes are important in all human and in some animal learning. Thus, **cognitive theorists** believe that learning is much more than behaving in a certain way. They want to explain learning in terms that cannot be observed or measured: They want to explain what actually goes on inside of us when we learn. Let us now take a closer look at the kinds of learning that cognitive theorists tend to study.

Conditioning has been seen as a process of pairing things together in time. In classical conditioning, an unconditioned and a conditioned stimulus are paired, while in operant conditioning a response is paired with reinforcement. In the late 1960s, psychologists took a major step toward refining these concepts when they began to ask if something more than simple pairing was behind conditioning. Did Pavlov's dogs salivate when they heard a bell only because the bell and food had appeared within a short time of one another? Or did the bell tell them something about the coming of food?

COGNITIVE PROCESSES AMONG ANIMALS

(Mary M. Thacher, Photo Researchers)

Humans do not have a monopoly on cognitive processes. In one experiment (Harlow, 1949), a monkey was shown two objects, a red square and a green triangle. If the monkey lifted the red square, it found a raisin underneath. There was no reward under the green triangle. The position of the two objects was changed at random. Sometimes the red square was on the right, sometimes on the left. This forced the monkey to choose on the basis of the objects themselves rather than according to their position. After the monkey had consistently learned to select the red square, it was presented with a new pair of objects, such as a large wood block and a small wood block. The monkey dealt with them much faster because it had *learned how to learn* or to form a **learning set.** In later experiments some chimps could discriminate among stimulus objects of five different dimensions, including size, color, and shape (Nissen, 1951).

Another psychologist, Edward Tolman, believed that animals operated according to what he called **cognitive maps** (1948). A cognitive map, like a road map, depicts spatial relationships in the environment. Tolman believed that in learning a maze the animal does not just learn a set of motor responses. Rather, it develops a cognitive map—an image of the maze—that helps it to find the reward at the end.

Olton (1977) placed rats at the center of a maze with eight radiating arms. Food pellets were put at the end of each arm. To get the most pellets, the rats had to visit each arm and get the food pellet, and then not return to that arm of the maze. Thus, the rats had to remember where they had been—showing a kind of "spatial memory." They learned this cognitive task quickly. Olton also found that the rats could keep their "spatial memory" for a long time. Confining the rats to the center of the maze for up to an hour between visits to the arms had little or no effect on their working memory!

According to Wickelgren (1977), animals display other cognitive processes besides spatial memory. He lists inference, such as problem solving and tool using, imitation of either human or animal behavior, and symbolic processes such as simple sign language. All these cognitive processes have been learned by animals.

Psychologist Robert Rescorla (1967) argues that the close appearance in time of two objects does not explain conditioning. In his view, the conditioned stimulus must be able to tell if the unconditioned stimulus is going to occur. The buzzer must signify contingency—that if one thing occurs, something else is likely to occur. This and related proposals have since been grouped under the heading of **contingency theory.** Rescorla tested his ideas by pairing a tone (the CS) with electric shocks (the US), which were administered in different ways to several groups of dogs. One group received the tone followed consistently by a shock, just as in classical conditioning studies. These dogs showed fear at the sound of the tone, much as Pavlov would predict. Another group received an equal number of tones and shocks, but the tone was never followed by a shock. The two were always unpaired. According to classical conditioning, no learning should occur, but Rescorla found that this was not so. Instead, the dogs learned that when the tone was not present shocks were more apt to occur, and that when the tone was present they were safe. In other words, although the CS and US were never paired, the dogs learned. For still another group, the tone and shock occurred randomly, entirely independently of one another. Occasionally, tone and shock were paired by chance. According to Pavlov's theory, this should have led to classical conditioning. But the dogs did not learn to fear the tone, apparently because it told them nothing about the likelihood of a shock. Thus, Rescorla concluded that a stimulus must "tell" the organism something about the other stimulus for classical conditioning to occur.

This same line of reasoning has also been extended to operant conditioning. It has been assumed that any behavior that is paired with a reinforcement will occur more often than it did before the reinforcement was introduced. As we saw when Skinner (1948) made food available on a random basis to caged pigeons, whatever the pigeons were doing at the time became more likely to recur in the future. The underlying assumption is that every time a behavior is paired with a reinforcement, some operant conditioning will occur.

Recent research suggests that pigeons—and other animals—are not as simple as psychologists thought. They seem to be able to distinguish situations in which they can control delivery of the reward from those in which they cannot. For example, while restrained in a harness, dogs received shocks at random. Skinner would argue that the harnessed dogs would learn only "superstitious" behavior, since none of the dogs' behavior had been consistently paired with a reward, or relief from pain. In fact the dogs seem to learn that nothing they can do will deliver them from their discomfort, that they have no control over the shocks. When they are placed in another context and given the chance to escape, these dogs whine and finally lie down, passively accepting shock after shock long after other dogs have learned to escape. Contingency theorists believe that this passivity, or **learned helplessness**, is learned in the harness and then mistakenly generalized to the new context in which escape is possible.

Contingency theory is a more cognitive approach to simple learning than traditional theories of conditioning. Contingency theorists believe that animals and humans continually collect, code, and distill information about their environment. Classical and operant conditioning procedures are simply two ways of providing that information to the subjects, and in this sense the distinction between classical and operant conditioning has been further reduced. Moreover, it suggests that there may be other, more effective procedures to provide this information and thus to cause learning to occur, at least for some organisms.

Albert Bandura has proposed that much human learning does not involve classical or operant conditioning. According to **social learning theory,** when we learn we do much more than just respond automatically and blindly to whatever is happening around us. Humans have not only sight but they also have insight, foresight, and hindsight. We use all three

(Drawing by Chas Addams; © 1981 *The New Yorker Magazine*, Inc.)

to interpret experiences (Bandura, 1962). Moreover, we can learn not only through direct experiences—conditioning—but also by watching what happens to other people and by just being told about something.

For example, imagine that you are going on a camping trip to Yellowstone Park. You remember a story your friend told you about the time he woke up to find a bear in his tent. The bear had come in for food. From this you learn that keeping food in your tent is a bad idea. So you buy a bear-proof locker to keep it in. You have also learned that learning from other people's experience—called *vicarious* or **observational learning**—can be very helpful. Much of what we learn in school is vicarious learning. In learning history, for example, you do not dig out all the original documents from the American Revolution and decide what happened for yourself. Someone does that for you and then tells you about it. The influence of such *models* on observational learning is central to the social learning viewpoint. By watching models, we can learn such things as how to start a lawn mower and how to be aggressive. We

can also learn how to show love or how to be prejudiced. Bandura stresses four essential mechanisms for observational learning:

1. *Attentional processes*—those factors that determine if you will pay attention to a model.
2. *Retention processes*—the various ways you file away observations for later use.
3. *Motor reproduction*—the translation from watching to doing.
4. *Reinforcement*—anticipating rewards as a motivational factor (Hilgard & Bower, 1975).

Bandura makes several points with these four mechanisms of learning. The nature of the models is more important than is mere exposure to them. Rehearsing modeled activities helps to retain them. We may learn a form of behavior, such as ballet dancing, without necessarily being able to perform it. And no matter how well we acquire or retain some skill, our learning of it will not manifest itself if we do not have enough incentives or social approval—that is, reinforcement.

Social learning theorists have a different view of reinforcement than traditional learning theorists do. As we said earlier, traditional learning theorists distinguish between primary reinforcers, such as hunger, sex, or relief from pain, and secondary reinforcers, such as money or the buzzer that tells a rat that food is coming. On the other hand, social learning theorists stress that our behavior is greatly affected by **symbolic reinforcers** such as compliments, affection, or attention from others. There is a debate about whether symbolic rewards can really be distinguished from secondary

HOW ETHICAL IS BEHAVIOR MODIFICATION?

In a society such as ours that places high value on freedom and civil rights, it is not surprising that the increasing use of behavior modification techniques brings with it an increasing concern for the ethics involved. Is it morally "right" to "control" other people's behavior by offering reinforcements and punishments? Supporters argue that we all practice behavior modification in our daily lives. Is it wrong, they ask, to encourage good manners in children by rewarding them with a "thank you" when they behave politely?

Of course, it is not that simple. Helping a person on their request to overcome some unwanted behav-

ior such as shyness or fear of flying is one thing; using behavior modification in school to keep children working quietly at their desks is another (Stolz, Wienckowski, & Brown, 1975). The latter situation raises questions such as: Is this a proven aid to the education process? Is the desired behavioral change meant to help the teacher rather than the pupils?

Clearly, anyone administering or supervising a behavior modification program has an ethical responsibility to evaluate the methods and the results from the viewpoint of all concerned. Procedures that protect people's rights should be built into all such programs (Stolz, Wienckowski, & Brown, 1975).

reinforcers. Some psychologists believe that secondary reinforcers are different because they do not seem to be directly related to primary reinforcers; other psychologists maintain that they can be related to primary reinforcers. For example, affection might be a secondary reinforcement for sex. In any case, symbolic reinforcers are social in origin—that is, they come from other people. Many symbolic rewards are fairly constant, such as the pleasure one may get from reading mystery novels. Others are more relative. A compliment may not flatter you quite so much if you hear another person being more highly praised. Still other rewards offer **vicarious reinforcement,** as when we modify our own behavior when we see others being rewarded or punished. Most important, in the standards and comparisons we set for ourselves, we have a great capacity for **self-reinforcement,** both positive and negative (Lazarus, 1977). "There is no more devastating punishment than self-contempt" (Bandura, 1973, p. 48).

Social learning theory deals with processes not explained by operant conditioning—self-reinforcement and observational learning, for example. It has great potential for widening our understanding not only of how people learn skills and abilities, but also of how attitudes, values, and ideas pass from person to person. Social learning theory can also teach us how *not* to pass something on. For example, suppose you want to teach a child not to hit other children. A traditional learning theorist might advise you to slap the child as punishment to make her change her behavior. But a social learning theorist might tell you that slapping this child only shows her a better way of hitting. It also supports her suspicion that hitting can be effective. You and the child would both be better off if you showed her a less antisocial model of dealing with other people (Bandura, 1973, 1977). Such advice, combined with traditional discrimination training and reinforcement, can indeed help people change their behavior. Because social learning theory takes the best from operant conditioning and combines it with the "human element" ignored by traditional learning theories, it is a major trend in learning research.

Application

MODIFYING YOUR OWN BEHAVIOR

Can people modify their own behavior? Indeed, yes. A remarkable instance of this is the case of a psychologist left confined to a wheelchair by an automobile accident (Goldiamond, 1973). While he was still in the hospital, he undertook a behavioral analysis of his daily life and the new contingencies—possibilities for reinforcement or non-reinforcement—that he faced. To keep busy, he kept careful logs of his exercises, muscle movements, medication, and emotional states. These logs proved to be extremely valuable. For example, when he suddenly developed insomnia, his nurse blamed it on worry and anxiety. But Goldiamond carefully checked his day-to-day records and discovered that he was having trouble sleeping simply because he had recently stopped taking a mild tranquilizer. Without his daily logs, he might have stayed up all night worrying about why he could not sleep. Goldiamond found his system so effective that he began to apply it to people who came to him for help in controlling some aspect of their lives.

As in any program designed to change behavior, the first thing to do is to decide what behavior you want to acquire—the "target" behav-

"Don't worry. If it turns out tobacco is harmful, we can always quit."
(Drawing by Garrett Price; © 1958 *The New Yorker Magazine*, Inc.)

ior. For example, you may wish to become more assertive, to sleep better, to become physically fit, or to get along better with your roommate. The next step is to define the target behavior precisely: What exactly do you mean by "assertive," or by "physically fit"? The next step is to monitor your present behavior, keeping a daily log of activities related to the target behavior in order to establish your present rate of behavior. The next step—the basic principle of self-modification—is to provide yourself with a positive reinforcer that is contingent on specifically detailed improvements in the target behavior. Watson and Tharp (1972) cite the example of a student who wanted to improve his relationship with his parents. He first counted the times he said something pleasant to them and then rewarded himself for improvement by making his favorite pastime, playing pool, contingent on predetermined increases in the number of pleasant remarks he made.

Behavior modification specialists particularly emphasize a positive approach called "ignoring." Much better results are achieved when the emphasis is on the behavior to be acquired rather than on the behavior to be eliminated. Also stressed is the need to analyze your own environment, because changing the environment is usually necessary if you are going to change behavior.

For example, say you are worried about gaining weight. You decide that you need to lose 10 pounds before summer comes. Picturing your slender new self—instead of telling yourself how fat you are and how badly you need help—is what behavior modifiers mean by "ignoring." Every time you eat something, you should write down in your daily log what you ate, where you were when you ate it, what you were doing at the time, who was with you, and so on. After a couple of weeks you should begin to see a pattern. Suppose that you usually study in your room and that most of your overeating is snacks that you nibble on while studying. Changing your environment by studying at a friend's house or at the library would be a good first step toward changing your eating behavior. Keeping the daily log until you have achieved your goal will help you discover other ways to change your environment, which in turn will help you change yourself.

Summary

1. *Learning* is the process by which relatively permanent changes in behavior are brought about through experience or practice. Some of the simplest kinds of learning are called *conditioning*— the acquisition of a particular pattern of behavior in the presence

of certain stimuli.

2. *Classical conditioning* involves learning to transfer a response from a stimulus that invariably elicits the response to some stimulus that does not normally produce such a response. Ivan Pavlov first demonstrated this process when he conditioned a dog to salivate when it heard a bell.

3. In classical conditioning, the stimulus that invariably causes the desired response is called the *unconditioned stimulus* (US). The reaction to the unconditioned stimulus is called the *unconditioned response* (UR). The neutral stimulus that the subject learns the response to is known as the *conditioned stimulus* (CS), and the response to the conditioned stimulus is called the *conditioned response* (CR).

4. A learned response will generally stop occurring if the conditioned stimulus fails to be followed by the unconditioned stimulus. This process is known as *extinction*. Extinction occurs because the subject has learned to *inhibit* the conditioned response. After a while, the inhibition weakens and the response may suddenly reappear on its own. This is known as *spontaneous recovery*.

5. Once a response has been conditioned to a particular stimulus, it may also be elicited by similar stimuli. This is *stimulus generalization*. The opposite of generalization is *discrimination*. This is the process by which a subject learns to respond to one specific stimulus and to inhibit the response to all other stimuli.

6. After a response to a conditioned stimulus has been learned, the conditioned stimulus itself can be used as the unconditioned stimulus in further training—a procedure known as *higher-order conditioning*.

7. In *operant conditioning*, subjects learn to operate on their environment in some way that will get them something they desire or allow them to avoid something unpleasant. The conditioning is done by reinforcing correct responses and ignoring or punishing incorrect ones.

8. For operant conditioning to occur, the desired response must be made. There are several ways to make the correct response occur. The most common method is to wait for the subject to hit upon the correct response. Another effective method is to *increase motivation*.

9. The direct intervention of the experimenter or teacher can also help the learner acquire the desired response. Such techniques as *forcing, verbal instruction,* and *modeling* are used.

10. Once the desired response has been made, *reinforcement* ensures that it will be repeated and learned. *Positive reinforcement* is something pleasant that is given to the learner after the correct response is made. *Negative reinforcement* after a correct response is made eases or ends a painful or unpleasant situation.

11. *Punishment* inhibits incorrect responses. Punishment is most

effective when paired with a reinforcement that teaches an alternative response that is incompatible with the undesirable response.

12. A *primary reinforcer* is one that is rewarding by itself. A *secondary reinforcer* is one whose value has to be learned through association with other reinforcers.

13. Reinforcing every correct response is less effective than some type of *partial reinforcement. Schedules of reinforcement* can be based either on the number of responses or the time lapse between responses. On a *fixed-interval schedule,* reinforcement is given for the first correct response after a specific time has passed. The amount of time always stays the same. On a *variable-interval schedule,* the amount of time between reinforcements varies. On a *fixed-ratio schedule,* reinforcement is given after a certain number of responses. The number of responses always stays the same. On a *variable-ratio schedule,* the number of responses between reinforcements varies.

14. *Stimulus generalization, response generalization,* and *discrimination* occur in operant conditioning, just as in classical conditioning. Operant responses are extinguished by withholding reinforcement, but they may recover spontaneously.

15. Complex as well as simple tasks can be learned by operant conditioning. A procedure known as *shaping* is used for teaching complicated patterns of behavior. Each simple part of the total behavior is built up step by step until the final behavior has been learned. Most operant behavior consists of chains of events. One response becomes the stimulus for the next response, and so on. *Behavior chains* are most easily learned if they are taught bit by bit in backward order.

16. Recent research has blurred the distinction between classical and operant conditioning to the point that many psychologists believe the two represent different methods of bringing about the same process of learning.

17. *Contingency theory* proposes that a simple pairing of the unconditioned stimulus (US) and the conditioned stimulus (CS) or of the desired response and reinforcement is not enough to explain learning. Only if one stimulus provides information about another does learning occur.

18. *Social learning theory,* proposed by Albert Bandura, combines elements of traditional operant conditioning and cognitive theory. One of Bandura's main departures from traditional learning theory is his emphasis on *observational learning*—the ability to learn by watching other people's behavior. Social learning theorists also have a different view of reinforcement than traditional learning theorists. They recognize *symbolic reinforcers* such as attention and approval, *vicarious reinforcers,* whereby other people's being rewarded or punished encourages us to change our behavior, and *self-reinforcers* such as pride or guilt.

Outline

Chapter 6

Information Processing and Memory

Suppose you and everyone else in your community not only forgot how to learn anything new, but also began to forget everything you had ever learned. This is exactly what happened to the people of Macondo, a fictional village described by the Colombian writer Gabriel Garcia Marquez in his novel *One Hundred Years of Solitude*. A plague that caused insomnia and gradual loss of memory spread through the village. After days of sleeplessness, the people began to first forget their childhood, and then to forget the names and uses of things and the identity of other people. Finally, the victims fell into a trance in which past and present had no meaning. The villagers tried to fight the effects of the disease by marking everything with its name and with detailed instructions about its use. A sign on a cow read, "This is the cow. She must be milked every morning so that she will produce milk, and the milk must be boiled in order to be mixed with coffee to make coffee and milk" (p. 53).

It was no use. Reality slowly dissolved as people forgot the meaning of letters and no longer even recognized their own parents or brothers and sisters. For relief from the strain of their illness, many turned to the village fortune teller, who reconstructed an imaginary world for them in the same way she had once foretold the future. Delivery from the plague came only when a gypsy appeared who dispensed a potion that restored the memory of those who drank it.

Marquez asks us to imagine what it would be like to remember nothing about what we have ever seen, heard, or otherwise experienced. It is a terrifying thought. Most of us would like to remember more than we do. Anyone who has ever sat in front of a blank examination book knows the experience of having a name, date, or fact fly out of his or her head. We may feel angry, frustrated, or afraid that our mental powers are vanishing. We expect that memory should be a simple, normal process that

169

anyone—except perhaps the very young or the very old—should be able to use all the time. In this chapter, we challenge these assumptions about memory.

Information Processing

How do we remember things? How do we take the information that surrounds us at any given moment and process some of it so that we can later find or *retrieve* it? Figure 6–1 shows us how this process takes place, beginning with the moment that an external stimulus enters our **sensory registers** and following it through to retrieval. Briefly, what happens is this: Information from our senses comes into our sensory registers, where it is kept for a second or two. If nothing more happens to this information, it drops out and is forgotten. But some of this information is matched up with what we already know (**long-term memory**), and the result is that we *recognize* the new information. Once it has been recognized, we can become *aware* of it (**short-term memory**). If the material is not processed further, within a few seconds it will fade or be replaced by new material. We can keep information in short-term memory indefinitely just by repeating it to ourselves over and over again. But if we want to store the information permanently, we must organize and *encode* it in long-term memory. When this has been done, we have added yet another piece of information to the huge storehouse of permanent knowledge that we carry around in our long-term memories. In the following sections, we will look at this sequence of activities in more detail.

Figure 6–1
The sequence of information processing.

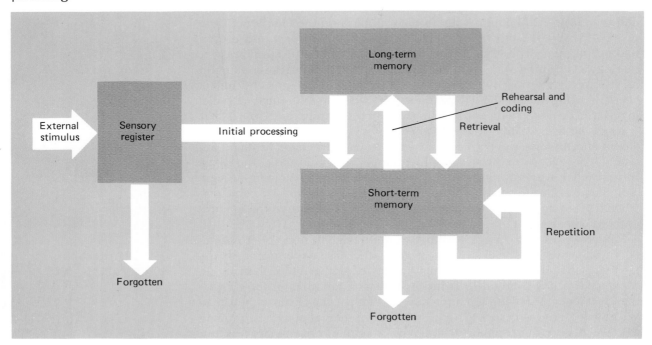

THE SENSORY REGISTERS

How do we begin to process information? First we must *register* some of the information that always surrounds us. If you look slowly around the room you are in, you will see that each glance—which may last for only a fraction of a second—takes in an enormous amount of visual information, including colors, shapes, textures, relative brightness, shadows, and so on. No matter how hard you concentrate, you cannot retain all that information for even a few seconds. And while you are doing that, you are not attentive to the sounds, smells, tastes, and other raw information that is also there.

All this raw information flows from our senses into what are known as the *sensory registers*. These are like waiting rooms. Information enters, stays for a very short time, and then is either lost or processed. Two sensory registers—visual and auditory—have been studied more extensively than any others.

To understand how much visual information we take in, and how quickly it is lost, take a Polaroid camera into a darkened room and take a photograph using a flashbulb. During the split second that the room is lit up by the flash, your sensory register will take in a surprising amount of information about the room and its contents. Try to hold on to that visual image, or icon, as long as you can. You will find that it fades rapidly and, in a few seconds, is gone. Then compare your remembered image of the room with what you actually saw at the time—as captured in the photograph. You will notice that there was far more information taken in by the sensory register than you were able to retain for even a few seconds. We are not sure how long this form of visual memory lasts, but in most cases information disappears from the visual sensory register very quickly.

By using the visual and auditory sensory registers together, information can be processed, organized, and stored in the memory at a faster rate.
(Michael Austin, Photo Researchers)

(Robert M. Mottar, Photo Researchers)

RECALL AND RECOGNITION

Studies of memory generally distinguish between two basic procedures for determining if information is in long-term memory: **recall** and **recognition.** If someone asks you to recite a poem you once learned, you may be able to do it word for word without help: You have perfect *recall* of the poem. But suppose you get stuck halfway through and cannot remember a line or phrase. When someone tells you what it is, you *recognize* it as soon as you hear it.

A multiple-choice test is a good example of a typical recognition test. There are several possible choices, but only one is correct. For example, if you are given a multiple-choice question about where the Arno River is and the choices are Germany, Italy, and France, you may be able to recognize Italy as the correct answer. Arno sounds more like Italian than German or French. By contrast, a recall test might ask, "Where is the Arno River?" Where indeed? Italy, Spain, South America? You are almost forced to recall an exact fact to answer correctly. Essay, short-answer, and fill-in-the-blank tests use recall to retrieve information from long-term memory.

In most cases, recognition is more sensitive than recall because it often provides evidence of **retention** when recall produces a blank. Performance on recognition tests also remains high even after much time has passed (Postman & Rau, 1957).

Why is it easier to recognize something than to recall it? One of the first explanations was the "threshold" hypothesis. According to this theory, items stored in long-term memory must have a certain amount of strength before they can be retrieved. To be recalled, an item must be stronger than it needs to be to be recognized. For this reason, proponents of the threshold theory argue, recognition testing pro-

duces better results than recall testing.

A more promising explanation of why it is easier to recognize than to recall information is the *dual-process* hypothesis which states that recognition and recall are two very different processes. Recall involves both conducting a search for an item in long-term memory and deciding if this is the item we want to retrieve. If it is not, the search goes on. Recognition, on the other hand, consists only of the second phase of recall, the decision. According to this view, recall is more difficult than recognition because, if the search fails, there is nothing to make a decision *about,* nothing to recognize. Recognition, since it involves only one step, is more likely to succeed.

But sometimes people can recall something that they do not recognize. This has led to a modified dual-process approach, which maintains that recognition, like recall, also involves searching our memories; but the two searches are carried out differently. Why would we go about retrieving information differently in order to recognize it than we would to recall it? New research suggests that how we retrieve something from long-term memory depends on how we first encoded it. When you see *cat* on a list of words and encode it for storage in long-term memory, you encode the word in the context of other items—such as your associations with the word *cat*—and also in the context of how you are feeling when you look at the list, what the weather is like, and your awareness that the person behind you keeps sniffling. So what you encode *and* retrieve is not only the word *cat* but also a whole package of information that makes up an *episode.* In a recognition test, unless the episode is duplicated, you retrieve only part of the package—the word *cat.* But in recalling the word,

The icon usually lasts only a second (Sperling, 1960), partly because it fades out by itself and partly because new visual information comes in and replaces or "erases" it. This erasure means that we can take in new images rapidly without overlapping or scrambling (Klatzky, 1980).

Auditory information fades more slowly than visual information. The auditory equivalent of the icon is the echo. The echo tends to last for several seconds, which, given the nature of speech, is fortunate. Otherwise, "*You* did it!" would be indistinguishable from "You *did* it!" because we would be unable to remember the emphasis on the first words by the time the last words were registered.

you can use more general cues to help retrieve the word. Suppose you take a paired-association test and are given the words *eye—cat*, with *cat* being the word to remember. You might be more likely to *recall cat* when given the cue *eye* than you would be to *recognize* the word *cat* by itself (Craik, 1979).

This last theory suggests that instead of encoding a single item, we actually encode a whole package of information. When it comes time to retrieve the item, we search out the whole package (Bower, 1967; Flexser & Tulving, 1978; Kintsch, 1974). For example, Bahrick, Bahrick, and Wittlinger (1974) studied people's ability to remember high school classmates. About 390 people who had graduated from 5 months to 48 years before the survey were given 6 tests, including tests for recall and recognition of classmates' names and photographs. Both recent graduates and those who had graduated 35 years earlier correctly recognized 9 out of 10 of their classmates' pictures. And even elderly adults who had graduated more than 40 years before recognized 75 percent of their classmates.

What about recall? When given enough time, adults could recall the names of many of their high school classmates. In one study, people were asked to recall the names of roughly 600 classmates during a series of testing sessions that extended over a number of weeks (Williams, 1976). One person recalled about 90 names by the end of the 1st hour, almost 120 by the end of the 2nd, approximately 160 by the end of the 4th, and nearly 220 names by the end of the 10th hour. Thus, in general, the ability to recall names did appear to improve over time. But even after many testing sessions, people could recognize more of their classmates than they could recall.

A good method of testing long-term memory recognition is through a multiple-choice test. Here several possible choices are presented which provide cues that significantly increase the chances of remembering.
(Teri Leigh Stratford)

RECOGNITION

The sensory registers are just the first step in the processing of information. At this point, the information that we register is meaningless, raw data. Look at the page in front of you. You will see a series of black lines on a white page. Until you recognize these lines as letters and words, they are just meaningless marks. To make sense of this jumble of data, the information in the sensory registers must be processed for *meaning* (see Figure 6–1).

How does this initial processing happen? How do we know what the word *fire* means, and that it is more important than the word *dog*? For

Whale

Whale

Whale

Whale

that matter, how do we recognize and understand any stimulus? When we read the word *important,* how do we know we are not reading *importune* or *deportment?* The simplest explanation is that we match the incoming information to a set of templates stored in our long-term memory. When a match is found, the stimulus is assigned the meaning that is associated with the template. For example, we receive a visual image of the word *whale,* and we find an appropriate template to fit it, and assign the corresponding meaning to the image. This is much like the child's toy that consists of a wooden board with holes of various geometric shapes and separate, matching wooden pieces, one of each shape. The child fits the square piece in the square hole, the round piece in the round hole, and so on. A more sophisticated illustration of a **template-matching** model is the account numbers printed on most checks, which are "read" by a computer.

But this model has its problems. First, there would have to be a huge number of templates for us to decode all the stimuli in the world around us. Not only can the word *whale* be printed in many different typefaces, but imagine the variations possible in presenting the same word in different handwritings. We would have to have a template for each possible version. Template matching is also complicated by the possibility that the stimulus may be rotated or changed in size. Is an upside-down letter *d* really a *p*, or should it still be recognized as a *d?* More templates are needed to meet these variations. Some theorists have tried to simplify these problems by suggesting an initial, rough, "cleaning-up" stage in which ill-defined images such as upside-down *d*'s or sloppily written letters are made to fit more closely to the standard templates. But such a cleaning-up stage will only work if we have already recognized the letter correctly! Otherwise, we would not know whether to convert a sloppy *d* into a *d* or a *p* or a *b* or some other letter.

All of these limitations of template matching suggest that it is probably not a very good explanation of how we recognize stimuli. Two other explanations seem more promising.

Before a furniture maker begins to make a certain chair in quantity, he builds a *prototype,* or rough model. The prototype is not an exact copy of the finished product but it is a rough approximation, with all of the essential features. Some theorists suggest that long-term memory does not contain exact templates but approximate, rough prototypes that identify new information and give it meaning. Suppose someone handed you a book that was round, with a large, round hole through the center, and with black pages with white type. According to template matching, you would be unlikely to recognize such an object as a book unless you already had a template for it in your long-term or permanent memory. In fact, you probably *would* recognize it as a book—though an unusual one—because it has certain basic elements that fit with our prototypical model of a book. It has a cover, perhaps a title printed on the outside, a "hinge" on one edge, and pages on which words are printed. Moreover, you probably would not identify it as a doughnut because despite its shape, it does not resemble the prototype of a doughnut that we carry in our long-term memory.

Prototype matching is especially helpful in explaining how we can iden-

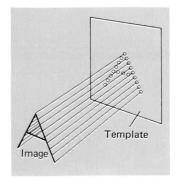

Figure 6–2
An instance of template matching.
(After P. Lindsay and D. Norman, *Human Information Processing.* New York: Academic Press, 1972.)

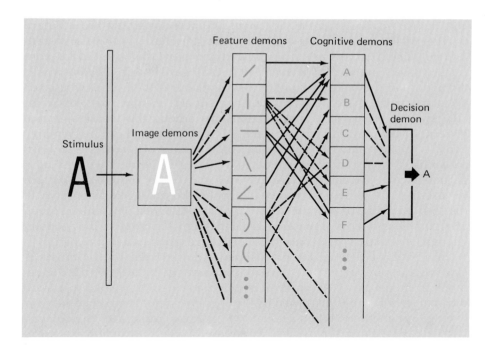

Figure 6–3

Selfridge's Pandemonium model. Image demons record the incoming signal. The signal passes to feature demons, which look for specific features of the signal. Cognitive demons then analyze the pattern of features. Finally, decision demons recognize the patterns by comparing them to patterns in long-term memory.

(From R. Klatzky, *Human Memory*. San Francisco: Freeman, 1980.)

tify stimuli, like the peculiar book, that do not exactly match anything that we have seen before. It also explains how we can process sensory information that is out of context—smelling cigar smoke during a church service, for instance, or tasting vanilla in tomato sauce.

A second alternative to template matching suggests that we break down the pattern of an incoming stimulus into its key elements, or *features*. These individual features are then matched with lists of features stored in long-term memory. The best match leads to pattern recognition (Klatzky, 1980).

A graphic illustration of the **feature analysis** model is known as Pandemonium (Selfridge, 1959). Selfridge developed the system as a computer program designed to identify handwritten characters through the use of a feature detection system. Information passes through a series of stages. At each stage, certain recognition tasks are performed by what Selfridge called demons. The first set of demons are called image demons. Their job is to record the incoming signal and perform basic "clean-up" chores. The image is then passed on to feature demons, which look for a specific feature, such as horizontal lines, partial curves, or particular angles. Feature demons are, in a sense, the key to the whole system, and there is evidence that such feature detectors—as they are usually called—do in fact exist. For example, consider the errors made in tests on the recognition of letters. People are much more likely to confuse a *C* with a *G* than with a letter of quite dissimilar features, such as an *M*. This kind of confusion is what would be expected from a recognition system based on feature detection.

Further evidence for feature detectors can be found in physiological research being carried out on the visual system of animals. There are neurons in the visual system that will respond to a specific feature: One might fire when a straight line is presented, another might fire for a curved

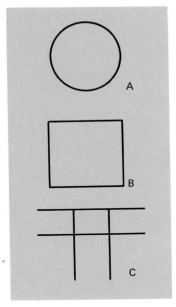

Figure 6–4
Feature detectors allow us to tell curved lines from straight lines.

line, and so on. For example, a straight line detector would fire if Figure 6–4B or 6–4C were shown to a person, but not if Figure 6–4A were shown.

If only line detectors are firing, how do we know the object is a square (Figure 6–4B) and not just a cluster of lines (Figure 6–4C)? Obviously, it is the pattern of the features and not just the features themselves that leads us to recognize the object and call it a square, a table, or a book. In other words, we consider the relationships among the features, or the pattern. In the **Pandemonium** model, this step is carried out by cognitive demons that respond to only certain combinations of features: two horizontal lines, two vertical lines, and four 90-degree corners would lead a particular cognitive demon to respond to Figure 6–4B; without this pattern (Figure 6–4C), the demon or detector would be quiet. We know that in the visual system of animals there are cells that respond only to such very complex patterns of features. Even incomplete stimuli, if they contain enough key features, can cause these cells to respond (see Figure 6–5).

Once we have defined the precise pattern of stimulation, we must decide what we are seeing—we have to recognize the pattern. In the Pandemonium model this is the task of the decision demons, which compare the pattern of features discerned by the cognitive demons to other patterns in long-term memory. When a match is found, we "recognize" the object—it now has meaning for us; it is a "square." This information is sent to short-term memory, where we experience a square or a circle or a dog or a house, not just unrelated features such as lines, edges, and angles.

Sometimes, though, even the pattern of features by itself is not enough to make an object recognizable; we need to consider the context of the pattern or the relationships between patterns. A straight, vertical line, for example, could be a lowercase "*l*" or the number "*1*" or even a capital "*I.*" By considering the context, we determine which one is being shown.

Recent research indicates that we can look for several matches in long-term memory at the same time. Thus, we can process information much more rapidly than if we had to make one laborious comparison after another. Other evidence suggests that processing information can also be hastened by how we apply our expectations—or previously stored knowledge—to the sensory data we receive (Klatzky, 1980). For example, if we see a feathered object in a nest, we do not have to match it up with a list of features that apply to dogs. Because we *expect* to see a bird in a nest, we can go right to the "bird list" in long-term memory. This recognition system also sends messages back to the sensory register, perhaps saying, "Look for wings." When we see that the feathered object does indeed have wings, we recognize it as a bird.

Figure 6–5
We can recognize letters if there are enough key features present.

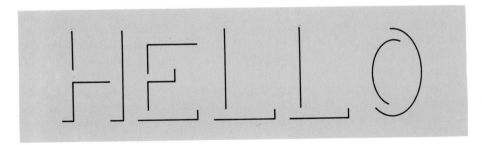

ATTENTION

No matter how hard we try, we simply cannot be aware of all the details that bombard our senses. We constantly select which information is chosen for further processing. This is what we call *attention:* the process of selective looking, listening, smelling, tasting, and feeling.

Suppose you are sitting at a desk reading this book. Your roommate is listening to a talk show on the radio. There are traffic sounds outside. The water you are heating to make tea starts to boil. What do you pay attention to? If you intend to study, you have to eliminate some of the other information. Some of it can be physically dealt with—you can turn off the kettle and ask your roommate to take the radio into the other room. But there will still be at least a vague hum from the radio, the traffic noises will continue, and you will taste the tea as you read.

How do we select which information to pay attention to? Broadbent (1958) was one of the first influential theorists on this subject. He suggested that there was a filtering process at the entrance to the nervous system. All incoming stimuli are accepted into the sensory registers where they are sorted out by physical properties such as color, size, loudness, location, shape, and so on. Only those stimuli that meet certain requirements are

The ability to screen out external stimuli and to concentrate on one particular matter is often not easy.
(Jan Halaska, Photo Researchers)

allowed through the filter, so that we can recognize them and figure out what they mean. If you are sitting at a restaurant table listening to a friend talk, you filter out all other conversations taking place around you. Although you may be able to describe certain physical characteristics of those other conversations, such as whether they were spoken by men or women, or spoken loudly or softly, normally you would be unable to describe what was being said. Because the conversations were filtered out, processing did not reach the point where you could understand the meanings of what you heard.

According to Broadbent's theory, information will draw our attention if it is made to stand out because of its physical properties—intensity, color, sudden starts or stops. Yet most of us have had the experience of reading a book only to have our attention swing to a particular meaningful word farther down the page—perhaps our own last name, or the name of our hometown. Or, to return to the restaurant example, if someone around us were to speak our name, in all likelihood our attention would shift to their conversation. This is called the cocktail-party phenomenon (Cherry, 1966). There is no physical reason why that one word should have stood out. In fact, since we were not attending to it and it was

presumably filtered out, we should not even have heard or seen the word.

Treisman (1965), among others, modified the filter theory to account for these exceptions. She suggested that the filter is not a simple on–or–off switch, but a variable control like the volume control on a radio that can "turn down" unwanted signals without rejecting them entirely. Instead of processing only one signal at a time, many signals are monitored at a low level at the same time. In this way, although we are not normally aware of these extraneous stimuli, we can shift our attention if we sense something particularly meaningful. This process works even when we are asleep: A classic example is the mother who wakes immediately to the sound of her baby crying yet sleeps through other, louder noises; another is that most of us would wake up immediately to the words "The house is on fire," while we would probably sleep through less important phrases such as "The car is for sale."

Other data also support the theory that apparently "unattended" messages are not completely filtered out. In an experiment, subjects wearing earphones are given separate messages in each ear at the same time and asked to *shadow*, or verbally repeat, one of these messages and to ignore the other. Cherry (1953) used this technique and found that subjects did pick up some information from the messages they were asked to ignore. They knew they were hearing *something*, and they noticed when the message changed from a male voice to a female voice. But they had no idea what any of the words were—or even what language they were in (Moray, 1959)!

In a similar experiment, however, Norman (1969) found that subjects could remember parts of a list of numbers that were fed into one ear as the irrelevant message, if they were interrupted during the experiment or asked to recall them immediately afterward. Moray (1959) also found that part of an unattended message could be remembered immediately after the message ended if it had been preceded by the subject's own name. But without this "signal," subjects could remember little or nothing of the unattended message. In another experiment, MacKay (1973) had subjects shadow vague sentences with one ear, while they were given information in the other ear that clarified the meaning of these sentences. For example, the vague sentences might concern a bank, while the unshadowed messages referred to *river* or *money*. Later, subjects tended to remember the meaning that fit the unshadowed message, although they could not recall the message itself. In other words, even "unattended" meaning filtered through.

To summarize, we know that we select very little information from the sensory registers to attend to, and that, in part, we select information for certain physical characteristics—such as color, a certain voice quality—and concentrate on those signals to try to recognize and understand them. But other, "ignored" signals get at least some processing, so that our attention can be shifted to focus on something particularly meaningful. We have seen how the sensory registers interact with long-term memory to help us recognize and pay attention to the information that enters the waiting rooms of our senses. Much of the information is discarded and lost. But what happens to the information that we recognize and attend to? It enters our short-term memory.

Short-Term Memory

Short-term memory (STM) is temporary, active, and conscious. It is our attention span, or **working memory.** STM is what we are "thinking about" at any given moment. It holds much less material than the sensory registers, though for a somewhat longer time. Material in short-term memory will disappear in 10 to 20 seconds if it is not repeated or practiced (Keele, 1973).

Psychologists generally believe that STM can hold on to, at most, 9 or 10 items at a time (Mandler, 1967; Miller, 1956). It may seem to us that we are holding more items than that—especially when we watch a circus or skim a book, for example. But psychologists explain this by comparing short-term memory to a purse. The purse will hold 7 coins, but it does not matter if the coins are pennies or silver dollars. It could not hold 700 pennies, but if each 100 pennies are grouped into 1 coin, each coin counts as a single item and the purse can hold the resulting 7 items. This way of grouping and organizing information to fit into meaningful units is called **chunking.**

Suppose you were asked to memorize 15 letters. That would be more than you could normally retain. But let us say you put together the first 3 letters, *S, U,* and *B,* into a single word—that is, you remember *SUB* as 1 item rather than as 3 separate ones. If you do this for each group of 3 letters, you will have 5 "words" instead of 15 letters. And your short-term memory can easily handle 5 items. As you can see, the critical factor for recall in short-term memory is the number of meaningful units involved (Murdock, 1961). It is just as easy to recall 3 separate words as it is to recall 3 separate letters. And by chunking words into clusters or sentences or sentence fragments, we can remember even more information (Aaronson & Scarborough, 1976, 1977; Tulving & Patkau, 1962).

Suppose that we are given a list of words to remember: *tree, song, hat, sparrow, box, lilac, cat.* One way to remember the words would be to cluster as many of them as possible into sentences. *Sparrow, song,* and *tree* can be easily associated with each other, as can *hat* and *box.* But is there a limit to this? If you put five words together into one sentence, and five others into another sentence, soon you might have five or six sentences to remember. Are five sentences really as easy to remember as five single words? Simon (1974) found that the size of the chunks—sentences in our example—does affect the ability to remember. Phrases and sentences are harder to remember than single letters and single words. As the size of each chunk increases, the number of chunks that can be recalled declines. And there are other limitations: Since short-term memory is also working memory, the ability to work on information constantly competes with the ability to store new information for a short time. In one experiment, subjects were given a simple reasoning task just after they had been given six numbers to remember. They performed their reasoning task more slowly than subjects who had simply been asked to repeat the numbers one through six throughout the task (Baddeley & Hitch, 1974).

While verbal information is being held in STM, most of it is stored acoustically, in sounds rather than in shapes. In other words, we *code* verbal information according to its echo rather than its icon, even if we see the word on a page rather than hear it spoken. For example, people are more likely to mix up *B* and *V* than they are to confuse *V* and *X*, because *B* and *V sound* alike, while *V* and *X* only look alike (Klatzky, 1980). But all verbal material in short-term memory is not stored acoustically. Some information appears to be stored in visual form, while other data is retained in terms of its meaning. For example, Posner and his colleagues (Posner, 1967) asked people to compare two letters and to press a button to denote whether they were the same or different. If subjects were shown a capital *A* and a small *a*, it took them longer to determine that the letters were the same than if the two letters were visually identical (*A A*). Since the tests were conducted so that any remaining icon in the sensory register would have faded, it would seem that we also code images in short-term memory according to their visual forms. Shepard and his colleagues (Shepard, 1978) have found that we can identify images by rotating them. If we are shown a ꞵ for example, we can turn it clockwise until we recognize it as a *B*. Since we cannot rotate sound, it appears that we do have a spatial, visual way of processing some information. Deaf people in particular use shapes rather than sounds to retain information in STM (Conrad, 1972; Frumkin & Anisfeld, 1977.

Up to this point, we have been discussing how short-term memory holds verbal information: letters, words, sentences, and so on. Until recently, most studies of short-term memory involved the use of these materials. But in the last decade there has been much interest in how we process nonverbal material in short-term memory. It may make sense to convert words into an acoustic code to hold them in short-term memory. But it would be odd if we had to convert things like maps, diagrams, and paintings into sound before we could store them. It seems obvious that this material also must be coded visually.

REHEARSAL IN SHORT-TERM MEMORY

To keep information in STM longer than 20 seconds, it must be repeated or practiced. In one form of practice, called **rote rehearsal,** you talk to yourself, repeating information over and over, silently or out loud. Through constant rote rehearsal, information can be held indefinitely in short-term memory (Klatzky, 1980). But if you stop repeating something you will quickly forget it. If a friend unexpectedly arrives at your door while you are on your way to the flour canister, there is a good chance that you will forget how much flour you need for the recipe. You can also lose information from short-term memory because other information interferes. If you are trying to remember a phone number by repeating it to yourself and someone else in the room is repeating another number, you may become confused and lose track of the number you were trying to keep in mind.

Generally, however, rote rehearsal is used to hold on to information that

It is through the process of chunking that information is organized into meaningful units that can be retrieved for later use.
(Joel Gordon)

EIDETIC IMAGERY

An **eidetic image** is an unusually sharp and detailed visual representation of something that has been seen—a picture, a scene, a page of text. Eidetic imagery is sometimes called "photographic memory," because it enables a person to see the features of an image in minute detail, sometimes even reading a page of a book that is no longer present. Eidetic imagery is much more common in children, but some adults also seem to have it.

Haber (1969) screened 500 elementary school-children before finding 20 with eidetic imagery. The children were told to scan a picture for 30 seconds, moving their eyes to see all its various parts. The picture was then removed, and the children were told to look at the blank easel and report what they saw. They needed at least 3 to 5 seconds of scanning to produce an image, even when the picture was familiar. Once the image had been described, it faded away. Imagery usually could not be prolonged or recalled, but the children could "erase" the images by blinking or looking away from the easel.

The quality of eidetic imagery seems to vary from person to person. One girl in Haber's study could move and reverse images and recall them several weeks later. Three children could produce eidetic images of three-dimensional objects, and some could superimpose an eidetic image of one picture onto another and form a new picture. However, the children with eidetic imagery performed no better than their noneidetic classmates on other tests of memory.

you only need for a moment or two. Once you discard information from STM without any further processing, it cannot be recalled (Peterson, 1977). If you repeat it long enough, however, you may recognize the information when you hear or use it again. In other words, if you are rehearsing a telephone number and someone asks you, 20 minutes later, "What was that number you dialed?" you are not likely to recall it. But if someone asks instead, "Were you dialing 555-1356?" you might recognize the number if you had rehearsed it previously (Glensberg, Smith, & Green, 1977). Whatever the cause, if we are distracted or interrupted when the material is still at the short-term memory level, we are unlikely to remember it later. What do we have to do to assure that information in STM will be remembered for longer than a few seconds? Most researchers believe that **elaborative rehearsal** is necessary (Postman, 1975).

Elaborative rehearsal involves organizing new information to relate it to something that we already know. This endows the information with more detail and makes it easier to remember. Suppose that you had to remember that the French word *poire* means *pear*. You are already familiar with *pear*, both as a word and as a fruit. *Poire*, however, means nothing to you. To remember what it means, you have to link it up with *pear*. To do this you might make up a sentence: *"Pear* and *poire* both begin with *p."* Or, you might associate *poire* with the familiar taste and image of a pear, a yellow-green, oval fruit that you have been eating for years. Psychologists call these techniques verbal and visual mediators, the use of words or images to link the unfamiliar with the already known (Bower, 1972; Delin, 1969).

How do we encode more complicated information, the kind that we encounter every day? Suppose a talkative neighbor tells you a long story about something that happened on his vacation. How do you incorporate his story into long-term memory so that you will be able to stop him from repeating it by reminding him that you already heard it? We encode large

(Alan Becker, Photo Researchers)

units of knowledge—like stories—by linking new material to structures or schemes already stored in long-term memory. In other words, we interpret new information in light of what we already know. If your neighbor's story is about a harrowing canoe trip in Colorado, you might link the story with things you already have stored in long-term memory: an uncle who lives in Denver, a story you read about mountain streams, a canoe you paddled as a child. All these connections will help you retain the new information your neighbor has given you. You will probably remember the information even better if you encode it in visual images as well as verbal ones—if you visualize the roaring water, the canoe, and so on.

What happens if elaborative rehearsal is interrupted or prevented? Frequently, a person who has suffered a concussion cannot recall what directly preceded the injury, even though he or she can remember what happened some time before the injury. A severe electric shock can have the same effect. This condition is known as **retrograde amnesia.** The events right before the accident were at the short-term memory level and had not been rehearsed enough to be transferred to the long-term level. Thus, they were completely forgotten.

A study by Cohen (1974*a*) shows how such interruptions of rehearsal can affect recall. One group of college students was instructed to call the weather report on the telephone immediately after they woke up and to write down the day's expected temperature. Then they were to write down anything they could remember about their dreams. A second group of students was instructed to lie still for 90 seconds upon waking—the approximate time the first group took to call the weather report—and then to write down their dreams. Only 33 percent of the first group could recall their dreams, while 63 percent of the second group remembered theirs.

Long-Term Memory

Everything that we "know" is stored in long-term memory: George Washington's birthday, the words to a song, how to drive a car, how to speak French. We have already seen that long-term memory contains what we need to make information meaningful. This includes rules for spelling and grammar and the kinds of knowledge we need to recall events and to solve problems; in other words, everything that we need to think. Like the sensory registers, long-term memory has a vast capacity for information. It holds the total sum of what we know.

Psychologists distinguish between two different kinds of information in long-term memory. On the one hand, we have general knowledge that lets us recognize Nevada when we see a map, add 2 and 2 to make 4, and know that George Washington was the first president of the United States. This is called **semantic memory.**

Our knowledge is not limited to general, impersonal facts, however. You may remember that you ate a hamburger last night, that a favorite aunt died in 1975, and that last week's *Time* magazine carried a cover story on the Super Bowl. This personal, specific kind of knowledge is called **episodic memory** (Tulving, 1972). Episodic memory is made up of specific events that have personal meaning for us. If semantic memory is like a dictionary, episodic memory is more like a diary.

Most of the research on long-term memory has involved verbal or *semantic* information—people are given tests based on lists of words, for instance. It is understandable therefore that most theories of semantic memory have focused on words and concepts and the associations between them. But there is recent evidence that semantic memory contains even more complex elements such as propositions—"a bird has feathers," for example—and "frames" or "scripts," which are general

Table 6–1
Differences Between the Three Stages of Memory

	Sensory Register	Short-Term Memory	Long-Term Memory
Entry of Information	Preattentive	Requires attention	Rehearsal
Maintenance of Information	Not possible	Continued attention Repetition	Repetition Organization
Form of Information	Literal copy of input	Auditory Probably visual Possibly semantic	Largely semantic Some auditory and visual
Capacity	Large	Small	No known limit
Information Loss	Erasure Possibly interference	Interference Decay	Possibly no storage loss Loss of access by interference
Trace Duration	¼ to a few seconds	Up to 30 seconds	

Source: Adapted from F.I.M. Craik and R. S. Lockhart, "Levels of Processing: A Framework for Memory Research." *Journal of Verbal Learning and Verbal Behavior,* 1972, *11,* 671–684.

THE ''TIP-OF-THE-TONGUE'' PHENOMENON

''It's on the tip of my tongue, but I can't quite remember.'' We have all experienced the frustration of almost, but not quite being able to recall a name or a familiar word. Now this problem has received an official scientific name: the ''tip-of-the-tongue'' phenomenon (TOT).

In the TOT state, people are likely to recall words that resemble the word they are searching for. Brown and McNeill (1966) gave some college students the definitions of words that are not in everyone's vocabulary—*sampan,* for example. The words the students came up with when trying to recall the right word sometimes resembled the word in meaning—junk, houseboat—but most often resembled it in sound—Siam, sarong.

To put it more scientifically, in the TOT state we have some information about the word we want; even, sometimes, the number of syllables or its first letter, but we cannot come up with the word itself. Why do we have this problem? Studies of TOT suggest that when we go to retrieve something, we do not necessarily pull it out whole. Instead, we may retrieve it in bits and pieces. Brown and McNeill believe that a word is stored in a specific location that contains information about both its sound and its meaning, so that we can retrieve words according to either characteristic. Someone can ask, ''What is a pet that barks?'' and you would go to a certain location in long-term memory and answer, ''A dog.'' Or, you could be asked instead, ''What is a dog?'' and the same spot in memory would give you the information you need to answer, ''A pet that barks.''

According to Brown and McNeill, long-term memory contains a whole complex of associations, or marked pathways, which are stored along with each word. These pathways lead to other, similar words, which is why we sometimes come up with a word that is almost, but not quite, the one we want (Brown & McNeill, 1966).

Because words are stored according to both sound and meaning, Brown and McNeill concluded that both phonetic—the sound of the word—and semantic—the meaning of the word—features are needed for word retrieval. By remembering such features, you can eventually recall a word that is on ''the tip of your tongue.''

Later research by Yarmey (1973) supports Brown and McNeill's findings, but also indicates that associations between words and events can help in the search for the correct word or name. For example, in identifying a well-known person from a photograph, we may realize: ''I saw him on the evening news last week. That's right; it's Dan Rather.'' Such situational cues may help the process of retrieval.

---

descriptions of things as we know them and which contain many pieces of knowledge (Klatzky, 1980).

This discussion makes it sound as if semantic memory is just information about words and their meanings. But it is also possible that some of the information in long-term memory is encoded in terms of sound—acoustic or phonetic coding—or visual images. For example, do you know what a trumpet sounds like? Can you picture the shape of Maine? Since most of us would probably say yes to both questions, we know that at least some long-term memories may be coded in terms of sight and sound as well as meaning.

But this still does not seem to explain why we remember the smell of lilacs or the taste of coffee. It may be that long-term memory is divided into several different stores of knowledge, some of which contain verbal information, some visual, and others that store information on sounds, tastes, and smells (Bourne, Dominowski & Loftus, 1979; Klatzky, 1980).

Long-term memory, then, is permanent. But how is it organized? There is some debate on this point, but most often long-term memory is compared to a library and its card catalog, or to a book and its index. Material is categorized or indexed. The card catalog or book index is then used

Long-term memory is a highly organized system and has an expanding capacity for information. It relates new ideas to categories that are already present.
(Will McIntyre, Photo Researchers)

to find what is needed. Similarly, information entering long-term memory is categorized or indexed according to its meaning. We can "look up" a piece of information by using the indexes. We may get to the word *Iowa* through thinking of corn, or hearing "Cedar Rapids" mentioned, or reading the word *Ionic* and recognizing the similarity of the initial sounds. The more indexes or associations an item has, the easier it will be to remember, just as it is easier to find a certain passage in a book if many of its key words and terms, rather than just one or two, are indexed. This is one reason why we tend to remember semantic material better than episodic (Tulving, 1972).

Episodic material is less easily retrieved since it is so quickly "dated." We code fewer cross-references for it. For instance, you may remember that you ate a hamburger last night, but there is no good reason to recall that fact 6 months, or even 1 week, later. On the other hand, it is semantic knowledge that hamburger is made of beef. This fact is stored in semantic memory according to an incredibly complex indexing system that makes it easier to retrieve.

It appears that coding is also the key to mnemonic skill. One study of a person highly skilled in **mnemonics** showed that he had a remarkable ability to code information quickly into accessible groups (Hunt & Love, 1972). This corresponds to skill at retrieving information. In a sense,

MNEMONIC DEVICES

Mnemonic devices are methods of encoding material that help us to remember. When we use mnemonic devices, we deliberately impose some sort of order on the material we want to learn. We may use rhyme, meanings, or groupings to organize separate items.

Some of the simplest mnemonic devices are the rhymes and jingles we often use to remember dates and other facts. "Thirty days hath September, April, June, and November," helps us recall how many days there are in a month. "*I* before *E*, except after *C*, or when sounded like *A*, as in *neighbor* and *weigh*," helps us spell certain words. Other simple mnemonic devices involve making words or sentences out of the material to be recalled. The colors of the visible spectrum—red, orange, yellow, green, blue, indigo, violet—can be remembered by using their first letters to form the name *ROY G. BIV*. In remembering musical notes, the spaces in the treble clef form the word *FACE*, while the lines in the clef may be remembered by "Every Good Boy Does Fine."

Greek and Roman orators used a topical system of mnemonics to memorize long speeches. They would visit a large house or temple and walk through the rooms in a definite order, noting where specific objects were placed within each room. When the plan of the building and its contents were memorized, the orator would go through the rooms in his mind, placing images of material to be remembered at different places in the rooms. To retrieve the material during the speech, he would imagine himself going through the building and, by association, would recall each point of his speech as he came to each object and each room.

A study by Bower (1973) shows that mnemonic techniques are more effective than rote learning. College students were asked to study 5 successive "shopping lists" of 20 unrelated words. They were given 5 seconds to study each word, and time to study each list as a whole. At the end of the session, they were asked to recall all 100 items.

Subjects using mnemonic devices remembered an average of 72 items, but the control group—generally relying on simple rote learning—remembered only 28. The subjects trained in mnemonic techniques were also much more successful at recalling the position of each item and the list on which it appeared.

mnemonic skill is like a filing system with only a few file folders. A person talented in mnemonics can take in information quickly and distribute it to the relevant folders. He or she can also retrieve this information from the folders with great speed and accuracy.

We have talked about retrieval mostly in terms of a conscious search for a piece of information. But retrieval processes can also be less deliberate. If a professor mentions Napoleon you may remember something about the Battle of Waterloo. But *Napoleon* may also conjure up a French pastry, a trip to Naples, or a man you know who is shorter than you are. The smell of an apple pie in the oven, the taste of apple pie, or the words *apple pie* printed in a book can all lead you to remember a particular experience of apple pie.

Can everything that is stored in memory be retrieved when we need it? All of us who have ever searched our memories during tests know the answer to that one. We have to distinguish between memory that is available and memory that is accessible (Mandler, 1967). A memory may be available—it is there if we know how to get to it—but inaccessible if we have not found out how or where to find it. Not all the information in long-term memory is accessible at any given time, though apparently most of it is always available, which is why we said LTM is relatively permanent. Is it true, then, that we never really "forget" anything, that information is always in memory if we could only retrieve it? Let us now look at what we call **forgetting**.

Forgetting

You are leaving for a weekend trip, suitcase in hand, but you are troubled by the vague feeling that you have forgotten something—and more often than not, you have. You panic at a final examination, groping

(Marc Anderson)

for the name of the Secretary of State, but it eludes you. An old relative inquires about the health of your grandfather, who died 5 years ago. You had something else on your mind when you put down your sunglasses, and now you cannot find them. You have not used a lawn mower in 2 years, and now you have no idea how to start it. A friend coldly informs you that you had said you would meet her yesterday at 4 o'clock—and you were not there. A year ago you lost an important tennis match to a friend and you became arch rivals, but now you have forgotten the anger you felt then and you are friends again.

All of these are instances of the same phenomenon, forgetting. Or are they? In all these examples, something once learned or experienced has "slipped the mind." But are all the causes the same? What happens when we forget something? Has it gone away forever, or is there just something standing in the way of remembering?

FORGETTING IN SHORT-TERM MEMORY

Our short-term memory could never remember all the facts and figures that are necessary to complete a tax form. This same information in long-term memory would become a jumble of illogical and confused data. Therefore, it is sometimes much easier to keep records on paper.
(Van Bucher, Photo Researchers)

Why do we lose material, or forget it? There are two basic explanations: *decay theory* and *interference theory*. According to the *decay theory*, the passing of time in itself will cause the strength of memory to decrease, thereby making it harder to remember. This theory has traditionally been applied to short-term memory, in which only a limited number of items can be held for a limited time. Most of the evidence for the decay theory comes from experiments known as *distractor studies*, which were first used by Brown (1958) and Peterson and Peterson (1959). The Petersons gave subjects a sequence of letters to learn, like *PSQ*. Then subjects heard a 3-digit number, like 167. They were then asked to count backward from 167 by 3s: 167, 164, 161, and so on, for up to 18 seconds. At the end of that period, they were given a recall cue and were asked to recall the 3 letters. The results of this test astonished the experimenters. The subjects showed a marked decline in their ability to remember the letters, the fastest forgetting that research had yet turned up. And since counting backward was assumed to be a noninterfering task, the fact that subjects forgot the letters seemed to prove that the letters had simply faded from short-term memory within its brief period of retention. Later experiments by Reitman (1974) and Shiffrin and Cook (1978) led to the same conclusion. Decay, then, seems to be at least partly responsible for forgetting in short-term memory.

But Shiffrin and Cook also found that interference can affect forgetting from STM. **Interference theory,** unlike decay theory, holds that information gets mixed up with, or pushed aside by, other information and thus becomes harder to remember. Interference can come from two places. New material can interfere with old material already in short-term memory. This is called **retroactive inhibition.** Or, old material in short-term memory can interfere with incoming information, which is called **proactive inhibition.** In both cases, the more similarity there is between the old and the new learning, the more interference there is likely to be.

Decay theory clearly points to a storage problem. If an item has faded away to nothing, it is simply not there. But interference could cause either storage or retrieval loss: Information could push other information out of

	Step 1	Step 2	Step 3
Experimental group	Learn List A	Learn List B	Recall List B
Control group	Rest or engage in unrelated activity	Learn List B	Recall List B

Figure 6–6
A diagram of the experiment used to measure proactive inhibition. The experimental group suffers the effects of proactive inhibition from List *A* and, when asked to recall List *B*, performs less well than the control group.

	Step 1	Step 2	Step 3
Experimental group	Learn List A	Learn List B	Recall List A
Control group	Learn List A	Rest or engage in unrelated activity	Recall List A

Figure 6–7
A diagram of the experiment measuring retroactive inhibition. The experimental group usually does not perform as well on tests of recall as the control group, which does not suffer from retroactive inhibition from the second list of words or syllables.

STM—storage loss—or simply make it harder to get at that information even though still in STM—retrieval loss.

It appears that proactive inhibition is due primarily to retrieval problems. Old information in STM makes it hard to retrieve new, similar information that is also in STM. To a lesser extent, the old information may actually push some new information out of STM completely. Retroactive inhibition appears to work largely by storage loss. To the extent that the new information interferes with the old, it is likely to push the old out of STM. In any case, forgetting in short-term memory appears to be due both to decay and to interference. Decay is a storage problem, while interference may be due to both storage and retrieval loss.

We have seen that the loss of information from STM is permanent. It is usually just as well that this sort of forgetting takes place. Not only does this give space in short-term memory for new information, but if every passing detail of our lives went into long-term memory, it would be a jumble of irrelevant, trivial, unrelated data. In this sense, short-term forgetting is not the "problem" that long-term forgetting is. Long-term forgetting can impair job performance because to do many jobs, we must permanently remember various facts, procedures, names, addresses, and dates. Our friends may become upset when we forget their birthdays, or take them to a restaurant that they hate, or smoke in their presence when this always makes them cough. And if long-term memory contains all that we know about the world, then forgetting from long-term memory can cause very serious problems indeed. Let us look at how it happens.

FORGETTING IN LONG-TERM MEMORY

We can only forget what we once knew. To forget information in long-term memory, it must first have been encoded there. Otherwise, we would be forgetting something that was never properly transferred to long-term memory in the first place (Klatzky, 1980). But even when something has been encoded, we may "lose" it.

We have seen that loss in short-term memory may be at least partly due to decay. But information once encoded in long-term memory does not seem to fade, as anyone who has listened to a grandparent's reminiscences will realize. In fact, with proper storage and retrieval procedures, we can dredge up an astonishing amount of information from long-term memory that seems as fresh to us as it did when we encoded it years ago. If decay is not a major factor in long-term memory, what causes such forgetting?

The most logical candidate is inhibition. And experiments show that competing information in long-term memory—both old and new—can contribute to forgetting. In one experiment, subjects were given lists of nonsense syllables to learn before going to sleep. Sometimes they went to sleep immediately after learning them. At other times, they carried on with their normal activities for various lengths of time. The subjects remembered more if they went to sleep soon after learning the lists (Ekstrand, 1972).

This suggests that new information interferes with information already in long-term memory—retroactive inhibitions. But what about proactive inhibition? Does old information cause us to forget new material coming into LTM? Apparently this does indeed happen. Subjects who learned nine successive lists of adjectives performed well when asked to recall items from the early lists, but they were unable to recall as many items from the later lists (Underwood, 1957).

Therefore it seems that the two kinds of interference that cause us to "lose" material from short-term memory also seem to influence forgetting in long-term memory. This brings us to our next question. Does interference in LTM cause a storage loss or a retrieval loss? We saw that interference may involve both kinds of loss in short-term memory. When it comes to long-term memory, however, there appears to be an important difference. Interference seems to cause errors in retrieval, but does not cause any significant loss of stored material (Klatzky, 1980). This means that the information that goes into long-term memory stays there permanently. If we have trouble remembering something, it is not because it is no longer there, but because we cannot reach it.

Unfortunately, there is still much about forgetting in long-term memory that is not understood. Much of what we know is based on experimental research involving single word pairings. But what happens in real life? Many of the things we know—or hold in long-term memory—are incredibly complex and meaningful. Information about such emotionally charged subjects as love and death, experiences that are painful and joyous, and knowledge of complicated issues like mortality, as well as information about the nature of physics, chemistry, and mathematics are all stored in long-term memory. Do the same processes affect the long-term memory of these higher levels of information as they affect simpler words or letters?

It stands to reason that interference should affect our ability to retrieve more meaningful information as well as the fact that one word appeared on a list next to another. But an important difference between "laboratory memory" and "real-world memory" is that in real life we seldom remember precisely how we heard or saw something. Instead, we remember the *content* or general idea, and so some "forgetting" of complex, meaningful material is due to the fact that it was poorly encoded in the first place (Klatzky, 1980). If someone tells you a long, rambling story, complete with flashbacks, you will not only not try to remember every word exactly, but you may even have trouble transferring all the major content from short-term memory into long-term memory. Moreover, if Jim tells you, "Yesterday I saw a blunderbuss," you will process that information in

EYEWITNESS TESTIMONY

"That's him!" exclaims the witness in the television drama, pointing to one of the five men in the police lineup. When this happens, we know the case is as good as closed. But is it? In real life, eyewitness testimony must be carefully monitored for errors. People who say, "I know what I saw" often mean, "I know what I *think* I saw." And they can be wrong.

In New York City, two Hasidic Jews were tried for attempted murder. Hasidic men stand out in a crowd. Most of them wear dark clothing, wide-brimmed hats, and have beards and long sidelocks. For this reason, the defense counsel feared that witnesses might identify the men on the basis of their group identity, rather than on their individual characteristics. The lawyers got permission to have the defendants sit in the spectator section, among a group of other Hasidic Jews, all identically dressed. The result was that nobody, not even the officer who arrested the two men, could distinguish the defendants from the people around them (Bazelon, 1980).

Cross-racial identification is one of the trickiest areas of eyewitness testimony. People appear to have more trouble recognizing faces belonging to people of other races than they do picking out someone of their own race. And whites tend to be less accurate than other racial groups in identifying minority members. Thus, the lawyers' ploy in the New York trial was a good way to protect their minority clients from the testimony of witnesses who think that "they all look alike."

This kind of error is most likely the result of improper coding of information in the first place. Someone who assumes that all blacks, or Chinese, or Puerto Ricans look alike is apt to record simply skin color, omitting vital information such as features. But errors can also be made because of faulty constructive processing. In one classic experiment, a group of students was shown a film of a car accident. They were then questioned about the film. Some were asked, "How fast was the white sports car going when it passed the barn while traveling along the country road?" A week later, all the students were asked whether there had been a barn in the film. Nearly 20 percent of the students who had been asked the initial question "remembered" the barn. In fact, there was no barn in the film (Bazelon, 1980; Loftus, 1975, 1977; Loftus, Miller, & Burns, 1978). Obviously, this has serious implications for eyewitness testimony in court cases. Some theorists believe that the use of psychologists to test the reliability of eyewitness accounts will help eliminate some of these errors, while others stress that an informed jury, aware of the pitfalls of human memory, will help cut down on tragic mistakes (Bazelon, 1980).

light of what you *think* you know about blunderbusses. If you are later asked, "What did Jim see yesterday?" you might reply that he saw a broken down bus. In fact, what he saw was a weapon! Clearly, **constructive processing** of complex or emotionally charged material is likely to be open to more errors than the processing of simple letters or short word lists.

Moreover, we may also distort or change information after we have encoded it in long-term memory. Again this is more likely with highly meaningful material that relates to all kinds of other knowledge in LTM. Sometimes, for instance, as we mull over something in our minds, we change it around a little until it is more to our liking and fits our other recollections.

Information in long-term memory, then, tends to stay put, though it may be distorted. If we "forget" something, it is generally because it was poorly encoded in the first place—never really in LTM at all—or because it is still available in LTM but inaccessible—retrieval loss. If we could encode information properly, leave it alone once it is stored, and avoid retrieval problems due to interference, we could have access to an awesome collection of virtually permanent memories and knowledge.

MOTIVATED FORGETTING

So far, our discussion has assumed that we want to remember things accurately. But go back to the beginning of this section and look at our examples of forgetting. Does this assumption apply to all of them? The date with your friend might have been forgotten because you had something unpleasant to tell her, or to "pay her back" for keeping you waiting 45 minutes last week. Your great-aunt might have been so grieved by your grandfather's death that she does not want to remember it. What you vaguely felt you had not put in your suitcase might have been the chemistry notes that were going to spoil your weekend. And forgetting how furious you were when you lost the tennis match helped save your friendship.

Without realizing it, we may blank out memories that are unpleasant or that conflict with our ideas of the people we want to be or the world we want to live in. **Repression** protects us from remembering things that are so painful that we would rather not think about them. There is a general desire on the part of human beings to see themselves—and to some extent, the world around them—as friendly, civilized, and reasonable. The memories that are in harmony with this view are acceptable to us, but those that conflict with it are often blotted out.

At its most extreme, repression can cause **hysterical amnesia.** Screenwriters have gotten a lot of footage over the years with amnesia victims, and we are all familiar with some form of the story: A man wakes up in a strange city, unable to remember his name or where he came from or how he got there, but perfectly capable of reciting the alphabet or frying an egg. The memory of any personal information is gone. It makes a good melodramatic story—and it does happen. In hysterical amnesia, there is no apparent organic reason for the failure of memory. Usually

REPRESSION

Freud often attributed the forgetting of names and places to repression. One of his patients, whom he called Mr. Y, fell in love with a woman who did not love him. She married another man, Mr. X. Although Mr. Y was well-acquainted with Mr. X and had business dealings with him, after the marriage he found himself unable to remember Mr. X's name and had to ask what it was every time he wrote to him about business. Since Mr. X was his rival and had married the woman he loved, Mr. Y, Freud believed, subconsciously did not want to know anything about him (Freud, 1928).

In another case reported by Freud, a philosophy student was tested about the teachings of Epicurus. When asked to name a latter-day follower of Epicurus, the student said Pierre Gassendi because he had overheard someone in a cafe mention that name. The professor was surprised and asked him how he knew this. Embarrassed to tell the truth, the student replied that he had been interested in Gassendi for a long time. This so impressed the examiner that he passed the student with high honors. Afterward, the student could never remember the name Pierre Gassendi because of his guilty conscience about the test.

Of late, Freud's theory of repression as a cause of forgetting has been attacked. For example, Freud suggested that repression causes many dreams to be forgotten. Cohen (1974*b*), however, found that the inability to recall dreams is not caused by repression. Instead, he points to two other factors that can limit dream recall: interference and salience. Interference occurs when events after waking draw attention away

"And then I say to myself, 'If I really wanted to talk to her, why do I keep forgetting to dial 1 first?'"
(Drawing by Modell; ©1981 *The New Yorker Magazine, Inc.*)

from the dream material; salience is the impact of the dream on the dreamer—its intensity, pace, and emotional force.

Mischel (1976) and Holmes (1974) argue more generally that despite much research, there has been no consistent evidence to support Freud's theory of repression. Holmes agrees that we do recall selectively, but he suggests that selective recall results more from selective attention, both during the experience and during later attempts at recall. For example, after watching two friends argue, you would not recall the same things that a trained therapist would recall. But you could not be charged with repressing information that you had never truly focused on.

something in the person's life has been so frightening or so unacceptable that he or she has totally repressed all personal memories rather than remember that one incident.

The conditions of hysterical amnesia have been approximated experimentally. In one study, college students were taught a list of word pairs. After learning the list of pairs, they were read a second list of words, some of which were consistently accompanied by a mild but unpleasant electrical shock. This second list was composed of words that appeared to be related to the word pairs in the first list. If the students had learned the pair *thief* and *steal,* for example, the corresponding word on the second list was *take.* When they were tested for their retention of the first list, the apparent association of the "shocked" word with the word pair led to a significant drop in their ability to remember the original pair even

Figure 6–8
The nonsense syllables and words used by Glucksberg and King in their experiment on repression. In the first stage of the experiment, subjects learned the syllable-word pairs in columns *A* and *B*. Then, they learned the words in column *D*, some of which were accompanied by mild electric shocks. The words in column *C* were links to the words in column *B*. The syllable-word pairs that were associated with shock were much harder to recall than the pairs that were not associated with shock.

		Inferred Chained Word	List 2
A	B	C	D
CEF	stem	flower	smell*
DAX	memory	mind	brain*
YOV	soldier	army	navy
VUX	trouble	bad	good*
WUB	wish	want	need
GEX	justice	peace	war*
JID	thief	steal	take*
ZIL	ocean	water	drink
LAJ	command	order	disorder
MYV	fruit	apple	tree*

* These words were paired with shock during the second stage of the experiment.

though the paired words had had no shock directly attached to them (Glucksberg & King, 1967).

Like other kinds of forgetting in LTM, repressing unpleasant memories does not mean that we erase them. Instead, we simply fail to retrieve them, often because we would rather not. This, at least, is what Sigmund Freud believed about repression, and this belief is the basis of psychoanalytic theory. In psychoanalysis, people are encouraged to "free-associate," to let one event trigger the memory of another, so that eventually we remember events or feelings that we have been repressing. When this is accomplished, psychoanalysts believe, we can begin to deal more effectively with those traumatic or unpleasant memories (see Chapter 14). **Hypnosis** appears to work in much the same way, helping people retrieve information that they otherwise cannot reach. Methods like psychoanalysis and hypnosis give us a dramatic idea of the extraordinary storage capacity of our long-term memories.

Biological Bases of Memory

Up to this point, we described memory as though it were something that could be seen, like a computer or the card catalog in a library. But what physiological processes take place inside of us when we are remembering something? What actually goes on inside the brain? Where and how is memory stored and retrieved?

THE LOCATION OF MEMORY

For the past 100 years, psychologists have been trying to find out if memory is localized in a certain part of the brain. In Chapter 2 we learned that some functions, such as vision and speech, are localized in this way. Early in the 19th century, it was believed that this was also true of memory. **Phrenology**—which held that specific mental operations took place in specific areas of the brain and could be determined by "reading" the shape of the skull—was fashionable then. Phrenologists believed that the "memory center" was located behind the eyes. A person with bulging eyes, they reasoned, would have a large memory center and thus would have a great capacity for remembering things. This theory of memory is no longer accepted. By the 1920s, it seemed apparent that no particular part of the brain was solely responsible for memory.

(Culver Pictures)

In a pivotal experiment (Lashley, 1950), parts of rats' cerebrums were removed. Although their memories were found to be weakened by losing any part of the brain, the memories were still present. The degree or amount of recall, therefore, seemed to depend on the mass of the brain, regardless of what specific part was missing. A single memory, it was surmised, can be stored in numerous parts of the brain, so that removal of a part can diminish but not erase the whole memory.

More recent experiments have supported this theory, although with some qualifications. In experiments with monkeys that had been trained to perform a certain task (Harlow, 1959), it was found that the removal of part of the brain affected the competency of some monkeys at the task, while other monkeys were entirely unaffected. This suggests that a given memory may lodge in one of many areas of the brain, but in no specific one. Recent experiments with rats indicate, however, that one form of memory, that of the location of objects, is localized in the region of the brain known as the hippocampus (Olton, 1977). Thus, evidence supports both notions: Memories are stored in specific regions of the brain, and memories are stored throughout many regions of the brain (Carlson, 1977).

One possible explanation for the widespread storage of memories is that several different senses seem to be involved in any one memory. A single experience might be stored in the brain's visual areas, auditory areas, and areas for smell and touch—all at the same time. Another explanation suggests that evidence for widespread storage of memory in the brain really suggests that the processing centers that retrieve the stored material are widely distributed. Damaging the brain may only interfere with some retrieval mechanisms. Evidence to support these two theories comes from studies in which one area of an animal's brain is damaged and retrieval cues are limited to the particular sense controlled by that area. For example, perhaps the visual area is removed and the retrieval cues are limited to only black–and–white visual images, with no sounds or smells to accompany them. In situations like this, retrieval does seem to be seriously impaired by specific brain damage. Even without brain damage, limiting the retrieval cues to only one sense can inhibit remembering. If you were to see a black–and–white silhouette of someone you know, you might have more difficulty recognizing her than if you simultaneously saw her profile, heard her voice, and smelled the particular brand of perfume that she always wore.

Finally, some evidence suggests that the formation of memory can be interfered with by damaging still other parts of the brain. At the base of the cortex is a section of the brain called the limbic system. It appears that the hippocampus—which is part of the limbic system—is instrumental in transferring verbal information from short-term to long-term memory. People damaged in this area can remember events that have just occurred, but often have to write everything down to remember it any longer, because the brain's ability to record this information is limited to the short-term span.

Some people experience memory loss after they have suffered brain damage. In 1959, Brenda Milner discovered a related group of behaviors associated with brain damage, which have come to be known as "Milner's syndrome." Milner studied one young man who had lost part of his temporal lobes and hippocampus in a brain operation. His IQ did not decline after the operation. He could remember events that preceded the operation as well as anyone else, but nothing that had happened *since* the operation stuck in his mind. His family moved to a new house shortly after his stay in the hospital, and although he remembered his old address perfectly well, the new one eluded him. He might use the lawn mower on a Tuesday, but on Wednesday his mother would have to tell him all over again where to find it. He read the same magazines over and over—and each time the material was new to him (Milner, 1966).

A person with this syndrome can remember events from the distant past before brain damage occurred. He or she can also retain new information for a short time if it is repeated. The person cannot transfer new material from short-term memory to long-term memory, however, even though long-term memory is still "working" well enough to retrieve "old" memories from the distant past (Klatzky, 1980). Thus, damage to different areas of the brain can interfere with different aspects of memory, from formation through storage to retrieval, supporting the idea that memory storage itself is widespread.

THE UNIT OF STORAGE

The second major aspect concerning the biological mechanisms of memory has to do with just what the individual unit of memory is. There is general agreement that long-term memory involves a permanent change in the structure of the brain (Doty, 1974). Yet, researchers still disagree about the nature of these changes.

One theory is that sensory experience produces a highly perishable response in the nervous system known as a **memory trace.** According to another theory, the sensory information coming into the brain stimulates one neuron, which in turn stimulates another, which in turn stimulates another, until the stimulation comes full circle and becomes a "reverberating circuit," which permanently records the new information (Hebb, 1949). Any part of this permanent assembly, when stimulated, sets off the entire circuit. Hebb's theory, then, would account for the "associative"

(Will McIntyre, Photo Researchers)

powers of memory. If several different units of information have been programmed into the same circuit, the stimulation of one would bring forth all the others.

Hebb's theory has been frequently attacked on physiological grounds, and Hebb has modified some aspects of it in the light of neurological findings. Yet Cermak (1972) argues that most evidence still contradicts the theory of specific circuitry in learning and memory. And McGaugh (1974) has questioned all of the prominent theories about the neural bases of memory. He claims that despite all the speculation, there is no clear empirical evidence to support these theories.

Other researchers have proposed a different view—that memory is carried by ribonucleic acid (RNA). As we saw in Chapter 2, RNA is vital in protein production in the body's cells. Since RNA can "remember" the DNA's instructions for making proteins, it is a likely candidate for storing other kinds of memory. These studies, too, have been criticized on various grounds, leaving future researchers to discover the answer to the question.

Application

HOW TO STUDY BETTER

So far in this chapter you have been reading about memory in the abstract, but how well have you been *learning* about memory? At the end of the semester, when you find yourself sitting face-to-face with the final exam and (presumably) this book is nowhere in sight, will you be able to recall in detail, say, the differences between short-term and long-term memory? If some of your classmates remember the material better than you do between now and the test, they may owe part of their success to their intelligence, but, in large part, it is also probably due to more effective learning strategies. What is the difference between effective and ineffective learning? A century of psychological research has produced some answers to this question.

Motivation

Common sense would suggest that highly motivated people learn most effectively, but research has qualified this assumption. To begin with, the intent to learn is not even necessary to learn. We acquire a great deal of information during an average day without trying to learn it. Not only is much learning unintended, but it is also downright unwanted. You may remember only too well the bad news that the repair bill for your car is high; or that your semester grades are *C*'s and *D*'s. Moreover, a person may have every intention of learning, but choose an ineffective strategy for carrying out that intention. Psychological research suggests that while a certain amount of motivation is usually necessary for effective studying, the most important difference between effective and ineffective learning is what happens during the learning process.

Rehearsal

Passive rehearsal, simply repeating the material over and over, is probably the most common learning strategy. Millions of students have learned their *ABC*'s and arithmetic by doggedly repeating letters, sums, and products; so, obviously, the technique works. Psychologists have confirmed this in experiments. For example, Hellyer (1962) presented a nonsense syllable to subjects 1, 2, 4, or 8 times. These repetitions were followed by intervals of 3, 9, 18, or 27 seconds. Hellyer found that the longer the interval, the more was forgotten, but the more repetitions, the less forgetting occurred. Mere repetition without any intent to learn, however, does not seem to enhance learning (Glenberg, Smith, & Green, 1977). A child may see the same mailboxes day after day for years on the way to school and still be unable to repeat the names on the mailboxes along the way. The mail carrier, however, probably could.

Suppose you have just finished reading an assigned chapter: What is the next step? You could simply reread the chapter until you have drummed it into your head. A more efficient approach, however, is active rehearsal, or recitation. After reading the chapter, close the book and try to remember what you have read. The more time that is spent recalling or attempting to recall the material, the better you will learn it within a given time. But there is an even more efficient strategy that begins *before* you have read the chapter.

The SQ3R Method

Probably the most effective system for studying written material is known only by the letters of its five stages: *SQRRR* (or *SQ3R*, for short).

Survey (1). Before you begin to read, quickly look at the chapter headings and at the chapter summary, if there is one. This will give you a sense of what you will read and make it easier to see how ideas are related.

Question (2). Before you start to read, translate each subhead into a question about the text to follow. This helps you compare the new material with what you already know. It gets you actively involved in thinking about the topic. It also helps to bring the main points into sharp relief. Presumably you have read the section on "Short-Term Memory" in Chapter 6, for example. Ask youself, "Why is it called 'short-term'?" "Is there another type of memory that lasts longer?" "What good is a short-term memory?" "Why do memories fade?" It is usually helpful to write these questions out.

Read (3). Read the appropriate part of the text. Look for the answers to the question you have just asked yourself. If you find major points not directly related to your questions, try either to revise or refine your old questions to include the new material, or to make up new questions specially for this material.

Recite (4). When you have finished the section, close the book and recite from memory the answers to your questions and any other major points you can remember. It may help to jot down your answers in outline form or even to recite them aloud to somebody. Then open the book and check to be sure you have covered all the major points in the section. Repeat steps 2, 3, and 4 for each section of the chapter.

Review (5). After you have completed the chapter, review your notes and then recite your questions and answers from memory. Relate the material to other ideas, thinking of particularly good examples or illustrations. Get involved. The *SQ3R* method forces you to react, to have a kind of dialogue with the text. This interaction makes the material more interesting and meaningful and improves your chances of recalling it. It also organizes the material and relates it to what you already know. As we have seen, this is important for transferring the material to long-term memory. Although this seems time-consuming, you will probably spend less time overall because studying for exams later should go much more quickly.

Recitation is really an organized way of giving meaning to what you have read. Making written material meaningful is the best way of remembering it. This involves putting together many bits of information that are already somewhat familiar to form a new pattern (Craik & Tulving, 1975). Very hard passages often have many unfamiliar or abstract words. It is a good idea to have a dictionary handy, so that you can learn what these words mean.

Imagery is also a great aid to understanding and recalling verbal material. In experiments, subjects who are taught to memorize word lists by forming mental pictures related to the meaning of each word show better recall than subjects who use other learning strategies. If you were asked to recall the word pair "man–horse," your best bet would be to imagine a horse and a man somehow interacting. You could visualize the horse trying to throw the man, for instance (Bugelski, 1979, p. 42). This strategy can also be applied to large pieces of writing. As you read, try to picture the people, events, and ideas described by the author. Sometimes a single image can bring meaning to an entire paragraph. The more you visualize, and the more dynamic your images, the better you will recall what you have read.

Summary

1. Memory is an active process that sifts, sorts, and reorganizes information, stores it, and makes it available to us for use at a later time.
2. Theorists now think of memory as an information-processing system with three levels: the sensory register, short-term memory, and long-term memory. At each level, information receives certain kinds of processing and is either discarded or stored.
3. The sensory registers receive sensory impressions from the external world and may be thought of as the "reception rooms" of memory. They have a huge capacity, but retention time is extremely brief and only a portion of what enters them passes to the next level—short-term memory.
4. For information to pass from the sensory registers to short-term memory, it must first go into long-term memory and be "matched" with information already there. In order to *recognize*

incoming information, we match it with material or patterns that are already encoded in long-term memory.

5. There are three *models of recognition: template matching, prototype matching,* and *feature analysis.* The *pandemonium model* is based on feature analysis and explains how we process new information. Processing is speeded up by the way we apply our expectations based on previously stored knowledge to sensory data.

6. Next, we must decide how much of the new information to *pay attention to.* According to Broadbent (1958), we pay attention to information that in some way stands out because of its physical properties. We tend to "filter" this material into our consciousness.

7. Short-term memory is temporary, active, and conscious. In everyday terms, it is our attention span. It is more selective, and slightly more permanent, than the sensory registers.

8. It is generally thought that short-term memory can hold on to only about 10 items at a time. Through the process of chunking, information is organized into meaningful units. A verbally coded item can be held indefinitely in short-term memory if it is repeated over and over again—either out loud or silently.

9. This is known as rote rehearsal. Rote rehearsal is generally used to hold on to information that we only need for a moment or two. Most information in short-term memory is coded acoustically, according to its sound, but some also appears to be coded visually and semantically according to its meaning.

10. Material is transferred from short-term memory to long-term memory through elaborative or constructive rehearsal. This process involves linking new material to facts and concepts in long-term memory. Coding—a way of compressing information into abbreviated form—must also take place.

11. Long-term memory has a vast capacity for information. It is highly organized and relatively permanent. It can be thought of as a dynamic, interdependent, continually shifting network. Whether something enters long-term memory or not depends mostly on how it can be organized.

12. It is convenient to divide long-term memory into two divisions: *semantic memory* and *episodic memory.*

13. Semantic memory contains all our general knowledge about the world. Most of the research on semantic memory has involved verbal information. Psychologists are not in agreement on its structure, but semantic memory seems to store words as well as concepts and the associations between them. Recent evidence suggests that there also may be more complex elements, such as *propositions* and *frames* or *scripts.*

14. Episodic memory is more personal, autobiographical, and more specific than semantic memory. The two kinds of memory may work together.

15. There is still debate concerning the exact manner in which long-term memory is organized, but it is often compared to a library and its card catalog, or to a book and its index. The information entering long-term memory is categorized or indexed according to its meaning, and perhaps in terms of sound or visual images.

16. *Retrieval* is the process by which we draw upon the information in long-term memory. We retrieve information through two basic processes: *recall* and *recognition.*

17. Recognition is generally more sensitive than recall because it often provides evidence of retention when recall produces a blank. A multiple-choice test is an example of a recognition test.

18. Recall involves the reproduction or repetition of learned material. According to the dual-coding hypothesis, people do better on recognition tests because recall involves two steps: search and decision. But it now appears that recognition, too, requires these two steps. People are sometimes better able to recall something than to recognize it.

19. We use cues to search for missing information. We check each of a number of categories to see if one of them contains the information we are looking for. The better the information in memory is organized, and the more categories it is filed under, the more successful the search is likely to be.

20. There are two basic explanations for forgetting in short-term memory: *decay theory* and *interference theory.*

21. The decay theory of forgetting holds that we forget isolated facts because time causes the strength of the memory to fade.

22. According to the interference theory of forgetting, we forget things because other things get in the way. Proactive inhibition occurs when earlier learning gets in the way of later learning. Retroactive inhibition is the result of later learning getting in the way of earlier learning.

23. It now appears that decay and interference both cause short-term memory loss. Decay is a storage problem, while interference may affect both storage and retrieval.

24. Decay does not appear to be responsible for long-term memory loss. Both retroactive and proactive inhibition seem to interfere with long-term memory, but they affect only retrieval, not storage. Most long-term memory loss occurs because of errors in encoding or retrieval. Otherwise, information is held in virtually permanent storage.

25. Memory of meaningful material is less susceptible to forgetting than is memory of isolated facts once encoded. We may forget the exact wording of information, but we frequently continue to remember the meaning. In the process of recollection, meanings are sometimes changed to conform to our own experiences and attitudes.

26. We may blank out memories that we want to forget. *Repression* is a form of motivated forgetting that protects us from painful memories. Its most extreme expression is *hysterical amnesia.*

27. Memories are stored both in specific regions of the brain and throughout the brain. Long-term memory involves a permanent change in the structure of the brain, but researchers disagree about the nature of the change.

Outline

Chapter 7

Cognition and Altered States

If someone were to ask you, "What is cognition or thinking?" your first response might be that thinking means pondering some deep problem, the way Rodin's sculpture *The Thinker* seems to be doing. Or you might say something as broad and vague as "Thinking is what goes on inside your head." The last answer, because it covers more, is probably more correct. Thinking is so complex a process and includes such a wide range of mental activities, that we can only hope to touch upon them. Sometimes, as when you rack your brain during an examination, you are aware that you are thinking; most often you think without noticing it.

A clue to the vast range of things that are involved in thinking can be seen in the different ways we use the word. "I think I will go to the store," indicates intention. "You were just not thinking!" is the same as saying that you were behaving absentmindedly. "I have thought it over," implies reflection or meditation. "What does he think of all this?" is a way of asking for an evaluation.

In Chapter 6, we saw that memory plays a central role in processing information. Long-term memory is so close to being the sum total of what we know that the words *remember* and *know* are almost interchangeable. When we say, "I know that September has 30 days," we mean that we remember that September has 30 days. But cognition or thinking involves more than the storage and retrieval of information. It involves manipulating that information in various ways. How does thinking take place?

Cognition

IMAGES

When we say we are "thinking about" something or someone, we sometimes mean that we have an **image** in our minds. When you think about your brother, for instance, you probably think of his face, or how he sounds when he talks. We often think of images as being visual—"pictures"—but they can also involve the senses of taste, of touch, of smell, and of sound.

Although we use more than one sense in forming images, images associated with different senses are not recalled with equal intensity (Lindsay & Norman, 1977). Most people experience visual, spatial, and motor (motion) images strongly. They report far fewer images of sound, taste, touch, and smell.

An image is our recollection or reconstruction of sensory experience; it need not contain every detail of the experience. As we saw in Chapter 6, our sensory registers are bombarded with information. From all this information, we select only a small amount for further processing. Most of it is lost almost immediately. After a vacation at the seashore, your visual images of a walk along the beach may include shells and driftwood lying on the sand, but not the old soft-drink cans that were also there. Your auditory images may include the sounds of waves and of sea gulls, but not the motorboats and radios that you also heard. Besides, images are not always recalled experiences of actual objects or sensations; we also recall dreams and hallucinations. Neither of these are real, but we can still have images of them.

It is difficult to study exactly how images function in our thinking. We must rely on people's reports of the imagery in their own thinking, and these reports, of course, are highly subjective. Still, studies have revealed much about imagery in thinking. For instance, it appears that while most people think more in visual images, some think more in auditory ones. According to Roe (1951), physical scientists are more apt to think in visual images—pictures, diagrams—and social scientists think more in auditory images—sounds.

Your visual image after a trip to this beach might include the footprints in the sand.
(Alexander Lowry, Photo Researchers)

LANGUAGE AND THOUGHT

Although we apparently can "think" using either visual or auditory images, most thinking involves words. Words shape how we think about something. Compare the reactions that the following statements produce:

Finest quality filet mignon.

The retirement of the French forces to previously prepared positions in the rear was accomplished briskly and efficiently.

First class piece of dead cow.

French armies in rapid retreat!

English

| purple | indi-go | blue | green | yel-low | orange | red |

Shona

| cips$^{\omega}$uka | citema | cicena | cips$^{\omega}$uka |

Bassa

| hui | z̃iza |

Figure 7 – 1
Different languages have different words for colors. English divides the visible spectrum into seven segments, while Shona speakers use only three terms, and Bassa speakers use only two. The difference in the verbal labels, however, does not mean that a person who speaks Bassa or Shona is unable to distinguish between what we call *purple* and *blue*.

(From H. A. Gleason, Jr., *An Introduction to Descriptive Linguistics*, rev. ed. Copyright 1955, 1961 by Holt, Rinehart and Winston, Inc. Reprinted by permission of Holt, Rinehart and Winston, Inc.)

The governor appeared to be gravely concerned and said that a statement would be issued in a few days after careful examination of the facts.

The governor was on the spot.

These examples (Hayakawa, 1949, p. 85) illustrate how we can use "loaded" words—or intentionally obscure and "neutral" words—to color facts and to stimulate certain desired responses in readers. The old baseball saying, "I call 'em as I see 'em," might very well be reversed: Sometimes we see things according to what we call them.

Moreover, words affect memory. As Lindsay and Norman (1977) point out, "Memory for single perceptual experiences is directly related to the ease with which language can communicate that experience" (p. 483). As we saw in Chapter 6, the easier something is to encode, the more likely we are to store it properly in long-term memory and to retrieve it correctly later. Brown and Lenneberg (1954) conducted a classic experiment in which subjects were asked to look at color patches and assign each one a name. Some colors were easily labeled with a single word, _blue_ for instance. Others took longer to name and were given less common labels, _pale blue_ or _sky blue_ for example. Colors that were quickly and easily named were rated high in codability. Next, the subjects were shown four color samples and, after a delay, were asked to pick those colors from among 120 different color patches. Highly codable colors were the ones that were recognized most accurately. The results of this experiment show that the ease with which we can name and encode colors is closely related to how easy it is for us to retrieve them—and thus to think about them. In other words, there is a link between language and cognition.

Words can also shape _what_ we remember. In an experiment conducted by Carmichael, Hogan, and Walter (1932), subjects were shown ambiguous pictures. Some of the subjects were told that the picture resembled curtains in a window. Others were told that it looked like a diamond in a square. When subjects later recalled what they had seen by drawing their own pictures, they drew them very differently. Some exaggerated the features so that their pictures looked like curtains. Others distorted the original picture to portray a diamond in a square. In other words, their memory of a picture was affected by what they had been told about it.

Apart from their effects on memory, do words and language generally affect how we think about things? One way to find out is to see if people with different linguistic backgrounds think differently. Benjamin Whorf (1956) believes that they do. According to his **linguistic relativity hypothesis,** the language that one speaks determines the pattern of one's thinking and one's view of the world. For Whorf, if a language lacks a particular expression, the thought that the expression corresponds to will probably not occur to the people who speak that language. Whorf notes that the Hopi Indians have only two nouns for everything that flies. One noun refers to birds. The other is used for everything else: airplanes, kites, or dragonflies. Thus, the Hopi would interpret all flying things in terms of either of these two nouns—something in the air would be either a bird or a nonbird.

One interesting experiment that supports Whorf's view involved Japanese women who had married American servicemen (Farb, 1974). The women spoke English when talking to other people, especially to their families and neighbors. When they talked together, however, the women spoke Japanese. Each woman was interviewed twice by a bilingual Japanese interpreter; the first interview was in Japanese, the second in English. The results showed that the women's responses to the same questions varied with each language they used. One woman completed the following sentences in these two ways (Farb, 1974, p. 184):

When my wishes conflict with my family's . . .
    it is a time of great unhappiness. (Japanese)
    I do what I want. (English)

Real friends should . . .
    help each other. (Japanese)
    be very frank. (English)

The drastic changes in the women's responses can be explained by the shift in language. The study thus appears to support the theory that people think differently within different language worlds.

Nevertheless, serious objections have been raised to Whorf's hypothesis. Some critics insist that a need to think about things differently may change a language, and not vice versa. For example, if the Hopi Indians had been subjected to air raids, they probably would have evolved a word to distinguish a butterfly from a bomber.

Another criticism of the linguistic relativity hypothesis asserts that while different languages encode experiences differently, any thought can be expressed in any language. In this view, words may affect interpretation,

Do you think these three people would talk about fishing in the same way?
(Left to right: Georg Gerster, Rapho/Photo Researchers; Bruce Roberts, Rapho/Photo Researchers; bottom: Leonard Lee Rue III, Photo Researchers, Inc.)

but not perception. People living in the city may call all types of snow *snow*, but they can perceive the differences between icy snow, slush, wet snow, and snow flurries. These critics say that culture, not language, accounts for different views of reality. Language merely expresses a type of knowledge that is native to a culture.

This criticism is borne out by Berlin and Kay (1969), who gave color tests to people with 20 different language backgrounds. First, the experimenters named the basic colors—red, blue, and so on—in each language. The subjects then had to decide which color was the best example of the basic or *focal* color term in their language. The subjects consistently selected the same focal colors. All the languages drew their basic color terms from a set of eleven colors: black, white, red, green, yellow, blue, brown, purple, pink, orange, and gray.

But can these basic colors influence cognition even among people who have no words to describe them? The Dani of New Guinea have no words for colors—everything is either "dark" or "light." Eleanor Heider (1972) used an experiment similar to the one of Brown and Lenneberg and found that the Dani, too, remember basic colors better than other colors. Furthermore, they learned the names of these focal colors faster than they learned the names of the others (Rosch, 1973). And they judged the similarity of colors much as English-speaking people do (Heider & Olivier, 1972).

These experiments demonstrate that colors are identifiable in a way that does not depend on language. In other words, contrary to Whorf's hypothesis, it appears that how we think about things also affects the words we use. People from different cultures with different languages seem to think about some things—like color—in remarkably similar ways.

Problem Solving

How do you get from Chicago to Des Moines? How can you keep a kite flying? What is the best way to treat a sprained ankle if you cannot get to a doctor? These are problems that have defined limits. All of them can be approached by problem solving, that is, using past experience, available information, and learned methods to reach a solution.

When we try to solve a problem, we *work* with information or manipulate it until we find a solution. This means that we have to operate within certain limits. For example, we must use short-term memory, since it is made up of what we are presently thinking about. But as we saw in Chapter 6, memory and task performance compete for space in short-term memory. If short-term memory is "full" of things we are trying to remember when we are also trying to solve a problem, either the task suffers or we lose some of the items we were trying to retain. We also saw that we sometimes have trouble retrieving information from long-term memory. Thus, the basic structure of memory and how information is processed set certain limits to our ability to solve problems (Bourne, Dominowski, & Loftus, 1979).

Attention span also limits our ability to solve a problem. It restricts

our capacity to work with more than a few problem-solving operations at the same time. As Lindsay and Norman (1977) point out, if we tried to plan out our whole strategy ahead of time, we could not even play tic-tac-toe. We would find it impossible to keep in mind all the possible moves and countermoves that are involved in the game from the first play.

How do we deal with these limitations and difficulties? We rely on external and long-term memory aids. External aids, like pens and pencils, let us record each step in the problem-solving process. We thereby overcome the obstacle imposed by short-term memory of not being able to remember the steps. Long-term memory aids provide ways of structuring large amounts of knowledge, so that they can easily be stored in long-term memory and retrieved, when necessary, to solve a problem. Look at the letters *ENCYCLOPEDIA* and the letters *FHJRSHKLEFGB.* You will have an easier time remembering the former because they are stored in long-term memory as a unit, a word (Lindsay & Norman, 1977). A little later in the chapter we will be looking at other strategies for getting around some of these limitations.

Despite these obstacles, we *do* manage to solve problems. How do we do it? There are several rough stages, but they do not necessarily occur in order. First, we generally *prepare* for the task. We do this differently for different kinds of problems. In a chess game, for example, an experienced player has already stored the rules and many of the possible moves in long-term memory. He or she must simply retrieve this information

The limitations of your attention span would make it impossible for you to plan out your whole strategy for this game beforehand.
(Bob S. Smith, Rapho/Photo Researchers)

An experienced chess player can retrieve moves from his long-term memory.
(F. B. Grunzweig, Photo Researchers)

while playing. But someone who is only playing chess for the second time will have to give the problem a lot more thought. We thus prepare to solve a problem by interpreting it, and this interpretation will vary from one person to another.

The next stage is to produce a solution. Sometimes we merely have to retrieve the solution from long-term memory. More complex problems, however, may require complex strategies. Two basic solution methods seem to be involved in problem solving. **Algorithms** are methods that guarantee a solution if they are properly carried out. For example, an algorithm for solving an anagram (a group of letters which can be re-arranged to form a word) entails trying every possible combination of letters until we come up with the hidden word. Suppose we are given the letters *ACB*. We try *ABC, BAC, BCA, CBA*, and finally come up with *CAB*, and the problem is solved.

Most of the problems we have to solve in everyday life, however, do not have one neat, guaranteed solution. A much more commonly used method of problem solving involves **heuristics.** Heuristics are "rules of thumb" that quickly tell us if we have solved a problem. Heuristic methods offer ways of simplifying problems (Bourne, Dominowski, & Loftus, 1979).

One heuristic method is called *means–end analysis.* This involves analyzing the difference between what currently exists and what the desired end is, and then doing something to reduce that distance. We can go through a series of actions with choices at various points about how to proceed further, and we can assess each choice in terms of whether it will bring us closer to our goal. We make the most likely choice and continue to the next point. Wickelgren (1979) notes, for example, that a woman driving toward a clear landmark—a mountain range—with no specific directions to guide her will probably choose roads that appear, from her present position, to be headed in that direction. The chosen route may prove to be false as she obtains more information. The road may curve and lead in a different direction than was expected, in which case the problem may have to be reassessed.

A second heuristic method involves *working backward*. In this case, the search for a solution begins at the goal and works backward toward the "givens." This method is often used when the goal has more information than the givens, and when the operations can work both forward and backward. If, for example, we wanted to spend exactly $100 on clothing, it would be difficult to reach that goal by simply buying some items and hoping that they totaled exactly $100. By working backward—starting with the $100 and breaking it down according to the various things we want—we are more likely to find the combination of clothing that costs $100.

Finally, by setting subgoals, we can break the problem into smaller, more manageable pieces, each of which is easier to solve than the problem as a whole. This part of the heuristic method is called the *planning process*. A student whose goal is to write a history paper might set subgoals in the following order: Decide on a topic; collect and read the research; prepare an outline; write a first draft; reread the draft; and write a second and final draft.

The last stage in problem solving is judgment. Is *our* solution really *the* solution to the problem? Sometimes the answer is obvious—CAB is an English word, for example, while BCA is not. So CAB is the word we want. But in real life, solutions are generally not so obvious. Instead, some solutions are better than others. Judgment in this kind of situation requires *evaluation*, and people often evaluate things differently. For example, one parent who is worried about her son's study habits may insist that he stay home until he has finished studying. Another may declare the television set off limits. And a third may take the time to go over her son's homework with him. These are all solutions, but some may work better than others.

This student might find writing easier if he broke his topic down into subgoals.
(Irene Springer)

FACTORS AFFECTING PROBLEM SOLVING

Problem solving is affected by many other influences other than simply the problem. These include anxiety, anger, and frustration resulting from the problem-solving process itself or from other sources in your life at that time. If these emotions are present to any extent, they may interfere with your finding a smooth solution to a problem. Severe anxiety may impair your ability to answer the questions on an exam, and frustration at not being able to work a crossword puzzle may block the right word from coming to you. Sometimes, however, these factors can help you solve a problem. For example, a very competitive person, anxious to succeed, might actually become more efficient when solving a problem.

Figure 7–2
To test the effects of functional fixedness, psychologists might give people the items shown on the table. They are asked to mount a candle on the wall. Can you see how it could be done? Figure 7–3 on page 214 shows a solution.

Different factors affect the ability to solve a problem, or even a crossword puzzle.
(Margot Granitsas, Photo Researchers)

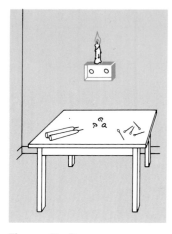

Figure 7–3
A solution to the problem shown in Figure 7–2. When the tacks are presented in the box, people tend to think of the box only as a container and to overlook that it can be used as a candleholder.

Research has also demonstrated that how a problem is *presented* affects the ease of difficulty with which it is solved (Bourne, Dominowski, & Loftus, 1979). In Figure 7–2, we see an example of a problem that is presented so that the solution (Figure 7–3) does not immediately occur to us. A related idea is **set,** which refers to our tendency to perceive and to approach situations in certain ways. This can be helpful if we have learned certain operations and perceptions in the past that we can apply to the present. For example, people tend to do better when they solve problems for the second—or third—time. This is not because they remember and repeat their previous actions, but because they have learned more effective strategies for *choosing* moves and understand the problem better (Reed, Ernst, & Banerji, 1974). When you find yourself with conflicting appointments—for example, a scheduled trip to the dentist and a casual tennis date with a friend—you might approach the problem with the set: "It is not polite to break formal appointments," and call your friend to set up another tennis date. Without that set, you might have spent much more time evaluating the situation and trying to decide how to solve the problem.

Because certain sets become habits, they do not always help solve problems. If a problem requires you to apply your previous experience in a new way, too strong a set could blind you to the possible solutions. This

INSIGHT

People sometimes report solving problems by using insight, a seemingly arbitrary flash that, "out of the blue," solves a problem. Most of us explain creative problem solving in terms of such inspiration. When we have an original idea and somebody says, "How did you arrive at that?" we realize that we did not get there step by step. We may answer with something like, "The idea just came to me while I was walking home." Henri Poincaré, the French mathematician, has described this process at work:

One evening, contrary to my custom, I drank black coffee and could not sleep. Ideas rose in crowds; I felt them collide until pairs interlocked, so to speak, making a stable combination. By the next morning, I had established the existence of a class of Fuchsian functions. . . . I had only to write out the results, which took but a few hours (Poincaré, 1924).

Many people have provided strikingly similar accounts of their own processes of creative thinking. In these cases, the solution does not, in any direct way, appear to follow logically from the preparation. Poincaré's thinking was directed. He knew what the problem was and what facts it involved. In his hours at his desk, he may have sought to solve the problem by normal means, but such a solution eluded him.

The way in which his thinking at his work table "led to" the sudden flash of insight that presented the solution is much less direct than the step-by-step method of problem solving. Note that Poincaré does not say that he brought the ideas together, but that he "felt them collide." Something other than logic appears to be involved, and that something is what we call "inspiration" or "insight."

Many psychologists are still unsure, however, if insightful or creative problem solving is much different from step-by-step problem solving. Some believe that the same processes are involved but are unrecognized by the person. We still do not know why people have sudden insights after "taking a vacation" from a task, as Poincaré did, but there are several possible explanations, none of which involve magic!

First, and most obviously, concentrating on a task for a long time can cause mental fatigue. We may do better after a break. Or, a rest may allow us to take a new approach when we return to the problem, to look at it from a new angle (Murray & Denny, 1969). Moreover, although we may think we are taking a break, we may actually be thinking—consciously or not (Neisser, 1967)—about the same old problem.

---

is why some psychologists believe that sets hamper creativity and make it harder to see new methods and possibilities. Yet much of our education involves learning sets and ways to solve problems, although it may seem that we are learning only specific information. We are taught to integrate new information into forms we already know, or to use methods that have proved effective in the past. In fact, the strategies we use in solving problems are themselves a set. We have learned that approaching a problem in a certain logical order is the best way to solve it. People who are most successful in solving problems are those who have many different sets at their disposal, and can judge when to change sets or when to give up the set entirely. Great ideas and inventions come out of such a balance. Copernicus was familiar with the sets of his time, but he had the flexibility to see that they might not be relevant to his work. Only by putting aside these sets could he discover that the earth revolves around the sun. The point is to use a set when it is appropriate, but not to let the set use you—not to be so controlled by learned ways of approaching a problem that you are closed to new approaches to solving it.

One set that can affect problem solving is **functional fixedness.** The more you use an object in one way, the harder it is to see new uses for it. When you get used to seeing something one way and only one way, you have assigned it a fixed function. To some extent, of course, part of the

A "foster grandparents" program is a positive, new solution to two old human problems.
(Paul Sequeira, Rapho/Photo Researchers)

learning process is assigning correct functions to objects. We teach a child that the "right" function of a spoon is stirring, not pounding. Much of how we form concepts involves learning the "right" functions of objects. But it is important to remain open enough to see that a coin can be used as an emergency screwdriver, or that a book can be used as a prop for a wobbly table leg.

We have been talking about functional fixedness in terms of objects, but the idea can also be applied to problems with people. For example, the problem of the elderly has been given much attention recently. Putting older people into institutions can make them feel useless and depressed. Unwanted children also live in institutions that cannot always give them the time and care that they need. Instead of seeing the elderly as people to be looked after, someone grasped the idea that they might serve as "foster grandparents" to the children in institutions. This was a case of suspending the fixed function of both groups. The "grandparents" gave the children love and attention, and the children gave the older people the feeling of being useful. Two human problems were solved with one wise, new, and compassionate solution.

Altered States of Consciousness

Friday night on a college campus is special. Late in the afternoon powerful sound-systems begin to pound out competing rhythms. By dinner time, most of the mental activity valued so highly by professors during the rest of the week—rational thought, problem solving, memorization—have become bad form. By mid-evening, many students have gone from a change of pace to a change of consciousness. This is especially true at bars, parties, and the more notorious fraternity houses. Early the next morning, however, the drinkers, the pot smokers, and almost everyone else share the same **altered state of consciousness** (ASC)—sleep.

Although we often assume that most people function in a "normal" state of consciousness, altered states seem to appeal to some people in all classes of all societies. For example, little children all over the world play at making themselves dizzy by turning rapidly in circles and eventually falling down to watch the world spin. Other people may experience sensory deprivation, meditation, hypnosis, or drug-induced experiences, all of which are ASCs. Other ASCs such as daydreams, sleep, and dreams are universal. The means to altering one's state of consciousness may vary, but the interest in doing so is commonplace.

An ASC has been broadly defined as any mental state caused by physiological, psychological, or pharmacological intervention that can be recognized either by the person experiencing it or by an objective observer as substantially different from a person's normal behavior when alert and awake. According to Ludwig (1969), most ASCs demonstrate one or more of the following general traits: an impaired ability to think clearly and to perceive reality; a distorted sense of time; a loss of self-control; a change in how emotions are displayed; a change in body image; perceptual distortions such as hallucinations and increased visual imagery; a change in the significance given to experience; a sense of having experienced something that cannot be verbalized or communicated; feelings of rebirth; and a very high degree of suggestibility. ASCs may vary not only in character but also in degree (Suedfeld & Borrie, 1978). At one extreme are mental states that are distinguished from normal ones only by an increase in the number of perceptions, intellectual activities, and emotional responses; at the other extreme are drastic qualitative changes.

Ludwig also lists three general functions of ASCs that have been traditionally socially acceptable: healing; gaining new knowledge; and providing a ritualized outlet for a group's conflicts and goals. Weil (1972) adds a controversial fourth function—counteracting the limiting effects of "straight," logical, uninsightful thinking. With this brief general introduction, let us now examine the major kinds of ASCs.

(Will McIntyre, Photo Researchers)

DAYDREAMING

You are sitting in class on a warm spring day, listening to a history lecture. The windows are open, and outside the birds are singing and the trees are budding. The urge to gaze out the window is irresistible. You think about what it would be like to be out there, sitting on the grass, relaxing in the sunlight. Then the professor interrupts her discussion of the Roman Empire to say, "Mr. Smith, just what is so interesting out the window?" You are jolted back to reality. Only what, exactly, have you come back from? There was no specific thing outside that interested you. Rather, the mood of the spring day set you **daydreaming.** Most people daydream every day, especially at bedtime. Interestingly, people who daydream a lot report that the content varies widely from one daydream to the next (Singer, 1974).

Such thoughts usually occur in situations in which you would rather be

THE HYPNAGOGIC STATE

One afternoon in 1865, the chemist Friedrich von Kekule turned his chair toward the fireplace and dozed off. For some time he had been trying to determine the shape of the benzene molecule. As he began to fall asleep, what looked like rows of atoms danced before his eyes, twisting like snakes. When one of the snakes seized hold of its own tail and whirled before him, von Kekule awoke immediately with the solution to his problem—the benzene ring. This discovery became a cornerstone of modern chemistry (Koestler, 1964).

Psychologists call the mental state from which von Kekule drew his inspiration the **hypnagogic state.** It occurs during the drowsy period between waking and sleeping and is marked by visual and auditory images that arise unwilled. They appear to the observer to be part of the external world. Also characteristic of the hypnagogic state are highly unusual patterns of thought and verbal constructions that sound at first as if they have a meaning, but dissolve into nonsense. The phenomenon seems to be quite common, with recent estimates of the proportion of people experiencing the hypnagogic state ranging from 72 to 77 percent (Schachter, 1976).

Like other ASCs, the hypnagogic state varies from person to person. According to Schachter (1976), visual imagery is most common. Typically, flashes of color, light, and geometric patterns appear first, then faces and other objects, and later landscapes or complex scenes. The faces often appear in vivid detail, and surprisingly, are usually those of complete strangers. Sometimes these faces are so grotesque that they scare children. Landscapes are typically described as unusually beautiful and striking.

Less commonly, people seem to hear sounds. Sometimes they hear their names called or see and hear someone speak to them. Music has also been reported. One subject heard Rachmaninoff's *Second Piano Concerto* so clearly that he felt his experience rivalled an actual performance (McKellar, 1957). Sometimes, people feel bodily sensations such as the feeling of falling. Bizarre sequences of thought and speech are also associated with the hypnagogic state. Archer, for instance, reported hearing the phrases, "A savory pudding—raw in the market," and "A little management of Killie-krankie," as he fell asleep (1935).

Is the hypnagogic state similar to or related to other ASCs? Hypnagogic experiences are clearly distinct from dreams in two ways: Dreamers usually dream about themselves, while people seldom participate in their own hypnagogic imagery; and dreams are usually longer and better organized than the "snapshot" imagery of the hypnagogic state.

Thus, although the contents of both experiences are often strange, hypnagogic imagery is probably not closely related to dreaming (Schachter, 1976). And although there seem to be some similarities in the form and quality of hypnagogic and drug-induced imagery, in general, the little research that has been done supports the unique nature of the hypnagogic state.

somewhere else, or doing something else—escaping from the demands of the real world for the moment—or when you are doing something that requires little conscious thought—like driving a car on a deserted highway. Sometimes you replay a scene from the past in your daydream, or you project into the future. Daydreams provide the opportunity to write, act in, direct, and stage manage a private drama of which you are the only audience.

Although the content of each daydream is unique, three daydream patterns have been identified by Singer. These patterns are closely linked to personality type. The first pattern of daydreams is marked by considerable mental wandering and short-lived rather than extensive daydreaming. The daydreams are often unpleasant and fearful. People whose daydreams fit into this pattern spend most of each day in idle thought, but, even so, they lack a clear idea of what their daydreams are about: They have trouble concentrating on particulars. The second pattern also involves unpleasant emotions such as self-doubt, guilt, fear of failure, or anger or aggression toward others. People who continually have day-dreams of this kind tend to brood and be full of self-doubt. The third pattern of daydreams identified by Singer involves a range of positive and accepting feelings. The daydreamers in this group focus on plans for the future and on the details of their personal lives. They appear to have no serious emotional problems and to use their daydreams con-structively. Most daydreams are of this last type.

Some psychologists believe that daydreams are a kind of wishful think-ing that occurs when inner needs cannot be expressed in actual behavior. We daydream, they claim, when the world outside does not meet our needs, or when we want to do something but cannot. Freudian theorists have traditionally held that daydreams reflect repressed desires, generally about sex or hostility, that make us feel guilty (Giambra, 1974).

By contrast, other psychologists have stressed the positive value of day-dreaming and of fantasy. Pulaski (1974) suggests that daydreaming can build cognitive and creative skills and can help people survive difficult situations. She notes that daydreaming helped prisoners of war endure torture and deprivation. Her view suggests that daydreaming and fantasy can provide relief from everyday—and often unpleasant—reality, and can reduce internal tension and external aggression.

Singer (1969) proposed that daydreams are not just a substitute for real-ity or an important form of relief, but part of the information-processing system we discussed in Chapter 6. Singer suggests that when we process the vast, potentially overwhelming array of information received through the senses, some of the material is singled out for later review. Whether asleep or awake, we work on this information and on the contents of long-term memory, coding or restructuring it.

Usually, we are unaware of this activity. But in dull moments, when we are only occupied with a few or with repetitive external stimuli, we can focus on the results of this mental activity, and "unfinished business" is the material most likely to emerge for reconsideration. By responding to these inner stimuli when daydreaming, you may briefly lose some contact with the outside world. But in the long run, shifting to an inner channel lets you organize and integrate pressing unfinished business and cope with the environment more effectively.

SLEEP AND DREAMING

We spend about one-third of our lives in an ASC, namely sleep. Through-out history, varying degrees of respect have been paid to sleep and to its product, dreams. Some societies believe that great universal truths are revealed in dreams, while others view sleep as an essential, but basically nonproductive, activity. Only recently have sleep researchers begun to analyze the fascinating complexity of sleep, its function, and its influence on human perceptual activity.

Scientists do not usually enter people's homes to study the ways in which they sleep. Instead, they find volunteers to spend some nights in what is called a "sleep lab." With electrodes that are painlessly attached to their skulls, the volunteers sleep comfortably while their brain waves,

Figure 7–4

A sensory deprivation chamber. The subject lies on a cot with cardboard cuffs over his hands and forearms and translucent goggles over his eyes. The only sound is the monotonous noise of the exhaust fan. A microphone allows experimenters to monitor his speech, and the wires attached to his head record his brain waves.

(After W. Heron, "Cognitive and Physiological Effect of Perceptual Isolation." In P. Solomon et al. [Eds.], _Sensory Deprivation._ Cambridge, Mass.: Harvard University Press, 1961, p. 9, Figure 2-1. Copyright 1961 Harvard University Press.)

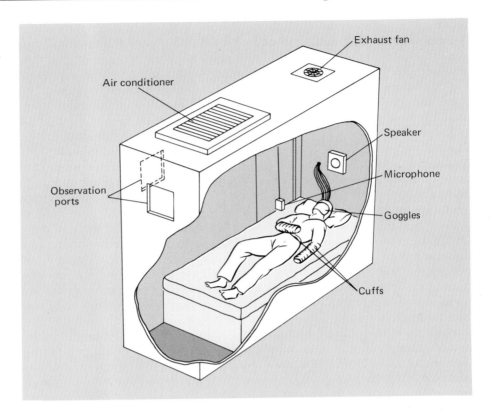

eye movements, and other physiological data are monitored.

Although there are significant individual differences, researchers using information gathered from these "sleep labs" have identified several stages that everyone goes through while sleeping (Kleitman, 1963). "Going to sleep" means losing awareness and failing to respond to a stimulus that would produce a response in the waking state. Often, this involves a floating or falling sensation, followed by a quick jolt back to consciousness, especially if the sleeper has entered Stage 1. Stage 1 is marked by irregular and low-voltage **brain waves,** slower pulse rate, muscle relaxation, and side-to-side rolling movements of the eyes. This eye movement is the most reliable indication of the initial sleep process (Dement, 1974). Stage 1 lasts only a few minutes. The sleeper is easily awakened at this point, and if awakened may be unaware of having been asleep. Stages 2 and 3 form a continuum of deeper and deeper sleep. In Stage 2, brain waves show bursts of activity called "spindles." In Stage 3, these disappear and brain waves become long and slow, about 1 per second. At this stage, the sleeper is hard to awaken and does not respond to stimuli. Heart rate, blood pressure, and temperature continue to drop. Stage 4 is **delta sleep,** the deepest stage, which is marked by slow, even brain waves. In young adults, delta sleep occurs in 15–20-minute segments—interspersed with lighter sleep—mostly during the first half of the night. Delta sleep lessens with age, but continues to be the first sleep to be made up after sleep has been lost.

About 30 or 40 minutes after going to sleep, the sleeper begins to ascend

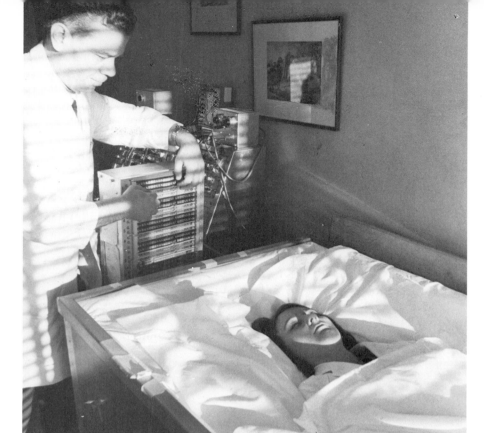

Figure 7–5
The brain wave patterns typical of the five stages of sleep. The brain waves in REM sleep closely resemble those of Stage 1 — but the person in REM is very deeply asleep, hard to wake up, and extremely relaxed.

(From *Sleep* by Gay Gaer Luce and Julius Segal. Reprinted by permission of Coward, McCann & Geoghegan, Inc. Copyright © 1966 by Gay Gaer Luce and Julius Segal.)

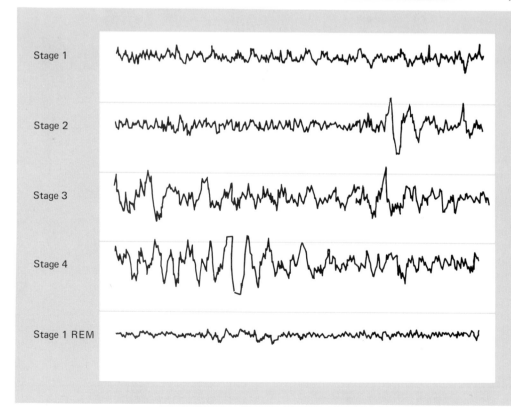

Stage 1

Stage 2

Stage 3

Stage 4

Stage 1 REM

from Stage 4, a process that takes about 40 minutes. At the end of this time, the brain waves exhibit a saw-toothed quality, the eyes move rapidly, and the muscles are more relaxed than they had been at any previous point. This is called **REM** (rapid eye movement) sleep, as opposed to the other four non-REM (NREM) stages. The first REM period lasts about 10 minutes and is followed by Stages 2, 3, and 4 of **NREM sleep.** This cycle continues all night long, averaging 90 minutes, but the pattern shifts. At first, NREM Stages 3 and 4 dominate, but as time passes, the REM periods gradually become longer, up to 60 minutes, with NREM Stage 2 the only interruption.

Dreams primarily occur during REM periods, although they also take place during NREM states. Subjects awakened from REM sleep report dreams 80–85 percent of the time (Berger, 1969). REM dreams are less like normal thought; they are more vivid, emotional, and distorted than NREM dreams (Dement, 1974; Foulkes, 1966). Thus, dreams become progressively more visual and less related to reality throughout the night as REM sleep becomes increasingly dominant (Broughton, 1975). There is

BIOLOGICAL CLOCKS

What does the birthrate have to do with crime? Not much—except that both are linked to inner body cycles that scientists are just beginning to understand.

One such cycle we all share is the 24-hour circadian cycle—from the Latin *circa diem:* "about a day"— of the body activity. The cycle seems to be inherited and to relate to hormones and body chemistry. At the high point of the cycle, functions like white cell formation, pulse, and the production of glycogen and other substances are greatest. People feel best at this high point, which occurs sometime during the day. The low point comes at night during sleep. Scientists have found that postsurgical deaths and the ability to withstand stress and illness are lowest at the low point of the cycle. Studies have shown that body temperature is highest around 5 P.M., and lowest between 4:00 and 5:00 A.M. (McFarland, 1975).

If our daily rhythm is upset, we may feel tired and irritable or may even become ill. Pilots, flight attendants, and frequent international travelers know that crossing time zones can cause physical problems, but people can adapt to these disruptions up to a point— night-shift workers, for example, can get used to sleeping during the day.

Scientists are certain that other cycles also affect our behavior, though all of them have not yet been fully identified and classified. The menstrual cycle clearly can affect mood, but there may be "mood

Disturbing our biological rhythms can make us irritable, or even sick.
(Omikron, Photo Researchers)

cycles" of varying lengths in all people. Depression or elation, accident proneness, and efficiency have all been shown to vary in cycles.

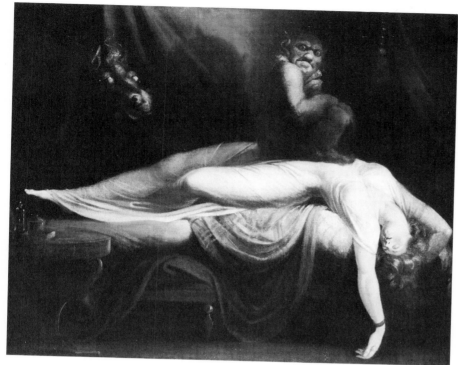

Throughout history, dreams were always thought to be significant, even if their meaning was unclear. The woman in this painting, entitled ''The Nightmare'' (by Henri Fuseli), is dreaming of monsters of her own creation.

(The Detroit Institute of Arts; Gift of Mr. and Mrs. Bert L. Smokler and Mr. and Mrs. Lawrence A. Fleischman)

also some evidence of dream activity during the day. In one experiment, subjects who were monitored during the day as if for sleep research reported a considerable amount of dreamlike activity when periodically interrupted (Foulkes & Fleisher, 1975). We may dream off and on, night and day, but only when competing external stimuli are minimal, however, do the dreams become coherent enough to recall (Koulack & Goodenough, 1976). People dream an average of 2 hours a night, even if they do not remember their dreams.

The dreams we have at night are in many ways like the daydreams we have while we are awake. They may be influenced by something in everyday waking life, but they reshape and recreate that material into new and ''illogical'' forms. A little boy who wishes his baby sister were dead knows it is unacceptable to have fantasies of killing her, much less to perform the act. When he dreams that she is dead, the dream is ''not his fault'' because he had no say in whether to have it. A dream may reflect a person's unconscious wishes, needs, and conflicts. It may draw on any part of one's history, from earliest childhood to events that happened the other day.

Dreams, like daydreams, can be a rich source of creative ideas. Franz Kafka got most of the material for his short stories from his dreams. René Descartes ''dreamed up'' the axioms of analytic geometry while sleeping one night. The high regard in which dreams have been held throughout history can be seen in such biblical stories as the pharaoh's dreams of ''fat and lean cattle,'' which Joseph interpreted as omens of 7 years of feast and 7 years of famine. Aristotle believed that dreams arose from the psychic activity of the sleeper. From ancient times, most people have felt that the content of their dreams was significant—even if they did not know what it meant.

Psychologists have spent considerable effort investigating the content and meaning of dreams. According to Freud, all dreams are symbolic expressions of repressed—and "forbidden"—desires that are hidden from awareness. Today, investigators of dreams rely on what dreamers remember about their dreams just after waking. Such recall of dreams shows that individual differences and daytime experiences help form the content of dreams, along with what happens during sleep itself. When you are closest to waking, your dreams are apt to be about recent events. In the middle of the night, when body temperature is lowest, more dreams involve childhood or past events. The last dream before waking is the one likely to be remembered.

Dreams vary according to age and sex. Children's dreams, like those of adults, seem to represent their waking life. Disturbed children have disturbed dreams, but most children dream about scary animals, while few adults, except in primitive cultures, dream about animals. Men dream more about men than about women. Women dream equally about both men and women. Men's dreams are more adventurous and aggressive and less emotional than women's dreams. Both sexes dream equally about being pursued or victimized. Before menstruation, women often dream about waiting. Before childbirth, they are likely to dream more about babies or their mothers than about their husbands. The dreams of women have more characters, warmer interactions, more indoor settings, and more family subjects than men's dreams.

Events near bedtime also affect a night's dreams. We may have dreams about snow when we are cold or about deserts when we are hot. But there is a general tendency for the content of dreams to contrast with the experiences that occurred just before we went to sleep. Eating salty food before bedtime made Freud dream of cold water. In one experiment, thirsty people who dreamed about drinking water drank less upon waking than those who did not dream about drinking. People who have been isolated tend to dream more about social interaction. It is difficult, however, to study how presleep experiences relate to dreams because people may respond to the same situation in terms of a different set of conflicts and defenses. These different conflicts and defenses affect the nature of dreams and must be understood before an experimenter can know if a subject's dreams are consistent with his or her waking emotional states (Webb & Cartwright, 1978).

Most dreams last about as long as the events would in real life; they do not flash on your mental screen just before waking, as was previously believed. Generally, they consist of a sequential story or a series of stories. Stimuli, both external and internal, may modify an ongoing dream, but they do not initiate dreams. One interesting experiment used three different external stimuli on subjects who were dreaming: a 5-second tone just below the waking threshold, a flashing lamp, and a light spray of cold water. The water was incorporated into 42 percent of the dreams, the light into 23 percent, and the tone into 9 percent (Dement & Wolpert, 1958). Another experiment by Dement and Wolpert (1958) showed that when a tape recording of the subject's voice was played back to the sub-

THE LONG AND SHORT OF SLEEP

If you are like most people, you need between 7 and 8 hours of sleep a night. If you get any less, you drag through the day hoping to get a good night's sleep the next night. If you get more sleep, you feel groggy from too much. Not everyone needs 7 or 8 hours of sleep; some people need a lot less and some need much more.

Ernest L. Hartman (1973) investigated the characteristics of long sleepers—those who need 9 or more hours of sleep a night—and short sleepers—those who need fewer than 6 hours—to learn whether their personalities as well as the quality of their sleep differed.

Short sleepers, according to Hartman, seem to take life as it comes. They rarely brood about their problems, spending their days in productive work. They are energetic and busy rather than introspective; they are conformist rather than seekers of political and social change; they are self-satisfied and relatively free from emotional problems.

Long sleepers, on the other hand, tend to be far less accepting of themselves and their lives than are short sleepers. They tend to be anxious and somewhat neurotic, but also artistic and creative. Political and social events arouse their passions as do day-to-day problems in their own lives.

When Hartman tested the sleeping patterns of long and short sleepers, he found that both got about the same amount of NREM sleep. But long sleepers spent more time than short sleepers in REM sleep. What is the value of these extra REM periods to the long sleeper? According to Hartman, "Longer sleep and more REM time may have some function in dealing with or restoring the brain and psyche after days of worry, depression, or disequilibrium or after difficult new learning—perhaps after any intrapsychic conflict" (Hartman, 1973). The research suggests that short sleepers do not have the same need to resolve conflicts as they sleep. Their easygoing nature carries on through the night.

ject while dreaming, the principal actor in the dream became more active and self-assertive. Thus, while these external stimuli are perceived during dreaming, their origin is often not perceived as being external. Their presence in the dream is usually personal and subjective, rather than literal. Interestingly, significant external stimuli such as the sleeper's name being spoken are most likely to spur awakening.

Are all the dreams dreamt in a single night related? Unfortunately, experimenters run into a methodological problem when they try to answer this question. Each time the subject is awakened to be asked about a dream, the natural course of the dream is interrupted and usually lost forever. If one particular problem or event weighs heavily on the dreamer's mind, however, it will often show up in dreams throughout the night (Dement, 1974).

Many desperate students have gone to sleep with a tape recorder conjugating foreign verbs in their ears in hopes of painlessly absorbing this material. Unfortunately, no study has yet proven that sleepers can learn complex material.

Attempts to influence dream content through presleep suggestions have had mixed results. Success seems to depend on subtleties such as the phrasing of the suggestion, the tone in which it is given, the relationship between the suggester and the subject, and the setting (Walker & Johnson, 1974). If these variables could be refined and controlled, the presleep suggestion technique could be important for both sleep researchers and psychotherapists.

People have often lamented about how much time we "waste" asleep.

Think what we must be missing! What we actually miss by sleeping are the following: visual, auditory, and tactile sensory disorders; vivid hallucinations; the inability to concentrate; withdrawal; the disorientation of self, time, and place; lapses of attention; an increased heart rate; more stress hormones in the blood; and the onset of psychosis. This alarming list, of course, refers to extreme cases—people who have stayed up, on a bet or for a television marathon, for over 200 hours. Among people who go without sleep for 60 hours or less the primary effect is, not surprisingly, sleepiness. A loss of sleep also affects the nervous system. Subjects perform certain tasks less efficiently; they experience hand tremors and lower pain thresholds. Reflexes and the autonomic nervous system seem to be affected very little by moderate deprivation. In the long run, however, the human body needs sleep to function, just as it needs food and water.

The need to dream appears to be less crucial than the need to sleep. Dement (1965) studied the effects of dream deprivation on people by awakening subjects just as they entered REM sleep. He found that subjects who went without REM sleep became anxious, testy, hungry, had difficulty concentrating, and even hallucinated in their waking hours. His assumption that eliminating REM sleep also eliminates dreams, however, was challenged by others who asserted that some dreams do occur in NREM sleep. Thus, in any one person it is difficult to tell how much REM deprivation eliminates dreams. While Dement found no evidence that REM dreams break through into other stages of sleep, he reversed his earlier findings about the lack of REM sleep on other grounds. In later experiments on the loss of REM sleep, Dement found no evidence of harmful changes in people who were kept from REM sleep for 16 days, nor in cats deprived for 70 days (Dement, 1974). "A decade of research," he wrote, "has failed to prove that substantial ill effects result even from prolonged selective REM deprivation" (Dement, 1974, p. 91).

This does not mean that stopping people from entering REM sleep does not affect them. When people have been deprived of REM sleep, and are then allowed to sleep undisturbed, the amount of REM sleep nearly doubles. This phenomenon is called "REM rebound." Interestingly, schizophrenics show little or no REM rebound. Persons who show signs of dreaming during the day also show less REM rebound (Cohen, 1976). This suggests that we can make up for the loss of dreamlike fantasy characteristic of REM sleep either in NREM sleep or in waking life (Dement et al., 1970). Many people who take drugs or drink alcohol, or who lose dreamtime because of illness or worry, say that when these inhibiting factors are removed they compensate by dreaming more intensely, often having nightmares (Dement, 1960). Studies of alcoholism indicate that REM deprivation caused by the disturbance of sleeping patterns may even break through to waking life. The result is delirium tremens, or d.t.'s, which are vivid hallucinations experienced during alcohol withdrawal (Greenberg & Pearlman, 1967).

REM sleep may also be essential to the normal operations of certain emotional and cognitive processes. There is some evidence, drawn mainly from studies of animals, that a loss of REM sleep may hinder the later storage and recall of information. Research has produced more definite results, however, about the information learned just before sleep. REM sleep helps us remember complex material and helps us adjust to emotionally disturbing events such as those that arouse anxiety. Dreams seem to help people cope more calmly with emotional situations in waking life. The learning of simple or irrelevant information, however, is not greatly affected by the amount of REM sleep (McGrath & Cohen, 1978).

SENSORY DEPRIVATION

All of us daydream and all of us sleep. But relatively few people experience another type of ASC, that connected with the drastic and systematic reduction of sensory stimulation from the environment. **Sensory deprivation** occurs under unusual circumstances such as those faced by fliers, sailors, prisoners, and the bedridden (Suedfeld & Borrie, 1978). Normally, our brains are continually aroused by sensory stimuli from the environment. But what happens when the number of stimuli is reduced? Is the brain thankful for the restful opportunity, or does it actually need stimulation to function?

These questions were probed extensively during the 1950s and 1960s in a series of experiments that by a variety of means carefully limited sensory input. The primary study was done at McGill University in Mon-

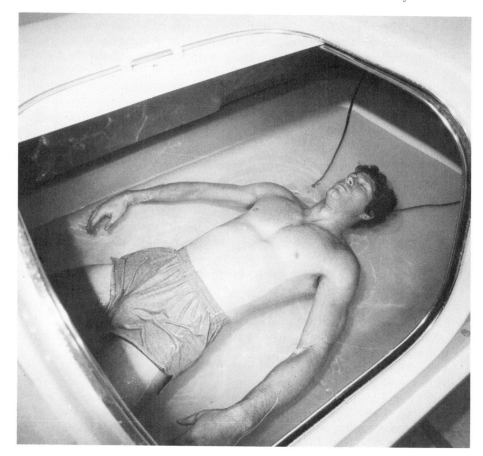

A subject undergoing sensory deprivation tests.
(Mark Perlstein/*The New York Times*)

treal in the late 1950s. Student volunteers were put in special cubicles. They were then masked and bandaged, severely restricting their visual, auditory, and tactile stimulation. The subjects were only released from these constraints for three meals a day and for trips to the bathroom. The results were dramatic. The subjects were increasingly unable to do the mental tasks that they had set for themselves. Some had planned to review their studies. Others had intended to think about a paper they had to write. The subjects grew increasingly irritable and eventually began to hallucinate. When released, they performed poorly on a number of tests, compared with the results of a control group on the same tests (Heron, 1957).

Other research has modified both the techniques for studying deprivation and the initial findings of the McGill study. Investigators learned to vary the mode of sensory deprivation in three ways. First, the patterns that normally characterize stimulation could be eliminated with translucent goggles or white noise. Second, the variability of sensory input could be reduced by immobilizing part or all of the subject's body in a frame. Third, the absolute level of sensation could be reduced by placing volunteers in dark, quiet chambers or by immersing them in water (Suedfeld & Borrie, 1978).

No matter how deprivation was induced, its effects were fairly similar. Subjects hallucinated, although not as often as first reported; experienced altered perceptions, both like and unlike those discovered among the McGill subjects; and dreamed, daydreamed, and fantasized. The term "hallucination" generally applies to the perception of apparently real visual and auditory stimuli in the absence of any real object. By this definition, most of the phenomena produced by sensory deprivation were not hallucinations. Instead, subjects reported flashes of light, geometrical forms, noises, and various complex images of objects or living beings that did not seem to be external. Some volunteers, confined to their deprivation chambers, also described nonexistent odors such as tobacco smoke and the feeling that the room or that they, themselves, were moving.

A second effect of sensory deprivation is to misinterpret real stimuli. Subjects emerging from their solitary confinement to face a battery of perceptual tests had impaired color perception and reaction time. Visual acuity and perception of brightness remained relatively unimpaired, and some faculties were actually heightened by systematic deprivation. Auditory vigilance, tactile acuity, pain sensitivity, and taste sensations all improved in this kind of experiment. Furthermore, the negative effects of deprivation were sometimes canceled out by countermeasures such as drugs, prior experience in isolation, and preisolation training (Zubek, 1973). Some of these effects, which are most powerful after about two days of deprivation, last for up to a day after the end of the experiment (Suedfeld & Borrie, 1978).

A third major component of the response of subjects to sensory deprivation consists of dreaming, daydreaming, and fantasy. By themselves in the chamber for a few hours, many subjects begin to pass through alternating states of drowsiness, sleep, and wakefulness. Suedfeld (1975) explains the resulting imagery as the subject's attempt to maintain a normal level of stimulation under deprived conditions. Because the distinctions among wakefulness, drowsiness, and sleep become blurred in the chamber, many of the "hallucinations" reported in the McGill research may in fact have been dreams or daydreams (Suedfeld, 1975). Bad dreams sometimes occur, but the tone of dreams and other imagery may depend on how a person reacts to deprivation.

MEDITATION

Like sensory deprivation, **meditation** brings about an unnatural ASC. Nevertheless, it is extremely common among human cultures, and is a part of almost all religions (Benson, 1975). Each form of meditation— Zen, yoga, Sufi, Christian, transcendental meditation (TM), and so on— focuses the meditator's attention in a slightly different way. Zen and yoga concentrate on respiration. The Sufi discipline, on the other hand, involves both frenzied dancing and a technique that is similar to the use of a mantra in TM (Schwartz, 1974). A mantra is an Indian sound specially picked for a student by the teacher. According to proponents of TM, concentrating on the mantra keeps all other images and problems at bay and lets the meditator relax more deeply (Deikman, 1973; Schwartz, 1974).

Meditation often creates a sense of unity between a person and his or her surroundings. The meditator may experience increased sensory awareness, euphoria, strong emotions, and a sense of timelessness and expanded awareness (Deikman, 1973). Peace of mind, a sense of well-being, and total relaxation have also been reported (Dean, 1970).

Meditation has been used to treat certain medical problems and drug abuse. Some studies found that a high percentage of meditators who had used drugs stopped using them. One survey of people who had practiced TM found a dramatic decrease in drug use among them (Benson & Wallace, 1972). The proportion using marijuana fell from 78 percent before practicing TM, to 12 percent after 21 months of meditation. Of all LSD users, 97 percent had ceased using the drug after an average of 22 months of meditation. The subjects of this study were already committed to TM when they were surveyed. Among another population—high-school drug users—meditation apparently was a less attractive alternative to drug use. Of 460 students offered the chance to learn TM, only 6 accepted. These 6, however, subsequently did tend to use fewer drugs (Benson et al., 1979). Meditation may also ease high blood pressure. TM and techniques related to yoga have lowered blood pressure among subjects matched by age, sex, and race (Stone & DeLeo, 1976). Relaxation techniques have also helped to make the heart beat more regularly (Benson, Alexander, & Feldman, 1975).

Despite its diverse forms, meditation seems to produce consistent physiological changes. These changes appear to be related to decreased activity of the sympathetic nervous system. In Chapter 2 we stated that this system of nerve fibers helps prepare the body for strenuous activity during an emergency. Meditation produces a lower rate of metabolism, which is shown by reduced absorption of oxygen in the bloodstream and elimination of carbon dioxide. Heart and respiratory rates also decrease. Alpha brain waves noticeably increase during meditation, and there is a decrease

Meditation is found among many cultures and religions; its benefits may be both physiological and psychological.
(Jean-Claude Lejeune, Stock, Boston)

in blood lactate, a chemical that may be linked to stress. Wallace and Benson (1972) have reported a sharp rise in skin resistance and interpret this as a sign of increased ability to cope with or shut out stressful occurrences, but other research (Schwartz, 1974) does not support this finding. These bodily responses are quite different from those of sleep or rest (Benson et al., 1979).

HYPNOSIS

Hypnosis first came to general attention in mid-18th-century Europe, when Anton Mesmer, a Viennese physician, fascinated audiences by putting patients into trances and by curing a variety of illnesses. Although some scientists studied and applied Mesmer's techniques to medical problems, for years hypnosis remained largely a sideshow amusement. When Freud successfully used hypnosis to cure symptoms of hysteria, however, scientific interest in the subject revived.

In an hypnotic trance, people may appear to be blind, deaf, or immune to pain. They may be able to perform seemingly impossible feats. For example, when told to relive their childhoods, people under hypnosis appear to be able to recite forgotten childhood memories. When awakened, they may be unable to recall anything that happened while they were hypnotized. The trance state thus seems unique and capable of giving extraordinary powers to ordinary people.

Hypnosis is one of the more controversial ASCs because psychologists cannot agree if it really is an ASC. Perhaps the most widely accepted criterion by which hypnosis is recognized is an increase in suggestibility. Under hypnosis subjects become more susceptible to the influence of suggestions made by hypnotists. But many people are highly suggestible even in a normal state of consciousness; some are just as susceptible as the best hypnotized subjects. Hypnosis cannot, therefore, be distinguished from a normal state solely by the degree of suggestibility.

Weitzenhoffer (1978) argues that hypnosis is indeed an ASC because under its influence subjects lose a sense of identity, which is retained in a normal state. According to him, hypnotized subjects reach a state of effortless, concentrated attention, free from distraction by sensations or random thoughts. This condition is somewhat like dreamless sleep. Subjects lose a sense of self and respond more or less automatically to the directions of the hypnotist.

The dispute over the nature of hypnosis is confusing and unresolved, in part because of two major research problems. First, unlike REM and NREM sleep, there is no physiological condition that can clearly be characterized as unique to a hypnotic state (Hilgard, 1974). Besides questioning if hypnosis is an ASC at all, this makes it hard to know when the hypnotic trance state has occurred, and thus makes it hard to study. Second, researchers must rely, at least in part, on the reports of people who have been hypnotized, and their reactions are subjective and varying (Dalal & Barber, 1970). Nevertheless, some objective measures of the perception and performance of people under hypnosis have been devised. While this research has not resolved the theoretical debate over hypnosis, it has

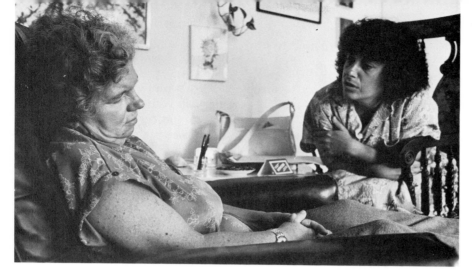

This woman is in an hypnotic trance. Whether the hypnotic state is truly an ASC is still being debated.
(Mark Antman, Stock, Boston)

shown that, for whatever reason, some people's perceptions can be dramatically altered by systematic forms of suggestion.

Some people are more susceptible to hypnosis than others. One leading researcher (Hilgard, 1975) finds that the best subjects are those with vivid imaginations, often those people who had imaginary childhood playmates or who use their imagination to escape from unpleasant realities. Hilgard hypothesizes that an active imagination enables the subject to create another world that shuts out stimuli from the external environment.

Differences among people to hypnotic susceptibility were demonstrated in a recent experiment by Hilgard (1974). First, the subjects, awake, immersed a hand and forearm in ice water and rated the intensity of the pain they felt. They next received hypnotic suggestions that their hand and arm were insensitive. They then immersed their hand and arm again and rated the pain a second time. Hilgard found that 67 percent of the "highly hypnotizable" subjects showed a 33 percent reduction in pain, while only 13 percent of the least hypnotizable subjects obtained such dramatic results.

DRUG-INDUCED EXPERIENCES

Since ancient times drugs have been used to alter consciousness for social, religious, medical, and personal reasons. Wine is mentioned often in the Old Testament. Marijuana first appeared in the herbal recipe book of a Chinese emperor in 2737 B.C. Today, with widespread education about psychology and much interest in—and misinformation about—drugs, many people take drugs in a conscious and deliberate effort to change their cognitive and perceptual styles, to get away from "straight" modes of thinking (Weil, 1972). The effects of some of these drugs may depend on the set—the expectations that people bring to the drug experience and their emotional state at the time—and the setting—the physical, social, and emotional atmosphere in which the drug is taken. Other drugs affect everyone in similar ways.

ALCOHOL. Are you surprised that alcohol is in this section? Our society recognizes many appropriate occasions for the use of alcohol: to celebrate important events, to reduce tension, to break down social isolation, and to promote group harmony. According to a government survey, 39 percent of American adults and 34 percent of American youths do not regard alcohol as a drug, and only 7 percent of the public regard alcoholism as a serious social problem—compared to 53 percent who hold this attitude toward all other drugs. Yet alcoholism is the most serious drug problem in the United States today. Users of alcohol outnumber users of all other drugs, largely because alcohol is readily available and aggressively marketed. It is also highly "reinforcing," that is, it tends to encourage repeated use and can result in both physical and psychological dependence. One out of every ten Americans uses it compulsively, and 50 percent of them are seriously dependent on it (National Commission on Marijuana and Drug Abuse, 1973*a*). Furthermore, there are signs of a sharp upsurge in alcoholism among adolescents.

Alcohol is a depressant and can lessen a person's normal inhibitions. Because people may feel more free to act in certain ways when drinking, they may think that the drug is a stimulant. It is not, but the excitement of feeling "free" certainly can be. During the euphoric period, a person's diminished self-control can result in social embarrassment, injury, or automobile accidents. Prolonged and excessive use of alcohol can damage the brain, liver, and other internal organs and can change the personality of the alcoholic.

Alcohol has mixed effects on visual perception. It heightens perception of dim lights, but it impairs perception of the differences between brighter lights, colors, and depth. The same is true of auditory perception. Some aspects of hearing, like perception of loudness, are not affected. The ability to discriminate between different rhythms and pitches, however, is impaired by a single dose of the drug. Smell and taste perception are uniformly diminished. Perception of time is also distorted. Most people report that time seems to pass more quickly when they are "under the influence" (NCMDA, 1973*b*).

In our society there are many occasions where drinking is acceptable and even encouraged. It should not be surprising, then, that alcohol is the most widely used drug in America.
(Will McIntyre, Photo Researchers)

MARIJUANA. Although marijuana use in the United States has risen markedly since the 1960s, there is no indication of significant compulsive use (NCMDA, 1973a). Moderate use seems to produce no mental or physical deterioration (Grinspoon, 1969). The most recent research, however, suggests some negative effects of long-term use, including damage to lung and brain cells and lowered sperm count among males (Zimmerman, 1979). On the positive side, marijuana also seems to relieve some of the symptoms of glaucoma and asthma, as well as the nausea resulting from chemotherapy. Repeated use of marijuana produces a reverse tolerance effect. Newcomers to the drug can absorb large quantities with little or no change in consciousness, while users with more experience are able to get high on much smaller amounts.

Marijuana is far less potent than the hallucinogens—LSD, peyote, mescaline, and psilocybin—and affects consciousness far less profoundly. A user who becomes "high" for the first time is likely to be anxious. This is usually followed by euphoria, a heightened sense of humor, a feeling of being bodiless, a rapid flow of ideas but confusion in relating them— due to impairment of short-term memory—heightened sensitivity, increased visual imagery, and a distorted sense of time. **Synesthesia** frequently occurs: Stimuli normally perceived in one mode are transformed into another—a person may "see" music or "feel" light. Cognitive tests administered to subjects after use of marijuana show mixed results: Some functions are unaffected, some are mildly impaired, and others may be slightly heightened (Grinspoon, 1969).

AMPHETAMINES AND BARBITURATES. Amphetamines (or "uppers") produce feelings of optimism and boundless energy. They are thus a highly reinforcing kind of drug. Compulsive use can eventually lead to psychosis, however.

Amphetamines have a stimulating effect, while barbiturates ("downers") are depressants. Barbiturates are pharmacologically similar to alcohol and have the same potential for creating physical and psychological dependence (NCMDA, 1973a). They relax all muscles—including the heart— and are therefore used to relieve anxiety. An overdose can relax muscle function so completely that death results.

Both amphetamines and barbiturates affect perception, primarily the perception of time. People's self-perceptions can also be affected—users of amphetamines may rate their abilities higher than they really are. Both drugs also affect memory. Barbiturates can cause **amnesia,** but they can also enhance long-term memory; "truth serums" are barbiturates (NCMDA, 1973a). Amphetamines can make it hard to concentrate and thus disrupt both attention and perception. When taken to excess, they may also cause a condition called "amphetamine psychosis" (Groves & Rebec, 1976). The symptoms of this condition, including fear, suspicion, paranoid delusions, and hallucinations, strongly resemble those associated with paranoid schizophrenia.

THE OPIATES. Heroin is the best-known member of the **opiate** family. Heroin use has tremendous social implications because the most likely addicts are young men in cities who would otherwise be seeking an

Marijuana is a nonaddictive and not very potent drug that has become widespread in the United States.
(Ed Lettau, Photo Researchers)

A person snorting cocaine.
(Charles Gatewood)

economic and social niche in society (NCMDA, 1973*a*). Because it is illegal and expensive, heroin, more than any other drug, generally results in criminal behavior. Most people who use heroin inject it intravenously, which leads relatively quickly to physical dependence and **addiction.** Overdoses can kill.

Heroin use produces a feeling of well-being and relaxation. Because of the rapid development of tolerance, however, the addict must take increasingly larger doses to achieve these effects. Smaller doses simply prevent the terrible pains of withdrawal. Because of the high cost, addicts must spend so much time and energy getting the drug that when they do get it, the primary feeling is generally one of relief rather than well-being. At this stage, it is less a means to alter consciousness than a medicine or a painkiller.

COCAINE. Cocaine is a stimulant and is the most reinforcing of all drugs. It has the greatest potential for psychological dependence. Cocaine's appeal is heightened because it is not physiologically addicting and because it has a mystique. It has become the drug of the elite.

Cocaine's immediate effects are similar to those of the amphetamines: increased alertness, impulsiveness, and suppression of hunger and fatigue. Moreover, cocaine results in a heightened sensitivity to sensory experience: colors are brighter, music is more beautiful, touch is more exciting. Self-perception may also be altered—a person may feel stronger and braver than usual. But, as with amphetamines, continued use of cocaine can result in psychosis, particularly paranoia.

HALLUCINOGENS. The **hallucinogens** include LSD ("acid"), mescaline, peyote, psilocybin, and other drugs. These drugs have a rather low dependency rate (NCMDA, 1973*a*). Contrary to some popular thinking, they seldom induce psychosis, and only rarely in people with no previous history of instability (Barron, Jarvik, & Bunnell, 1964). The effects of hallucinogens last considerably longer than those of most drugs—12 hours or longer is common. This length of time can cause unstable people to panic unless reminded and reassured that the effects are temporary. Pahnke and Richards (1966) feel that the sense that the experience is only temporary is one of the important distinctions between the psychedelic experience and psychosis.

The problem with studying hallucinogens is that more than with most drugs, their effects are determined not only by the properties of the drug itself but by a person's set and the setting in which the drug is taken. Moreover, subjects under the influence of these drugs often find a researcher's questions hilarious or irrelevant and either refuse or are unable to answer (NCMDA, 1973*a*).

Hallucinogens have profound effects on visual and auditory perception. At a minimal level, colors seem more vivid and surface details stand out more. With a higher dose of the drug or more sensitivity to it, a person may see kaleidoscopic patterns and images, or fully integrated and often bizarre scenes (Barron, Jarvik, & Bunnell, 1964). Spatial distortions and changed body images are also common. Sometimes these visual effects are described as breathtakingly beautiful, at other times as extremely un-pleasant and upsetting.

Auditory perception also changes in a fascinating variety of ways. Some people report hearing imaginary conversations, or fully orchestrated and original symphonies, or foreign languages previously unknown to them. Auditory acuity may be increased, making the person keenly aware of low sounds like breathing, heartbeats, or the light rustle of leaves in the wind (Barron, Jarvik, & Bunnell, 1964).

Some students of hallucinogens view all of the above as the shallow aspects of the drug experience, compared with the mystical and transcen-dental qualities that are often noted. For example, Pahnke and Richards (1966) say that the synesthetic experience of music as a series of visual images is insignificant compared with the consciousness attained when one goes through the drug pattern toward a mystical sense of harmony, unity, and serenity. Deikman (1973) cites the LSD experience as another means of achieving "deautomatization," the abolition of psychological structures that normally limit, select, and interpret sensory stimuli. In conclusion, it should be noted that scientists are still debating whether any or all of the hallucinogens have harmful physiological effects.

Application

ALTERED STATES AND THE "NEW RELIGIONS"

In the 1960s, drugs were the thing. Young people—and not-so-young people—popped LSD and mescaline and smoked marijuana. Some used psychedelic drugs just to get high, but for many others, hallucinogens were a means to a sense of "cosmic consciousness." In other words, people were using psychedelic drugs for what we might call religious purposes.

By the late 1960s, the drug culture had begun to wane. People put aside their psychedelic drugs and put on the robes of a bewil-dering variety of religious groups, which came to be known as "the new religions." The new religions often took the symbols and cere-monies of Oriental religions and adapted them to fit American needs. Alan Watts described them as a search for experience that contains "the conviction that this entire unspeakable world is 'right,' so right that our normal anxieties become ludicrous, that if only men could see it [that the world is right] they would go wild with joy" (in Raschke, 1980, p. 229).

The recruitment and indoctrination techniques used by many of the cults involved behavioral manipulations that had far-reaching effects. Prayer, chanting, and frequent lectures induce altered states of con-sciousness and submission. Cults provide seekers with "instant fam-ilies" and relieve them from having to make their own decisions about sex, marriage, and careers. Cults literally interpret everything in the world to their followers.

The new religions thus offered a form of "salvation"—but at a price. Sociologist Robert Bellah wrote that "out of the shattered hopes of the 1960s there has emerged a cynical privatism, a narrowing of sympathy and concern . . . that is truly frightening" (Raschke, 1980, p. 237). Christopher Lasch used the word "narcissism" to describe the new self-fulfillment religions. And Tom Wolfe dubbed the 1970s the "Me Decade." Raschke warns that *gnosticism*—from the ancient Gnostic sect that turned inward and sought salvation in their own visions—"flourishes wherever there is a death of common purpose, a dread of the future, and a mad rush for personal legitimacy in a psychic war of all against all" (Raschke, 1980, p. 239).

By the 1980s, the new religions were no longer new. People began dropping out of the cults of the 1970s. Because many cults demand total obedience, members who become disenchanted often find that it is harder to leave the cult than it is to join it. What happens to these people, which some estimate at two to three million, most of them young adults? Margaret Thaler Singer, who has worked with ex-members of the Children of God, Unification Church, Krishna

(Yan Lukas, Rapho/Photo Researchers)

Consciousness, and the Divine Light Mission, points out that these drop-outs face unique problems in readjusting to the outside world. Ex-cult members are suddenly faced with the dilemmas they left behind when they entered the cloistered world of the cult. For people who had serious emotional problems *before* they joined—a study of one cult put this number at nearly 40 percent—returning to the "real world" can be overwhelming. Leaving adopted families and rigorous routines can cause loneliness, aimlessness, and depression. Some ex-members report that they slip back into the altered states of consciousness they experienced when they were in the cult. These trancelike states may recur in response to stress, depression, or contact with certain words or ideas. Some ex-members report episodes of "floating" months after they leave the group. "Weeks after I left," said one man, "I would suddenly feel spacey and hear the cult leader saying, 'You'll always come back. You are one with us. You can never separate' ... I got so frightened once that I slapped my face to make it stop" (Singer, 1979, p. 76).

Others report loss of reasoning skills, passive acceptance of demands from others, and even a fear of harassment from their former "families" and feelings of guilt about betraying their former ideals. "People just can't understand what the group puts into your mind," said one ex-member. "How they play on your guilts and needs." One of the hardest things to accept is that in the real world, they are no longer members of an elite, no longer "chosen people." But Margaret Thaler Singer suggests that by working with therapists and with other ex-members who are also trying to readjust to life outside the cult, many people find the support they need to begin to lead their own lives again (Singer, 1979).

Summary

1. *Cognition* involves manipulating the information that we have processed and stored in long-term memory.
2. One of the ways we think is by using *images*.
3. *Images* are recollections or reconstructions of sensory experience and may employ sight, taste, touch, smell, and sound. They may be incomplete or even inaccurate, concrete or abstract, dim or vivid.
4. Most images are lost immediately. We select only a few for further processing.
5. Most thinking involves verbal images or *words*. Words affect what we remember and how we remember it.
6. The *linguistic relativity hypothesis* maintains that thinking is pat-

terned by language and that the language one speaks determines one's view of the world. This theory has been criticized; there is also evidence to suggest that the way we think also affects the words we use. People from different language backgrounds appear to think about some things—like color—in very similar ways.

7. Various factors can affect problem solving. Anxiety, anger, and frustration may make a problem more difficult to solve, or they may increase efficiency in working out a solution to a problem. The limitations of short-term and long-term memory can also affect the way we approach problem solving.

8. There are three rough stages in problem solving, which do not necessarily occur in chronological order: *preparation, production,* and *judgment.*

9. We generally use two methods of finding solutions to problems in the production stage: *algorithms* and *heuristics.*

10. *Algorithms* are methods that guarantee a solution if they are properly carried out.

11. *Heuristics* are "rules of thumb" that tell us quickly whether or not we have solved a problem. *Means–end analysis, working backward,* and *planning processes* are three heuristic methods.

12. *Set* refers to a habit or the way we are used to perceiving situations. Set can be helpful in problem solving, since we benefit from past experiences in learning certain operations and ways of perceiving. But if we rely too heavily on set, rather than looking for new methods to solve problems, we may overlook more creative strategies. *Functional fixedness* occurs when we get used to perceiving something in one way and cannot perceive it in any other way.

13. People sometimes solve problems through creative problem solving, which is characterized by insight. It is unclear whether the processes involved in creative problem solving greatly differ from those in step-by-step problem solving.

14. *Altered states of consciousness* include daydreaming, sleep, dreaming, sensory deprivation, meditation, hypnosis, and drug-induced experiences.

15. *Daydreaming* allows you to escape from the demands of the real world and be somewhere else for the moment. Daydreams may be a way of processing "unfinished business," which is permitted by a reduction of external stimuli.

16. There are four stages of *sleep.* Stage 1 lasts only a few minutes and is a borderline between true sleep and waking. Sleep becomes progressively deeper in Stages 2 and 3.

17. Stage 4, *delta sleep,* is the deepest stage. After Stage 4, *REM* (rapid eye movement) *sleep* begins. The other stages of sleep are referred to as *NREM* (nonrapid eye movement) *sleep.*

18. *Dreams* occur in both REM and NREM sleep, but are more frequent and detailed in REM sleep. Dreams reshape and recreate

material into new and often illogical forms and can be a source of creative ideas. A dream may reflect the dreamer's unconscious wishes, needs, and conflicts.

19. *Sensory deprivation*, an induced ASC, results in occasional hallucinations, altered perceptions, dreams, daydreams, and fantasies. Research indicates that hearing, touch, sensitivity to pain, and taste become more acute, while other sensory capacities are either unaffected or reduced.

20. *Meditation* involves an identifiable cluster of physiological changes. Successful meditation produces deep relaxation and has proved useful in reducing drug use and certain circulatory problems.

21. Psychologists disagree about whether the trance induced by *hypnosis* is a true altered state of consciousness. One reason for this is that there are no consistent physiological signs that accompany the hypnotic state. Hypnosis has been shown to alter some people's perceptions and behavior.

22. The use of *drugs* to alter consciousness has a long history. The effect any drug has on consciousness depends on *set*—the person's state of mind at the time the drug is taken—and *setting*—the physical, social, and emotional atmosphere in which the drug is taken.

23. The most commonly used drug is *alcohol*. Alcohol is a depressant and can lessen the person's normal inhibitions, which has a temporary stimulating effect. Alcohol impairs some kinds of perception.

24. *Marijuana*, if used moderately, does not appear to cause mental and physical deterioration. Long-term use, however, may cause physical harm. Its effects include euphoria, a heightened sense of humor, impairment of short-term memory, heightened sensory sensitivity, increased visual imagery, and distortion of the sense of time.

25. *Amphetamines* produce feelings of optimism and boundless energy. Amphetamine use can become compulsive and may eventually lead to psychosis. *Barbiturates* are depressants and have the same potential for creating physical and psychological dependence that alcohol does. Both drugs affect perception of time, self-perception, and memory.

26. *Heroin* use results in physical and psychological dependence. Its users become tolerant of the drug and need larger doses to achieve the same effects after using it for a period of time.

27. *Cocaine* is a stimulant and has the greatest potential for psychological dependence of all drugs. Its effects are similar to those of the amphetamines.

28. The *hallucinogens* include LSD, mescaline, peyote, and psilocybin. They have a low dependence rate and rarely cause psychosis. Hallucinogens have profound effects on visual and auditory perception.

Outline

Chapter 8

Sensation and Perception

How do we know when it is morning? This is a simple question, yet the answer is complex. In part we depend on our **sensations**—what we see, what we hear. In part we also depend on our **perceptions**—how we interpret these sensations. Thus sensation is raw sensory data, while perception is the organization and interpretation of that data. We may conclude that it is morning when we perceive the dawn's light, or hear birds singing or the sounds of traffic, or simply hear an alarm go off and see the familiar time on the clock.

We continually use our senses to inform ourselves about the world. Usually, we do not even know that we are doing it. When we get up in the morning, we do not say to ourselves, "I hear a sound that must be birds singing." We know the difference between singing birds and ringing alarm clocks. We take these perceptions for granted. But sometimes our senses can be "confused." Coming from the bright sunlight into a dark theater, we accept a few moments of "blindness." After a loud concert, it may seem funny, but not frightening, that our ears still ring with the music. Sitting in a train, we suddenly perceive that we are moving only to discover that it is the train next to us that is really moving.

Psychologists are interested in how information about the outside world gets through to us, and why we perceive what we do. How do we know that one thing is farther away than another? How does the vibration of our eardrum become the familiar sound of a police siren? How does the brain enable us to see and hear the world around us?

All of our senses do not work the same way—the way we see is very different from the way we hear. Before we turn to the specific characteristics of sight and hearing,* let us look at the general characteristics common to both of them.

*The minor senses—including taste, touch, and smell—are discussed in Chapter 2.

241

The Nature of Sensation

Psychologists are interested in how information about the outside world gets through to us, and why we perceive what we do.
(Weiss, Rapho/Photo Researchers)

THE GENERAL CHARACTER OF SENSATION

Described in general terms, the sequence of events that produces a sensation seems quite simple. First, some form of energy, either from an external source or from within the body, stimulates a receptor cell in one of the sense organs—such as the eye or the ear. A receptor cell is specialized to respond to one form of energy—light waves, for instance, or air pressure. Obviously, the energy must be intense enough or the receptor cell will ignore it.

All receptors can change the energy they receive into a coded, electrochemical impulse. This process is known as **transduction** and **coding.** The brightness of a light might be coded by how fast a particular nerve cell fires. As the neural impulses pass along the sensory nerves to the central nervous system, they are processed further, so that when they reach the brain the message is precise and detailed. Without this coding process, the receptors could only tell the brain, "Hey, you! Pay attention!" The coding that occurs along the way lets the brain know exactly what to pay attention to.

All sensation, then, occurs as a result of the same sequence of events. Yet each of the body's sensory systems is unique. The receptor cells are different and respond to different kinds of stimulation. The way they convert energy into neural impulses varies. The pathways to the brain are direct and indirect. And, most obviously, the sensations we have are quite different.

Until the 19th century, most theories of perception were still based on ancient ideas. The Greek natural philosophers were extremely influential. For example, Empedocles in the 5th century B.C. theorized that objects gave off invisible *effluvia*, which acted upon our senses to provide our images of the world. Another ancient Greek, Democritos, supposed that objects gave off projections, faint images of themselves called *simulacra*, which acquainted the mind with what these images represented.

Johannes Müller was the first man to successfully challenge these ancient ideas, and thus to begin the modern study of sensation. In 1826, Müller argued that since the mind is inside the body, it can only be in direct contact with its own nerves, not with what it perceives. Therefore, he

HOW SENSITIVE ARE YOUR SENSES?

Each of our sense organs is remarkably sensitive. The absolute thresholds are much lower than you probably realize. McBurney and Collings (1977) gave the approximate absolute thresholds for the senses:

Vision: A candle flame seen from 50 kilometers (31 miles) on a clear, dark night.

Taste: One gram (.035 ounce) of table salt in 500 liters (529 quarts) of water.

Smell: One drop of perfume diffused throughout a three-room apartment.

Touch: The wing of a bee falling on your cheek from a height of 1 centimeter (.39 inch).

observed, the mind perceives only its nerves, and these nerves are what the real world affects.

Later, Müller formulated his doctrine of specific nerve energies. He stated that we are not aware of sensory stimuli, as such, only of the state in our nerves that the sensory stimuli cause. Moreover, he stated, when a given nerve is stimulated, the sensation that results is determined by the nature of the nerve, not by what stimulated it. Stimulating the visual nerves either by pressing on the eye or looking at a pretty landscape will both cause us to see something. Stimulating the auditory nerves either by listening to a symphony or by trickling water into the ear will both cause us to hear something.

It is important to understand that, in a way, any sensory experience is an illusion created by the brain. The brain sits isolated within our bodies, listening to the "clicking" of neural impulses coming in over millions of nerve fibers. The clicks on the optic fibers are not any more "visual" than the clicks on the auditory fibers. But the clicks on the optic fibers have somehow been arbitrarily specified as "visual nerve energy," and thus they give rise to visual experience. This is one of the many natural mysteries of our brain and nervous system.

THE MEASUREMENT OF SENSATION

How much sensory stimulation is needed to produce a given sensation or a noticeable difference in sensation? Answering this question involves isolating one kind of stimulation from another and measuring the effect on the particular sense being tested. This process has led to the development of the science of **psychophysics.** How intense does a sound have to be, for example, for a person to hear it? How bright does a "blip" on a radar screen have to be for the operator to see it? This minimum intensity of physical energy that is required to produce any sensation at all in a person is called the **absolute threshold.** Any stimulation below the absolute threshold of the person being tested will not be reported. (See Figure 8–1.)

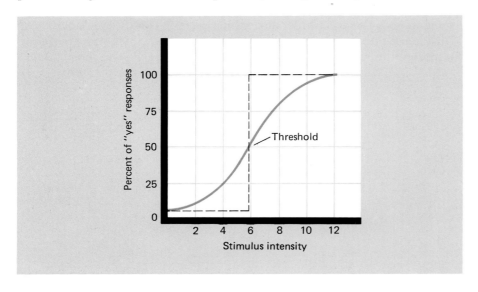

Figure 8–1
Determining a sensory threshold. The dotted line represents an ideal case—at all intensities below the threshold the subject reports no sensation or no change in intensity; at all intensities above the threshold the subject does report a sensation or a change in intensity. In actual practice, the ideal of the dotted line is never realized. The threshold is taken at the point where the subject reports a sensation or a change in intensity 50 percent of the time.

Other tests measure the **difference threshold**—the smallest change in stimulation that a person can detect. This is also called the **just noticeable difference,** or **j.n.d.** For example, how much stronger does a sound have to be before you actually notice that it has become louder? Like the absolute threshold, the difference threshold will vary from person to person and from time to time. Difference thresholds also vary with the absolute level of stimulation. For example, a match struck in a dark room is much more noticeable than one struck outside at noon on a sunny day.

Vision

A human eye.
(Danny Brass, Photo Researchers)

Animals vary in their relative dependence on the different senses. Dogs rely heavily on the sense of smell, bats on hearing, some fish on taste. But for humans, vision is probably the most important sense, and has thus been most thoroughly studied by psychologists and physiologists.

The physical stimulus for the sense of vision is light—a small part of the spectrum of electromagnetic energy. The total spectrum extends from the range of energy used in radio communication at one end, all the way down to minute cosmic rays at the other (see Figure 8–2). The receptors in the eye are sensitive to only one small segment of this spectrum—known as **visible light.** (See Figures 8–3 and 8–4.)

THE EYE

The structure of the human eye is shown in Figure 8–5. Light enters the eye through the **cornea,** the transparent protective coating over the front part of the eye. Then it passes through the **pupil,** the opening in the center of the **iris,** the colored part of the eye. In very bright light, the muscles in the iris contract to make the pupil smaller and protect the eye from damage. This also helps us to see better in bright light. In dim light the muscles extend to open the pupil wider and to let in as much light as possible.

Inside the pupil the light passes through the **lens,** which focuses it onto the **retina,** the inner lining of the back of the eyeball. The lens changes

Figure 8–2
The electromagnetic spectrum. The eye is sensitive to only a very small segment of the spectrum, known as visible light.

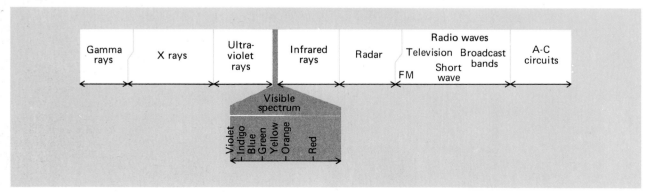

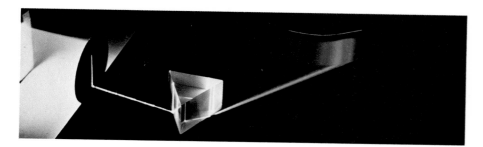

Figure 8–3
Sunlight contains the wavelengths for all the colors we can see. When it is passed through a prism, the wavelengths are bent at different angles and the light is separated into a color spectrum.
(Fritz Goro, *Life Magazine*, © Time Inc.)

Figure 8–4
A natural spectrum, a rainbow, occurs when sunlight is bent by the atmosphere.
(Fritz Henle, Photo Researchers)

shape to focus on objects that are closer or farther away. Normally, the lens is focused on a middle distance, at a point neither very near nor very far away. To focus on an object that is very close to the eyes, tiny muscles around the lens contract and make the lens rounder. To focus on an object that is far away, the muscles make the lens flatter. The retina contains the receptor cells that respond to light. But before the light can reach the receptor cells, it must pass through a layer of nerve cells and blood vessels and a layer of neurons, which make the connections between the receptor cells and the nerve pathways to the brain (see Figure 8–6).

RODS AND CONES. There are two kinds of receptor cells in the retina— **rods** and **cones**—named for their characteristic shapes. Cones are less

Figure 8–5
A cross section of the human eye.

Figure 8–6
The layers of the retina. Light must pass through the ganglion cells and the bipolar neurons to reach the rods and cones. The sensory messages then travel back out again from the receptor cells, through the bipolar neurons, to the ganglion cells, the axons of which gather together to form the optic nerve.

(From "The Visual Cortex of the Brain" by David H. Hubel. Copyright © 1963 by *Scientific America*, Inc. All rights reserved).

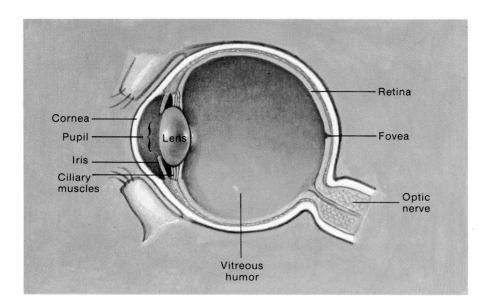

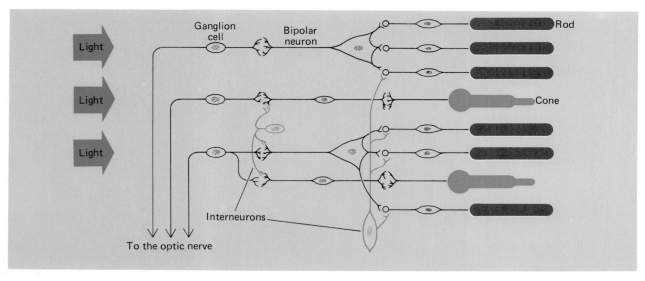

sensitive to light than rods are (MacLeod, 1978). Cones mainly operate in daylight and respond to colors. The better the lighting, the more cones will be stimulated; when more cones are stimulated, **visual acuity**—the ability to distinguish fine details and small spatial separations—is increased. Rods are mainly responsible for night vision, when there is not enough light to stimulate the cones. Rods only respond to varying degrees of light and dark, not to colors. Each eye contains about 130 million rods and cones.

The depressed spot on the retina, directly behind the lens, is called the **fovea.** The fovea corresponds to the center of the visual field. Thus, the words that you are now reading are hitting the fovea, while the rest of what you see—a desk, walls, or whatever—are hitting other areas of the eye.

The fovea is packed with nearly 100,000 cones, but contains no rods. Daytime vision is most acute when light is focused directly on the fovea. One reason for this is the high density of cones in the fovea; another reason is that on the fovea light reaches the receptor cells directly. Rods predominate around the edge of the fovea. As we move outward from the fovea, toward the edges of the retina, both rods and cones get sparser. At the extreme edges there are no cones and only a few rods. Since the rods are more sensitive to light than are the cones, we can often see things better at night by looking out of the sides of our eyes so that the light is focused on the rods just outside the fovea.

The rods and cones differ from one another in more than just shape. For one thing, they contain different chemical pigments. The pigment found in rods is called **rhodopsin.** When light strikes a rod, rhodopsin breaks down into retinene and other chemical substances. The chemical activity in the rod is thought to stimulate the neurons connected to it, thus starting the sensory message on its way to the brain. Then the chemicals get back together again—the retinene recombines with the other substances to form rhodopsin. Vitamin A is essential to this recombination, which is why a deficiency in vitamin A often causes "night blindness."

The chemical activity in the cones, though similar, appears to be more complex than that in the rods. The chemical make-up and activity of the cones has been intensely studied, but even the pigment in the cones is still unidentified. In general, the cone pigments seem to be close in structure to rhodopsin, but different in the spectrum of light wavelengths that they can absorb. As we shall see, three different kinds of cones enable us to distinguish color: red-absorbing, green-absorbing, and blue-absorbing cones (Cornsweet, 1970). Light striking the cones causes a chemical breakdown similar to that in the rods, but the recombination occurs much faster in the cones.

NEURAL CONNECTIONS. Rods and cones also differ in how they connect to the nerve fibers that carry their messages to the brain. Both rods and cones connect to what are called "bipolar neurons."* Some bipolar neurons connect to both rods and cones. In the fovea, however, cones generally connect with only one bipolar neuron, a sort of "private line" arrangement. Rods are usually on a "party line": Several rods share a single bipolar neuron. This explains why the rods operate better in dim light than the

---

*A bipolar neuron has only one axon and one dendrite.

●

cones do. Each rod gets very little light, but the combined effect of all the rods is enough to cause the bipolar neuron to fire off a message.

The situation gets complex as rods and cones combine with bipolar neurons in different numbers and in different combinations. It becomes more complicated when the two layers of cells that form lateral connections—the ones between different receptor cells and the ones between different bipolar neurons—become involved. These lateral connections allow complex processing to occur in the retina itself (Michael, 1969). Although the maze of connections is very intricate, the neural impulses somehow find their way out of the eye. The bipolar neurons connect to the ganglion cells, whose axons make up the **optic nerve** and carry the neural messages to the brain. The place on the retina where the axons of all the ganglion cells join to leave the eye is called the *blind spot*—it contains no receptor cells. We are not normally aware of the blind spot. When light from a small object is focused directly on it, however, the object the light is coming from will not be seen (see Figure 8–7).

After they leave the eyes, the fibers that make up each optic nerve separate, and some of them cross to the other side. The nerve fibers from the right side of each eye travel to the right hemisphere of the brain; the fibers from the left half of each eye travel to the left hemisphere. The place where the fibers cross over is called the **optic chiasma** (see Figure 8–8).

Figure 8–8
The neural pathways of the visual system. Messages from the left visual field of each eye travel to the right occipital lobe; those from the right visual field of each eye go to the left occipital lobe. The crossover point is the optic chiasma.

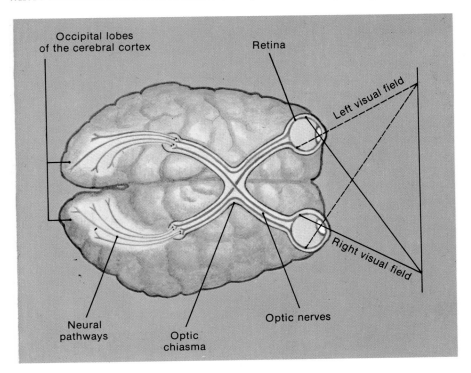

Occipital lobes of the cerebral cortex

Retina

Left visual field

Right visual field

Neural pathways

Optic chiasma

Optic nerves

Having crossed over, the fibers of the optic nerves carry their messages to several different parts of the brain. Some of the messages reach the part of the brain that controls the reflex movements that adjust the size of the pupil. Others reach the part of the brain that directs the eye muscles to change the shape of the lens. But the main destinations for the messages from the retina are the visual projection areas of the cerebral cortex, where the pattern of stimulated and unstimulated receptor cells is registered, integrated, and interpreted.

The ability to see colors depends on the eye's capacity to send different messages to the brain in response to different wavelengths of the visible spectrum, but the question of exactly how we see colors is much debated. In the early 19th century, Thomas Young, an English physicist, mixed three lights, red, green, and blue. He found that almost any hue that the human eye can detect could be produced by adjusting the relative intensities of the three lights. He surmised that this is what the eye must do. A German physiologist, Hermann von Helmholtz, added to this theory. He argued that we see colors because the eye contains three different kinds of color receptors—cells that respond to red, those that respond to green, and others that respond to blue–violet. Other colors, he believed, result from mixtures of the three reception systems. This is known as the **trichromatic theory.**

The ability of these bathers to see the July Fourth sky show in color may depend upon specific color receptors in their eyes.
(Catherine Noren, Photo Researchers)

In 1878, Ewald Hering asserted that color vision depends not on a mixture of the three basic colors, but rather on a combination of opponent processes. Hering agreed that there are three separate kinds of color receptors. He believed, however, that we see color through a pairing of opposite receptors, and that certain receptors cannot combine. A yellow–blue receptor cannot send messages about yellow and blue at the same time, nor can a red–green receptor send both red and green messages at the same time. This, Hering maintained, is why we never see a reddish green or a bluish yellow. Hering's theory is known as the **opponent-process theory.**

Neither trichromatic nor opponent-process theories are completely satisfactory by themselves. The opponent-process theory, however, is somewhat more successful in explaining **color blindness.** People with normal vision are **trichromats**—given three hues, their visual system can reproduce all the colors of the spectrum. At the other extreme are **monochromats**—the rare people who see no color at all and respond only to shades of light and dark. Much more common than monochromats are **dichromats**—people who respond to only two hues and can see only those colors that result from mixing those two. Red–green color blindness, a sex-linked inherited trait, is the most common form of dichromatism. People with this form of color blindness may see red and green as a kind of yellowish gray, or they may confuse red and green a bit because they do not see them very vividly (see Figure 8–9). The problem with the Young–Helmholtz theory of color vision is that it maintains that yellow is produced by the combined activity of the red and green receptors, yet the person who can see neither red nor green can still see yellow. The opponent-process theory, on the other hand, explains red–green color blindness by saying that the set of receptors that responds to either red or green simply does not work in the retina of the red–green dichromat.

The two theories have coexisted for over 50 years and there is still no

Figure 8–9
The Dvorine Pseudo-Isochromatic Plates are used to detect color blindness. People who are color-blind cannot see the figure inside the circle (below). To show what this means in everyday life, we have printed a photo of a butterfly both in normal color (left) and as someone with red-green color blindness would see it (lower right).

(Color-blindness test reproduced by permission of the Scientific Publishing Co., Baltimore, Maryland; photo by Karl Maslowski, Photo Researchers)

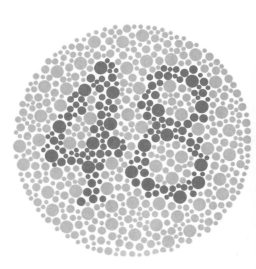

resolution in sight. Modern investigations have found evidence that both theories may, in fact, be valid, but at two different stages in the visual process. Measurement of the responses of individual receptor cells has revealed cells with distinctly different responses to wavelengths in the blue, green, and red–yellow areas of the spectrum (Brown & Wald, 1964; Marks, Dobelle, & MacNichol, 1964). Young and Helmholtz, it seems, were not altogether wrong after all.

Other studies, however, recording the electrical activities of the bipolar neurons and the ganglion cells in the retina, indicate that colors are coded neurally in an opponent-process way. The first indication that the ganglion cells played an active role in coding visual messages came when it was discovered that they always showed some level of electrical activity. They do not just sit there and wait for a message to come from the bipolar neurons. Rather, since they are constantly conducting nerve impulses, they can respond in two opposite directions. They can turn "on" by increasing their rate of firing, or they can turn "off" by decreasing it. Some cells have been found, for example, that turn "on" to yellow or green, but turn "off" to blue. These cells are paired with others that respond in the opposite way—"on" to blue, "off" to yellow or green (Hurvich & Jameson, 1974). So, Hering was not completely wrong either.

It seems plausible now that there are, as Young and Helmholtz believed, three kinds of receptor cells for color. The messages they transmit, how-

COLOR PROPERTIES AND COLOR MIXING

Physicists can describe colors quite precisely in terms of wavelengths and amplitudes. But most of us, when we describe what colors we see, use terms that are much less exact. When we talk about colors, we generally refer to three basic dimensions, which are represented spatially on the color solid shown in Figure 8–10.

The first dimension that usually comes to mind is *hue*—the particular name of the color, like green or blue. This is what physicists mean when they refer to different wavelengths. Then we might mention the *saturation* of the color—how pure it is. Pink is usually less saturated than fire-engine red. A grayish blue is usually less saturated than a pure blue. Pastels generally are less saturated than vivid colors. Light waves that are made up of different elements result in colors that are low in saturation. The third dimension of a color is its *brightness*—how dark or light it is. Sky blue is brighter than navy blue. The brightness of a color depends mainly on the strength of its energy source. The more light an object reflects the brighter it will be.

To mix colors, artists usually start with red, yellow, and blue pigments and combine them to create the colors they need. Psychologists also start with three colors, but they use lights instead of pigments. Any three colors that are widely separated on the spectrum can be combined to produce all the other colors. The psychologist usually starts with red, green, and blue.

The reason that the artist and the psychologist start with different colors is that the artist's color mixing is a *subtractive process*. Each of the artist's pigments absorbs a different part of the spectrum, thus subtracting some wavelengths from the total range of wavelengths reflected to the eye. Mixing red and green pigments, for example, results in a mixture that absorbs both the green and the red wavelengths and reflects only gray. Mixing lights, on the other hand, is an *additive process*—the wavelengths of one color are added to the wavelengths of another to produce a third. Projecting red and green lights together onto a white surface, for example, will result not in gray, but in yellow (see Figure 8–11).

Figure 8–10
The color solid. The dimension of hue is represented around the circumference. Saturation ranges along the radius from the inside to the outside of the solid. Brightness varies along the vertical axis.
(Photo courtesy of Inmont Corporation)

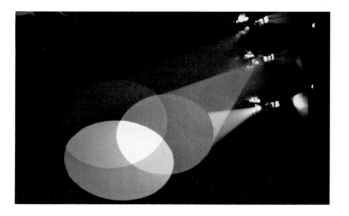

Figure 8–11
Mixing light waves is an additive process. When red and green are combined, the resulting hue is yellow. When all three basic colors are mixed, we see white.
(Fritz Goro, *Life Magazine*, © Times Inc.)

ever, seem to be translated by the bipolar neurons or by the ganglion cells into opponent-process form. These patterns of "on" and "off" firing of certain groups of neurons then carry the messages to the brain, and we see the colors of all the separate areas in our field of vision.

Hearing

There is an ancient question that asks, "If a tree falls in the woods and there is no one there, is there a sound?" A psychologist would answer, "There are sound waves, but there is no sound or noise."

SOUND

The physical stimuli for the sense of hearing are sound waves—the changes in pressure caused when molecules of air or fluid collide with one another then move apart again, transmitting energy at every bump. The simplest sound wave—what we hear as a pure tone—can be pictured as a sine wave (see Figure 8–12). The tuning fork vibrates, causing the molecules of air to first compress and then expand. The **frequency** of the waves is measured in cycles per second, expressed in a unit called **hertz (Hz).** Frequency primarily determines the **pitch** of the sound—how high or how low it is. The human ear responds to frequencies from about 20 Hz to 20,000 Hz. A bass viola can reach down to about 50 Hz, a piano to as high as 5,000 Hz. The height of the wave represents its **amplitude,** which, together with pitch, determines the *loudness* of a sound. Loudness is measured in **decibels** (see Figure 8–13).

The sounds we hear, however, seldom result from pure tones. Most fundamental tones also carry with them a load of **overtones**—accompanying sound waves that are different multiples of the frequency of the basic tone. A violin string, for example, does not only vibrate as a whole; it also vibrates in halves, thirds, quarters, and so on, all at the same time. Each set

Figure 8–12
The tuning fork, as it vibrates, alternately compresses and expands the molecules of air, creating a sound wave.

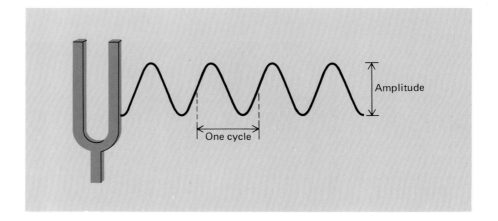

Figure 8–13

A decibel scale for several common sounds. Prolonged exposure to sounds above 85 decibels can cause permanent damage to the ears. As a further point of reference, one Rolling Stones concert was measured at 136 decibels.

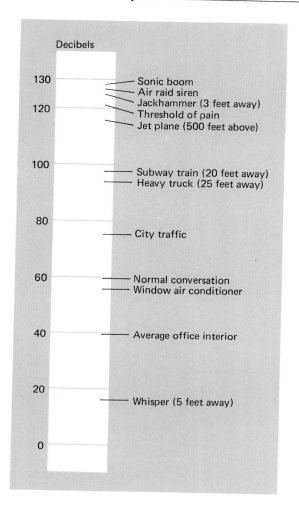

Decibels

130	Sonic boom
	Air raid siren
120	Jackhammer (3 feet away)
	Threshold of pain
	Jet plane (500 feet above)
100	Subway train (20 feet away)
	Heavy truck (25 feet away)
80	City traffic
60	Normal conversation
	Window air conditioner
40	Average office interior
20	Whisper (5 feet away)
0	

We would probably describe the sound made by this drill as "loud" and the sound made by the triangle as "high."

(Top: L. L. T. Rhodes, Taurus Photos; bottom: Jeffrey Foxx, Woodfin Camp & Associates)

of vibrations produces a tone. The complex pattern of overtones determines the **timbre**—or "texture"—of the sound.

THE EAR

Hearing begins when sound waves bump up against the eardrum (see Figure 8–14) and cause it to vibrate. The quivering of the eardrum causes three tiny bones in the middle ear—called the **hammer,** the **anvil,** and the **stirrup**—to hit each other in sequence and to carry the vibrations to the inner ear. The last of these three bones, the stirrup, is attached to a membrane called the **oval window.** Just below the oval window is another membrane, called the **round window,** which equalizes the pressure in the inner ear when the stirrup hits against the oval window.

The air waves are magnified during their trip through the middle ear. Thus, when the oval window starts to vibrate at the touch of the stirrup, it

Figure 8–14
The structure of the human ear.

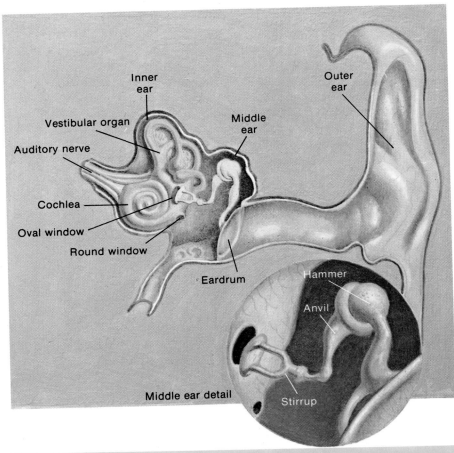

Figure 8–15
If the cochlea were uncoiled and stretched out, it would look something like this.

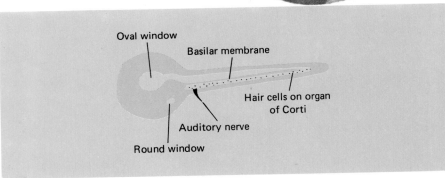

has a powerful effect on the inner ear. There, the vibrations are transmitted to the fluid inside a snail-shaped structure called the **cochlea.** The cochlea is divided lengthwise by the **basilar membrane.** The basilar membrane is stiffer near the oval and round windows, and gets gradually more flexible as it coils inward toward its other end. When the fluids in the cochlea begin to move, the basilar membrane is pushed up and down, bringing the vibrations deeper into the inner ear.

Lying on top of the basilar membrane, and moving with it, is the **organ of Corti** (see Figure 8–15). It is here that the messages from the sound waves finally reach the receptor cells, creating the sense of hearing. The receptors—millions of tiny hair cells—are pushed and pulled by the vibrations of the fluid inside the cochlea. The hair cells cause their adjacent bipolar neurons to fire, sending out a coded message through the auditory nerve about the pattern of vibrations the sound wave has created.

NEURAL CONNECTIONS. The sense of hearing is truly bilateral. Each ear sends messages to both cerebral hemispheres. The switching station where the nerve fibers from the ears cross over is in the medulla, part of the hindbrain. From the medulla, other nerve fibers carry the messages from the ear to the higher parts of the brain. Some messages go to the brain centers that coordinate the movements of the eyes, head, and ears. Others travel through the reticular activating system, which probably tacks on a few special "wake-up" or "ho-hum" postscripts to the sound messages. The primary destinations, of course, are the auditory projection areas in the **temporal lobes** of the two cerebral hemispheres. Along the way, the auditory messages pass through at least four levels of neurons, a much less direct route than in the visual system. At each stage, auditory information becomes more precisely coded.

As we grow older, we lose some of our ability to hear low-intensity sounds (McBurney & Collings, 1977). We can hear high-intensity sounds, however, as well as ever. This is why elderly people may ask you to speak louder and then, when you oblige by speaking much louder, tell you, "There's no need to shout!"

THEORIES OF HEARING

So far we have said nothing about how the different sound-wave patterns that reach our ears are coded into neural messages—how the tiny organ of Corti can tell the brain how loud a sound is or what pitch it has. The millions of tiny hair cells send messages about the infinite variations in the pitch, loudness, and timbre of sounds, as well as their location and duration. The loudness of a sound seems to depend on how many neurons are activated—the more neurons that fire, the louder the sound seems to be.

The coding of messages about pitch is more complicated. There are two basic views on pitch discrimination: **place theories** and **frequency theories.** The place theory states that the brain determines pitch by noting the *place* on the basilar membrane where the message originates. Helmholtz—the same man who helped develop the trichromatic theory of color vision—believed that fibers located at different places on the basilar membrane reacted to different tones. More recently, Georg von Bekesy alternatively proposed that as the sound waves travel through the cochlear fluid, they cause different places on the basilar membrane to move in direct proportion to the pitch of the sound wave.

The second type of theory of pitch discrimination states that the *frequency* of vibrations of the basilar membrane is translated into an equivalent *frequency* of nerve impulses. Thus, if a hair cell is pulled or pushed rapidly, it fires off a high frequency message to the brain. Neurons cannot fire, however, as rapidly as the frequency of the highest pitched sound that can be heard. This problem has led theorists to suggest a **volley principle.** The nerve cells, they maintain, fire in sequence: One neuron fires, then a second one, then a third. By then, the first neuron has had time to recover and can fire again. If necessary, the three neurons together can send a rapid series of impulses to the brain. Neither the place theory nor the frequency theory alone, however, fully explains pitch discrimination, so some combination of the two is needed. The volley principle, for example, works quite well to explain the ear's responses to frequencies up to about 4,000 Hz. Above that, however, the place theory provides a better explanation of what is happening.

Sensory Adaptation

Each of our senses undergoes constant change—from no stimulation to stimulation, from less stimulation to more, and vice versa. But when the intensity of stimulation stays the same for a while, we get used to that constant level. For example, when you first get into a bath the water may feel unbearably hot. Your skin soon adapts to the heat, however, and you feel comfortably warm. This phenomenon is known as **adaptation.** When the receptor cells adapt to a constant level of stimulation, they become less sensitive. Then, when the level of stimulation is increased or decreased, the receptor cells become sensitive again. Sensory adaptation may complicate the task of the psychologist who is trying to measure sensations, but it is really one of the body's most important mechanisms for adjusting to and surviving in the world. For example, miners do not lose their way in the semidarkness of mine shafts.

The most rapid sensory adaptation probably occurs in the sense of smell. We get accustomed to smells quickly, especially strong ones. People who live in a paper mill town rarely notice the putrid smell that would repel a passing visitor. The rate of adaptation, however, appears to differ in degree for various odors. And while women's senses of smell are generally more acute than those of men, this sensitivity in women may change from day to day. Sensitivity to odor also seems to decrease with age (Engen, 1973).

The sense of taste, too, adapts quickly, more quickly than the sense of hearing or the sense of vision. Taste adaptation is complicated. For instance, adaptation to one kind of salt lowers the threshold of sensitivity to other salts, and adaptation to one kind of acid usually affects the sensitivity to other acids. This kind of cross-adaptation in the sense of taste is not fully understood. More information is needed about the activities of the taste cells and about how their messages are coded and interpreted by the nervous system.

Visual adaptation is slower than adaptation to tastes or smells. Obviously, it is important for our safety and our pleasure that visual adaptation occur slowly and rarely be complete. Visual adaptation is only partial because light stimulation is rarely focused on the same rods and cones long enough for them to become wholly insensitive. In fact, research has shown that objects vanish from perception when their images on the retina are held perfectly still. Small, involuntary eye movements cause the image on the

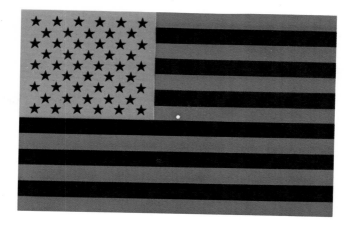

Figure 8–16
Stare at the white spot in the center of this flag for about 30 seconds. Then look at a blank piece of white paper and you will see an after-image.

(Photo courtesy of Inmont Corporation)

retina to drift slowly from the fovea, and then to bring it back again with only a tiny flick. At the same time, the eyes continually show a slight, extremely rapid tremor. This tremor is so minute that it goes completely unnoticed. Yet it is almost impossible to stop these movements without damaging the eye. All these movements together keep the image moving around the retina which stops the receptors from completely adapting to the image.

The receptors of the eye also partly adapt to overall levels of light and dark. Adaptation to the dark after bright daylight takes place in two stages. The cones recover first. After about 10 minutes, they become as sensitive as they are going to be at detecting objects in the dark. The rods, on the other hand, do not reach maximum sensitivity until about 30 minutes after encountering darkness. But even with **dark adaptation,** there is not enough energy in dim light to stimulate the cones to respond to colors. As a result, you see a black–and–white world of different brightnesses—except, as observed earlier, for some familiar objects, where we tend to "add on" the known color of the object despite the lack of color information that we receive from the environment.

When you first go out into bright light, your eyes will be very sensitive, sometimes painfully so. In the dark, both the cones and the rods have had a chance to build up a good supply of light-absorbing pigments, which the light affects immediately. All the neurons fire at once, overwhelming you. You squint and shield your eyes, and use up some of the pigment stored in the cones. It was once thought that this bleaching of the cone's pigment was the major part of light adaptation. It now seems that the changes in the bipolar cells are far more important. The intensity of the background or adapting light is also important to the ease of adaptation.

Afterimages are one of the odder phenomena associated with visual adaptation. If you look at Figure 8–16 for about 30 seconds, and then look at a sheet of white paper, you will see an afterimage. This is one of the effects that caused Hering to question the trichromatic theory of color mentioned earlier in this chapter. Hering's explanation for afterimages is that the receptors in the red–green set have reversed themselves. When you were looking at the figure, they were sending "green" messages; but when the stimulation was withdrawn they readjusted, and in the process now send "red" messages. Hering claimed that the opponent-process system was designed to reestablish equilibrium when neural activity had been "disturbed."

Perception

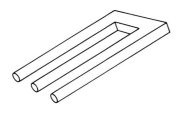

The eye records patterns of light and dark, but it does not "see" a red light. The eardrum vibrates in a particular fashion but it does not "hear" a symphony. Seeing and hearing meaningful patterns in the jumble of sensory information is what we mean by *perception*. In Chapter 6 we discussed how information from the sensory registers is selected, attended to, and identified. Here we will examine the immediate results of that process: our perceptual experiences.

Ultimately, it is the brain that shapes the complex flow of information from the senses. This is true even when information fed to the brain is contradictory—as in some optical illusions. The many familiar "impossible objects," such as the "two-pronged trident" at the left, are often seen at first glance as ordinary figures, owing to the brain's tendency to organize sensory input into familiar, acceptable patterns.

Gestalt psychologists were among the first to systematically study how sensory impressions are organized by the brain. This school of psychological thought developed in Germany in the early 20th century. The word *gestalt* has no exact English equivalent, but essentially means "whole" or "pattern." The Gestalt psychologists believed that the brain creates a coherent perceptual experience that is more than simply the sum of its various sensory perceptions.

The most fundamental principle identified by Gestaltists is probably the perceptual distinction between a **figure** and the **ground** it appears against. A colorfully upholstered chair stands out against darker furniture in a room. A marble statue is perceived as a whole figure standing out from the ground of a red brick wall.

Sometimes, however, the contrast between figure and ground does not give us enough cues to decide which is which. In those instances, we have a **reversible figure** like those shown in Figures 8–17, 8–18, and 8–19. At first glance, we may see white figures against a black background, but a second glance may present just the opposite image. It should also be noted that the figure–ground relationship extends to other senses besides the visual sense. It helps us to distinguish a violin solo against the ground of a symphony orchestra, or a single voice amid cocktail party chatter.

Some studies have reached interesting conclusions about figure and ground:

1. The contour—or outline—appears to belong to the figure, not to the ground.
2. The figure seems to have form, while the background appears to be formless.
3. The figure always appears to be in front of the ground, while the ground extends behind the figure.
4. The figure has the nature of a thing, while the ground is often perceived as nothing in particular.
5. The figure is more easily remembered.

An optical illusion: The perspective in this photo makes the people in the foreground seem to be much bigger in relation to the Eiffel Tower than they really are.
(Peter Buckley)

Figure 8–17
Figure and ground are clearly distinguished at the top and bottom of this woodcut by M. C. Escher, but in the middle, they alternate.
(Haags Gemeentemuseum, The Hague)

Figure 8–18
The reversible figure and ground cause us to see first devils and then angels in each of the rings.
(Haags Gemeentemuseum, The Hague)

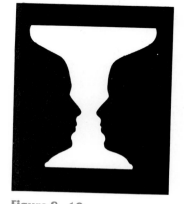

Figure 8–19
This figure can be seen either as a white cup against a blue background, or as two blue faces against a white ground.

Figure 8–20
We tend to perceive all these figures as ''closed'' objects, not as separate lines.

(Lisa Osta)

Even if this sign read STTOP or STOPP, we would still most likely see it as STOP.
(Susan McCartney, Photo Researchers)

Another important principle of sensory organization is **closure.** This refers to our inclination to overlook incompleteness in our sensations and to perceive a finished unit even where none really exists. If we see only partial outlines, as in Figure 8–20, for example, we tend to fill in the missing lines and perceive the objects as a whole. The same thing happens with aural sensations. Often, during long distance telephone calls, we hear only bits and pieces of sentences, but we can, nonetheless, fill in the gaps and perceive the sounds as whole words and sentences.

Gestaltists also identified the principle of **continuity.** That is, objects that continue a pattern or a direction tend to be perceived as a group. Closely allied to this is the principle of **proximity.** When objects are close to each other, we tend to perceive them together rather than separately. This principle also extends to aural sensations. "Did he tell you what the night rate is?" means something quite different from, "Did he tell you what the nitrate is?" Both sentences contain the same sounds, but how the speaker groups the sounds—where he or she pauses—will usually determine how the sounds are perceived.

Similarity is another principle of grouping. Objects that are of a similar color, size, or shape are usually perceived as part of a pattern. Gestalt theorists also recognized the principle of **common fate.** Objects that are in motion together—a precision flying team, runners in a marathon race—are perceived as distinct from the objects around them.

Gestalt psychologists also recognized that past experience and expectations about how the world operates affect how a person perceives things. For example, in a well-known children's game, a piece of cardboard with a red stop sign is flashed in front of you. What did the sign say? Nearly everyone will say that the sign read "STOP." But, in fact, the sign is misprinted "STOPP" or "STTOP." Because we are used to stop signs reading "STOP," we tend to perceive the familiar symbol rather than the misprint.

For the most part, Gestalt psychology as a separate school of thought no longer exists, but contemporary psychology has built on many of the Gestalt principles in trying to understand how we create perceptual experiences out of sensory information.

PERCEPTUAL CONSTANCIES

Perceptual constancy refers to the tendency to perceive objects as relatively stable and unchanging, despite changing sensory information. Without this ability, the world would be completely confusing. Once we have formed a stable perception of an object, we can recognize it from almost any position, at almost any distance, under almost any illumination. A white house is perceived as a white house by day or by night and from any angle. We see it as the same house. The sensory information changes, but the object is perceived as constant.

Objects tend to be perceived as being their true size, regardless of the size of the image they cast on the retina of our eyes. As Figure 8–21 shows, the farther away an object is from the lens of the eye, the smaller the retinal image it casts. For example, a 6-foot-tall man standing 20 feet away casts a

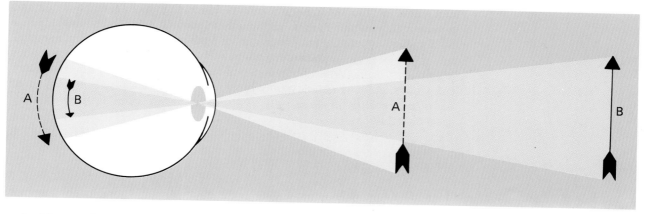

retinal image that is only 50 percent of the size of the retinal image he casts at a distance of 10 feet. Yet he is not perceived as having shrunk to 3 feet. **Size constancy** depends partly on experience—information about the relative sizes of objects is stored in long-term memory—and partly on distance cues.

When there are no distance cues, size constancy has to rely solely on what we have learned from our previous experience with an object. Naturally, more errors occur when there are no distance cues, but fewer than one would expect in view of the radical changes in the size of the retinal image. We might guess that a woman 20 feet away is 5'4" instead of 5'8", but hardly anyone would perceive her as being 3 feet tall, no matter how far away she is. We know from experience that adults are seldom that short.

Familiar objects also tend to be seen as having a constant shape, even though the retinal images they cast change as they are viewed from different angles. A dinner plate is perceived as a circle, even when it is tilted and the retinal image is oval. A rectangular door will only project a rectangular image on the retina when it is viewed directly from the front. From any other angle, it casts a trapezoidal image on the retina, but it is not perceived as having suddenly become a trapezoidal door. These are examples of **shape constancy.**

Two other important constancies are **brightness constancy** and **color constancy.** In the former, although we observe that the amount of light available to our eyes varies greatly, the perceived brightness of familiar objects hardly varies at all. We perceive a sheet of white paper as white whether we see it in candlelight or under a bright bulb. Likewise, we perceive a piece of coal as black whether we see it in a dark cellar or in noon-day sunlight. This may seem obvious, but bear in mind that coal in sunlight reflects more light than white paper in candlelight, yet we always perceive white paper as being brighter. The explanation for brightness constancy is that a white object—or a black or gray one—will reflect the same percentage of the light falling on it, no matter if the light is from a candle, a fluorescent lamp, or the sun. What is important is not the absolute amount of light the object reflects but how the relative reflection compares to the surrounding objects.

Similarly, we tend to perceive familiar objects as keeping their color,

Figure 8-21
The relationship between distance and the size of the retinal image. Object A and Object B are the same size, but A, being much closer to the eye, casts a much larger image on the retina.

regardless of the information that reaches the eye. If you own a red automobile, you will see it as red whether it is on a brightly lit street, or in a dark garage, where the small amount of light may send your eye a message that the color is closer to brown or black than red. But color constancy does not always occur. When objects are unfamiliar or there are no customary color cues, color constancy may be distorted—as when we buy a pair of pants in a brightly lit store, only to discover that in ordinary daylight they are a different shade.

OBSERVER CHARACTERISTICS

Clearly, our perceptual experience depends on more than just the immediate information we receive from our sense organs. As we saw, perceptual constancy depends greatly on experience and learning. Several other factors can also affect perception, such as a person's particular motivations and values, expectations, cognitive style, and what he or she has experienced growing up in a certain culture.

MOTIVATION. Our desires and needs may strongly influence our perceptions. People in need are more likely to perceive something that they think will satisfy that need.

Several interesting experiments have tested the influence of hunger on perception. Sanford (1937) found that if people were deprived of food for some time and were then shown vague or ambiguous pictures, they were apt to perceive the pictures as being related to food. Similarly, McClelland and Atkinson (1948) showed blurred pictues to people who had not eaten for varying times. Some had eaten 1 hour before; others had gone as long as 16 hours without food. Those who had not eaten for 16 hours perceived the blurred images as pictures of food more often than those who had eaten just 1 hour before.

Another experiment showed how strongly perceptions can be affected by a person's values. Nursery-school children were shown a poker chip. Each child was asked to compare the size of the chip to the size of a circle of light until the child perceived the chip and the circle of light as being the same size. The children were then shown a machine with a crank. When a child turned the crank, he or she received a poker chip, which could be exchanged for candy. Thus, the children were taught to value the poker chips more highly than they had before. After the children had been rewarded with the candy for cranking out the poker chips, they were again asked to compare the size of the chips to a circle of light. This time the chips seemed larger to the children (Lambert, Solomon, & Watson, 1949).

EXPECTATIONS. Knowing in advance what we are supposed to perceive can influence our perception. Siipola (1935) showed how prior expectations affected people's responses to certain words. He told one group of people that they would be shown words related to animals. For a brief moment, he showed them combinations of letters that really did not spell anything—like "sael," "dack," and "wharl." Most of the group perceived the letters as the words "seal," "deck," and "whale." He then told a second group that he was

Figure 8–22
Look first at the drawing on the left and ask a friend to look at the one on the right. When you both look at the one in the middle, you will probably perceive it differently, because your expectations are different.

(From R. W. Leeper, "A Study of a Neglected Portion of the Field of Learning: The Development of Sensory Organization." *Pedagogical Seminary and Journal of Genetic Psychology*, 1935, *46*, 41–75. Courtesy of Journal Press.)

going to show them words about boats, and showed them the same letter combinations. This group, expecting to see nautical terms, perceived the same letter combinations as the words "sail," "deck," and "wharf."

PERSONALITY AND PERCEPTION. As we mature, we develop a *cognitive style*—our own general method of dealing with the environment. Some psychologists distinguish between two general approaches people use in perceiving the world (Witkin et al., 1962). The first is the "field-dependent" approach. A person perceives the environment as a whole and does not clearly differentiate the shape, color, size, or other qualities of individual items. If field-dependent people are asked to draw a human figure, they usually do not draw the figure so that it stands out clearly against the background. People who are "field independent," on the other hand, tend to perceive the elements of the environment as separate and distinct from each other and to draw each element as standing out from the background.

Another way of defining cognitive styles is to distinguish between "levelers" and "sharpeners"—those who level out the distinctions between objects and those who magnify them. To investigate the differences between these two approaches, Klein (1951) showed people sets of squares of varying sizes and asked them to estimate the size of each of the squares. One group, the "levelers," failed to perceive any difference in their size. The "sharpeners," however, were aware of the differences in the size of the squares and changed their size estimates accordingly.

CULTURAL BACKGROUND. Cultural background can also influence people's perceptions. As noted in Chapter 6, the language people speak can affect how they perceive their surroundings and their experiences. Other cultural differences can influence how people use perceptual cues.

In the West, for example, the square and the rectangle are the most common shapes. Most buildings are built on rectangular lines; the round church, house, or barn is the exception. Furniture is usually square or rectangular: rectangular beds, tables, and desks are made to fit into rectangular rooms. Streets usually run at right angles to one another. Farmers plow their rectangular fields in neat, straight furrows.

In other societies, however, other shapes predominate. Among the Zulu, for example, the circle is much more prevalent than the rectangle. The

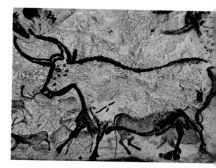

Our perceptions depend a great deal on our cultural cues and experiences. For example, we would probably not perceive animals the way our paleolithic ancestors did.
(Peter Buckley)

Zulus arrange their huts in circles. The huts themselves are round with round doors. They plow in curved furrows that follow the contours of the land. Their language has no words for squares or rectangles.

Other perceptual judgments depend on cues that may be more prevalent in one culture than in another. The Mbuti pygmies of Zaire, for example, seldom leave the forest and rarely encounter objects that are more than a few feet away. On one occasion, Colin Turnbull (1961), an anthropologist, took a pygmy guide named Kenge on a trip out onto the plains. When Kenge looked across the plain and saw a herd of buffalo, he asked what kind of insects they were. He refused to believe that the tiny black spots he saw were buffalo. As he and Turnbull drove toward the herd, Kenge believed that magic was making the animals grow larger. Because he had no experience of distant objects, he could not perceive the buffalo as having constant size.

Let us now look at two basic perceptual phenomena—distance and depth, and movement—to see how we use both stimulus information and past experience to create perceptual experiences.

PERCEPTION OF DISTANCE AND DEPTH

We constantly have to judge the distance between us and other objects. When we walk through a classroom, our perception of distance helps us to avoid bumping into desks or tripping over a wastebasket. If we reach out to pick up a pencil, we automatically judge how far we extend our arms. We also constantly judge the depth of objects—how much total space they occupy. In doing so, we seem to ask ourselves—often without being aware of the question—"How big is this object? How thick or thin is it?"

We use many of the same cues to determine the distance and the size of objects. Some of these cues depend on visual messages that one eye alone can transmit and are called *monocular cues*. Others—called *binocular cues*—require the use of both eyes.

MONOCULAR CUES. Having two eyes allows us to make more accurate judgments about distance and depth, particularly when objects are relatively near. But the monocular cues for distance and depth often let us judge distance and depth successfully by using only one eye.

We depend upon the visual images sent by either one or both eyes to determine the distance and size of objects.
(Peter Buckley)

Figure 8–23
Because the king of clubs has been superimposed on the blank card, we perceive it as being closer. When the cards are spaced out, however, we can see that the cards have been notched to create an illusion, and that the king of spades is actually no farther away than the king of clubs.

Superposition, when one object partly blocks a second object, is an important relative distance cue. The first object is perceived as being closer, the second as more distant (see Figure 8–23).

As all students of art know, there are several ways *perspective* can help in estimating distance and depth. Two parallel lines that extend into the distance seem to come together at some point on the horizon. This cue to distance and depth is known as **linear perspective.** In **aerial perspective,** distant objects have a hazy appearance and a somewhat blurred outline. On a clear day, mountains often seem to be much closer than they do on a hazy day when their outlines become blurred. The **elevation** of an object is another perspective cue to depth. An object that is on a higher horizontal plane seems to be farther away than one on a lower plane.

Figure 8–24
Because of its higher elevation and the suggestion of depth provided by the road, the tree on the right is perceived as being farther away and therefore larger.

Texture is a monocular cue that helps us to determine the distances and depths of objects.
(Kazuyoshi Nomachi, Photo Researchers)

Still another helpful monocular cue to distance and depth is **texture gradient.** An object that is close seems to have a rough or detailed texture. As distance increases, the texture becomes finer until finally the original texture cannot be clearly distinguished, if at all. A man standing on a pebbly beach, for example, can distinguish the gray stones and gravel beside his feet. As he looks off down the beach, however, the stones will seem to become smaller and finer until eventually he will be unable to note individual stones.

Shadowing can provide another important cue to distance and to the depth and solidity of an object. Normally, shadows appear on the parts of objects that are farther away. The shadowing on the outer edges of a spherical object, such as a ball or globe, gives it a three-dimensional quality. Without this shadowing, the object might be perceived as a flat disk. The shadow an object casts behind itself can also give a cue to its depth. And the presence of shadows either before or behind objects can help to indicate how far away they are.

People traveling on buses or trains often notice that the trees or telephone poles that are close to the road or the railroad tracks seem to flash past the windows, while buildings and other objects that are farther away seem to move slowly. You can observe the same effect if you stand still and move your head from side to side. The objects close to you are perceived as moving very quickly; those that are farther away seem to move more slowly. These differences in the speeds of *movement* of images across the retina as you move give an important cue to distance and depth. Also, you will notice that if you fix your gaze on an object in the middle distance, as you turn your head from side to side, images closer to you than your focusing spot tend to move in opposition to your head while images farther from your focusing spot tend to move with your head. This distance cue is known as **motion parallax.**

In the process known as **accommodation,** the lens of the eye changes its curvature to focus different objects on the retina. If the object is close, the lens is made rounder; if the object is farther away, the lens is flattened. Sensations from the muscles that cause these changes provide another cue to how near or far an object is. This is a weaker cue than convergence, however, one of the binocular cues discussed in the next section.

BINOCULAR CUES. All the cues discussed so far depend on the action of only one eye. Many animals, such as horses, deer, and fish, depend entirely on monocular cues, although they have two eyes. Because their eyes are set on the sides of their heads, the two visual fields do not overlap. But humans, apes, and many predatory animals—such as lions, tigers, and wolves—have a distinct physical advantage over these animals. Because both eyes are set in the front of the head, the visual fields overlap. The **stereoscopic vision** obtained from combining the two retinal images makes the perception of depth and distance more accurate.

Because our eyes are set approximately 2½ inches apart, each one has a slightly different view of things. The difference between the two images the eyes receive is known as **retinal disparity.** The left eye receives more information about the left side of an object, and the right eye receives more information about the right side. You can easily prove that each of your

Because the lion's visual fields overlap, he can discern distances more accurately than the horse.
(Left: Tom McHugh, Photo Researchers; right: Elizabeth Weiland, Rapho/Photo Researchers)

eyes receives a different image: Close one eye and line up a finger with some vertical line, like the edge of a door. Then open that eye and close the other one. Your finger will appear to have moved a great distance. When you look at the finger with both eyes, however, the two different images become one.

Another binocular cue to distance comes from the muscles that control the **convergence** of the eyes. When we look at objects that are fairly close to us, our eyes tend to converge—to turn slightly inward toward each other. The sensations from the muscles that control this movement of the eyes provide another cue to distance. If the object is very close, such as the end of the nose, the eyes cannot converge and two separate images are perceived. If the object is more than 60 or 70 feet away, the sight lines of the eyes are more or less parallel and there is no convergence.

VISUAL ILLUSIONS

False distance or depth cues explain many visual illusions. We perceive objects that cannot exist because we are led to believe false things about distance and depth. Figure 8–25 shows examples of some visual stimuli that give misleading depth cues. For example, the strange triangle is constructed so that a fake depth cue seems to signal a three-dimensional figure that clearly cannot exist. Other figures that fool us by presenting false depth cues are Figure 8–26E, where the top line is perceived as shorter; the visual illusion in Figure 8–26F; and the Ames room in Figure 8–27, in which there are three-dimensional illusory cues.

The effects of a misleading distance cue can even be seen in nature. The full moon seems larger when it first rises over the horizon than later on when it is higher in the sky. Yet, photographs prove that its size does not change at all. If you wish to test this for yourself, hold a pencil at arm's length and measure the moon when it is in different positions in the sky. Why the moon, the sun, and the constellations all seem larger when they are nearer the horizon has puzzled people for thousands of years. Today, most researchers explain it with the *apparent-distance theory* proposed by Kaufman and Rock (1962). This theory is based on the fact that an object appears smaller when it is farther away and seems to grow larger as it approaches us. To most people, the horizon seems farther away than the sky, which seems to be directly overhead. Thus, we perceive the moon at the horizon as larger to make up for its apparently greater distance from us. When the terrain is blocked out, the moon at the horizon does not appear larger than the moon at the zenith. The impression of distance is apparently created by the terrain.

In other illusions, the visual information is ambiguous, so that without better distance and depth cues we cannot decide which perception is correct. In Figure 8–26A, is the cube facing to the left or to the right? Which way can you pass through the coils—left or right? Do you see a flight of stairs or an overhanging cornice in Figure 8–26C? The answer here is always "both." Moreover, the more you stare at the figures, the more confusing they become—shifting first one way, then another. Reversible figures like these clearly show that without adequate information from the

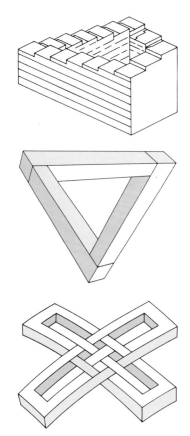

Figure 8–25
In these "impossible figures" each individual part seems acceptable to us, but as we follow along the surface lines, we must continually form new interpretations to adapt to the everchanging apparent distance of the object.

visual stimulus, we must search for the best way to interpret them.

According to R. L. Gregory (1966), the sensory information from a reversible figure can come from either of two different stimuli. Since the visual information does not provide enough clues to tell us which hypothesis is correct, we keep shifting from one to the other. In other situations,

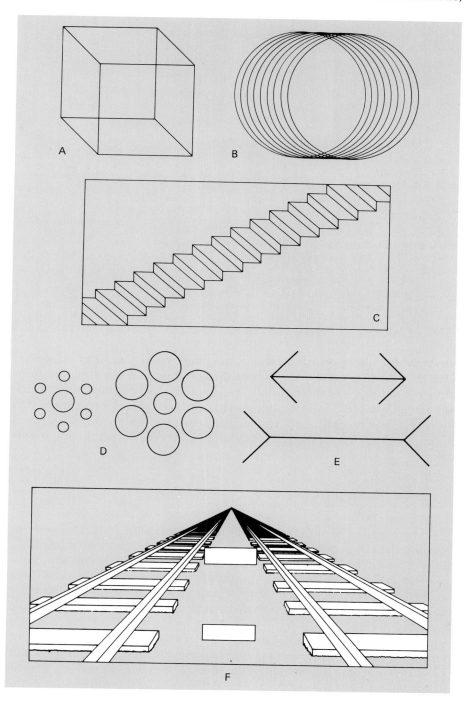

Figure 8–26
A, B, and C are examples of reversible figures. Each drawing can be interpreted in two different ways. D, E, and F show that through the effect of misleading contexts we misjudge the size of objects.
(Adapted from R. L. Gregory, *Eye and Brain*, New York: McGraw-Hill, 1966.)

Figure 8–27
The Ames room. Most people watch with disbelief as the man seems to grow taller as he crosses the room. But the room actually has a tilted floor, and that is what misleads us.

(William Vandivert/*Scientific American*)

we may turn to contextual clues—the context of size and shape for example. Some visual illusions—like those in Figure 8–26—rely on deliberate manipulation of these contextual clues. It is clear from all of this that we use all available information to create a perceptual experience that makes sense of the information available to us, even if sometimes the result is "impossible." The same process can be observed in perceiving movement.

PERCEPTION OF MOVEMENT

The perception of movement is also a complicated process, involving both the visual messages from the eye as an image moves across the retina, and the messages from the muscles around the eye as they shift the eye to follow a moving object. At times, our perceptual processes play tricks on us and we think we perceive movement when the objects we are looking at are really not moving at all. We must distinguish, therefore, between real and apparent movement.

Real movement means the physical displacement of an object from one position to another. The perception of real movement depends only in part on the movement of images across the retina of the eye. If a man stands still and moves his head to look around him, the images of all the objects in the room will pass across his retina. Yet he will probably perceive all these objects as stationary. Even if he holds his head still and moves only his eyes, the images continue to pass across the retina. But the messages from the eye muscles seem to counteract those from the retina, and the objects in the room are perceived as motionless.

Therefore, the perception of real movement seems to be determined less by images moving across the retina than by how the position of objects change in relation to a background that is perceived as stationary. When we perceive a car moving along a street, for example, we see the street, the buildings, and the sidewalk as a stationary background and the car as a moving object. Remarkably, the brain can distinguish between these retinal images of an object moving against an immobile background and all the other moving images on the retina.

It is possible, under certain conditions, to see movement in objects that are really standing still. One form of *apparent movement* is the **autokinetic illusion**—the perceived motion created by a single stationary object. If you stand in a room that is absolutely dark except for one tiny spot of light and stare at the light for a few seconds, you will begin to see the light drift. In the darkened room, your eyes have no visible framework. There are no cues to tell that the light is really stationary. The slight movements of the eye muscles, which go unnoticed all the time, make the light appear to move.

Another form of illusory movement is **stroboscopic motion**—the apparent motion created by a rapid series of images of stationary objects. A motion picture, for example, is not in motion at all. The film consists of a series of still pictures, showing people or objects in slightly different positions. When the separate images are projected in sequence onto the screen, the people or objects seem to be moving because of the rapid change from one still picture to the next.

Stroboscopic motion also causes a perceptual illusion known as the **phi phenomenon.** When a light is flashed on at a certain point in a darkened room, then flashed off, and a second light is flashed on a split second later at a point a short distance away, most people will perceive a single spot of light moving from one point to another. Of course, the distance between the two points, the intensity of the two lights, and the time interval between them must be carefully controlled for the illusion to succeed. The same perceptual process causes us to see motion in neon signs or theater marquees, where words appear to move from one side to the other as different combinations of stationary lights are flashed on and off.

When this filmstrip is projected onto a screen, the people will appear to be moving. This illusion of movement is known as stroboscopic motion.
(Anita Duncan)

_____

Application

PERCEPTION AND THE BLIND

A woman who had been blind from birth finally had the operation that would enable her to see. One of her first sights after the operation

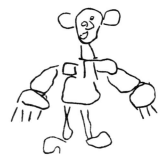

Drawn by people blind from birth, these illustrations portray, from top to bottom, crossed fingers, a figure running (one leg is foreshortened), and a boy.

(From Nancy Hechinger, "Seeing Without Eyes," _Science 81,_ March, p. 41)

was her own reflection in a mirror. Her response: "I thought I was better looking."

This story illustrates what many people have always suspected: Blind people have visual images, though they may never have actually seen anything. The question of _how_ blind people visualize the world and where they get their information is of great interest to psychologists and researchers in the field of perception and sensation.

In the 1930s, Marius von Senden, a German scientist, studied the perceptions of people who had been born blind and were later cured. One patient thought that people and trees looked alike, because they both have a central trunk that you can put your arms around, no sharp edges, and limbs that emerge from the trunk. She was quite surprised to discover, upon being cured, that people and trees look so different.

John Kennedy, a psychologist at the University of Toronto, has studied how blind people perceive by asking them to draw various objects. Since the blind perceive objects only through touch, Kennedy wished to see if they could convey their sense of objects through line drawings. He was surprised to note that the blind people in his study quickly realized that some aspects of reality must be sacrificed in a drawing—that you cannot draw all sides of an object, for example. The blind artists devised ways to represent objects, such as a cup or a table, that were readily understood by people who could see. Kennedy was especially fascinated to find that his blind subjects understood the idea of occlusion—that objects in front will partly or totally obscure objects behind them.

Apparently, when blind people are cured, their initial sense impressions are very much like a newborn baby's—they see patches of brightness and darkness, but can barely perceive the details of objects. One blind man who, at 53, was cured, could not discern what a lathe was—although he had worked with one every day for years while blind—until he could touch and handle it. In the blind, touch appears to fill much of the void left by the lack of sight. It also seems that active blind people who are finally cured learn to see more quickly than passive blind people. Active exploration is vital to learning. Held and Hein (1963) performed some famous experiments in the 1960s with newborn kittens. The kittens were raised in total darkness, except for 1 hour a day, when they were allowed to see. During that hour, one group was allowed to move around a patterned cylinder, while the other group sat passively in a gondola pulled by a kitten from the active group. Later, both groups were released. The active kittens learned to see normally, the passive kittens did not.

Another fascinating aspect of visual perception is "blindsight." This is the apparent ability of a person whose blindness is the result of a damaged cortex to perceive light without actually "seeing" it. Normally, the eyes send messages to the visual cortex where we consciously "see." When the cortex is damaged, we can no longer "see." But it seems that the eyes also send information to certain subcortical centers that usually remain unaffected by cortical damage. These areas of the brain function below our awareness. They are part of the more primitive, so-called "reptilian brain," which also controls our senses of orientation and coordination. As a result, blind people with blindsight can point at or turn their heads toward a flash of light without "seeing" or being "aware" of it (Hechinger & Lewin, 1981).

Summary

1. The study of sensation is the study of how the body's various receptor cells translate physical energy into neural messages; how those messages reach the central nervous system; and the experiences that result. Perception is the interpretation of this data by the brain.

2. In all sensory processes, some form of energy stimulates a receptor cell in one of the sense organs. The receptor cell then changes the energy it receives into an electromechanical neural impulse in a process known as *transduction and coding*. As the neural impulse travels through the sensory nerves to the central nervous system, it is processed further. By the time it reaches the brain its message is quite precise. The brain creates the "illusion" of sensory experience by interpreting the clicks on the optic and auditory fibers.

3. *Psychophysics* deals with the measurement of sensation. One measure of sensation is the *absolute threshold*—the minimum intensity of physical energy required to produce any sensation at all in a person. Another is the *difference threshold*—the smallest change in stimulation that a person can detect, also called the *just noticeable difference (j.n.d.)*.

4. The physical stimulus for the sense of vision is light. Light enters the eye through the *cornea* and passes through the *pupil*, which expands or contracts to let more or less light through. Inside the pupil, the light passes through the *lens*, which focuses it onto the *retina*.

5. There are two kinds of receptors in the retina—*rods* and *cones*. Cones operate mainly in daylight and respond to colors. Rods are primarily responsible for night vision when there is not enough light to stimulate the cones. The *fovea*—the depressed spot on the retina directly behind the lens—contains thousands of cones but no rods.

6. Rods and cones differ in shape, chemical pigments, and neural connections. The pigment in rods is *rhodopsin*. The pigment in cones has not yet been identified. Both break down into retinene and other chemical substances when struck by light, then recom-

bine. The chemical activity is thought to stimulate the *bipolar neurons*, which connect to the ganglion cells, whose axons make up the *optic nerve*. The nerve fibers from the right side of each eye travel to the right hemisphere of the brain, and vice versa. The fibers cross over at the *optic chiasma*.

7. When the intensity of stimulation remains constant for a time, the receptor cells become less sensitive. This phenomenon is known as *adaptation*, and it is important for adjustment and survival in the world. Adaptation happens more quickly in the sense of smell and taste than in the other senses.

8. There are two main theories of color vision. According to the *trichromatic theory*, the eye contains three different kinds of color receptors that respond to red, green, and blue light, respectively. By mixing these three basic colors, the eye can detect any color in the spectrum. The *opponent-process* theory accepts the notion of three different kinds of receptors, but claims that each receptor responds to either member of three basic color pairs: red and green, yellow and blue, and black and white (dark and light).

9. The physical stimuli for the sense of hearing are *sound waves*. The frequency of the waves determines the *pitch* of a sound; their *amplitude* determines *loudness;* and their *overtones* determine *timbre*.

10. There are two major theories of pitch discrimination. *Place theories* state that sound waves, depending on their pitch, cause different places on the basilar membrane to move. *Frequency* theories say that pitch is determined by the frequency of the firing of the nerve cells. Neither theory by itself fully explains pitch discrimination.

11. Perception is seeing and hearing meaningful patterns in the information our senses take in.

12. The brain tends to give form to the things it perceives, to organize sensory input into familiar patterns.

13. *Gestalt* psychologists distinguished between a *figure* and the *ground* against which it appears. They recognized the principle of *closure*, which refers to the tendency of the brain to overlook incompleteness in sensations and to perceive a finished unit where none really exists. The concept of *continuity* states that objects that continue a pattern or a direction tend to be perceived as a group. Likewise, the principle of *proximity* supposes that objects seen or heard close together tend to be perceived as a group. The principle of *similarity* states that objects that look alike are perceived as part of a pattern. According to the principle of *common fate*, objects that are in motion together are perceived as distinct from the objects around them.

14. *Perceptual constancy* refers to the tendency to perceive objects as relatively stable and unchanging, despite changing sensory images. Experience seems to compensate for the changing sensory images, leading to *size constancy, shape constancy,* and

brightness and *color constancy*. *Color constancy* is more easily thwarted than the others, as when we buy a pair of pants in a brightly lit store and discover that they are a different color in daylight.

15. Our desires and needs may strongly influence our perceptions. We tend to perceive things as we expect them to be. How an object is interpreted also depends on a person's values, expectations, cognitive style, and cultural background.

16. We can perceive *distance* or *depth* through *monocular cues*—from one eye—or *binocular cues*—which depend on the interaction of both eyes.

17. Monocular cues include *superposition, aerial* and *linear perspective, elevation, texture gradient, shadowing, movement, motion parallax,* and *accommodation.*

18. Binocular cues increase the accuracy of depth and distance perception. Each eye has a slightly different view of things. The difference between the images that the two eyes receive is called *retinal disparity.* Other binocular cues include *stereoscopic vision* and *convergence.*

19. At times, our senses mislead us into perceiving objects that cannot exist. This is particularly true in visual perception. Objects of this sort—impossible objects—are known as *visual* or *optical illusions.* Most illusions involve fake distance and depth cues, or ambiguous information.

20. Perception of *movement* is a complicated process involving both the visual messages from the retina and the kinesthetic messages from the muscles around the eye as they shift to follow a moving object.

21. The perception of *real movement*—the physical displacement of an object from one position to another—seems to be determined chiefly by changes in the position of objects in relation to a background that is perceived as stationary.

22. *Illusory movement* involves the perception of movement in objects that are actually standing still. The *autokinetic illusion* refers to the apparent motion created by a rapid series of images of stationary objects. *Stroboscopic motion* is the apparent motion created by a rapid series of images of stationary objects. It is responsible for the perceptual illusion known as the *phi phenomenon.*

Outline

Chapter 9

Motivation and Emotion

To watch the manipulation of motivation and emotion at a sophisticated level, we might turn to a detective story. At the beginning, all that we know is that a murder has been committed: After eating dinner with her family, sweet little old Miss Jones collapses and dies of strychnine poisoning. "Now, why would anyone do a thing like that?" everybody asks. The police ask the same question, in different terms: "Who has a *motive* for killing Miss Jones?" In a good mystery, the answer is, "Practically everybody."

The younger sister—now 75 years old—still bristles when she thinks of the tragic day 50 years ago when Miss Jones stole her sweetheart. The next-door neighbor, a frequent dinner guest, has been heard to say that if Miss Jones's poodle tramples his peonies one more time, he will. . . . The nephew, a major heir, is deeply in debt. The parlor maid has a guilty secret that Miss Jones knows. All four people were in the house on the night that Miss Jones was poisoned. And all four had easy access to strychnine, which was used to kill rats in Miss Jones's basement. All of these people had emotional reactions to Miss Jones: envy, anger, shame, and guilt. And all of them had motives for killing her.

These are the first things that come to mind when we think of a murder mystery. But look at some of the day-to-day happenings in the same story. Motivated by hunger, the family gets together for meals. The next-door neighbor is lonely and visits because he wants company. The parlor maid's guilty secret involves her sex drive. The poodle's presence in the peonies may spring from its need to eliminate wastes or from sheer curiosity. When Miss Jones dies, the tragedy draws the family together; their need for affiliation makes them seek one another out. Yet, they quickly become fearful; the drive for self-preservation makes each one wonder if the other is actually the killer. In all these less spectacular acts, motivation and emotion are also present. In this chapter, we shall discuss all these motives and emotions, from the most basic to the most complex.

Figure 9–1

The stages of motivation. First a stimulus (a bodily need, a cue in the environment) triggers a motive. The motive leads to behavior. When the behavior results in goal attainment, the organism achieves a state of rest, or freedom from tension, until the next stimulus.

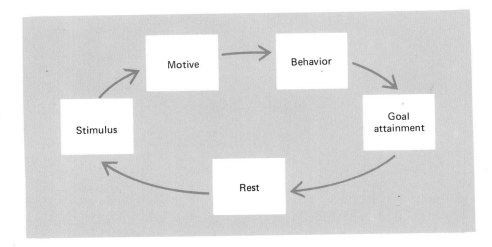

Both emotions and motives take their names from the Latin root meaning *to move*. At their most basic level, both motives and emotions move us to some kind of action—whether it be as dramatic as murder, or as mundane as drumming our fingers on a table because we are nervous. The relationships between emotions and motives are complex. Sometimes emotions are the bases of motives and vice versa. Anger can cause aggression, for instance, and hunger can lead to resentment. We shall begin this chapter by looking at motivation.

We might best think of **motivation** as a series of stages that we continually go through. Each series begins with a stimulus—perhaps a bodily need or an external cue in the environment. The stimulus triggers a **motive**—an arousal to action of one kind or another. The motive, in turn, activates and directs *behavior*. When this behavior attains its *goal*, the motive is satisfied and the chain of motivation is complete.

This process takes place whether we are aware of it or not. We do not have to know we are feeling hungry to go to the refrigerator, or to be conscious of a need for achievement to study for an exam. Moreover, the same motivation may produce different behaviors. Ambition might motivate one person to go to law school and another to join a crime ring. On the other hand, the same behavior may spring from different motives: You may buy liver because you like it, because it is cheap, or because your body "knows" that you need iron.

Primary Drives

We saw in Chapter 2 how several very basic motives, such as hunger and thirst, depend heavily on biological processes in the body. These motives are unlearned and are common to every animal, including humans. Thus, they are called **primary drives.**

Sometimes even these primary drives are triggered by stimuli outside of the body. For example, all of our hunger does not stem from our bodies' nutritional needs. External cues like the smell of a cake baking in the oven or a magazine picture of a juicy steak can trigger the hunger drive at almost any hour of the day. In fact, sometimes just looking at the clock and realizing it is "dinnertime" can make us hungry.

Although there is controversy over the causes of hunger, responses to hunger vary greatly with experience. For example, most people learn to eat three meals a day at more or less regular intervals, and to a large extent what they choose to eat is governed by learning. Most Americans, for example, love milk, but the Chinese have a strong aversion to it (Balagura, 1973). A cola drink may provide the sweetness of orange juice and the stimulation of coffee, but you would probably not have it with bacon and eggs for breakfast. Emotional factors can also affect hunger. You may sit down to the table and be starving, but then have an argument that "turns off" your desire to eat. Social factors can make a meal a ceremony, and elaborate rituals have grown up around the offering and accepting of food.

Thirst, too, can be a response to cues in the environment. On a hot summer day, seeing a glass of lemonade can make us feel thirsty. And what we drink is greatly affected by learning and experience. Water is water, but in chic restaurants people pay $2 a glass for water imported from France. Some people avoid coffee, having been raised to believe that stimulants are harmful. As magazine advertisements indicate, our self-image may be linked to what we choose to drink. One beer may be said to appeal to a "man's thirst," another to someone who wants to "stay on the light side."

In Chapter 2 we saw that there are differences in the physiological ways people respond to pain. But if physiological responses differ from one person to another, our psychological experiences of pain and the behaviors of escaping or avoiding pain are even more varied. To illustrate this, Melzack and Scott (1957) raised one set of puppies under normal circumstances. A second set grew up isolated in cages that made the usual sensory stimuli, experience, and learning impossible—especially the normal bumps and scrapes from puppy play. When full grown, both groups were exposed to pain: shock, a match held under the nose, a prick of a needle. The dogs that had been raised normally showed an awareness of pain by yelping or wincing, and they tried to avoid its source. The isolated group, on the other hand, did not seem to know how to avoid the pain and often did not even seem to feel it. When a needle was jabbed into the leg of one of these dogs, a localized twitch was the only sign of pain.

In humans, also, responses to pain are conditioned by learning and experience. Some people are more sensitive to pain than others, as dentists surely know. And some groups are more sensitive to pain than other groups. Differences in pain tolerance have been found among people of different ages, sexes, and ethnic backgrounds (Woodrow et al., 1972).

The motivation for sexual behavior is even more complex. As we pointed out in Chapter 2, human sexual activity depends less on hormones and unlearned responses to specific external stimuli than on learning and experience. For example, many adult males whose testes have been removed for medical reasons continue to lead normal sex lives (Thompson, 1975).

What kinds of stimuli activate the human sex drive? It need not be

This child's hunger drive may well have been stimulated by an external clue rather than a biological one.
(Jean-Claude Lejeune, Stock, Boston)

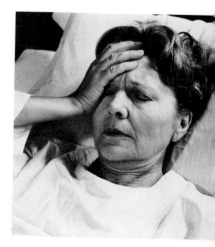

(Stan Levy, Photo Researchers)

anything as immediate as a sexual partner. People respond sexually to fantasies, pictures, words, and to things they see, touch, or hear. Magazines stress the aphrodisiac effects of soft lights and music. One person may be unmoved by an explicit pornographic movie, but aroused by a romantic love story. If we look at popular music, we see that people can be sexually "turned on" by all kinds of things. The Beatles sang about "something in the way she moves." Fred Astaire told Audrey Hepburn, "I love your funny face." And Cole Porter admired "the way you sing off-key." Human sexual behavior is also affected by social experience, sexual experience, nutrition, emotions—particularly one's feelings about the sex partner—and age.

Therefore, even the most basic, primary drives can be aroused and satisfied in many ways. It should come as no surprise, then, that there are other motives that are more heavily influenced by learning and experience. It is to these that we now turn.

Stimulus Motives

All people and animals need to be active.

(Ellis Herwig, Stock, Boston)

Stimulus motives seem to be largely innate, but in all species these motives depend even more on external stimuli—things in the world around us—than primary drives do. Moreover, unlike the primary drives, their function extends beyond the bare survival of the organism or species to a much less specific end—dealing with information about the environment in general. Motives such as *activity, curiosity, exploration, manipulation,* and *contact* push us to investigate, and often to change, the environment. Most often, external stimuli set these motives in action. We, in turn, respond with stimulus-seeking behavior.

ACTIVITY

People need to be active. Most people get bored when they are confined to a small space with nothing to do: They wander around, drum their fingers on the table, or study the cracks in the wall. Of course, age, sex, health, genetic makeup, and temperament affect the need for *activity* to various degrees. One person may be comfortable sitting in the same position for hours, while another may begin to fidget in 5 minutes. A normally active, energetic person may become lethargic and droopy with a bad cold.

Although all animals need activity, scientists are not sure if it is a motive in itself or a combination of other motives. Most of the experiments to determine if there is a separate "activity motive" have been done with rats. A rat put into a cage so small that it cannot move around will be more active than normal when it is released (Hill, 1956). But before we conclude that activity is an innate motive, we should consider other experiments. Food deprivation increases activity, but running increases more than restlessness (pawing, climbing, moving around aimlessly). Experiments with female rats (Wang, 1923) show that peak activity coincides with peak sexual receptivity. So it is still unclear whether boredom and the need for activity is a separate motive by itself or simply the result of other motives.

EXPLORATION AND CURIOSITY

Where does that road go? What is that dark little shop? How does a television set work? What is that tool used for? Answering these questions has no obvious benefit for you. You do not expect the road to take you anywhere you need to go, or the shop to contain anything you really want. You are not about to start a TV-repair service or use an unknown tool. You just want to *know*. Exploration and curiosity appear to be motives activated by the new and unknown and directed toward no more specific goal than "finding out." Even animals will learn a behavior just to be allowed to explore the environment. The family dog will run around a new house, sniffing and checking things out, before it settles down to eat its dinner.

Animals also seem to prefer complexity, presumably because more complex forms take longer to know and are therefore more interesting (Dember, Earl, & Paradise, 1957). Placed in a maze that is painted black, a rat will explore it and learn its way around. The next time, given a choice between a black maze and a blue one, it will choose the blue one (Dember, 1965). Apparently the unfamiliarity of the unknown maze has more appeal. The rat seems to be curious to see what the new one is like.

There are, of course, reservations. At times we have all found the unknown more distressing than stimulating, or found something—an argument, a symphony, or a chess game—too complex for us. A young child accustomed only to her parents may withdraw from a new face and scream with terror if that face has a beard. Unusual clothing or a radical piece of art or music may be rejected, scorned or even attacked. But here again learning is important. Familiarity may reduce the face, the clothing, or the symphony from the unacceptable to the novel and interesting. A child who at age 2 is only up to "Three Blind Mice" welcomes the complexity of a

Although this child is too young to use the contents of the purse, she is very curious about them.
(Erika Stone, Photo Researchers)

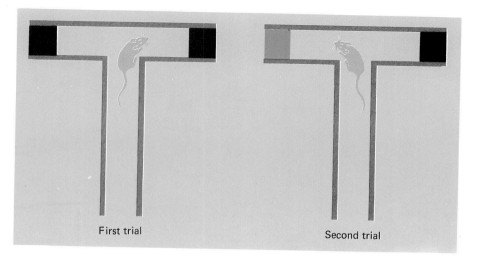

First trial

Second trial

Figure 9–2
On the first trial, a rat explores either black arm of the maze at random. On the second trial, however, given a choice between black and blue arms, a rat will consistently choose the unfamiliar blue one.
(After W. N. Dember, "The New Look in Motivation," *American Scientist*, 1965, *53*, 409–427.)

IS WORK A STIMULUS MOTIVE?

Studies suggest that rats, pigeons, and children sometimes work to gain rewards even if they can get the same rewards without working (D'Amato, 1974, p. 95):

Rats will run down an alley tripping over hundreds of food pellets to obtain a single, identical pellet in the goal box, . . . and pigeons will peck a key, even on intermittent schedules of reinforcement, to get exactly the same food that is freely available in a nearby cup. Given the option of receiving marbles merely by waiting an equivalent amount of time for their delivery, children tend to prefer to press a lever . . . to get the same marbles.

Why would animals or humans work for food or other rewards when they can get the same payoff without working? Isn't there an inherent tendency to "freeload"? Apparently just the opposite is true: There seems to be an inherent need to work. Both animals and people prefer to earn their rewards. In fact, external rewards may even undermine the *intrinsic* motivation to perform a task. In one experiment, monkeys manipulated puzzles without any reward until the puzzles were baited with a raisin. Once they realized they could get a raisin by manipulating a puzzle, the monkeys lost interest in the unbaited puzzle (de Charms, 1968).

Why would people and animals prefer to work for their rewards? Working for rewards may help us control our environment. Such control is necessary for survival and is basic in both animals and human beings. In a number of experiments, animals that could not control their rewards and punishments became passive, apathetic, and simply "gave up." This "learned helplessness" has recently received considerable attention as an explanation for some cases of severe depression (see Chapter 13).

popular song at age 12, and perhaps of a Mozart string quartet at age 22. As we learn—and as we continually explore and learn about our environment—we raise our threshold for the new and complex, and our explorations and our curiosity become much more ambitious.

MANIPULATION

Could you resist touching this exhibit, if it were not under glass?
(Jan Lukas, Photo Researchers)

Why do you suppose that museums have "Do Not Touch" signs everywhere? It is because the staff *knows* from experience that the urge to touch is irresistible. Unlike curiosity and exploration, manipulation is directed

toward a specific object that must be touched, handled, played with, and felt before we are satisfied. Manipulation is a motive that seems to be limited to primates, which have agile fingers and toes.

The desire to manipulate seems to be related to two things: a need to know about something at a tactile level, and sometimes a need to be soothed. The Greek "worry beads"—a set of beads on a short string that are moved back and forth during a conversation—are examples of this second type of manipulation. Under stress, people "fiddle" with a cigarette, a paper napkin, a fountain pen. Children are always manipulating the objects around them. Eyeglasses, earrings, flowers, dogs' tails—everything must be touched and played with. The brighter the object, the more mixed its colors, the more irregular its shape, the more appealing it is as a potential object for manipulation.

CONTACT

People also want to touch other people. The need for contact is broader and more universal than the need for manipulation. Furthermore, it is not limited to touching with the fingers—it can involve the whole body. Manipulation is active, but contact can be passive.

In a famous series of experiments (Harlow, 1958; Harlow & Zimmerman, 1959), newborn baby monkeys were separated from their mothers and given two "surrogate mothers." Both were the same shape, but one was made of wire and offered no soft surfaces. The other was cuddly—layered with foam rubber and covered with terry cloth. A nursing bottle was put in the wire "mother," and both "mothers" were warmed by means of an electric light placed inside them. Thus the wire "mother" fulfilled two physiological drives for the infant monkeys: the need for food and the need for warmth. But it was to the terry-cloth "mother," which did not provide food, that the babies went. When they were frightened, they would run and cling to it as they would to a real mother. Since both mothers were warm, it seems that the need for affection, cuddling, and closeness goes deeper than a need for mere warmth.

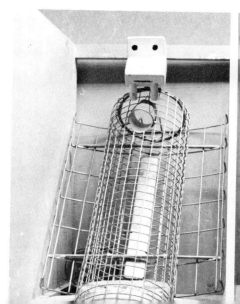 

An infant monkey with its "surrogate mothers"—one made of wire, the other covered with terry-cloth. The monkey prefers the terrycloth "mother," even though the wire mother provides both warmth and food.

(Courtesy Harry F. Harlow, University of Wisconsin Primate Laboratory)

Social Motives

We are not born with all of our motives. We have already seen that even motives that appear to be unlearned—such as hunger, pain, and sex—are actually learned in part. As we develop, our behavior becomes governed by new motives that are almost entirely learned. Although these new motives are learned, not innate, they can control our behavior just as much as unlearned drives and motives can.

One particularly important class of learned motives centers around our relationships with other people. Our discussion will focus on some of the most important of these **social motives.** (Another important social motive, aggression, is covered in Chapter 16.)

ACHIEVEMENT

Climbing Mount Everest "because it is there," sending rockets into space, making the dean's list, rising to the top of a giant corporation are all actions that probably have mixed underlying motives. Of course, achievement can be sought because of motives such as curiosity, fear of failure, and so on. But in all the activities just mentioned, there is a desire to excel. It is this interest in achievement for its own sake that leads psychologists to suggest a separate achievement motive. Need for achievement, or **nAch,** varies widely from person to person. McClelland (1958) developed techniques to measure *nAch* experimentally. For example, one picture in the Thematic Apperception Test (see Chapter 11) shows an adolescent boy sitting at a classroom desk. An open book lies on the desk, but the boy's gaze is directed outward toward the viewer. Subjects are asked to make up stories about this picture. One person responded:

FUNCTIONAL AUTONOMY

Dog owners know that their pets will sometimes pick up something and shake it—just what they would do if they wanted to kill prey. But dogs do not shake things only when they are hungry. Besides, how long has it been since Rover killed rabbits for food? People, too, may keep on doing things even when the original motives for doing them seem to have disappeared—for example, misers count their money over and over again, even though they know how much they have.

R. W. Woodworth (1918*a*) was the first to suggest that some of the skills we learn can become motives of their own, no longer reflecting any basic motive. A woman learns to play bridge because she is curious, for instance, and the skills she develops become, in effect, drives that propel her to play bridge again and again.

Gordon Allport (1937) described behavior with no apparent motive beyond itself as having **functional autonomy.** Such behavior, he said, may originally have been a response to a biological need or a secondary drive, like the need for approval, but it continues even though the original motivation no longer exists. Moreover, it has no present motive beyond itself. (Thus, if the bridge player plays to win money, her behavior cannot be called functionally autonomous.)

The boy in the picture is trying to reconcile the philosophies of Descartes and Thomas Aquinas—at the tender age of 18. He has read several books on philosophy and feels the weight of the world on his shoulders.

Another response was in sharp contrast:

Ed is thinking of leaving home for a while in the hope that this might shock his parents into getting along.

The first response comes from someone who scored high in the need for achievement, the second from someone who scored low (Atkinson & Birch, 1970; Atkinson & Raynor, 1975).

The man on the left is taking the Thematic Apperception Test. Analysis of these tests may depend on the objectivity of the examiner and the approach used in questioning.
(Van Bucher, Photo Researchers)

Atkinson and his colleagues see achievement motivation as a fluid, dynamic process. They believe that motivation is affected by how a given task is related both to future goals and to experiences. In other words, a pre-med student's motivation to do well on an anatomy test is affected by current class standing and by how he or she perceives the test performance will affect getting into medical school (Atkinson, Bongort, & Price, 1977). Moreover, at any given time the presence or absence of other motives or emotions may add or subtract from achievement motivation. For instance, a desire for parental approval may add to achievement motivation and cause a student to study harder. A need to be popular with friends, on the other hand, may cause this same student to put down the books and go to a party.

People who have a high need for achievement are usually competitive and have high personal standards of performance.
(Bill Bachman, Photo Researchers)

From tests and personal histories, psychologists have discovered some general traits of high *nAch* people. These people do best in competitive situations and are fast learners. They are driven less by the desire for fame or fortune than by the need to live up to a high, self-imposed standard of performance. They are self-confident, take on responsibility willingly, and are relatively resistant to outside social pressures. They are energetic and let little obstruct their goals. But they are also apt to be tense and to have psychosomatic illnesses.

How does high *nAch* relate to occupational choice? In a study of 55 college graduates who were tested for achievement levels while in college, McClelland (1965) found that 83 percent of those who had high *nAch* scores went into "entrepreneurial occupations" (p. 389). These occupations, which include sales, owning and operating a business, management consulting, and the like are marked by a high degree of risk and challenge, decision-making responsibility, and objective feedback on job performance. McClelland also found that 70 percent of those who chose professions that were not entrepreneurial had low *nAch* scores.

Why do people have a high need for achievement? McClelland et al. (1953) suggest two reasons. First, children must see that their actions or efforts can change the world around them for the better. Second, the success of these actions must be measured and reinforced by adult standards of excellence. Children who are exposed to such standards will soon learn how to tell a good performance from a bad one. They know that they will be praised for achievement. This may lead to a desire to excel.

It is important to remember that our standards of achievement are often biased by our culture (Maehr, 1974). On many tests, lower-class, black children show a low achievement motivation. Yet these same children may demonstrate an intense achievement drive on a basketball court. Similarly, disadvantaged children who have problems learning English grammar in school may speak familiar dialects fluently among their own groups. Any serious study of the achievement needs of various Americans should avoid *ethnocentrism*—the attitude that one's own culture is superior to others. If white, middle-class standards are the only yardstick for measuring achievement motivation, we can expect that white, middle-class children will consistently appear more achievement oriented. Such studies will not help us to understand the ambitions and desires of many children who are not from the white middle class.

AVOIDANCE OF SUCCESS

Is there a motive to *avoid* success? According to Matina Horner (1969), both men and women develop the need to achieve, but women also develop a fear of success. Horner asked undergraduate men at the University of Michigan to finish a story that began: "After first-term finals, John finds himself at the top of his medical school class." Undergraduate women got the same story, but with "Anne" substituted for "John." Only about 10 percent of the men revealed doubt or fear about success. But the women worried about social rejection, picturing Anne as "acne-faced," lonely and dateless, and "unsexed."

Horner attributed this fear of success to how women are raised in our society. A girl grows up hearing women who achieve outside the home called "sexless," "unfeminine," or "hard," so that achievement—or the prospect of it—makes her feel guilty and anxious. Horner believes that unless these feelings can be resolved, women will not make full use of their opportunities.

Horner's work has received widespread publicity, but some of her methods and conclusions have been questioned. Tresemer (1974) noted the small size of Horner's sample and various inconsistencies and problems in the coding of fear of success (FOS). Tresemer was also skeptical of Horner's connection between FOS imagery and women's actual behavior. He claims that Horner's work has not shown that fear of success is a clear motive for the lack of achievement in women. For example, nonachievement imagery in women subjects may represent "fear of sex-role inappropriateness" rather than "fear of success."

A more serious problem is that the situations that arouse the motive to avoid success have never been identified. Do the situations occur only when women compete with men, or only when sex roles are involved? Or is this motive aroused by any situation in which it is possible to succeed? Studies have been inconclusive (Zuckerman & Wheeler, 1975).

Interestingly, other studies using the "Anne" story showed that men rated high on FOS too. This indicates that men and women with high FOS may simply be responding to cultural stereotypes about appropriate sex roles (de Charms & Muir, 1978). Women may fear becoming doctors because "men are supposed to be doctors"; but men may fear becoming nurses or librarians because these activities are traditionally "women's

Some women fail in business because they fear success or because they feel that being a successful businesswoman is an inappropriate sex role. The woman in this picture is a successful architect, a job often thought of as a man's occupation.

(Ray Ellis, Photo Researchers)

work." These people may be less afraid of success than of reversing sex-roles.

Whatever its cause, this fear of success may be changing. Using undergraduates from the University of Michigan once again, Hoffman (1974) repeated Horner's study several years later with some surprising results. She found that about 65 percent of the women showed fear of success—about the same percentage Horner found. However, 77 percent of the men also expressed this fear, a dramatic increase from Horner's study. Hoffman suggests that this turnaround may relate to men's questioning of the value of achievement—something they would have been less likely to do 6 years earlier. Moreover, the wide publicity that Horner's original study received may have influenced the subjects of the later studies (de Charms & Muir, 1978).

POWER

One important type of achievement motivation is the power motive. Generally, we think of achievement in terms of specific skills: the ability to write a poem, to throw a football, or to argue a legal case. Yet for some people, achievement means dominating others. According to researchers, the power motive may be defined as the need to win recognition or to influence or control other people or groups.

Winter (1973) studied the power motives of 12 American presidents, from Theodore Roosevelt to Richard Nixon. He scored the concerns, aspirations, fears, and plans for action of each president as revealed in his inaugural speech. The highest scorers in terms of power drives were Theodore Roosevelt, Franklin Roosevelt, Harry Truman, Woodrow Wilson, John Kennedy, and Lyndon Johnson. Except for Theodore Roosevelt, all were Democrats, and all six men were action-oriented presidents. All also scored high in the need for achievement. By contrast, Republican presidents—such as Taft, Hoover, and Eisenhower—were more restrained and scored much lower in power motivation and in the need for achievement. Richard Nixon scored quite high in the need for achievement but relatively low in power motivation. According to Winter, the effect of this is a tendency to vacillate in the exercise of power. Winter (1976) studied Jimmy Carter when he was still a presidential candidate and found his power motive to be about average and his need to achieve somewhat above average—about the same as Theodore Roosevelt's. Winter suggests a number of interesting relationships between the power motive and specific presidential policy decisions and actions:

1. Those presidents in power when the country entered wars tended to score high on power motive.
2. Power motive scores of presidents seem to be related to the gain or loss of territory through wars, expansion, treaties, and independence struggles.
3. Presidents with high power motive scores tended to have the highest turnover in cabinet members during their administration.

Presidents who score high in power motive (like John Kennedy) are action-oriented and have a high need for achievement. (UPI)

AFFILIATION

Sometimes you want to get away from it all—to spend an evening or a weekend alone, reading, thinking, or just being by yourself. But generally, people have a need for affiliation, a need to be with other people. If people are isolated from social contact for a long time, they may become anxious. Why do people seek each other out? How are groups formed, and why do a handful of isolated people become a group?

For one thing, the **affiliative motive** is aroused when people feel threatened. Esprit de corps—the feeling that you are part of a sympathetic group—is important among troops going into a battle. A football coach's pregame pep talk is also important to the team. Both are designed to make people feel they are working for a common cause or against a common foe.

Often, affiliative behavior results from another motive entirely. For example, you may give a party to celebrate getting a job because you want to be praised for your achievement. It has also been suggested that fear and anxiety are closely linked to the affiliative motive. When rats, monkeys, or humans are put in anxiety-producing situations, the presence of a member of the same species who is not anxious will reduce the fear of the anxious one. If you are on a plane during a bumpy flight and are nervous, you may strike up a conversation with the calm-looking woman sitting next to you, because the erratic flight of the plane does not seem to be worrying her. In a study of two groups of female college students (Schachter, 1959), one group—the high-anxiety group—was told that they would receive a severe electric shock and the other group—the low-anxiety group—was told that the shock would merely tickle. Over two-thirds of the high-anxiety group, given the choice of waiting alone or with others, chose to wait with others. Only one-third of the low-anxiety group chose to wait with others.

How does the motive for affiliation develop in people? Many conclusions about how the affiliative motive develops are still tentative, but the desire to be with others clearly goes back to the family, the first group we were ever

"Esprit de corps" can be the key to a group's success.
(Photo courtesy Dick Cox and Charles Taddo)

UNCONSCIOUS MOTIVES

A new car is advertised, and a man decides he would like to own one. Why? He may tell you that his old car was running down and this one looks "pretty good" to him. But there may be other reasons why he wants this new car of which he is unaware.

Theories of **unconscious motivation** vary. Freud's is probably the most extreme. Freud believed that every act—however trivial—derives from a host of unconscious motives. A Freudian might see the man's choice of a car as the desire to conquer a sexual object—a desire encouraged by advertisements touting it as "sleek," "purring," and "packed with power." Or Freudian theory cites aggression as a reason, the man's need to zoom down Main Street with as much horsepower as possible under his control.

Some psychologists maintain that not only is behavior influenced by unconscious motives, but also that some kinds of behavior occur *only* when we are unaware of our motives (Brody, 1980). This is in line with the Freudian theory of the unconscious.

But we do not need to explain all acts in Freudian terms to realize that they can spring from unconscious motives. The man who buys a car may be expressing a desire for social approval—"Be the first one on your block to own one!"—or he may be rewarding himself for hard work. He could be trying to bolster a sagging self-image, or he could be consoling himself for the loss of a promotion or a girlfriend.

It should be emphasized that unconscious motives are not a particular *class* of motives, as physiological, learned, and stimulus motives are. As we pointed out in the discussion of physiological drives, we do not have to be aware of hunger and thirst to act to satisfy them. An unconscious motive is one that we are acting to satisfy without quite knowing why.

It is difficult to learn about unconscious motives because we have to rely on what people *say* about their motives. For example, when people report their motives they are recalling something that has already occurred, and their memories may be inaccurate. People may also experience things on different levels of consciousness, and these experiences may be too subtle to put into words.

In one experiment, for example, people were hypnotized and told that they would experience no pain. Subsequently they said they had felt no pain, but other behaviors indicated that they were indeed suffering (Hilgard, 1973, 1977).

in. It has been found (Sarnoff & Zimbardo, 1961) that firstborn or only children have stronger affiliative motives than those born later, perhaps because they were used to receiving more parental attention during their early years. Children who are brought up to be dependent, or who are raised with close family ties, show stronger affiliative motives than those coming from families that encouraged early independence.

A Hierarchy of Motives

You have probably noted that our discussion has gradually moved from primitive motives, shared by all creatures, to motives that are more sophisticated, complex, and human. Maslow (1954) arranged all motives in such a hierarchy, from lower to higher. The lower motives are relatively simple; they spring from bodily states that *must* be satisfied. As the motives become higher, they arise from other things: the desire to live as comfortably as possible in our environment, to deal as well as we can with other human beings, and to make the best impression on others that we can. Maslow's hierarchy of motives is shown in Figure 9–3.

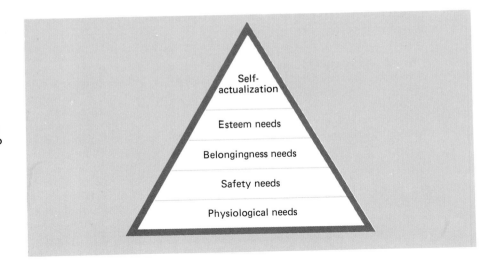

According to Maslow's theory, higher motives appear only after the more basic ones have been satisfied. This is true on both an evolutionary and an individual scale. If you are starving, you will probably not care what people think of your table manners.

Maslow believed that the most highly "evolved" motive in the hierarchy is self-actualization. This may be described as a desire to make the best one can out of oneself. It does not concern the respect of other human beings and their judgments of us, but rather what we ourselves want to be. People differ in how important self-actualization is in their behavior, but to some extent all of us are motivated to live according to what is necessary for our personal growth. The people who are the most self-actualizing, Maslow said, think of themselves as whole beings, not as parcels of hunger, fear, ambition, and dependency.

Although Maslow's hierarchy theory is useful as a way of thinking about motives, it is extremely difficult to test (Wahba & Bridwell, 1976). Research has questioned the evidence supporting the classification of human needs into five separate categories, and the placement of these categories in a hierarchical structure.

Emotions

In the first part of this chapter we saw that motives can both arouse and direct our behavior. Emotions do the same. "She shouted for joy," we say, or, "I was so angry I could have strangled him." The fact that emotions arouse and shape behavior provides a rich source of profits for advertising agencies. By manipulating our emotions, advertisers can get us to buy everything from cars to mouthwash.

To some extent, we can classify emotions in terms of whether they cause us to turn to or away from objects (Arnold, 1960). On this basis, there appear to be three basic categories of emotion. Imagine that you overhear this conversation between three people whose television set has just gone out during a midsummer thunderstorm:

A. Just when the movie was getting good! I've wanted to see it for years and now *this* happens. (*Fiddles with set, to no avail, and switches it off disgustedly.*) Things like this always happen at the worst time. It makes me furious.

B. I *hate* thunderstorms, I always have. Don't you think we ought to turn off all the lights, so we won't attract the lightning? My grandmother used to hide in a closet till it stopped, and I don't blame her. She used to say it was God's vengeance for our sins.

C. (*Going to window.*) Look at it, it's fantastic—the way the blue flashes light up everything. It makes the whole world different. I've always loved thunderstorms—they're so wild and happy. They make me feel liberated and crazy.

(Will McIntyre, Photo Researchers)

"A" is frustrated and angry. This category of emotions moves us to approach something, but in an aggressive or hostile way. "B" is fearful and anxious. These emotions make us want to avoid something. "C" is happy and experiencing a sense of release and joy. These emotions make us want to approach something.

But emotions, like motives, can begin a chain of fairly complex behavior that goes far beyond simple approach or avoidance. If we are anxious about something, for instance, we may collect information about it, ask questions, and then decide whether to approach it, to flee it, or to stay and

EMOTION: PRO AND CON

Traditionally, psychologists—and our society in general—have held emotion in low esteem (Leeper, 1948). Even in the laboratory, psychologists usually regard emotional responses as a disorganized—and disorganizing—aspect of behavior. "Don't let your feelings run away with you," we are told. "Get yourself under control." "Don't get carried away." Our emotions are seen as wild horses that will drag us headlong into disaster if we do not control them with the firm hand of reason.

Why has Western culture so often viewed emotions as nasty, frightening, and destructive? One reason may be that Western society is committed to rationalism, which sees reason as the only thing that sets humans apart from the other animals. Recently, however, our culture shows signs of moving in the opposite direction. Evangelicals have resurrected fervent revival meetings. Teachers, bankers, and business executives undergo sensitivity training. It has become so popular to "get in touch with your feelings" that

journalist Tom Wolfe dubbed the 1970s the "Me Decade" (Wolfe, 1976).

Strupp (1976) feels that the pendulum has swung too far. Anti-intellectualism and irrationalism are threatening an "erosion of excellence." He fears that we are replacing reason and rational inquiry with gut reactions, encounter groups, and the simplistic belief that "all we need is love." The biggest danger, in Strupp's view, is that this approach implies that reason and emotion are mutually exclusive. Ideally, they work together. For example, competent therapists must be aware of their own emotional responses and their causes to deal effectively—and rationally—with their clients.

Perhaps for all of us Alfred North Whitehead's observation is true: "Intellect is to emotion as our clothes are to our bodies; we could not very well have civilized life without clothes, but we would be in a poor way if we had only clothes without bodies" (Whitehead, 1977).

to fight it. Leeper (1948) gives the example of a family who heard that an arsonist was in the neighborhood. First the family saw how the situation related to them, finding that one of their rooms was a firetrap. They learned about possible protective devices and had them installed. Their anxiety about fire focused their performance.

Sometimes, our emotions seem like uninvited guests. Most of us have been in situations where we desperately wanted to think rationally but could not because our emotions had disrupted our concentration. Under what circumstances does emotion hinder what we do? When does it help? There seems to be no single, simple answer. It is largely a question of degree—of both the strength of the emotion and the difficulty of the task. The **Yerkes–Dodson law** puts it this way: The more complex the task, the lower the level of emotion that can be tolerated without interfering with performance. You may feel very angry while boiling an egg, and it may not make much difference, but the same degree of emotion may interfere with your ability to drive safely. Moreover, although a certain minimum level of emotional arousal is necessary for good performance, a very high level of emotional arousal may affect your performance for the worse.

BASIC EMOTIONAL EXPERIENCES

As we saw earlier, emotions can be broadly grouped according to how they affect our behavior—whether they motivate us to approach or to avoid something. But within these broad groups, how many different emotions are there?

One of the most influential attempts to identify and classify emotions was

Figure 9–4
Plutchik's three-dimensional model of the emotions. Intensity is represented on the vertical dimension, ranging from maximum intensity at the top to a state of deep sleep at the bottom: The model tapers inward at the bottom to indicate that emotions are less distinguishable at low intensities.

(From _The Emotions: Facts, Theories, and a New Model_, by Robert Plutchik. Copyright © 1962 by Random House, Inc.)

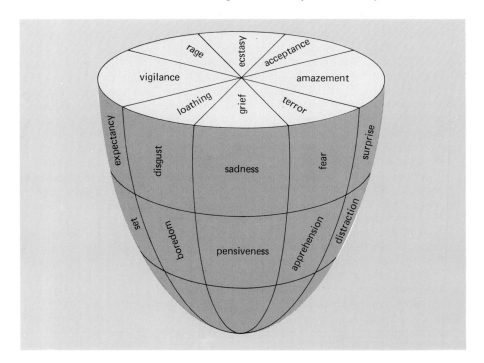

The disappointment of losing at the race track is clearly reflected in the emotional intensity felt by these bettors.
(UPI)

made by Robert Plutchik (1962). He proposed that human beings have eight basic emotions founded on basic human and animal instincts (Figure 9–4). Emotions that lie next to each other on the circle are more similar than those that lie opposite each other, or that are farther away from each other. Terror and fear are likely to lead to avoidance, while rage and anger—on opposite sides of the model—lead people to attack or destroy the thing that makes them angry—or, sometimes, to attack or destroy a substitute for that thing. Acceptance makes people incorporate, or embrace, something, while loathing causes them to reject it.

Within any of the eight categories, emotions vary in *intensity* (represented by the vertical dimension of the model). At the top—or at the most intense—end of the spectrum lie ecstasy, acceptance, amazement, terror, grief, loathing, vigilance, and rage. As we move down toward the bottom, each emotion becomes less intense. Anger, for example, is less intense than rage, and annoyance is even less intense than anger. But all three emotions—annoyance, anger, and rage—are closely related. In general, the more intense the emotion, the more *motivation* it supplies. If you want to mail an important letter and you get to the post office one minute after it closes, your basic emotion might be "anger," and you might respond with a muttered expletive. If you only wanted to buy some stamps, you would probably feel "annoyed," and you might just walk away. But if you wanted to mail an income tax form that had to be postmarked by midnight that night, you might feel "rage," and end up banging on the post office door, or, perhaps, even kicking it.

Thus, although Plutchik claims there are only eight categories or families of emotions, within any category emotions vary in intensity, and this greatly expands the range of emotions we experience. Moreover, different emotions can combine to produce an even wider range of experience. Anger and joy, for example, combine to become pride. Joy and acceptance make us feel love. Curiosity is a blend of surprise and acceptance. And guilt or despair are the likely result of experiencing fear and sorrow at the same time (Plutchik, 1962).

As we pointed out earlier, emotion and motivation are controversial areas. Plutchik's model is widely used to describe emotions and to account for how they arouse and direct behavior. His model helps us understand the basic dynamics of emotion, but it is only one way of looking at them.

295

Theories of Emotion

Why do we feel on top of the world one minute and down in the dumps the next? What causes emotional experiences?

In the 1880s, William James formulated the first modern theory of emotion, and almost simultaneously a Danish psychologist, Carl Lange, reached the same conclusions. The **James–Lange theory** reversed what had been believed about how emotions are aroused. Before, it had been thought that the sequence of arousal was: *you see a bear, you feel afraid, you run.* According to the new theory, the order was changed to: *you see a bear, you run, you feel afraid.* According to James and Lange, the perception of the stimulus (the bear) causes your muscles, skin, and viscera (internal organs) to undergo changes: faster heart rate, enlarged pupils, deeper or shallower breathing, flushed face, increased perspiration, butterflies in the stomach, and a gooseflesh sensation as the body's hairs stand on end. Emotion is simply our awareness of these changes (Strongman, 1978). All of this, of course, happens almost instantaneously and in a reflexive, automatic way. But, according to James and Lange, if the bodily responses were bypassed, no emotion would be felt. You would see the bear without fear.

We now know that the James–Lange-type theories are partly right. It is clear that peripheral body changes are important in experiencing emotion. When 25 men with lesions in their spinal cords were asked to describe their feelings of anger, sex, and fear, they reported that these *feelings* were decreased, although they could *act* emotional (Hohmann, 1966).

But if peripheral body changes alone *cause* specific emotions, then we should be able to pinpoint different body changes for each emotion. Perhaps butterflies in the stomach make us afraid of fear or anxiety and blushing causes shame or guilt. In fact, there is some evidence that the body changes associated with fear are different from those associated with anger. In one experiment (Funkenstein, King, & Drolette, 1953), a group of college students was told to solve a set of very difficult problems without using paper and pencil. They were then accused of stupidity when they failed the tasks. Three different kinds of reactions occurred. Some of the students showed fear and anxiety at being unable to solve the problems and at being scolded by the experimenters. Others expressed anger at the experimenters. A third group also expressed anger, but they blamed themselves for their failure. The cardiovascular pattern—the heart and pulse rate, and the circulation of blood—of all three groups was then tested. The students who had expressed anger at the experimenters showed the physiological changes that would have occurred if they had received an injection of norepinephrine. The students who had become anxious showed an exaggerated epinephrine pattern.*

In another study, urine samples were taken from professional hockey players before and after a game. In general, norepinephrine levels were six times higher after the game, as one might expect if the players were angry. But there were some exceptions. Two players who sat out the game and

In this statue of Saint Teresa in ecstasy, Bernini captured all three aspects of basic emotional experiences. The stimulus that Saint Teresa is responding to is very approachable and has aroused intense pleasant emotions.
(Alinari—Editorial Photocolor Archives)

---

*Epinephrine and norepinephrine are transmitter substances that are discussed in Chapter 2.

worried about their injuries had no increase in norepinephrine, but a considerable increase in epinephrine. Other studies of astronauts in training have reached the same conclusion: norepinephrine production is associated with aggressive action, while epinephrine production is linked to fear, anxiety, and flight (McGeer & McGeer, 1980).

Beyond these studies, psychologists have had little success in finding distinct body responses that fit the various emotions. Your pulse may race when you are feeling a strong emotion, but a rapid pulse rate does not tell you which emotion you are feeling. Most of the physiological "signs" of emotion say only that emotion is there and tell how intense it is. They cannot tell us if we are trembling from terror or from joy.

If the same visceral changes—increased heartbeat and sweating, for example—are experienced for emotions as different as fear, anger, and excitement, how can we explain the differences between these emotions? Nearly 70 years ago an alternate theory of emotions, the **Cannon–Bard theory,** proposed that emotions and bodily responses occur simultaneously, as a result of brain activity, not one after another. Thus, *you see the bear, you run-and-are-afraid,* with neither reaction preceding the other. Since the Cannon–Bard theory was introduced, a number of other theories have also stressed the role of the central nervous system—particularly the brain—in emotion, each theory differing in detail from the others. We know now that the external stimulus is registered by the reticular activating system, whose function is simply arousal. At this point, only the dimension of intensity is involved. It is immaterial to the reticular activating system whether you just cut your hand or got an *A* in chemistry. But as the message of arousal reaches the limbic system, the emotion is defined.

For example, an important experiment by Olds and Milner (1954) located points in the brain that register pleasure and pain. The researchers implanted electrodes in the hypothalamus of rats' brains. They then placed the rats in Skinner boxes and allowed them to stimulate themselves electrically by pressing a lever. The rats found the stimulation very rewarding: They would press the lever up to several thousand times an hour. Further research (Olds, 1956) revealed that the intensity of the shock was more important than how often it occurred. The rats would press the bar far more eagerly for strong shocks, even if they occurred less often. Later experiments located nearby regions in the rats' brains that produced pain. The rats would press the lever for hours to avoid the stimulus, finally developing ulcers if the experiment continued.

Further self-stimulation studies support the idea that the limbic system is at the physiological center of emotion. Delgado (1969) produced a variety of emotional reactions in humans by electrically stimulating various areas of the limbic system. He found that stimulating the posterior hypothalamus creates the most intense pleasure sensations. Stimulating the septal region produces sexual sensations that can approach orgasmic intensity. Higher brain centers also seem to be involved in emotional experiences. If the cerebral cortex is separated from lower brain structures, the result is unfocused emotional reactions that come and go very quickly (Strongman, 1978).

The exact connections between these physiological components are not yet known in detail. We know the functions of various areas of the brain

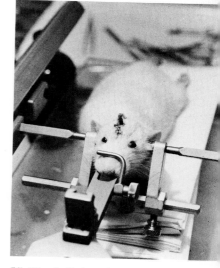

(Mimi Forsyth, Monkmeyer)

and nervous system, and the circumstances that bring them into play. Someday we may be able to diagram them as we would a computer circuit, but that day has not yet come. Part of the problem is that research on the central nervous system involves experiments with animals, while studies of the role of peripheral mechanisms can only be conducted with human beings who can put their emotions into words (McGeer & McGeer, 1980).

Up to this point we have seen that both the central and peripheral nervous systems play a part in emotion. It seems likely that peripheral nervous system arousal is important, but it is the central nervous system that somehow determines what the emotions will be. A number of theorists suggest that one important contribution of the central nervous system is *cognition*. According to this view, physiological arousal, together with perception and judgment of situations (cognition), jointly determine which emotions are felt. All emotional states consist of a diffuse and general arousal of the nervous system. The situation we are in when we are aroused—the environment—gives us clues as to what we should call this general state of arousal. Thus, our cognitions tell us how to label our diffuse feelings in a way suitable to our current thoughts and ideas about our surroundings.

Schachter and Singer (1962) tested the interaction of cognition and physiological arousal to study how emotional states are labeled. The experimenters told a group of subjects that they would be injected with a dose of "Suproxin"—a fictitious vitamin compound that affected vision— and that they would be tested for its effects. They divided the subjects into two groups. They gave one group a placebo that produced no physiological effect whatsoever. Then they injected the rest of the subjects with epi- nephrine, which produces general physiological arousal similar to that of emotional states. They divided these latter subjects into three subgroups. They told the first subgroup about epinephrine's real effects. They told the second subgroup nothing. And they misinformed the third subgroup by telling them to expect side effects other than those epinephrine would produce. The placebo group was not told to expect any side effects.

The experimenters then exposed each subject separately to a stooge, supposedly another subject, who pretended to be either euphoric and friendly or angry and resentful. The experimenters observed the subjects through a two-way mirror to determine how much they appeared to adopt the stooge's emotional state. Afterward, they gave the subjects a self-report questionnaire to find out how angry and irritated or happy and contented they felt.

Schachter and his co-workers discovered that those who were ignorant or misinformed about the effects of epinephrine–Suproxin were much more emotionally aroused—that is, more euphoric or angry—than those who knew what the drug would do and knew what to expect. These data support Schachter's idea that if there is little physiological difference between emotional states, then our cognitions—perceptions and expecta- tions—must tell us what emotion we are experiencing.

Additional support for Schachter's theory comes from the fact that people have to learn from others which emotions to experience when smoking marijuana. In a way marijuana is similar to epinephrine. It produces vague, diffuse physiological arousal that first-time users find hard

TRUTH IS SKIN-DEEP: THE LIE DETECTOR

Our skin, superficial covering that it is, indicates emotions inside of us. This is because the skin undergoes changes in resistance to electrical current due to changes in blood vessels and sweat glands. These telltale changes, along with heart rate and breathing, are registered by a polygraph machine, commonly called a lie detector. Despite individual differences in the electrical conductance of the skin, all skin "talks," as psychologist Barbara Brown put it.

Although polygraphs are used in business, most of us are more familiar with its use as a police tool. But are polygraphs being used as well as they could be? David Lykken (1975) thinks that they are not. The changes in our skin in response to the polygraph—known as galvanic skin response—fluctuate in response to all kinds of emotions. When someone is asked if he or she committed a murder, the lie detector is likely to jump.

Of course this may reflect guilt, but it may also reflect anxiety, fear, or loathing—all possible reactions to being questioned about a crime. If a suspect were questioned about marital problems, relationships with parents, or even attitudes toward work, the polygraph might record the same kind of jump in emotional response.

In fact, the best the police can do with the results of a polygraph test is to *infer* the emotion that is reflected. And the only fair way to do this is to phrase questions so that the police can be sure the response indicates guilt rather than another emotion. For example, if a list of names of banks is read, a guilty suspect should react strongly to the name of the bank he actually robbed. According to Lykken, if a suspect shows such "guilty knowledge" on 6 of 10 such "crime-detail" items, the chances that he is innocent will be "only one in 1,000."

This multiple-choice approach also avoids broad incriminating questions that can make an innocent person respond emotionally, causing him to "fail" the test. Since the multiple-choice approach requires knowledge of many details, it is also harder to "beat" the lie detector if you are really guilty.

to describe. Beginning smokers learn to label their physiological symptoms as a "high"—that is, other people teach them to label and interpret the physiological changes.

In a related line of work, Stuart Valins (1966) showed how even minor cues appear to control a person's emotions. Valins showed a group of male subjects pictures of female nudes and arranged his equipment so that the subjects could hear their own heartbeats as each slide was shown. He deceived one group by substituting a recording that contained first increasing heart rates and then decreasing heart rates. He found that his deceived subjects found those nudes most attractive that had been accompanied by what they thought were their own increasing heart rates.

Later studies have questioned Valins's work, however. Valins, for example, did not monitor the subjects' real heart rates. Yet, tests have shown that the real heart rate is as closely related as the fake heart rate to ratings of attractiveness. Beck (1978) concludes that Valins may have merely shown that subjects are aware that heart rate changes are supposed to be related to emotion.

Magda Arnold (1960) also believes that cognitive processes control how we interpret our feelings and how we act on them. She emphasizes the function of appraisal: We first decide if an incoming stimulus is "good," "bad," or "indifferent." If it is good, we approach it; if it is bad, we avoid it; if it is indifferent, we ignore it. Our appraisal of any new stimulus is determined by our memories of past experiences and our simultaneous imagining of various ways of coping with the situation and of whether it will be good or bad for us. These appraisals are thought to be almost instantaneous. They precede any emotional feelings or actions. For example, if you are picnicking in a field and see a bull coming toward you, your appraisal will be based on memories of being told that bulls are dangerous, of crossing traffic intersections in front of fast-moving trucks, of seeing accident victims or wounded matadors, of imagining what will happen if you stay where you are, and so on. This appraisal will produce a direct action: You will run for your life and simultaneously experience fear.

A fascinating test of the **cognitive theory of emotion** was undertaken by Joseph C. Spiesman (1965). People were shown a gory film that aroused strong emotional responses in American viewers, both as measured by autonomic responses like heart rate and skin conductivity, and as reported by the viewers in interviews.

Spiesman decided to explore how different kinds of sound tracks would affect the level of emotional response to this stress-inducing film, as measured by skin conductivity. He compared the arousal effects of the original silent film with three different sound tracks. The first he called the *trauma* track. This track simply narrated what was happening in the film. The second tract was *intellectual*. Its description was detached and clinical. It allowed the viewer to maintain emotional distance from the events on the screen. The third sound track was the *denial* track. It tended to gloss over, deny, or speak in glowing terms about what was depicted.

The subjects were selected from two groups: university students and business executives. Each person saw the film alone, seated in a comfortable chair, with the device to measure skin conductivity attached through-

Figure 9–5

A summary of the four major theories of emotion. According to the James-Lange theory, the body first responds physiologically to a stimulus, and then the cerebral cortex determines which emotion is being experienced. In the Cannon-Bard theory, impulses are sent simultaneously to the cerebral cortex and peripheral nervous system. Thus the stimulus is responded to and the emotion is experienced at the same time, but independently. Stanley Schachter proposes that the cerebral cortex and the peripheral nervous system work jointly to determine which emotions we feel. Magda Arnold emphasizes our appraisal of the situation and thus feels that the emotions we experience and our physiological responses are both determined by the cerebral cortex.

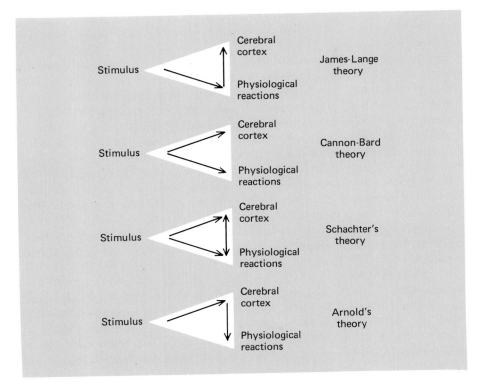

EMOTIONS AND ATTITUDES

Cognitive theories of emotion are generally described in terms of how cognition affects emotion. But that question can be reversed. How does emotion affect how we think? Some men, for instance, are embarrassed, ashamed, or contemptuous when they go to a ballet and watch a man dance an exquisite solo.

How do these feelings affect how such men *think* about sex roles? How does emotion in general affect thinking?

One interesting study by Rosenberg (1960) explored the relationships between emotions and attitudes. Rosenberg took a group of people whose attitudes toward blacks' moving into their neighborhoods were very negative. Then he hypnotized the people and told them:

You will be very much in favor of Negroes moving into white neighborhoods. The mere idea of Negroes moving into white

neighborhoods will give you a happy, exhilarated feeling (Rosenberg, 1960).

After the subjects were brought out of the hypnotic trance, Rosenberg found significant changes in their values and in their beliefs about blacks. The same people who had previously reacted negatively to the suggestion of blacks' moving into white neighborhoods now vigorously defended their new belief that blacks would not cause a lowering of property values. When confronted with their earlier beliefs, they indicated that they had simply been wrong. Rosenberg got the same results with people's attitudes toward United States foreign aid. Again, he found that changing people's feelings or emotions led to a change in their beliefs and attitudes. In both cases, after the posthypnotic suggestion was removed and the original emotions returned, the beliefs shifted back toward what they had been before the experiment.

out the showing. The results clearly show that the different verbal settings provided by each sound track affected the people's emotional response. Those who heard the trauma track were much more emotional than those who had seen the film with no accompanying narration. Those who heard the intellectual and denial tracks were much less emotional. These results show quite clearly that our emotional reponses are directly and sharply affected by how we interpret a situation.

Finally, C. E. Izard (1972) developed a theory that seeks to provide a complete picture of emotional processes. He believes that we have nine basic, innate emotions—very similar to Plutchik's model of eight—that are at the root of all human motivation. What makes these emotions unique and forceful is the feedback that our brains receive from our facial expressions and body postures. In other words, we experience surprise, for instance, once a complex pattern of muscular—and especially facial activity—has "told" the brain that we are feeling surprise, rather than anger or shame. According to Izard, peripheral factors and cognitive factors unite in a complex system that involves an incredible number of mechanisms and interactions.

As we have moved from one kind of theory to another, we have seen that the relationships between physiology and emotion are far more complicated than was believed a century ago. And we have also seen that these relationships are now thought to involve a third element, cognition. What we know and how we interpret the present situation directly affect the emotional experience. Finally, if Izard is right, one important element in determining our emotional experience is our expressive behavior, which is the next—and final—topic in this chapter.

The Expression of Emotion

Sometimes you are vaguely aware that a person makes you feel uncomfortable. When pressed to be more precise, you might say, "You never know what he is thinking." But you do not mean that you never know his opinion of a film or what he thought about the last election. It would probably be more accurate to say that you do not know what he is _feeling_. Almost all of us conceal our emotions to some extent to protect our self-image or to conform to social conventions. But usually there are some clues to help us determine another person's emotions.

VERBAL COMMUNICATION

It would be simplest, of course, if we could just ask people what they were feeling. Sometimes we do, with varying results. If your roommate finishes washing the dishes and says acidly, "I hope you are enjoying your novel," her words are quite clear, but you know very well that she is not saying what she means. If she were to say, "I am furious that you did not offer to help," she would be giving you an accurate report of her emotions at that moment.

For many reasons, we may not be able or willing to report our emotions accurately. In some situations, people simply do not know what their emotions are. The father of an abused child may sincerely profess affection for the child, yet act in ways that reflect another set of emotions that are

CULTURAL PATTERNS OF EMOTIONAL EXPRESSION

Some Americans speak loudly and wave their arms when they are angry. Others speak softly, and carry the proverbial "big stick." Most of us are aware that different persons and groups in our culture have different ways of physically expressing their emotions. Physical expressions of emotions also vary among cultures.

Psychologist Otto Klineberg (1938) became interested in these cultural differences and devised a unique method to study them. His "novel" approach was to take several classic and modern Chinese works of fiction and examine how the emotions of the characters were represented in physical descriptions. He discovered both similarities to and differences from Western styles of expressing emotion.

For example, fear is described in a similar fashion in both Chinese and Western literature. Chinese examples include, "Everyone trembled with a face the color

of clay," "All of his hairs stood on end, and the pimples came out on the skin all over his body."

Other emotions, however, were manifested quite differently. "They stretched out their tongues," conveys surprise to the Chinese, not the insolence or teasing it suggests to us. In Chinese fiction, anger is exhibited by the eyes growing round and also opening wide.

Fainting is as common in Chinese novels as in Western fiction, but the Chinese faint in anger. From the Chinese viewpoint, the delicate Victorian maidens who cultivated the fine art of fainting from fear were responding inappropriately.

Klineberg's study revealed the cultural variability of overt expressions of emotion. Similar gestures, body postures, or physical movements often convey drastically different emotional meanings in different cultures. We express our emotions in the style we have learned.

hidden from his own awareness. Even when we are aware of our emotions, we sometimes diminish the degree of emotion we are feeling, as when we say we are "a little worried" about an upcoming exam, when in fact we are terrified. Or we may deny the emotion entirely, especially if it is negative. This may be done out of politeness or out of self-protection, as when we claim to like someone either because we do not want to hurt that person or because we feel we should like him or her.

(Van Bucher, Photo Researchers)

NONVERBAL COMMUNICATION

"Actions speak louder than words," and people are often more eloquent than they realize or intend. We transmit a lot of information to others through our facial expressions, body postures, vocal intonations, and physical distance, and our bodies often send emotional messages that contradict our words.

At a county fair, a political rally, or a football game, a pickpocket goes to work. Standing behind someone, the nimble-fingered thief prepares to relieve him of his wallet. Slowly the hand moves toward the back pocket, is almost touching the wallet when, suddenly, it pulls back empty. The pickpocket moves casually through the crowd, whistling unconcernedly. What went wrong? What gave the thief a clue that his intended victim might have been about to reach for his wallet? It could have been any one of many signs to any pickpocket skillful enough to stay out of jail. The hairs on the back of the intended victim's neck might have bristled slightly; there might have been a slight stiffening of the back, a twitch in a neck muscle, a subtle change in skin color, a trickle of sweat. The man might not yet have been aware that his pocket was about to be picked, but these physiological signals showed an awareness that something was afoot.

As we noted earlier, these physiological changes are not normally under our control. They tend to function independently of our will, and often, indeed, against it. *Facial expressions* are the most obvious emotional indicators. We can tell a lot about a person's emotional state by observing whether he or she is laughing, crying, smiling, or frowning. Many facial expressions are innate, not learned. Children who are born deaf and blind use the same facial gestures to express the same emotions as normal children do. Charles Darwin observed that most animals share a common pattern of muscular facial movements. For example, dogs, tigers, and men all bare their teeth in rage. Some human facial expressions of emotion are universal; others are unique (Izard, 1971).

While most people can recognize widely differing emotions in facial expressions, they tend to confuse some emotions with others, such as fear with surprise (Tomkins & McCarter, 1964). Thompson and Meltzer (1964) designed an experiment to see if certain emotions were easier to express facially than others. They found that most people have no trouble expressing love, fear, determination, and happiness, but suffering, disgust, and contempt are significantly more difficult to express—and to recognize.

The rest of the body also sends messages, particularly through position and posture. This has been called *body language.* When we are relaxed, we tend to sprawl back in a chair; when tense, to sit more stiffly with our feet

(Suzanne Szasz, Photo Researchers)

together. Slumping, crossing of the arms and legs, straightness of the back, all these supply clues about which emotion someone is feeling. Birdwhistle (1952) has made the study of body language into a science called *kinesics*. He believes that every movement of the body has a meaning, that no movement is accidental, and that all of our significant gestures and movements are learned. Moreover, these body gestures may contradict our verbal messages about what we are feeling (Birdwhistle, 1974). In a family, for example, one might first notice that the mother verbally defers to her husband and children by asking for and taking their advice. But a closer inspection reveals her to be the true leader when she crosses her legs and all the other family members unconsciously imitate her (Fast, 1970). And in some cases, we may fail to communicate emotions effectively simply because we are not very good at deliberately controlling emotional expression. Beier (1974) videotaped subjects acting out six emotions: anger, fear, seductiveness, indifference, happiness, and sadness. He found that most of his subjects could successfully portray two out of the six and that the rest of their portrayals did not reflect their intentions. One girl appeared angry no matter what emotion she tried to project; another was invariably seductive.

Just as people send out complex and contradictory emotional messages by nonverbal cues, they also show considerable variety in their ability to read such messages. Rosenthal and his colleagues (1974) developed a test of sensitivity to nonverbal cues—the Profile of Nonverbal Sensitivity (PONS)—that assesses people's ability to judge the meaning of vocal intonations and face and body movements. In the test, the subjects watch a film that shows an actress or actor portraying various emotional states. Sometimes the portrayal is accompanied by spoken phrases, but certain tones and rhythms that identify them as distinct words have been removed. The viewer then picks one of two possible interpretations of the scene.

The study showed that women were consistently better than men at understanding nonverbal cues, although men in the "nurturant" professions—psychiatrists, psychologists, mental hospital aides, and teachers—along with artists, actors, and designers, scored as highly as women. The study also showed that sensitivity to nonverbal cues increases with age, probably because the young have not had the necessary experience in judging vocal tones and observing body movements.

Another kind of body communication is *distance*. The normal distance between people definitely differs from culture to culture. Two Swedes standing around and talking would ordinarily stand much farther apart than two Arabs or Greeks. Within every culture, there seems to be a distance that is generally thought appropriate for normal conversation. If someone is standing closer than usual to you, it may indicate aggressiveness or sexuality; if farther away than usual, it may indicate withdrawal or repugnance.

Explicit *acts*, of course, can also be nonverbal clues. When we receive a 2:00 A.M. telephone call, we expect that what the caller has to say is urgent. A slammed door tells us that the person who left the room is angry. If friends drop in for a visit and you invite them into the living room, you are probably less at ease with them than you are with people you would ask to sit down at the kitchen table. *Gestures* such as a slap on the back or an embrace can

LEARNING TO EXPRESS EMOTIONS

How do we become emotional beings? A newborn baby seems to experience only one emotion, a state of general excitement. A baby will react with this diffuse excitement to a red rattle, a large dog, a loud noise, or a mother's breast. A newborn girl smiles and her delighted aunt says, "Oh look, she's happy!" Someone else says grumpily, "It's only gas." Apparently, it is neither. Instead, smiles in newborns indicate fluctuations in central nervous system activity (Ekman & Oster, 1979).

More specific emotional responses follow, but they seem to be modified by learning and experience. Bridges (1932) suggested that after the first generalized excitement, babies start to show separate emotions of distress—unpleasantness, avoidance—and of delight—pleasantness, approach. Between 3 and 6 months of age, emotions such as anger, disgust, and elation are displayed. Others, such as affection, jealousy, and joy come later.

We have learned, however, that the sequence of emotional development is not as simple or as clear-cut as Bridges suggested. From day to day, the emotions shown by a baby greatly differ. Emotions in both infants and adults are the result of many simultaneous processes—all of which determine the emotions that are displayed (Haith & Campos, 1977). As the range of emotions increases, the number of stimuli that trigger the emotions increases too. Much of this occurs simply because the child's capacity to assimilate experience increases. His or her world gets larger every day. Children learn which stimuli produce which emotion, either directly or by imitation. A child bitten by a snake will, of course, be afraid of snakes (direct experience). But a child whose mother screams at the sight of a wriggling garter snake will probably also learn this response (imitation).

Aronfreed (1968) suggests that being able to internalize emotional stimuli may be the first step toward emotional self-control and is thus a milestone in a child's development. As Aronfreed describes the process, children learn to associate their behavior with how other people respond to it and how that makes them feel. Children internalize this sequence and may begin to feel pleasure or fear when they only think of doing something that they have learned will be praised or punished.

For example, a little boy wants to take a toy away from his sister but decides not to because his fear of punishment outweighs the pleasure he might get from playing with the toy. Aronfreed notes that internalization is easier when the child has a close and rewarding attachment to an adult.

Figure 9–6

The situations that cause fear in children. Note the change in the kinds of stimuli that evoke fear as children grow older.

(After A. T. Jersild, F. V. Markey, and C. L. Jersild, "Children's Fears, Dreams, Pleasant and Unpleasant Memories." *Child Development Monongraphs*, No. 12. New York: Teachers College Press, 1933.)

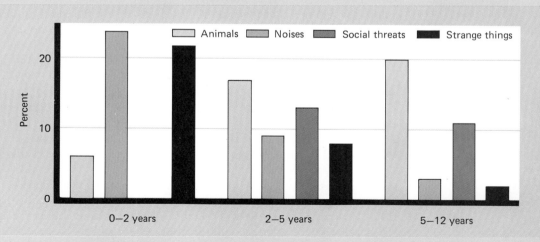

also indicate feelings. Whether a person shakes your hand briefly or for a long time, firmly or limply, can tell you something about what he or she feels toward you.

A word of caution is needed here. Although overt behavior can be a clue to emotion, it is not always infallible. Laughing and crying sound alike, for example, and we bare our teeth in smiles as well as in snarls. Crying can "mean" sorrow, joy, anger, nostalgia, or that you are slicing an onion. Moreover, as with verbal reports, it is always possible that someone is putting out false clues. And we all have done something thoughtlessly—turned our backs, frowned because we were thinking about something else, laughed at the wrong time—that has given offense because these acts were taken to express an emotion that we were not, in fact, feeling at that time.

Application

OBESITY

"California slim," croons a voice. We watch enviously as lithe, suntanned young bodies surf, swim, jog, and ride bikes in various states of undress. It is only a television soft-drink commercial, but it reflects a social reality. Fitness is America's obsession; people now worry about cellulite the way they used to worry about crabgrass. Thin is in, and the generous proportions so admired in the past by artists like Rubens and Renoir are decidedly not chic today.

But unfashionable or not, many people *are* overweight, and some are heavy enough to be considered obese. Why do people become fat? One explanation, offered by Donald Thomas and Jean Mayer (1973), presents obesity as an internally controlled, physiological phenomenon. According to Thomas and Mayer, the obese person is unable to rely on normal internal signals of hunger and satiety. They believe that surplus energy—mainly due to inactivity—is an important cause of weight problems. One of their studies found that overweight girls ate several hundred calories *less* per day than girls of normal weight. The cause of their obesity seemed to be a lack of exercise; the overweight girls were only about one-third as physically active as the girls of normal weight.

But more recent research seems to support an alternative view, stressing the importance of food as a powerful stimulus affecting obesity. According to Schachter and his colleagues (1971*a*, 1971*b*), fat people are particularly sensitive to environmental food cues. External or environmental cues—like the sight or smell of food—can trigger hunger in all of us, but Schachter believes that fat people are particularly vulnerable to such stimuli.

Schachter's theory is supported by several important studies. In one, subjects were given either a vanilla milkshake or one with bitter-

(Rhoda Galyn, Photo Researchers)

tasting quinine. Obese subjects drank more of the vanilla milkshakes than did normal-weight subjects, but they drank less than normal subjects when the milkshakes were filled with quinine. In other words, obese people seem to be more sensitive to such external stimuli as the taste of food. In another study, subjects were offered some almonds with shells and some without. Normal subjects ate nuts more or less equally from both batches. But while 19 of the 20 obese subjects ate almonds without shells, only 1 ate the almonds that had shells. This suggests that obese people do not like to work very hard for food and will eat only when food is easily available.

More recent research (Rodin et al., 1977) also supports Schachter's view that obese people are more sensitive to external food cues, even though they are no more sensitive than people of normal weight to *internal* cues, such as stomach activity (Stunkard & Fox, 1971). Of course, fat people may be more sensitive to external food cues *because* they are fat. Since our fitness-conscious culture considers obesity deviant, people who are fat often restrict their food intake. Paradoxically, this restraint may make them more aware of external cues, which they then depend on more than do people of normal weight (Costanzo & Woody, 1979). Anyone who has ever been on a diet knows that a hot fudge sundae is even more tempting and distracting when it is taboo!

Scientists today understand more about obesity than they used to, but are still unsure of its causes. Although evidence supporting Schachter's theory seems to be mounting, there are still some puzzling inconsistencies. For example, some studies have shown that the *very* obese—people 50 percent or more above ideal body weight—are no more sensitive to external food cues than people of normal weight (Rodin, 1973).

Summary

1. *Motivation* consists of a series of stages. First a stimulus triggers a motive, which in turn leads to behavior. If the behavior results in the attainment of the goal, the motive is satisfied and the chain is complete.
2. *Primary drives* are unlearned and are common to every animal. They include hunger, thirst, pain, and sex. They are triggered by physiological stimuli and by both internal and external cues. All of them are subject to learning and experience. Of the four drives, sex is the least dependent on physiological factors.
3. As the stimuli that motivate these drives become more complex, so do the behaviors that satisfy them.

4. A second set of motives that is largely innate depends more on external stimuli than on internal physiological states. These *stimulus motives*, such as curiosity, activity, exploration, manipulation, and contact, push us to investigate, and often to alter, our environment.

5. All animals seem to need *activity*, but we do not know if activity is a motive in itself or a combination of other motives.

6. The motives of *exploration* and *curiosity* appear to be activated by the new and unknown and to be directed toward finding something out. Unfamiliar and complex things seem to have more appeal to animals than the familiar or simple, but sometimes the unknown can be distressing or even frightening.

7. *Manipulation* is directed toward a specific object that must be touched, handled, played with, and felt. Manipulation appears to be limited to primates, who have fingers and toes. The desire to manipulate expresses a need to know something at a tactile level and sometimes a need to be soothed.

8. The need for *contact* with others is much broader and more universal than the need for manipulation. It can involve the whole body and can be passive.

9. Some motives are learned as we develop. One important class of learned motives are *social motives*, which center around our relationships with other people. Social motives include achievement, power, and affiliation.

10. The need for achievement—*nAch*—varies from person to person. If children see that their actions lead to successful changes in the environment and then have these actions reinforced, they are more likely to develop a high need for achievement. People with a high *nAch* are more likely to choose self-directed occupations than those with a low *nAch*.

11. Horner found that women have a *motive to avoid success*. This may relate to how women are raised in our society. A later study found that men also have this motive. In both men and women, this fear may simply be due to a desire to avoid inappropriate sex behaviors.

12. The *power motive* is the need to control or influence other people or groups.

13. The *affiliation motive*—the need to be with others—is usually aroused when people feel threatened. Fear and anxiety are closely linked to the affiliation motive.

14. Abraham Maslow proposed that all motives can be arranged in a *hierarchy*, from lower to higher. According to this theory, higher motives will appear only after the more basic ones have been satisfied. The most evolved motive in Maslow's hierarchy is *self-actualization*.

15. Emotions, like motives, arouse and direct our behavior.

16. No single classification has succeeded in dealing with the richness and complexity of emotional experiences. There are, however,

several categories, or families, of emotion that may help us distinguish among them: emotions that cause us to approach something, those that cause us to avoid something, and those that cause us to approach something aggressively.

17. The *Yerkes–Dodson law* says that the more complex the task at hand, the lower the level of emotion that can be tolerated without interfering with performance. On the other hand, emotions can organize and direct behavior just as motives can.

18. One influential model that helps us understand emotion was designed by Robert Plutchik. His main categories of eight emotions also vary in intensity. The more intense the emotion, the more motivation it supplies. Different emotions also combine to produce even more complex emotions.

19. There are three basic theories about emotion. The *James–Lange theory* maintains that emotion is the result of visceral, or *peripheral*, reactions. The perception of a stimulus causes the body to undergo certain physiological changes, and these changes are the cause of emotion.

20. The *Cannon–Bard theory*, unlike the James–Lange theory, holds that emotions and bodily responses occur simultaneously, not one after the other. When a stimulus is perceived, nerve impulses pass through the thalamus, where they are split, some going to the cortex—where the stimulus is perceived and the emotional response is experienced—and some to the muscles and viscera—where the physiological reactions take place.

21. *Cognitive theories* state that emotion results from the interaction of cognitive and physiological processes. Most emotional states are quite diffuse, and many emotions are accompanied by essentially the same physiological reaction. Cognitive theorists believe that our interpretation is affected by events and people in the environment, by memories, by our predisposition to look for and respond to certain stimuli, and by our culture.

22. It appears that peripheral mechanisms interact with cognitive processes in the brain and produce what we call emotion.

23. *Verbal reports* do not always give a complete picture of what a person is feeling, because people may be unable or unwilling to report their emotions accurately. Research into people's descriptions of various emotions has, however, found wide agreement about what emotional labels mean.

24. *Nonverbal communication*—facial expressions, position, posture, distance between people, explicit acts, and gestures—can be a useful clue to emotion. In many cases, nonverbal communication contradicts a person's verbal message. Many facial expressions do not appear to be learned, and many are universal. Although each culture has its own distinct "vocabulary" of facial expressions and gestures, most people have only minor problems recognizing many emotions when they are nonverbally displayed by people from other cultures.

Outline

Chapter 10

Measuring Intelligence and Creativity

Test A
Describe the difference between laziness and idleness. Which direction would you have to face so your right hand would be toward the north?

Test B
What does *obliterate* mean?
In what way are an *hour* and a *week* alike?

Test C

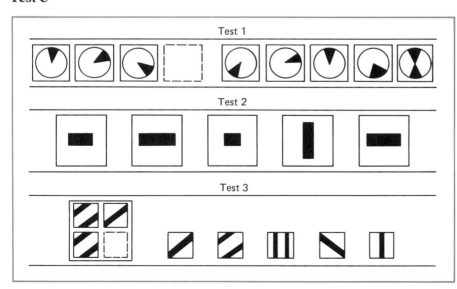

1. Test 1. Select the item that completes the series.

2. Test 2. Mark the one item in each row that does not belong with the others.

3. Test 3. Mark the item that correctly completes the given matrix, or pattern.

Test D

Choose the numbered block which best completes the pattern in Figure A.

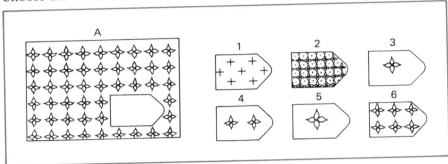

Test E

	Answer

1. The opposite of hate is:
   1. enemy, 2. fear, 3. love, 4. friend, 5. joy .... ( )
2. If 3 pencils cost 25 cents, how many pencils can be bought for 75 cents? .... (9)
3. A bird does not always have:
   1. wings, 2. eyes, 3. feet, 4. a nest, 5. a bill .... ( )
4. The opposite of honor is:
   1. glory, 2. disgrace, 3. cowardice, 4. fear, 5. defeat ...... ( )

Test F

1. Choose the lettered word or phrase which is most nearly *opposite* in meaning to the word in capital letters:

SCHISM: (A) majority   (B) union   (C) uniformity
         (D) conference   (E) construction

2. Choose the one word or set of words which, when inserted in the sentence *best* fits in with the meaning of the sentence as a whole:

From the first the islanders, despite an outward _____, did what they could to _____ the ruthless occupying power.
(A) harmony .. assist   (B) enmity .. embarrass
(C) rebellion .. foil   (D) resistance .. destroy
(E) acquiescence .. thwart

3. Select the lettered pair which best expresses a relationship similar to that expressed in the original pair:

CRUTCH: LOCOMOTION: (A) paddle: canoe   (B) hero: worship
(C) horse: carriage   (D) spectacles: vision   (E) statement: contention

Test G

Write a title for this short-story plot: "A new clerk in a department store, in anticipation of winter, ordered 10 dozen gloves, but forgot to specify that they should be in pairs. The store now has 100 left-handed gloves."

What would be the results if people no longer needed or wanted sleep?

List the possible jobs that might be symbolized by a "light bulb."

Test H

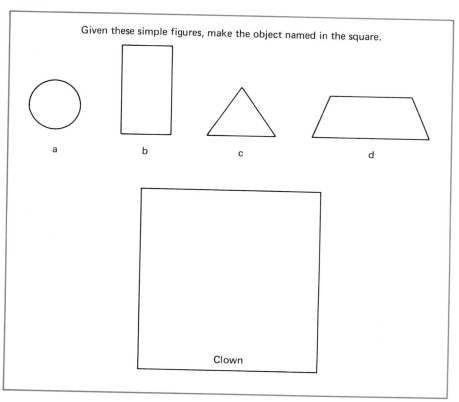

Given these simple figures, make the object named in the square.

a   b   c   d

Clown

Test I

1. The first three figures are alike in some way. Find the figure at the right that goes with the first three.

A   B   C   D   E

2. Decide how the first two figures are related to each other. Then find the one figure at the right that goes with the third figure in the same way that the second figure goes with the first.

A   B   C   D   E

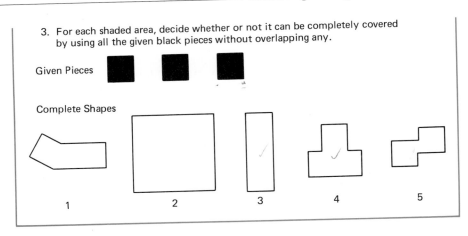

3. For each shaded area, decide whether or not it can be completely covered by using all the given black pieces without overlapping any.

These questions have been taken from various psychological tests, and except for Test G, all of them claim to measure different facets of "intelligence." Obviously, we cannot see the complex mental processes that are involved in intelligence. We have to approach the subject indirectly—by watching what people do when situations require the use of intelligence. But what do these tests actually tell us? If you could answer one of the questions above, does it mean that you should be able to answer all of them? What do your answers say about you? Do they tell us anything about your background or motivations? Can they be used to predict how successful you will be in school, in a job, or in your personal life?

Intelligence Tests

THE STANFORD–BINET INTELLIGENCE SCALE

The first "intelligence test" was designed by Alfred Binet—director of the psychological laboratory at the Sorbonne—and his colleague, Theodore Simon, for the French public school system. Binet and Simon developed a number of questions and tested them on schoolchildren in Paris to find out which children were retarded, or had trouble learning in school.

The first *Binet–Simon Scale* was issued in 1905. It consisted of 30 tests arranged in order of increasing difficulty. With each child the examiner started at the top of the list and worked down until the child could no longer answer questions. By 1908, they had tested enough children to predict what the normal average child could do at each age level. From these average scores, Binet developed the concept of *mental age*. A child who scores as well as an average 4-year-old has a mental age of 4; a child who scores as well as an average 12-year-old has a mental age of 12.

In the next 10 years a number of Binet adaptations were issued, the best known of which was prepared at Stanford University by L. M. Terman and issued in 1916. Terman introduced the now famous term **IQ** (*intelligence quotient*), and set the score of 100 for a person of average intelligence.

The Stanford–Binet Scale has been revised twice since 1916, for two reasons. First, any test must be updated as word meanings and styles change. Second, Terman and his colleagues found that some questions were easier for people from one part of the country than from another, that some were easier for boys than for girls—and vice versa—and that some failed to discriminate between age levels since nearly everyone tested could answer them. Such questions were replaced. Test A at the start of the chapter is drawn from the revised Stanford–Binet.

The Stanford–Binet test is not simply passed out to a roomful of students. Instead, each test is given individually, by trained examiners. The test resembles an interview. It takes about 30 minutes for young children and up to 1½ hours for older ones. For instance, 3-year-olds are asked to identify a toy cup as something "we drink out of," and to name objects such as "chair" and "key"; 6-year-olds are asked to define words such as "orange" and "envelope" and to complete a sentence such as, "An inch is short; a mile is _____." A 12-year-old might be asked to define "skill" and "juggler" and to complete the sentence: "The streams are dry _____ there has been little rain" (Cronbach, 1970).

The standard procedure is to begin by testing just below the expected mental age of the subject. If a person fails a test, he or she is then given the test at the next lowest level, and so on, until the test is passed. This level is then established as the person's *basal age*. Once the basal age is established, the examiner continues testing at higher and higher levels until the person fails *all* the tests. Then, the tests stop. After scoring the tests, the examiner determines the subject's mental age by adding to the basal age credits for each test passed above that age level.

This preschool child is taking the pictorial identification part of the Stanford-Binet intelligence test.
(Nancy Hays, Monkmeyer)

THE WECHSLER ADULT INTELLIGENCE SCALE

The individual test most often given to adults is the *Wechsler Adult Intelligence Scale* (WAIS). The WAIS was published in 1939 by David Wechsler, a psychologist at Bellevue Hospital in New York. Wechsler objected to using the Stanford–Binet for adults on three grounds. First, the problems had been designed for children and seemed juvenile to

This high school student is taking the Wechsler Adult Intelligence Scale which measures both performance and verbal skills.
(Sybil Shacleman, Monkmeyer)

adults. Second, the mental age norms of the Stanford–Binet did not apply to adults. Finally, the Stanford–Binet overemphasizes verbal skills. Wechsler felt that adult intelligence consists more in the ability to handle the environment rather than in the skill to solve verbal and abstract problems.

The WAIS is divided into two parts. One part stresses verbal skills, the other stresses performance skills. The *verbal scale* includes tests of information—"How many nickels make a dime?" "Who wrote *Paradise Lost*?"—tests of simple arithmetic—Sam had three pieces of candy, and Joe gave him four more. How many pieces of candy did Sam have then?"—and tests of comprehension—"What should you do if you see someone forget a book on a bus?" The *performance scale* also measures routine tasks. People are asked to "find the missing part"—buttonholes in a coat, for example—to copy patterns, and to arrange three to five pictures so that they tell a story (Cronbach, 1970). Test B at the start of this chapter is taken from the WAIS.

Although the questions and instructions might be more sophisticated on the WAIS than on the Stanford–Binet, the problems are not especially adult ones. Wechsler's chief innovation was in scoring. First, the subject is given verbal and performance scores, and an overall IQ score. Usually scores on the two scales are similar, but high performance scores and low verbal scores might mean that a person had little education. Second, on some items the subject can earn one or two extra points, depending on the complexity of his or her answer. This gives credit for the reflective qualities we expect to find in adults. Third, on some tests, both speed and accuracy affect the score.

GROUP TESTS

The Stanford–Binet and the WAIS are individual tests. The examiner takes the subject to an isolated room, spreads the materials on a table, and spends from 30 to 90 minutes giving the test. The examiner may then spend another hour or so scoring the test according to detailed instructions in the manual. Obviously this is a time-consuming, costly operation. Moreover, the examiner's behavior may influence the score.

For these reasons, test-makers have devised written intelligence tests that a single examiner can give to large groups. Instead of a person sitting across the table asking you to name an object, the test booklet gives you a choice of four words. Instead of building a design with blocks, you choose one of four shapes that will complete a design. Tests C–F and Test I in the introduction to this chapter are all from group tests.

When people talk about intelligence tests, they most often mean group tests, because this is how they were tested in school. Schools are among the biggest users of group tests. From fourth grade through high school, tests such as the *School and College Ability Tests* (SCAT) and the *California Test of Mental Maturity* (CTMM) are used to measure students' specific abilities. The *Scholastic Aptitude Tests* (SAT)—Test F in the introduction—and the *American College Testing Program* (ACTP) are designed to measure a student's ability to do college-level work. The *Graduate Record Examination* (GRE) plays the same role on the graduate level. Group tests are also widely used in different industries, the civil service, and the military.

Group tests have some distinct advantages. They eliminate bias in the examiner. A computer or a clerk who never saw the subject can score marks on an answer sheet quickly and objectively. More people can be tested in this way and thus better norms can be established. There are also some distinct disadvantages of group tests, however. There is less chance that the examiner will notice if a student is tired, ill, or confused by the directions. Those students not used to being tested tend to be more handicapped on group tests than on individual tests (Anastasi, 1976). Emotionally disturbed children also seem to do better on individual tests (Bower, 1969; Willis, 1970).

Another problem of group tests involves the kinds of items that are used. In particular, multiple-choice questions may not be a fair way to measure those who have an original, innovative way of looking at things. One person may decide, for example, that a horn-shaped object looks more like a flower than a musical instrument. Group tests have also been called inflexible since they prevent subjects from concentrating on those items that most suit their level of ability. On the Stanford–Binet, as we saw earlier, people are tested on the basis of previous performance. This means that to some extent the tests are tailored for each person. On group tests, people may be bored by those questions that are too easy and frustrated by those that are too hard (Anastasi, 1976).

(Mimi Forsyth, Monkmeyer)

PERFORMANCE AND CULTURE-FAIR TESTS

Deaf children take longer to learn words than children who can hear. Immigrants, who may have been lawyers or teachers in their own countries, may need time to learn English. Infants and preschool children are too young to understand directions or answer questions. How can we test these people? One way is to use problems that minimize or eliminate the use of words, that is, **performance tests** or nonverbal tests of various sorts.

One of the earliest performance tests, the *Seguin Form Board*, was devised in 1866 to test the mentally retarded. The form board is essentially a puzzle. The examiner removes the cutouts, stacks them in a predetermined order, and asks the person to replace them as quickly as possible. Another performance test, the *Porteus Maze*, consists of a series of increasingly difficult printed mazes. The examiner asks the person to trace his or her way through the maze without lifting the pencil from the paper. This test gives the examiner the equivalent of a mental age based on the most difficult maze a person negotiates.

One of the most effective tests used for very young children is the *Bayley Scales of Infant Development*. The Bayley Scales are used to evaluate the developmental abilities of children from ages 2 to 2½. One scale tests perception, memory, and the beginning of verbal communication. Another scale measures sitting, standing, walking, and manual dexterity. The Bayley Scales can detect early signs of sensory and neurological defects, emotional problems, and troubles in a child's home (Anastasi, 1976).

Culture-fair tests try to measure the intelligence of people who are outside of the culture in which the test was devised. Like performance tests, culture-fair tests minimize or eliminate the use of language. Culture-fair tests also try to eliminate skills and values—such as the need for speed—that vary from culture to culture. A good example of this is the *Goodenough–Harris Drawing Test*. The subject is asked to draw the best picture of a person that he or she can. The drawing is scored for proportions, correct and complete representation of the parts of the body, detail in clothing, and so on. It is not scored for artistic talent.

Cattell's *Culture-Fair Intelligence Test* comes in three levels and can be used from 4 years of age to "superior adults." At each level, one test demands verbal comprehension and specific cultural knowledge, and a second test is "culture-fair." By comparing these two tests, cultural factors can be isolated from "general intelligence." Examples of culture-fair items from the Cattell test can be found in Test C in our introduction. Cattell claims that the instructions for these tasks can be given in a foreign language, or by pantomime, without affecting test performance. But these tests have not always produced the desired results. In some countries with cultures very different from ours, test performance was lower. And American black children from poor homes did no better on the Cattell test than they did on the Stanford–Binet (Willard, 1968).

Another culture-fair test developed in England by Raven is the *Progressive Matrices* (Test D in our introduction). This test consists of 60 designs, each with a missing part. The subject is given 6 to 8 possible choices to replace the part. The test involves various logical relationships and requires discrimination. It can be given to one person or to a group. Like the Cattell Test, the accuracy of the Progressive Matrices has been questioned for groups whose cultural background is not American middle-class (Anastasi, 1976).

What Makes a Good Test?

All the tests we have mentioned claim to measure the same thing: intelligence. How do we know if they really do? Is one test better than another? Psychologists answer these questions on the basis of a test's **reliability** and **validity.**

RELIABILITY

By reliability psychologists mean whether a person's score is dependable and consistent. If your alarm clock is set for 8:15 and goes off at that time every morning, it is reliable. But if it is set for 8:15 and rings at 8:00 one morning and 8:40 the next, you cannot depend on it; it is unreliable. Similarly, if you take the same test twice and get roughly the same score each time, the test can be said to be reliable. The results are consistent. If, however, you score 90 on a verbal aptitude test one week and 60 on

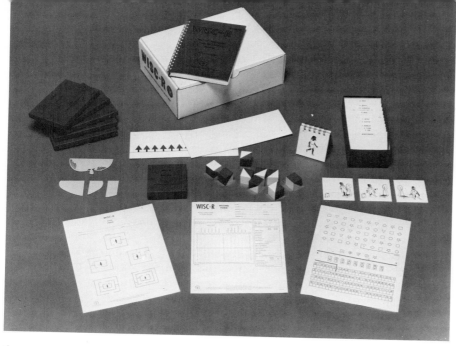

(The Psychological Corporation)

the same or an equivalent test a week or two later, something is wrong.

How do we know if a test is reliable? Before any test is published or released, its reliability is measured by at least one of several techniques. The simplest way is to give the test to a group and then, after a short time, give the same people the same test again. If they score the same each time, the test is reliable. For example, look at these scores from eight people tested one year apart:

Person	First Testing	Second Testing
A	130	127
B	123	127
C	121	119
D	116	122
E	109	108
F	107	112
G	95	93
H	89	94

This is a very reliable test. Although the scores did change slightly, none changed by more than six points.

There are some potential problems with this test of reliability. Most people, for example, improve and do better when they retake the same test. In fact, they may even remember answers from the first testing and simply repeat them the second time around (Anastasi, 1976). To avoid this, *alternate forms* of the test are often used. In this method, two equivalent tests are designed to measure the same ability or subject. If a person gets the same score on both forms, the test is reliable. One way to create alternate forms is to split a single test into two parts, for example, to assign odd-numbered items to one part and even-numbered items to the other. If scores on the two halves agree, the test is said to have **split-half reliability.** Most intelligence tests do have alternate equivalent forms—for example, there are many versions of each college admission test.

319

These methods of testing reliability can be very effective. But is there some way of being more precise than simply calling a test "very reliable"? Psychologists express reliability in terms of correlation coefficients, which measures the relationship between two sets of scores.* If test scores on one occasion are absolutely consistent with those on another occasion, the correlation coefficient would be 1.0. If there is no relationship between the scores, the correlation coefficient would be zero. In the example given above, where there was a close, but not perfect, relationship between the two sets of scores, the coefficient is .96.

How reliable are intelligence tests? For the Stanford–Binet there is only a 5 percent chance that a child's true IQ score is more than 10 points from the score obtained on any one occasion. On the WAIS, there is only a 5 percent chance that a person's true IQ score is more than 5 points from the score obtained on any one occasion. Performance and culture-fair tests are somewhat less reliable.

Scores on even the best tests vary a bit from one day to another, however. Many testing services, therefore, now report a person's score along with a range of scores that allow for variations due to chance. The person might be told that his or her score was 105, with a range of 95–115. This implies that the true score almost certainly lies somewhere between 95 and 115, but is most likely within a few points of 105. It should be clear, then, that even with the *best* intelligence tests, differences of a few points in IQ scores have little meaning, and should not be the basis for major decisions, such as putting a child in an accelerated or remedial program.

We have seen that some intelligence tests are reliable. The person who has an IQ score of 110 on one test is not likely to score much above 120 or below 100 on the same test taken on some other day. But does the test really measure "intelligence"? In fact, intelligence tests—or any other kind of test—can only measure *behavior*. These tests show that people will behave fairly consistently from one day to the next when tested, but how do we know that the consistency is due to "intelligence" and not to something else? This is what psychologists mean by test validity.

VALIDITY

Reliability involves the consistency of test scores. Validity focuses on their accuracy. A valid test is one that measures what it sets out to measure. There is, however, more than one way to determine if a given test actually measures what it claims to measure.

CONTENT VALIDITY. Does a test contain an adequate sample of the skills or knowledge that it is supposed to measure? If it does, it has *content validity*. Consider, for example, an achievement test on U.S. history. All of the items on the test must relate to the main topic. The different aspects of the field must also be covered in correct proportion. The test

*For more information on correlation coefficients, consult the appendix on measurement and statistical methods at the end of this book.

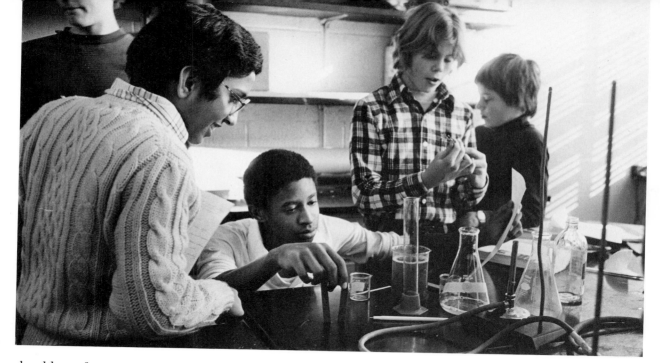

should not, for example, overemphasize the Civil War and ignore the Revolution. Nor should the test include too many questions that can be answered too easily.

To design a test with high content validity, then, you must know ahead
of time what you want to measure. But "intelligence" is so vague, that
it is much more difficult to know if a given test over- or underemphasizes
some aspect of it. Do the questions in Tests A–F and Test I adequately
sample what is meant by intelligence? What, in fact, is "intelligence"?

Psychologists have developed more and more complicated ideas of what
"intelligence" is, and, therefore, about what the proper content for intelligence tests should be. Charles Spearman, a British psychologist, began
working on a theory of intelligence around 1900. It struck him that people
who are bright in one area often seem to be bright in other areas. So
Spearman argued that intelligence is more than an accumulation of specific skills. Instead, he maintained, intelligence is quite general, a kind of
well, or spring, of mental energy that flows into every action. The intelligent person understands things quickly, makes good decisions, carries on
interesting conversations, and so on. He or she behaves intelligently in
various situations. All of us are quicker in some areas than in others.
We may find math easy, for example, but will spend hours writing an
essay. But Spearman saw these differences as simply ways in which the
same underlying general intelligence was revealed in different activities.
To return to the image of a well or spring, general intelligence is the fountain from which specific abilities flow like streams of water in different
directions. If this is correct, an intelligence test should have a variety of
questions, but exact content is not terribly important, since all questions
measure the same underlying intelligence.

L. L. Thurstone, an American psychologist, partly agreed with Spearman,
but he thought the differences between various abilities needed more
attention. From the results of various intelligence tests, Thurstone made a
list of seven primary mental abilities (Thurstone, 1938):

321

S–Spatial ability*
P–Perceptual speed
N–Numerical ability
V–Verbal meaning

M–Memory
W–Word fluency
R–Reasoning

To read a book, you need verbal meaning, word fluency, and reasoning.
(Ed Lettau, Photo Researchers)

Thurstone believed that these abilities are relatively independent of one another. A person with high spatial ability might be low on word fluency, for example. But together, Thurstone felt, these primary mental abilities are what we mean when we speak of general intelligence. According to Thurstone, one or more of these abilities can be found in any intellectual activity. To read a book, you need verbal meaning, word fluency, and reasoning. To study that same book for an exam, you also need memory. Thurstone thus presented a somewhat more complex model of intelligence than Spearman's. According to Thurstone's model, a valid intelligence test should cover all seven primary abilities about equally.

J. P. Guilford found both Spearman's and Thurstone's models of intelligence incomplete. Guilford distinguished three basic kinds of mental ability: **operations,** the act of thinking; **contents,** the terms in which we think—such as words or symbols; and **products,** the ideas we come up with (Guilford, 1961). Each of these categories can be broken down further. The result is the three-dimensional model shown in Figure 10–1. At least one factor from each category of the three major categories, Guilford claimed, is present in all intellectual activities.

For example, you are reading a newspaper column on the candidates in a mayoral election. Reading involves three operations: cognition, memory—you recall the candidates' speeches and ads—and evaluation: Does the columnist make sense? Do the candidates make sense? In performing these operations you use two kinds of contents: semantic—the words—and behavioral—the activities or behavior described. The products of your reading are inferences—this person would make a good mayor, that person would not—and classes—two candidates are liberal, the third is conservative. You may also discover some relationships. Perhaps the candidate born in the central city understands its problems better than the two who were raised in the suburbs. According to this model, a valid intelligence test might be expected to sample all 120 combinations of operations, contents, and processes.

We have seen that as the meaning of "intelligence" becomes more complex, it is harder to decide if a given intelligence test has content validity, that is, if its items adequately represent what is meant by "intelligence." Let us look at some of the standard intelligence tests and try to determine if they have content validity.

Alfred Binet specifically designed his test to measure qualities like judgment, comprehension, and reasoning. The test was more heavily verbal than perceptual or sensory. Binet himself felt that his intelligence test did not measure a single entity called "intelligence." Instead, he believed that his test sampled various different mental operations, all of which are part of intelligence. As we saw earlier, Binet's original test has been revised and updated several times. At the earliest age levels, the test now

*Spatial ability is the ability to perceive distance, recognize shapes, and so on.

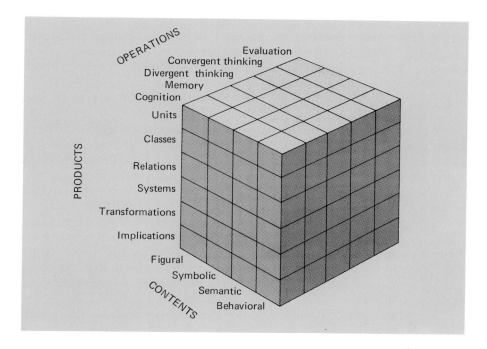

Figure 10–1
Guilford's three-dimensional model of the structure of the intellect. The model is made up of 120 small cubes, or factors. Each factor can be classified according to operation, product, and content.
(From J. P. Guilford, "Factorial Angles to Psychology," *Psychological Review*, 1961, *68*, 1–20. Copyright © 1961 by the American Psychological Association. Reprinted by permission.)

requires eye–hand coordination, discrimination, and the ability to follow directions. Children build with blocks, string beads, match lengths, and so on. Older children are tested on skills they learn in school, like reading and math. The tests still rely heavily on verbal content: vocabulary, sentence completion, and interpreting proverbs, for instance. And the tests that are not strictly verbal require understanding of fairly complex verbal instructions.

Most people would agree that the content of the Stanford–Binet is at least part of what we commonly consider "intelligence," so that we can conclude that the Stanford–Binet does have at least some content validity. But the heavy emphasis on verbal skills suggests that the test may not adequately sample all aspects of intelligence equally well.

As we saw earlier, it was partly the Stanford–Binet's emphasis on verbal skills that prompted Wechsler to devise the WAIS. Wechsler believes that his 11 subtests together do adequately measure what we call "intelligence," which he defines as "the aggregate or global capacity of the individual to act purposefully, to think rationally, and to deal effectively with his environment." If you look back at Thurstone's theory of intelligence, you can see that the WAIS covers many of the primary abilities that Thurstone included under "intelligence."

So far, we have looked at the validity of the two major individual intelligence tests. What about group tests? How valid is *their* content? They rely on written questions and answers, and do not require any non-verbal behavior, like moving blocks around. But they do include tests that ask people to make *quantitative* decisions—for example, to decide if 5 x 0 is greater, less than, or equal to 5—to work with geometric figures, and to solve mathematical tasks. Of course, to solve a math problem, the

The Stanford-Binet now measures the eye-hand coordination of younger children.
(Alice Kandell, Photo Researchers)

subject must also be able to read and understand verbal instructions.

In general, then, most intelligence tests do include content that seems relevant to "intelligence," though some—like WAIS—may be more representative than others. But as we shall see later in this chapter, there are many critics who are far from convinced that intelligence tests have *sufficient* content validity.

CRITERION-RELATED VALIDITY. Is test content the only way to determine if an intelligence test is valid? Fortunately, it is not. If both the WAIS and the SAT measure intelligence, high scores on one should go with high scores on the other. If school grades reflect intelligence, then students with good grades should be high scorers on the Stanford–Binet, or on the WAIS, or on any other intelligence test. In each case we can compare scores on the test with some other "direct and independent measure of that which the test is designed to predict" (Anastasi, 1976, p. 140). The independent measure against which the test is evaluated is the criterion. This "criterion-related validity" may be more appropriate than "content validity" for determining if aptitude and personality tests are, in fact, valid.

Using this measure of validity, various intelligence tests do relate well with each other, despite the differences in their content. People who score high on one test do tend to score high on the others. Again, we can use the correlation coefficient to describe the strength of the relationship. The Stanford–Binet and WAIS correlate around .80. The SAT and WAIS have a correlation coefficient of about .60 to .80. Raven's Progressive Matrices and the Porteus Maze Test correlate .40 to .80 with other intelligence tests. The Goodenough–Harris Drawing Test correlates about .50 or better with other tests. Thus, despite their differences in surface content, most intelligence tests do seem to be measuring similar things.

But the real question about IQ tests is if they predict academic achievement. As we shall see later, even the strongest critics agree that this is one thing that IQ tests do well. The Stanford–Binet was designed specifically to predict school performance, and it typically does this quite well. Correlations between grades and IQ of .50 to .75 are quite common. Like the Stanford–Binet, the WAIS also correlates highly with school grades, especially the verbal IQ score.

Group "aptitude" tests were also specifically designed to predict school achievement. Many are used for admission to colleges and graduate schools. The SCAT—used in elementary and high school—correlates .40 to .70 with grades. The SAT and ACT college admissions tests correlate around .50 with college grades. The GRE is also a good predictor of performance in graduate school. Evidence on the various performance and culture-fair tests is scanty but suggests that these tests do not predict school grades as well as other intelligence tests (Blum, 1979).

It seems, then, that IQ tests are reasonably reliable and valid measures of "intelligence." But in the past decade IQ tests have been heavily criticized despite this. In large part, this criticism has arisen because of research on the determinants of intelligence—research that often uses standard IQ tests such as those we have been discussing. Let us look at some of the research and then at the criticisms of IQ tests it has triggered.

Research on Intelligence

HEREDITY

About 30 years ago, R. C. Tryon began wondering if the ability to run mazes could be bred into rats. Horse breeders and cattle farmers have long known that selective breeding—for example, crossing a fast horse with a strong one—can change the physical characteristics of animals. Could the same technique alter mental abilities? Tryon isolated eligible pairs of "maze-bright" rats in one pen and "maze-dull" rats in another. The animals were left free to breed. Within a few generations the difference between the two groups was astounding: The maze-dull rats made many more mistakes learning a maze than their bright counterparts (Tryon, 1940; see Figure 10–2).

It is difficult to explain how maze ability was transmitted. Perhaps the brighter rats inherited better eyesight, larger brains, quicker reflexes, greater motivation, or a combination of these things. Still, Tryon did show that a specific ability can be passed down from one generation of rats to another.

Obviously, laboratory experiments in selective breeding of humans are impractical. Nature, however, gives us nearly perfect experimental subjects for measuring heredity in humans: identical twins. Unlike siblings and fraternal twins, whose genes come from the same parents but have combined differently, identical twins have exactly the same genetic inheritance. If, as Tryon's experiment suggests, intelligence is inherited, they will have identical IQs. Any difference between them can be attributed to environment.

Studies of twins begin by comparing the IQ scores of identical twins who have been raised together. The correlation, shown in Figure 10–3, is very high. But these twins grew up in the same environment: They shared parents, home, schoolteachers, vacations, and probably friends and clothes too. These common experiences may explain their similarity. To check this possibility, researchers look for identical twins who were

Figure 10–2
Errors made in learning a maze by the rats Tryon bred to be maze-dull. The colored line shows what percentage of the parent group made each number of errors. The black lines show the results of the eighth generation of rats. Notice that almost all of the maze-dull rats made more errors than the maze-bright rats.
(After R. C. Tryon, "Genetic Differences in Maze-Learning Abilities in Rats," In *39th Yearbook, Part I, National Society for the Study of Education.* Chicago: University of Chicago Press, 1940, 111–119.)

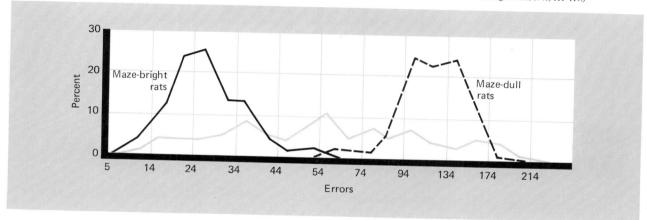

separated early in life—generally before they were 6 months old—and raised in different families. The correlation between IQs of separated twins is nearly as high as that between twins raised together, but there is some evidence of environmental influence.

Heredity clearly affects IQ scores. But what about fraternal twins, brothers and sisters, parents and their new child? The correlation between their IQs is not nearly as high as that for identical twins. Finally, researchers compare the IQs and intellectual development of unrelated children raised in the same home and of adopted children and their foster parents: The correlations here are very low (Munsinger, 1975).

At this point the case for heredity seems to be won: Identical twins have about equal IQ scores, even when they have not been raised together. For several reasons, however, twin studies are not "final proof." First, it is so difficult to find identical twins who were separated at birth that very few such pairs have been studied. Second, adoption agencies tend to match natural and foster parents. If the twins were born to middle-class, educated parents, it is highly likely that the adopted twin was placed with middle-class, educated foster parents. Finally, even if the twins grew up in radically different environments, for 9 months they lived in the same

According to Tryon, these identical twins should have the same IQ. Any difference between them is the result of environment.

(Bettye Lane, Photo Researchers)

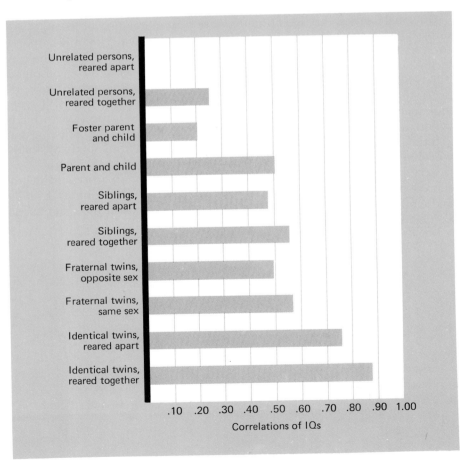

Figure 10–3
Correlations of IQ scores and familial relationships.

(Adapted from L. Erlenmeyer-Kimling and L. F. Jarvik, "Genetics and Intelligence: A Review," *Science*, 1963, *142*, 1477–1479. Copyright 1963 by the American Association for the Advancement of Science.)

mother: Their prenatal experiences were identical. Therefore, at least some of their similarity may actually be due to similar environment. It is here that the environmental case begins.

ENVIRONMENT

Environmentalists do not deny that some part of intelligence is inherited, but they feel this is only the start. Each of us inherits a certain body build from our parents, but our actual weight depends on what we eat and how much we exercise. Similarly, environmentalists argue, we inherit certain mental capacities, but how our intellectual abilities develop depends on what we see around us as infants, how our parents respond to our first attempts to talk, the schools we attend, the books we read, the TV programs we watch—and even what we eat.

The environmental case begins even before birth. A number of studies show that prenatal nutrition affects IQ scores. For example, one group of psychologists studied a group of pregnant women who were poor and therefore rarely got "three square meals a day." Half the women were given a dietary supplement, and half were given placebos—to guard against the possibility that merely taking pills would make the women feel better and that this, not nutrition, would affect their babies. When given intelligence tests between the ages of 3 and 4, the children of the mothers who had taken the supplement scored significantly higher than the other children (Harrell, Woodyard, & Gates, 1955).

Extreme malnutrition during infancy can lower IQ scores and may lead to retardation that cannot be cured by improved diet in later years.

For example, severely undernourished children in South Africa averaged 20 points lower in IQ than similar children with adequate diets (Stock & Smythe, 1963). If children do not get an adequate diet early in their development, both their mental and their physiological growth will be stunted.

None of this is surprising: Common sense tells us that we need food to grow. But is that all we need? Apparently not. Many psychologists think that surroundings are as important to mental development as diet. The first hint of this came from studies of the effect of light deprivation on sight. Chimpanzees, kittens, rabbits, and other animals raised in total darkness for 16 to 18 months and then moved to a normal environment could never see as well as animals exposed to daylight since birth. There was nothing wrong with these animals' eyes at birth. It seems the cells and nerves we use to see do not develop without stimulation (Wiesel & Hubel, 1963).

Even more revealing was a further study of Tryon's maze-bright and maze-dull rats conducted in the 1950s. Psychologists raised one group of mixed bright and dull rats in absolutely plain surroundings, and another group in a stimulating environment that contained toys, an activity wheel, and a ladder. When the rats were grown, they were tested on the mazes. There was no difference between formerly bright and dull rats that had been raised in a restricted environment—indicating that the inherited abilities of the bright rats had failed to develop—and little difference between the rats raised in the unusually stimulating environment—indicating that the maze-dull rats could make up through experience what they lacked in heredity. The researchers performed autopsies on both groups and found that the rats brought up in a stimulating environment had heavier brains than the others, whether or not they had inherited maze-brightness (Cooper & Zubek, 1958).

Quite by chance, one researcher found evidence that IQ scores also depend on stimulation. In the 1930s, psychologist H. M. Skeels was investigating orphanages for the state of Iowa. Then, as now, the wards were terribly overcrowded: Often 3 or 4 attendants were responsible for washing, dressing, feeding, and cleaning up after as many as 35 children. There was rarely time to play with the children, to talk to them or to read them stories. Many of the children were classified as subnormal. It was fairly common for the state to transfer them to institutions for the mentally retarded when the orphanages ran out of space. Skeels became interested in two such children who, after 1½ years in an orphanage, were sent to a ward for severely retarded adult women. When Skeels first tested these girls, they did seem retarded, but after a year on the adult ward their IQs were normal (Skeels, 1938). This was quite remarkable. After all, the women they had lived with were themselves severely retarded. Skeels decided to repeat the experiment and placed 13 slow children as houseguests in adult wards (Skeels, 1942). Within 18 months the mean IQ of these children had risen from 64 to 92 (within the normal range), all because they had had someone to play with them, to read to them, to cheer when they took their first steps, to encourage them to talk. During the same period the mean IQ of a group of children who had been left in orphanages dropped from 86 to 61. Such dramatic changes

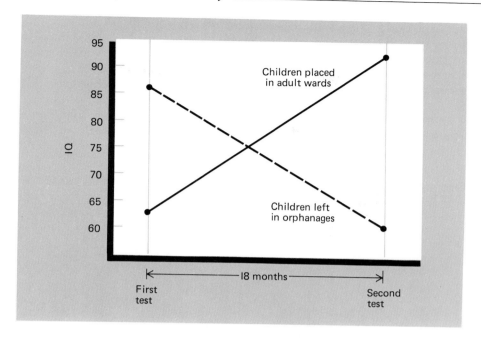

Figure 10–4

Changes in IQ of the institutionalized children studied by Skeels.

(Adapted from H. M. Skeels, "The Study of the Effects of Differential Stimulation on Mentally Retarded Children: A Follow-up Report," *American Journal of Mental Deficiencies*, 1942, *46*, 340–350.)

could not occur if intelligence were stable and hereditary. Skeels found 30 years later that all 13 of the children raised on adult wards were self-supporting, their occupations ranging from waitresses to real estate sales people. Half of the contrasting group were unemployed; four were still in institutions, and all those who had jobs were dishwashers (Skeels, 1966).

Taking their cue from Skeels, some researchers suggest that child-rearing patterns explain class differences in IQ. They point out that lower-class mothers, especially mothers with large families, often do not play with their children as much as middle-class mothers do. Nor do they reward them consistently for achievements—such as learning to crawl or to tell time. Middle-class parents encourage their children to talk. They ask them to describe what they are building with blocks, to identify shapes, colors, and sizes. Those who claim that intelligence depends on stimulation explain the lower IQs of some poor children in terms of thwarted curiosity, an underdeveloped attention span, and a general mistrust of adults.

This is the essence of the environmentalist case. True, some general abilities are inherited, but without stimulation a child's intelligence will not develop. The effects of early deprivation—whether the extreme loneliness of the institutionalized child or the relative isolation of some lower-class children—may not be reversible in later life.

THE JENSEN CONTROVERSY

The recent furor over IQ testing was triggered by a 1969 article by psychologist Arthur Jensen that criticized compensatory education programs such as Head Start. The purpose of Operation Head Start was to

Environmental psychologists would claim that the IQ of this girl was positively affected because of the encouragement she received from her mother.

(Erika Stone, Photo Researchers)

act as a kind of foster middle-class environment for disadvantaged children. Its purpose was not only to teach children basic concepts, but also to encourage them to put their perceptions into words. The program sought to teach children to trust adults, to feel comfortable in a schoolroom, and to exercise their curiosity: in other words, to get children ready for school.

In the first part of his article, Jensen examines the evidence that intelligence is inherited and concludes that heredity accounts for at least 80 percent of the variation in IQ. He then turns to the question of the effect

IQ SCORES, FAMILY SIZE, AND BIRTH ORDER

Zajonc (1975) presents some striking findings about the relationship between IQ scores, family size, and birth order. After reviewing research conducted by Belmont and Marolla (1973), who collected IQ and birth-order statistics on 386,114 young men in the Netherlands, Zajonc concluded:

Intelligence declines with family size; the fewer children in your family, the smarter you are likely to be. Intelligence also declines with birth order; the fewer older brothers or sisters you have, the brighter you are likely to be.

Zajonc and Markus (1975) constructed a model of the intellectual environment of a family in order to account for these findings. Their model suggests that when a newborn baby enters a family, the average intellectual environment of the family is lowered. Each parent is arbitrarily given an "intellect score" of 100. But the zero score assigned to the newborn baby lowers the average intellectual environment in the family to a level of 67. If a second child is born 2 years later, the family's average score will drop to nearly 50. One simple way to explain this is to imagine the intellectual capacity of the parents being spread among a number of young children. The more children there are, the smaller the amount that will be passed to each child.

To maximize the intellectual environment of your children, Zajonc suggests that you have no more than two children and that you have them at least 3 years apart. One of the benefits firstborn children have is the opportunity to teach things to their younger siblings. Contrary to popular belief, Zajonc has found that only children are not better off intellectually. This is probably because they lack this teaching opportunity.

There is some doubt about Zajonc's conclusions. Other studies have suggested that when we look at *individual* families, rather than aggregate statistics, the results are very different. In fact, family size

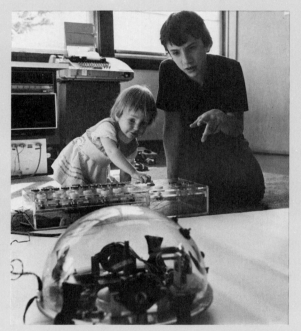

One of the benefits firstborn children have is the chance to teach their younger siblings.
(Hella Hammid, Photo Researchers)

appears to be much less important in determining mental abilities than social class and ethnic background. Although there is not enough research on the question, the *origins* of these influences may be related to such factors as education and environment. Children with well-educated parents who provide a rich intellectual climate are likely to have a better chance to develop their intellectual skills than children whose parents cannot provide them with these benefits (Page & Grandon, 1979).

of race differences on intelligence: Black Americans average 15 points lower than whites on IQ tests. Jensen claims that socioeconomic class does not explain these differences. Blacks in the upper and middle classes, as well as those in the lower class, have lower IQ scores than their white counterparts. American Indians, who are worse off in every way, score higher on IQ tests than blacks. Jensen concludes that discrimination and prejudice cannot explain the gap. According to Jensen, one must conclude that the gene pool of blacks differs from that of the general population. Although Jensen concluded that heredity is strongly implicated in IQ differences between groups, he did caution against drawing conclusions about any one person's IQ on the basis of such group generalizations.

Jensen's work caused a furious controversy among educators and social scientists over the validity of IQ testing, the heritability of intelligence, and the relationship between race and intelligence. Between 1969 and 1973 alone, 117 articles were published in response to his original piece in the *Harvard Educational Review* (1969). Critics have pointed out that for generations blacks were told that they belonged to an inferior race. The effects of such discrimination show in the fact that IQ scores for blacks from the northern part of the United States are significantly higher than those for southern blacks, suggesting that a higher level of discrimination in the South depresses IQ scores.

Second, teachers tend to expect less from black students and will communicate this, however subtly. The effects of low expectations and low self-esteem mount over the years.

Jensen assumes that blacks and whites from the same class live in the same environments. Few researchers would agree. In housing, for example, the average white construction worker owns his own home. His black co-worker, with the same salary and references, finds it much more difficult to find a home and to get a mortgage.

It is difficult to sort out the conflicting data and claims involved in the argument over Jensen's work. This is especially true since most of the participants, including Jensen and many of his critics, agree that *both* hereditary and environmental factors affect IQ. Dobzhansky (1973) insists that we simply do not have conclusive evidence to prove that there is, or is not, a genetic basis for racial differences in IQ scores. Moreover, as Jensen himself points out, we should remember that comparisons of average scores of any group tell us very little about what we can expect of any *one* member of the group. While these criticisms are directed specifically at Jensen's arguments, other critics have gone further and questioned the very nature of IQ tests themselves.

(Top: Myron Wood, Photo Researchers; bottom: Monkmeyer Press)

CRITICISMS OF IQ TESTS

TEST CONTENT AND SCORES. One major criticism of IQ tests is directed at their content. Many critics believe that intelligence tests not only do not measure all aspects of intelligence, but that intelligence tests are actually concerned with only a very narrow set of skills: passive, verbal understanding, the ability to follow instructions, common sense, and, at best, scholastic aptitude (Ginsberg, 1972; Sattler, 1975). For example, one critic observes: "Intelligence tests measure how quickly people can solve relatively unimportant problems making as few errors as possible, rather than measuring how people grapple with relatively important problems, making as many productive errors as necessary with no time factor" (Blum, 1979, p. 83).

These critics suggest that if there is just one thing that all intelligence tests measure, it is the ability to take tests. This would explain why people who do well on one IQ test also tend to do well on others. And it would also explain why intelligence tests correlate so closely with school performance, since academic grades also depend heavily on test scores. But whether this ability applies to other, real-life situations that require thinking is questionable (Blum, 1979).

A related criticism is that intelligence tests do not measure creative thinking, which may be far more important than the ability to follow instructions and to take tests. Guilford's complex model of intelligence (Figure 10–1) includes five kinds of operations, one of which is "divergent thinking." Divergent thinkers expand on the facts, letting their minds go wherever each piece of evidence leads. Instead of looking for the "right" answer, divergent thinkers develop all possibilities, producing different solutions that can then be evaluated or combined into an active decision. Although Guilford considers such divergent thinking a part of "intelligence," it is not reflected in the content or instructions of standard IQ tests. And there is some evidence that creativity is not closely related to IQ as it is usually tested.

In one study, Getzels and Jackson (1962) gave creativity and IQ tests to a group of fifth- through twelfth-graders. In subsequent comparisons between those who scored high in creativity and those with high IQ scores, they found distinct personality differences. The high-IQ children were conscientious, careful, and self-controlled. Their personal and career goals seemed to match those of their teachers. The creative children, on the other hand, were playful, expressive, and independent. Although they often worked harder than the children with high IQs, doing more than was expected of them, they did not get along well with their teachers.

A few years later, Wallach and Kogan (1965) conducted a similar investigation but divided the students into four groups. The students who were high on both creativity and IQ performed well in both free and controlled

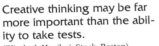

Creative thinking may be far more important than the ability to take tests.
(Elizabeth Hanilori, Stock, Boston)

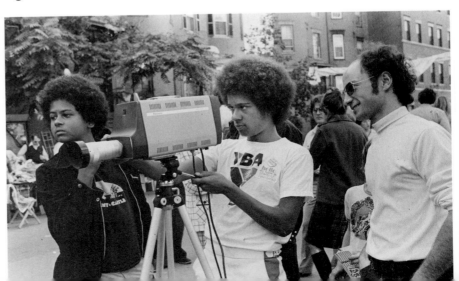

situations and with both childlike and adult behavior. The high-creative, low IQ children were most frustrated in the school environment, but were able to perform well in a freer context. The third group, those with low creativity but high IQ, placed high value on achievement in school and

CREATIVITY TESTS

To many people, the idea of testing creativity seems absurd. How can we measure imagination with a question that can be answered true or false, *a* or *b*? The answer is that we need not measure creativity with such questions. Creativity tests can be open-ended. Instead of asking for the right answers to a problem, the examiner asks how many solutions the subject can see. Scores are based on the number and originality of the subject's answers.

For example, in the *Torrance Test of Creative Thinking* the examiner shows the subject a picture and asks what questions he or she would ask to learn about what is happening in the picture, to explain how the scene came about, and to predict its consequences. The *Christensen–Guilford Test* asks the subject to list as many words with a given letter as possible; to name things belonging to a class—such as liquids that will burn; and to write four-word sentences beginning with the letters *R, D, L, S*—Rainy days look sad, Red dogs like soup, Renaissance dramas lack symmetry, and so on. The sample items on Test H in the introduction are taken from the Christensen–Guilford Test.

One of the most widely used creativity tests, Mednick's (1962) *Remote Associates Test* (RAT), asks the subject to produce a single verbal response that relates to a set of three apparently unrelated words. For example, the three stimulus words may be ''poke,'' ''go,'' and ''molasses.'' The person must answer with a single ''creative'' response. In the example given, the desirable response—though not the only possible one—is ''slow'': *slow*-poke, go *slow, slow* as molasses. Arriving at such responses is not easy, especially since the stimulus words have no apparent connection to each other.

A more recent test is the *Wallach and Kogan Creative Battery,* which is based on Mednick's definition of creative thinking: ''the forming of associative elements into new combinations which either meet specified requirements or are in some way useful'' (Mednick, 1962). Children are asked to ''name all the round things you can think of'' and to find similarities between objects—for example, a potato and a carrot.

(The Psychological Corporation)

It is possible for people who do not have high IQs to receive high scores on this test. The Torrance test, on the other hand, seems to require a reasonably high IQ for adequate performance. But the validity of the Wallach–Kogan test is not conclusive, nor is the Torrance test (Crockenberg, 1972; Anastasi, 1976).

Another problem with creativity tests is that unique or novel ideas may not be *good,* or useful ones. Until we can measure the *quality* of creative thinking, it will be hard to judge just how ''creative'' any test response is (Crockenberg, 1972).

How creative are people who do well on creativity tests? The correlation between test scores and the products we associate with creativity—paintings, poems, operas, inventions, cures for cancer—is low. Many psychologists explain these disappointing results by pointing out that creativity appears to depend on more than just certain kinds of intellectual abilities. For example, Tryk (1968) sees *motivation* as a critical factor in creative output. Great artists, scientists, or writers have more than simple ''talent'' or ''genius.'' They have intense dedication, ambition, and perseverance.

worked hard to excel at their studies. The students who scored low in both creativity and IQ tended to avoid their schoolwork and either concentrated on social activities or displayed regression or psychosomatic symptoms.* Like the earlier study by Getzels and Jackson, Wallach and Kogan's investigation suggested the existence of two somewhat different modes of thinking. Wallach and Wing (1969) studied the divergent thinking ability of a sample of college freshmen and compared this to the students' scores on Scholastic Aptitude Tests as a measure of intelligence. Again, there seemed to be little direct relationship between scholastic aptitude and divergent thinking ability.

All of these studies rely heavily on ways of testing creativity. Any conclusions from them must be qualified by what many experimenters regard as the dubious relationship between test scores and real-life creativity. But other studies at least partially avoid this problem by studying adults who have demonstrated outstanding creativity in their lives. In one, IQ tests were given to 64 eminent scientists. While some of them scored very high, many had such modest scores that there was not "the slightest clue that the subject was a scientist of reknown" (Roe, 1956). The most comprehensive study of IQ scores and creativity was conducted by Donald MacKinnon (1966). An IQ test was given to groups of mathematicians, creative writers, architects, research scientists, and electronic engineers. Test scores for each group were then compared with ratings of creative accomplishment. There was a low positive correlation between the two scores for mathematicians, but for all of the other groups there was no correlation at all. And when the IQ scores of two groups of architects— one outstanding, the other undistinguished—were compared, there was no difference in the average IQ scores of the two groups.

Still other critics suggest that the content and administration of IQ tests actually discriminate against minorities. In part this may be because minority children tend to see such tests as "just a game" and so make less of an effort to do well (Palmer, 1970). But it is also suggested that the unique language skills of black and minority children are not measured by most IQ tests (Blum, 1979). Moreover, examiners often complain that they "cannot understand" how poor black children talk, and this obviously does not encourage good test performance (Sattler, 1975).

Certain questions may have very different meanings for a white, middleclass child and for a black ghetto child. The Stanford–Binet, for instance, asks: "What's the thing for you to do if another boy hits you without meaning to do it?" The "correct" answer is, "Walk away." But for a ghetto child, whose survival may depend on being tough, the logical answer might be, "Hit him back." This answer, however, receives zero credit on the Stanford–Binet (Williams, 1970).

Even the culture-fair tests may accentuate the very cultural differences they were designed to minimize. Nonverbal tests, for example, may even be more culturally loaded than verbal ones. For example, when given a picture of a head with the mouth missing, one group of Oriental children responded by saying that the body was missing, thus receiving no credit.

---

*Regression—returning to behavior patterns characteristic of an earlier stage of development—and psychosomatic illnesses—physical disorders that have psychological origins—are discussed in more detail in Chapters 13 and 14 respectively.

The unique skills of minority children may not be measured by IQ tests.
(UPI)

To them, the absence of a body under the head was more remarkable than the absence of the mouth (Ortar, 1963). And nonverbal tests often require abstract thinking styles that are typical of Western, middle-class cultures (Cohen, 1969). Cattell's Culture-Fair Test, for example, may be easier for those cultural groups accustomed to working with pencils and paper or who are motivated to do well on tests.

There are many other reasons why minority children may do less well on IQ tests than middle-class whites (Sattler, 1975). Studies suggest that minority children are more wary of adults, more anxious for adult approval, less motivated to get "the right answer" just for the sake of being right, and less driven to achieve. These emotional and motivational deficits cannot help but be reflected in test performance. Finally, IQ scores—whatever test they come from—tend to oversimplify. An IQ score is really a very simplistic way of summing up an extremely complex set of abilities. The score may hide more than it shows. Maloney points out that we do not describe a whole personality with a two- or three-digit number. Why, then, he asks, should we try to sum up something as complex as intelligence by labeling someone "90" or "110"? (Maloney, 1978)

CHANGES IN IQ

Another criticism of IQ tests is that IQ scores change with time. People are sometimes tested only once, and this score follows them through life. But, in fact, IQ scores from early childhood have very little relationship to later IQ scores. It is not until children are about 3 years old that scores begin to stabilize (Bayley, 1970), but even then, IQ scores can change significantly, either spontaneously or because of various learning techniques.

Studies have linked large shifts in IQ to a number of factors (Bradway, 1945; Honzick, Macfarlane, & Allen, 1948; Rees & Palmer, 1970). Children in culturally disadvantaged environments tend to lose ground as they age; those with superior environments tend to gain (Anastasi, 1976). One child, whose score fluctuated dramatically, was shy and withdrawn when she was very young, and was part of a family in which there was a good deal of illness. After the age of 10, however, she began to develop various interests and become more outgoing (Honzick, Macfarlane, & Allen, 1948).

335

Changes have also been attributed to how much schooling a person receives between one test and another (Harnquist, 1973). And a follow-up long-term study of adults showed that how people cope with problems or frustrations seems to be associated with changes in IQ. The IQs of those who cope realistically and constructively tend to rise; the IQs of those who withdraw from problems or rationalize them away tend to fall (Haan, 1963).

These data raise the question of whether it is deliberately possible to change a person's IQ. In 1961, Heber launched the Milwaukee Project. Its purpose was to see if intervening in a child's family life could alter the effects of cultural and socioeconomic deprivation on IQ. Heber and his associates worked with 40 poor, mostly black families in the Milwaukee area in which the average IQ of the mothers was under 75 on the WAIS. The women were split into two groups. One group was given job training and sent to school. As they found jobs, they were also instructed in child care, home economics, and personal relationships. When all 40 women had had their babies, the research team began to concentrate on the children. The children of the mothers who were being given special training were taken to an infant education center at the age of 3 months. For the next 6 years, these children spent the better part of each day at the center. They were given nourishing meals and an educational program that included a wide range of educational toys. The children were cared for by paraprofessionals who behaved like nonworking mothers in affluent families.

All of the children were periodically given IQ tests. Those in the experimental group ended with an average IQ score of 126—51 points higher than the scores of their mothers. The average score of the children in the control group whose lives had not been changed as much was 94, still much higher than their mothers' average scores, probably because they had become accustomed to taking tests, an experience their mothers had never had.

Sandra Scarr-Salapatek and Richard A. Weinberg went a step further than Heber and his associates. They studied black children who had been adopted by white, well-educated families with moderate incomes. They found that children who had been adopted early in life and who had warm, intellectually enriched family environments got higher IQ scores than the national average score for blacks, and also did better in school (Scarr-Salapatek & Weinberg, 1976).

IQ AND SUCCESS. We have seen that the content of IQ tests has been heavily criticized. Critics complain that the content is limited and fails to test important abilities like creativity, that it is racially and ethnically biased, and that it greatly oversimplifies "intelligence." But despite these limitations, IQ tests do predict school performance. What does this fact mean and how important is it?

IQ scores should correlate well with academic performance, because both involve some intellectual activity and stress verbal ability. Moreover, both academic achievement and high IQ scores require similar kinds of motivation, attention, and continuity of effort (Ginsberg, 1972). And since academic success depends largely on test-taking ability, the correlation is not surprising. But critics suggest that there may be another, less attractive, reason for the relationship between school performance and IQ test scores. If teachers expect a student to do well in school—on the basis of his or her IQ scores—they may encourage the student. By the same token, a student with a low IQ score may not be expected to perform as well, and may be neglected as a result.

Whatever the reason, IQ scores do predict success in school with some accuracy. Moreover, people with high IQ scores get into high-status occupations: Doctors and lawyers tend to have high IQs; truck drivers and janitors tend not to have high IQs. But critics point out that this can be explained in various ways. For one thing, because people with higher IQs tend to do better in school, they stay in school longer; they get advanced degrees, which in turn open the door to high-status jobs. Moreover, children from wealthy families are more likely to have the motivation and the money needed for graduate school and occupational training. They also tend to have helpful family connections. Perhaps most important, they grow up in an environment that encourages academic success and rewards good performance on tests (Blum, 1979).

Studies have shown, however, that IQ scores and grades in college have very little to do with later occupational success (McClelland, 1973). We saw earlier that creative scientists, for instance, are no more likely to have high IQs than less gifted ones. In fact, we now know that when education and social class are held constant, in a wide range of jobs people with high IQs do not perform better than people with lower IQs. As early as 1921, Thorndike observed that the Stanford–Binet test was useful in predicting a child's academic achievement, but less helpful in determining "how well he will respond to thinking about a machine that he tends, crops that he grows, merchandise that he buys and sells and other concrete realities that he encounters in the laboratory, field, shop, and office. It may prophesy still less accurately how well he will succeed in thinking about people and their passions and in responding to these" (Sattler, 1975, p. 21).

USE OF IQ SCORES. If IQ tests were just used for some obscure research purposes, perhaps the criticisms would carry less weight. But because IQ tests have been used for so many significant purposes, their evaluation is very important.

Alfred Binet developed the first IQ test to help the French public school system identify students who needed to be put in special classes. Binet's test was designed as a diagnostic instrument—not as a means of distinguishing between genetic and environmental effects on intelligence. In fact, Binet believed that courses of "mental orthopedics" could be used to help those with low IQ scores.

But when the Binet–Simon test was imported to America and put to use by Lewis Terman, Henry Goddard, and Robert Yerkes, among others, it underwent some strange changes. These psychologists who were interested in eugenics believed that the test measured "innate intelligence" and could be used to detect people who were genetically inferior. When Terman published his Stanford–Binet test in 1916, he wrote, "in the near future intelligence tests will bring tens of thousands of . . . high grade defec-

IQ tests do predict success in school with some accuracy.
(Guy Gillette, Photo Researchers)

These immigrants came to the United States in 1906. Although it is hard to believe today, at one time the mental testing movement was used to discriminate against certain groups of immigrants.
(E. Levick, Prentice-Hall Photo Archives)

tives under the surveillance and protection of society." The surveillance and protection he had in mind extended to people with IQs in the 70–80 range, "very, very common among Spanish–Indian and Mexican families of the Southwest and also among negroes. Their dullness seems to be racial, or at least inherent in the family stocks from which they come" (Kamin, 1974).

Terman was writing at a time when some people believed that sterilizing the "unfit" would benefit society. The first modern sterilization law was passed by Indiana in 1907, and applied to crime, "in which heredity plays a most important part." Other states followed suit. Those in favor of sterilization used the genetic arguments of the IQ test pioneers to support their position. In 1917, Terman wrote, "If we would preserve our state for a class of people worthy to possess it, we must prevent, as far as possible, the propagation of mental degenerates."

Fortunately, sterilization was seldom enforced, but the mental testing movement was used for another discriminatory piece of legislation, the Johnson–Lodge Immigration Act of 1924, which established racial quotas for immigrants and largely excluded Orientals, Italians, Jews, Slavs, and refugees from Asia and southeast Europe who were believed to be genetically inferior. Supporters of the Immigration Act got much of their fuel from a book published by Carl Bughaim, with a foreword written by Yerkes (Kamin, 1974), that warned of the dangers of immigration: "Immigration should not only be restrictive but highly selective." Francis Kinnicutt, of the Immigration Restriction League, recommended to the U. S. Senate Committee on Immigration in 1923 that immigration from southeast Europe should be further restricted since "the evidence is abundant ... that ... it is largely of a very low degree of intelligence." Dr. Arthur Sweeney testified that "we have been overrun with a horde of the unfit. . . . The psychological tests . . . furnished us with the necessary yardstick. . . . We cannot be seriously opposed to immigrants from Great Britain, Holland, Canada, Germany, Denmark, and Scandinavia. . . . We can, however, strenuously object to immigration from Italy . . . Russia . . . Poland . . . Greece . . . Turkey. . . . The Slavic and Latin countries show a marked contrast in intelligence with the western and northern European group. . . . Being constitutionally inferior they are necessarily socially inadequate. . . . We shall degenerate to the level of the Slav and Latin races . . . pauperism, crime, sex offenses, and dependency" (Kamin, 1974).

Today such ideas seem almost unbelievable to many people. But critics point out that IQ tests continue to be misused in more subtle ways. For example, using IQ tests to put a person into a "track" or "slot," as in school classes, can backfire. To the extent that a child gets a low score on an IQ test because of test bias, language handicap, or disinterest, labeling the child "slow" or "retarded" and putting him or her into special classes apart from "normal" students can have a disastrous effect, one that may get worse, not better, with time. Although the American Medical Association's Council on Mental Deficiency defines mental retardation as "subaverage general intellectual functioning . . . associated with impairment in adaptive behavior," Jane Mercer found that 42 percent of children labeled retarded by public schools had IQs above 70 and suffered from no physical disabilities (Mercer, 1972). Mercer and her colleagues also found that most of the adults who were considered retarded were competent in their social roles for people their age. Almost all of them could take care of themselves; 65 percent of them were employed. Mercer concludes that *adaptive behavior* is as important as IQ scores in judging if a person is retarded, but that very often IQ tests alone are used to make this decision.

In this section, we have looked at the various criticisms that have been leveled at IQ tests and their use. But criticism does not always mean that the critics want IQ tests to be altogether eliminated. Instead, these criticisms may serve to make IQ tests more useful. For example, Mercer has developed a "System of Multicultural Pluralistic Assessment" (SOMPA), which can be used to test children between the ages of 5 and 11. SOMPA takes into account both the dominant school culture and family background, and IQ scores (based on the WAIS) are then adjusted accordingly (Rice, 1979).

In any event, it is important to remember that an IQ score is *not* the same as intelligence. Tests measure a person's ability level at a certain point in time, in relation to the norms for his or her age group. IQ scores do not tell us why someone performs poorly or well. Moreover "intelligence" is not a single entity. Rather it is "a combination of abilities required for survival and advancement within a particular culture" (Anastasi, 1976). Obviously, these abilities will vary from culture to culture and from one age to another. Those abilities most important in one culture will tend to increase; abilities that are deemphasized will tend to decrease (Levinson, 1959).

Although IQ tests are useful for predicting academic performance and for reflecting past learning, there is much that they do not measure—motivation, emotion, and attitudes, for example. In making vital decisions, it is important that we know as much as possible about a person. IQ tests cannot tell us all that we need to know.

Application

THE GIFTED CHILD

Children with low IQ scores may be assigned to special classes for "slow learners." But what about children with high IQ scores? Recently, there has been a national movement to establish special programs for "the gifted," based largely on their performance on standard IQ tests. In 1979, over 600,000 public school students were designated as "gifted," and one in every four school districts now has special provisions for these children, from enriched activities in their regular classes to separate classes altogether. The United States government has allocated funds to help states underwrite such programs. By 1983, the federal government may be spending $50 million on

There has been a recent movement to establish enriched educational opportunities for children of high intelligence.

(Dan Hogan Charles, *The New York Times*)

these programs. The states themselves spent $110 million in 1979.

The Ann Arbor, Michigan, public school system joined the "gifted revolution" in 1979, launching a pilot program for fourth, fifth, and sixth graders identified as gifted primarily by achievement test scores, but supplemented by information from parents and teachers about the children's creativity, motivation, and intelligence. The children labeled "gifted" will spend two half-days each week in special classes where they will engage in learning activities based on their own interests. This "pullout" program with an "enrichment room" is the most common approach, although schools use various methods to provide special attention for exceptional students.

Anne Remley (in the *Ann Arbor Observer*, October, 1980) points out that this emphasis on gifted students is often based on certain assumptions which may not be true. One assumption is that the gifted are a distinct group, demonstrably superior to other people in intelligence and creativity. People who are "gifted" in one area, however, may not be gifted in others. For this reason, lumping "the gifted" together may do them all a disservice, says Jeffrey Zettel of the Council for Exceptional Children. Since students have diverse talents, some of these abilities are bound to be overlooked. A chess prodigy may have trouble with spelling, while a virtuoso violinist may be unable to write a complete sentence. To the extent that the selection of "gifted" students embraces a broad range of abilities and that programs allow for individual differences, this criticism is less valid.

A second assumption behind the argument for many gifted programs is that today's gifted child is tomorrow's natural leader. As we have seen, there is no evidence that high IQ scores by themselves predict such things as leadership. Whether "giftedness," defined in terms of a broader range of abilities, motives, and attitudes, is the mark of a future leader remains unproven.

Some advocates of gifted programs argue that gifted students are bored and unhappy in regular classes. But critics point out that students do not have to be bright to be bored! The gifted movement also assumes that if gifted students are labeled as such and given special treatment, they will more likely fulfill their unique potentials. This assumption also is untested, and like other "special classrooms," the idea may backfire. Even Jeffrey Zettel, who lobbies for aid to

(Drawing by Leonard Dove; © 1963 *The New Yorker Magazine, Inc.*)

exceptional students, admits that "labeled children are often victimized by a stigma associated with the label." Some children, it seems, would rather not be thought of as "brains." And gifted children may chafe under the pressure to perform. One "gifted" Ann Arbor student remarked, "I never felt so dumb in math in my life as when I was in the high math track." Psychologist Jacquelynne Parsons found that Ann Arbor junior high school students in advanced math classes feel that they do less well than students in mixed ability math classes. Perhaps most important is how "gifted" and "nongifted" children feel about themselves. We simply do not know yet how children react when they are divided up to fit into these special programs.

Finally, there is concern that special attention for one group—the gifted—will come only at the expense of other groups that could perhaps profit even more from the imaginative, individual attention that children in gifted programs receive. Why, ask some critics, cannot *all* children be treated as if they were gifted and be given a chance to develop skills such as creative thinking and problem solving? (Anne Remley, *Ann Arbor Observer*, October, 1980)

Summary

1. Since intelligence cannot be seen directly, psychologists concern themselves with what they view as intelligent behavior.
2. The first test of intelligence was the *Binet–Simon Scale*. This was adapted by Terman into the *Stanford–Binet Scale*. Terman also introduced the term IQ (intelligence quotient) and established the score of 100 for average intelligence. The test is administered individually, by a trained examiner.
3. The *Wechsler Adult Intelligence Scale* (WAIS) was designed especially for adults. It includes a verbal scale and a performance scale; it yields separate scores on the two scales, as well as an overall IQ. Like the Stanford–Binet, it is administered individually.
4. Group tests, like the *Scholastic Aptitude Tests*, are designed to be administered to many people at one time. Two advantages of group tests are efficiency in testing and the elimination of bias on the part of the examiner. One disadvantage is that of keeping the examiner from discovering specific problems the subject might have at the time of the test.
5. Performance tests are used to test people who are unable to take standard intelligence tests, such as infants, the handicapped, non-English-speaking people, and preschool children. These tests generally substitute puzzles or mazes for word questions. The *Bayley*

Scales of Infant Development, for example, are used to measure the development of very young children.

6. Culture-fair intelligence tests are designed to measure the intelligence of people who are not part of the test-maker's own culture, for example, immigrants or members of subcultures. They attempt to include only materials that will be equally unfamiliar to all cultural groups. Culture-fair tests include the *Goodenough–Harris Drawing Test, Cattell's Culture-Fair Intelligence Test,* and *Raven's Progressive Matrices.*

7. Psychologists judge intelligence tests on the basis of two factors: *reliability* and *validity.*

8. *Reliability* means that an individual's test score is dependable and consistent. Reliability can be measured by *retesting* people at different times and comparing the results, by using *alternate forms* of the same test, or by dividing the test into two parts and checking for *split-half reliability.* Reliability is expressed in terms of *correlation coefficients.* If test scores correlate perfectly, the correlation coefficient is 1.0; if there is no relationship between the scores, the coefficient is zero.

9. The most widely used tests—the Stanford–Binet, WAIS, and group tests—are very reliable. IQ scores vary only about 5 or 10 points in either direction.

10. Another way to measure intelligence tests is to evaluate their *validity. Content validity* means that a test contains an adequate sample of the skills or knowledge it is supposed to measure. Since "intelligence" is so difficult to define, it is hard to determine the content validity of IQ tests.

11. Various psychologists have sought to define intelligence. Spearman felt that intelligence is like a well, or spring, from which specific abilities flow. Intelligence itself is quite general; people who are bright in one area tend to be bright in others.

12. Thurstone compiled a list of seven primary mental abilities, making his model somewhat more complicated than Spearman's.

13. Guilford devised a three-dimensional *model of the intellect* to show the interactions of three classes of mental ability.

14. Over the course of time, psychologists have come to see intelligence as more and more complex. This is why it is hard to evaluate an IQ test's content validity. In general, however, most IQ tests appear to have a certain amount of content validity, although there are critics who do not agree with this assessment.

15. To assess personality and aptitude tests, it is more useful to look at their *criterion-related validity.* This is done by comparing scores on different tests or relating IQ scores to grades. If the scores correlate well, the test is considered valid. Most IQ tests do relate well, despite differences in content. With the exception of various performance and culture-fair tests, most IQ tests are good predictors of school grades.

16. Psychologists have long debated the question of whether intelligence is primarily inherited or developed by environmental

influences. Selective breeding experiments with rats and comparative studies of identical twins suggest that intelligence can indeed be passed on from one generation to the next. Further studies have shown, however, that without the proper environmental stimulation, inherited capacities will not develop to the fullest extent. Thus, the low IQs of poor children can be explained by the childrearing practices of poor families, which often cannot give children the attention and encouragement they need to stimulate their intelligence. The effects of early deprivation may not be reversible.

17. In 1969 Arthur Jensen suggested that the 15-point difference between the IQs of black and white Americans could be attributed primarily to inheritance. Jensen's critics, however, have argued that the effects of racial discrimination must be taken into account, no matter how similar black and white environments appear to be.

18. In the past decade or so, IQ tests have been criticized for a number of reasons. Critics attack the *content* of tests, claiming that they test only a limited number of abilities, many of which are not relevant to real-life situations. Some feel that the tests measure only the ability to take tests, and fail to tell us why or how someone arrived at his or her answers. IQ tests fall short in measuring creative thinking. Creativity and the kind of "intelligence" measured by IQ tests appear to have little in common.

19. Another objection to the content of IQ tests has to do with the fact that many people feel the tests are racially biased, discriminating against those who are not white, Anglo-Saxon, and middle class. IQ tests are also criticized for oversimplifying a very complex set of abilities.

20. IQ scores change over the course of time, becoming relatively stable by age 5, but remaining subject to change because of environmental, emotional, and learning factors. Several studies have been done on the effects of intervening in a child's family life in order to alter the effects of deprivation on intelligence. It appears that IQ scores can be dramatically improved by improving people's environments.

21. IQ tests have also been attacked on the grounds that there is no evidence that people with high IQ scores do better in their careers than those with lower scores, although they are more likely to hold high-status jobs. There is also no clear evidence that personal fulfillment and IQ scores are linked.

22. Critics are also concerned with the use, or misuse, of tests. Scores are sometimes used to put people into "slots," often with tragic results. Children with language handicaps, for example, may be labeled "retarded" simply on the basis of IQ scores. Critics argue that we should look at people's *adaptive behavior* before deciding whether or not they are retarded. Others feel that IQ tests are simply a convenient way of pigeon-holing people, and advocate doing away with the tests altogether.

Outline

Chapter 11

Personality

People often talk about **personality** as if it were a commodity, like a bright tie that adds life to an old suit. We sometimes also talk as if personality consisted only of appealing, admirable traits: affection, charm, honesty. But as we shall see in this chapter, to a psychologist personality is much more complex than the ordinary use of the word implies. For one thing, it includes negative as well as positive personal qualities.

It is easy to talk about aspects or traits of personality without defining the term itself. And we often do: "I don't trust that man. He isn't honest." Or, "I love Anne. She's goodhearted," are typical comments. But a broad definition of personality is difficult, partly because personality is not one characteristic or ability, but a whole range of them. Personality is a person's psychological signature: the behavior, attitudes, motives, tendencies, outlooks, and emotions with which he or she responds to the world. Personality, however, is not just individuality. It is consistency of individuality. It is reflected in our usual behavior.

Whether we are reflecting on our own behavior or interpreting the actions of someone else, we expect to find consistency. If a person is friendly one day, we would be surprised if he or she is unfriendly the next. If a relative who is usually quiet and mannerly suddenly turns loud and disrespectful, we are concerned and seek explanations. We know that life is not as predictable as a television serial, but we do expect a degree of consistency, a pattern of behavior that reflects each person's unique personality. And when we are faced with inconsistency, we suspect that something is wrong.

Thoughtful people have always tried to comprehend the variety of human personality. But it was only a century ago that scientists began to make systematic scientific observations of personality and to draw conclusions from them. The attempt to define personality continues. Some theorists emphasize early childhood experiences; some stress heredity. Others attribute the key role to environment. In this chapter, we will look briefly at some of the major personality theories in contemporary psychology, and at ways to assess personality.

345

Psychoanalytic Theory

A woodcut of Sigmund Freud by Jean Cocteau.
(The Bettmann Archive)

SIGMUND FREUD

To this day, Sigmund Freud is the best known and most influential personality theorist. Freud opened up a whole new route for the study of human behavior. Up to his time, psychology had focused on consciousness. Freud, however, stressed the **unconscious.** Although many of his views were modified by later research—Freud himself revised and expanded his theories throughout his life—his ideas are still the basis of **psychoanalysis** and influence our language, literature, customs, and child-rearing practices.

Freud came upon the technique that inspired his theory indirectly. After receiving his medical degree from the University of Vienna, Freud studied with Jean Charcot in Paris. Charcot was a French psychiatrist who used hypnosis to treat patients with hysteria. When Freud began to practice on his own as a specialist in nervous disorders, he became dissatisfied with the results of conventional treatment. At the suggestion of Dr. Josef Breuer, he used hypnosis to induce his patients to talk about their problems. Freud encouraged those patients whom he was unable to hypnotize to talk directly about their problems. From this he developed his psychoanalytic technique of the "free association of ideas."

Freud found that as patients described their thoughts and dreams, they began to remember things that they had forgotten. Once these were remembered, the patients could deal with them successfully. Thus, from his clinical work in the early 1900s, Freud developed his theory to explain the structure of the personality.

THE THREEFOLD STRUCTURE OF THE MIND. Freud believed that personality is composed of three interrelated parts: the **id,** the **ego,** and the **superego.** Unfortunately, popular usage has given each of these terms an identity of its own, making them seem like three separate forces vying to control a person. The three are really parts of one integrated whole: They interact so closely that few of their functions can be separated.

Freud considered the id the basic storehouse of energy from which the ego and the superego develop. It consists of all of the basic instincts that we are born with, such as hunger, thirst, sex, self-preservation, and aggression. Because the id is completely unconscious, it is only revealed indirectly through our dreams, actions, and behavior. For example, the absent-minded mistakes known as "Freudian slips" arise from the unconscious, and Freud believed that they revealed the workings of the id.

Freud also believed that the instinctual drives of the id are the source of the energy for personality. This energy is set in motion by deprivation, which results in discomfort or tension. The id has two means of relieving discomfort. One is by reflex actions, such as coughing, which relieves unpleasant sensations at once. Another is by what Freud termed "wish fulfillment," or **"primary process thinking."** A person can form a mental image of an object or situation that will relieve the uncomfortable feeling.

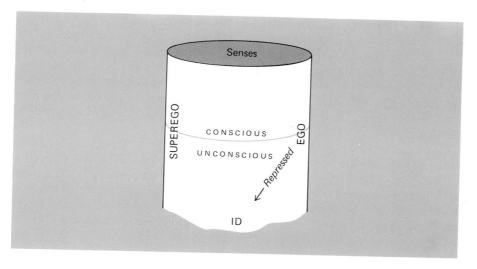

Figure 11–1
The structural relationships of the systems of the mind. The ego is partly unconscious, partly conscious, and receives knowledge of the external world through the senses. Thoughts repressed by the ego are kept unconscious. The superego is also partly conscious and partly unconscious. But the id is entirely unconscious. The open space at the bottom of the diagram indicates the limitlessness of the unconscious id.

(Adapted from a diagram from *The Complete Introductory Lectures on Psychoanalysis* by Sigmund Freud. Translated and edited by James Strachey. With the permission of W. W. Norton & Company, Inc. Copyright © 1966 by W. W. Norton & Company, Inc. Copyright © 1965, 1964, 1963 by James Strachey. Also by permission of The Hogarth Press Ltd. in *New Introductory Lectures on Psychoanalysis* by Sigmund Freud.)

Primary process thought is most clearly evident in dreams, but a person may also have a mental picture of a wish-fulfilling object or situation. On a hot, dusty day, for example, you may have a mental picture of yourself lying under a shady tree, sipping a cool drink. Although a mental image may give fleeting relief, however, it cannot actually satisfy a need. Just thinking about water does not quench your thirst. Therefore, the id by itself is not very satisfactory in gratifying instincts. It must ultimately have contact with reality if it is to relieve its discomfort. The id's link to reality is the ego.

Freud thought that the ego controls all thinking and reasoning activities. Through seeing, hearing, and touching, the ego learns about the external world. The ego also controls the ways of satisfying the id's drives in the external world. In seeking to replace discomfort with comfort, the id acts according to the **pleasure principle.** In contrast, the ego operates by the **reality principle.** That is, it protects the person against dangers that might result from the indiscriminate satisfaction of the cravings of the id. For

Figure 11–2
The pleasure principle expresses the basic tendency in human nature to avoid unpleasant experiences and seek only pleasant ones. The reality principle modifies the pleasure principle by using rational thought to find a safe means of satisfying the desire for pleasure.

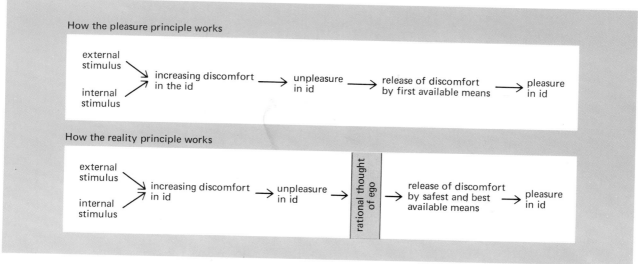

example, a thirsty person who sees a bottle filled with liquid would be apt to pick up the bottle and drink the liquid. It does not occur to the id to see first what is in the bottle. The id only knows that it is thirsty and wants a drink now. It is the ego that says, "Wait! That's poison! Let's go to the kitchen and drink water instead." Thus, by intelligent reasoning the ego tries to delay appeasing the id's desires until it can satisfy those desires safely and successfully. Freud called this type of realistic thinking **secondary process thinking.**

The ego, then, directs the personality. It gets its energy from the id, and its task is to satisfy the id's desires. But it must control the id and direct its energy into effective, realistic channels. Freud, who was very fond of analogies, compared the relation of ego and id to a rider trying to guide a spirited horse. A personality consisting only of ego and id, however, would be completely selfish. It would behave effectively, but unsocially. Fully adult behavior is governed not just by reality but also by morality, that is, by the **conscience** or the moral standards that people develop through interacting with their parents and society. Freud called this moral guardian the superego.

The superego is not present in a child at birth. As young children we are amoral and go for whatever appears pleasurable. As we mature, we assimilate, or adopt as our own, the judgment of our parents about what is

"Who needs a super ego with 'Him' around?"

"good" or "bad." In time, the external restraint applied by our parents is replaced by our own internal self-restraint. The superego, then, acting as conscience, takes over the task of observing and guiding the ego, just as the parents observe and guide the child.

According to Freud, the superego also compares the ego's actions with an **"ego ideal"** of perfection and then rewards or punishes the ego. Unfortunately, the superego may be too harsh in its judgments. Dominated by such a punishing superego, an artist, for example, knowing that he or she can never equal Rembrandt or Michelangelo, may just stop trying.

Ideally, the id, ego, and superego work in harmony. The ego satisfies the demands of the id in a reasonable, moral manner approved by the superego. We are then free to love and to hate, and to express our emotions sensibly without guilt. When our id is dominant, our emotions are unbridled and we are apt to be a danger to ourselves and to society. When the superego dominates, our behavior is checked too tightly and we cannot enjoy a normal life.

When our id is dominant, our emotions are unbridled.
(UPI)

DYNAMIC FORCES. Freud maintained that the id's energy arises from unconscious forces, or instincts, which are inborn needs. He distinguished two classes of instincts, **life instincts** and **death instincts.** Little is known about the death instincts, which reveal themselves chiefly in self-destruction or suicidal tendencies when they are directed against the self, and as aggression or war when they are directed toward others. Freud included under life instincts all those instincts involved in the survival of the individual and of the species: hunger, pain, self-preservation, and especially sex. Among the sexual instincts, however, Freud also included not only the genital sexual function but also impulses arising from other areas that are sensitive to erotic stimulation, such as the mouth, lips, and anus. He regarded sexual instincts as the most important drives in personality development. Freud called the energy generated by the sexual instincts libido.

There are four aspects of an instinct: its source, its aim, its object, and its intensity. The source of an instinct is bodily need or excitation (felt as tension). Its aim is to satisfy the need (to reduce tension). Its object is how to satisfy the need. Its intensity is the strength of the compulsion to satisfy the need. With hunger, for example, the source of the instinct is the body's need for food, which is felt as tension. The aim is to reduce the tension. The object is usually food. And the intensity is the energy used to get the food. A starving person will seek food much more eagerly than someone who ate a big meal an hour ago.

Freud believed that the source and aim of our instincts stayed the same throughout our life, except for natural changes that occurred as we matured. The object and intensity of our instincts, however, can change greatly. For example, a person may choose to substitute a different object to satisfy a given need. The energy generated by that need is then displaced onto a new object. This **displacement** of energy is the chief cause of differences in human behavior. According to our own interests, tastes, attitudes, and talents, each of us chooses different objects on which to expend our energy. The only instincts that cannot be displaced or deferred for long are hunger and thirst. **Sublimation,** which is a special kind of displacement, occurs when a person gives up one object for a higher cultural or social object. A person may choose, for example, not to marry and to have a family, but to stay single and to help others. Very often, Freud believed, artistic achievements result when sexual drives are sublimated into creative activities. Sublimation and displacement are examples of **defense mechanisms**—processes that can alter the object of an instinct. Other defense mechanisms will be discussed in more detail in Chapter 12.

Freud theorized, then, that all energy originates in the urges of the id. Some energy passes into the ego, where it is used in interactions with the external world. The ego stores up the excess energy it receives from the id and uses it for its rational processes: thinking, remembering, choosing, and acting. Part of the id's energy is also channeled into the superego, which uses it to oppose the id's "improper" urges.

PSYCHOSEXUAL STAGES. Freud believed that the sexual instinct is the most important instinct. He also believed that the sources and objects of this instinct change as humans develop. Freud explained these changes in his **psychosexual stages** of personality development. According to Freud (1949), our sexual instinct goes through critical developmental stages during childhood. In each of these stages, the libido is localized in a different erogenous zone. No two people experience these psychosexual stages in quite the same way, but what happens during the infantile period—up to the age of 5 or 6—greatly influences our adult personality.

During the **oral period,** the first of these ages, sexual activity is centered around the mouth. This is where the baby has the most contact with his or her environment. The id gets pleasure from biting, sucking, and spitting things out. In later life, such actions may be reflected in aggression, acquisitiveness, and contempt, respectively. An adult's habit of chewing gum or smoking may be caused from having been weaned too early or too late as a child. A person who does not easily trust other people may have been fed in infancy less than he or she wished, or may have been fed on an undependable schedule.

The **anal stage** is the second of the infantile stages. In this stage the child finds pleasure in expelling or in retaining feces. In learning bowel control, the child has its first significant encounter with authority and social pressure. Freud suggests that if parents are very strict in their toilet training, their children will learn to value holding back and may become stingy, miserly adults. If parents push their children to control themselves before they really can, the children may use expulsion to express hostility. As a result a child may become a cruel and bad-tempered adult.

During the **phallic period**—after the age of 3 or so—children discover their genitals and the pleasure of masturbation. It is at this time that the child develops a marked attachment for the parent of the opposite sex and becomes jealous of the parent of the same sex. Freud called this the **Oedipus complex** for a boy and the **Electra complex** for a girl. In Greek mythology, Oedipus killed his father and married his mother; he is thus a model for boys, who, Freud believed, sexually desire their mothers and would like to kill their fathers, who block this goal. Because our society prevents children from killing their fathers, the boy has no choice but to repress these unacceptable impulses. Moreover, he is afraid that his father

Sigmund Freud
(UPI)

knows what he is thinking and is going to punish him. This situation—where the boy is attracted to but repelled by his mother, and afraid of but violently jealous of his father—is the crux of the Oedipus complex. The Electra complex follows more or less the same pattern. In either case, the child eventually resolves the conflict by identifying with the parent of the same sex. At this point, Freud believed, the **latency period**—when children avoid intimate contact with the opposite sex—begins.

At puberty we enter the last stage, which Freud called the **genital stage.** In this stage our sexual impulses reawaken. In lovemaking, the adolescent and adult can satisfy unfulfilled desires from infancy and childhood. But it is during the three infantile stages—oral, anal, and phallic—Freud said, that the die of adult personality is cast (Hall & Lindzey, 1970).

Freud's beliefs, particularly his emphasis on sexuality, were not completely accepted even by those who were members of the psychoanalytic school. Carl Jung and Alfred Adler were two early followers of Freud who later broke with him and formulated their own theories of personality.

CARL JUNG

Carl Jung became a close associate of Freud in 1909. He left Freud's circle in 1913, however, and founded his own school of analytical psychology.

Jung's beliefs differed from Freud's in many ways. Jung contended that libido, or psychic energy, represents all the life forces, not just the sexual ones, and that it arises in the normal course of body metabolism just as physical energy does. Both Freud and Jung emphasized the role of the unconscious in determining human behavior. But where Freud saw the id as a "cauldron of seething excitations" that the ego had to control, Jung saw the unconscious as the ego's source of strength and vitality. Jung believed that there were two distinct levels of the unconscious: a **personal unconscious** and a **collective unconscious.** The personal unconscious contains our repressed thoughts, forgotten experiences, and undeveloped ideas. These ideas may rise again to consciousness if some incident or sensation triggers their recall.

The collective unconscious, which is perhaps Jung's most original concept, consists of the memories and behavior patterns inherited from past generations. Jung believed that just as the human body is the product of a million years of evolution, so over the centuries the human mind has developed "thought forms" or collective memories of experiences that people have had in common since prehistoric times. He called these thought forms **archetypes.** The archetypes are not mental images themselves. They do give rise, however, to certain typical mental images or mythical representations. Since all people have mothers, the archetype of "mother" is universally associated with the image of one's own mother, with Mother Earth, with a protective presence. The archetype of the hero who rallies his people can be equally represented in a primitive tribal chieftain, in Joshua at the battle of Jericho, or in John F. Kennedy, depending on the particular moment in history.

Jung proposed that there are two general attitude-types of personalities in people: the **introverted** type and the **extroverted** type. Extroverts are

Carl Jung
(Culver Pictures)

concerned with the external world. They are "joiners," interested in other people and in events. Introverts are more concerned with their own private worlds. They tend to be unsociable, and lack confidence in their dealings with people. Everyone, Jung felt, has some of both attitude-types, but one is usually dominant, while the other is largely submerged.

Besides these two general types, Jung further divided people into rational or irrational categories. Rational people regulate their actions by the psychological functions of thinking and feeling. In making decisions, they may be guided principally by thought, or they may give more weight to emotional factors and value judgments. In contrast, irrational people base their decisions on perception either through the senses (sensation), or through unconscious processes (intuition). Most people show some of these four psychological functions: thinking, feeling, sensing, and intuiting. Jung felt, however, that one or more of the four functions usually dominates the others. Thus, a predominantly thinking person is rational and logical and decides on the basis of facts. The feeling person is sensitive to his or her surroundings, acts tactfully, and has a balanced sense of values. The sensing type relies primarily on surface perceptions, rarely using imagination or deeper understanding. And the intuitive type sees beyond the obvious facts to predict future possibilities.

While Freud emphasized the sexual instincts, Jung stressed rational and spiritual qualities. While Freud considered development to be set in childhood, Jung thought that full psychic development occurred only at middle age. And while Jung had a sense of historical continuity, believing that the roots of the human personality extended back through our ancestral past, he also contended that a person moves constantly toward self-realization, toward blending all parts of his or her personality into an harmonious whole. Because Jung broke with Freud, whose theories have dominated the study of personality, and because of the symbolism and mysticism that characterize his theory, Jung's ideas have been somewhat neglected by psychologists. Recently, perhaps because of the popular interest in mysticism, Jung has been "rediscovered," and there is renewed interest in his theories.

ALFRED ADLER

Alfred Adler broke with Freud in 1911 and founded his own school of psychology. He, too, believed that behavior is shaped by unconscious, inborn forces. But, according to Adler, these forces are social urges. Adler considered people essentially social beings, exposed to personal relationships from birth and having to adjust to society constantly throughout life. Adler also stressed the role of consciousness in shaping personality and considered the ego more important than Freud did. He believed that people are not at the mercy of instinctual urges; each person is free to choose their own destiny, to create their own life plan, and to develop those traits, attitudes, and abilities that will help them to achieve their goals. Thus, a musician may organize a timetable allowing uninterrupted hours for daily practice; a gossip columnist may try to see as many people as possible.

Adler also believed that the driving motivation is a striving toward superiority, based, in part, on feelings of inferiority. Infants depend on adults for food, shelter, and protection. Throughout their early development, they are constantly reminded of their inferior position as parents, teachers, and other adults point out their faults and correct them. A physical defect, the presence of older brothers and sisters, or an unhappy home life may strengthen the inferiority reaction. To compensate for this "inferiority complex," Adler said, the child sets personal goals whose achievement brings a sense of superiority or fulfillment or a feeling of power over others. The goal may be realistic, such as becoming a teacher, a scientist, or a bank president; it may also be unrealistic, as when a person with scant musical ability aspires to be a concert pianist, or when someone with poor eyesight wants to be an airline pilot. In some cases, the striving for power may be neurotic, as with the person who uses illness to dominate others. But once a goal is chosen, all the person's actions consciously and unconsciously are oriented toward reaching it. The striving toward the goal provides the momentum of his or her life.

Two of the more prominent neo-Freudians, or "new Freudians," who accepted many of Freud's principles but developed their own theories of the motivation for human behavior, are Karen Horney and Erik Erikson.

Alfred Alder
(The Granger Collection)

KAREN HORNEY

Karen Horney, while admitting her great debt to Freud, disagreed strongly with some of his ideas, particularly with his analysis of women and with his stress on the sexual instincts. From her experience as a practicing psychoanalyst in both Germany and the United States, she concluded that environmental factors are the most important influence in shaping personality, and that the most vital of these factors are the human relationships with which the child grows up.

Horney believed that overemphasizing the sexual drives gave a distorted picture of human relationships. Feelings and drives do indeed arise from sexual desires, she said, but they may also arise from nonsexual sources. A mother, for example, may have purely maternal and protective feelings for her child. For Horney, **anxiety** is a stronger motivating force than sexual drives. (Anxiety is a disproportionate reaction to real and/or imagined danger; fear is a reasonable reaction to real danger.) Anxiety originates in childhood, when children depend on others for survival and cannot defend themselves against critical adults and a generally hostile world. Children therefore build defenses that allow them some satisfaction but that also keep them "safe." The child of domineering parents may adopt a submissive attitude, which frustrates his or her own desires somewhat but keeps the parents from getting angry. Children learn that if they are "good," their parents may reward them. They feel safe as long as they do not disobey. Alternatively, if they feel neglected, they may act aggressively to attract their parents' attention. Horney identified three general "neurotic trends," all of which attempt to resolve emotional problems and to secure safety at the expense of personal independence: moving toward people (submission), moving against people (aggression), and moving away from people (detachment).

Karen Horney
(Association for the Advancement of Psychoanalysis of the Karen Horney Psychoanalytic Institute and Center)

ERIK ERIKSON

Erik Erikson
(© Jill Krenentz)

Erik Erikson, who studied with Freud in Vienna, takes a more social view of personality development and stresses the workings of the ego more than Freud did. While he agrees with Freud's theory of sexual development, Erikson believes that this is only part of the story. Equally important is the child's sense of trust—self-trust and trust in others. Erikson points out that different societies value different characteristics. In some cultures mothers ridicule male children who cry. In others boys are encouraged to express their emotions. For Erikson, the quality of parent–child relationships is what counts. A child can be disciplined in a way that leaves a feeling of being loved or in a way that leaves the child feeling hated. The difference is largely in the atmosphere of the home. The important point is that children should feel that their own needs and desires are compatible with those of society. Only if children feel competent and valuable, in their own and society's eyes, will they develop a sense of identity. This, in Erikson's view, is crucial.

In contrast to Freud's emphasis on the childhood years, Erikson feels that personality continues to develop throughout life. In explaining this view, he outlined "eight stages of man," and suggested that success in each stage depends on a person's adjustments in the previous stages (Erikson, 1963).

1. Trust versus mistrust. In infancy, babies must acquire an "inner certainty" that their mother will love and care for them. They must also learn that they can rely on themselves. These are the bases of social trust and identity.
2. Autonomy versus shame and doubt. During their first 3 years, when children learn to walk and begin to talk, they are exploring their own powers. If their parents ridicule them—if they laugh when they fall down, taunt them for bed-wetting—the children will lose the sense of being competent, autonomous beings.
3. Initiative versus guilt. Between the ages of 3 and 6, children acquire motor skills, practice being adults in play and fantasy, and develop a conscience. It is also when they learn self-control. If their parents are too restrictive, if they discourage explorations, children lose the will to try. Failure in this stage is felt more as the loss of self-esteem than as the loss of parental love.
4. Industry versus inferiority. During the next 6 or 7 years, children learn the skills and values of their culture—in school, or at play. All children receive formal instruction in this stage. The need for self-discipline increases. If children have learned to trust themselves and their world in the earlier stages, they identify themselves with the goals of their society and find great satisfaction in their own accomplishments. If they have not learned trust, their feelings of inadequacy and mediocrity may be confirmed.
5. Identity versus role confusion. At puberty, childhood comes to an end. The responsibilities of adulthood loom ahead. Adolescents question the feelings and beliefs they have depended on through childhood. They compare their image of themselves with how others see them, their role

at home with their role among peers. They must work out a sense of inner continuity, an identity.

6. Intimacy versus isolation. Trusting young men and women who have a firm sense of identity can risk themselves in associations with others, can commit themselves to relationships and affiliations, and can maintain these commitments. If they cannot, they feel isolated.

7. Generativity versus stagnation. Adulthood is marked by expanded interests and concerns. People can give themselves over to guiding the next generation, directly and indirectly. They raise offspring and work to improve the world, to contribute to their society. If they are still struggling against mistrust, still unable to establish intimate relationships, they stagnate.

8. Integrity versus despair. Only the person who has been able to trust, to adapt to "triumphs and disappointments," to contribute to his or her world, feels what Erikson calls "ego integrity" in old age. Others fear death, having lost the chance for self-fulfillment.

Young adults, for example, often find themselves going through the life stages that Erikson calls identity vs. role confusion and intimacy vs. isolation in which identity and intimacy are crucial issues. Erikson claims that a person must achieve a sense of identity before he or she can have intimate personal relationships. "True engagement with others is the result and the test of firm self-delineation" (Erikson, 1959). Is it necessary to achieve identity in order to achieve intimacy? The answer would seem to be yes. Orlofsky, Marcia, and Lesser (1973) found that the college men who were the least isolated socially were also those with the highest sense of self. Some of the men were "rebels." They did not identify with the system. But they had a strong personal philosophy that seemed to help them succeed at forming open and intimate relationships with others. Orlofsky called these types "alienated achievers."

In a follow-up study of the same group of college men 6 years after the initial interviews, Marcia (1976) observed that identity was still related to intimacy: Achieving a sense of personal identity makes it possible to have successful personal relationships. Interestingly enough, Marcia made no reference to the alienated achiever group in the follow-up study, prompting one psychologist to suggest that this identity category may have been a temporary phenomenon of the 1960s. If this is true, it would lend further support to Erikson's assertion that personality is in part a reflection of one's cultural milieu.

The earliest study of identity status among college women (Marcia & Friedman, 1970) found that women who chose foreclosure—conventional identities accepted from others—were more likely to achieve intimacy than men who foreclosed. But later studies (Schenkel & Marcia, 1972) failed to support this difference between the sexes. It may be that a decade ago young college women could find an identity by accepting conventional norms. If so, one would expect that today more women will have begun to seek identity achievement. A more recent study, in fact, found that the relationships between identity and intimacy are now quite similar for both sexes. Both men and women now believe that a positive sense of identity is the basis for satisfying personal relationships (Orlofsky, 1978).

Self Theory

The **self theory** of Carl Rogers is similar to the theories of Freud, Jung, and others of the psychoanalytic school in that it develops out of Rogers' work with troubled people (see Chapter 14). The basic idea behind the self theory is that people know more about themselves and their problems than anyone else. Each person is thus the best one able to find ways of solving his or her problems. Rogers (1959) has carried this basic idea over to his theory of personality.

ORIGIN OF PERSONALITY

According to Rogers, infants have certain basic attributes. First, they create their own environment. What they experience constitutes their reality. Second, they have an inborn tendency to protect and maintain themselves and to develop their capacities. This tendency involves not only what is basic for life such as eating and sleeping, but all that leads to personal growth, reproduction, creativity, and movement toward personal goals. This inborn tendency is the motivating power of personality. Third, everyone exercises this inborn tendency within their own private world and makes value judgments about their experiences. People value as good those experiences that satisfy their needs or help them grow. They react negatively toward those that hinder growth or are unpleasant.

DEVELOPMENT OF THE SELF

As infants mature, Rogers believes that they gradually become aware of being and of functioning. Part of their private world is then distinguished as "me," and becomes the conscious self. The infants' awareness of self probably starts when they feel they have control over some part of their body or some part of their private world. At the same time, they make value judgments about what is pleasant and unpleasant.

However, the values that children develop are of two kinds: they make some values themselves; they take others over from other people but erroneously perceive them as their own. When people take over other people's values that are opposed to their own, they in effect lose touch with a part of themselves. For example, a child may like to tear up the daily newspaper, particularly before her father and mother have read it. For her, this is a very pleasant experience, which she values highly. But her father and mother indicate by words, gestures, and facial expressions that they do not approve of this behavior. The child then begins to view herself and her behavior in the same way her parents do. In effect she says to herself, "When you tear up the newspaper, you are a bad girl." But yet she knows "I like to tear up newspapers—it is fun." If the child responds by denying her own feelings, then she may lose touch with them and become "estranged" from herself.

Carl Rogers
(Courtesy of Carl R. Rogers)

Ideally, this distortion of the child's feelings need not occur. The parents could explain to the child that they respect her feelings but also have regard for their own, and that they cannot let her express herself when her wants cut across the feelings of others. The child could then have her destructive feelings wihout guilt, but could also choose to please her parents by leaving the newspaper intact, rather than to please herself by destroying it. Which ever course of action she chose, she would stay in touch with her feelings of satisfaction or of dissatisfaction. Once children begin to adopt disorienting values, however, their concept of self becomes distorted and the pattern continues through adulthood.

Constitutional and Trait Theories

One of the earliest theories of personality is **constitutional theory,** which asserts that body type and personality are related. The most fully researched and documented version of this theory, that of William Sheldon, divides the human physique into three types: *endomorphs* (round, soft bodies and large abdomens), *mesomorphs* (a sturdy upright body with strong bones and muscles), and *ectomorphs* (thin, small-boned and fragile). Most people have some of the characteristics of all three **somatotypes,** with one type dominant.

Sheldon also divided temperament or personality into three types: *viscerotonia,* characterized by sociability, fondness for food and people, and love of comfort; *somatotonia,* characterized by love of physical adventure, risk, and vigorous activity; and *cerebrotonia,* characterized by restraint, self-consciousness, and love of privacy.

Sheldon asserted that chubby endomorphs were likely to be high in viscerotonia, athletic mesomorphs high in somatotonia, and thin ectomorphs high in cerebrotonia. Sheldon also believed that personality type is caused by body type. Although the details of both his theory and his

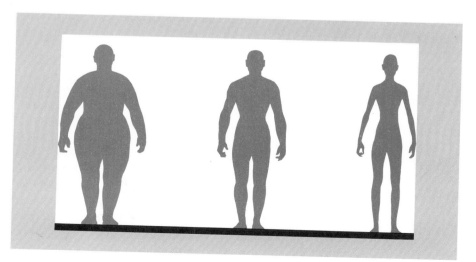

Figure 11–3
Sheldon's three basic somatotypes. The person on the left ranks high in endomorphy, the person in the center is high in mesomorphy, and the person on the right is high in ectomorphy.
(After W. H. Sheldon, *The Varieties of Temperament.* New York: Harper & Row, 1942.)

methods have been attacked, his work does suggest at least some relationship between physique and personality.

Trait theorists differ from constitutional theorists in several ways. First, they do not believe in clearcut types of people, but rather in dimensions or traits of personality within people, which vary to greater or lesser degrees. Second, they assert that there are not just three, but many possible personality traits, such as dependency, anxiety, aggressiveness, and extraversion. Third, most trait theorists reject body build as a determinant of personality.

We cannot observe traits directly. We cannot see sociability in the way we can see long hair, blue eyes, or a taste for loud colors. But we can _infer_ a trait from how a person behaves. If a person consistently throws parties, goes to great lengths to make friends, and is regularly seen in a group, we might conclude that he or she has the trait of sociability.

Psychologists have identified many traits. Allport and Odbert (1936) drew up a list of 17,953 English words for personal behavior traits. But Digman (1977) has shown that this long list can be boiled down to only a few key traits that show up repeatedly in research: friendly vs. hostile, active–gregarious vs. passive–withdrawn, emotionally stable vs. neurotic, self-monitored vs. unorganized, and creative vs. stereotyped.

According to trait theorists, traits are relatively permanent and consistent behavior patterns that a person exhibits in many situations. They are only relatively permanent because personality constantly develops and changes as one matures. They are only relatively consistent because the same person may show contradictory traits in different situations. An army sergeant who is meek and mild toward colonels, for example, may be aggressive and rude to privates. The usually calm and methodical person may become flustered when rushing to catch a plane.

Traits are considered to be general because they appear in many situations and provoke a wide range of related responses. There may be no simple one-to-one relationship, however, between a single trait and a given behavior. In two apparently similar situations, the same person might respond with anxiety and hostility in one case, and with anxiety and dependency in the other. This seemingly inconsistent behavior might reflect different combinations of traits that already exist within that person (Allport, 1966).

Two trait theorists in particular have supported their ideas of the existence of traits with extensive research data. R. B. Cattell (1965) identified 16 major dimensions of personality by studying and analyzing the data from thousands of questionnaires, objective tests, and life histories. H. J. Eysenck (1970), however, believes that there are only three personality dimensions: introversion–extroversion, neuroticism, and psychoticism.

There has been much controversy over trait theories. Many psychologists believe that a trait theory of personality, if not actually wrong in focus, is at least too simple. A human being is more complex, they say. He or she cannot be labeled as someone who is, was, and always will be a certain way because of stable personality traits. We all act differently in different situations, around different people, at different times in life. Moreover, trait theory suggests that a personality characteristic has always existed, even though it may not have overtly appeared. One may, for example, be a "latent" homosexual or a "potential" criminal (Byrne, 1974).

Is the average person really a patchwork of traits? Or are these specific personality characteristics only descriptive shortcuts for psychologists? It is important to remember that traits can only be inferred; they are not definite and observable like laboratory data. For that reason, many psychologists question their validity.

Interactionism

The dispute over the validity of traits has centered on whether consistencies in behavior are due to consistencies in people (trait theory) or in the environment **(situationism),** or whether the consistencies are due to the interaction of the person with the environment **(interactionism).** For example, let us say you get angry when your parents do not seem grateful enough for a gift you have carefully chosen for them. Is your anger due to some general trait of hostility? Does it arise just because of your parents' behavior? Or does it reflect both your need for appreciation and your parents' behavior?

Interactionism claims that to understand a person's behavior, an observer must know something not only about the person and the situation, but also about the relationship between the two, and how the situation is perceived. One early interactionist, whose theories have recently received renewed attention from psychologists, is Henry Murray. Because a person's reason for doing something is important to the meaning of the act, Murray's theory stresses motivation. For example, breaking a window in order to help a heart attack victim in a locked house is not the same thing as

(Drawing by Lippman; © 1972 *The New Yorker Magazine, Inc.*)

To understand a person's actions, we need to know something about the environment or situation in which those actions occur.
(Hugh Rogers, Monkmeyer)

breaking a window for the purpose of annoying a neighbor.

But Murray notes that motives or "needs" can be either conscious or unconscious. According to Murray, a full explanation of behavior must include how a person perceives the environment and the extent to which it stimulates his or her needs. For example, being rejected by another person can trigger the need for aggression, counteraction, or self-defense. These needs, in turn, direct a person's behavior until they are satisfied. Murray's followers find Murray's theory comprehensive yet simple enough to permit in-depth studies (Epstein, 1979).

An example of a more recent interactionist theory is Walter Mischel's social behavior theory (1968, 1976). According to Mischel, behavior is the result of five "person variables": people's ability to make an intended response; how they label situations, themselves, and others; what they expect from specific actions or stimuli; the subjective values they place on expected outcomes; and the self-regulatory systems and plans that they use to control their own behavior (Mischel, 1973, 1977). Situations affect behavior through one or more of these variables. If a situation is so broad or simple that it requires only those skills that everyone has, and if everyone interprets the situation in the same way and has the same expectations and values, then all people will behave very similarly and "personality" will scarcely affect behavior. But if a situation demands particular skills, is ambiguous, or provides no common incentives, then people will behave in many different ways.

Mischel does not suggest that we are all pawns whose behavior is controlled entirely by the circumstances in which we find ourselves. Not only do we react to and modify situations in highly personal ways, but, more importantly, we pick many of the situations in which we find ourselves (Mischel, 1977). In this respect Mischel—and other interactionists—differ sharply from the more extreme situationist theories.

Situationism

A more extreme reaction to trait theory is situationism, which puts even more emphasis on environment and less on personality. For situationists, it is not internal personality variables but the particular situation that determines behavior. Traits are not real entities, but labels we create for behavior patterns. Moreover, the situationists believe that behavior is not necessarily consistent, despite temptations to see it as such. You yourself, for example, may be buoyant and outspoken with some friends but reserved and cautious with others. Other people may seem to act consistently because we only see them in certain situations. Situationists also recognize that personality varies over time. An outgoing child does not always become an outgoing adult.

It is small wonder, then, that we hesitate on a personality test when faced with a yes–or–no question such as, "Would you rather go to a sporting event or to a concert?" (What kind of sport? What kind of concert? On what day of the week? With whom?)

LOCUS OF CONTROL: WHO'S IN CHARGE OF WHO GETS WHAT?

Most situationist approaches to personality emphasize how reinforcements influence behavior. From this perspective comes the concept of the **locus of control.** Are our reinforcements controlled by our own behavior (internal control), or by outside events, people, and chance (external control)?

Many people believe, for example, that success depends on "being in the right place at the right time." Such people have an external attitude toward control. They tend to emphasize chance or fate. They are the buyers of lottery tickets, the readers of horoscopes, the owners of lucky charms. In the extreme, they see promotions as going to whomever the boss happens to like, marriage as depending on who chances to fall in love with them, and life itself as a case of "whatever will be, will be."

Other people, with an internal attitude, tend to see themselves as masters of their own fate, as the source of their reinforcements and rewards. Rather than lottery tickets, they buy self-improvement books. They believe that promotion depends on hard work, on what you know rather than who you know.

Rotter (1966) developed an internal–external test that has been widely used by other experimenters. Few people, of course, can be classified as 100 percent "internal" or "external." As with many personality characteristics, most of us seem to be both. But people who score more toward the "internal" side tend to be more intelligent, more success oriented, and less conforming and compliant; to support political positions that stress personal responsibility; and to take more reasonable risks (Strickland, 1977).

In an extensive survey of locus-of-control studies, Lefcourt (1976) suggested that there are advantages to being internally oriented, even if a person is sometimes at odds with reality. Phares (1976) reached many of the same conclusions, but it would be a mistake to conclude that it is always "best" to be

(UPI)

internally oriented. People who are internally oriented often handle problems more effectively, but externally oriented people may perceive external obstacles to success more quickly and cope with those obstacles more efficiently.

Do internals or externals fare better in school and in college? Prociuk and Breen (1977) found that internals outperformed externals in academic subjects. Phares (1978) observed that internal grammar-school students received higher grades than their external classmates, but he found no differences among college students.

RADICAL BEHAVIOR THEORY

An example of a situationist analysis of personality is the **radical behavior theory** of B. F. Skinner and others. Trait theorists believe that, "You do what you are." Skinner and other behavior theorists believe just the opposite: "You are what you do." For radical behaviorists, only observable and measurable behavior is relevant. Skinner therefore concentrates on

(UPI)

finding the ties between a person's observable behavior and the conditions that controlled or caused it (Mischel, 1976). For example, Skinner does not consider drives, such as thirst, to be a cause of behavior, as Freud would (Hall & Lindzey, 1970). Thirst, for Skinner, simply describes a relationship between a stimulus condition and the drinking behavior to which it leads. In other words, a hot day and a dry throat are stimuli that result in a behavioral response: drinking water. In the same way, our behavior toward another person is determined by aspects of that person and the situation in which we find ourselves.

Skinner also points out that although the situation leads to the response, this does not mean that we all react in the same way to the same situation. Hall and Lindzey (1970) illustrate this concept with the example of two people seeking a raise from the same employer. One person may approach the situation aggressively, the other passively. It all depends on what has worked for each of them in the past.

Behavior theorists do not deny that biology can determine behavior—such as the effects of being taller or shorter than other people, for example. But they reject structural or body-type theories, such as Sheldon's; they also reject the trait theories that see us as a collection of certain characteristics. Although behaviorists reject Freud's idea of a self divided into several parts, they agree with Freudian personality theory in emphasizing _development_. Both Freud and Skinner would say that what happens to us in our early life greatly affects our later behavior. Behavior theorists also agree that there are periods of life that are crucial to personality development. An example of this would be the stage when we form attachments to others. Specifically, behavior theory recognizes that behavior patterns learned in infancy may be carried into adulthood, and that the effects of deprivation or punishment at that state are strong and long-lasting.

For example, one behavioral response that humans share with animals is escape. Removing heavy clothing when it is hot, putting our fingers in our ears when a train passes, squirming when we are uncomfortable are all attempts to escape unpleasant stimuli. But escape is not always that simple, and as we mature, we adopt subtle and sometimes habitual escape mechanisms. We may "arrange" our behavior to avoid certain people or situations. Thus, a child who fears being questioned in school may learn to say, "I don't know," whenever he or she is afraid. This response may result in a shy, evasive, and escape-oriented adult (Lundin, 1974).

Because the study of personality developed more from clinical and case histories than from laboratory research, behavior theorists want to see a more scientific approach to personality. "The early study of personality has distinguished itself from other branches of psychology by being more speculative and less subject to careful controls, that is, based more on intuition than experience" (Lundin, 1974, p. 2). Behavior theorists believe that data based on free association, dream content, or personal observation are scientifically unreliable and that the hypotheses of Freud—and his successors—are conjectural and unprovable. But behavior theorists face the same problem that all personality theorists face: the difficulty of gaining actual experimental data about human beings under controlled conditions. The problem is even greater when the psychologist wants to study human behavior over a long period.

The personality theories we have discussed represent the efforts of various psychologists to explain, in an orderly and coherent manner, the characteristic behavior of people. But interest in personality centers not only on how and why people behave as they do, but also on how to evaluate and measure characteristic behavior patterns.

Personality Assessment

Our assessments of people are informal and subjective, based largely on our own experience or on hearsay. They are apt to be strongly influenced by our own biases. But there are many occasions when an objective, unbiased, and accurate assessment of someone's personality is valuable. A reliable measure of personality is extremely helpful, for example, in a firm's hiring of staff.

There are special difficulties in measuring personality, however, that are not found in measuring intelligence and academic ability (see Chapter 10). As we mentioned earlier, personality reflects *characteristic* behavior and how a person *consistently* reacts to his or her environment. In assessing personality, then, we are not interested in someone's *best* behavior. We want to find out what his *typical* behavior is. How does he usually behave in ordinary situations? To the extent the behavior is not due simply to traits but also to situational influences, a person may not have a typical way of behaving. All of us can act differently under special conditions. Any measurement of personality, therefore, must include the possibility that the person being assessed may be behaving oddly.

Another problem lies in the subject matter of personality testing. To get an accurate picture of a person's personality, the psychologist must often ask questions about sensitive areas, such as the person's emotional adjustment, relationships with other people, intimate family history, and attitudes. The question of privacy arises. How far, in the interests of science, may a psychologist delve into the personal life of another person? The privacy of the person being evaluated must be respected and protected.

In the intricate task of measuring personality, psychologists use four basic tools: the personal interview, the direct observation of behavior, **objective tests,** and **projective tests.** Most of our knowledge about personality comes from the tools and procedures we are about to discuss.

THE INTERVIEW

Essentially, an interview is a conversation. The interviewer asks another person questions to evaluate him or her in general terms. Ideally, the interviewer should try to direct the conversation over a wide range of subjects, encouraging the person to discuss his or her experiences, feelings, and attitudes. The interviewer also watches the other person's behavior, such as his or her way of speaking, poise, or tenseness about certain topics.

The success of an interview depends largely on the skill of the inter-

(© 1959 United Feature Syndicate, Inc.)

viewer. For example, he or she should build a sympathetic relationship with the person being interviewed but not become too emotionally involved. The interviewer's own personality should not affect the person's answers. The interviewer should also be sensitive to the person's unconscious cues, such as unexpected changes in the tone of voice or a clenching of the fists at the mention of certain topics.

OBSERVATION

Another way to find out how a person usually behaves is to *observe* his or her actions in everyday situations over a long period. Behaviorists and other personality theorists who question the concept of traits prefer this method. Observing behavior in different situations gives a much better view of the role that situation and environment have on behavior and the range of behaviors a person might show. Since most people tend to be self-conscious if they suspect they are being watched, observation works best with young children or with people who have problems with language. But observation can be used successfully with people of almost any age and in many settings: a company cafeteria, an assembly line, or wherever people work or play together.

Direct observation lets the observer see the person's behavior firsthand. It does not have to rely on how a person says he or she acts. And if several, careful observers give unbiased, factual accounts of a person's behavior over time, the composite picture of that person's personality can be quite accurate. An observer, however, may misinterpret the true meaning of some act. For example, he or she may think a child is being hostile when the child is merely protecting himself against the class bully. Also, observation must be selective. Relatively few people can be observed for a limited period.

364

OBJECTIVE TESTS

In an attempt to devise measuring instruments that do not depend on the skill of an interviewer or the interpretive abilities of an observer, psychologists have created objective tests, or personality inventories. Generally, these are written tests that are given and scored according to a standard procedure. The tests usually are constructed so that the person merely chooses between a "yes" and "no" response or selects one answer among many choices. Since the administration and scoring procedures are standardized, the test results are less apt to be affected by the biases of the people giving them and by variations in how they are given. Because of their efforts to create a way of accurately measuring personality traits, trait theorists in particular have favored objective tests. But how can the thousands of traits observable in a person be reduced to a number reasonable enough to be measured? Some trait theorists, particularly Cattell and H. J. Eysenck, have tried to do this by statistical factor analysis.

Cattell (1965) believes that there are a few basic traits, which he calls source traits, that are essential to a personality, just as chemical elements form the basic structures of the physical world. To identify these source traits, Cattell had a few hundred young men and women rated on about 60 different trait elements by people who knew them well. When the ratings were related to each other, between 12 and 20 clusters of traits were found. Tests were then devised to measure these traits. With this research, Cattell built several personality inventory scales. The most comperehensive is the *Sixteen Personality Factor Questionnaire (16PF)*, to score the 16 source traits Cattell identified.

The value of a direct questionnaire, however, depends on the honesty and frankness with which it is answered. The "right" answers can be faked. To overcome this shortcoming, some tests include rating scales to show if a person is distorting his or her answers. One of the most widely used tests with built-in correction scales is the **Minnesota Multiphasic Personality Inventory.**

Minnesota Multiphasic Personality Inventory. The Minnesota Multiphasic Personality Inventory (MMPI), published in 1942 by Hathaway and McKinley, was originally developed to help diagnose psychiatric disorders. The test consists of 550 items to which the person answers "true," "false," or "cannot say." Some typical items are: "Once in a while I put off until tomorrow what I ought to do today"; "At times I feel like swearing"; "There are persons who are trying to steal my thoughts and ideas." Some of the items repeat almost the same question in different words: "I tire easily"; "I feel weak all over much of the time." This is done for ease of scoring and to check on the possibility of false or inconsistent answers. The test is scored according to 10 personality scales.

The MMPI also has four scales that check on the validity of the responses. The *?*, or question, scale consists of the total number of items the person has put in the "cannot say" category. If the "cannot say" responses are too numerous, the test is invalid. The *L*, or lie, scale is scored on 15 items scattered in the test. Sample items rated on this scale are: "I do not always tell the truth" and, "I gossip a little at times." Most people would admit that

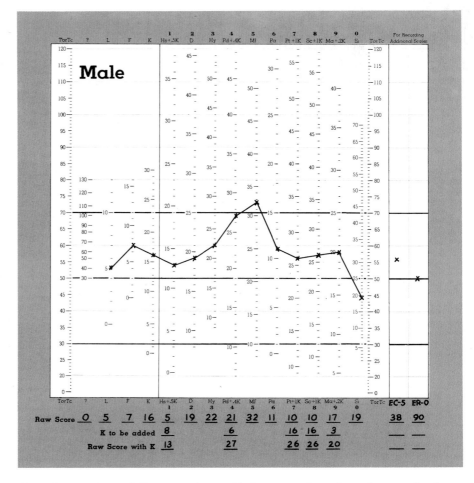

they do gossip and lie sometimes. If they say that they do *not* do these things and mark a number of the items this way, they are believed to be consciously or unconsciously distorting the truth to present themselves in a more favorable light.

PROJECTIVE TESTS

Most projective tests of personality consist of a simple unstructured task that can elicit an unlimited number of responses. People may be shown some essentially meaningless material or a vague picture and be asked to tell what the material means to them. Or they may be given two or three words, such as, "My brother is . . . " and be asked to complete the statement. They are given no clues as to the "best way" to interpret the material or finish the sentence. It is believed that in devising their own answers, they will "project" their personality into the test materials.

Projective tests have several advantages in testing personality. Since the tests are flexible and can be treated as a game or puzzle, they can be given in a relaxed atmosphere, without the tension and self-consciousness that sometimes accompany written tests. Sometimes the true purpose of the test can be hidden, so that responses are less likely to be faked. The person may be told, for instance, that he is being measured on his powers of imagination. The projective test, it is believed, can uncover unconscious thoughts and fantasies, such as latent sexual or family problems. The accuracy of the tests, however, depends on the skill and the bias of the examiner.

RORSCHACH TEST. The **Rorschach Test** is probably the best known of the projective personality tests. It is named for the Swiss psychiatrist who in 1921 published the results of his research on interpreting inkblots as a key to personality. Much work on the inkblot technique had already been done when Rorschach began to practice, but he was the first to use the technique to evaluate a person's total personality. For 10 years he tested thousands of blots and finally chose 10 that seemed to arouse the most emotional response in people.

Each inkblot design is printed on a separate card and is unique in its form, color, shading, and white space. Five of the blots are black and gray; two have red splotches; three blots have patches of several colors. The cards are given to the subject one at a time and in a specific order. The subject is asked to tell what he or she sees in each blot. The test instructions are kept to a minimum, so that the subject's responses will be completely his or her own. Although no specific permission is given, the subject may turn the card and look at the blot from any angle and may make as many interpretations of each blot as he or she wants. After the subject has interpreted all the blots, he or she goes over the cards again with the examiner and tells which part of each blot determined each response.

The Rorschach test was designed to measure personality traits. Here a subject views a series of ten inkblots and interprets each blot for the examiner.

(Van Bucher, Photo Researchers)

THEMATIC APPERCEPTION TEST. Somewhat more demanding is the **Thematic Apperception Test** (TAT), developed at Harvard by H. A. Murray and his associates. It consists of 20 cards picturing one or more human figures in various poses. Some of the pictures suggest a basic story; others give few plot hints. A person is shown the cards one by one. He or she has to make up a complete story for each picture, including what led up to the scene depicted, what the characters are doing at that moment, what their thoughts and feelings are, and what the outcome will be.

Although various scoring systems have been devised for the TAT, the examiner usually interprets the stories in the light of his or her personal knowledge of the subject. An important part of the evaluation is to determine if the subject seems to identify with the hero or heroine of the story or with one of the minor characters. Then the examiner must determine what the attitudes and feelings of the character reveal about the storyteller. The examiner also assesses each story on its content, language, originality, organization, and consistency. Certain themes, such as the need for affection, repeated failure, or parental domination may recur in several plots.

Application

FEMINISTS vs. FREUD

Freudian thought and feminism are two of the most important movements of this century, and both have inspired fierce controversy. The championship bout may be the battle between Freud's followers and feminists who believe that his psychoanalytic theory has been one of the most powerful tools used to oppress women. Feminist Eva Figes wrote that, "of all the factors that have served to perpetuate a male-oriented society, that have hindered the free development of women as human beings in the Western world today, the emergence of Freudian psychoanalysis has been the most serious" (Figes, 1970, p. 148).

What is it about Freud's work that has inspired this contention? Freud believed that sexual impulses had to be sublimated to some extent in the interests of society, and that these energies could then be directed to other, more creative ends. Management of sexuality was especially difficult for women in Freud's time—the late 19th and early 20th centuries—with its double standard of sexual behavior. Though frowned on, male sexuality was accepted as natural. Women, on the other hand, were expected to smother their sexual urges before marriage, and limit them after procreation. Moreover, civilization represents the realm of the superego—morality and order—and civilization as Freud knew it, and as we still largely know it today, was male-dominated.

Perhaps the single most controversial aspect of Freud's theory is his notion of "penis envy" in women. As we have seen, around the ages of 4 or 5 stirrings of sexual feelings lead to the Oedipal conflict in boys. When boys make the traumatic discovery that girls do not have penises, they conclude that girls must have been castrated as punishment for having unacceptable feelings about their parents, and they fear that this might happen to them, too. Consequently, they repress their incestuous feelings for their mothers and their hostility toward their fathers, and they *internalize* their father's standards and position of authority, at which point the superego gains control over the id.

Freud coined the term "penis envy" to describe the corresponding feeling that little girls have when *they* first notice the anatomical difference between themselves and boys. Girls, he claimed, also decide that their lack of a penis means that they have already been castrated, though in their case it is too late to avoid the catastrophe. They blame their mothers for their loss and develop feelings of inferiority. At this point, according to Freud, they turn to their fathers for love and reassurance, becoming submissive and "lovable." The desire for a penis is repressed, but it does not go away. Instead, it becomes expressed as the desire for a child—preferably a son. Moreover, because girls do not fear castration—believing that it has already happened—they do not develop superegos as strong as those of boys, and consequently they do not become the authority figures that boys become. Women learn to find fulfillment in the role of wife and mother because of a pattern of inferiority and submission begun in childhood.

Freud summarized his views on sex differences in his famous—and most controversial—statement: Anatomy is destiny. Feminist critics, however, take issue with this statement, and with the whole concept of penis envy. Psychologist Karen Horney (Tavris & Offir, 1977) agreed that biological factors affect our psychological states, but pointed out that in Western society women are at a profound disadvantage. Horney claimed that women are dependent on men primarily because of how society is set up. In fact, Horney turned Freud's argument around and argued that men envy women their ability to bear children. Men also fear women's biological powers and try to maintain their superior status by glorifying "machismo." In other words, while Freud felt that women accept their subordinate status because they stand in awe and envy of the anatomical symbol of male power, Horney felt that men fear and envy women, and to conquer this dread of female power they make sure that women "stay in their place."

In *The Feminine Mystique* (1963), Betty Friedan asks why bright, well-educated American women of the 1940s stayed trapped in subordinate sex roles. Part of the answer, she feels, is Freud's theory, which helps justify the patriarchal status quo and women's subordinate position in it. Friedan respects some of Freud's discoveries but feels that, in many respects, he was a prisoner of his own time. Victorian women, she points out, had plenty of reason to envy men: Men had freedom and power; women had neither. It was not the male penis that women wanted, just the privileges that went along with it. Popularizers of Freudian theory in America preached that a "normal" woman should be perfectly happy to fulfill herself through her husband and family. Freudian thought permeated all the social sciences. Magazines told women to be content with their roles. And intelligent women, listening to the voice of science, bought a bill of goods and then wondered why they felt so unhappy. As Clara M. Thompson put it: "It seems clear that envy of the male exists in most women in this culture. . . . The attitude of the women in this situation is not qualitatively different from that found in any minority group in a competitive culture" (Thompson, 1950). Since the publication of *The Feminine Mystique*, writers like Germaine Greer (1971) and Kate Millett (1970) have taken an even more aggressive stand against Freudian thought.

But there are other feminists who do not take issue with Freud. Juliet Mitchell writes that Freud's psychoanalytic theory "is not a recommendation *for* a patriarchal society, but an analysis *of* one" (Mitchell, 1974). Freud himself was always more tentative in his conclusions about women than he was in his thinking about men. He called for more investigation of his theories, and wrote that "it is not always easy to distinguish what should be ascribed to the influence of the sexual function and what to social breeding" (Strouse, 1974).

Summary

1. *Personality* refers to the characteristic behavior patterns, emotions, motives, thoughts, and attitudes with which a person consistently reacts to his or her environment.

2. Sigmund Freud proposed the first major *psychoanalytic theory* of personality. He believed that personality is composed of three interrelated parts—the id, the ego, and the superego—that form an integrated whole.

3. The *id* is the storehouse of energy from which the ego and superego develop. The energy from the instinctual drives of the id is set in motion by a state of deprivation, which causes discomfort or tension. The id relieves this discomfort by reflex actions or by wish fulfillment, which Freud called *primary process thinking*. The id acts according to the *pleasure principle*. The *ego* operates on the *reality principle*. It controls thinking and reasoning and directs the personality. The ego derives its energy from the id. It also controls the id and directs its energy into effective, realistic channels, a process known as *secondary process thinking*. The *superego*, the moral guardian of behavior, compares the ego's actions with an ego ideal and then rewards or punishes the ego.

4. The dynamic forces of this threefold structure arise from two classes of unconscious drives or instincts: *life instincts* and *death instincts*. Freud placed great emphasis on the *libido*—energy generated by the sexual instincts. The source and aim of our instincts are the same through life—except for natural changes as we mature. But their object and intensity can change a great deal.

5. As part of his theory of personality development, Freud identified five *psychosexual stages* through which children must pass: the *oral, anal, phallic, latent,* and *genital* stages. Strong attachment to the parent of the opposite sex and jealousy of the parent of the same sex—which develops during the phallic stage—is called the *Oedipus complex* in boys and the *Electra complex* in girls.

6. Carl Jung stressed the rational and spiritual qualities of humans. According to Jung, the libido represents all the life forces, not just the sexual ones. It arises during normal body metabolism just as physical energy does. Jung saw the unconscious as the ego's source of strength and vitality and divided it into two parts: the *personal unconscious* and the *collective unconscious*. Jung proposed two general attitude-types of personalities: the *introverted* and the *extroverted*.

7. Alfred Adler believed that our unconscious, inborn forces are social urges. Adler placed more importance than Freud did on the ego in shaping personality. He believed that we are not at the mercy of instinctual urges. Each of us is free to choose our own destiny and to develop in any way that will help us reach our goals.

Adler believed that a person's motivation is a striving toward _superiority_, based in part on feelings of _inferiority_.

8. Karen Horney believed that environment—especially the human relationships with which a child grows up—is the most important influence in shaping personality. She felt that anxiety is a stronger motive than sexual drives. She rejected Freud's theory that a woman's emotional life is governed by her desire for a penis. Horney claimed instead that if women want to be masculine, it is probably because they want the same social rights that men have.

9. Erik Erikson's view of personality is more socially oriented than Freud's and stresses the workings of the ego. In contrast to Freud, Erikson feels that personality continues to develop during the life span. He describes eight stages of personality development, each of which involves the resolution of a crisis: _trust versus mistrust, autonomy versus shame and doubt, initiative versus guilt, industry versus inferiority, identity versus role confusion, intimacy versus isolation, generativity versus stagnation,_ and _integrity versus despair._

10. The _self theory_ of Carl Rogers asserts that every person is the center of his or her own private world. According to Rogers, all infants possess certain attributes. They all create their own environment. They have an inborn tendency to protect and maintain themselves and to develop their capacities. And they each exercise this inborn tendency within their own world of reality, where they form value judgments about their experiences. As they mature, they gain an awareness of being and a consciousness of _self_. As children they develop two kinds of values: those experienced directly and those taken over from others but misperceived as their own.

11. The oldest theory of personality is probably the _constitutional_ or _type theory,_ which suggests that there is a relationship between physique and behavior. Sheldon identified three basic dimensions of a person's _somatotype: endomorphy, mesomorphy,_ and _ectomorphy._ He found that somatotype ratings were often related to temperament.

12. _Trait theorists_ maintain that a unique pattern of traits exists within each person and that they dominate the person's behavior. They define traits as relatively permanent and consistent behavior patterns that a person shows in many situations.

13. There has been much controversy over trait theory. The central dispute is whether consistencies in behavior are due to consistencies in a person, to consistencies in the environment, or to the person and the environment interacting.

14. _Interactionism_ holds that knowledge both of a person and of the environment are needed to understand a person's behavior. Mischel's _social behavior theory,_ which involves the influence of the situation on five "person variables," is an interactionist theory.

15. Situationists believe that the environment governs behavior.

Radical behavior theorists particularly tend to this view and are the most critical of trait theory. Situationists point out that behavior does not have to be consistent and that personality changes with time.

16. Psychologists use four basic tools to assess personality: personal interviews, direct observation of behavior, objective tests, and projective tests.

17. During an *interview*, an interviewer seeks to evaluate another person by listening to what the person says and observing his or her behavior.

18. *Observation* can be used to study general behavior and behavior in special situations. The observer must see enough to get a good average of a person's behavior. The main advantage of direct observation is that the observer does not have to rely on a person's own description of his or her behavior.

19. *Objective tests* of personality are given and scored according to a standardized procedure. One type of objective test is a direct questionnaire requiring yes–or–no responses or the selection of one answer among multiple choices. The effectiveness of this type of test depends on the honesty with which it is answered. One of the most widely used is the *Minnesota Multiphasic Personality Inventory* (MMPI).

20. *Projective tests* of personality are simple, unstructured tasks that can elicit an unlimited number of responses. It is believed that a person will project his or her personality into the test material. Two well-known projective tests are the *Rorschach Test*—consisting of 10 inkblot designs, which subjects are asked to interpret— and the *Thematic Apperception Test* (TAT)—consisting of 20 pictures, which subjects are asked to make up stories about.

Outline

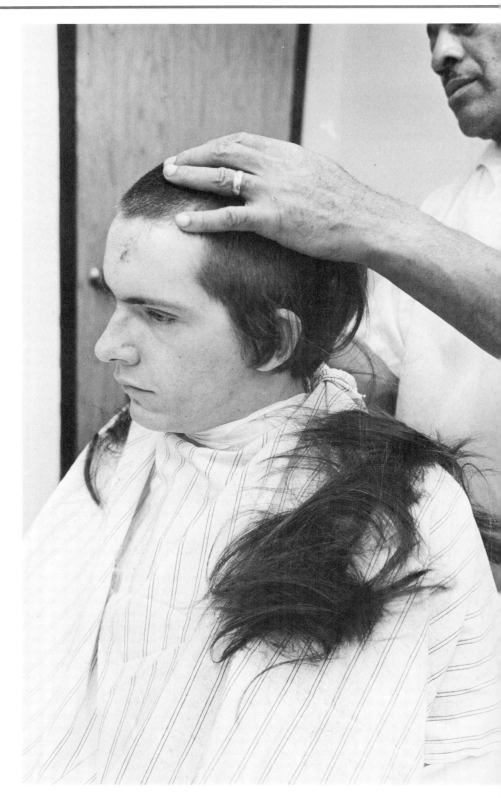

Chapter 12

Adjustment

One of the hard lessons that we all learn in childhood is that we cannot always get our way. We demand ice cream now, but we must settle for enjoying it later, or not at all. We want to win the games we play, but sometimes the dice or the cards favor our opponent. We audition for a part in the school play or interview for a part-time job, but the part or position goes to someone with more poise or experience.

All through our lives, therefore, we learn to adjust to a life that is less perfect than our dreams. As children, we "adjust" to school, our friends, our families. As we grow older, we adjust to the demands of our careers, the responsibilities of our families, to the joys and burdens of freedom to choose our way of life, and finally, to the strain of illness, old age, and impending death.

Every **adjustment** is an attempt—successful or not—to balance our desires with the demands of the environment, to balance our needs with what is possible. Adjustment is not just learning to live with bad news; it is more a sort of psychological belt-tightening. The student who fails to get the lead in the school play, for example, may quit the production altogether, accept a smaller role, join the debating team, or even criticize the production in the school paper. Each of these responses is an adjustment, but some are more constructive than others.

The variety of our responses to new and recurring problems in our environment is the subject of this chapter. Because the problems we face are numerous and complex, maintaining balance in our lives is often difficult. We shall begin by examining the various problems people face and then describe how they cope with them. Finally, we will examine how psychologists determine who is "well-adjusted."

What Do We Have to Adjust To?

When we feel unable to cope with the demands of our environment, when we are threatened with physical or psychological harm, we begin to feel tense and uncomfortable. We are experiencing **stress.** This term describes both the situations in which we feel in conflict or threatened beyond our capacity to cope or endure, and our emotional and physiological reactions to such situations. Psychologists have found that coping with psychological stress puts as much burden on the body as coping with physiological stress.

Some things, of course, are inherently stressful—such as wars and natural disasters. Here the danger is very real: Lives are threatened, and there is little or nothing people can do to save themselves. Some people fall apart in such situations; others are shaken but regain their composure almost immediately; still others refuse to admit the danger. Rescue workers invariably find families who have simply ignored hurricane or flood warnings.

But stress is not limited to life–and–death situations. The person who loses a job may feel as threatened as the soldier who is caught behind enemy lines. The person dying of cancer may feel less anxious than one who suspects a spouse of infidelity. How much stress we feel depends on how much danger we perceive, and this, in turn, depends on learning. The boy who has been frightened by a large, vicious dog has learned to be terrified every time he sees a dog; the girl whose beagle sleeps in her room every night has not learned this fear of dogs.

Stress also depends on how we rate our ability to cope with whatever threatens us. Students who know they can study when they have to and have done well in the past are calmer the night before an exam than those who are on the verge of flunking out of school.

How people respond to stress depends in part on whether they believe they have some control over events or whether they feel helpless. Some studies have concluded that having some control or responsibility makes situations even more stressful; other studies claim that lack of control or helplessness makes stressful situations worse. Porter and his colleagues (1958) provided the classic example of the relationship between responsibility and stress in a series of experiments with "executive monkeys."

Two rhesus monkeys with similar backgrounds were strapped into adjacent chairs. Both were given painful shocks every 20 seconds. One of the monkeys, the "executive," could delay the shocks to both itself and its partner by pressing a lever. The other monkey was also given a lever, but it did not work; there was nothing this monkey could do to avoid pain. The executive monkey soon developed severe stomach ulcers. Apparently, the strain of being responsible for its own conduct and that of its companion was too much for it. The nonexecutive monkey, who did not undergo the same stress, did not develop ulcers.

A later study by Weiss (1971), however, reversed these findings. Weiss found that those rats that were *deprived* of control were the most likely to develop ulcers. His study raises questions about the methods used by

"As we feared, Harkness was stunned by the news."
(Reprinted with permission of Charles Scribner's Sons from *Good News/Bad News,* by Henry R. Martin, Copyright © 1977 Henry R. Martin)

Porter and his colleagues. The researchers pretested all their monkeys, and those monkeys that had the highest response rates were assigned to the "executive" category (Lefcourt, 1973). These monkeys may have been more anxious to begin with than the other monkeys. Thus, their ulcers may have occurred despite—rather than because of—the control they had over the shocks.

When Brady and his colleagues (1958) varied the time the monkeys were strapped in the chairs and the length of the rest periods, they noticed that the executive monkeys had more stomach acid during the rest periods. Apparently, anticipating danger was more stressful for these animals than danger itself.

Seymour Epstein (1962) studied the effects of anticipating stress on a group of 28 parachutists and found much the same pattern. Each man was asked to describe his feelings before, during, and after his jump. All reported an increase of fear and of the desire to escape as the jump approached. Once they were in line and realized they could not turn back,

STRESS AND EVERYDAY LIFE

Which situation is harder to overcome: the death of a spouse, or a serious illness coupled with a marital reconciliation? Is it harder to cope with a single major source of stress—for example, losing one's job—or several minor stresses occurring at once, such as disagreements with family members, new living conditions, and financial problems?

The first method for measuring the stress of life experiences was devised by Holmes and Rahe (1967). Their Social Readjustment Rating Scale (SRRS) questionnaire focuses on events and experiences that require a person to adapt to or cope with changes in his or her life pattern.

The stressfulness of each experience is rated on the SRRS system according to the number of "life change units" (LCUs) it entails. The most severe of the more than 40 stressful life events on the scale is the death of a spouse. It has a rating of 100. At the bottom of the scale, a minor brush with the law is rated 11.

Not all experiences included in the Holmes and Rahe scale are unpleasant. Marriage, for example, is rated 50, and Christmas is rated 12.

Many of the items may be either positive or negative. For example, a change in financial state, rated 38, may be a change for the better or for the worse. What is important is that each experience—either good or bad—changes the person's life pattern and requires adaptation.

Some of the other items on the SRRS are:

Divorce	73	Son or daughter leaving home	29
Death of a close relative	63	Outstanding personal achievement	28
Personal injury or illness	53	Change in living conditions	25
Marital reconciliation	45	Change in schools	20
Gain of a new family member	39	Change in social activities	18
Mortgage over $10,000	31	Vacation	13

An analysis of life stress in a person can focus upon a period as brief as 6 months or as long as 3 years. Within that period, the scale value of each event is multiplied by the number of times the same event recurred, and a total score for all events and recurrences is obtained. A score of 150 or less is normal; 150–199 points to mild stress; 200–299 suggests a moderate crisis; and 300 or higher indicates a major life crisis. Thus, according to the SRRS, it would be slightly more difficult to cope with the death of one's spouse (100) than to adjust to being seriously ill (53) and to reconcile with one's spouse during the same period (45). And the birth of a child (39) combined with a new mortgage (31), the revision of one's personal habits (24), a change in residence (20), and a change in social activities (18) altogether would pose a more serious threat to one's well-being than the death of one's spouse.

(David R. Frazier, Photo Researchers)

however, they began to calm down. By the time they reached the most dangerous part of the jump—when they were in free-fall and waiting for their chutes to open—their fears had subsided.

Psychologists are interested in stress in part because people generally perform less well when upset than when confident. Lazarus and Erikson (1952) showed this with a group of students. All were given an intelligence test and told that their scores would indicate how well they would do in college. A few days later the students were called back for more testing. Some were told they had done very poorly and would be given another chance; others were told that they had done well and that the experimenters wanted to know if the tests truly measured their ability. On the second test the students who felt threatened made many more mistakes than those who had been encouraged and praised. Clearly, the students in the first group were unable to deal with the test: Stress interfered with their normal performance.

Stress is a general term that covers a range of situations and feelings. Four of the most common sources of stress are pressure, anxiety, frustration, and conflict. We will now take a closer look at these four sources of stress before discussing how to adjust to stress.

PRESSURE

Pressure occurs when we feel that we must live up to a particular standard of behavior or adapt to rapid change. Our *internal pressures* are often related to maintaining self-esteem. Because of our feelings about our intelligence, appearance, popularity, or talents, we may push ourselves to reach an ever higher standard of excellence. Internal pressure can be constructive. It may lead, for example, to a serious effort to learn to play a musical instrument, which can ultimately bring us great pleasure. On the other hand, internal pressure can also be destructive if our ideals are impossible to achieve.

External pressures hit us from all sides. Among the most significant and consistent are the pressure to compete, the pressure to adapt to the rapid rate of change in our society, and the pressure to live up to what our family and close friends expect of us. The pressure to compete affects all relationships in American life. We compete for grades, jobs, sexual and marital partners, and popularity. We are taught to see failure in terms of shame and worthlessness; thus the pressure to "win" can be intense.

Our society is very complex and is changing quickly. For example, television scarcely existed in the 1940s. But today, nearly every family in the United States has at least one television set. Our patterns of family life are also changing rapidly, and our divorce rate is skyrocketing. But it is not change alone that is hard to adjust to. It is also the constancy and pervasiveness of change. Alvin Toffler (1970) coined the term "future shock" to describe the deep emotional trauma that results from living in the midst of a rapidly changing society. Another source of pressure is the changing roles that we must adopt as we age (see Chapter 4).

We also often face pressures from our family and from our close friends. People who are emotionally involved in our lives are especially

The amount of stress we feel in a situation depends on our ability to deal with it. This ability to cope varies among people.

(Rapho, Photo Researchers)

ETHICS OF STRESS RESEARCH

A group of students assembled for a discussion suddenly notice that smoke is seeping under the door of their seminar room. When they attempt to leave the room, they discover that the door is locked. Is this the prelude to a campus tragedy? No, it is a psychology experiment designed to investigate the effects of prior organization on group behavior.

Psychologists agree that how people respond to stress and how they behave in stressful situations are important issues. Research, moreover, has yielded valuable insights in these areas. There is, however, considerable controversy whether scientists should be permitted to disturb the emotional states of their research subjects to study the effects of these states. Subjects are made to believe that their lives are in danger, that they failed important tests or other tasks, that they have latent homosexual tendencies, or that they have caused pain or injury to others. Furthermore, subjects are sometimes misinformed or deceived about the true nature of the research, coerced into participating, or even completely unaware that they are participating in a research project (Cook, 1976).

At one extreme in the ethics controversy are those scientists who stress the obligation to protect human participants in research projects. They argue that subjects should never be misled about the nature of the research in which they participate, that emotionally or physically stressful situations should be avoided, and that subjects should be thoroughly briefed before they agree to participate in an experiment.

Many other scientists, however, insist that these procedures would not really minimize the harm or distress to subjects but would severely hamper the efforts of scientists to conduct critical research. Against the obligation to preserve human dignity and self-determination, these scientists balance the rights of science to investigate, and of society to profit from, the fruits of those investigations. Sometimes friction between these ideals can be eliminated, as in situations where emotional stress occurs naturally. For example, one can interview people who are about to undergo surgery, patients in a dentist's waiting room, or students worrying about an impending examination.

Most researchers now agree that, if possible, the scope and nature of an experiment should be explained to prospective subjects and their informed consent should be obtained before the experiment begins. Loftus and Fries (1979) warn, however, of the "dark side of the placebo effect." Subjects participating in a drug study were told in advance of possible side effects from the drug. These subjects often reported dizziness, nausea, and depression even when they were in a control group to which no drugs were administered! It would appear that at least in this case disclosure may have done more harm than good.

A number of protections are now generally recommended for participants. If an experiment induces physical or psychological stress, medical or psychological experts should be consulted. If subjects are misinformed or deceived before the experiment, they should be debriefed afterward and helped to overcome any negative effects. If questionable practices are employed, they should be reasonable and necessary, and the researcher must balance the right to conduct research with the obligation to preserve the freedom and dignity of research participants.

likely to make demands on us and to expect them to be met. Being a spouse or a parent is especially stressful. These roles constantly require us to face demands from others that we may not always be able or willing to satisfy.

ANXIETY

Anxiety is a very difficult and puzzling source of stress. In the examples we have discussed of people under stress or pressure, those involved knew *why* they were frightened or upset. Anxious people do not know why they feel this way. They experience all the symptoms of stress—"butter-

(Rapho, Photo Researchers)

flies" in the stomach, shallow breathing, muscle tension, inability to think clearly, and so on—but they do not know why. They feel angry when their roommate says "good morning," guilty for not calling their parents even though they called last week, depressed even though they have saved enough money to go to Europe. In short, their feelings seem to contradict a rational evaluation of their situation. Anxiety is thus very private, disturbing, and hard to cope with since it is difficult to identify a cause or a cure.

Many psychologists use psychoanalytic theory to explain anxiety. According to this view, anxiety is a sign of internal, unconscious conflict. Some wish or desire that conflicts with the person's conscious values is trying to surface. For example, a girl is furious with her mother but firmly believes it is wrong to feel angry with one's parents. If her inhibitions are particularly strong, she may use all her energy to keep from realizing just how angry she is. But the emotion persists. She feels depressed and tired, blows up at her friends, or goes on a shopping spree.

Other psychologists distinguish between trait anxiety and state anxiety. According to Spielberger (1966), *trait anxiety* is a relatively stable personality characteristic that stays with us. Levels of trait anxiety, like levels of intelligence, vary from person to person. We all carry a certain amount of anxiety into every situation. *State anxiety,* on the other hand, is tied to particular situations and may change in intensity from moment to moment.

Martinez-Urrutia (1975) found that surgical patients felt more state anxiety before surgery and less state anxiety after surgery. Their level of trait anxiety, however, remained stable throughout. Thus, trait anxiety—a personality characteristic—does not respond to specific conditions of threat, while state anxiety does.

Do some stressful situations lead to more anxiety than others? In general, the longer and more severe the stressful event, the greater the state anxiety. Moreover, warning that a stressful situation is about to occur lessens the state anxiety in some people, but increases it in others. Finally, studies have shown that we react with less state anxiety when we know the kind of stress we can expect than when we are unsure of it.

FRUSTRATION

Still another source of stress is **frustration.** Frustration occurs when a person is somehow prevented from reaching a goal—something or someone is in the way (see Figure 12–1). A teenager with a crush on a singer may learn that he is happily married. A high-school student who does poorly on his College Boards may not get into his father's alma mater. These persons' goals are unattainable. They must either give them up or find some way to overcome the obstacles in their way.

The teenager with a crush will probably recover quickly. The student may face a more complex problem. Most likely, his first reaction will be to get angry—angry at himself for not having studied more, angry at his father for pushing him to apply to that college, angry at the admissions board for not considering that he had a bad cold the day he

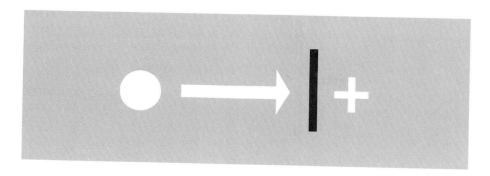

took his College Boards. He may not be able to express his anger directly— society does not approve of sons punching their fathers. He may not even realize or admit how disappointed he is. In any case, he must either find a new way to reach his goal, or change it and be satisfied with another school.

Coleman and Hammen (1974) identified five basic sources of frustration. *Delays* are hard for us to accept because our culture stresses the value of time. Anyone who has been caught in a traffic jam is familiar with the frustration of delay. Also, because advertising makes consumer goods so attractive, we may become frustrated if something we would like to own is out of our immediate economic reach. *Lack of resources* is especially frustrating to low-income Americans who cannot afford the new cars or vacations that TV programs and magazine articles suggest everyone should have. *Losses*, such as the end of a cherished friendship or a love affair, are frustrating because they often make us feel helpless and may affect our sense of worth and importance. *Failure* is a constant source of frustration in our competitive society. The aspect of failure that is hardest to cope with is guilt. We feel that we should have done something differently and thus feel responsible for our own or someone else's pain and disappointment. Finally, some people feel that life is *meaningless*. Building a meaningful and fulfilling life is often harder than we expect. This can cause frustration, particularly if we blame society and feel unable to do anything about it. This source of powerlessness can cause alienation, despair, and a feeling that nothing we do is really important.

The quest for consumer goods can be a major cause of frustration.
(General Motors)

CONFLICT

Of all life's troubles, *conflicts* are probably the most common. A student finds that both of the required courses she wanted to take this year meet at the same time. In an election, the views of one candidate on foreign policy reflect our own, but we favor the domestic programs proposed by his or her opponent. A boy does not want to go to his aunt's for dinner, but also does not want to listen to his mother complain if he stays home.

Conflicts arise when we face two incompatible demands, opportunities, needs, or goals. There is no complete resolution of conflicts. We must either give up one of our goals, modify one or both, delay one, or learn to accept that neither is going to be fully satisfied.

In the 1930s, Kurt Lewin described conflict in terms of two opposite tendencies: *approach* and *avoidance.* When something attracts us, we want to approach it; when something frightens us, we try to avoid it. Lewin (1935) showed how different combinations of these tendencies produce three basic types of conflict.

The first, diagrammed in Figure 12–2, he called **approach/approach conflict.** A person (the circle) is simultaneously attracted (the arrows) to two desirable goals (the plus signs). For example, a woman may want to pursue a career but also to raise a family. As a rational person, she considers the alternatives. She could accept a job now and delay having children, or she could have children now and look for work when they go to school. Alternatively, she could modify both goals by hiring a housekeeper and working part-time. Or she and her husband could share child care duties. Here the solutions are numerous, but this is not always the case. Suppose the same woman wanted a career that required frequent, often prolonged travel, for example in international sales. She might conclude that her career would mean neglecting her family. If she is right, it might in fact be impossible for her to attain both goals simultaneously.

The reverse of this dilemma is **avoidance/avoidance conflict,** when a person is faced with two undesirable or threatening possibilities (Figure 12–3). When faced with an avoidance/avoidance conflict, people will usually try to escape it. If escape is impossible—if other factors keep them in the situation—they will cope with it in a number of ways, depending on how severe the conflict is. The student who must choose between studying something he or she finds terribly boring and failing an exam

Figure 12–2
A diagram of approach / approach conflict. The person is attracted to two incompatible goals at the same time.

Figure 12–3
A diagram of avoidance / avoidance conflict. Repelled by two fears or threats at the same time, the person is inclined to try to escape (the black arrow), but often other factors prevent such an escape.

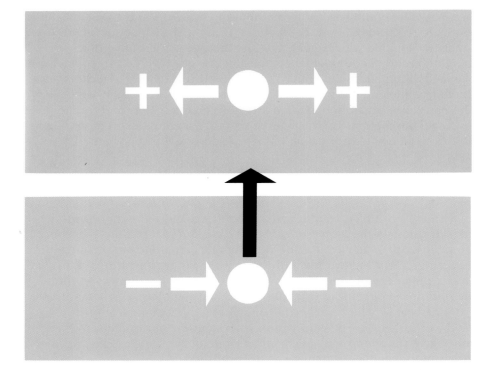

will probably decide to study, at least for a time. Otherwise the course might have to be repeated, an even more unpleasant alternative. But the choice is not always easy. The police officer in a high crime area who knows he risks his life each time he answers a radio call, but risks his fellow officers' lives—and his own self-esteem—if he does not respond, has a more difficult decision.

People caught in avoidance/avoidance conflicts often vacillate between one threat and another, like the baseball player caught between first and second base. He starts to run, then realizes he will be tagged and turns around, only to realize he will be tagged on first if he tries to go back there. In no-exit situations like this, many people simply wait for events to resolve their conflict for them.

Approach/avoidance conflicts (see Figure 12–4), in which a person is both attracted to and repelled by the same goal, are also difficult to resolve. A football player recovering from an operation may want to return to his team, but knows he may limp for the rest of his life if he is injured again. A woman may know she will hurt a man she really likes if she

(Will McIntyre, Photo Researchers)

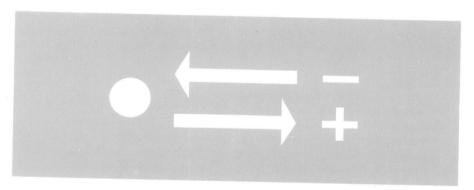

Figure 12–4
A diagram of approach/ avoidance conflict. The person is both repelled by and attracted to the same goal.

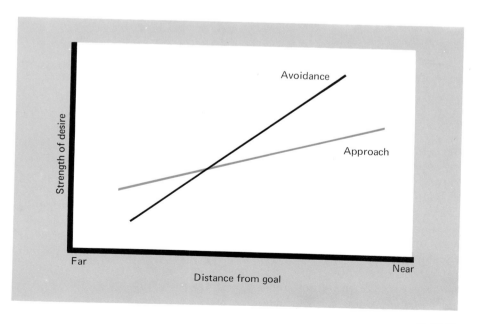

Figure 12–5
Both approach and avoidance increase as the distance to the goal decreases. At the point where the two lines cross, the person will begin to waver, unless he or she is forced to decide or the situation changes.

Figure 12–6
A diagram of double approach/avoidance conflict. We are caught between two goals, each of which simultaneously attracts and repels us.

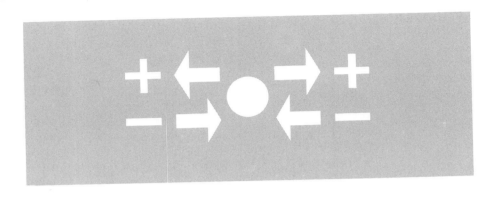

goes out with others, but realizes she will feel resentful toward him if she does not. Children whose parents have taught them that sex is dirty and sinful may find themselves simultaneously attracted to and repelled by members of the opposite sex.

The desire to approach a goal grows stronger as we get nearer to it, but so does the desire to avoid it. The avoidance tendency usually increases in strength faster than the approach tendency. Thus, in an approach/avoidance conflict, we will approach the goal until we reach the point where the two lines cross (see Figure 12–5). Afraid to go any closer, we will stop, fall back, approach again, vacillating until we have to make a decision or until the situation changes.

Often approach/avoidance conflicts are combined in complex patterns. A mother who loves classical music may dream that her son will be a great pianist. His father might want him to be an athlete. If the child practices on the piano, he pleases his mother but upsets his father; if he stays after school for football practice, he disappoints his mother but pleases his father. *Double approach/avoidance conflict,* as Lewin called this, is diagrammed in Figure 12–6.

Ways of Adjusting

THE GENERAL ADAPTATION SYNDROME

Hans Selye (1976) defined stress as "the nonspecific response of the body to any demand." He pointed out that stress has no single cause and can be produced by both positive and negative events or conditions. The stress of happiness or success is as real as the stress of sorrow or failure. Likewise, the effects of stress upon a person may be good or bad, depending upon how he or she responds to a given situation. For example, the stress of a student's academic success would have a positive effect if it inspired continued efforts to excel, but it would have a negative effect if it led to isolation from less gifted schoolmates and a sense of insecurity or ostracism. On the other hand, the stress someone feels after an unsuccessful audition for the school orchestra can have positive effects

STRESS AND DISEASE

Psychological stress has been linked to numerous illnesses, including insomnia and stroke, but in recent years most attention has focused on heart disease. Stress or frustration on the job or in personal or family life seem to increase the risk of coronary disease. The connection between stress and illness is especially marked when the source of stress—for example, being laid off from a job or the death of a close relative—is one over which a person has little or no control (Glass, 1977).

According to various studies, the person who should be expected to run the highest risk of falling victim to heart disease is a man in his 50s who weighs too much and exercises too little; smokes more than a pack of cigarettes a day; has a high level of blood cholesterol; suffers from hypertension and/or diabetes; and has a history of heart disease in his family (Glass, 1977; Jenkins, 1971).

Underlying the various conditions that trigger heart disease is what Friedman and Rosenman (1974) call "Type A behavior." The extreme Type A person is obsessed by a sense of the urgency of time and constantly tries to do several things at once. He is often hostile and impatient, speaks in staccato, and often finishes other people's sentences for them. He usually drives himself harder at work than he does his employees, but he is competitive and difficult to get along with. The Type B person, by contrast, is rarely driven to increase the amount of his output. Instead, he is concerned with the quality of achievement and experience. Often as intelligent and ambitious as his Type A counterpart, he frequently prevails over the more aggressive Type A.

Friedman and Rosenman found that the Type A men first studied in 1960 were nearly three times as likely to get heart disease during the next 10 years as the Type B men. Glass has suggested that Type A's are especially sensitive to negative sources of stress that threaten their control over their environment, and it appears to be the response of Type A's to such stressful life events that increases their likelihood of heart disease (1977).

The relationship between stress and disease in human beings is still controversial. Some researchers continue to seek only physical causes of disease, but recent findings strongly suggest that both psychological and physical factors lie at the root of some of mankind's most troubling afflictions.

---

if the person then decides to spend more time studying or working for the school paper.

Selye observed that the body reacts to stress in three stages that he has called the "general adaptation syndrome." These three stages are the alarm reaction, the stage of resistance, and the stage of exhaustion. The three phases may be repeated several times in a single day, as new demands arise. Each phase corresponds to one of the stages of life: "alarm" corresponds to childhood and is characterized by flexibility and learning; "resistance" corresponds to adulthood and is characterized by stability and resistance to change; and "exhaustion" corresponds to old age and is characterized by fatigue and the final exhaustion of death.

The alarm reaction is a person's first response to stress. The signs of this stage include heightened emotions and tension, increased sensitivity and alertness, and the start of a defense against the source of stress. As the body's resistance drops, physical and psychological symptoms of stress may occur so that one may become mentally disoriented or physically ill. If the stress is too severe, death may result. More often, however, people find a way first to resist stress, at least partially or temporarily, and then to begin to adapt or cope. During the second stage (resistance), the body's resistance rises above normal, although some symptoms of distress may persist. If resistance succeeds, the person returns to normal,

HYPERTENSION

One out of three American adults suffers from high blood pressure, the primary cause of stroke and a frequent contributor to heart attack and coronary artery disease (Hassett, 1978). Although drugs can be used to markedly reduce blood pressure and to increase life expectancy, medicines have side effects and do not completely control blood pressure (Jacob, 1977).

Since stress is generally thought to be a key contributor to these problems, several other treatments have also been explored, of which relaxation training and biofeedback are perhaps the most interesting. Both relaxation training and biofeedback are intended to reduce anxiety and achieve a relaxed state. They both require regular practice, promote muscle relaxation, and involve mental focusing and task awareness (Jacob, 1977).

Perhaps the most widely used and best publicized technique is Benson's "relaxation response." This is designed to induce a state that is distinct from normal relaxation or sleep (Hassett, 1978), and which is accompanied by feelings of peace of mind, being at ease with the world, and well-being (Benson, 1977). To achieve this state the person needs a quiet environment, a comfortable position, a "mental device" such as a repeated word or phrase, and a passive attitude (Hassett, 1978).

Biofeedback is a very different procedure for getting relaxation. As we saw in Chapter 5, it has recently been discovered that people can control all sorts of physiological processes that were previously considered involuntary. Sensitive recording devices record brain waves, blood pressure, and other bodily functions; this information is fed back to the person by means of auditory signals or visual displays so that the person knows which part of his or her body is doing what, and thus can gain some control over bodily functions (Coleman, 1978). Biofeedback has been applied to a wide range of disorders, including hypertension, headache, backache, muscle spasms, teeth grinding, asthma, epilepsy, and sexual impotence.

Both relaxation training and biofeedback have limitations and drawbacks. Both require that the person be trained and this takes more time than is needed to write a prescription. Many physicians are unwilling or ill-equipped to use biofeedback, and there is a shortage of trained specialists. Biofeedback equipment is complex and costly. Moreover, since many hypertension patients do not take their prescribed medication regularly, they may not be willing to undergo behavioral treatment. Also, behavioral therapy may not be equally effective for everyone. Intensive, carefully monitored behavioral treatment is not a miracle cure. But it may well supplement conventional medicine for many people.

but if the stress continues, he or she enters the third stage—exhaustion. Bodily resources are depleted causing coping measures to fail. Some features of the alarm reaction may reappear, but now they are both ineffectual and irreversible. If the stress continues, exhaustion can lead to irreparable physical and psychological damage—or even death (Coleman, 1979; Selye, 1976).

Selye emphasizes that "stress cannot and should not be avoided" (1976). Everyone undergoes some stress at all times, even when asleep. Often, stress is part of physical and emotional growth, learning, and pleasure. Therefore, according to Selye, to say that someone is under stress is to say the obvious. Stress is part of living; only death provides complete freedom from stress.

Stress, from whatever source, calls for adjustment. Psychologists distinguish between two general types of adjustment: direct coping and defensive coping. *Direct coping* refers to any action we take to change an uncomfortable situation. When our needs or desires are frustrated, we attempt to remove the obstacles between ourselves and our goal, or we give it up. Similarly, when we are threatened, we try to eliminate the source of the threat—either by attacking it or by escaping from it.

Defensive coping refers to the different ways people convince themselves that they are not really threatened, that they did not really want something they could not get. A form of self-deception, defensive coping is characteristic of internal, often unconscious conflicts. We feel unable to bring a problem to the surface and deal with it directly—it is too threatening. In self-defense, we avoid the conflict.

DIRECT COPING

"This toy is designed to hasten the child's adjustment to the world around him. No matter how carefully he puts it together, it won't work."
(Drawing by Mirachi; © 1964 *The New Yorker Magazine*, Inc.)

When we are threatened, frustrated, or in conflict, we have three basic choices for coping directly: We can try to change the situation in which we find ourselves; we can try to change ourselves; or we can withdraw from the situation. For example, a woman who has worked hard at her job for 5 years is not promoted. She learns that the reason is her stated unwillingness to relocate temporarily from the company's main office to a branch office in another part of the country in order to get more experience. Her unwillingness to move is an obstacle between her and her goal of advancing in her career.

She has several choices. She can change herself: If she wants to move up in the company badly enough, she might indicate that she is willing to relocate. Or she can change her goals, perhaps deciding that she has advanced as far as she wants to go. But what if she does not want to spend a year or two in another part of the country, yet still wants to continue working for the company and to receive the promotion? In this case she might attempt to change the situation. She might begin by pointing out to her supervisor that although she has never worked in a branch office, she has enough experience to handle a better job in the main office. She may also remind her supervisor of the company's need to have more women working in its top level positions. Or, she might challenge the assumption that the branch office will provide the kind of experience that her supervisor wants her to have.

Compromise is one of the most common ways of directly coping with a conflict or with frustration. The woman could work out a compromise with her supervisor: "I will relocate if you will agree to send me to a branch office which is less than 100 miles away." Each of them gives something up to reach a satisfactory solution.

AGGRESSION. Often, people who are forced to adjust get angry. Few would blame the woman in our example for feeling angry about having to deal with these conflicts and frustrations. But she is likely to control her anger until it is time to go home. Then she might walk out to her car and kick one of the tires with all her might. Afterward, she will probably feel better. Why? As we note in Chapter 16, some psychologists feel that human beings are innately aggressive, that it is part of our nature to want to defend ourselves and our territory, to destroy our enemies and to demolish anything that stands in our way. But society says we cannot, so, frustrated, we kick tires, honk our horns and yell in traffic jams, cheer on football teams, and start wars.

Much of the aggression that people express is the result of the competition for limited resources, in this case, space.
(Photo Researchers)

The theory that aggression is innate is debatable, as we shall see in Chapter 16. But even if aggression is an innate response to frustration, social inhibitions usually prevent our acting on this impulse. Direct expression of anger is more common than direct attack.

Whether physical or verbal, direct or indirect, the success of aggressive action depends on two conditions. First, we must know who or what threatens us or stands in our way. This is not always possible. The man who gets an incorrect computerized bill may fold, spindle, and mutilate the bill, but with little effect. He will have difficulty finding out who is responsible for the mistake. Riots often provide examples of aggression with no clearly defined adversary. Rioters attack what are for them symbols of oppression—police officers and stores—sometimes hurting members of their own community.

Second, aggression will succeed only when we are at least equal to our enemy. People seldom attack—even verbally—when they know their adversary can reciprocate effectively. The student who argues vehemently with a graduate assistant over grades or an assignment would probably be more timid if the course were taught by the head of the department. A consumer may yell at the grocer—there are always other stores to go to—but not at the landlord—who may put off making needed repairs. If the student, however, has been elected to a committee on the curriculum, and the consumer is a leader of a neighborhood action group, each will feel stronger.

WITHDRAWAL. In many situations the most effective solution is to withdraw. When our anxiety or frustration is particularly related to a stressful event—our car stalls in the middle of a highway, for example—we can deal with it through avoidance behavior. That is, we physically escape from the stress. By abandoning our car and waiting for help on the side of the road, we reduce the amount of stress we experience. The woman in our earlier example could quit her present job and join a new firm. The boy whose parents argue about whether he should play the piano or football might end up spending his afternoons in the woods with his dog. Often we equate withdrawal with simply refusing to face problems. But when we realize that our adversary is more powerful than we are, that there is no way we can effectively change ourselves, alter the situation, or reach a compromise, and that any form of aggression would be self-destructive, withdrawal is a positive and realistic adjustment.

388

Perhaps the greatest danger is that withdrawal will turn into avoidance of all similar situations: We may refuse to travel in any car again, the woman who did not want to move to a branch office may quit her job and not get a new one. At this point, effective coping by withdrawal becomes maladaptive avoidance, and we begin to suspect that the adjustment is not really effective.

Withdrawal, in whatever form, is therefore a mixed blessing: It can be an effective method of coping, but it has built-in dangers. The same tends to be true of all forms of defensive coping.

DEFENSIVE COPING

Defensive coping is characteristic of two kinds of situations. One of these is ambiguous situations, when people cannot tell who or what is threatening them. The other is internal conflicts that threaten a person's sense of identity and self-esteem. A high-school girl wants to go camping with a group of classmates, but her parents refuse to let her go. She runs to her room in tears and slams the door. She knows that if she defies her parents and goes without their approval, she will feel guilty, but that if she does not go, she will disappoint her friends and lessen her own sense of independence. Still, part of her is glad that her parents said no. Some of the girls who went the year before have been talking about couples going off alone to sleep together, and she feels threatened by this because she does not feel sure of herself sexually. She turns on the radio and tries to forget the whole thing.

Resignation or apathy is another way of coping defensively. It is an extreme form of withdrawal. In seemingly hopeless situations, such as submarine and mining disasters, few people panic (Mintz, 1951). Realizing that there is nothing they can do to save themselves, they give up. If the situation is in fact hopeless, resignation may be the most effective way of coping. But people who have given up are in a poor position to take advantage of a more effective solution—should one come along. Research cited by Seligman (1975) shows that people who are put into seemingly hopeless situations not only become apathetic and depressed, but when the situation changes, they fail to learn that they can cope more effectively. They continue to be helpless, apathetic, passive, and depressed even when there are, in fact, opportunities for improving their situations.

Seligman and his colleagues first identified *learned helplessness* in animal experiments (Overmier & Seligman, 1967; Seligman & Maier, 1967). They placed dogs in experimental chambers from which they could not escape. Then they gave them a series of electric shocks. Most dogs soon learned that nothing they could do would stop the shocks and they gave up trying to escape. When these dogs were transferred to experimental chambers from which it was possible to escape, their helplessness continued. They did not try to find a way out of their new environment. Even when the experimenter picked them up and showed them how to escape, they did not seem to understand. They just went back to their corners and endured the shocks. They had learned to be helpless (see Chapter 5).

(Mimi Forsyth, Monkmeyer)

Dweck and Reppucci (1973) demonstrated one effect of learned helplessness in humans. A group of fifth-grade students were given unsolvable problems by one teacher and solvable problems by another. When the "unsolvable" teacher later presented the students with problems that could be solved, they were unable to solve them, even though they had solved nearly identical problems given by the other teacher.

Forgetting is one way that people cope with complex problems they feel unable to solve. By denying that a threat exists, blocking out painful memories, and repressing unacceptable impulses—like wanting to hit a child or sleep with a friend's spouse—people protect their self-image and integrity. No one is perfect, but it is often painful to admit to a particular trait or desire. Moreover, admitting it will also force a person to deal with it, which can be even more painful. To avoid the pain, therefore, people will deny that something—a situation or a problem—exists.

Sometimes, of course, a problem cannot be ignored. In such a situation people may distort their perception of things, translating the problem into a form they can handle. For example, a high-school girl talks her boyfriend into sneaking away together for the weekend. It is a bad experience for both of them. Days later she insists that it was *he* who had pushed her into it. She is not lying—she really believes that he did. Probably she feels guilty for insisting that they sneak away, angry with him for not talking her out of it, disturbed by what she felt during the experience. To pull herself back together, she locates the responsibility outside of herself. **Projection**—as this is called—is a form of defensive coping.

The self-deceptive element in such adjustments led Freud to conclude that they are entirely unconscious. Freud was particularly interested in distortions of memory and in irrational feelings and behavior, all of which he considered symptoms of the struggle against unconscious impulses. Suppose a man quite suddenly develops a chronic fear of falling. Perhaps as a child he had fantasies about pushing a younger brother out of a window; perhaps he feels guilty about wanting to unseat his superior—who has an office with a window on the twentieth floor—and unconsciously wants to punish himself; perhaps he is afraid of "falling" in love. All of these explanations are oversimplified. The point is that Freud believed that defensive ways of coping always spring from unconscious conflicts, and that we have little or no control over them.

Not all psychologists accept this interpretation. Often we realize that we are pushing something out of our memory or transferring emotions. We all have blown up at one person when we knew we were really angry with someone else. The transfer is conscious: If questioned, we could explain our behavior quite clearly. Despite this difference in approach, psychologists agree in describing certain basic types of defensive coping, called **defense mechanisms**—how people react to stress by deceiving themselves about their real desires and goals in an effort to maintain their self-esteem and to avoid anxiety.

DENIAL. One common defense mechanism is denial—refusing to acknowledge painful or threatening circumstances. Lazarus (1969) cites the example of a woman who was dying from severe burns. At first she was depressed and frightened, but after a few days her attitude began to change. She felt sure that she would soon be able to return home and care for her children, although all medical evidence was to the contrary. By denying the extent of her injuries, this woman was able to stay calm and cheerful. She was not merely putting on an act for her relatives and friends—she *believed* she would recover. In a similar situation, C. T. Wolff and his colleagues (1964) interviewed the parents of children who were dying of leukemia. Some parents denied their children's condition, others accepted it. But physical examinations revealed that those who were denying the illness did not have the physiological symptoms of stress, such as excessive stomach acid, that those who accepted it were suffering.

Most psychologists would agree that in these situations denial is a positive solution. But in other situations, it clearly is not. Students who deny their need to study and instead spend most nights at the movies may well fail their exams. Heroin addicts who insist that they are merely experimenting with drugs are also deluding themselves.

REPRESSION. Perhaps the most common mechanism for blocking out painful feelings and experiences is repression. Repression, as we saw in Chapter 6, is a form of forgetting. The most extreme form of this defense is *amnesia*—the total inability to recall a part of the past. Soldiers who break down in the field often block out the experiences that led to their collapse (Grinker & Spiegel, 1945). But forgetting that you are supposed to go for a job interview Thursday morning, or forgetting the embarrassing things you said at a party last night, may also be instances of repression. Repression is never entirely successful; repressed material may cause anxiety and irrational behavior.

Many psychologists believe that repression is a sign that people are struggling against impulses that their conscious values prevent them from expressing. A teenage girl who has been taught that "nice" girls do not have sexual desires may flirt with a boy and then be shocked when he becomes sexually aroused. She may not be conscious of the conflict between her values and her actions.

Denial and repression are the most fundamental defense mechanisms. Both involve blocking out virtually all of our painful experiences or feelings. In denial, we block out situations that we cannot cope with. In repression, we block out unacceptable impulses or thoughts. These mechanisms form the bases for other defensive ways of coping.

INTELLECTUALIZATION. This defense mechanism is a subtle form of denial. We realize that we are threatened but detach ourselves from our problems by analyzing and intellectualizing them. Parents who sit down to discuss their child's difficulties in a new school and hours later find themselves in a sophisticated discussion of educational philosophy may be intellectualizing. They appear to be dealing with their problems but may, in fact, have cut themselves off from their emotions.

Like denial, **intellectualization** can be a valuable defense. Doctors and nurses see pain and suffering every day of their working lives. They must keep some degree of detachment if they are to be objective and clear-headed. Psychologist Bruno Bettelheim, once a prisoner in a Nazi

Repression is a form of locking out painful feelings and experiences.
(Rapho, Photo Researchers)

REACTION FORMATION: AN EXAMPLE

Jules Masserman, a psychologist who used cats as experimental subjects for research on alcoholism, once received the following letter from an ardent antivivisectionist. The woman's concern for the welfare of the cats appears to be a coverup for her very bitter and hostile attitudes toward people:

I read . . . your work on alcoholism. . . . I am surprised that anyone who is as well educated as you must be to hold the position that you do would stoop to such a depth to torture helpless little cats in the pursuit of a cure for alcoholics. . . . A drunkard does not want to be cured—a drunkard is just a weakminded idiot who belongs in the gutter and should be left there. Instead of torturing helpless little cats why not torture the drunks or better still exert your would-be noble effort toward getting a bill passed to exterminate the drunks. They are not any good to anyone or themselves and are just a drain on the public, having to pull them off the street and jail them, then they have to be fed while there and it's against the law to feed them arsenic so there they are. . . . If people are such weaklings the world is better off without them. . . . My greatest wish is that you have brought home to you a torture that will be a thousand-fold greater than what you have, and are doing to the little animals. . . . I'm glad I am just an ordinary human being without a letter after my name. I'd rather be just myself with a clear conscience, *knowing I have not hurt any living creature,* and can sleep without seeing frightened, terrified dying cats—because I know they must die after you finish with them. No punishment is too great for you and I hope I live to read about your mangled body and long suffering before you finally die . . . and I'll laugh long and loud (Masserman, 1946, p. 35).

---

concentration camp, reports that he felt completely detached on the journey to prison. He simply did not feel that it was happening to him (Bettelheim, 1943).

REACTION FORMATION. The term **"reaction formation"** refers to a behavioral form of denial: The person expresses exaggerated emotions that are the opposite of what he or she really feels. Exaggeration is the clue. Examples of this behavior are common. The man who praises a rival extravagantly may be overreacting—covering up hostility about his opponent's success. Reaction formation may also be a way of convincing oneself that one's motives are pure. The woman who feels ambivalent about being a mother may devote all her time to her children in an attempt to prove to *herself* that she is a good mother.

DISPLACEMENT. Displacement is the redirection of energy from unsatisfied drives onto other objects. It is closely related to repression. With displacement, repressed feelings find a new outlet. The man who has always wanted to be a father and learns he cannot have children may feel inadequate. As a result, he may become extremely attached to a pet or to a neighbor's child. Loving the pet or the child may not be a totally satisfactory substitute for a child of his own, but it enables him to carry on.

Displacement often occurs when we cannot defend ourselves directly. The woman who must smile and agree with her boss all day may come home and yell at her children or her husband. Bettelheim cites an interesting example of this type of defensive coping in his study of former concentration camp prisoners. At one point during the war, English and

President Carter and Senator Edward Kennedy were rivals at the 1980 Democratic Convention. But after Carter completed his acceptance speech, Kennedy joined him on the podium, as a sign of party unity.
(UPI)

American journalists began to report on the inhumane treatment of prisoners in Nazi Germany. Learning of this, camp guards punished the prisoners severely. In later years the former prisoners blamed the journalists rather than the guards for the bad treatment they had received. Bettelheim suggests that this is because the prisoners had been completely at the mercy of their captors. So they blamed the journalists, who were "safer" targets (Bettelheim, 1960).

SUBLIMATION. Freud believed that **sublimation,** the transformation of drives into more socially acceptable forms, is essential to personality development—and to civilization. Sexual curiosity may become a desire for knowledge; unexpressed hostility toward the mother or father may become the driving force behind a hammer or a surgical knife; the need for approval may lead to a talent for acting. Without these transformations, Freud argued, people would continue to live on a very primitive level and could never build societies.

According to psychoanalytic theory, then, sublimation is at times both necessary and desirable. The conflict between a person's desires and society's demands is inevitable. Only when people find an acceptable way to express and release these drives can they find inner peace.

SUBLIMATION: A CASE HISTORY

An infant was seen to have considerable aggression and hostility. This was quite evident in his later ideas, his behavior, his fantasies, and in repeated incidents with his playmates. There were also several episodes of cruel and sadistic treatment of pets. His reading and hobbies also confirmed these trends.

As he grew older, he became quite interested in hobbies, first in guns, and later in knives and sharp instruments. His hostility, sadistic trends, and his aggressive trends met with overwhelming parental and social disapproval and, almost inevitably, he disapproved of them, too. By the time he had traversed the latent stage of development there appeared to be little outward trace of these drives left.

There was, however, some growing interest in the work of physicians in the field of medicine. In adult life this man became a highly successful and respected surgeon.

The repressed, instinctual, aggressive strivings had been successfully sublimated into surgical work of a high caliber. The process of sublimation had not only been successful, but had also proved highly valuable from personal, cultural, and social standpoints (reprinted from Laughlin, 1963, p. 98).

PROJECTION: A CASE HISTORY

A 36-year-old elementary schoolteacher was best known by her colleagues for her bitter condemnations of anyone in whom she observed signs of poor organization, lack of orderliness and meticulousness, or an inability to cope with difficult situations. It was anathema to her if someone became easily emotional or unnerved.

It had been for a long time painfully obvious to her friends that she herself possessed the attributes she so readily ascribed to others, and which she censured so much. Her appearance was unkempt; her desk was generally in disarray; and she readily "flew off the handle" when things did not go smoothly.

Her fellow teachers implicitly recognized that she was projecting her inadequacies and shortcomings onto others. This projecting spared her the anxiety and intolerable burden of self-censure that would otherwise result if she were to consciously recognize these faults in herself (reprinted from Laughlin, 1970, p. 227).

PROJECTION. Projection is the displacement of one's own motives onto others. We attribute feelings we do not want to someone else, thus locating the source of conflict outside of ourselves. A corporation executive who feels guilty about her unscrupulous rise to power may project her own motives onto her colleagues. She is simply doing her job, she believes, but her associates are all two-faced connivers.

Dana Bramel (1962) demonstrated projection with an experiment in which male subjects were exposed to a homosexual advance. Each subject was given a partner, and both were connected to a machine they were told would measure sexual arousal while they looked at a series of pictures. Actually, the machine was a fake—the experimenter controlled the dial. Some of the subjects were led to believe they had measurable homosexual tendencies; others were not. In interviews after the experiment, the subjects in the first group were more inclined to attribute homosexual feelings to their partners than were the control subjects. Bramel feels that this was because they could not deny evidence about themselves from the machine. Trapped, they projected the self-image they found unacceptable onto their partners.*

IDENTIFICATION. The reverse of projection is **identification.** Through projection, we rid ourselves of undesirable feelings by attributing them to someone else. Through identification, we take on the characteristics of someone else to share in that person's triumphs and to avoid feeling incompetent. The admired person's actions become a substitute for our own. Identification is considered a form of defensive coping because it enables people to resolve conflicts vicariously. A parent with unfulfilled career ambitions may share emotionally in a child's professional success. When the child is promoted, the parent may feel as if he or she had triumphed.

Identification is a very natural part of growing up. All children imitate

---

*This study provoked considerable ethical controversy. The ethics of psychological research are discussed in Chapter 1 and in a box on p. 379 of this chapter.

adults in their play, often with disturbing accuracy. A game of cowboys and Indians, for example, allows children to practice the moral values they are learning. Sex roles are also developed in part through play.

But identification is more than imitation. Children internalize values long before the values have any direct meaning for them. A 6-year-old may not care about his mother's collection of china figurines, but he warns his friends to stay away from the shelf because he identifies with his mother and wants her approval. He feels it is wrong to play with them, even though he has no sense of their artistic or sentimental value. Identification is thus a primary source of moral values.

Freud felt that in part children identify with their parents in self-defense. He believed that children go through a stage of considering the parent of the same sex a rival. They want to do away with that parent and fear reprisal for their fantasies. Identification with that parent resolves the conflict and removes the fear (see Chapter 11).

Identification is also important in adolescence. Young teenagers are no longer satisfied with games and make-believe success. Their goals are adult, but society says they are not yet ready to function as full members. Both sex and full-time work are prohibited. Adolescents typically resolve the conflict between what they think they can do and what society and their parents allow by identifying with rock musicians, movie stars, politicians, and other public figures.

(Photo Researchers)

Of course, identification goes both ways in the parent–child relationship. Even if parents do not have ambitions for their children, they may identify with them in certain ways. A mother may enjoy her daughter's popularity or political activism; a father may share his son's bent for poetry, science, or motorcycles. These adults regain their youth and hope by identifying with their children. Identification is thus a way of coping with being too young or too old to do things one wants to do.

Identification is also a way of coping with situations in which a person feels utterly helpless. Bettelheim describes how prisoners in concentration camps gradually came to identify with the Nazi guards. Unable to retaliate against their captors, prisoners turned on each other. Over the years they began to copy the speech and mannerisms of the guards, and sometimes even their values.

Bettelheim explains this puzzling behavior in Freudian terms. The prisoners were completely dependent on the guards, who could treat them however they liked. The relationship between prisoner and guard was similar to that between son and father. Bettelheim suggests that the guards may have consciously made the prisoners feel like children. For example, prisoners had to ask permission to go to the bathroom. Sometimes that permission was denied, forcing on grown men the indignity of wetting their pants. Reduced to a childlike, helpless condition, prisoners reverted to a pattern developed in childhood—identification with the aggressor (Bettelheim, 1943, 1960). Like boys in conflict with a stern and cruel father, they grew to admire their enemy.

REGRESSION. People under severe stress, like the concentration camp victims described by Bettelheim, may revert to childlike behavior and primitive defenses. No form of adult behavior would have worked for the

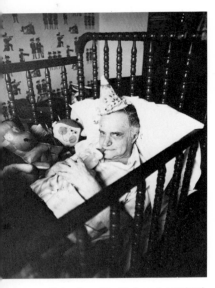

(Arthur Tress, Woodfin Camp & Associates)

concentration camp prisoners; they could not have argued with their oppressors or appealed to their humanity. Direct action would certainly have made the situation worse. With no recourse, these victims found some relief in regressing to immature behavior patterns. **Regression,** however, may also occur in less extreme circumstances.

Why do people regress? Some psychologists feel that it is because an adult cannot stand feeling helpless. Children, on the other hand, are made to feel dependent every day. Becoming more childlike can make total dependency or helplessness more bearable.

But regression is not always the result of imposed dependency. Adults who cry when their arguments fail may expect those around them to react sympathetically, as their parents did when they were children. Others may use temper tantrums in a similar way. In both examples the persons are drawing on experiences long past to solve current problems, in the hope that someone will respond. Inappropriate as it may seem, such behavior often works—which brings up the final point in this section.

Is defensive coping a sign that a person is immature, unstable, on the edge of a "breakdown"? The answer is no. Everyone uses defense mechanisms to cope with real problems and internal conflicts. As Coleman and Hammen (1974) point out, defenses "are essential for softening failure . . . alleviating anxiety, repairing emotional hurt, and maintaining our feelings of adequacy and worth" (p. 138). We could not get along from day to day if we allowed ourselves to fully realize the dangers of flying in an airplane or driving on an expressway. Sublimation and identification, at least according to the psychoanalytic view, are essential to growing up. And as we saw in Chapter 4, denial is one of the first reactions of people who learn that they are going to die. When any of these defenses interferes with a person's ability to function, however, or creates more problems that it solves, psychologists consider the defense maladaptive. But what is successful adjustment?

The Well-Adjusted Person

Psychologists have different opinions about what constitutes effective adjustment. Some base their evaluation on a person's ability to live according to social norms. All people have hostile and selfish wishes; all people dream impossible dreams. Those who learn to control such impulses and to limit their goals to those society allows and provides for are, by this definition, "well-adjusted." The woman who grows up in a small town, attends her state university, teaches for a year or two, then settles down to a peaceful family life might be considered "well-adjusted" to the extent that she is living by the predominant values of her community.

Other psychologists disagree strongly with this "conformist" viewpoint. Barron (1963), for example, argues that "refusal to adjust . . . is very often the mark of a healthy character." Society is not always right. To accept its rules blindly—to say, for example, "My country, right or wrong"—is to give in. Barron suggests that well-adjusted people _enjoy_ the difficulties

and ambiguities of life—rather than avoiding them by conforming. They can accept challenges and feel pain and confusion. Confident of their ability to deal with problems in a realistic and mature way, they can admit primitive or childish impulses into their consciousness. Temporary regression does not threaten them. Barron sees flexibility, spontaneity, and creativity as signs of healthy adjustment.

This view is based primarily on the psychoanalytic theory that over-control produces anxiety. Antisocial impulses do not disappear when we push them out of our minds. People who live by a strict code of values and work simply to meet society's demands are very likely repressing their own needs. Unable to feel or express their emotions, they are tense, defensive, overly anxious to please—and probably uncomfortably neurotic. The man who really wanted to be an artist but yielded to pressure to go into business—and at age 50 develops a heart condition—may be an example.

But not all psychologists feel that how people cope with their lives

THE SELF-ACTUALIZING PERSON
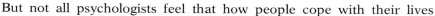

Another view of the well-adjusted person was provided by Abraham Maslow. People who are well-adjusted attempt to "actualize" themselves. That is, they live in a way that they believe is best for their own growth and fulfillment regardless of what others may think. Studying a number of famous people and a group of college students, Maslow (1954) compiled a list of 15 traits that he believed were characteristic of self-actualizing people:

1. *More efficient perception of reality.* They judge people and events realistically and are better able than others to accept uncertainty and ambiguity.
2. *Acceptance of self and others.* They take others for what they are and are not guilty or defensive about themselves.
3. *Spontaneity.* This quality is shown more in thinking than in action. As a matter of fact, self-actualizing people are frequently quite conventional in behavior.
4. *Problem centering.* They are more concerned with problems than with themselves and are likely to have what they consider important goals.
5. *Detachment.* They need privacy and do not mind being alone.
6. *Autonomy.* They are able to be independent of their environment.
7. *Continued freshness of appreciation,* even of often-repeated experiences.
8. *Mystical experiences, or the oceanic feeling.* This

feeling, which Maslow includes under the heading of "peak experiences," frequently involves wonder, awe, a feeling of oneness with the universe, and a loss of self.
9. *Gemeinschaftsgefuhl,* or social interest. This is a feeling of unity with humanity in general.
10. *Interpersonal relationships.* Deep, close relationships with a chosen few characterize self-actualizing people.
11. *Democratic character structure.* Self-actualizing people are relatively indifferent to such matters as sex, birth, race, color, and religion in judging other people.
12. *Discrimination between means and ends.* They enjoy activities for their own sake, but also appreciate the difference between means and goals.
13. *Sense of humor.* Their sense of humor is philosophical rather than hostile.
14. *Creativeness.* Their creativity in any field consists mostly of the ability to generate new ideas.
15. *Resistance to enculturation.* They are not rebellious, but they are generally independent of any given culture.

Maslow did not consider self-actualizing people perfect—disregard of others is one possible fault, for example. Moreover, having the characteristics on this list does not mean that you are self-actualizing, only that self-actualization is important to you and that you are the type of person who tries to achieve it.

determines if they will be happy and fulfilled. All that matters, according to one view, is that they learn how to get along. One woman finds happiness in marriage; another in working her way to the top of a corporation; still another tends her garden in the evenings and on weekends. In this view, the absence of tension indicates healthy adjustment.

Not content with this negative definition, still others suggest the following pattern. Well-adjusted people have learned to balance conformity and nonconformity, self-control and spontaneity. They can let themselves go, but can also control themselves in situations where acting on their impulses would be damaging. They can change when society demands it, but also try to change society when this seems the better course. One explanation of this flexibility is that these people can realistically judge both the world around them and their own needs and capabilities. They both know their strengths and admit their weaknesses. As a result, they have chosen a role in life that is in harmony with their inner selves. They do not feel they must act against their values in order to be successful. This self-trust enables them to face conflicts and threats without excessive anxiety and, perhaps more important, to risk their feelings and self-esteem in intimate relationships.

Another means of evaluating adjustment is to use specific criteria, such as the following (Coleman & Hammen, 1974):

1. *Does the person's behavior really meet the stress, or does it simply postpone resolving the problem?* Various forms of escapism—drugs, alcohol and even endless fantasizing through books, movies, and television— may divert us from our pain. But they do not eliminate the causes of our difficulties. Thus completely relying on escapism can never be a truly effective adjustment to a stressful situation.
2. *Does the action satisfy the person's own needs?* Often we act to eliminate external pressures in our lives without considering our own needs. People may abandon personal career goals because of the goals of a spouse. In the short run, external pressure on them may be reduced, but they may be frustrated and disappointed for the rest of their lives. A solution that creates such inner conflict is often not really an effective adjustment.
3. *Is the action in harmony with the person's environment?* Some people satisfy their needs in a way that hurts others. The young executive who uses people and manipulates co-workers may "get ahead" through such actions. But even if he does succeed in becoming vice-president of his company, he may find himself without friends. He may become afraid that others will treat him as he treated them. Ultimately, this situation can become quite stressful and frustrating. An effective adjustment must take into consideration both individual needs and the well-being of others.

We have seen that there are many different standards for deciding if a person is well-adjusted. A person who is considered well-adjusted according to one standard, however, may or may not be considered well-adjusted according to others. As you might expect, the same holds true when we try to decide what behaviors are "abnormal"—the topic of the next chapter.

THE STOCKHOLM SYNDROME

One of the clearest illustrations of how people cope with extraordinary stress is the reactions of the hostages and their captors. The stress is sudden, unexpected, and intense; hostages, captors, and outside authorities often have little control over events as they unfold. What kinds of adjustment mechanisms do people use in such situations?

One of the most striking coping procedures is known as "The Stockholm Syndrome," in which hostages actually side with their captors—and the captors come to sympathize with the captives. The term "Stockholm Syndrome" derives from a 1973 bank robbery in Stockholm, Sweden, where the robbers held four hostages captive for six days. By the end of the ordeal the hostages found themselves more loyal to the bank robbers than to the police. They ultimately refused to testify against their former captors. One woman hostage became so emotionally attached to one of the robbers that she broke her engagement to another man after the incident. Psychologists define three stages of the syndrome:

1. The hostages begin to feel positive about their captors.
2. The hostages develop negative feelings toward the authorities trying to rescue them.
3. The captors develop positive feelings toward their victims. Both groups are isolated and terrorized and come to believe, "We are in this together."

Why would a hostage come to like or even love a captor? Dr. Frank Ochberg, director of the Michigan Department of Mental Health, explains, "When someone captures you and places you in an infantile position, he sets the stage for love as a response to infantile terror—he could kill you but he does not and you are grateful" (*Time*, 1979).

Richard Dudman and two other reporters following American and South Vietnamese troops once blundered into a Cambodian war zone held by Communist-led guerrillas. Dudman recalls his "exaggerated gratitude toward the five guerrillas who were put in charge of us. For not killing us. For promising not to mistreat us any more. [They had been beaten on the first day of capture.] For giving us the same food they had, and for saving our lives three times, when U. S. war planes attacked our area" (McCarthy, 1980).

Dr. Robert J. Lifton of Yale University writes of the "psychology of the pawn" (Lifton, 1961). Manipulated through constant fear of death or harm to act as instructed, the pawn adapts to events beyond his or her control. The pawn adopts certain behaviors for coping, such as submissiveness. Like any human being, pawns are deeply sensitive to their limitations and unfulfilled potential. They are vulnerable to any guilt the captors may want them to feel in their effort to affect their outlook.

Lorraine Berzins, an officer with the Canadian Penitentiary Service, offers other insights into why a hostage develops a positive feeling toward a captor. In 1970 she was taken hostage at knifepoint by an inmate. She had been professionally trained to deal with violent behavior and she got her captor to trust her. She observes:

There may be a clash between our different perceptions of a person's 'good' qualities alongside his criminal behavior. . . . If a person is not trained or experienced enough to be able to accommodate the seeming contradiction of the two, he may need to deny one in order to preserve the other. The hostage, to preserve the trust that his survival depends on, may need to see his captor as 'all good' to resolve the dissonance and maintain harmony between them (Schreiber, 1978).

There is also sympathy. Berzins saw that her captor was "very, very frightened" and cared about his life while at the same time he was quite aware that he was endangering her life.

Why do the hostages develop negative feelings toward the authorities trying to rescue them?

For the authorities the desired outcome is the capture of the kidnappers and the recovery of persons and property. Having been on the outside and indulged in some of those same calculations himself as he followed other kidnap episodes in the news, the hostage is deeply distrustful of the negotiators. Suppose they overreact. . . . "I had this very strong feeling that my life wasn't as important to the negotiators as it was to me," says Berzins (Schreiber, 1978).

Berzins also states, "If your way of coping with anxiety is to project blame onto other people, you're obviously not going to project it onto the hostage-taker because it's too dangerous. . . . The easiest target is the outside authorities."

The prisoner can feel that he or she and the hostage-taker are a small group facing a hostile world when outside events appear to reaffirm the hostage-taker's viewpoint. Isolated from outside information, Patty Hearst, for example, was told that her parents and society no longer cared about her. This lie was seemingly confirmed when her six captors burned to death in a police raid on their Los Angeles hideout (Conway & Siegelman, 1980).

The hostage may be unclear as to exactly what principles of the outside authorities he or she is defending. Lifton points out that one of the ex-hostages in Iran viewed his resistance to his captors partly as a matter of suffering for the sake of the Shah, whom he did not wholeheartedly support. The Iranians led him to focus on a questionable cause and overlook the fact that he was being held illegally (*U. S. News & World Report*, 1979/1980).

Why would the captors develop positive attitudes toward their victims? Confronted by authorities who want to set the example that hostage-taking does not succeed, the captors know they may very well die. Concern about the pain and discomfort of their victims helps keep their minds off the stress. Also, despite their proclamations of being willing to die for their cause, they often compromise their ideals. To survive themselves, they often do not harm their hostages.

The Stockholm Syndrome does not always occur. According to Lifton, if hostages have a "relatively strong belief system" or a "varied knowledge and a fluid kind of identity," they can withstand shocking challenges to their viewpoints (*U. S. News & World Report*, 1979/1980). Moreover, the captors may overmanipulate their victims, causing those who had been initially fearful to become angered by their humiliating treatment. The manipulations may be heavy-handed and easily perceived and countered by hostages who can reflect upon them and discuss them with each other.

Resentment of overmanipulation led the Iranian hostages to develop strategies that maintained their pride. Resourceful secret communication systems and humorous cartoons mocking the Iranians enabled the Americans to enjoy outwitting their captors. Other strategies used by these hostages to uphold their individuality included demanding better food, maintaining a neat appearance, observing a busy daily schedule, and attempting escapes.

The effects of captivity on a hostage continue after liberation. They can include:

1. feelings of guilt about hostages who have died or those who are still hostages;
2. lack of any feelings, which gives way periodically to an intense need to talk;
3. suspicion of deceptive behavior, especially by established authorities;
4. hostility, in particular toward employers who may expect ex-hostages quickly to return to normal;
5. loss of confidence in the world, requiring continual reassurances from family and friends that the ex-hostage's life will not be violently interrupted again; and
6. need to find meaning in the ordeal, which leads some hostages to feel a sense of rebirth or the need to "turn over a new leaf."

Comparing these aftereffects to material in the rest of this chapter, you will notice that they are all normal responses to extreme stress and are all attempts to cope effectively with overwhelming pressure. Thus they illustrate, in exaggerated form, the same coping processes we all use in less extraordinary situations.

(UPI)

(UPI)

Summary

1. The way people attempt to adapt to their physical and social environment, and attempt to achieve harmony between their desires and motives and the demands and constraints placed on them by their environment, is called *adjustment*.

2. *Stress* describes situations in which people feel threatened, frustrated, or in conflict, and their reactions to such situations. It occurs in pleasant and unpleasant situations, and cannot be entirely avoided or eliminated.

3. *Pressure* is a form of stress in which people feel they must live up to a particular standard of behavior or adapt to rapid change. We may pressure ourselves to live up to some *internal* standard of excellence. *External* pressures include competition, change, and the demands of family and friends.

4. *Anxiety* is a form of stress in which people experience all the symptoms of stress but cannot identify what is frightening or upsetting them.

5. *Frustration* occurs when people are somehow prevented from achieving their goals. They must either give up their goal, find some new way to achieve it, or adjust to living with their disappointment.

6. *Conflicts* are probably the most common problems to which people must adjust. Conflicts occur when a person is faced with two incompatible demands, opportunities, needs, or goals.

7. One way of describing conflict is in terms of two opposite tendencies: *approach* and *avoidance*. Developed by Kurt Lewin, this theory says that we want to approach things that attract us and avoid things that frighten us. These contradictory feelings produce three basic types of conflict.

8. In an *approach/approach conflict*, we are attracted to two goals at the same time and must either make a choice between them or modify one or both of them in some way.

9. In an *avoidance/avoidance conflict*, we face two undesirable or threatening, yet unavoidable, alternatives and must either choose the one that causes the least discomfort or, in certain extreme instances, sit the situation out and wait for the inevitable.

10. In an *approach/avoidance conflict*, we are both attracted to and repelled by the same goal.

11. Hans Seyle believes that people react to stress in three stages that he calls the *General Adaptation Syndrome:* alarm, resistance, exhaustion.

12. There are two general types of coping: *direct coping* and *defensive coping*. Direct coping refers to any action people take to alter an uncomfortable situation: trying to change the situation, trying to change themselves, or withdrawing from the situation. *Aggression,*

compromise, and *withdrawal* are all ways of coping directly.

13. Defensive coping is one way that people deal with complex situations that they feel unable to solve. They may deny that a threat exists, block out painful memories, or repress unacceptable impulses. *Learned helplessness*, an extreme form of withdrawal, refers to people's feelings that their actions will have no effect in changing their lives; they learn how not to cope.

14. Defensive coping can take several forms, called *defense mechanisms*. In using defense mechanisms, people react to frustration or conflict by deceiving themselves about their real desires and goals in order to maintain their self-esteem and avoid anxiety.

15. *Denial* is the refusal to acknowledge that a painful or threatening situation exists. *Repression*, a form of forgetting, is probably the most common means of blocking out painful situations. *Intellectualization* is a subtle form of denial by which we detach ourselves emotionally from our problems by analyzing them in purely rational terms. *Reaction formation*, a behavioral form of denial, is exhibited when we express emotions that are the opposite of what we really feel.

16. *Displacement* is the redirection of energy from unsatisfied drives onto other objects. *Sublimation* is the redirection of primitive drives into acceptable forms of behavior that allow us to develop our personalities and build societies.

17. *Projection* involves the displacement of one's own motives onto others. The reverse is *identification*—assuming the characteristics of someone else in order to share that person's successes and avoid feelings of personal incompetence.

18. *Regression* refers to the reversion to childlike, even infantile behavior in situations where no form of adult behavior will work.

19. Some psychologists believe that healthy adjustment depends on people's ability to live according to social norms, to control their drives and direct their goals to those society allows. Others feel that people are well-adjusted when they are able to face the difficulties and ambiguities of life by demonstrating flexibility, spontaneity, and creativity. Some claim that the absence of tension indicates effective adjustment, while others suggest that the well-adjusted person is able to balance conformity and nonconformity, self-control and spontaneity.

Outline

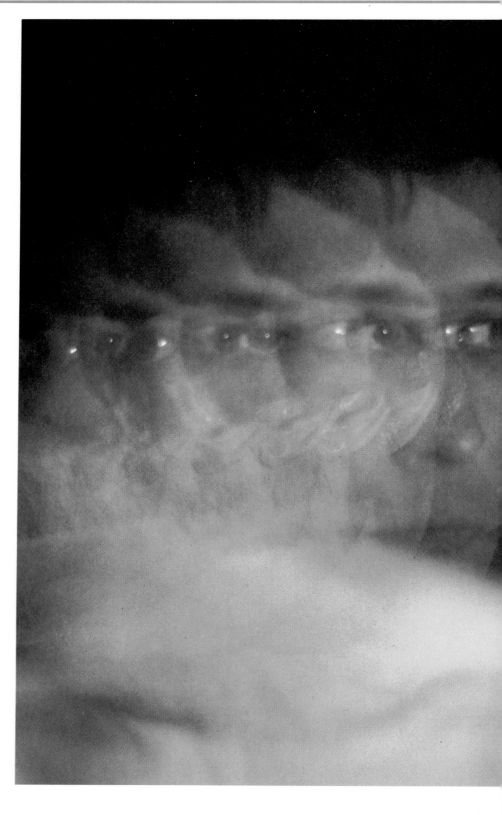

Chapter 13

Abnormal Behavior

When does behavior become abnormal behavior? The answer to this question is harder than it may seem. There is no doubt that the man on a street corner who claims to be George Washington or the woman who insists that elevators are trying to kill her are behaving abnormally, but what about the 20 students who cram themselves into a telephone booth, or the business executive who has three martinis every day for lunch? Defining these behaviors as abnormal depends upon whose standards and system of values are being used: society's, the individual's, or the mental health professional's.

As you can see from Table 13–1, these three parties have different views on mental health; they use different standards to judge normal and abnormal behavior. Society's main concern is whether behavior conforms to the existing social order. A person is concerned with his or her own sense of well-being. The mental health professional is concerned with theories of personality. Because these views are often at odds, it is difficult for psychologists to derive a single definition of normal and abnormal behavior that includes them all.

To some extent psychologists turn to *intrapersonal standards* of normality, that is, they try to evaluate people in terms of their own lives. Consider the following examples:

A bookkeeper falls behind in her work because no matter how often she erases stray pencil marks on her ledger, she cannot get the page clean enough. Her employer does not understand. Finally, one morning, she cannot get up to go to work.

The adolescent son of a wealthy suburbanite has a substantial allowance of his own, yet one night he is arrested for trying to hold up a gas station. He insists that there is nothing wrong with his actions.

405

A quiet, well-behaved child suddenly covers the living-room walls with paint. When questioned, she explains that "Johnny" did it. Within a few weeks, the child is spending all her time alone in her room talking with her imaginary friend.

Each of these people is acting in an impaired, self-defeating manner. The bookkeeper has set herself an impossible task. Her need for neatness is so exaggerated that she cannot possibly succeed. The young man is surprised at the reactions of people to his robbery attempt. "Why all the fuss?" he asks. "So I got caught." His failure to accept certain basic social values is a psychological problem. All children use their imaginations—they invent people when they play and make excuses for unacceptable behavior. But the girl in the previous example is unable—or unwilling—to turn her imagination off. Perhaps Johnny protects her from punishment, loss of love, loneliness. Johnny does all the things she cannot.

The behavior of these people is considered abnormal because their perception of reality is distorted and their ability to cope is impaired. The bookkeeper is struggling to reach an impossible goal: perfection. The

**Table 13–1
Viewpoints on
Mental Health**

	Standards/Values	**Measures**
Society	Orderly world in which people assume responsibility for their assigned social roles (e.g., breadwinner, parent), conform to prevailing mores, and meet situational requirements.	Observations of behavior, extent to which a person fulfills society's expectations and measures up to prevailing standards.
Individual	Happiness, gratification of needs.	Subjective perceptions of self-esteem, acceptance, and well-being.
Mental Health Professional	Sound personality structure characterized by growth, development, autonomy, environmental mastery, ability to cope with stress, adaptation.	Clinical judgment, aided by behavioral observations and psychological tests of such variables as self-concept, sense of identity, balance of psychic forces, unified outlook on life, resistance to stress, self-regulation, ability to cope with reality, absence of mental and behavioral symptoms, adequacy in love, work, and play, adequacy in interpersonal relationships.

Source: Adapted from H. H. Strupp and S. W. Hadley, "A Tripartite Model of Mental Health and Therapeutic Outcomes: With Special Reference to Negative Effects in Psychotherapy." *American Psychologist*, 1977, *32*, 190. Copyright © 1977 by the American Psychological Association. Reprinted by permission.

young man grasps neither the effects of his action on his intended victim nor the basic immorality of his behavior. The child, on the other hand, perceives her own normal impulses as terribly wrong, but since she cannot control them, she invents a second self. In each case, the important point about abnormal behavior is that the person's *interpretation of reality* makes adjustment impossible. Within that interpretation of reality, the person is trying to cope effectively. But each person's behavior creates more problems than it solves. Distorted perception, inappropriate behavior, and discomfort are three criteria of abnormal behavior.

A fourth criterion is danger—to oneself or to others. The person who is likely to attempt suicide or to harm someone else in a sudden outburst is an obvious threat. So, in a more general—though usually less dangerous—way, is the person who behaves irrationally. We all depend on being able to predict how people will act. We expect drivers to stop for red lights, grocers to give us food in exchange for money, friends to respect our feelings and be sympathetic. When people violate these written and unwritten rules, they create problems for themselves and for those around them. When these violations are extreme, we think such people need help. But this has not always been so.

What Is Abnormal Behavior?

HISTORICAL VIEWS OF ABNORMAL BEHAVIOR

No one knows for sure what was considered abnormal behavior thousands of years ago. Based on studies of contemporary primitive tribes, however, we can hazard a general description: In such cultures, nearly everything was attributed to supernatural powers. Madness was a sign that the spirits had possessed a person. Sometimes, people who were "possessed" were seen as sacred, and their visions were considered messages from the gods. At other times the tribal wise men diagnosed the presence of evil spirits. Presumably, this supernatural view of abnormal behavior dominated early societies.

The ancient Greeks viewed strange behavior differently. Hippocrates (c. 450–c. 377 B.C.), for example, maintained that madness was like any other sickness, a natural event arising from natural causes. Epilepsy, he reasoned, was caused by the brain melting down into the body, resulting in fits and foaming at the mouth. Hysteria was a woman's disease that occurred when the womb wandered from its natural place in the body in a frustrated search for sex and children; marriage was the obvious cure. Melancholia, an imbalance in the body fluids, was cured with abstinence and quiet. Because of the influence of Hippocrates' ideas, the mentally disturbed were treated with kindness for centuries.

Then, in the Middle Ages, under the influence of the Church, abnormal behavior was considered the work of demons. The ravings of madmen, the curses of old women, the sudden impotence of soldiers, the melancholy of young girls were often blamed on the Devil and his agents.

"Witches" in Salem, Massachusetts: A supernatural view of abnormal behavior tended to prevail before the eighteenth century.
(The Bettmann Archive)

Philippe Pinel removing the chains from patients in the Bicêtre Hospital in Paris.
(The Bettmann Archive)

Charcot demonstrating hypnotism to his students. This picture hung in Freud's study. Freud trained under Charcot, and much of his early work was based on the effects of hypnosis on his patients.
(The Bettmann Archive)

Over the years, sincere and pious men developed a range of cruel techniques for combatting the Devil, the most common of which was burning at the stake.

The 15th and early 16th centuries, however, saw a return to the humanistic ideals of Greek culture. Writers suggested that some practices were cruel and inhuman. Some argued that madness was an illness and should be treated as such. Major cities gradually built asylums, where the insane—as they were called—were confined instead of tortured. By the late 1700s, pressure was mounting for a further reevaluation of attitudes.

Most contemporary views of abnormal behavior derive from this revolutionary period in the history of psychology and medicine. In 1793, Philippe Pinel unchained the patients in a mental hospital in Paris—only 11 years after the last witch-burning incident in Switzerland. He argued that disturbed people should have pleasant surroundings, enjoyable occupations, kind treatment, and a chance to discuss their problems. The "moral cure," as this was called, maintained that abnormal behavior was the result of problems in living.

At about the same time, Franz Anton Mesmer achieved considerable fame for his success in curing everything from melancholy to blindness through hypnosis. Mesmer himself was something of a showman, but a number of doctors took him seriously—among them the neurologist Jean-Martin Charcot. Charcot sought connections between the workings of the brain and the miraculous effects of hypnosis. Sigmund Freud, who studied under Charcot, based much of his early psychoanalytic work on the effects of hypnosis on disturbed people.

Meanwhile, in America, Dorothea Dix launched a crusade against the imprisonment and mistreatment of the insane in state institutions. It was largely through her efforts that people began to think of disturbed people as "mentally ill." This country's asylums were gradually turned into hospitals that were staffed by doctors, nurses, and attendants.

One of the earliest hints that abnormal behavior might have an organic or physiological basis came in 1875. In that year, Fournier published an explanation of *paresis*—an overall breakdown of the mind and the body that was common among 19th-century merchants and soldiers. He found that most of them had at some point contracted syphilis. Fournier determined that syphilis caused the massive mental deterioration that characterized paresis. Thus began the search for medical cures for all forms of madness.

CURRENT VIEWS OF ABNORMAL BEHAVIOR

By the 1920s, three explanations of abnormal behavior had a substantial following—explanations that still influence psychological research and theory today. At one end is the **organic model:** Abnormal behavior has a biochemical or physiological basis. In part, this view rests on the evidence that a tendency to schizophrenia can be inherited (see Chapter 2). Over the years a number of researchers have found chemical differences between normal and disturbed people. Some types of mental retardation have been traced to dietary deficiencies. The extensive use of drugs in mental institutions also rests on the organic model of abnormal behavior.

At the opposite extreme is the **psychoanalytic model** of abnormal behavior that was developed by Freud and his followers. According to this model, behavior disorders are symbolic expressions of internal conflicts. To recover, people must trace their problems to their origins in childhood and infancy.

The **medical model** of abnormal behavior has adherents from both the physiological and psychoanalytic camps. More a perspective than a theory, the medical model suggests that people who behave abnormally are sick. This approach has led to the classification of psychological symptoms and the naming of diseases—a procedure that enables doctors to compare cases and methods for treating them. It also claims that disturbed people are not responsible for their behavior—that they are fundamentally different from normal people.

In recent years, new views on behavior disorders have appeared. The medical model has been attacked by learning theorists who argue that abnormal behavior, like all behavior, is the result of learning. By reversing this process, fear, anxiety, frigidity, hallucinations, and so on can be *unlearned* without the probing of the analyst—which can take years— or the use of drugs. By implication, the **learning theory model** suggests that only experience separates the normal person from the "sick" one.

Thomas Szasz has also attacked the medical model, claiming that the idea of mental illness is a myth equivalent to the demonic myth of the Middle Ages. Because most of us find it difficult to deal with people who are deviant, when people behave in a way that society disapproves of, society simply disposes of them by labeling them sick and putting them in an institution. Szasz (1974) particularly deplores the government's use of the medical model as an excuse to create laws that determine what is mentally healthy behavior.

R. D. Laing takes an even more radical view. According to Laing, most of us refuse to admit our own craziness, preferring to live in an artificial world of logic, neat explanations, and happy endings. The so-called mentally ill, Laing says, have dared to step over the boundaries of this world into their minds. Laing sees their journey into the unknown and chaotic parts of the self as an act of heroism (Laing, 1967).

Whether these new views of abnormal behavior will replace the traditional models remains to be seen. At present, most psychiatrists think of mental disturbances partly in terms of the medical model, and partly in terms of "problems in living." Many psychological disorders start as social problems: loss of love or self-esteem, frustration, unresolved conflicts. But when people cope with these problems in a way that makes them feel more nervous and unhappy, or escape them by distorting reality and cutting themselves off entirely from other people, a problem in living has become a psychological problem.

As you read the descriptions of the various disorders summarized in this chapter, you may feel an uncomfortable twinge of recognition. This is only natural. Much abnormal behavior is simply normal behavior that is greatly exaggerated or displayed in inappropriate situations. Moreover, the similarities between yourself and a person with psychological problems are likely to be as instructive as the differences.

Classification of Abnormal Behavior

The Shriek by Munch.
(Editorial Photocolor Archives)

For the past three decades, the APA (the American Psychiatric Association) has classified abnormal behavior. To help clarify and simplify the job of diagnosing such behavior, the APA has published three editions of its *Diagnostic and Statistical Manual of Mental Disorders*. The first edition appeared in 1952, and heavily relied on the then popular "psychobiological" view, which held that mental disorders were reactions to psychological, social, and biological factors. The second edition in 1968 classified mental disorders without giving any one theoretical view as their cause. Both society and psychiatry, however, changed greatly in the late 1960s and in the early 1970s. As a result, many professionals felt that a new manual was needed. In 1974, a task force was appointed by the APA. The new manual—which we shall refer to as *DSM-III*—appeared in 1980. It has greatly altered how mental disorders are classified and diagnosed, and it reflects society's changed attitudes toward sex roles, social roles, and social behavior (APA, 1980).

BASIC CONCEPT OF *DSM-III*

The authors of *DSM-III* classify mental disorders according to significant behavioral patterns. In other words, a diagnosis is largely based on the clinical observation of behavior. There are no sharp boundaries among categories. The authors felt that distinctions among certain mental disorders, and among some cases of mental disorders and some cases where there were no mental disorders, were too hard to define. The authors avoid classifying people solely on the basis of these disorders. They refer to "a person with schizophrenia" rather than "a schizophrenic." This is an effort to take a more humane view of mental disorders (APA, 1980).

CONTROVERSY SURROUNDING *DSM-III*

Despite—or perhaps because of—the care and attention devoted to the new methods of classification, *DSM-III* is very controversial. Many traditionally minded psychiatrists believe that *DSM-III* goes too far in its attempts to update abnormal behavior. The reclassification of certain psychosexual disorders has especially come under fire, as you will see. Many psychologists also argue that *DSM-III* includes too many types of behavior that have nothing to do with mental illness—such as dependence on marijuana or alcohol. These critics charge that in trying to be comprehensive, *DSM-III* has become a grab bag of poorly defined types of behavior.

Moreover, many psychologists feel that the classification method reduces people to a series of symptoms, and since many of these symptoms are defined in medical terms, the usefulness of nonmedical specialists, such as psychologists, is downplayed.

Despite the many criticisms aimed at *DSM-III*, the manual clearly establishes certain professional standards and is now widely used in diagnosing abnormal behavior. Although the new edition of the diagnostic manual lists more than 230 types of disorders, many of these only concern specialists. The major types of disorders are of interest to students of psychology, however, and will be discussed next.

Neurotic Disorders

The term **neurosis** comes from the now discarded theory that behavioral patterns such as anxiety and depression stem from a disease of the nervous system. The concepts of neurosis and of a neurotic person have achieved wide recognition in our society: "I cleaned my room three times this week. I guess that's pretty neurotic." At the same time, neurotic disorders have lost credibility among professionals.

Today, there is no consensus among mental health professionals about what "neurosis" means. *DSM-III*, in fact, has eliminated "neurosis" altogether as a general category. The authors write instead of specific neurotic

Head of a Man by Pablo Picasso.
(Editorial Photocolor Archives)

INDIVIDUAL DIFFERENCES AND NEUROTIC BEHAVIOR

White and Watt (1973) pose an interesting question about the many different styles of neurotic behavior:

Why does one person have plain anxiety attacks, another a circumscribed phobia, a third a crippling set of obsessions and compulsions, a fourth an amnesia for personal identity, while a fifth blossoms forth with an hysterical paralysis of the lower limbs? (p. 231)

Eysenck (1970) made the most extensive studies of how personality is related to neurotic disorders. After much research, he concluded that people's choice of a disorder depends on whether they are extroverted or introverted. As Eysenck described it, the extrovert is sociable, changeable, and spontaneous. Such a person may develop somatoform disorders and dissociated states under extreme conditions. By contrast, the introvert is quiet, introspective, and reserved. When stress occurs, the introvert is apt to lapse into phobias and obsessive disorders.

Korner (1971) also related personality factors to how people respond to stimulation, but he used the terms "reflection" and "action" instead of introversion and extraversion. Thus, reflective people mull things over, dislike new or excessively strong stimulation, and analyze and sort out their experiences. On the other hand, active people like novelty and react to strong stimulation with impulsive and excited movements and emotions. When threatened, reflective people defend themselves by intellectualization and isolation, while active people get even more excited. What is most interesting is Korner's conclusion, reached after studying 2- to 4-day-old infants, that these personality differences are present at birth.

Are neurotic responses also present at birth? Coleman (1980) points out that the role genetic and biological factors play is not yet known. Although studies have shown that neurotic disorders tend to occur in families, no link has been established between these findings and heredity. The link between neurotic disorders and socioeconomic status, however, seems to be clear. According to Coleman, "The social environment influences both the individual's likelihood of adopting a neurotic reaction and the particular form that reaction is most likely to take" (p. 245). Neurotics from lower socioeconomic levels have a higher incidence of conversion disorders—aches, pains, and other somatic symptoms—while neurotics from the middle and upper socioeconomic classes are more likely to be anxious and obsessive–compulsive (Coleman, 1980).

disorders such as "anxiety disorders," and some kinds of affect and psychosexual disorders. In general, these **neurotic disorders** are all marked by relatively long-lasting symptoms that have no known organic cause. The person remains in touch with reality and finds the symptoms disturbing, but these symptoms are not gross departures from what is socially acceptable or permissible (APA, 1980).

People with neurotic disorders are not "crazy," and they usually function fairly well in society. Neurotic disorders can cause significant problems, however, such as a crippling fear of being enclosed in a small space, or even memory loss.

What causes such behavior? Although we will discuss causes of the major disorders in more detail when we get to them, most psychoanalytic theorists believe that neurotic disorders are generally reactions to internal threats. People suffering from them are fighting impulses that contradict their self-image and values. When their usual defense mechanisms fail to control these impulses, they resort to more extreme behavior. For example, take a woman who suddenly begins to suffer from amnesia. After working in the same company for 10 years, she has her first serious argument with her boss. As she storms out of the office, she feels the same hatred toward her boss that she felt toward her father as a child.

This hatred of her father overwhelms her with guilt. When this guilt is coupled with a fear of losing her job, the woman can no longer cope with the situation. She develops amnesia as a form of self-protection, to shield her from feeling crippling levels of fear and guilt. Thus, according to psychoanalytic theory, neurotic disorders are symbolic, indirect expressions of unconscious conflicts. As we shall see, this kind of amnesia—not amnesia that stems from physical injury—is classified in *DSM-III* as a "dissociative disorder."

Behavior theorists, on the other hand, believe that people who behave "neurotically" have learned to associate fear and anxiety with an apparently harmless situation or object. The woman who suffers amnesia after arguing with her boss may have been punished as a child for showing anger. Perhaps this experience was reinforced in later life, when a close friend also rejected or abused her for showing bad temper. These incidents could lead to an overwhelming fear of displaying anger, which might cause the woman to avoid even painful thoughts associated with her anger.

Whatever the source of neurotic behavior, most psychologists agree that the behavior itself becomes a trap. People suffering from neurotic disorders are often anxious, unhappy, ineffective, and guilt-ridden. Moreover, the disorder itself often makes it even more difficult to cope effectively. They know their behavior is unreasonable but find it difficult or impossible to change. They are often tired, irritable, tense, and depressed, though these feelings are by no means restricted to those with neurotic disorders. Let us describe some of the more common neurotic disorders.

Anxiety Disorders

Disorders in which anxiety is the predominant symptom are classified in *DSM-III* as anxiety disorders. Although everyone is afraid from time to time, most people know why they have these feelings. As we saw in

POST-TRAUMATIC STRESS DISORDERS

Psychologists recognize that some anxiety disorders—called *post-traumatic stress disorders*—occur when a person suffers a trauma—something so severe that almost anyone would be significantly distressed by it. Even the best adjusted of us would suffer anxiety and fear after rape, military combat, a flood, or an earthquake (Sarason, 1980). These kinds of events tend to be outside the realm of ordinary grief and loss (APA, 1980).

These disorders are "reactive" to specific events and often include reduced responsiveness to the outside world and reduced social involvement, including even complete withdrawal. Often a person suffering from a reactive disorder relives the experience in nightmares and repeated thoughts and images that intrude on everyday thoughts. Sometimes the disorder sets in immediately, sometimes only after several months; sometimes the period of distress is brief but recurrent, sometimes it is prolonged. An important factor in determining the results of such disorders is how much emotional support a person receives from his or her family, friends, and community.

(Arthur Tress, Woodfin Camp & Associates)

Chapter 12, a person suffering from anxiety does not know why he or she is afraid, and so cannot take effective action against this fear. Of course, knowing why you are afraid does not always mean you can do something about it. A student who does not like to go home because she always fights with her parents, but does not want to spend Christmas alone, can neither attack the problem nor escape it comfortably. But at least she knows why she is apprehensive. Most sufferers of anxiety disorders simply do not know why they are so terribly afraid.

Anxiety can be unfocused panic or fear, or it can show up as phobic or obsessive–compulsive disorders.

Phobic Disorders

A phobia is an intense, paralyzing fear of something in the absence of any real danger—a fear of something that most other people find bearable. This fear is often recognized by the person suffering from it as unreasonable, but the fear stays uncontrolled.

Of course, many people have irrational fears. But when people are so afraid of snakes that they cannot go to a zoo, walk through a field, or even look at pictures of snakes without trembling, they may be said to have a phobic disorder. Fears of heights, water, closed rooms, and cats are all common phobias. Perhaps the most common phobic disorder, however, is "agoraphobia," "a marked fear of being alone, or being in public places from which escape might be difficult" (APA, 1980, p. 226). Sufferers avoid such things as elevators, tunnels, and crowds, especially crowded stores or busy streets.

Psychoanalytic theorists see phobias as displacement. Those suffering from phobic disorders are frightened by their own unconscious wishes and thus avoid situations that might trigger those wishes. In other cases, people feel threatened for unknown reasons, and by converting their vague anxiety into a fear of something specific like elevators or spiders, they gain at least the temporary illusion of controlling their fears. After all, you can avoid elevators, but how do you avoid the real source of your anxiety if you don't even know what it is?

Other psychologists believe that some phobias are learned more directly. For example, a young boy is savagely attacked by a large dog. Because of this experience, he is now terribly afraid of all large dogs. As we saw in Chapter 5, because phobias are often learned after only one such event and are extremely hard to change, some learning theorists see them as *prepared responses*—responses built into us biologically through evolution. Seligman (1972) suggests that this is why there is a relatively limited range of phobic objects. Common objects of phobias—darkness, snakes, open spaces—were once real threats to our survival. Few people develop phobias about electrical outlets, hammers, and knives, although many of us have had unpleasant childhood experiences with them. But note that now driving and flying in airplanes are also relatively common objects of phobic disorders.

Most people would recoil from being covered with crabs. But an uncontrollable fear of these animals could be a phobia.
(Arthur Tress, Photo Researchers)

414

One way that people deal with phobias is to confront and conquer what frightens them. A woman who fears heights may climb mountains to conquer her fear. Counterphobic behavior such as this may restore the person's self-esteem, but it can lead to real dangers by persuading people to push themselves beyond their real abilities, and, in some cases, by exposing the person to extraordinary fear and anxiety that they cannot handle. In Chapter 14, we will see a number of more effective ways of dealing with this and other neurotic disorders.

Obsessive–Compulsive Disorders

Obsessions are involuntary thoughts or ideas that keep recurring despite the person's attempt to stop them. *Compulsions* are repetitive, ritualistic behaviors that a person feels *compelled* to perform. Common obsessive thoughts are of violence—for example, of killing somebody—contamination—becoming infected—and doubt—repeated worry that one has not done something. Common compulsive behaviors involve hand-washing or counting (APA, 1980).

At times, even normal people act this way. Occasional violent fantasies do not mean that you have an **obsessive–compulsive disorder.** A husband who checks his watch every 5 minutes when his wife is late coming home is merely being normally anxious. By contrast, a woman who feels she must go through her house every day checking every clock every hour may, indeed, be showing signs of an obsessive–compulsive disorder. We think of the behavior as disordered when it dominates the lives of those involved, and when the person becomes tense or anxious if he or she tries to resist it.

Psychoanalysts suggest that obsessive–compulsive behavior begins when repression fails and the person must deal with an uncomfortable, unconscious emotion or fantasy. For example, a young man who is about to finish his medical internship is repeatedly tortured by the thought that he has made a mistake. He cannot help thinking about the life he might have had if he had not gone to medical school and had not married early. Fantasies about murdering his wife begin to surface. Then, he dis-

(Timothy Eagan, Woodfin Camp & Associates)

covers that if he concentrates on a list of symptoms of an illness that he memorized years ago in school, he can escape his worries about his life. Reciting lists becomes more and more frequent. Later, he realizes that his wife is hinting that they should start a family. Every time the topic comes up, he becomes tense and anxious and goes to the bathroom to wash his hands. This, too, may reduce his anxiety, and he increasingly responds with this kind of behavior as a means of escaping tension and worry. Soon, these trivial rituals—reciting lists, washing his hands—hold his life together and also eat up more and more of his time and energy. In other words, repeated thoughts and actions—obsessive–compulsive behavior—that once helped control the tension and anxiety have now become problems themselves.

On the other hand, learning theorists believe that obsessions and compulsions are a learned response to trauma. The behavior may be learned by trial–and–error—as when the intern in our example discovered that reciting lists reduced his anxiety. It can also be an exaggerated version of behavior that succeeded when we were children—washing our hands is a "good" thing that parents praise (Dollard & Miller, 1950). If the behavior reduces anxiety, it is reinforced and becomes more likely to recur.

Carr (1974) suggests that personality is critical in the development of this disorder. People with obsessive–compulsive disorders are abnormally cautious, afraid of risks, and always expect the worst from every situation. These traits account for their extreme anxiety and explain why their behavior, though excessive, is so oriented to the real world. Their ritualistic behavior is simply an overdeveloped superstition, and like all superstitions (see Chapter 5) lets them feel that they control events in some magical way.

Dissociative Disorders

The horrors of war can cause memory loss.
(Steve Northup, UPI)

Dissociative disorders are among the most puzzling forms of mental disorders, both to the observer and to the sufferer. Dissociation means that part of a person's personality is separated or dissociated from the rest, and for some reason, the person cannot reassemble the pieces. It usually takes the form of memory loss, a complete—but usually temporary—change in identity, or even the presence of several distinct personalities in one person.

Loss of memory without an organic cause may be a reaction to intolerable experiences. People block out an event or a period of their lives. During World War II, some hospitalized soldiers could not recall their names, where they lived, when they were born, or how they came to be in battle. But war and its horrors are not the only causes of amnesia. The person who betrays a friend to complete a business deal, or the unhappily married man who reserves a single ticket to Tahiti may also forget—selectively—what they have done. They may even assume an entirely new identity. Total amnesia, in which people forget everything, is quite rare, however, despite its popularity in novels and films.

Multiple personality also occurs less often than is suggested by popular fiction. In this disorder, a person has several distinct personalities that emerge at different times. The shift among personalities is sudden and generally occurs after great stress (APA, 1980). Of course, we all play different roles: We behave differently with our parents, for example, than we do with our friends. But through it all we remember who we are. In a multiple personality disorder, one personality often does not know what the other personality says or does. This disorder is usually attributed to conflicting values and desires. A man who always suppresses anger and frustration may periodically go "berserk," acting out his violent impulses. A quiet, modest young woman may suddenly change her posture and voice, and go to bars to pick up men. In each case, the two personalities are incompatible, so each is acted out independently.

Depersonalization is a more common dissociative disorder. Its essential feature is that the person suddenly feels changed or different in a strange way. Some people feel they have left their bodies; others feel that their actions are mechanical or dreamlike. A sense of losing control of one's own behavior is common, and it is not unusual to imagine changes in one's environment. This kind of feeling strikes most people at one time or another. It is especially common during adolescence and young adulthood, when our sense of ourselves changes rapidly (see Chapter 4). Only when the sense of depersonalization becomes a long-term or chronic problem, or when the alienation impairs normal social functioning, can this be classified as a dissociative disorder (APA, 1980).

In the dissociative disorder of depersonalization, a person can feel changed and alienated from his own body.
(Timothy Eagan, Woodfin Camp & Associates)

Somatoform Disorders

Somatoform disorders involve physical symptoms of serious bodily disorders without any physical evidence of organic causes for them. Sufferers from these disorders do not consciously seek to mislead people about their physical condition: The symptoms are real and not under voluntary control (APA, 1980).

In some cases, the person feels recurring, multiple physical symptoms for which medical attention has been repeatedly sought but no organic cause found. Complaints often involve back pains, dizziness, partial paralysis, or abdominal pains.

Less often, people complain of more bizarre symptoms such as paralysis, blindness, deafness, seizures, loss of feeling, or false pregnancy. Sufferers from such **conversion disorders** are healthy; their muscles and nerves are intact. Although these extreme symptoms are relatively rare today, they used to be very common. They were noted by the ancient Greeks and Romans and referred to in the Middle Ages and the Renaissance. In the late 19th century, a few hypnotists gained recognition for curing what was then called "hysteria." In fact, Freud began to develop his "talking cure" on cases of hysteria.

Psychoanalysts see somatoform disorders as a displacement—or conversion—of emotional problems to physical problems. Freud concluded that the physical symptoms were always related to traumatic experiences buried in a patient's past: A woman who, years earlier, saw her mother seduced by a traveling salesman suddenly loses her sight; a man who was punished for masturbating later loses the use of his hand.

By unconsciously developing a handicap, people punish themselves for forbidden desires or behavior, prevent themselves from acting out these desires or repeating this forbidden behavior, and regress to an earlier stage when others took care of them. Although there is no real physical cause for the handicap, the symptoms can cause physical damage. For example, when muscles are not used for a long time, they become weak and atrophy.

Sometimes it is easy to determine that there is no organic cause for a disorder. Some symptoms are anatomically impossible, as in "glove anesthesia," which is a lack of feeling in the hand from the wrist down. There is no way that damage to the nerves running into the hand could cause such a localized pattern of anesthesia. Another clue that the disorder has psychological causes is that the person may be quite cheerful about it! Most people would be very upset if they suddenly discovered that they could not see or move. The hysteric, however, is not. Psychologists call this attitude **la belle indifference.**

A related disorder is **hypochondriasis.** Here the person interprets some small sign or symptom—perhaps a cough, bruise, or perspiration—as a sign of a serious disease. Although the symptom may exist, there is no evidence that it reflects a serious illness, though repeated assurances of this sort have little effect. As a result, the person is likely to visit one doctor after another looking for one who will share his or her conviction.

PSYCHOSOMATIC DISORDERS

Psychosomatic disorders are real physical disorders with organic explanations but that seem to have psychological causes, at least initially. Many cases of ulcers, migraine headaches, asthma, high blood pressure, and heart disease are thought to be psychosomatic. In each case the complaints have a valid physical cause but psychological factors are also involved.

It is important to distinguish between psychosomatic disorders and *hypochondria*. Hypochondria refers to the continued belief that one is seriously ill *in the absence of any substantial symptoms*. People suffering from psychosomatic disorders, however, really are ill—they are not imagining their problem. But the problem seems to stem originally from stress, anxiety, or other psychological causes.

"Hypochondriacs get sick too, you know!"
(Drawing by Dedini; © 1958 *The New Yorker Magazine*, Inc.)

Affective Disorders

With phobias, dissociative disorders, somatoform disorders, and obsessive–compulsive rituals, people reject internal problems by projecting their anxieties onto objects, by separating off a part of themselves that they dislike, by translating fears into physical symptoms, or by blocking disturbing thoughts with rituals and mind-absorbing chores. In many **affective disorders** this process is reversed. People acknowledge, and even exaggerate, their sense of guilt and helplessness. The result is depression, feelings of worthlessness, and varying degrees of inactivity. Such people feel that they have failed utterly. Their ability to become involved with other people and to work or study declines. They blame their troubles entirely on themselves and feel tired and apathetic. The depressed person may be too filled with self-doubt and pessimism to restore his or her self-confidence.

Although we use the word *depression* every day, it is important to distinguish between a "normal" depressed state and a true affective disorder. Everyone gets depressed, sometimes when we least expect it. Christmas and New Year's Day, for example, are well known to psychologists as periods when normally happy people suffer from "the blues." We also get depressed at the death of a loved one, the break-up of a love affair, or if we move far from friends and family. This grieving can last a long time, but gradually the guilt, hostility, feelings of loss, and physical symptoms of depression disappear. It is only when this depression gets continually worse, or when it is unconnected to any event in a person's life, or when it persists for more than two years without much relief, that it can be classified as an affective disorder (APA, 1980; Sarason, 1980).

Sometimes the depressed state is followed by its opposite, the manic state, in which the person becomes excessively talkative, outgoing, and confident. People in a manic state have unlimited hopes and schemes, but often have little interest in carrying them out. They sometimes become aggressive and hostile toward others, as their self-confidence becomes more and more unrealistic. In an acute state, manic persons may become wild, incomprehensible, or violent, until they collapse from exhaustion. Oddly enough, while nearly all people suffering from a manic episode will later experience depression, the opposite is not true. Very often, people suffering from depression do not have the extreme mood swings that have been called **"manic-depressive."** The reason appears to be that manic behavior is a defense against depression. Manics sense deep despair just below the surface and do everything to deny their feelings.

Explanations of depression vary greatly. Psychoanalysts believe that as children, depressed persons were never sure that they were loved and wanted. They felt angry about the lack of warmth in their family, but were afraid that if they expressed their hostility, they would only drive their parents farther away. They grew up doubting that they were lovable and mistrusting the affection and confidence others offered them. In later life, a sudden loss or a slow accumulation of disappointments taps this well of need and anger, and depression follows. According to this view,

(Sylvia Johnson, Woodfin Camp & Associates)

depression expresses mixed feelings. Depressed persons want love, but they never believe that anyone loves them, and they resent those on whom they depend for affection and attention.

Psychoanalysts stress the self-punishing side of depression. This self-punishment may be payment for fantasies and behavior considered sinful. Depressed persons may also feel that if they punish themselves, then no one else will hurt them. In effect, they internalize and act out the parental role. As children, they knew that they would be punished for certain acts. If they sent themselves to their rooms without waiting for their parents to tell them, they felt more in control. This combination of self-assertion and self-punishment continues into adulthood. Other theorists believe that depression is displaced aggression. Depressed persons, they feel, are furious at someone, but cannot express their anger. By turning their hostility against themselves, they eliminate the possibility of punishment.

Behavior theorists agree that mistrust causes depression, but they offer a somewhat different interpretation. Over the years, they say, some depressed people have come to believe that they have little or no control over the successes and failures in their lives. They are pessimistic about their ability to improve their lives or environment. They lack aggressiveness and competitive drive. All of these symptoms resemble the behavior of dogs and rats in *learned helplessness* studies. In such a study, no matter what the animal does, it gets an electric shock. When the animal later gets electric shocks, it behaves passively and does not attempt to escape even if given the chance. In fact, even when shown how to escape, such animals learn very slowly, and some never learn how to get away. Thus, say behavior theorists, human beings may respond in the same way to continual or perceived failure (see Chapters 5 and 12).

Psychosexual Disorders

Ideas about what is normal and what is abnormal in sex vary with the times—and with the individual. As Kinsey showed years ago, most Americans enjoy sexual activities forbidden by laws that do not recognize current sexual mores. For years, most sex laws were based on the idea that the sole purpose of sex was procreation. Any act that did not lead to conception was thus unnatural. Today many people consider sex a source of pleasure, intimacy, and personal fulfillment and feel that good sexual relationships are a sign of physical and mental health.

Among psychologists today there are two main schools of thought about what is normal and abnormal in sex. On the one hand are those who regard any activity not associated with heterosexual intercourse as deviant. On the other hand are those who prefer not to judge specific activities. Instead, they focus on people's feelings about what they do. According to this view, if people are compulsive or guilty about their sex life, or if they cannot enjoy sex fully, then—and only then—are they sexually maladjusted.

DYSFUNCTION

Sexual dysfunction refers to an inability to function effectively during sex. In men, this often takes the form of **impotence,** the inability to achieve or keep an erection. In women it is often **frigidity,** the inability to become sexually excited or reach orgasm. These dysfunctions are common, especially in their milder forms. Most people undergo periods of sexual dysfunction caused by a lack of interest in their partner, or over-excitement, or anxiety about their sexual "performance." Only when such dysfunction becomes typical, when enjoyment of sexual relationships becomes impaired, should it be considered serious. Most truly impotent men and frigid women, for example, cannot have satisfying sexual relations, even after repeated attempts with a partner whom they desire.

Many psychologists feel that sexual dysfunction is based on fear of heterosexual intimacy. The impotent man may have been warned as a child about venereal disease or domineering females, and may feel threatened by women. Frigidity may result from a fear of pregnancy, fear of male domination, an overall fear of letting go, or a lingering sense—leftover from childhood—that sex is somehow dirty or disgusting.

Sexual dysfunction in men often takes the form of impotency.
(Kenneth Karp)

PARAPHILIAS

A second group of sexual disorders involves the use of unconventional sex objects. Most people have unconventional sexual fantasies at some time, and this fantasizing is often a healthy outlet that stimulates normal sexual enjoyment. The repeated use of nonhuman objects, however— a shoe, for instance, or a belt—as the preferred or exclusive method of achieving sexual excitement is considered a psychosexual disorder. Fetishes, for example, often involve articles of clothing, and the fetish is often associated with someone a person was close to in childhood. Other deviations in the choice of sex objects include **pedophilia**—sexual relations with children—and **zoophilia**—sexual relations with animals. Other unconventional ways of enjoying sex are **voyeurism,** watching other people have sex or spying on people who are nude instead of having sex oneself; **exhibitionism,** the compulsion to expose one's genitals in inappropriate situations; and **transvestism,** wearing clothes of the opposite sex. **Sadomasochism** ties sexual pleasure to aggression. To attain sexual gratification, sadists humiliate or physically harm their sex partners. Masochists cannot enjoy sex without emotional or physical pain. As with sexual dysfunction, most psychologists see the choice of unconventional sexual objects as indicating fear of heterosexual intimacy.

HOMOSEXUALITY

Our society has traditionally considered **homosexuality** a mental disorder. Recent studies, however, indicate that homosexuals are no more maladjusted than heterosexuals, and the view of homosexuality as a mental disorder has increasingly been challenged (Coleman, 1980).

Homosexuality is now viewed as a disorder only if it causes a person undue, persistent stress and anxiety.
(Yan Lukas, Photo Researchers)

The controversy over whether to include homosexuality as a mental disorder in *DSM-III* was so heated that it generated over 180 pages of correspondence between members of the various committees involved in the American Psychiatric Association's efforts to classify mental disorders. The compromise was to list homosexuality in *DSM-III* as a disorder *only* when a person has persistent distress or anxiety because of his or her sexual orientation, has negative feelings about homosexuality, and wishes to be more heterosexual.

The prevalence of homosexual behavior—documented by Kinsey—is one of the reasons for the change in classification. His studies showed that 37 percent of white males had a homosexual experience resulting in orgasm sometime between their adolescence and old age. The frequency of homosexual behavior in women was about half that found in men (Kinsey et al., 1948).

Many children and adolescents have homosexual experiences, often because intimate physical contact with the opposite sex is forbidden. This is also true in prisons and mental institutions, where the sexes are segregated. Some people who engage in homosexual activity enjoy relations with both sexes. Others are exclusively attracted to their own sex.

ORIGINS OF HOMOSEXUALITY. There are many conflicting theories about the origins of homosexuality. Psychoanalysts consider homosexuality the result of unresolved oedipal conflicts. They say that the young boy who wants exclusive rights to his mother fears retribution from his father in the form of castration. To win his father's affection and to convince his father that he is not a rival, he begins imitating his mother. His sexual identity becomes confused, and in adulthood he seeks to restore his self-image through a "magical unity" with other men. The dynamics are somewhat different with girls. Psychoanalysts explain homosexuality in women as fixation in the mother-attached stage, as an inability to transfer love for the mother to love for the father. In both sexes, psychoanalysts say, homosexuality seems to develop most often in homes where one parent seems domineering, the other passive and ineffectual.

Many psychologists do not fully accept the psychoanalytic explanation; there are differing interpretations of the data even among those who place the roots of homosexuality in early parent–child relationships. Irving Bieber and his associates (Bieber et al., 1962) found that mothers of homosexual males behaved seductively toward their sons from infancy, engaging them in an unusual degree of intimacy. (This mother–son relationship is referred to as "close-binding.") But the mothers were domineering and derogatory toward their husbands. In turn, the fathers were indifferent and often hostile toward their sons. The Bieber hypothesis is that any male child exposed to this pattern in his childhood, or to one of several variations of it, is likely to have homosexual conflicts.

The data of the Bieber group were drawn from homosexual males undergoing psychotherapy. Immediate objections were raised about the risks of generalizing from people in therapy to wider populations. Evans (1969) studied a group of homosexuals who were not in therapy and compared them with a control group of heterosexuals, using the questionnaire devised by Bieber. The homosexual males reported more often that they had been fearful of physical injury, had avoided physical conflicts, and had been loners who did not engage in competitive sports. The mothers of the homosexuals had encouraged "feminine" rather than "masculine" attitudes, allied with the son against the father, and behaved seductively toward the son. The homosexuals had spent less time with their fathers, were more hostile toward and more fearful of them, and felt less accepted by and less accepting of their fathers than did the heterosexuals.

Evans, while confirming some of the results of the Bieber study, nonetheless rejected Bieber's interpretation of the cause–and–effect relationship. He pointed out that the father of a son who ultimately becomes homosexual may be withdrawn from and hostile to his son because of childhood signs of the son's homosexual tendency. He also noted that some homosexuals were raised without a father.

Gundlach (1969) found that the behavior of female homosexuals often had an emotional content quite different from that of male homosexuals. Homosexual women tend to seek warmth and affection from their partners, whereas homosexual men often search for domination and power. This significant difference, as well as the early family origins of female homosexuality, is hard to fit into the Bieber theory.

Hooker, a psychiatrist who has conducted many studies of homosexuals, concludes that "it can no longer be questioned that faulty, disturbed, or pathological parental relationships in early childhood are more commonly reported by male homosexual patients than by a comparable group of male heterosexuals" (Hooker, 1969). She goes on, however, to warn that the origins of homosexuality cannot be established from psychiatric samples alone and that no conclusive pattern of causal relationships between early childhood relationships with parents and subsequent homosexuality has been determined. White and Watt (1973) suggest that the most important factor may be the mother's attitude that sex is ugly, nasty, and degrading. This is generalized by children to mean that all intimate, heterosexual relationships are likewise ugly, nasty, and degrading. But as children grow up, their sexual needs must be satisfied. Because they have learned to avoid the opposite sex they may become homosexual. Thus, we have several hypotheses, but as yet no firmly established set of conclusions about the origins of either male or female homosexual behavior.

Personality Disorders

There are certain types of mental disorders that are not neurotic disorders, nor are they classified among the more serious psychotic disorders. *DSM-III* refers to them as **personality disorders.** In these cases, a personality trait is so exaggerated and inflexible that it causes serious social problems. These people attribute the source of their problems to others; thus, they see no reason to change, and as a result they cause the same problems to recur, even though they are not happy about the results. It follows that they seldom seek therapy.

A **schizoid personality** is characterized by a persistent inability and little desire to form social relationships and the absence of warm or tender feelings for others. Such "loners" cannot express their feelings and are perceived by others as cold, distant, and unfeeling. Moreover, they often appear vague, absentminded, indecisive, or "in a fog." Because their withdrawal is so complete, schizoids seldom marry and may have trouble holding a job that requires them to work with or relate to others (APA, 1980).

Paranoid personalities also appear to be "odd." They are suspicious and mistrustful even when there is no reason to be, and are hypersensitive to any possible threat or trick. They refuse to accept blame or criticism even when it is deserved. They are guarded, secretive, devious, scheming, and argumentative, though they often see themselves as rational and objective.

Persons suffering from an **antisocial personality disorder** used to be called "sociopaths" or "psychopaths." They lie, steal, cheat, and show little or no sense of responsibility, although they are often intelligent and charming on first acquaintance. The "con man" exemplifies many of the features of the antisocial personality. Other examples might include: the man who compulsively cheats his business partners because he knows their weak points; the imposters who appear in the papers after their deceit is discovered; and various criminals who show no guilt. The antisocial personality rarely shows the slightest traces of anxiety or guilt over his or her behavior. Indeed, these people blame society or their victims for the antisocial actions that they themselves commit.

Some psychologists feel that antisocial behavior is the result of emotional

Lee Harvey Oswald.
(UPI)

deprivation in early childhood. Respect for others is the basis of our social code, but if you cannot see things from the other person's perspective, rules about what you can and cannot do will seem to be only an assertion of adult power, to be broken as soon as possible. The child for whom no one cares, say psychologists, cares for no one. The child whose problems no one identifies with can identify with no one else's problems. Other psychologists feel that inconsistent parental behavior may explain many antisocial personality disorders. Sometimes the parents of these people punished them for being bad, sometimes they did not. Sometimes the parents worried over them and lavished attention on them, sometimes they ignored them and forced them to be prematurely independent. Thus, these children felt that their actions had no influence on how others behaved toward them.

Borderline personality disorders are less clearcut than other disorders. The basic characteristic is "instability"—of mood, behavior, attitude, or emotion. The person is noticeably unpredictable or impulsive, particularly in areas that are potentially self-damaging, such as alcohol or drug abuse, sexual hyperactivity, gambling, suicide, overeating, or shoplifting (APA, 1980). They continually question their self-image, wondering who they are and why they behave as they do. Unlike antisocial people, they are often beset by anxiety and guilt over their life choices. The personal relationships of people with this kind of disorder are extremely turbulent, and they may have no tolerance for frustration.

Narcissism, or the total love of oneself, has been the subject of much recent clinical interest and research. The word *narcissism* comes from a character in Greek mythology named Narcissus, who fell in love with his own reflection in a pool, and pined away because he could not reach the beautiful face he saw before him.

While we all love ourselves to some extent, a person with a narcissistic personality disorder has near total self-absorption, a grandiose sense of self-importance, a preoccupation with fantasies of unlimited success, a need for constant attention and admiration, and an inability to love or really care for anyone else (APA, 1980). But Otto Kernberg, who has devoted considerable study to narcissism, observes that the self-esteem of the narcissistic person is really very fragile: "The pathological narcissist cannot sustain his or her self-regard without having it fed constantly by the attentions of others" (Wolfe, 1978).

Many psychologists believe that narcissism begins early in life. While all infants tend to be narcissistic, most grow out of it. But for reasons that we do not yet understand, the narcissistic person never makes the change. Some social critics assert that certain tendencies in modern American society—such as our worship of youth and beauty, and our disregard for old age—have contributed to an apparent "boom" in narcissistic personality disorders (Lasch, 1979). Clinical data, however, do not support this speculation. While acknowledging that our society stimulates narcissism, Kernberg argues that this cannot be the root of the disorder: "The most I would be willing to say is that society can make serious psychological abnormalities, which already exist in some percentage of the population, seem to be at least superficially appropriate" (Wolfe, 1978).

Narcissus pining away for himself.

(The Bettmann Archive)

Substance Use Disorders

In our society, the use of some substances to alter mood or behavior is, under certain circumstances, regarded as normal behavior. This includes moderate intake of alcohol and of the caffeine in coffee, tea, or cola. It also includes tobacco and, in various subcultures, such illegal substances as marijuana, cocaine, and amphetamines. (In other subcultures, the use of any or all of these substances is frowned upon.) In recent years, there has been increasing concern that our society is much too dependent on such substances.

DSM-III classifies the abuse of these substances and dependence on them as a disorder. *Substance abuse* is determined by three things: (1) a pattern of pathological use such as intoxication throughout the day, an inability to cut down or stop, a need for its daily use in order to function adequately, and the continuing use of the substance even if it makes a physical disorder worse; (2) disturbance in social relationships or the deterioration of occupational functioning; and (3) signs of disturbance lasting for at least 1 month. *Substance dependence* is more serious and requires evidence of tolerance—increasing amounts required to achieve the same effect—or *withdrawal*—physical and psychological symptoms that appear if a person reduces or stops using the substance (APA, 1980).

Dependency on alcohol may occur in stages. People drink to unwind or to ward off anxiety—a few drinks at a party or at lunch or before dinner make them feel better. They then feel that they cannot cope without those few drinks. Sometimes this dependency is followed by a phase of drinking sprees, in which they drink themselves unconscious for days or even weeks. After drinking regularly for some time, these people find that if they do not drink heavily they feel withdrawal symptoms: depression, nausea, the shakes. Continued overuse of alcohol usually causes severe physical harm, mainly to the brain and the liver.

No one is sure if alcohol dependency is a physical addiction or a psychological habituation. In **addiction,** body chemistry changes, and dependence on the drug becomes a biological need. People need larger amounts of the drug to get high, cannot feel normal without it, and become physically sick on withdrawal. On the other hand, psychological **habituation** is an emotional dependence on a drug: People feel they need a drug and feel sick when they do not use it, but the need is psychological, not biological.

Heroin, opium, and other narcotics affect the central nervous system. They relieve pain—hence their use in medicine—cause drowsiness—"nodding out"—and produce a feeling of euphoria and well-being. Narcotics are physically addictive. The body gradually builds up a tolerance to these drugs, and a person must take larger amounts to relieve pain or to get high. Withdrawal is accompanied by severe muscle cramps, vomiting, hot and cold flashes, depression, and restlessness.

Narcotics themselves do not usually cause physical deterioration, but addicts usually lose interest in food, sex, work, and family. The chief danger is that people will suffer severe physical reactions from an over-

Alcohol dependency may become both physical and psychological.
(Arthur Tress, Photo Researchers)

DRUGS IN SOCIETY

Today most people believe that drugs such as heroin, cocaine, and opium are harmful and dangerous, and that drugs such as alcohol, nicotine, and caffeine are less harmful—but this was not always so.

Actually, the history of drug use in various societies is somewhat surprising, given our current biases (Freedman, 1973). In 1634 the Tsar of Russia forbade the smoking of tobacco—which contains nicotine—and decreed that persistent violators were to be executed. Tea—which contains caffeine—was once believed to be a dangerous drug that would end family life, among other evils. Its introduction in England, where it is now a national drink, was violently opposed. In the United States, opium and morphine were widely used for medical and therapeutic purposes in the late 1800s. Each was widely sold in grocery stores and pharmacies. Many respectable, middle-class citizens became addicted to opium, yet this addiction did not lead to crime, since opium could be openly purchased.

These examples show that the evaluation of a drug is primarily determined by current social mores and taboos. Drugs that were once considered dangerous are now commonplace, while drugs that were once commonplace are now considered dangerous. Moreover, in our society, there is a growing trend to view drugs as the solution to many medical, social, and personal problems.

Freedman argues that why people take drugs is more important than whether the drugs are "good" or "bad." In his view, taking any drug is a person's attempt to deal with the ambiguities of modern life. For example, the mass atrocities committed in our century have convinced many people that human beings are not innately good. At the same time, since the American, French, and Russian Revolutions, we have come to think of all forms of social deprivation as injustice rather than as being the misfortune of birth. Freedman thus sees widespread drug use in our society as a response to the anger, frustration, and powerlessness caused by these conflicting ways of looking at ourselves and our society.

dose. The substances used by drug dealers to "cut" the drugs before selling them can also harm the user, and the social costs of supporting an addiction are immense—from robbery and prostitution to broken families and ruined lives.

The classification of substance abuse in *DSM-III* is controversial. Some psychologists complain that it makes no sense to exclude homosexuals who do not wish to change their life-style, but to include tobacco smokers who do not wish to quit smoking (Coleman, 1980). Nevertheless, it is clear that substance dependence and abuse is of considerable concern to our society, and will continue to generate much clinical interest and research.

Schizophrenic Disorders

Most people think **schizophrenia** refers to multiple personalities, but as we have seen, "split personality" is a dissociative disorder. Schizophrenic disorders are marked by disordered thought, inappropriate emotions, and bizarre behavior. Schizophrenics are out of touch with reality. They may hear voices when no one is speaking, may see things that others cannot see. They often have delusions and false beliefs, which distort their relationships with their surroundings and with other people. They may think that a doctor wishes to kill them, or that they are receiving radio waves from outer space. They often regard their own bodies—as well as the outside world—as hostile and alien. Because their world is utterly different from the one most people live in, they usually cannot function socially or professionally. Often they are unable or unwilling to communicate.

Psychologists divide schizophrenic disorders into several categories. **Disorganized schizophrenia** includes some of the more bizarre symptoms such as delusions and hallucinations accompanied by grimacing and frantic gesturing. These people show a childish disregard for social conventions, and may urinate or defecate at inappropriate times. They are active, but aimless, and are often given to childish laughter and inexplicable gestures.

The primary feature of **catatonic schizophrenia** is a severe disturbance of motor activity. People in this state may remain immobile, mute, and impassive. At the opposite extreme they become extremely excited, talking and shouting continuously. They behave in a robot-like fashion when ordered to move, and some have even let doctors mold their arms and legs into strange and uncomfortable positions, which they then can maintain for hours.

Paranoid schizophrenia is marked by extreme suspiciousness and delusions or hallucinations. People in this state often believe that they are persecuted for "knowing" something that others do not want them to know. They appear "normal" at first, but gradually their fear of persecution totally absorbs their attention, and they become hostile and aggressive toward anyone who questions their thinking or tries to contradict their delusions (Sarason, 1980).

Some researchers believe that schizophrenic disorders are hereditary. The incidence of schizophrenia is higher among children of schizophrenic parents than in the general population. Moreover, if one of two identical twins is schizophrenic, the chances are high that the other will be too. But in most of these studies, the twins have been raised in the same

Schizophrenic disorders are marked by bizarre behaviors.
(Arthur Tress, Woodfin Camp & Associates)

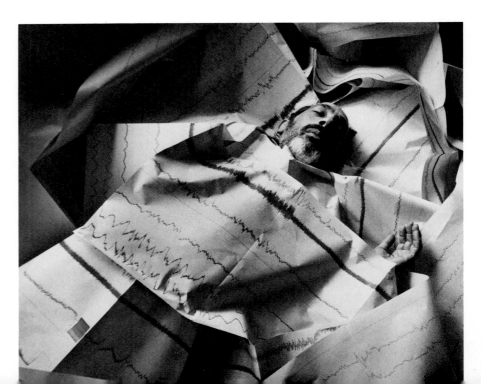

THE SCHIZOPHRENIC EXPERIENCE

Schizophrenia is frightening, and difficult to grasp from the outside. A third-year medical student gave this account of a paranoid schizophrenic episode:

"I decided that I was having heart failure and that people felt I wasn't strong enough to accept this, so they weren't telling me. I thought about all the things that had happened recently that could be interpreted in that light. I looked up heart failure in a textbook and found that the section had been removed, so I concluded someone had removed it to protect me. The thought occurred that I might be getting medicine without my knowledge, perhaps by radio. I began to think I might have a machine inside of me that secre-

ted medicine into my bloodstream. Then I began to have the feeling that other people were watching me. I said to myself that the whole thing was absurd, but when I looked again, the people really were watching me. Conversations had hidden meanings. When someone later told me that I was delusional, I seemed to know it. There was a sequence: first panic, then groping, then elation at having found out. Involvement with the delusions would fade in and out. One part of me seemed to say, 'Keep your mouth shut, you know this is a delusion and it will pass.' But the other side of me wanted the delusion, preferred to have things this way" (Bowers, 1974).

home, making it impossible to rule out the influence of environment. (See Chapter 2 for a more detailed discussion.)

Other researchers look for a biochemical explanation of schizophrenia. Gjessing (1966) related periodic schizophrenic episodes to a malfunction in the thyroid gland. Heath (1960) injected raraxein—a protein that affects the central nervous system—from schizophrenics into monkeys and found that the monkeys' behavior and brain waves changed dramatically. Other researchers point to the similarities between mescaline (a hallucinogenic drug) and epinephrine, which is a normal body chemical involved in the control of nervous system activity (Hoffer & Osmond, 1959). Perhaps schizophrenics have some metabolic disorder that releases the hallucinogenic potential in epinephrine. Dopamine is another chemical involved in the transference of neural impulses from one neuron to another. According to Carlson, studies with schizophrenics have shown that when the action of dopamine is retarded by antipsychotic drugs, schizophrenic symptoms diminish, and when the action of dopamine is stimulated, so are the symptoms (Carlson, 1977).

All of these findings are hotly disputed. Critics point out that most experiments dealt with hospitalized schizophrenics. There is no way of telling if the inactivity and institutionalization affected their emotional and biochemical make-up. Moreover, it is impossible to determine if the biochemical differences just mentioned are the causes or the effects of schizophrenic behavior.

Psychoanalysts reject a purely biological explanation for schizophrenia. They believe that schizophrenia stems from childhood trauma. Psychoanalysts claim that at some point in their early years schizophrenics faced a crisis in their family relationships that they could not resolve—for example, the real or imagined loss of a parent. Terrified, they began erecting defenses. Their maladjustment was not noticed—their defenses worked. But later—usually in late adolescence—new crises revived the early, unresolved conflict. Their overstrained defenses collapsed; impulses,

William Blake, *Self-Portrait.* Blake claimed to be "under the direction of messengers from Heaven," and his hallucinations provided much of the material for his poetry and engravings. Considered a mystic in his own time, Blake might well be classified as a paranoid schizophrenic today. (The Bettmann Archive)

fears, memories, and fantasies flooded their consciousness, making rational behavior impossible. According to this view, schizophrenics live in a nightmare from which they cannot awaken. Their egos are overwhelmed and cannot function effectively.

Other theorists see schizophrenia as a severe information processing problem. They maintain that schizophrenics cannot tell what is meaningful from what is not. Unable to screen out extraneous information—the ticking of a clock, a conversation on the other side of the room—they overload their senses. The schizophrenic may also be listening to both internal and external signals at once. Most of us turn off the daydreams to concentrate on a conversation or some other stimulus from the outside world. But the schizophrenic may not have learned this skill.

Still other theorists suggest that schizophrenics have learned to respond to reality in bizarre ways. The **double-bind theory** (Bateson et al., 1956) is an interesting example of this view. It suggests that as children schizophrenics were taught to act in ways that contradicted their perception of reality and their own feelings. For example, because a little boy's mother resents him, she is stiff and remote when she holds him. Since she cannot accept her feelings of resentment, however, she demands that he react as if she were warm and loving. The boy knows that if he hugs her, she will pull away, but that if he does not, she will reproach him for not showing affection. This is the double-bind: He is damned if he does and damned if he doesn't. The child grows up mistrusting others and distorting the expressions of his own feelings.

In an article on schizophrenia, Brown (1973) criticized this double-bind theory. He noted that "there are plenty of ways of responding to double-binds without losing your grip on rationality" (p. 402). He denied that the existence of the bind itself is the cause of mental illness. If it were merely the bind itself, he asked, why would some people be overwhelmed by double-bind messages and others respond in a more ordinary way?

Sociological theorists insist that schizophrenia is also a social problem. Society makes many demands on us, and sometimes these demands are contradictory or exceed our ability to understand and absorb them. Sociologists point out that schizophrenic disorders usually occur in late adolescence or middle age; both are critical periods when people face many changes in their roles and self-perceptions (see Chapter 4). According to this view, crises that lead to extreme social isolation—that is, problems in living—are the chief causes of schizophrenic breakdown. People become so cut off from others that they develop the withdrawn, shut-in personality common among schizophrenics. The process begins when children with low self-esteem withdraw from social relationships to avoid anxiety and stress. A vicious cycle ensues: The more the children withdraw, the less feedback they get from other people, the lower their social skills sink, and the less they can successfully relate to their environment. This, in turn, further lowers their self-esteem and increases their anxiety.

Although quite different in emphasis, the various views of schizophrenic disorders are by no means mutually exclusive. Many theorists believe that a combination of some or all of these factors produces schizophrenia, and in practice, many psychologists use a combination of drugs and therapy to treat schizophrenia, as we shall see in the next chapter.

MENTAL ILLNESS AND THE LAW

When David Berkowitz, better known as "Son of Sam," was arrested in New York in August 1977, he was taken into custody by a cordon of some 30 police officers wearing bullet-proof vests and carrying shotguns. Public emotions were running high. Berkowitz was suspected of murdering six young people and wounding seven others in a killing spree that had attracted headlines around the world. Two court-appointed psychiatrists decided that the suspect was not fit to stand trial. But the psychiatrist appointed by the prosecutor's office later declared that Berkowitz could understand the proceedings against him and assist in his own defense, and the judge agreed with him. Berkowitz was tried, but was acquitted on grounds of insanity and sent to a state psychiatric hospital.

Since criminals who are declared legally insane are not subject to punishment for their actions, the court system has devised various legal tests of "insanity." They use the advice and testimony of "forensic psychiatrists," who help determine the mental state of suspects before trial and during trial, as well as in deciding questions about rehabilitation, parole, or fitness to stand trial at a later date (Robitscher & Williams, 1977).

Insanity is rarely an issue in serious criminal cases—less than 1 percent according to some estimates (*U.S. News & World Report*, May 7, 1979, p. 42). More often, it is used in civil cases, in suits based on automobile accidents, wills and contracts, divorce, guardianship, and admission to mental hospitals, for instance.

The influence of forensic psychologists and psychiatrists on the outcome of court cases—both the murder trials that make headlines and the less dramatic but more common civil cases involving lesser issues—is increasingly controversial. How large a part, if any, should these mental health experts play in deciding the fate of people who have violated the law? Some, like Thomas Szasz, feel that psychiatrists should stay out of the legal arena altogether. He points to the danger of a "therapeutic state," in which dependence on psychiatric opinion might lead to a massive loss of personal liberties. Other critics are concerned that psychiatrists are under pressure to testify as defense or prosecution attorneys want them to. At the other extreme, psychiatrist Bernard Diamond feels that psychiatry should play a larger role in the judicial process and in some cases even determine guilt. He believes that forensic psychiatry is an important way to educate the public, reform the law, and change social attitudes toward mental illness. In the middle lies a skeptical public, which may distrust psychiatric jargon and feel that psychiatrists "let off" dangerous criminals who still pose a threat to the community. Trial lawyer

David Berkowitz.
(UPI)

F. Lee Bailey claims that jurors often say, "I know this guy is nuts, but we're not going to put him in some institution where some psychiatrist can let him out" (_Newsweek,_ August 29, 1977, p. 28). And still other mental health experts, like Karl Menninger, believe that psychiatrists should stay out of the courtroom, but should be consulted after the trial on such matters as length of sentence, rehabilitation methods, and parole (Robitscher & Williams, 1977).

Despite the controversy, psychiatric involvement in court cases is rising. At its beginnings in the 19th century, it was mainly used to define insanity. The M'Naghten decision of 1843 set a precedent that is still the rule in most parts of the country today. Daniel M'Naghten was a Scot who believed he was being persecuted by Sir Robert Peel, England's prime minister. He tried to shoot Peel, but killed his secretary by mistake. M'Naghten was acquitted on the grounds that a "mental defect" was responsible for his act. The M'Naghten rule provides that people cannot be prosecuted if they did not understand what they were doing at the time of the act or did not understand that the act was legally wrong.

While the M'Naghten rule is still often used, it is difficult for psychiatrists to determine precisely what a defendant's state of mind was when the criminal action took place. For this reason, other rules have been formulated to clarify the issue of competence to stand trial. The Durham decision of 1954 provides that "an accused is not criminally responsible if his unlawful act was the product of a mental disease or defect" (_Durham vs. United States,_ 214 F. 2d 862, 874–875, D. C. Cir. 1954.) The American Law Institute's Model Penal Code attempts to distinguish between offenders who can control their conduct and those who cannot. "Mental disease" alone does not erase responsibility—the defendant must also show that this disorder made it impossible to obey the law or to appreciate that his or her conduct was wrong. Many states also allow for "irresistible impulse": If a defendant is uncontrollably impelled by his or her mental condition to perform a criminal act, he or she is not held accountable (George, 1968). All of these rules invite psychiatric evidence.

Once an accused person is found unfit to stand trial, he or she is usually sent to a security mental hospital until psychiatrists and the judge agree that the defendant is competent to return to the courtroom. In some cases, this means never. It is possible for an accused person to spend the rest of his or her life in an institution. In effect, they _have_ been sentenced. If an accused criminal, like David Berkowitz, _is_ found mentally fit to stand trial, he or she may still be found not guilty by reason of insanity.

But what is insanity? Critics claim that clever defendants can even fool the experts and, in some cases, be set free to kill again if psychiatrists and the judge agree that they are no longer dangerous. Thomas Vanda, a Chicago man acquitted in 1975 after stabbing a teenage girl, later advised a fellow inmate to "act crazy" in front of psychiatrists. When Vanda offered this advice, it was 1979, and he was back in jail, charged with stabbing another young woman. And once again, he was pleading insanity.

Such cases lead critics to question the validity of psychiatric testimony, not only before a trial, but afterward. To help guard against errors of this sort, about half of the states now require that a defendant who pleads insanity must prove that the claim is valid. (In the past, the prosecutor had to show that the claim was *invalid*.) And before they are released from mental institutions, people acquitted on grounds of insanity must prove they are no longer a threat to the community.

Other critics of forensic psychiatry argue from the opposite point of view—the criminal's. It is almost impossible for someone to get a fair trial, say some, once he or she has been hospitalized as "incompetent." Patients held in prisons disrupt prison routine and may be victims of cruelty from other inmates. Reform is difficult because it is cheaper to maintain a "hospital prison"—where care is simply custodial—that it is to run a real treatment hospital. Moreover, a treatment hospital system requires out-patient facilities, and many communities are afraid of having "lunatics" loose in their towns. But efforts are underway in some areas to develop a single state hospital system for patients and the legally incompetent or insane. Those who are "criminally insane" will be so judged early in the legal process so that they can be sent to facilities where they will get the kind of care they need (George, 1968).

Summary

1. The distinctions between normal and abnormal behavior are unclear. Four criteria that are widely used to distinguish normal from abnormal behavior are: a distorted perception of reality, an ineffectiveness within one's social surroundings, an inability to cope, and danger to oneself or to others.

2. Abnormal behavior was treated in different ways throughout history, ranging from the brutal to the gentle and concerned. By the 1920s, there were four major ways of regarding mental illness: The *organic model* holds that abnormal behavior has a biochemical basis; the *psychoanalytic model* says that mental and personality disorders are a result of childhood traumas and unconscious conflicts; the *medical model* suggests that mental disorders are a sickness that can be codified and cured; the

learning model implies that only experience separates the normal person from the sick one. Most mental health professionals regard abnormal behavior as a combination of these models.

3. For the past 30 years, the American Psychiatric Association has classified abnormal behavior in its *Diagnostic and Statistical Manual of Mental Disorders*. The most recent edition—*DSM-III*—was published in 1980, and reclassifies many mental disorders.

4. Although the term *neurosis* is out of favor with mental health professionals, it still has wide usage. It refers to behavior characterized by inappropriate emotions, by misuse of defense mechanisms, and by distressing patterns of behavior that a person cannot overcome alone. Psychoanalysts believe that neurotic disorders are reactions to impulses that a person cannot accept. Behavior theorists believe that these disorders stem from an association of fear and anxiety with an otherwise ordinary situation.

5. *Anxiety disorders* are mental disorders in which a direct experience of anxiety is the predominant symptom. This may also occur in *phobias*—intense fear of an object or situation in the absence of real danger—or *obsessive–compulsive* behavior, in which people obsessively focus on certain thoughts—violence, fear of contamination—or repetitive, ritualistic behavior—reciting lists, continual washing.

6. *Reactive disorders* are regarded as a separate category of *anxiety disorders*. They are the result of one or more life events or circumstances of such magnitude that they would cause suffering and distressed behavior in people with the soundest mental health. Such circumstances as rape, torture, war, and serious accidents are often the cause of reactive disorders.

7. *Dissociative disorders*, such as *amnesia* and *multiple personality*, are among the most puzzling of mental disorders. They feature a temporary dislocation from the person's perceptions of his or her identity. Amnesia involves a partial memory loss, while multiple personality involves the existence of two or more separate personalities within the same person. Another common dissociative disorder is *depersonalization*, in which people feel alienated from their minds and bodies.

8. *Somatoform disorders* are mental disorders in which the body is affected. Such a disorder may feature recurring, multiple, physical symptoms for which there is no apparent organic cause. Conversion disorders, which used to be called "hysteria," involve partial paralysis, blindness, and deafness. Psychoanalysts see somatoform disorders as a displacement of emotional problems to physical symptoms; patients are simultaneously punishing themselves and crying out for help. *Psychosomatic illnesses* differ in that they are actual physical disorders prompted by psychological problems. Ulcers, headaches, asthma, and high blood pressure are all ailments that may be caused by psychosomatic disorders.

9. *Affective disorders* are characterized by feelings of failure, worthlessness, and detachment. Although many people with this disorder are involved in a cycle of *manic-depressive* behavior—in which their moods are subject to sudden and violent changes—many others are subject to major depression without any accompanying manic period. The reverse—mania without depression—is almost never seen. It is important to distinguish between common depression, which affects everyone, and a more severe chronic depression that can cripple people emotionally. Most psychologists see manic behavior as a defense against depression. Psychoanalysts stress the self-punishing side of depression, in which people internalize and act out parental disapproval of their fantasies or behavior. Behaviorists stress that depressed people feel that they have lost control of their lives.

10. Ideas about what is and what isn't normal in sexual relationships change as society changes. Today, most psychologists stress the person's feelings about his or her sexual relationships. *Sexual dysfunction* refers to a person's inability to feel a complete cycle of sexual response. This is called *impotence* in men and *frigidity* in women. While nearly everyone experiences sexual dysfunction at one time or another, serious and prolonged inability to enjoy or experience sexual activities is usually regarded as a fear of intimacy. *Fetishism* refers to the use of nonliving objects for sexual excitement. *Pedophilia* (sexual relations with children) and *zoophilia* (sexual relations with animals) are also seen as representing a flight from heterosexual intimacy, and are often characterized by severe guilt and anxiety. *Sadomasochism* refers to the need for pain and suffering to bring about sexual pleasure.

11. Homosexuality per se is no longer classified as a mental disorder in *DSM-III;* instead, a new classification was devised. Now homosexuals are classified as exhibiting abnormal behavior only if they are distressed by their sexual orientation. This classification has caused considerable controversy but was deemed necessary by the authors because of the great changes in social attitudes toward homosexuality in the past decade. There are many conflicting theories about the origins of homosexuality, and while most theorists seem to believe that disturbed family relationships are in some way responsible, there is no consensus as to how this takes place, why it takes place in some cases and not in others, or even if it is the primary factor involved.

12. *Personality disorders* are characterized more by their effect on other people than on the person in question. These disorders often take the form of antisocial behavior, fractured relationships, an inability to take responsibility for actions, and a manipulative attitude toward others. *Schizoid* behavior is characterized by an inability to form social relationships and a lack of interest in doing so. *Paranoid* personalities are secretive, superstitious, and mistrustful. People suffering from an *antisocial personality*

disorder are often charming and intelligent on first acquaintance, but in reality are often deceitful and openly contemptuous of the feelings of others. Antisocial personalities rarely exhibit any guilt or anxiety about their activities. Some psychologists feel that this kind of behavior is the result of emotional deprivation in childhood; others feel that inconsistent parental behavior may act upon children in such a way that they feel that their actions have no influence on other people's opinions of them. Other personality disorders include *borderline personality disorder*, in which there is a variety of unstable types of behavior, and *narcissistic personality disorder*, characterized by a near total self-absorption and an inability to love or care for anyone.

13. *Substance use disorders* are another recent category of abnormal behavior. While there is no consensus on how much consumption of or dependence on various substances—alcohol, marijuana, tobacco, cocaine, and so on—is abnormal, *DSM-III* classifies the abuse and dependence on these substances as a mental disorder. *Substance abuse* is defined by *DSM-III* as including a pattern of pathological use—intoxication throughout the day and impairment of social and occupational functioning. *Substance dependence* is defined as tolerance of the substance—requiring greater amounts for the same effect. This may lead to *withdrawal*— a specific set of physical and psychological symptoms brought about when a person tries to cease his or her dependence on the substance. This category of mental disorder is among the most controversial in *DSM-III*.

14. *Schizophrenia* is the most common psychotic disorder. Schizophrenics are absorbed in fantasies and hallucinations, and are subject to delusions of grandeur and feelings of persecution. There are three main categories of schizophrenia: *Disorganized schizophrenia* is often accompanied by visual hallucinations and strange and childish grimacing and gesturing; *catatonic schizophrenia* includes a severe disturbance of motor activity—either complete or partial immobility, or extremely agitated movements with stiff, robot-like steps; *paranoid schizophrenia* is characterized by extremely suspicious behavior and dramatic shifts from delusions of grandeur to delusions of persecution. Paranoid schizophrenics may become hostile and aggressive to anyone who tries to question their delusions.

15. Doctors have been seeking a medical explanation for schizophrenic disorders for over a century. Some researchers look for a genetic or a biochemical explanation of schizophrenia. Considerable research has been done in this field but no conclusions have been reached. Psychoanalysts consider schizophrenia to be an extreme reaction of a person to an emotional disorder stemming from childhood traumas. Some learning theorists suggest that schizophrenics have learned to respond to reality in bizarre ways through a *double-bind*, in which they are taught to act in ways

that contradict their perception of reality. Sociological theorists insist that schizophrenia is a social as well as a personal problem, attributable to problems in living in a stressful society. Most psychologists view schizophrenia from a combination of these approaches.

Outline

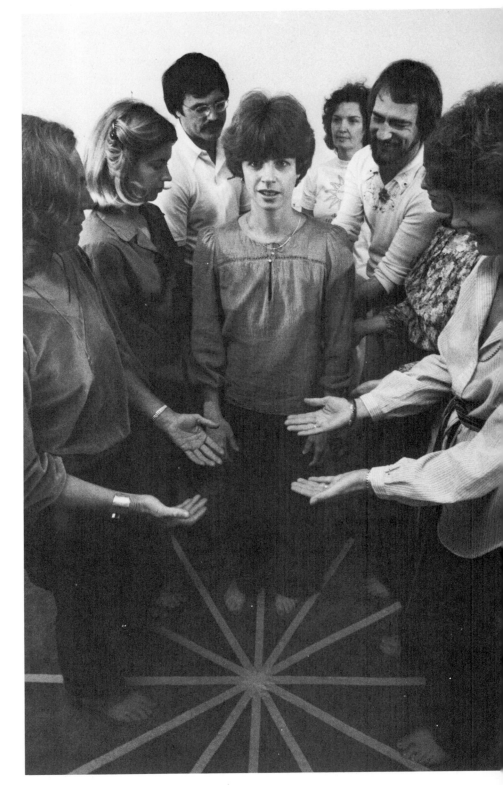

Chapter 14

Therapies

For most people, the term "psychotherapy" evokes an image of a bearded man with a pipe sitting silently in a chair while a client, reclining on a sofa, stares at the ceiling and recounts a traumatic event in his or her life. As the anxious client reveals dreams, fantasies, fears, and obsessions, the therapist scribbles a few words in a notebook or, perhaps, even asks a question or two. The therapist rarely advises the patient and never reveals details of his or her own personal life.

This cliché of psychotherapy has some truth to it; scenes like this do occur. But there are also other forms of therapy. In fact, although many therapies have much in common, others bear little or no resemblance to one another. To understand the nature of therapy generally, one must understand the nature of different therapies.

Americans seek therapy for many reasons. Some are troubled by chronic problems: anxiety, tension, sexual difficulties. Some consult a psychologist during a crisis—when their family is falling apart, or because of trouble at work or in school. Still others go into therapy because they want to learn more about themselves and want to enjoy life more fully. Many others depend on tranquilizers, stimulants, or sleeping pills to "solve" their problems.

Nonetheless, relatively few Americans know what psychotherapy is. Some families consider it a disgrace to see a therapist; others see psychotherapy as self-indulgence. They feel that people should work out problems on their own. Asking for help—and paying for it—are signs of a weak character. Family and friends, however, often turn severely disturbed people over to doctors and admit that their problem is mental illness.

Surprisingly, psychotherapy is as controversial among psychologists as it is among lay people. Many experimentally oriented psychologists view therapy as a vague and poorly defined art. The say that it is practically

439

impossible to measure the effectiveness of one treatment over another. In the summer of 1972, confusion over the use and effectiveness of therapy made national headlines: Democratic vice-presidential nominee Thomas Eagleton revealed that on three occasions he had been treated for depression with shock therapy. Reporters interviewed psychiatrists and found little agreement on how shock treatment works, when to use it, and if severe depression can be cured.

Most psychotherapies developed as professionals treated neurotic behavior. Thus, most therapies are problem oriented. In recent years, however, new therapies have been designed to help people develop skills rather than to solve problems. These therapies—for example, assertiveness training—seek to help a person who is basically well-adjusted handle other people or stress better. Thus, these new therapies emphasize growth rather than cure.

This chapter surveys the various therapies used in private practice and in institutions and describes some of their new directions, particularly in community programs. Most therapists today do not strictly adhere to one technique, but borrow from several to meet the needs of their clients, as recent studies indicate that no one therapy is "best." In any therapy, however, the more flexible the therapist, the more likely that the therapy will succeed. Indeed, the personal qualities of the therapist are more important to successful therapy than the particular technique. And, in most cases, any therapy seems to be better than none at all (Di Loreto, 1971; Sloane et al., 1975).

Individual Psychotherapies

PSYCHOANALYSIS

Psychoanalysis, the classical approach to psychotherapy, is based on the belief that the anxiety and problems that cause a person to seek help are symptoms of repressed feelings from childhood. Usually these repressed emotions are aggressive or sexual drives that the child thought were dangerous or forbidden. Psychoanalysis reverses this process and brings these repressed feelings to consciousness, so that the person can more effectively deal with them.

Successful psychoanalysis depends on two conditions: First, the person must not inhibit or control thoughts and fantasies. Slips-of-the-tongue and associations between seemingly unrelated thoughts are clues to underlying problems. This procedure is called **free association.** Second, the analyst must remain completely neutral and mostly silent. Usually, the client lies on a couch, and the analyst sits behind him or her, so that the analyst cannot be easily seen. The analyst's silence becomes a blank screen on which the client projects feelings that might otherwise be suppressed.

Analysis typically proceeds in stages. After the initial awkwardness wears off, most people enjoy the chance to talk without interruption and like having someone interested in their problems. After a few sessions, they may test their analysts by talking about desires and fantasies they have never revealed before. When their analysts are not shocked or disgusted, clients are reassured and see their analysts as warm and accepting. At this point, many people feel they are getting better and express confidence in their analysts' ability to help them. Good feelings for one's analyst, which psychoanalysts see as reflecting positive feelings toward one's parents, are called **positive transference.**

This euphoria gradually wears off. People expose their innermost feelings and feel terribly vulnerable. They want reassurance and affection, but their analysts remain silent. Their anxiety builds. Threatened by the analyst's silence and by their own thoughts, clients may feel cheated and accuse their analysts of being money-grabbers. Or they may feel that their analysts are really disgusted by their disclosures, or that their analysts laugh about them behind their backs. This **negative transference** is a crucial step, for it reveals people's negative feelings about authority figures and their resistance to uncovering repressed emotions.

At this point in therapy analysts begin to interpret their clients' feelings. The goal of interpretation is **insight:** People must see why they feel and act as they do and how their present state of mind relates to childhood experiences. Analysts encourage clients to confront events they have only mentioned briefly and to recall them fully. In this way analysts help their patients to relive their childhood traumas and to resolve conflicts that they could not solve in the past. *Working through* old conflicts provides people with a second chance to review and to revise the feelings and beliefs that underlie their problems.

This description applies to traditional, or orthodox, psychoanalysis. But only a handful of people who consult psychologists go into traditional analysis. For one thing, as Freud himself recognized, analysis depends on people's motivation to change and on their ability to deal rationally with whatever analysis uncovers. Schizophrenics freely talk about their fantasies and unconscious wishes, but they often cannot use the analyst's interpretations effectively. Psychoanalysis is best suited to "potentially autonomous" people (Hersher, 1970)—not to psychotics. Moreover, analysis may take 5 years or more, and most analysts feel that at least 3 and sometimes 5 sessions a week are essential. Thus, few people can afford psychoanalysis, and many others need immediate help for immediate problems.

Some psychologists also believe that orthodox psychoanalysis itself is outdated. Freud invented this technique in the late 19th century. He worked primarily with upper-class people who were struggling with the strict moral and social codes of a Victorian society. But society has changed. Today, it may be harder for people to *find* guidelines for behavior than it is for them to break through them.

Other critics of psychoanalysis point out that there is little research on the effects of the process itself, how and why it works. Many contemporary psychologists feel that this lack of scientific validity is a major weakness and reject psychoanalysis because of it.

Finally, as we saw in Chapter 11, the neo-Freudians—Alfred Adler, Otto Rank, and Karen Horney—proposed theories of personality that differ from Freud's, and these differences are reflected in their approaches to

An artist's conception of free association. You can see how each figure seems to grow out of the one before it.
(Picture Collection, The Branch Libraries, The New York Public Library)

"Has the possibility occurred to you, Senator, that you're a Democrat and don't know it?"
(Drawing by Dedini; © 1955 *The New Yorker Magazine*, Inc.)

therapy. For example, although Freud felt that to understand the present one had first to understand the past, most neo-Freudians try to get their clients to cope with current problems, rather than with unresolved conflicts from the past.

Adler, for example, felt that the therapists' job was to assure their clients that they could take charge of their own lives, that they were adequate and did not need to hide from life. Rank felt that classical analysis merely encouraged people to feel dependent, and that within the therapeutic relationship therapists should refuse clients' attempts to lean on them and should encourage them to be strong. Horney felt that the purpose of therapy was to teach people to give up their illusions and to accept their real self. Once this was accomplished, people did not need to make excuses for themselves. Also, and perhaps most importantly, neo-Freudians favor face-to-face discussions, and most take an active role—they interpret clients' statements freely, suggest topics for discussion, illustrate comments by role-playing, and so on.

Some psychoanalysts feel that Freud did not give enough attention to the ego. These ego psychologists—for example, Heinz Hartmann, Erik Erikson, and Anna Freud (Sigmund Freud's daughter)—emphasize the ego's effects on the personality, and thus on behavior. Hartmann (1964) notes that at times the ego functions independently of the id, and thus ego psychology can lead to a more comprehensive understanding of how the different layers of human motivation interrelate. Concentrating on the id also implies concentrating on conflicts and problems, while concentrating on the ego makes it easier for analysts to support people's successes as well as to

A person undergoing Freudian analysis. Most therapists today favor face-to-face discussions with their clients.
(Van Bucher, Photo Researchers)

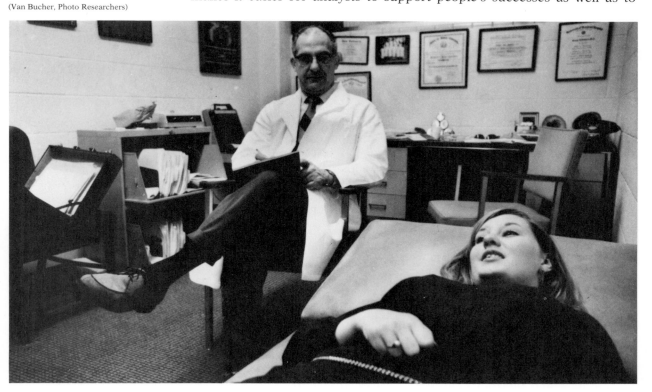

explore their failures. In recent years, several distinct schools of psychotherapy have developed from, and in addition to, these early rebellions
against Freud: client-centered therapy, rational therapy, and reality therapy.

CLIENT-CENTERED THERAPY

Carl Rogers, the founder of **client-centered therapy,** took bits and pieces
of the neo-Freudians' views and revised and rearranged them into a new
theory of personality development with a radically different approach to
therapy. Rogers agrees with Adler and Rank that infants often feel inadequate and dependent, but he does not believe that this is a necessary fact of
the human condition. He agrees with Horney that there is often a difference among who people actually are, who they think they are, and who they
would like to be. But Rogers expands the concept of the "ideal self" to
include both positive and negative feelings. The gap between the real self
and the ideal self, says Rogers, is the source of anxiety. Healthy or "fully

CLIENT-CENTERED THERAPY: AN ILLUSTRATION

Patient: I guess I do have problems at school.
. . . You see, I'm Chairman of the Science Department, so you can imagine what kind of a department
it is.

Therapist: You sort of feel that if you're in something
that it can't be too good. Is that . . .

Patient: Well, it's not that I . . . it's just that
I'm . . . I don't think that I could run it.

Therapist: You don't have any confidence in yourself?

Patient: No confidence, no confidence in myself. I
never had any confidence in myself. I—like I told
you that like when even when I was a kid I didn't feel
I was capable and I always wanted to get back with
the intellectual group.

Therapist: This has been a long-term thing, then, it's
gone on a long time.

Patient: Yeah, the *feeling* is—even though I know it
isn't it's the feeling that I have that—that I haven't
got it, that—that—that—people will find out that
I'm dumb or—or . . .

Therapist: Masquerade . . .

Patient: Superficial, I'm just superficial. There's nothing below the surface. Just superficial generalities,
that . . .

Therapist: There's nothing really deep and meaningful to you.

Patient: No—they don't know it, and . . .

Therapist: And you're terrified they're going to find
out.

Patient: My wife has a friend, and—and she and the
friend got together so we could go out together
with her and my wife and her husband. . . . And
this guy, he's an engineer and he's, you know—
he's got it, you know; and I don't want to go, I don't
want to go because—because if—if we get together he's liable to start to—to talk about something I don't know, and I'll—I won't know about
that.

Therapist: You'll show up very poorly in this kind of
situation.

Patient: That I—I'll show up poorly, that I'll—that I'll
just clam up, that I . . .

Therapist: You're terribly frightened in this sort of
thing.

Patient: I—I'm afraid to be around people who—who
I feel are my peers. Even in pool—now I—I play
pool very well and—if I'm playing with some guy,
that I—I know I can beat, *psychologically,* I can run
50, but—but if I start playing with somebody that's
my level, I'm done. I'm done. I—I—I'll miss a ball
every time.

Therapist: So the . . . the fear of what's going on
just immobilizes you, keeps you from doing a good
job (Hersher, 1970, pp.29–32).

functioning" people do not judge themselves or others and therefore have no reason to act defensively. They know themselves, they are open to new experiences, and they possess "unshakable self-esteem." The goal of therapy, in Rogers' view, is to help clients become fully functioning, to open them up to all of their experiences and to all of themselves.

Rogers calls his approach to therapy "client-centered" because he does not feel that the image of a patient seeking advice from an expert, the doctor, is appropriate. The best experts on individual people are the people themselves.

Rogers' ideas about therapy are quite specific. First, therapists must offer their clients *unconditional positive regard,* that is, therapists must show that they truly like and accept their clients—no matter what the clients say or do. Rogers feels that the therapists' acceptance is the first step toward getting clients to accept themselves. Instead of waiting silently for the clients to reveal their life stories or offering expert, objective interpretations, Rogerian therapists try to understand things from the client's point of view. Second, Rogerian therapists are emphatically *nondirective.* They do not suggest why clients feel as they do, how they might handle a difficult situation, or how they should interpret their dreams. Instead, they try to reflect the clients' statements, sometimes asking questions and sometimes hinting at feelings clients have not put into words. Rogers feels that when therapists provide this open atmosphere and genuine respect, clients can find themselves.

RATIONAL THERAPY

Unlike Rogerians, *rational therapists* see themselves as experts and their clients as people who do not know how to help themselves. According to Ellis (1973), most people rate themselves against other people and then label themselves. This is a mistake that prevents them from accepting their natural faults and usually results in self-contempt, or in a pose of defensive superiority. Regardless of what may have happened in the past, rational therapists assume that people are solely responsible in the present for how they feel about themselves and for their happiness. The goal of **rational therapy** is to show clients that their misinterpretations of events are causing their problems and to teach them to see themselves more rationally.

Rational therapists believe that people seek help when they habitually act in self-defeating ways. For example, some people feel that something is wrong with them if everyone they meet does not love and admire them. Others "beat their brains out" trying to solve a problem that is beyond their control. Still others simply refuse to examine obvious evidence and persist in thinking they are weak, sinful, or stupid. To correct these illogical and self-defeating goals and beliefs, rational therapists use a variety of techniques, including persuasion, confrontation, challenge, commands, and even theoretical arguments. They do not "baby" their clients, and some people may find their toughness hard to accept. They may go as far as to give "homework" assignments, encouraging clients to argue with their bosses, to ask the girl down the hall for a date, to pat the dog that frightens them. In short, rational therapists are very directive.

COMPUTER THERAPY

Computers can sometimes act as therapists. Computerized therapy is used to desensitize phobias, to administer positive and negative reinforcements, and to conduct a psychotherapeutic dialogue in everyday language.

In the 1970s, Lang developed a computerized Device for Automated Desensitization (DAD) to treat phobias. The device instructs patients to relax while showing them a program of pictures related to the things they are afraid of. Comparisons indicate that DAD is about as effective as a human therapist in administering this type of treatment (Arieti, 1975). In other cases, computerized devices teach children to speak. The children "play" with the computer, which is programed to reward their success in speaking.

The most interesting use of computers, however, is in simulating traditional therapist–patient conversations. In 1974, Weizenbaum created ELIZA, the first program for therapeutic communication between people and computers using natural language (Arieti, 1975). The client types in any message and ELIZA types out its response. The resultant dialogue has many of the properties of spoken conversation:

Program: Was there much friction between you and him (your father) when you were growing up?
Person: Yes, we fought all the time.
Program: Perhaps you were afraid of him.
Person: I certainly was. He used to really blow up.
Program: Perhaps you are still a little fearful of older men.
Person: Let's talk about something else.

Program: Okay. Go ahead. I will try to follow what you have to say about it (Hilgard et al., 1971, p. 514).

Psychotherapists are quick to point out that emotions such as empathy, sympathy, and understanding lie outside the realm of any machine. The therapeutic significance of pauses, silences, and confrontations may also be missed by a computer. Moreover, computers cannot deal effectively with bizarre conversation, as is illustrated by the following "dialogue":

Program: Do you say that because no one else will listen to you for some special reason?
Person: Etcetera.
Program: I'm not sure I fully understand you.
Person: Abracadabra. Heresahellofafunnybobo.
Program: Earlier you said your brother beats you up all the time . . . (Spero, 1978, p.282).

Yet, while the general use of computerized psychotherapy lies in the future, mechanized therapists could help to fill the gap created by the present shortage of trained professionals. Many severely distressed people, who never receive professional psychotherapeutic attention, could be helped by special computer scripts that focus on their characteristics and needs. Moreover, certain patients become closer to an always available, infinitely patient computer than to a human therapist. While some of the technology needed for such computerized therapy lies in the future, limited, supervised use of computers as therapists is possible.

REALITY THERAPY

Developed by William Glasser (1965), **reality therapy,** like rational therapy, also assumes that people bear a significant responsibility for their own problems. The primary goal of this therapy is to help people develop responsible behavior. Reality therapists follow five basic principles:

1. They encourage clients to judge their own behavior.
2. They encourage clients to plan for some desired goal.
3. They ask clients to commit themselves to that plan.
4. They ask clients to make no excuses if they fail to keep that commitment.
5. For their part, therapists make it clear they will inflict no punishment on their clients, that is, they will never reject them (Barr, 1974, p. 64).

Both reality therapy and rational therapy are highly directive. In each one the therapists are frank and sometimes blunt with their clients. The main difference between the two is that reality therapy is more concerned with *behavior* than with *belief*. While rational therapists encourage their clients to *view events* more rationally, reality therapists want their clients to *act* more responsibly.

EFFECTIVENESS OF PSYCHOTHERAPIES

Many studies have tried to determine if psychotherapy works. The results of these studies are mixed. In a classic survey of 19 studies covering more than 7,000 cases, H. J. Eysenck (1952) concluded that individual psychotherapy is no more effective in bringing about change in people with neurotic disorders than no therapy at all. According to Eysenck, "Roughly two-thirds of a group of neurotic patients will recover or improve to a marked extent within about 2 years of the onset of their illness whether they are treated by means of psychotherapy or not" (p. 322). Eysenck's conclusions, however, have not been universally accepted. Bergin (1966) questions the "spontaneous recovery" of the control subjects in the studies. According to Bergin, although these people did not receive any formal therapy, many sought help for emotional problems from other sources, including friends, clergy, physicians, and teachers. This informal therapy undermines Eysenck's comparison of these subjects with subjects in treatment.

Other studies attest to the effectiveness of individual psychotherapy in bringing about positive change. Meltzoff and Kornreich (1971) point to the 80 percent positive results yielded by 100 studies comparing clients in therapy with controls. Gomes-Schwartz, Hadley, and Strupp (1978) conclude that clients in therapy often improve more than control subjects do. They emphasize, however, the need to clarify what "improvement" means in psychotherapy. Is it measured in terms of the client's sense of personal satisfaction or well-being, the therapist's assessment of the client's state of mind, or society's judgment of the client's social functioning? As you recall from Chapter 13, these perspectives yield different definitions of mental health and different expectations of what constitutes successful therapy.

People receive informal—and often very effective—therapy from friends, the clergy, physicians, and teachers.
(Timothy Eagan, Woodfin Camp & Associates)

Behavior Therapies

Behaviorists do not consider behavior disorders symptoms of hidden emotional conflicts that must be uncovered and resolved. Behaviorists argue that the behavior disorder is the problem, not a symptom of the problem. They feel that if therapists can teach people to respond more appropriately, they have "cured" them.

Behavior therapies are based on the belief that all behavior, normal and abnormal, is learned. Hypochondriacs learned that they get attention when they are sick; catatonics learned that they are safe when they completely withdraw from reality. The therapists' job is to teach people more satisfying ways of behaving; they do not need to know how or why people learned to behave as they do. Behaviorists use several techniques to build new habits.

OPERANT CONDITIONING

Operant conditioning techniques are based on the idea that a person learns to behave in different ways if new behaviors are rewarded and old behaviors are ignored. For example, Kennedy (1964) had a hospital staff disregard the irrational behavior of three chronic schizophrenics. When the patients said something rational and appropriate, they were rewarded with smiles and attention. When their communications were unintelligible or irrational, they were ignored. All three patients improved markedly within a few months.

Isaacs, Thomas, and Goldiamond (1960) used a similar approach with a mute patient who was extremely fond of chewing gum. Using gum as a reinforcer, they gave it to him every time he moved his mouth. When the patient learned to move his mouth in order to get the gum, they began to withhold the gum until he made a sound. They gradually increased their demands, so that the patient had to say words to get the gum. In this way, they taught him to speak.

Operant conditioning works best when the therapists completely control the rewards and the punishments. If the mute patient had lived at home and his family gave him gum whenever he wanted it, the therapy would have failed.

In another form of operant conditioning called **contingency contracting,** the therapist—or anyone trying to help someone change a behavior pattern—and client agree on behavioral goals and on the reinforcement the client receives when the goals are reached. These goals and reinforcements are often written in contract form, binding both the client and the therapist as if they were involved in a legal agreement. The contract specifies the behaviors that are its goals, the penalties if the agreed-upon behaviors are not complied with, and any expected privileges (Harmatz, 1978). For example, a father and daughter might agree that she will study at least 1 hour each night. In return, the father agrees to buy her a new pair of ice skates when she has kept to her study schedule for 1 month. If she fails to

Cigarette smoking can be reduced or eliminated through operant or aversive conditioning.
(Frank Siteman, Stock, Boston)

meet her contractual requirement, the daughter agrees not to watch television that day. Similar contracts are used to control substance abuse and absenteeism among high school students.

AVERSIVE CONDITIONING

Aversive conditioning is a technique to eliminate specific behavior patterns. Therapists teach clients to associate pain and discomfort with the response clients want to unlearn. This form of behavior therapy has successfully treated alcoholism, obesity, and smoking.

Sometimes therapists use real physical pain. Dent (1954) treated alcoholics by giving them a drug that produces extreme nausea when mixed with alcohol in the stomach. The people were encouraged—in fact, instructed—to drink. Each time they did, they became violently sick. Soon they felt sick just seeing a bottle of whiskey. Convicted child molesters have been cured by showing them pictures of naked children and giving them electric shocks (Knight, 1974). More recently, behaviorists found that pain is not necessary. People can be taught to block behavior with unpleasant fantasies. For example, without undergoing shock treatment, the child molesters could learn to associate things they feared with pictures of children, and to associate things they enjoyed with pictures of adults.

BEHAVIOR THERAPY IN INSTITUTIONS: AN ETHICAL ISSUE

A chain smoker who decides to use aversive conditioning to break her smoking habit is acting on her own initiative. So is an alcoholic who enrolls in a behavior therapy alcohol detoxification program. But inmates of prisons and patients in mental hospitals who are subjected to a range of behavior modification techniques, including aversive conditioning, often have very little choice in their treatment. This has raised serious ethical questions about exactly whom the therapy is serving: the patient or the institution and society.

As Stolz, Wienckowski, and Brown (1975) point out, many people equate using behavior modification techniques on "captive" subjects with mind control. If some mental patients are institutionalized for the convenience of society, then the treatment these patients receive can be seen as an attempt to make them change their deviant behavior and to conform to society rather than to express their own character. The problems are especially acute in prisons, where, instead of helping the inmate, the therapist may be enforcing conformity to the prison's rules.

As Feshbach (1976) points out, the danger of be-

havior modification in these institutions arises from the tremendous difference in power between the therapist who controls the treatment and the involuntary subject. "The options of patients and of prisoners," Feshbach explains, "are far more restricted than those of the institutional behavior change agents. The latter, if a particular reinforcer is ineffective, can vary the amount of reinforcement, the schedule of reinforcement, and the type of reinforcement. What choices do patients or prisoners have other than to conform to the requirement for reinforcement?" (p. 540). Cotter (1967) contends that therapists must recognize that patients have the right to participate in their own therapy and to decide what is best for themselves, even if their behavior is not in the best interest of the society.

The social regulation of individual behavior through behavior modification has also become a legal concern. The courts have recently declared that aversive behavior modification inflicted on unwilling prisoners and mental patients is cruel and unusual punishment and is thus unconstitutional (Davison & Stuart, 1975; Perlin, 1976).

DESENSITIZATION

In some cases, aversive conditioning may be harmful. For example, if a little boy who is afraid of dogs were taken by the hand and urged to approach the dog that bit him, he might well be terrified the next time someone took his hand. In such cases, **desensitization,** a method for gradually reducing irrational fear, would be a more useful technique. A therapist gives the child cookies and milk if he sits by a window and watches a chained dog outside. Once he seems calm in this situation, the therapist gives him cookies only if he goes out into the yard and plays 30 feet away from the chained dog. Waiting at each stage until the child seems relaxed, the therapist gradually moves the child closer to the dog. Behaviorists have used desensitization to cure phobias about snakes, heights, closed rooms, and sex. These examples indicate that behaviorists can successfully treat specific problems and fears, from psychotic behavior to a child's fear of dogs. But many of the people who consult psychotherapists are vague about their problems—they feel anxious and unhappy most of the time. Can behaviorists treat such diffuse anxiety?

Wolpe (1973) believes they can. Chronically anxious people may not know why they feel tense, but they can distinguish between different levels of anxiety. For example, in his first session a politician tells the therapist that he is very anxious about speaking to crowds. The therapist looks for more details. She asks if the man is more threatened by an audience of 500 than by an audience of 50, more tense when he is addressing men than when he is speaking to both men and women, and so on. Perhaps this politician feels more anxious talking to adolescents than to small children. Thus, the therapist establishes a *hierarchy,* from the least to the most anxiety-provoking situations.

After establishing a hierarchy, therapists teach clients to clear their minds, to release tense muscles, and to relax. In some cases, drugs or mild hypnosis help the client to relax. Once clients have mastered the technique of deep relaxation, they begin to work at the bottom of their anxiety hierarchy. Therapists ask the clients to imagine the least threatening situation and to signal when they begin to feel tense. At the signal, the therapists tell the clients to forget the scene and to concentrate on relaxing. After a short time, they instruct them to return to the scene. This process is repeated until the clients feel completely relaxed. Eventually, the clients imagine the situation they are most afraid of without anxiety. Wolpe reports that most clients transfer what they learn in his office to real-life situations.

In recent years, cognition has become increasingly important to behavior therapy. Many behavior therapists argue that behavior cannot be explained solely in terms of stimulus–response learning theory. People reward and punish themselves through their own thinking, which has nothing to do with external stimuli (Lazarus, 1977). Phobias, for example, may be more than the conditioned avoidance responses proposed by strict behaviorists. They may also be used as manipulative ploys, face-saving devices, and symbolic withdrawals. As Lazarus points out, the general acceptance of both a cognitive basis and a stimulus–response basis for behavior has freed behavior therapy from ties to any one point of view.

EFFECTIVENESS OF BEHAVIOR THERAPIES

Some psychologists think that behavior therapies oversimplify psychology by only treating behavior. These psychologists believe that patterns of thought are as important in therapy as is overt behavior. The chief opposition to behavior therapies comes from traditional psychoanalysts. Analysts, as noted earlier, believe that neurotic and psychotic behavior are symptoms of unconscious problems. They argue that if you teach people to give up their symptoms without resolving the conflicts that caused them, new symptoms—perhaps even less desirable—will appear. Wolpe (1969) defends his approach with follow-up studies: Of 249 people he treated for neurotic problems, only 4 developed new symptoms.

Is behavior therapy more effective than psychotherapy in bringing about positive changes in people? Sloane and his colleagues (1975) studied 94 people with anxiety or personality disorders. They randomly divided these people into 3 groups: 31 clients were assignd to behavior therapy, 30 to psychotherapy, and 33 to a waiting list.

Clients in behavior therapy were treated with several behavior techniques, including systematic desensitization, assertiveness training, and avoidance conditioning. Those in psychotherapy were treated with short-term insight therapy. And those on the waiting list received no specific therapy; they were told that they would have to wait 4 months before their therapy would begin.

After 4 months, the researchers found that all 3 groups had improved, but those in the 2 groups receiving therapy had improved the most. When the subjects were asked if they *felt* better, those who had received behavior therapy reported more improvement than either of the other groups. The researchers concluded, however, that despite people's feelings of well-being, "there is no clear evidence for the superiority of behavior therapy over psychotherapy" (p. 376). Many therapists believe that combining these two forms of treatment may be the best form of therapy for many clients (Gomes-Schwartz et al., 1978).

Group Therapies

By definition, psychotherapy is limited to the interaction of the client and the therapist. Many psychologists think this less than ideal. People may attach great importance to their therapists' real and imagined reactions. Therapists are human, so there is always some degree of **countertransference** (therapists' projecting their own emotions onto clients). Furthermore, therapy sessions are unlike everyday life. People seldom find the psychoanalyst's neutrality or the Rogerian analyst's unconditional positive regard among their friends and family. They may find it hard to transfer the insight and confidence they have gained in therapy to other situations.

Group therapies allow both therapist and client to see how the person acts with others. They also let people shed inhibitions and express themselves in a safe setting. Finally, groups are a source of reinforcement.

TRADITIONAL GROUPS

Traditional therapy groups are an extension of psychotherapy. The participants are usually also seeing the therapist individually. Such groups meet once or twice weekly, for about 1½ hours. These sessions often emphasize uncovering ghosts that haunt people from the past and influence their behavior in the present. For example, John, an older man, is extremely hostile toward a younger student, Tim. Is John projecting the image of a younger brother onto Tim, or perhaps acting out his frustrations with his son? When he attacks Tim's appearance, is he speaking for himself or echoing his father's values?

GESTALT GROUPS

Gestalt therapy is largely an outgrowth of the work of Frederick (Fritz) Perls at the Esalen Institute in California. Perls began his career as a psychoanalyst, but later turned vehemently against Freud and psychoanalytic techniques. Perls felt that "Freud invented the couch because he could not look people in the eye" (1974, p. 118). Gestalt therapy emphasizes the here-and-now and encourages face-to-face confrontations.

Gestalt therapy is designed to make people self-supporting. It can be used with individuals, but it is more frequently used in a group setting. The therapist is active and directive and usually concentrates on one person at a time. The emphasis in Gestalt therapy is on the *whole* person, and the therapist's role, as Perls describes it, is to "fill in the holes in the personality to make the person whole and complete again" (Perls, 1969, p. 2). Gestalt therapists try to make people aware of their feelings, to awaken them to sensory information they may be ignoring. Many techniques may be

451

GESTALT THERAPY

Therapist: Try to describe just what you are aware of at each moment as fully as possible. For instance, what are you aware of now?

Bill: I'm aware of wanting to tell you about my problem, and also a sense of shame—yes, I feel very ashamed right now.

Therapist: Okay. I would like you to develop a dialogue with your feeling of shame. Put your shame in the empty chair over here (*indicates chair*), and talk to it.

Bill: Are you serious? I haven't even told you about my problem yet.

Therapist: That can wait—I'm perfectly serious, and I want to know what you have to say to your shame.

Bill (*awkward and hesitant at first, but then becoming looser and more involved*): Shame, I hate you. I wish you would leave me—you drive me crazy, always reminding me that I have a problem, that I'm perverse, different, shameful—even ugly. Why don't you leave me alone?

Therapist: Okay, now go to the empty chair, take the role of shame, and answer yourself back.

Bill (*moves to the empty chair*): I am your constant companion—and I don't *want* to leave you. I would feel lonely without you, and I don't hate you. I pity you, and I pity your attempts to shake me loose, because you are doomed to failure.

Therapist: Okay, now go back to your original chair and answer back.

Bill (*once again as himself*): How do you know I'm doomed to failure? (*Spontaneously shifts chairs now, no longer needing direction from the therapist; answers himself back, once again in the role of shame.*) I know that you're doomed to failure because *I* want you to fail and because I control your life. You can't make a single move without me. For all you know, you were *born* with me. You can hardly remember a single moment when you were without me, totally unafraid that I would spring up and suddenly remind you of your loathesomeness.

Bill: You're right; so far you *have* controlled my life—I feel constantly embarrassed and awkward. (*His voice grows stronger.*) But that doesn't mean that you'll continue to control my life. That's why I've come here—to find some way of destroying you. (*Shifts to the "shame" chair.*) Do you think *he* can help you? (*Bill, as shame, points to the therapist.*) What can he do? He hardly knows you as I know you—besides, he's only going to see you once or twice each week. I am with you every single moment of every day!

Therapist: Bill, look how one hand keeps rubbing the other when you speak for shame. Could you exaggerate that motion? Who does that remind you of?

Bill (*rubbing his hands together harder and harder*): My mother would do this—yes, whenever she was nervous she would rub her hands harder and harder.

Therapist: Okay, now speak for your mother (Shaffer, 1978, pp. 92–93).

---

used—people are told to talk about themselves in the first person ("I keep looking away" instead of "My eyes keep looking away"). By this method, therapists remind clients that they alone are responsible for everything they do. If they want to discuss a third person, they must speak directly to that person or act out a conversation if that person is absent. Gestalt therapy, like psychoanalysis, uses people's dreams to help uncover information. Often clients are asked to act out all parts in their dreams—both people and objects.

SENSITIVITY AND ENCOUNTER GROUPS

Sensitivity groups, like the groups conducted at the Esalen Institute, seek to enhance *awareness* by focusing on nonverbal communication and the senses. Often the participants are well-adjusted—in their own minds, too well-adjusted. They feel they have lost touch with simple things. How many people rush around and never pause to look into a stranger's eyes or smell the air on a spring day? How many people never touch anyone except for their lover, spouse, or children? Sensitivity groups use exercises to reawaken the senses.

Encounter groups take this process one step further. They demand that participants *respond* to the immediate situation and express themselves directly. By stripping away the social pretenses of everyday life, encounter groups force people to give up their inhibitions and to stop acting in ways they think others expect. For example, Susan attacks John and he responds by saying, "You're projecting." This may be correct, but John is avoiding his own feelings about being attacked. How does he feel? Threatened? Hurt? Angry? By coming to grips with such feelings, participants feel better and less anxious. Many people who do not feel anxious enough for individual therapy join encounter and sensitivity groups because they want to grow. Sometimes these groups are conducted in *marathon sessions*. Participants meet all day, every day, for a weekend or more, either in the therapist's office or at a vacation retreat.

One purpose of encounter groups is to enable people to get in touch with their feelings.
(Mimi Forsyth, Monkmeyer)

TRANSACTIONAL ANALYSIS

Originated by Eric Berne (1957, 1964), **transactional analysis** claims that people are always acting out one or another of three ego stages: the Child, the Parent, or the Adult. The *Child* represents people's behavior and attitudes at an earlier stage of development; the *Parent* represents the attitudes, responses, and behavior absorbed from their own parents and other authority figures; and the *Adult* represents their ability to act and think independently, without being influenced by the demands of the Child and the Parent. Berne suggests not that people should always act as Adults, but that they should learn to recognize communication directed to the Adult in them and to respond to it. The primary goal of transactional analysis is to improve communication between people by making them more aware of what they are communicating.

Transactional analysis aims at understanding which ego states people are acting from by studying transactions between two or more people. Thus, transactional analysis is more effective as a group therapy. Therapists try to minimize "crossed transactions"—when one person acts as Adult and the other responds as Child—and "ulterior transactions"—when one person acts as Adult because he or she feels that is the best way to draw out the other person's Child (Berne, 1968).

FAMILY THERAPY

This therapy claims that if one person in the family has problems, it is often a signal that the entire family unit needs assistance. Family therapists believe that most psychotherapists treat people in a vacuum. Most of them never meet the person's parents, spouse, and children. The primary goals of **family therapy** include improving communication, encouraging family members to become more empathetic, getting them to share the respon-

Family therapy is called for when problems exist between a husband and wife, parents and children, or other family members.
(Linda Ferrer, Woodfin Camp & Associates)

sibilities of leadership, and reducing conflict. To achieve this, all family members must see that they will benefit from changes in their behavior. Family therapists must thoroughly understand the family and must concentrate on changing how its members satisfy their needs rather than changing those needs or the people's personalities (Horn, 1975).

Family therapy is indicated when problems exist between husband and wife, parents and children, and other family members. It is also indicated when people's progress in individual therapy seems to be slowed by their family, or when a family member has trouble adjusting to another member's improvement. Goldenberg (1973) notes, however, that all families may not benefit from family therapy. Some problems are too entrenched; important family members may be absent or unwilling to cooperate; or one family member may monopolize the session, so that the therapy becomes unworkable. In such cases, a different therapeutic approach might work better.

EFFECTIVENESS OF GROUP THERAPIES

With therapy groups, psychologists reach more people at lower costs and, with marathons, in less time. But are such short-term groups therapeutic? They seem to fulfill some people's needs for openness, intimacy, and physical warmth. But how effective are they?

Goldenberg (1973) identifies several important criticisms of encounter and sensitivity groups: Their benefits may be only short-term. After the "high" feeling passes, people may be no better off than they were before. Not all groups are run by trained psychotherapists. The number of untrained, self-styled group leaders is increasing, and this can be dangerous in view of the intensity of emotion expressed by members in the group.

Often group leaders are not careful enough about whom they accept into the group. They should interview applicants at length to ensure that they will have a positive influence on the rest of the group and that they are strong enough to stand the strain of intense, undefended interactions with other people. Some leaders have been criticized for not taking responsibility for the members of their groups. For example, most leaders of "weekend workshops" neglect to make follow-up studies to see how participating in the group has affected the group's members. As some people have become seriously disturbed by their experiences in such groups, the responsibility of the group leader should not end when the marathon is over.

These groups emphasize emotions and play down the intellect. "Gut-level feelings are in, while head trips are out. . . . Yet lasting change probably requires some integration of the intellect with the senses" (Goldenberg, 1973, p. 407). Hartley, Roback, and Abramowitz (1976) share this view. They feel that many objections to encounter groups could be overcome and the number of "casualties" reduced if effective screening methods excluded psychotics, certain neurotics, hysterics, and people in crisis; if potential group members were adequately informed about group goals and behavior; if leaders were specifically trained to deal with recurring problems; and if leaders were certified by a regulatory body.

Lieberman (1976) studied the effectiveness of various groups in two ways. First, he reviewed research on groups whose members were compared to people not involved in any formal therapy. The results were generally positive: Groups seemed to help. According to Lieberman, however, these studies often had serious methodological problems, including what evidence they relied on to measure attitude change, and the use of volunteers who shared similar values. In analyzing a second group of studies that compared two or more forms of treatment—token versus nontoken environment, leader-controlled versus peer-controlled groups, and so on—Lieberman found that structured, directing groups seem to produce more changes than unstructured, less directive groups. Lieberman also found that a strong therapist or group leader was not needed to bring about change.

Meyer and Smith (1977) take a more positive stance than Lieberman on the effectiveness of group therapy. In their view, group therapy gives participants immediate, realistic feedback, a range of behavioral models, and group validation of decisions and future plans. Moreover, they contend that group therapy helps clients with a range of disorders.

Physical Treatment

Sometimes therapists find they cannot "reach" people with any of the therapies we have described because they are extremely agitated, disoriented, or totally unresponsive. In these cases, therapists may decide to use **physical treatment** to change clients' behavior so that they can benefit from therapy. Physical treatment is also used both to restrain clients who are dangerous to themselves and to others and in institutions where there are only a few therapists for many patients.

SHOCK TREATMENTS

Shock treatment is most often used for sudden and severe depression, especially in psychotics. In **electroconvulsive shock therapy** (ECT), one electrode is placed on each side of the person's head and a mild current is turned on for a very short time. This produces a brief convulsion, followed by a temporary coma. **Insulin shock treatment** consists of an intramuscular injection of insulin, which lowers the level of sugar in the blood and produces a brief coma.

Shock is a stimulant. After treatment the person is happier, more responsive, and more active. No one knows exactly why shock treatment works the way it does, but most researchers believe that convulsions produce both physiological and psychological changes (Ullman & Krasner, 1975).

Because of the negative side effects, insulin shock therapy is rarely used today. Muscle relaxants to prevent dislocations and fractures during the convulsions produced by ECT have made it more manageable, but its use is also declining. Both treatments can temporarily impair a person's memory, and both are risky with people who have other medical problems, such as heart disease.

PSYCHOSURGERY

As we saw in Chapter 2, changing a person's behavior and emotional state by brain surgery is a drastic step, especially since the effects of *psychosurgery*, particularly prefrontal lobotomies, are difficult to predict. One procedure may work with one person, but fail completely with another, perhaps producing undesirable, permanent side effects. Lobotomies are rarely performed today. Instead, new areas of the brain—particularly in the limbic system—are being tested as possible sites for psychosurgery. The more recent techniques seek to reduce aggressive, violent impulses. Doctors have cured schizophrenia and reduced the incidence of "homicidal rage" in many of their patients. But researchers consider psychosurgery a "desperation measure" that destroys part of a person's personality.

DRUG THERAPY

Most psychiatrists—and only medical doctors are allowed by law to prescribe drugs—prefer drugs to either shock treatment or psychosurgery. Drugs produce only temporary changes in body chemistry, their effects are reversible, the dosage can be varied from one person to another, and the side effects are easier to predict.

Until the mid-1950s drugs were not widely used—the only available sedatives induced sleep as well as calm. Then, *reserpine* and the *phenothiazines* were introduced. Both of these drugs are antipsychotic, major tranquilizers. They reduce anxiety and aggressive behavior, and sometimes alleviate delusions and hallucinations. How do they work? Research with animals indicates that they inhibit the functioning of the hypothalamus,

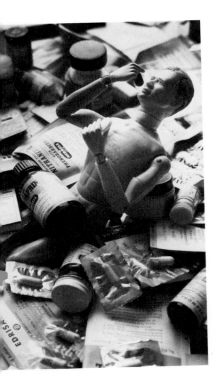

While drugs may be useful in treating people with neurotic disorders and can help relieve stress and tension, they do not *cure* psychological problems and may easily be abused.

(Arthur Tress, Photo Researchers)

which controls arousal. Brain wave studies suggest that this prevents internal arousal signals from reaching the higher portions of the brain (Sarason, 1980). Psychiatrists sometimes also prescribe antidepressants, which speed up all physiological processes and thus reduce severe depression.

Besides these major tranquilizers, minor tranquilizers, such as Valium, Librium, and Miltown, are prescribed as antianxiety drugs to treat people with neurotic disorders. These drugs are primarily used by normal people for stress-related tension and anxiety. But they are also given to psychotics and former addicts as part of a treatment program. Their effect is to help patients relax and sleep.

Of course, drugs do not cure psychological problems. If the medication is stopped, people return to their original conditions. But drugs calm agitated and depressed people, and in some cases enable people who might otherwise be confined to institutions to return to their homes and families.

VALIUM

Valium, known in scientific circles as diazepam, is an antianxiety drug or minor tranquilizer. After its introduction in 1963, Valium rapidly became the most widely prescribed drug in the United States. In 1978, about 68 million prescriptions were written for Valium, Librium, and other related tranquilizers at a wholesale market value of $360 million (Clark & Hager, 1978).

The benefits of Valium do not come without substantial costs, however. Side effects of drowsiness and motor impairment are sometimes responsible for car accidents. Valium is often mixed with other drugs or alcohol, causing negative effects when the different substances combine. Valium may interfere with serotonin, a natural brain chemical that is an antidepressant and aids in normal sleep, thereby increasing depression and sleeplessness. Dr. E. H. Uhlenhuth of the University of Chicago warns that "if a doctor does not recognize a depressed patient and pulls out Valium, he may make the patient more depressed and even suicidal" (*Newsweek*, November 12, 1979, p. 101). Valium, with its anxiety-easing properties, may also mask clinically important symptoms and could prevent a person from seeking needed psychotherapy (Coleman, 1980).

But perhaps the worst possibility is that Valium users will become dependent on the drug. When use is abruptly stopped, serious withdrawal symptoms can occur, such as tremors, nervousness, weakness, weight loss, nausea, retching, abdominal pain and cramping, insomnia, muscle twitches, facial numbness, and muscle cramps (Pevnick et al., 1978). According to Dr. Conway Hunter, Jr. of Atlanta's Peachform Hospital, withdrawal from Valium "is more prolonged and often more difficult than [withdrawal from] heroin" (Clark, Gosnell, & Whitmore, 1979). Addiction can develop even when the doctors' orders are obeyed, because many physicians, unaware of the drug's addictive potential, prescribe it freely.

Defenders of Valium, however, argue that its negative effects are exaggerated. According to them, the people who have trouble with the drug are those who disobey the doctor's orders. Valium proponents view the large percentage of people using the drug as "reasonable evidence of consumer satisfaction" rather than as a sign of overprescription or increased dependence (Cole & Davis, 1975).

Despite the arguments against it, Valium's value should not be overlooked. Although side effects and dependency may develop, even with the prescribed dosage, Valium is relatively safe and helps people deal with profound anxiety. Caution and restraint, however, should be exercised by physicians in prescribing the drug. It should not be regarded as a cure for all the stresses and strains of everyday life. It should be reserved for those seriously affected by anxiety. Also, Valium is not a cure in itself. Whenever possible, it should be used in combination with psychotherapy to help people deal with the root of their problems.

Institutionalization

How and why are people committed to mental institutions? People are usually committed at the request of family members, either acting alone or on the recommendation of a physician. Others enter hospitals voluntarily. Still others are committed by the courts, either because of violent behavior or a suicide attempt.

Most people are first placed on a psychiatric ward in a general hospital. During their first few days in the hospital, the patients are interviewed and tested by the staff psychologists. Then, the staff meets to decide how to proceed. They ask, first, if the patients are potentially dangerous to themselves or to others; second, if they would benefit from hospitalization; third, if they could get along by themselves if they were released from the hospital.

In most states, two psychiatrists must certify that a person is "mentally ill" before he or she can be committed. The final decision rests with the

ON BEING SANE IN INSANE PLACES

D. L. Rosenhan (1973) wanted to study the quality of care in mental hospitals. Eight sane people—Rosenhan himself, three psychologists, a pediatrician, a psychiatrist, a painter, and a housewife—applied for admission at twelve different psychiatric hospitals. The hospitals were a mixed group—old and new, public and private, understaffed and adequately staffed. The "pseudopatients" told the admitting doctor that they heard voices that said "empty," "hollow," and "thud." (These words were chosen because they suggest _existential psychosis_—a feeling that life is meaningless—no cases of which have ever been reported.) The voices were the only problem the pseudo patients said they had, and all gave their authentic life histories to the doctor. They all "passed" and were admitted. Seven of them were diagnosed as schizophrenic, and the eighth was labeled manic-depressive.

Once they were in the hospitals, they all behaved normally. They talked to the patients and openly took notes about what they saw on the wards. They told the staff they no longer heard voices and tried to get discharged. Many of the real patients knew at once that the pseudopatients were sane. One said, "You're not crazy. You're a journalist, or professor [referring to the constant note-taking]. You're checking up on the hospital." The staff, on the other hand, knew the

pseudopatients were psychotic because the admitting diagnosis said so. One staff nurse described the note-taking—recognized by the patients as a sign of sanity—as, "Patient engages in writing behavior."

The pseudopatients found the hospitals to be highly dehumanizing. They had no privacy, their direct questions were ignored, and they were treated as though they did not exist. On a men's ward, one nurse showed how little attention she gave to the patients by unbuttoning her blouse to adjust her bra. In over 3 months of hospitalization, 6 of the pseudopatients estimated that they talked with a doctor for about 7 minutes a day. They also noted that the doctors did not openly respond to their direct questions and avoided looking them in the eyes. Rosenhan concluded that "the consequences to patients hospitalized in such an environment—the powerlessness, depersonalization, segregation, mortification, and self-labeling—seem undoubtedly countertherapeutic" (p. 252).

This study caused a lot of controversy among the psychiatric community. Rosenhan's critics said that his sample was too small, and that his judgment should not be generalized to all mental hospitals. Most doctors did agree, however, that hospital care could be improved if hospitals were staffed with more qualified people, and if more money were available.

courts (Lazarus, 1969). If people are to be institutionalized, they are usually sent to a state mental hospital, since few people can afford private hospitals. Most state institutions are isolated from the community, either by walls or by their location. People who are committed lose their legal rights—they cannot come and go as they please, and they have few opportunities to petition for their freedom.

The patient in a state institution has many problems. Most large institutions cannot afford enough staff to give all the patients intensive therapy. In such cases, the patients who are judged to have the best chance of being cured, or at least of improving, receive therapy. Others are given only custodial care—the staff looks after them, sees that they are washed, dressed, fed, and that they take their medicine; these patients may see a psychologist for only a few minutes a week. Some hospitals have good recreational and vocational facilities; others have only a television set. Not surprisingly, the patients on many wards are apathetic.

Recently some psychologists have felt that such institutions are not only inadequate, but that they have a negative effect on patients. Some argue that the hospitals merely teach people how to be "good patients," thus promoting the behavior they are supposed to cure. In the last decade, the emphasis has moved away from custodial care toward returning people to their families and homes as soon as possible.

TOKEN ECONOMIES

Token economies are based on the behavioral approach to therapy: If you consistently reward people for desirable behavior, they will behave appropriately. In life the chief reinforcement is money. People work and are rewarded with money, which enables them to buy things they want. If their work improves, their salary increases.

Ayllon and Azrin (1968) recreated this incentive system on a ward for chronic psychotic patients. All the patients were women, and all had been in the hospital a long time. Ayllon and Azrin's chief aim was to encourage the patients to behave so that they could return to society—to care for themselves and their rooms, to relate to other people in an appropriate way, and to work at jobs around the hospital. Each time a patient behaved in a desirable way, she was given tokens that could be exchanged for candy and cigarettes, extra TV time, the right to choose where to sit for dinner, a chance to see the psychologist or chaplain, a pass to go out on the grounds, and so on.

Ayllon and Azrin chose the token system of reinforcement for two reasons. First, tokens resemble money and thus create a bridge back to society. (Some of these patients had been hospitalized for 20 years and had forgotten what life was like "on the outside.") Second, tokens are a concrete reward. On the average ward a patient may strive for smiles and attention. But these rewards are ambiguous, particularly to disturbed people who have trouble interpreting other people's signals. Tokens enable the staff to establish a definite, reliable scale for rewards. The patients could see and touch evidence of "good social behavior."

Patients in this program improved dramatically. Some who had spent years sitting by themselves took an interest in hospital activities. Many performed useful jobs and some even "paid" for their rooms with the tokens they had earned. Staff morale also increased throughout the hospital. In the past, doctors and attendants alike were pessimistic about helping their patients. Now they had a workable method. However, many psychologists have reservations about token economies. They feel that people learn how to earn tokens, not new behavior, and that when the tokens stop, so does the learning. Thus, although token economies may encourage patients in an institution to change their behavior, these psychologists caution against applying such a program to other situations.

Repucci and Saunders (1974) have been particularly outspoken about the limits of behavior modification techniques. They write that "even minimal conditions necessary for behavior change are difficult to obtain" (p. 659). They describe eight types of problems or constraints that behavior modifiers face when they try to work in less than ideal settings. Among these are *institutional constraints*, such as bureaucratic stalling and "red tape"; *external pressure*, such as newspapers and the police insisting on tight security in a reform school; and *limited resources*—in one such school, it took 1½ years to build desired sleeping alcoves for the boys, primarily because of the lack of cooperation from the campus maintenance people. Such problems have led Repucci and Saunders to caution against accepting the more extravagant claims of behavior modification supporters.

Community Psychology

In recent years, drugs have been developed that allow many psychotics to return to their families, and the public has become more sophisticated about emotional problems and mental health care than it was 15 or 20 years ago. As a result, many people seek treatment for themselves and for family members *before* they need hospitalization (Satloff & Worby, 1970). Moreover, psychologists are reaching out—looking for those in need instead of waiting for people to come to them. This new approach is the result of a developing school of research and practice—**community psychology.**

Applied community psychology seeks to prevent mental illness and to *educate* the public—particularly those people who have only limited access to psychotherapy. How can psychologists prevent mental illness? By establishing closer links with the community, so that teachers, members of the clergy, and neighbors recognize the signs of psychological crises. Education has two purposes: to let people know that there is help for emotional problems—that there is some place they can go—and to teach people how to cope with psychological problems themselves.

One of the pilot studies in community approaches to mental health was conducted in Susanville, a small town in northern California. Until the late 1960s, Susanville depended on visiting professionals who were called in when local officials found a person with psychological problems. (About 12 people were committed to state mental hospitals from this town each year.)

DEINSTITUTIONALIZATION

The process of rehabilitating people within their own communities is called "deinstitutionalization." It is the result of widespread and effective use of antipsychotic and antidepressant drugs that enable many seriously disturbed people to function outside the institutional walls. The desire to reduce the financial burden of the state mental hospitals has also contributed to such programs (Bassuk & Gerson, 1978).

For the most part, however, deinstitutionalization has not worked well. Discharged patients are confronted with poorly funded community mental health centers, lack of adequate follow-up care, ineffective outpatient therapy, and negative responses from the general population. There is little guidance available to help ex-patients cope with the mechanics of daily life. Patients who return home are often a burden to their families, especially without close follow-up care. Residential centers, such as **halfway houses,** often provide inadequate medical and psychological care, and minimal contact with the outside world. In any case, the dearth of sheltered housing forces many former patients into nonpsychiatric facilities often located in dirty, unsafe, and isolated ghettos. Former patients are further burdened by social stigma, which is perhaps the largest single obstacle to their rehabilitation (Bassuk & Gerson, 1978).

The problems of deinstitutionalization, however, are not insurmountable. Innovative programs providing total care for discharged patients have been successful. In one example, 130 former patients were relocated to a residential hotel on West 87th Street in New York City. Community residents established a lunch program, contributed books, clothes, furniture, money, and enlisted the aid of social workers. Patients participated in social events and neighborhood activities. Besides helping the ex-patients, the program was a kind of therapy for the neighborhood (Bassuk & Gerson, 1978).

For deinstitutionalization to succeed, there must be decent housing, improved services and programs, and more trained community workers. These goals can only be reached by proper planning, increased funding, and community support.

Then some concerned citizens decided that instead of hiring outsiders when someone needed help, they would hire professionals to teach local people how to deal with personal and family problems. The group was primarily concerned with deviant behavior, "school phobia," and family breakdowns.

Eighteen adults, most of whom worked in the community's social agencies, and 14 high-school students were selected as trainees. All attended lectures on the basic principles of behavior therapy and practice sessions in which some trainees would act out the parts of members of a family in crisis. Then, "problem families" were selected from a list of those whose children were often in trouble at school.

The lay therapists met with individuals and entire families about once a week. The purpose of these sessions was to show the clients how they interacted, and to teach them that if they behaved differently, they might solve their personal problems. All the participating families reported that their home life improved during the 8 weeks of the program. Nearly half the lay therapists planned to continue seeing "their" families after the program ended (Beier, Robinson, & Micheletti, 1971).

The community can involve itself in several areas. Two of the most important types of community action are:

1. *Prevention of mental illness.* The final report of the Joint Commission on Mental Health of Children in 1970 called for a new focus for mental

Community psychology seeks to prevent mental illness.
(Jim Anderson, Woodfin Camp & Associates)

health work. The commission found a need for the *prevention* of mental disorders rather than *treatment* after the disorders were already obvious (Hamm, 1974). But vigorous community action is needed to promote relevant research efforts and appropriate and innovative programs aimed at preventing mental illness in children. A crucial step in such an approach involves using school systems to monitor the physical and mental health of children.

2. *Crisis intervention.* Goldenberg (1973) characterizes this psychotherapeutic approach as "prompt, brief, here-and-now, and action-oriented" (p. 344). Among the clients of crisis intervention programs are adults with suicidal tendencies, adolescents with serious drug problems, and young children who are nervous about going to school. Crisis intervention is important in a community approach to mental health because "crisis centers" become involved in the most pressing social problems.

Iscoe (1974) stresses that community psychology should seek to create the *competent community*. In such a community, members can make sound and rational decisions about critical issues after carefully weighing all the available alternatives. They are not problem-free, but they are better able to cope with their community problems. The competent community fully develops all of its resources—especially the untapped human resources of its members. Ideally, it is as self-sufficient as possible and functions well without help from community psychologists. According to Iscoe, the goals of the competent community are not necessarily those of the mental health professionals; the community's goals might not conform to white, middle-class standards, for example. The community's goals spring from its own members and are related to their needs.

Application

HOW TO FIND HELP

As we have seen in this chapter, there is no such thing as *therapy* in a definitive sense; there are only *therapies*. There are probably as many approaches to therapy as there are practicing psychologists. While we have referred to a number of them in this chapter, there are others—many of them developed through a synthesis of various techniques and practices. Whole books could be—and have been—written to list the many people and organizations dedicated to helping people who feel they need some kind of counseling.

It should be clear by now that therapy and psychological counseling are not just intended to help "crazy" people. Unfortunately, the notion that seeking help for your problems is a sign of weakness or mental illness is hard to dispel. But the fact is that tens of thousands of people have been helped though psychological counseling and therapy. These people include business executives, artists, sports heroes, celebrities, and students. They are, in short, people like you and me. Problems are nothing to be ashamed of, and therapy—once considered a dark family secret—is today a common, useful aid in coping with daily living.

College is a time of stress and anxiety for many students. The pressure of work, the competition for grades, the exposure to different people with different views, the tension of relating to your peers—these and other factors add up to considerable emotional and physical stress. These problems can be made worse because many students are away from home for the first time. Most colleges and universities have their own counseling services—many as sophisticated as the best clinics in the country. Most communities also have a community mental health program. As an aid to a potential search for the right counseling service, however, we are including a list of some of the available resources for people seeking mental health professionals. Many of these services have national offices which, if contacted, will provide you with local branches and the appropriate people to contact in your area.

Alcohol and Drug Abuse

Alcohol and Drug Problems
  Association
1130 17th St. NW
Washington, D.C. 20036

National Clearinghouse for
  Alcohol Information
P.O. Box 2345
Rockville, Maryland 20852

National Clearinghouse for Drug
  Abuse Information
Room 110
1400 Rockville Pike
Rockville, Maryland 20852

Veterans Administration
Alcohol and Drug Dependency
  Services
810 Vermont Ave. NW
Washington, D.C. 20005

Association of Halfway Houses
Alcoholism Programs, Inc.
786 E. 7th St.
St. Paul, Minnesota 55106

General Service Board
Alcoholics Anonymous, Inc.
P.O. Box 459
Grand Central Station
New York, N.Y. 10017

For those with a friend or relative who has an alcohol problem:

Al-Anon Family Group Headquarters, Inc.
P.O. Box 182
Madison Square Station
New York, N.Y. 10010

Smoking

The National Congress of Parents
   and Teachers
700 North Rush St.
Chicago, Illinois 60611

Weight and Smoking Counseling
   Service
400 E. 59th St.
New York, N.Y. 10022
212–755–4363

Depression and Suicide

Rescue, Inc.
Room 25
Boston Fire Headquarters
115 Southampton St.
Boston, Massachusetts 02118
617–426–6600

International Association for
   Suicide Prevention
Suicide Prevention Center
1041 S. Menlo Ave.
Los Angeles, California 90006
213–381–5111

Payne Whitney Suicide
   Prevention Program
525 E. 68th St.
New York, N.Y. 10021
212–472–6162

National Save A Life League
815 Second Ave.
Suite 409
New York, N.Y. 10017
212–736–6191

Sexual and Sex-Related Problems

Community Sex Information, Inc.
P.O. Box 2858
Grand Central Station
New York, N.Y. 10017

Sex Information and Education
   Council of the United States
(SIECUS)
137–158 N. Franklin St.
Hempstead, New York 11550
516–483–3033

Mary Ann Largen
National Rape Task Force
   Coordinator
National Organization of Women
   Legislative Office
1107 National Press Building
Washington, D.C. 20004
202–347–2279

Association of Women in
   Psychiatry
Women's Studies Dept.
University of Delaware
34 W. Delaware
Newark, Delaware 19711

Association of Gay Psychiatrists
P.O. Box 29527
Atlanta, Georgia 30359
404–231–0751

Homosexual Community
   Counseling Center, Inc.
30 E. 60th St.
New York, N.Y. 10022
212–688–0628

Stress and Neurosis

American Academy of Stress
  Disorders
8 S. Michigan Ave.
Chicago, Illinois 60603
312–263–7343

Neurotics Anonymous
1341 G. St. NW
Room 426
Washington, D.C. 20005

National Commission Against
  Mental Illness
1101 17th St. NW
Washington, D.C. 20036
202–296–4435

For Help in Selecting a Therapy

Psychiatric Service Section
American Hospital Association
840 N. Lake Shore Drive
Chicago, Illinois 60611

Mental Health Help Line
789 West End Ave.
New York, N.Y. 10024
212–663–4372

Psychotherapy Selection Service
3 E. 80th St.
New York, N.Y. 10021
212–861–6387

General Information on Mental Health and Counseling

Mental Health Association
1800 N. Kent St.
Arlington, Virginia 22209
703–528–6405

The American Psychiatric
  Association
1700 18th St. NW
Washington, D.C. 20009

The American Psychological
  Association
1200 17th St. NW
Washington, D.C. 20036

The Mental Health Materials
  Center
419 Park Ave. South
New York, N.Y. 10016

The National Institute of Mental
  Health
1400 Rockville Pike
Rockwall Bldg.
Room 505
Rockville, Maryland 20850

Community Psychology Division
The American Psychiatric
  Association
c/o Barbara Dohrenwend
CUNY Graduate Center
33 W. 42nd St.
New York, N.Y. 10036

Counseling Division
The American Psychiatric
  Association
c/o Norman I. Kagan
Department of Education
Michigan State University
East Lansing, Michigan 48823

Rehabilitation Psychiatry Division
The American Psychiatric
  Association
c/o Durand Jacobs
VA Hospital
10701 East Boulevard
Cleveland, Ohio 44106

There are, in addition, several comprehensive guides to therapies, services, and practitioners. They should be available at your school or local library:

Allen, Robert D., ed. *The Mental Health Almanac.* New York: Garland STPM Press, 1978.

Detlefsen, Ellen Gay, ed. *The National Directory of Mental Health.* New York: Wiley, 1980.

Norback, Judith, ed. *The Mental Health Yearbook Directory.* New York: Van Nostrand Reinhold, 1980.

Park, Clara Claiborne, ed. *You Are Not Alone.* Boston: Little Brown, 1976.

Summary

1. Psychotherapy is a general term that covers a variety of therapies used in private practice, institutions, and in community programs. While psychotherapies are problem oriented, in recent years new therapies have been designed to help people develop skills, rather than to solve problems.
2. *Psychoanalysis,* as developed by Freud, is based on the belief that the anxiety and problems that cause a person to seek help are symptoms of repressed feelings from early childhood. Psychoanalysis brings these repressed feelings to consciousness, so that the person can directly deal with them by *working through* them. Successful analysis depends on the person's effort not to inhibit or control his or her thoughts and fantasies, but to express them in a process of *free association.* The analyst remains neutral and, for the most part, silent.
3. Many psychologists disagree with Freud's approach to psychotherapy. Alfred Adler felt that therapists must assure clients that they can take charge of their own lives. Otto Rank felt that

therapists should refuse clients' attempts to become dependent on them and encourage them to be strong. Karen Horney felt that therapy should teach people to give up illusions about themselves so that they don't have to make excuses for themselves. All these neo-Freudians believe that therapists should take an active role as they try to get their clients to focus on coping with current problems rather than on resolving past conflicts.

4. According to Carl Rogers' *client-centered therapy*, the gap between the real self and the ideal self is the source of anxiety. The goal of client-centered therapy is to help people to become fully functioning, to open them up to all of their experiences and to all of themselves so that they have no reason to act defensively. The client-centered therapist is *nondirective* and tries only to reflect the client's statements.

5. *Rational therapy* assumes that people are solely responsible for their feelings about themselves and thus for their happiness. Rational therapists directly show their clients how their misinterpretations of events are the cause for their problems and teach their clients to see events more rationally.

6. *Reality therapy* is also very directive and assumes that people are responsible for their own problems. Its primary goal is to help people behave responsibly.

7. There is debate about the effectiveness of psychotherapies. Eysenck found them to be as effective as no therapy at all. Other researchers have found psychotherapies to be highly effective.

8. Behaviorists reject the idea that behavior disorders are symptoms of hidden emotional conflicts and argue that the behavior disorder is the problem, not a symptom of the problem. *Behavior therapies* are based on the belief that all behavior is learned. The behavior therapist seeks to teach the client more satisfying behavior.

9. In *operant conditioning*, people learn to behave in different ways if new behaviors are rewarded and old behaviors are ignored. It works best when the therapist completely controls rewards and punishments.

10. *Aversive conditioning* eliminates specific behavior patterns by teaching clients to associate pain and discomfort with the undesirable response. When aversive conditioning might be harmful, *desensitization*, which gradually reduces irrational fear, can be more useful.

11. Wolpe believes that chronically anxious people may not know why they feel tense, but that they can distinguish between different levels of anxiety. The therapist establishes a *hierarchy* from the least to the most anxiety-producing situations and then teaches the person to relax. The therapist begins with the least threatening scene and works up to the most threatening one.

12. *Group therapies* allow both the therapist and the client to see the person interacting with others, give people a chance to shed

inhibitions and express themselves in a safe atmosphere, and provide a source of reinforcement.

13. *Traditional therapy groups* are an extension of individual psychotherapy and emphasize uncovering repressed feelings and conflicts. *Gestalt groups* emphasize the whole person and attempt to reawaken a person to his or her feelings. *Sensitivity groups* stress the here-and-now and are designed to enhance awareness by focusing on nonverbal communication and reawakening the senses. Encounter groups also stress the here-and-now. They demand that participants respond to the immediate situation and try to strip away the social pretenses of everyday life.

14. *Transactional analysis* is based on the assumption that people have three ego states: the Child, the Parent, and the Adult. By studying the communication between two or more people, the transactional analyst determines which ego state they are operating from, and helps to improve the communication by making them more aware of what they are communicating. *Family therapy* is based on the assumption that when one family member has problems, the whole family may need help. Family therapy is indicated when problems exist between husband and wife, parents and children, or other family members; when the gains a person makes in therapy are undermined by problems at home; or when a family member has trouble adjusting to another member's improvement

15. There is disagreement over the effects of group therapies. Encounter and sensitivity groups are criticized because their effects may be only short-term and because groups are often run by untrained "leaders" who may be unable to cope with the emotional intensity in the groups.

16. *Electroconvulsive shock therapy (ECT)* and *insulin shock treatment* are most often used to alleviate sudden and severe depression, especially in psychotics. After shock treatment the person is happier, more responsive, and more active; but shock can be harmful, and its use is declining. *Psychosurgery* is a drastic step to change a person's behavior and emotional state. Most therapists prefer *drug therapy* to either shock treatment or psychosurgery. Drugs do not cure psychological problems, but they do calm agitated and depressed people, help them to function more easily on a daily basis, and sometimes enable people to benefit from other forms of therapy.

17. People are institutionalized at their own request or that of family members, or by court order. State institutions are usually isolated from the community. Patients lose their legal rights, and may or may not receive therapy. Many institutions provide only custodial care. This level of care deprives patients of their personal identity and merely teaches them to be good patients. Some institutions return a patient to the community as soon as possible. The "dumping" of patients into communities without adequate re-

sources for their support and follow-up care, however, has also become a problem. In some cases, *halfway houses* enable ex-patients to work their way back into society.

18. *Token economies* seek to encourage patients to behave in ways that enable them to return to society. Psychologists reward patients for desirable behavior by giving them tokens that can be exchanged for various items or privileges.

19. The aims of *community psychology*, a developing school of research and practice, are to look for those in need instead of waiting for people to come for help, and to reach people for treatment before hospitalization becomes necessary. The goals of community psychology are to prevent mental illness and to educate the public. *Crisis intervention* programs are an important element of the community approach to mental health.

Outline

Chapter 15

Social Psychology

Imagine that you are about to go off on a vacation by yourself. It seems like a great idea: to get away from the people you have to live and work with, to be accountable just to yourself, to do just what you want to do and nothing more. But now imagine that this is a permanent situation. Just you. No one else. Chances are this scares you. We all crave privacy. Often, we want the crowds we meet every day to disappear. But the prospect of *no* social interaction with others profoundly disturbs most people. No matter how independent we think we are, our identity and our responses to the world are so bound up with other people that just imagining a world without them is chilling—if not absurd.

Our relationships with other people serve many functions. They test our own ideas and give us ideas and models of behavior that we would never have been able to find on our own. They also give us a sense of well-being and belonging, for the support we get from friends helps determine how we feel about ourselves.

Social psychology studies how people relate to and are affected by other people. How do we perceive them? Why do we like or dislike them? How do the groups we belong to influence us? What are the patterns of communication and leadership in groups? These are some of the questions social psychologists try to answer.

Life in groups is almost synonymous with human life. We meet people, we size them up, they size us up. We like or dislike them. They like or dislike us. We influence their attitudes and behavior. They influence ours. It is safe to say that humans have behaved this way for as long as our species has been on earth.

Interpersonal Relationships

PERSON PERCEPTION

How do we form our first impressions of people? What cues do we use? How accurate and reliable are we?

When two strangers meet for the first time, they notice each other's way of dressing, gestures, manner of speaking, tone of voice. They use these and other easily observable cues to make assumptions. We judge people by the look in their eyes, the firmness of their handshake, and so forth. No matter how little information we may have, no matter how contradictory it may be, no matter how many times we may have been wrong in the past, we still classify and categorize people.

We form our first impressions of people through external cues that fit them into particular categories. Then, on the basis of these categories, we draw inferences about people and adjust our own behavior accordingly. Our culture and the social groups that we belong to provide us with a range of "ready-made" inferences from particular, external cues: Fat people are jolly; people with long, thin fingers are sensitive; a person who is carefully dressed and groomed has an orderly mind, and so on. Our impressions of other people are also influenced by their emotions. As we noted in Chapter 9, we find emotional clues in facial expressions, posture, gestures, and the tone of voice. In most situations, our judgments from first impressions are reasonably accurate.

Undoubtedly, our perceptions about other people differ from our perceptions about inanimate objects. We may infer from looking at a car that it is new, needs repairs, or is expensive. We do not have to bother with moods

How do we form first impressions?

(Jim Anderson, Woodfin Camp & Associates)

and emotions. In meeting a person for the first time, however—no matter how accurate we feel our "first impressions" are—it is impossible to be sure about what that person is like. Is she acting the way she normally does? Is she reacting to pressures and forces we can't see? Our first impressions may be subject to biases which can mislead us about others.

INSUFFICIENT INFORMATION. This is a common cause of error in our first impressions of others. We often lack the time to form a reliable impression. For example, at a large party there may be so many people, so much noise, smoke, and general distraction, that the cues we perceive through the social and atmospheric haze are minimal and inadequate. If we categorize people under these circumstances, we often do so with qualifications: "I didn't really have a chance to get to know her." "It's hard to say what I think of him." Since we usually tend to categorize people rapidly, these reactions indicate that we did not have even the minimal cues.

MANIPULATION. People often give out false cues on purpose to reach a goal, to get power, and to influence others. These people are often referred to as *Machiavellian,* after Niccolò Machiavelli, a 16th-century Italian political philosopher. This is the attitude of the used-car dealer who acts like your best friend while selling you a lemon; of the politician who promises slum dwellers a new start and then complains about "welfare cheats" to wealthy audiences; and even of the classmate who becomes your confidante because he or she wants your answers to the history exam (Christie & Geis, 1970).

STEREOTYPING. Sometimes, we mislead ourselves by referring to general categories of behavior or personality that do not take sufficient account of the variations among people. This is called *stereotyping.* It results in the

INGRATIATION

Ingratiation is the process of managing the impressions you make on someone else in order to increase his or her feeling for you. Edward E. Jones (1972) extensively studied this kind of "impression management." He found three main reasons for people to be ingratiating:

1. *Acquisition,* or self-gain, such as a student "buttering up" a teacher to get a good grade.
2. *Protection,* as when a prisoner curries favor with a guard to be treated more kindly.
3. *Signification,* or a desire for the esteem of others. This is linked to the belief that if others like us, we must be worthy of their liking, and therefore must be worthy of our own self-esteem.

There are several ways to ingratiate. One tactic is outright flattery or compliments; this assumes that people find it hard to resist those who think highly of them. A second tactic is to conform to another person's opinions or behavior; this assumes that people find it hard to resist liking others who think and act like themselves. A third tactic is to present a favorable self-image; this assumes that people will respond positively to those who strongly present a positive view of themselves—though this can often backfire. Finally, one can do favors; this assumes that people are attracted to those who give them gifts or other rewards. It is important to note, however, that people are often repelled by gifts and rewards that they view as unsuitable. There is a big gap between "liking" someone and feeling socially indebted to him or her.

Stereotypes can be misleading. The man on the left, Charles Gordone, is a well-known playwright.
(Sherry Suris, Photo Researchers)

rigid categorizing of people on the basis of group membership, and the assumption that the stereotyped person has many traits associated with that group. For example, if we meet a 20-year-old college man and assume that he is a rock-and-roll fan and an avid beer drinker, we are stereotyping. Many 20-year-old college men prefer Bach to rock and milk to beer. Although some stereotypes have a kernel of truth—many college men do like rock and beer—they mostly distort facts.

LOGICAL ERROR AND DESIRE FOR CONSISTENCY. Perceptions of others may be distorted by *logical errors.* When people display one trait, we assume they have other traits that we associate with that first one. Because a man is intelligent, we also assume that he is competent. But this is not always true.

People evaluate other people according to their own biases. If we value a sense of humor, or a warm and generous manner, then we are likely to value a person with these traits. If we mistrust people who do not make eye contact it is because we may doubt their honesty and sincerity, even if they avoided our eyes because of shyness.

Certain traits influence our perceptions of people more than other traits do. Asch (1946) found that the traits "warm" and "cold"—as they relate to personality—are particularly influential, though their effects often depend on the context. If a person is described as "obedient, weak, shallow, unambitious, and vain," it makes no difference if that person is also described as warm. The negative picture of that person is not improved by his or her "warmth" (Freedman, Sears, & Carlsmith, 1981).

We also perceive people as behaving consistently over time. This is partly because we want to see our own behavior as consistent over time. It is also a human trait to seek—often in vain—for consistent behavior and responses. In fact, when we perceive two inconsistent aspects of another person—or ourselves—we strive to bring these two factors into a consistent balance. (See the discussion of dissonance theory later in this chapter.) For instance, if we learn that a trusted salesman who regularly tries to give us a bargain also robbed the store he works for, we may change our perception of his earlier kindness—"He was just buttering me up"—or we may see his dubious actions in a better light: "He was having money problems."

The so-called **halo** and **devil effects** are special cases of the desire for consistent behavior. If we like people, we see everything they do in a favorable light and attribute positive characteristics to them. If we dislike them, the reverse is true: We judge even their most unselfish acts harshly. This is true of our evaluations of both public figures—such as politicians—and of our friends and colleagues.

Although person perception is often inaccurate, inconsistent, and incorrect, we get by socially without major difficulties. One reason is that except in our most intimate and sustained personal relationships, we usually interact with others on the basis of assigned social roles. For example, there are certain broad patterns that define relationships between student and teacher. Once we identify the situation and the roles proper to it, the bulk of our interaction is determined. Although personal preferences may shape and color performances of a given role, as long as the basic obligations are met the relationship is accepted as satisfactory.

Indeed, in playing roles, it is sometimes wiser *not* to behave according to accurate perceptions of the personal qualities of those with whom we have to interact. The army private who correctly perceives that the platoon sergeant is stupid is well advised not to act on this accurate perception. Relationships between sergeant and private are defined by the military, and those who want to get along will go along with the rules. The same is true of most large groups such as schools, hospitals, businesses, or government agencies. Most social relationships in these groups do not depend on accurate personal perceptions.

ATTRIBUTION THEORY

We judge people's actions as well as their personalities. These inferences about the causes and effects of actions are also often based on limited external cues: facial expressions, gestures, language. How do we use these cues to make decisions about people's actions?

For one thing, we look for factors that accompany their behavior and that seldom occur in its absence. If, for instance, your mother is usually pleasant and in good spirits, but is invariably annoyed if you stay out all night, you might attribute her mood to your actions. If a close friend is usually shy but has a wild time at large parties, you might well attribute the craziness to the party environment. Whenever a cause *invariably* accompanies an effect, and in the absence of the cause the effect does not occur, we tend to attribute the effect to that cause. This is called the principle of **invariance.**

Kelley (1967) suggested that there are three different criteria of cause–effect relationships. First, does the behavior occur only in the presence of the stimulus object, or does the behavior occur with other objects too? For

Our inferences about people's behavior are often based on external clues like facial expressions and body posture.

(Michael Hanulak, Photo Researchers)

PEOPLE DO JUDGE BOOKS—AND PEOPLE—BY THEIR COVERS

Although many people hate to admit it, physical attraction seems to have a big effect on how we perceive and relate to others. If you asked a teacher or an employer if a certain man's or woman's good looks influenced that person's grade, position, or salary, you would probably get laughed at. But if you were to ask these same teachers and employers if they were *aware* of that person's physical attractiveness, most—if they're honest—would say that they were. The same holds true for most of our personal relationships.

In one study, college students were shown photographs of three other students. One was physically attractive, one was average, one was relatively unattractive. The subjects were asked to rate each of these people on 27 different personality traits, and were asked to predict each future happiness. The physically

attractive person was given the most desirable personality traits and the most uniform predictions of future happiness. Another study found that nursery-school children were more responsive to attractive than to less attractive peers. Moreover, teachers tend to be more lenient toward the bad behavior of an exceptionally attractive child, and to have higher expectations about his or her intelligence and grades.

This almost universal attitude toward physical attractiveness can become a "self-fulfilling prophecy." Physically attractive people may come to think of themselves as good or lovable because they are continually being treated that way. Conversely, "homely" people may begin to see themselves as bad or unlovable because they have always been regarded that way—even as children (Aronson, 1980).

example, to understand why Joan cries throughout a movie, you would consider the *distinctiveness* of the behavior: Does Joan cry often or is this rare? If the behavior is unique, then we attribute the cause to the stimulus object—the film—rather than to Joan. But we also consider other information: Does everyone else react in the same way to the stimulus object? What if Joan is the only person crying during the film? What if everybody else is crying too? If there is a *consensus* among others—everyone reacts the same way—we confirm that Joan is crying because the film is sad. Finally, we consider the *consistency* of Joan's behavior: If she cries every time she sees this film we again confirm that the film—the stimulus object—is the culprit. On the other hand, if Joan often cries at films, few other people find the film sad, and Joan always cries at this particular film, then we attribute the behavior to something in Joan herself: Perhaps she is "an emotional person," or "depressed," or whatever. Finally, if she seldom cries, nobody else cried, and she has never cried at this film before, then we conclude that something particular is causing her behavior—perhaps personal problems or a piece of bad news.

It is revealing that when we judge the causes of other people's behavior we underemphasize the effects of stimulus objects and context, and overemphasize factors internal to the person. But when we judge our own behavior, we do just the opposite (Jones & Nisbett, 1972). In other words, if a husband and wife are at a cocktail party, and the husband spends most of the evening chatting with an attractive young woman, the wife is likely to attribute this to personal qualities of her husband—perhaps his lack of esteem for her, his selfishness, his childishness, and so on. The husband, however, is more likely to attribute his actions to such external factors as the young woman's dynamic personality, her fascinating conversation, and so forth.

We are also inclined to make *defensive* attributions about the causes of behavior. That is, we are inclined to be biased in ways that preserve our self-esteem. Kingdon (1967) interviewed winning and losing political candidates in Wisconsin. He found that the winners attributed their victory to their own superior characteristics (internal factors). The losers, however, invariably attributed their defeat to their party label or to a misinformed public (external factors).

Another aspect of attribution is the tendency to blame events on the victim. If a person is in a car accident, we suspect that he or she may have been driving carelessly. Many people still believe that if a woman is raped, she must somehow have provoked it. Lerner (1965) suggests that this is because we wish to believe in a "just world," where goodness is rewarded and evil punished. This belief is demonstrably false. But that does not change how observers morally judge the events that affect others. This may be a defensive posture based on the human desire to avoid the random horrors of life. The unspoken idea is: This awful thing can't happen to me because it only happens to bad people who deserve it (Freedman, Sears, & Carlsmith, 1981).

Attribution processes are also involved in our judgments of social groups. Are the causes of delinquency internal—do some young people just have trouble adjusting to the world? Or are they external—the result of social deprivation, frustration, or the lack of good models? Do children in

(Hugh Rogers, Monkmeyer)

the ghetto grow up to be poor because they are not very smart? Or do they start with two strikes against them because of their subculture (Ashmore & McConahay, 1975)? Because our tendency to find external or internal causes for people's actions colors many of our political opinions and social attitudes, the attribution of cause has attracted much recent research.

ATTRACTION AND LIKING

So far we have seen how people form impressions of each other and judge the causes of their behavior. When people meet, what determines if they will like each other? This is the subject of much speculation and not a little mystification, with popular explanations running the gamut from fate to compatible astrological signs. Romantics believe that irresistible forces propel them toward an inevitable meeting with their beloved, but the people who run computer dating services, for example, take a more hardheaded view of the matter. Their criteria are *proximity, similarity of interests, complementary expectations,* and *rewardingness.*

PROXIMITY. Sheer proximity is decisive in determining who will become friends. Our friends are likely to live nearby. Although absence is said to

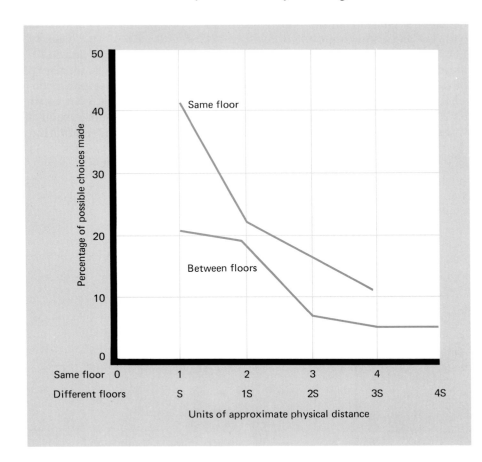

Figure 15–1
The relationship between proximity and liking. "Units of approximate physical distance" means how many doors apart the people lived—2S means 2 doors and a stairway apart. As you can see, the closer together people lived, the more likely they were to become friends.

(Reprinted from *Social Pressures in Informal Groups,* by Leon Festinger, Stanley Schachter, and Kurt Back, with the permission of the publisher, Stanford University Press. © 1950 by Leon Festinger, Stanley Schachter, and Kurt Back.)

Friendship often depends upon proximity.
(Ellen Pines Sheffield, Woodfin Camp & Associates)

make the heart grow fonder, it also causes friendships to fade. While relationships may be kept up through letters, they usually have to be reinforced by periodic visits or they will dissolve.

Festinger, Schachter, and Back (1950) investigated the effects of proximity on friendship. They chose a two-story apartment complex with five apartments to a floor. People moved into the complex randomly, so previous social attachments did not influence the results of the study. Forty-four percent of the residents said they were most friendly with their next-door neighbors. Twenty-two percent saw the people who lived two doors away the most often socially. Only 10 percent said that their best friends lived as far away as down the hall. People were even less likely to be friendly with those who lived upstairs or downstairs from them (see Figure 15-1).

One way to explain the effects of proximity is that the more people see each other, the more they like each other. This has also been shown with photographs (Zajonc, 1968). People were shown groups of photographs of other people. Some of the photographs were repeated at random. The more often people saw these particular faces, the more they came to like them. Familiarity, it seems, does not always breed contempt; sometimes it leads to liking.

SIMILARITY. Given proximity, similarity of interests is the basis for most friendships. We are more likely to want to develop deeper relationships with people who share our interests, attitudes, and values. The more we have in common, the greater the chance of our getting to know and to like another person. When we know that people share our attitudes, we tend to have more positive feelings toward them and to be more complimentary when evaluating them (Byrne, 1961). The weight and the subject of the issue of agreement do not seem to matter as much as the proportion of shared attitudes (Byrne & Nelson, 1964). No matter how many similarities

It is easier to be friends with those who share our interests, attitudes, and values.
(Rohn Engh, Photo Researchers)

we share with other people, however, we may not be attracted to them if we view ourselves negatively. According to Leonard (1975), if we feel good about ourselves, we are attracted to others with similar traits. If we have a negative self-concept, we move away from people who are similar to ourselves.

Sometimes *perceived* similarity is more important than actual similarity (Marsden, 1966). We often believe or assume that we share attitudes with people who attract us in other ways. Some findings (Rosenblood & Goldstein, 1969) indicate that similarity in intelligence is more important than shared attitudes or opinions in determining if people will like each other. And agreement following prior disagreement leads to more attraction than does agreement from the start (Sigall & Aronson, 1967).

COMPLEMENTARITY. Opposites do sometimes attract. Such relationships are based on complementarity rather than similarity. Quiet people are generally more comfortable around other quiet people, but often two friends or a married couple seem to be made up of an extravert and an introvert. One person's need to talk is met by the other person's need to listen. Perhaps this is why we sometimes like people in one role but dislike them in another. If you are used to your friend's playing straight man to your jokes, you may not like it if he starts telling his own jokes.

REWARDINGNESS. We all like people who say nice things about us, and being liked by a person generally increases the chances that we will like him or her in return. Being praised and being liked are *rewarding*. But the tendency to like someone who speaks well of you is not that simple, as some recent research has shown.

Aronson (1980) postulates a theory of interpersonal attraction that he calls the gain–loss theory. This theory suggests that *increases* in rewarding behavior influence our perception of someone more than constant positive behavior does. In other words, if a man were to meet and talk with the same woman at three successive parties, and if, during these conversations, her attitude toward him changed from polite indifference to overt flattery, he would be inclined to like this woman more than if she had immediately started praising him during their first conversation and continued the praise each time they met. The reverse is also true. You are more likely to take seriously a person's bad opinion of you if it slides from positive to negative than if it is immediately negative. You will also tend to like that person less than one who simply expressed a lack of interest in you from the start.

The gain–loss theory also postulates that people close to us are less likely to provide us with strong rewards in love and esteem precisely because we have come to expect this kind of behavior from them. They also can deal the worst blows to our esteem, however, because we expect this constant level of affection and appreciation.

LOVING

Although psychologists have long studied why people like each other, the study of love, and of why people fall in love with each other, was largely

Psychologists have only recently begun to study why people fall in love.
(Ellen Pines Sheffield, Woodfin Camp & Associates)

ignored until recently. There are many reasons for this. One is that studying love requires more than the kind of quick testing and random sampling that are sufficient to measure simple attraction or stereotyping. Also, love is a concept that is much discussed but seldom defined. Finally, like the study of human sexual response, love was considered too intimate, personal, and mysterious to study scientifically and systematically. With the coming of the "sexual revolution," however, and with the rapid rise in the divorce rate, many psychologists decided that studies of love are not only pertinent but important.

Rubin (1973) defined love as the combination of three elements:

1. *Caring.* The feeling that another person's emotions and gratifications are as important to you as your own.
2. *Attachment.* The need or desire to make physical contact with the other, to be approved of and cared for.
3. *Intimacy.* The bond or link between two people.

Having defined love, Rubin made a scale to measure it, and to distinguish it from *liking.* Subjects were asked to complete questions such as, "If I could never be with _____, I would feel miserable." They answered the questions first about lovers, then about friends. The results showed that while friends and lovers were both liked, they were distinguished from each other on the "love scale." The very existence of this measuring instrument has encouraged research on love.

Some research on love indicates, for example, that there is such a thing as a "Romeo and Juliet" effect. That is, the intensity of love increases when faced with parental opposition. Similarly, lovers of different religions score higher in the intensity of their love. While this accords with the popular belief that love flourishes in adversity, this effect may be only temporary. Rubin found that the strength of interfaith relationships was enhanced for couples who were together for less than 18 months, but the pattern was reversed for couples who were together longer. They scored lower in intensity on the "love scale" than did lovers of the same faith (Rubin, 1973).

INTERPERSONAL INFLUENCE

Just the presence of other people affects our behavior and attitudes. We compare our ideas and feelings with those of others, we rate our performance against them, we conform with or resist their attitudes and expectations, and we behave differently with others than when we are alone.

SOCIAL COMPARISON. The theory of **social comparison,** first elaborated by Leon Festinger (1954), proposes that people need to evaluate themselves. Without objective scales, they compare themselves with other people. When we want to know where we stand against the competition, we usually pick people we feel are close to us in attitudes or skills and compare ourselves with them. For example, a graduate student in physics rates her performance against that of her fellow students, rather than against a poet or against Albert Einstein.

CONFORMITY. **Conformity** is not simply the act of doing what others do. For instance, millions of Americans drink coffee in the morning, but they do not do so to conform. Conformity implies that a person has yielded his or her own preferences or beliefs to those of a larger group. Conformity implies conflict between what a person wants or thinks and what a group expects.

Of course, we all conform in some ways to what society wants from us. We wear clothes in public and drive on the right side of the road. But conformity varies from person to person and from situation to situation. Often, disdain for conformity leads not to individuality but to *counterconformity*. This is seen in rebellious children who do just the opposite of what their parents want. Thus, even in opposition to conformity, most people are still bound in some ways by the rules of a larger group.

Many factors influence conformity. In a group where no one knows how to proceed, conformity is usually high. There is "safety" in going along with the group. Also, if the group seems sure about something that a person is not, the chances for conformity are increased. Both implicit and explicit pressure are also important in causing conformity. That is, the threat of punishment or the fear of being rejected or shunned by the group is also important in causing conformity. Indeed, fear in general—of punishment, of isolation, of appearing foolish, of being disliked—is one of the strongest contributors to conformity. *Identification* is also important. If someone or some group you respect and consider important to you acts or thinks in a certain way, you will also be influenced to think and act in that way (Kelman, 1961). (See the discussion of reference groups later in this chapter.)

In a series of experiments, Asch (1951) demonstrated the importance of group pressures to conform, even when this resulted in the denial of physical evidence. The study ostensibly tested visual judgment. People were asked to choose from a card with several lines of differing lengths the line most similar to the line on a comparison card (see Figure 15–2). The

Even in opposition to conformity, most people are bound by the rules of a group.
(Jim Anderson, Woodfin Camp & Associates)

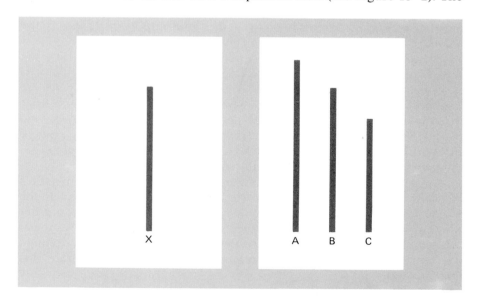

X   A   B   C

Figure 15–2
In Asch's experiment on conformity, subjects were shown a comparison card like the one on the left, and were asked to indicate which of the three lines on the card on the right was the most similar.

lines were deliberately drawn so that the comparison was obvious and the correct choice was clear. All but one of the subjects were planted by the experimenter. On certain trials, these people deliberately gave the same wrong answer. This put the subject on the spot. Should he conform to what he knew to be a wrong decision and agree with the group, thereby denying the evidence of his own senses, or should he disagree with the group and not conform?

Most subjects chose to conform about 35 percent of the time. There were large individual differences, however. Some subjects never conformed. Others conformed most of the time. A variety of experiments using different stimuli have confirmed this result.

OBEDIENCE TO AUTHORITY. Conformity and obedience are related, since people look at the opinions and beliefs of others for guidance. But obedience differs from conformity in two ways. First, conformity implies compliance to a *group*, while obedience refers to compliance with the orders or guidelines of a single person (a leader) or of a *symbolic* person (a government). Second, conformity often involves only implicit pressure by the group to move someone in a desired direction. But obedience to authority is usually explicit. The authority figure commands, a person obeys. There is often no attempt to explain, rationalize, or persuade.

Several studies by Milgram that were mentioned in Chapter 1 showed how far many people will go to obey someone in authority (Milgram, 1963). When "teachers" were told to give "learners" an electric shock for each wrong answer, almost 67 percent of them obeyed and gave what they thought was a near lethal shock. Other research supports Milgram's findings. A survey showed that 67 percent of Americans felt most people would act as William Calley did when he carried out an order to shoot women and children in the Vietnamese hamlet of My Lai (Kelman & Lawrence, 1972).

What factors influence the degree to which people will do what they are told? Studies in which people were asked to put a dime in a parking meter by people wearing uniforms showed that one important factor is the amount of power vested in the person giving the orders (Brickman, 1974). A guard whose uniform looked like a policeman's was obeyed more often than either a man dressed as a milkman or a civilian. Another factor is surveillance. If we are ordered to do something and then left alone, we are less likely to obey than when we are being watched. This seems to be truer when the order involves an unethical act. Most of Brickman's subjects still put a dime in the meter when the policeman–impersonator was out of sight, but Milgram found that his "teachers" were less willing to give severe shocks when the experimenter left the room.

Milgram's experiments showed other factors that influence a person's ability to follow orders. When the victim was in the same room as the teacher, obedience dropped sharply. When another "teacher" was present who refused to give shocks, obedience also dropped. But when responsibility for an act is shared, so that the person is only one of many doing it, obedience is much greater. Executions by firing squads illustrate this principle.

What makes people willing to obey an authority figure, even if it means violating their own principles? Milgram (1974) thinks that people feel obliged to those in power. First, because they respect their credentials and assume they know what they are doing; and second, because often they have established trust with the people in authority by agreeing to do whatever they ask. Once this happens, subjects may feel conflict about what they are doing, but through rationalization can "forget" about it and thus minimize the conflict.

These experiments show people's willingness to obey someone in authority. But obedience doesn't just extend to specific authority figures. We are so socialized to following the norms of our culture that we sometimes find it impossible to go against them. Try singing at the top of your lungs on a crowded bus, for example, or asking a total stranger for his or her subway seat without saying that you feel faint or have a twisted ankle. Milgram had his own students try this (Tavris, 1974), and they found that while they could easily envision themselves doing such things, it was virtually impossible to do them. The words stuck in their throats when they came face-to-face with a seated subway passenger or when they settled into their seat in the bus. It's not easy to go against authority, in the form of a person or a custom.

SOCIAL FACILITATION. How does the presence of other people affect performance? Does it make a difference? And if so, what difference and under what conditions? On many tasks, research shows that subjects do work faster in groups than alone, even when the tasks are explicitly noncompetitive and the results are not compared. Energy output increases and, for relatively simple tasks, productivity also goes up. In some cases, it does not seem to matter if the people in the group are working with the subjects or just observing them—their presence alone stimulates subjects to perform better (Zajonc, 1965, 1966).

But the effects of competition and of having an audience vary. Often a simple task goes slower (Cottrell, Rittle, & Wack, 1967). Competition can produce anxiety and the sort of motivation that interferes with performance. In some experiments, women performed better when they worked alone than when they worked with men. The presence of others can be distracting, especially when people have to learn something. Zajonc (1965, 1966) found that the presence of an audience improved people's performances of tasks they knew well, but interfered with their doing something unfamiliar.

DEINDIVIDUATION

People sometimes act differently in a group than they would by themselves. Perhaps the most striking and frightening instance of this is *mob behavior*. Some well-known violent examples are the beatings and lynchings of blacks, the looting that sometimes accompanies urban rioting, and the wanton destruction of property that occurs during otherwise peaceful protests and demonstrations. After a power blackout in New York City in 1977 during which considerable looting took place, some of the looters were interviewed. These interviews indicated that many people would

(Alon Reininger, Woodfin Camp & Associates)

never have thought of looting had they been alone, and that others were later shocked by their own behavior.

One reason for such behavior is that people lose their personal sense of responsibility in a group, especially in a group subjected to intense pressures and anxiety. This is called **deindividuation** because people respond not as individuals, but as anonymous parts of a larger group. In general, the more anonymous people feel in a group, the less responsible they feel as persons.

In one study, groups of four women were recruited to take part in a study supposedly involving responses to strangers (Zimbardo, 1969). In one group, the women were greeted by name, wore name tags, and were easily identifiable. In another group, they wore oversized white lab coats and hoods over their heads. They resembled members of the Ku Klux Klan and were not identifiable at all. The groups were given an opportunity to deliver electric shocks to a woman not in the group. The subjects who were "deindividuated" gave almost twice as many electric shocks as did the subjects who were clearly identifiable. Apparently, being "deindividuated" produced more aggressive and hostile behavior. This supports the idea that a loss of a feeling of individuality may be a major cause of the violent, antisocial behavior sometimes shown by groups.

Deindividuation partly explains mob behavior. Another factor is that, in a group, one strongly dominant and persuasive person can convince people to act through a "snowball effect": Convince a few, and they convince others. Moreover, large groups provide *protection*. Anonymity makes it difficult to press charges. If two, or even ten people start smashing windows, they will probably be arrested. If a thousand people do it, very few of them could be caught or punished.

It is important to note that the behavior of large groups is *not* always negative. Groups have helped victims of disasters, have rebuilt houses destroyed by fires or floods, and have collected money for the needy. In other words, groups can influence people to behave both negatively and positively.

ALTRUISTIC BEHAVIOR. Our treatment of others is often motivated by our own self-interest. We offer our boss a ride home from the office because we know that our next promotion depends on how much he or she likes us. We

Residents and volunteers helped to sandbag the flood waters threatening this town on the Illinois River. Without their efforts, damages would have been much worse. (UPI)

volunteer to water our neighbors' lawn while they are away because we want to use their pool. But if this kind of behavior is *not* linked to personal gain, it is called **altruistic** or **helping behavior.** A person who acts in an altruistic way does not expect any recognition or reward in return, except perhaps the good feelings that come from helping the needy. Many altruistic acts, including many charitable contributions, are directed at strangers and are made anonymously (Freedman, Sears, & Carlsmith, 1981; Hoffman, 1977).

Under what conditions is altruistic behavior likely to occur? According to Moriarty (1975), increasing the amount of personal responsibility one person feels for another also increases the likelihood of altruistic support. In his experiment, subjects were more likely to try to stop the theft of a stranger's property if they had promised to watch the property while the stranger was away than if they had had no contact with him or her. The amount of empathy we feel with another person also affects our willingness to act in an altruistic way. Krebs (1975) found that when subjects felt that their values and personalities were similar to a victim's, they were more likely to try to help even if their own safety were jeopardized. The ambiguity of a situation also affects the likelihood of altruistic help. When bystanders are sure that there is an emergency, they will usually try to help the person in need. When they are less certain, their rate of response decreases (Clark & Word, 1974).

The ambiguity of an emergency partly explains certain instances of bystander apathy. One of the most infamous examples of apathy occurred during the killing of Kitty Genovese:

Kitty Genovese is set upon by a maniac as she returns from work at 3 A.M. Thirty-eight of her neighbors in Kew Gardens come to their windows when she cries out in terror; none come to her assistance even though her stalker takes over half an hour to murder her. No one even so much as calls the police. She dies. (Latane & Darley, 1970)

Kitty Genovese's neighbors were not indifferent to her cries. But some of them mistook them for a lovers' quarrel into which they had no right to intrude. Are there other reasons why bystanders might refuse to help in an emergency?

485

To further study the issue of bystander apathy, Latane and Darley questioned people who did not help a subject who staged a "fit" during an experiment. Nonhelpers were nervous and emotional, not apathetic. Most seemed to doubt that the emergency was real. Conflict between the costs of helping—especially if there is no real emergency—and the guilt of not helping causes anxiety. Unfortunately for the victims, guilt is not enough to make most people risk making fools of themselves.

The failure to help in an emergency is increased by the presence of others who are passive. In one experiment, subjects completing a questionnaire heard a taped "emergency" in the next room, complete with a crash and screams. Of those who were alone, 70 percent offered help, but of those who were with an experimenter who did nothing, only 7 percent offered help (Latane & Rodin, 1969).

Although people are often unwilling to help in an emergency, they may help in situations that are not urgent, especially if the help is minor and costs little. Most will give strangers the time or directions. And in another study, 34 percent of those interviewed would give a stranger a dime (Latane & Darley, 1970).

RISK-TAKING. Another interesting aspect of the psychology of group behavior is that people are more willing to take risks in a group than on their own. We are often confronted with choices between acts that are less risky but yield lower returns, and acts that are more risky but yield higher returns. Alone, we choose the less risky situation. In a group, however, people pick the higher risk.

In a series of studies, subjects were exposed to many complex business and political decisions. They carefully considered the situations and were given a list of options, with a numerical estimate of the risk involved. ("The chances are 3 in 10 that the foreign country will remain politically stable.") First subjects made their decisions alone. They were then brought into a group, asked to discuss the situation, and to reach a unanimous decision. There was a strong tendency for the group decision to involve more risk than the decisions made by the individuals (Freedman, Sears, & Carlsmith, 1981).

Researchers proposed four reasons to explain increased risk-taking in groups (Davis, Laughlin, & Komorita, 1976). First, those group members who are more likely to take risks may persuade others to join them. Second, reluctant group members become more aware of new arguments in favor of the higher risk, which may change their minds. Third, as we just noted, deindividuation in a group diffuses responsibility for the consequences of an act. Finally, the pressure to conform, as we have also seen, is often too much for people to resist, thus moving them toward the greater risk demanded by the group.

A last point about taking risks is that people in our society admire risk-taking skill. Brown (1965) asked people to rate themselves on their risk-taking. Then he told them how high another group of people had been rated. A significant number of Brown's subjects then revised their own rating to show even more risk-taking than before. This suggests that comparisons between group members may help shift them toward riskier decisions.

Group Structure and Dynamics

Although the group's influence on a person's behavior is an important aspect of group behavior, there are numerous other aspects that are equally complex and equally important to social psychology. Let us now turn to group structures and processes. How is leadership exerted? How do group members communicate with one another? How do groups solve problems?

LEADERSHIP

A group may be formal or informal, task oriented or purely social, but it is sure to have a leader. The leader may be a formal leader—the chairman of the board, for instance—or merely the member who exerts the strongest influence on the group. Group leadership can be self-perpetuating, or it may change, as in a parliamentary system when a vote of "no confidence" causes the government to fall.

There are many theories about the emergence of group leaders. The dominant theory for many years was the so-called "great man theory." This theory states that leaders are extraordinary people who assume positions of influence and then shape events around them. In this view, Washington, Napoleon, and even Hitler were "born leaders" who would have led any nation at any time in history.

Most historians and psychologists now regard this theory as naive, and claim that it ignores social and economic factors. For instance, had Germany not lost World War I and suffered a crippling depression, its people might not have been open to the nationalistic fervor that Hitler preached. Moreover, had Hitler been born in America, his chances of becoming a world leader in the 1930s would have been much less.

A more popular theory suggests that leadership is the result of the right person being in the right place at the right time. For instance, in the late 1950s and early 1960s Dr. Martin Luther King, Jr. emerged as the leader of the black civil rights movement. Dr. King was clearly a "great man": intelligent, dynamic, eloquent, and highly motivated. Yet, had the times not been right, it is doubtful that he would have been as successful as he was (Wrightsman & Deaux, 1981).

Status also appears to be a prime factor in leadership. A high-status person is likely to become a leader even if this status is totally unrelated to the group in question. Strodtbeck, Simon, and Hawkins (1958) conducted mock trials in which participants were asked to act as a jury and to pick a foreman. There was a strong tendency to pick someone who was of a relatively high professional status. Proprietors—management level professionals—were chosen almost twice as often as laborers. Thus, even in a nominally democratic group such as a jury, socioeconomic status proved to be a major deciding factor in picking a leader.

Many physical and intellectual attributes may also be important in determining a leader. But with rare exceptions, leaders must not stand out from the group too strongly. A well-known nonconformist is unlikely to

Dr. Martin Luther King.
(Dan Budnik, Woodfin Camp & Associates)

become a group leader. More often, a leader is a strong representative of the group—someone who typifies the status quo and embodies the qualities that the group likes to think it possesses.

PATTERNS OF COMMUNICATION

No group exists without communication: the exchange of information, feelings, and attitudes among its members. Group effectiveness often depends on the effectiveness of its communications. A group works out various mechanisms so that its leaders and its members are reciprocally informed about what is happening in the group and between the group and its external environment.

In an *authoritarian* system, communications are directed from the leader to the members. A *democratic* system emphasizes discussion and consensus on decisions. In almost any group, leaders talk more than other members. Some members may be consulted extensively about their area of expertise, but otherwise do not enter into the communication system. Still others may specialize in communicating feelings and emotions, and thus help relieve group tensions.

Psychologists have identified various communication patterns or *networks* and have explored their consequences for group effectiveness and member satisfaction. Among the common patterns (illustrated in Figure 15–3) are the *circle*, the *chain*, the *Y-shape*, and the *wheel*.

These communication networks are studied by arranging people so that they can communicate, using written notes or an intercom, only in the pattern under investigation. The group is then given a task, and as the members work, the observers study how the communication network operates. The results clearly show that the structure of the communication

A democratic system emphasizes discussion and consensus.
(Dick Hanley, Photo Researchers)

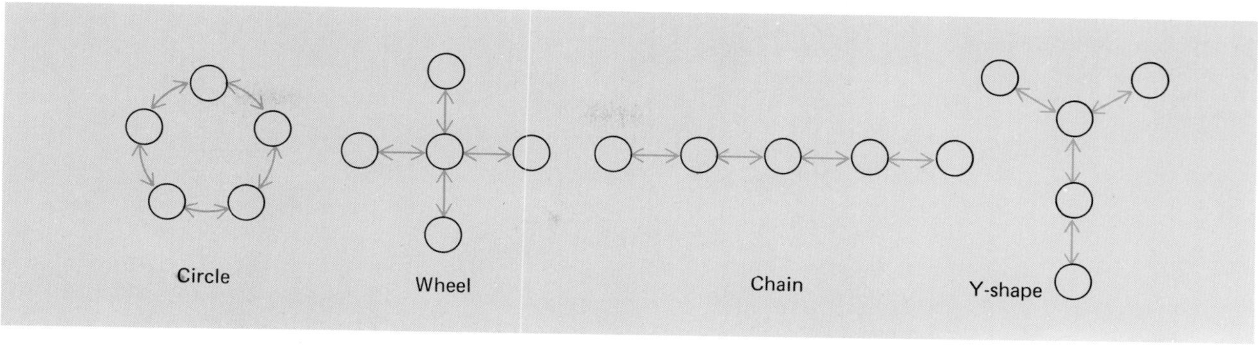

Figure 15–3
Common communication net-
works. Arrows indicate who
can talk to whom and the
overall flow of discussion.

Circle Wheel Chain Y-shape

network affects the group's ability to solve problems and the satisfaction of its members.

In the circle arrangement, the leader is not set apart, but is an equal member of the group. In the wheel arrangement, only the leader, the person at the center, can talk to everyone else. The others can communicate only through the leader. In the chain network, the people at the end have access to only one other person. In a five-person Y-shaped arrangement, the person in the center position has more access to others than those at the ends.

In general, those at the centers of the communications networks are named most often as leaders by the members of the group. The more a position in a network allows its occupant to communicate, the more satisfaction the occupant expresses. The decentralized circle network seems to be best at solving complex problems. The tightly centralized wheel is more effective in solving simple problems that are easily directed by the person at the center.

Communication networks become less rigid as the members get to know one another better. Less formal patterns of communication—and hence of influence and leadership—develop in time. Even where, as in many large organizations, the communication system is defined by a formal organizational chart, there are often informal systems of communication that bypass the formal pattern. In almost every academic department, the chairman's secretary has more to say about what goes on than do most of the instructors. The secretary is at the center of the network of communication and controls access to the boss. The secretary may not exercise it, but will have considerable informal power by virtue of holding a strategic position in the communication network.

PROBLEM SOLVING

We have already noted the phenomenon of the **risky shift,** the tendency of persons acting together in groups to take more risks than they would alone.

Is it better to try to solve a problem alone or in a group? One study compared people working alone with people working with others to produce creative ideas in response to open-ended questions (Taylor, Berry, & Block, 1958). Each group of five was measured against five individuals.

Group problem solving may be less effective than individual problem solving.
(Sylvia Johnson, Woodfin Camp & Associates)

The latter got 68.1 ideas in all, compared with 37.5 for the group. Those working alone had 19.8 creative ideas versus 10.8 from the group. When alone, people let themselves go more, worried less about competition, were freer of criticism. When people express their own ideas and follow their own impulses, the result is more productivity, creativity, and concentration.

Janis (1972) shares this negative view of group decision-making. Strong pressure to conform, he believes, prevents people from expressing critical ideas. In a group, amiability and morale take precedence over judgment. As group cohesiveness increases, self-criticism decreases, and members seem more willing to act at the expense of nonmembers. Members with doubts may hesitate to express them. The result may be bad decisions—the Bay of Pigs invasion or the Watergate coverup, for example.

Group problem solving is inferior to individual problem solving even when the group is told to "brainstorm." In brainstorming, subjects put aside their inhibitions and say what is on their minds, no matter how silly or out of line. Despite the belief that group brainstorming produces more ideas than individual brainstorming, evidence shows otherwise. When groups and individuals were asked to determine the possible consequences of a hypothetical event, more ideas were produced by subjects who brainstormed by themselves than by those who worked in small groups (Lamm & Trommsdorff, 1973). The researchers point out, however, that the complex political, business, and scientific problems of everyday life may be better dealt with in group settings. The solution of these problems benefits from the organizational ability of the group, including its ability to assign specific activities to group members according to their skills. Moreover, a group may have resources that a person lacks. In devising ways to stop airplane hijackings, for example, a group composed of an engineer, a pilot, a flight attendant, a passenger, and a bomb expert will come up with more ideas than any one person could.

Where different skills and a division of labor are useful, mixed groups do better than homogenous ones. When group members are of different sexes, ages, and backgrounds, the group is usually more effective. Groups also seem to be more efficient when the members know each other well. Each member's specific strengths and weaknesses are known to the group. Abilities can thus be used effectively, and shortcomings can be compensated for.

We learned earlier that people take more risks in a group than when acting alone. But Myers and Lamm (1975) found that this is not always true in group discussions and problem solving. The tendency toward a risky shift in problem solving may be affected by the initial dominant point of view of some of the group members. Group discussion, according to the researchers, is likely to enhance the group members' initial responses rather than change them. If the prediscussion consensus was toward greater risk, then the group discussion is likely to shift the response further in that direction. But if caution dominated the group's initial viewpoint, the group problem-solving process is likely to increase it.

Attitudes

The phrase "I don't like his attitude" is a telling one. We may be drawn to someone on various levels yet be unable to relate to his "attitude." This may be a major factor in how well we can work with, live with, or socialize with this person. People are often told to "get a better attitude." What does this mean? Just what are *attitudes* and how are they defined and measured? How are they formed? Can they be changed?

THE NATURE OF ATTITUDES

An attitude toward something has three major components: *beliefs* about the object, *feelings* about the object, and a *tendency to behave* in certain ways toward the object. Beliefs include facts, opinions, and our general knowledge about the object. Feelings include love, hate, like, dislike, and similar sentiments. The tendency to behave implies the likelihood—though not the conviction—that certain actions toward the object will occur, given our feelings and beliefs.

Suppose a man believes that all the members of the women's movement are wild-eyed radicals who want to overturn the social order. This attitude may be supported (rationalized) by facts and reasons that he has derived from the news media. The man's attitude, however, probably stems not from the news coverage but from an emotional response. Thus, his beliefs are strongly influenced by his feelings of fear and dislike. This, in turn, influences his behavior toward members of the women's movement. He might, for example, avoid contact with any women he considered a part of the movement. He might ridicule them in conversation, or even work against them.

(Timothy Eagan, Woodfin Camp & Associates)

ATTITUDES AND BEHAVIOR

Most people would probably agree that attitudes directly influence behavior. This, of course, explains why social psychologists have spent so much time and energy measuring attitudes—to be able to predict behavior. But evidence indicates that behavior does not always relate directly to attitudes.

In a classic study in 1934, R. T. LaPiere demonstrated this differential between attitudes and behavior. LaPiere traveled through the United States with an Oriental couple—at a time when prejudice against Orientals was still high in this country. LaPiere discovered that they were refused service at only 1 of the 250 hotels and restaurants they stopped at. Later, LaPiere wrote to each of the establishments they had visited and asked if they would provide service for Chinese people. Of those who replied, 92 percent said they would refuse to accept Chinese guests. A similar study was carried out with a black woman and two white women (Kutner, Wilkins, & Yarrow, 1952). Again, although the women were not refused service in any of the 11 restaurants they selected, over 50 percent of the establishments later stated they would refuse to serve such a group.

Attitudes may have little influence on behavior because the relevant attitude may be weak; other attitudes may also be involved in influencing the behavior; the general attitude measured may not have much to do with the specific behavior being studied; and, as we have seen, behavior is also influenced by conformity and obedience (Freedman, Sears & Carlsmith, 1981). It is clear, however, that where a strong, relevant attitude is closely related to the behavior under study, where few other attitudes are relevant, and where few facts contradict the attitude, behavior does in fact closely match the attitude. In other—more realistic—situations, the relationship, however, is likely to be less impressive.

THE DEVELOPMENT OF ATTITUDES

How do we acquire our attitudes? Where do they come from? Many of our most basic attitudes come from early, direct personal experience. A toddler, for example, is likely to enjoy her first bowl of ice cream because of its sweet, cool taste, and because her mother connects the ice cream with pleasure. Children are reinforced with positive smiles and encouragement when they please their parents, and they are punished through disapproval when they displease them. These early experiences give the child enduring positive and negative attitudes toward objects (Oskamp, 1977). Attitudes are also formed by imitation. Children ape the behavior of their parents and peers, and thus acquire attitudes even when no one is trying to influence their beliefs.

Moreover, children are exposed to highly selective information, even on controversial issues. Thus, children adopt the same beliefs as those around them. This is particularly true of simple, recurrent, concrete issues, such as presidential elections. A national survey of high-school seniors and their parents revealed that 83 percent agreed on their choice of presidential candidate. Parents, however, appear to have a smaller influence on more

(William Hubbell, Woodfin Camp & Associates)

complex issues, such as civil liberties or personal trust (Freedman, Sears, & Carlsmith, 1981).

REFERENCE GROUPS. But parents are not the only source of attitudes, and often they are not even the most lasting influence in our lives. Our teachers, friends, and even famous people can be more important. If a young man joins a fraternity, for example, he may model his behavior and attitudes on those of the members. If a young woman idolizes one of her teachers, she may adopt many of her attitudes toward controversial subjects, even if they run counter to attitudes expressed by her parents.

In a famous study done in 1943, Theodore Newcomb researched the beliefs and attitudes of students at Bennington College in Vermont. The Bennington students, largely from upper-class, conservative families, generally arrived as freshmen with conservative values. By graduation, however, their attitudes had been greatly liberalized (see Figure 15–4). The largely liberal faculty and a student body which constantly reinforced these attitudes—the most popular women were the more liberal students—became the new reference group for the freshmen. These liberal attitudes persisted 20 years later. In other words, the attitudes developed from the college **reference group** became the dominant attitudes of these women's lives.

This tendency for basic political attitudes to persist in adult life is widespread. Melville (1972) surveyed students who were arrested for participating in the Free Speech Movement of the late 1960s at the University of California. These students five years later still retained their

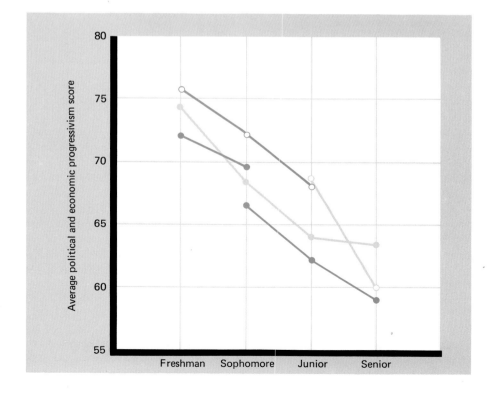

Figure 15–4
The changes in political attitudes during the college years in five classes at Bennington College. The lower the score, the more liberal the attitudes.
(Adapted from data in T. M. Newcomb, *Personality and Social Change.* Copyright 1943 by T. M. Newcomb. Reprinted by permission of Holt, Rinehart, and Winston and Theodore M. Newcomb.)

Berkeley, 1966.
(UPI)

radical political beliefs, although few of them were as politically active as they had been in college.

MASS MEDIA. Television and newspapers also have a great impact on the formation of attitudes in our society. Television bombards us with messages—not merely through commercials, but in more subtle ways: Violence is a commonplace in life . . . women are dependent on men . . . without possessions your life is empty, and so on.

Gerbner and Gross (1974) found that the attitudes of people who often watch television are more consistent with the stereotypes that are seen on television than are the attitudes of those who seldom watch it. They also found that black teenagers who watch television a lot perceive white people more positively than they perceive other blacks. This apparently reflects the fact that middle-class whites are shown on television much more than middle-class blacks are.

Similarly, Hartmann and Husband (1971) found that, without experience of their own, children rely on television to form their social attitudes. They found that white children in England who had little contact with nonwhites tended to associate race relations with conflicts and hostility more often than white children who lived in integrated neighborhoods. The first group of children were informed exclusively from TV news reports that focused on the problems caused by integration.

Does the tremendous use of mass media influence the attitudes of voters during a political campaign? According to Atkin (1973), while political ads have some impact on the attitudes of undecided voters, they will not influence people whose attitudes are already formed. This brings us to the issue of how to change existing attitudes.

494

Attitude Change

During the Korean War, the Chinese and the North Korean Communists took great pains to try to convert American prisoners to their cause (Schein, 1956). The prisoners were obviously under great stress. Their captors tried to manipulate their beliefs by rewarding compliant behavior with food and privileges and by punishing resistance with deprivation of food, loss of freedom, and various forms of harassment. Group structure was also manipulated to secure compliance. Prisoners were segregated by rank, race, and nationality. Collective punishments were administered to whole groups of prisoners if one member did not conform to the captors' demands. Officers were ordered to report to enlisted men. Models for behavior were provided. Prisoners who had "converted" were cited as examples of desirable attitudes and behavior. Some of the prisoners became confused. Some became ill or died under the stress. But most complied only enough to ensure their survival, making enough mental reservations so that on their release they returned to their previous attitudes. Only a handful of men became genuine "converts" to the communist cause. Although people may derive comfort from the relative strength of the human spirit under such conditions of extreme stress, we must also note that the Chinese and North Koreans used relatively unsophisticated techniques.

What makes one attempt to change attitudes fail and another succeed? More generally, just how and why do attitudes change? When do we resist change? How successful is our resistance likely to be?

Although we are all bombarded with attempts to change our attitudes on subjects ranging from abortion to toothpaste, few of the methods used by interest groups and advertising agencies succeed. Doubtless, one of the major reasons for this is our ability to tune out what we do not want to hear. This is true both for politics and for products. Not only do we often fail to pay attention to editorials and discussions of public affairs, but we also simply do not hear much of the information directed at us, even if we seem to be paying attention. This is partly unintentional, but there is also an element of motivated selection on our part. Brock and Balloun (1967) found that subjects were more likely to tune into *supportive* messages than into *nonsupportive* ones. Kleinhessilink and Edwards (1975) took this a step further. They found that people listen to even nonsupportive messages as long as they are easy to refute. But they block out any nonsupportive messages that are hard to refute. Attention is highest for those arguments that least threaten the subject's own position.

We have a tendency to try to make the three aspects of an attitude consistent: the belief (or cognitive) component, the feeling component, and the behavior tendency. When one of these three is out of line, the discrepancy causes tension. The greater the discrepancy is, the greater the tension will be. Suppose you think that Truman was a great president. Your political science teacher, whose opinions you usually respect, believes that Truman was an average president. Because the discrepancy is not great in this situation, the pressure to change your attitude would be minor. You would probably change your opinion slightly because it requires only a little modification, and this is easier than dismissing your teacher's opinion entirely. If your teacher asserts that Truman was a mediocre president, however, it becomes harder for you to modify your opinion. From *great* to *good* is a relatively simple modification. From *great* to *mediocre* is a much harder attitude moderation. Nonetheless, research shows that under these circumstances, most people will still try to change their attitude to reduce the discrepancy. If, however, your teacher asserts that Truman was a terrible president, the discrepancy becomes too great. Instead of changing your attitude, the communicator (your teacher) begins to lose credibility. You might begin to suspect that this teacher is misinformed. As discrepancy grows, it becomes easier to dismiss an attitude or information that does not agree with your own (Freedman, Sears, & Carlsmith, 1981).

THE INFORMATIONAL APPROACH

Attempts to change attitudes by changing their belief components are usually discussed in terms of a source–message–audience model. The *source* may be a television program, a billboard, a newspaper editorial, a teacher, a friend, a group—in short, anyone or anything that produces a *message*, new or additional information about an object or event. The *audience,* of course, is the person or persons whose attitudes the source is trying to change. The most obvious example is the television commercial.

Several factors influence the effectiveness of attitude change. Some of these factors have to do with the source of the new information. One such factor is the *credibility* of the source. We are less likely to change our attitude toward the oil industry's antipollution efforts if the president of a major refining company tells us about them than we are if we hear the same information from an impartial commission appointed to study the situation. Another factor is the *prestige* of the source. A source that is high in prestige is likely to cause more change in attitudes than one with lower prestige. In one experiment, for example, people were asked to evaluate nine stanzas of modern poetry (Aronson, Turner, & Carlsmith, 1963). After they had rated the stanzas, they were given another person's favorable evaluation of one of the stanzas they had severely criticized. Some were told that the evaluaton had been written by the poet T. S. Eliot, others that it was by a student at a state teachers' college. Not surprisingly, when asked to reevaluate the stanzas, those who thought they had read a favorable evaluation by T. S. Eliot changed their own evaluations more than those who thought they had read an essay by a college student. The *intentions* of a source also determine the effectiveness of an attitude change. If we know from the outset that people are out to change our attitudes—if they come on with a "hard sell"—we are more likely to resist or dismiss their message. Moreover, our knowledge of people and their attractiveness and similarity to us all affect how much our attitudes change in response to their message.

Another set of factors deals with the message itself. How is the material presented? How much discrepancy does it arouse? Up to a point, it seems that the higher the *discrepancy* between a message and our attitude, the greater the likelihood and magnitude of the attitude change. We say "up to

Most Americans regarded Walter Cronkite as a highly credible source.
(UPI)

THE FOOT-IN-THE-DOOR TECHNIQUE

If you have ever been approached by a door-to-door salesman, you know about "the foot-in-the-door technique." A salesman can enter your house by first getting you to agree to a small request, and then use that as the basis for a salespitch aimed at a larger request. For instance, many people have been approached over the years by young men and women who claim to be working their way through college by selling magazines. Their initial "pitch" is that they receive a bonus from their employer even if you simply let them in to discuss the subscriptions they offer. It is not easy for many people to turn down this request. We approve of hard-working youths trying to better themselves. Once we have complied with the first request, it is often harder to resist subscribing to their magazines.

This approach is used by many people and groups, often in subtle ways. Political groups that first ask you to sign a petition and then flood you with pamphlets and position papers use this technique, as do many charities and "public interest" groups, which first engage your sympathy or interest in some small way, and then ask you for money or volunteer time. Advertising is filled with examples of the foot-in-the-door method. For instance, many products offer "sweepstakes" for which you just have to send in a card—no purchase necessary—to qualify. The idea is that if you perform any act connected with the product, you will be more likely to buy it in the future.

Freedman and Fraser (1966) researched this phenomenon. Certain residents of Palo Alto, California, were approached by experimenters posing as a Committee for Safe Driving. Residents were asked to place a large, ugly sign, reading "Drive Carefully," in their front yards. Only 17 percent agreed to do it. Then, other residents were approached and asked to sign a petition to California legislators requesting more laws designed to promote safe driving. Almost all those approached agreed to sign this petition. These same people were then asked to place the same sign in their yards. The results were striking: 55 percent agreed to do so. Apparently, the initial small request more than tripled the rate of compliance with the larger request.

Why this technique works so strongly is not clear. The most common explanation is that people who agree to a small request become involved and feel committed either to the issue in question or just to what they did—*appearing* to be involved. Another explanation is that those involved in this phenomenon undergo a mild change in self-image. In this experiment, a woman might see herself as someone aloof from social issues, who does not post signs or even relate to those who come to her door and ask for something. But the signing of a petition for such a noncontroversial position as safe driving may have changed her self-image. She may have come to see herself as one who could—under the right circumstances—become involved.

Similarly, the reverse tactic is equally persuasive. In other words, asking for a large favor and then "softening" the request to a smaller favor can often be very effective. In one study (Cialdini, 1975), subjects were asked to contribute a huge chunk of time to a worthy cause. Most refused. They were then asked to donate a very short period of time. Fifty percent of those asked complied with this second request. This technique of persuasion is well known to anyone who has been involved in collective bargaining or in a lawsuit, where plaintiffs always sue for enormous sums, anticipating that this will be pared down to a smaller, more acceptable amount (Freedman, Sears, & Carlsmith, 1981).

It is also possible to increase someone's tendency to comply with a request by removing the reasons for saying no. If, for example, you are approached at your home by representatives of a charitable organizaton, it is usually not hard to find reasons not to donate money: You're broke. You already gave to another charity this week. You don't know enough about the organization, and so forth. But if, besides the standard plea for money, the solicitor adds, "Please give something. Even one penny would help," you might find it much harder to resist. After all, do you want to be thought of—or to think of yourself—as a person who wouldn't even give a *penny* to help a worthy cause? Another study by Cialdini (1978) researched this very phenomenon. The results: the "even-a-penny-would-help" routine resulted in more people giving, and they also donated *more* money than people who were asked to contribute only what they could afford. Apparently, the "foot-in-the-door technique" not only encourages people to give, but once they decide to give, they see themselves as people who give to good causes; larger donations are more consistent with their new self-perception of being concerned and generous.

a point" because if the discrepancy is too great, there is a good chance that the person will reject the new information altogether. Usually, a *two-sided message* is more effective than one that presents only one side of an issue. Other evidence indicates that a message is more effective if the pleasant part of the information comes first (McGuire, 1957).

Perhaps the most important factors in changing attitudes are those that have to do with the audience. Because of the immense variations among people, these factors are often the most difficult to control. One consumer is convinced by a television commercial to buy laundry detergent, while another is not. One voter is persuaded by a political speech to vote for John Doe for mayor, while another stands firm in her intention to vote for his opponent. Yet, certain general conclusions can be drawn about how different attributes of an audience affect the likelihood that their attitudes will be changed. One is the *commitment* of people to their present attitudes. A man who has just gone on a speaking tour advocating liberalized abortion laws is less likely to change his attitudes toward the subject than someone who has never openly expressed an opinion one way or the other and is thus not "on the record." If people have had an attitude imposed on them or have merely adopted the attitudes of their parents or friends, they are more susceptible to change than someone who has considered the alternatives and made a *free choice* among them. McGuire (1964) identified certain "cultural truisms"—attitudes that are so universal that they are rarely challenged in our society. These cultural truisms—like "Democracy is good" or "You should brush your teeth after each meal"—are, he feels, highly susceptible to change, because we have never been "inoculated" against persuasive attempts to change them. An attitude that is interwoven with many of our other attitudes is harder to change because we would have to change or adjust a whole complex of attitudes. When we are given *advance warning* that another person is going to try to change our attitudes, we are less likely to change. Forewarned, it seems, *is* forearmed. Another personal characteristic that can affect attitude change is the level of our *self-esteem.* If we are highly self-confident, we will resist change more than if we doubt our own worth or adequacy.

Traditionally, women are thought to be more easily influenced than men. In a review of the relevant research, Eagly (1978) questioned this belief. She found that the evidence supporting this view can be explained by the tendency of researchers to use materials unfamiliar to women. Eagly's review, however, reaffirmed the belief that women in group settings are more likely than men to change their expressed opinions. Whether this reflects a genuine attitude change or is a mere mouthing of words to promote group harmony is not clear.

In theory, our attitudes are dynamic. As we interact with people, objects, and ideas, we test and reevaluate our original attitudes. But, in fact, we seldom easily change our attitudes, for our biases limit how we interact with the objects of our attitudes (Kelman, 1974). A woman may have concluded from her reading and from what others tell her that all drugs produce harmful effects. This opinion prevents her from trying out drugs and testing her attitudes for herself.

Faced with a message, we can resist changing our attitude in several ways. We can downgrade the source of the message—"What does he know

Women are usually thought of as being more susceptible to influence, including advertising, than men are.

(Peter Yates, Editorial Photocolor Archives)

about it anyway?" We can draw on other facts or beliefs to refute the message. We can reject the message altogether. We can distort the message as being less different than it really is. All these alternatives reduce the amount of discrepancy, without our having to change our attitude very much, if at all.

THE COGNITIVE CONSISTENCY APPROACH

One of the more fascinating approaches to the study of attitudes and attitude change derives from the theory of **cognitive dissonance,** developed by Leon Festinger (1957). Cognitive dissonance theory claims that unpleasant discord arises when one cognition that a person holds follows from the opposite of another cognition that that person holds. We are motivated to do something to bring the two (or more) cognitions into some sort of consistency.

With respect to attitudes, cognitive dissonance occurs when we are faced with two incompatible beliefs—"Nice girls don't engage in premarital sex." "My best friend is sleeping with her boyfriend."—when our beliefs and feelings are discrepant—"I believe that blacks and whites are equal." "I feel uncomfortable in an integrated social situation."—or when we behave in some way that is inconsistent with what we have previously expressed as our beliefs or feelings—such as when we visit the dentist, even though we hate and fear the visit.

This last situation implies that a change in behavior sometimes leads to a change in attitude, just as a change in attitude sometimes leads to a change in behavior. If, for instance, we visit the dentist despite our fears and discover that the treatment is not as painful or unpleasant as we thought, it may modify our attitude toward the next visit. This aspect of cognitive dissonance theory is behind much of the government's efforts to legislate desegregation. The idea is that if citizens are forced to treat blacks and whites equally, then they may begin to believe in equality.

We have already seen that there are various ways in which people reduce the dissonance caused by actions that disagree with their beliefs. We tend to see ourselves as rational, but in fact we are often more prone to rationalization than to rational behavior (Aronson, 1980). We can reduce dissonance by adding more consonant elements to outweigh the dissonant elements. For example, the famous incident of survivors of a plane crash in the Andes Mountains is a classic illustration of cognitive dissonance. To stay alive, the survivors ate their dead comrades. The dissonant elements here are pretty clear: "Cannibalism is abhorrent"; yet, "I must eat human flesh to live." One of the survivors later described how he justified his actions: "It's like Holy Communion. My friend has given us his body so that we can have life" (Read, 1974, p. 83). In this case, we see how the three parts of an attitude system became consistent: the new belief that cannibalism is not only pragmatic but actually has religious significance, followed by the disappearance of revulsion toward the act, followed by the actual behavior—the eating of human flesh.

We can also reduce dissonance by telling ourselves that the dissonant behavior is not that significant. For instance, a cigarette smoker who knows

(Philip Jon Bailey, Stock, Boston)

that cigarette smoking causes cancer persuades herself that she does not smoke *that much*, or that her brand is low in tar, or that she will quit soon. Still another alternative is to change or minimize the dissonant element, so that it is no longer incompatible with our attitudes. Recall the earlier example of a girl who believes only "bad" girls have premarital sex, and who then discovers that her best friend is sleeping with her boyfriend. She counters this dissonance by minimizing her friend's activity—"She's not being promiscuous; she's in love"—or by changing her perception—"It's really only wrong if you do it with just anybody." This alternative only works when the dissonance is the result of two incompatible beliefs or feelings. If the dissonance is aroused by an action that has already been taken—"Only bad girls have premarital sex," yet, "I am sleeping with my boyfriend"—we have to change our attitude completely to reduce the dissonance.

Several factors affect the amount of attitude change that results from cognitive dissonance. One factor is *choice*—if people feel personally responsible for a dissonant act, they are more likely to change their attitudes than if they feel they were forced to act in a way that contradicts their beliefs (Cooper, 1971; Kelman, 1974). For instance, during the late 1950s, when desegregation caused turmoil throughout the South, North Carolina remained calm and was almost a model of smooth desegregation. Why? Many people believe that it was because the state government appeared to be offering a choice to its citizens. It ordered the public school system desegregated, but it also offered state aid to families who wished to send their children to private schools. Because the application process for this aid was extremely complex, most families chose to continue to send their children to the public schools. In doing so, they were actively *choosing* to change their behavior, thus increasing the dissonance and increasing the attitude change (Worchel & Cooper, 1981).

Another factor that affects the amount of attitude change is reward. People who are paid to behave in ways that violate their attitudes experience less dissonance than those who are not, and thus they are less likely to change their attitudes. The opposite situation also occurs. When people are rewarded for behaving consistently with their beliefs and feelings, the reward actually makes them value their behavior *less* than they did before.

A third factor affecting attitude change is *justification*. If people are convinced that there is a good reason to perform a discrepant act, they will experience little dissonance and their attitudes are not likely to change, though their behavior may shift for a time.

FACTORS INFLUENCING ATTITUDE CHANGE

As we have seen, people rationalize their attitudes to justify themselves and their behavior, and tune out what they do not want to hear. All of these factors act against the possibility of attitude change. Yet, attitudes are sometimes changed. Under what circumstances do they change? First, let us state the two circumstances under which they are *least* likely to change. The first is when people have built an environment for themselves in which their beliefs are rarely if ever challenged. The other is when people are so deeply, psychologically committed to their beliefs that even massive assaults on them are ineffective.

Now, when do circumstances favor attitude change? Well, one favorable environment is a sudden immersion in an atmosphere of strong opinions at a young age. The study done at Bennington College, mentioned earlier in this chapter, is a prime example of this type of situation. But while young people in an intellectual atmosphere would seem to be ideally suited for changes in attitude, if their attitudes are deeply rooted they may change little. Stuart Cook (1970) tested the radical attitudes of a group of white southern college girls. He selected the most prejudiced. Then, in a completely different setting—another college—he put each of these highly prejudiced girls through an experiment that involved about 40 hours of close contact with a black co-worker. Most of the time was spent working on a task that required complete cooperation. A few months later, the girls were retested for racial prejudice in surroundings completely removed from the experiment. Cook found that 40 percent of the subjects had become less negative toward blacks. Yet about 20 percent had become *more* prejudiced. In general, it appears that attitudes that have been socialized early in life and to which one is highly committed do not change very much with time (Freedman, Sears, & Carlsmith, 1981).

When attitudes do change, it is most likely because the source of the new information is both expert and trustworthy. If the source is a person, his or her trustworthiness is enhanced by arguing a position apparently opposed to his or her own self-interest. For example, the vice-president of a tobacco company is not effective in urging you to disregard medical reports and to go on smoking. But a nuclear scientist who argues against the use of nuclear power could be deemed highly trustworthy and effective (Aronson, 1980).

Other elements also promote attitude change; one of these is *fear*. Arousing fear is a common way of trying to influence someone. These efforts range from a mother convincing a child not to touch a hot stove, to mobsters persuading a merchant to buy "protection."

Dabbs and Leventhal (1966) researched how effective fear was in getting students to obtain tetanus inoculations. The disease was described in vivid, ugly detail, and it was pointed out how easy and effective the inoculations were. The message was delivered with various degrees of fear arousal. The descriptions of the disease were extremely vivid and frightening in one group, moderately frightening in another, and not very frightening in a third. The findings were quite impressive. The more fear aroused, the more the subjects were determined to get the inoculations. The greater fear not only aroused *intentions* but actually changed behavior. More students from the high-fear group got the inoculations.

Fear is not always this effective. If fear is aroused out of proportion to the actual situation, then the subjects tend to be turned *off* rather than persuaded. Causing people to be too frightened may simply paralyze them or cause them to deny the danger.

Is there a personality type that seems more inclined toward attitude change? People with a low sense of self-esteem seem more inclined to change their attitudes. But the effect of trying to change the attitude of someone with low self-esteem may not be what is desired. Such people may change their opinions easily, but there will be little sense of commitment to the change. There is a good chance that their attitudes may change yet *again*. Interestingly enough, intelligent people are more inclined to change their attitudes than less intelligent people. This may not be what you might expect, but remember that intelligent people are more likely to *understand* information than less intelligent people. Moreover, people who are insecure about their intelligence often cling to their opinions and beliefs even in the face of very persuasive evidence to the contrary.

The fact remains that attitudes are extremely difficult to change, as politicians, marketing experts, and public interest groups have all found out. In general, it seems simpler to change people's overt behavior than to change their attitudes. Because people's attitudes toward minorities, toward civil liberties, toward war and peace, and a host of other issues are so important to our lives—and indeed, to the lives of thousands of others throughout the world—there is no doubt that the study of attitudes and how to change them will continue to be important for social psychology.

Application

SUCCESS AND SEX

In 1942, a movie called *Take a Letter, Darling* was released. Audiences guffawed as a struggling artist, played by Fred MacMurray, swallowed his pride and became the secretary to a female advertising tycoon, played by Rosalind Russell. Of course (since it was 1942), this role reversal didn't last, and by the fadeout the boss had fallen in love with her secretary and was quitting her job to follow him to Mexico where he planned to paint.

Times have changed. Today, women are competing with men for high level jobs in business and industry. Many men, on the other hand, are functioning as something other than breadwinners. But sexual stereotypes die hard, and there is still a double standard of success for men and women. In the 19th century, the successful man braved the evils of the active life to "bring home the bacon." The successful woman was an "angel of the hearth" who devoted her life to her husband and her children. The women's movement actually began more than a century ago, but as recently as the 1950s the successful man was still the one with the most earning power, and the successful woman derived most of her status from her husband.

The acceleration of the women's movement in the 1960s and 1970s posed serious challenges to traditional concepts of male and female success. Men are now told that success also encompasses such human—and traditionally "feminine"—qualities as nurturance, tenderness, and sympathy, besides a willingness to take out the garbage. Women are exhorted to raise their consciousness, realize their potential, and compete in the marketplace. For both men and women, this redefinition of sex roles promises great rewards, but in the short run it causes anxiety and confusion. Many women used to feel guilty about "neglecting" their families for their jobs. Today, the shoe is frequently on the other foot. Those who choose domesticity often feel guilty that they are not achieving outside the home. And whether single or married, working women face a "Catch-22" situation in the job market: No matter how much they want professional success, they are thwarted by a male-dominated "good old boy" network (Kanter, 1975).

Some women pursue careers and manage households at the same time, which generally means sacrifices on both ends. Unfortunately, we still know very little about how women feel about themselves when they give up or defer careers to raise families. But early studies show that such women are more prone to depression and have less self-esteem than women who work (Yorburg, 1974).

Men, too, have trouble juggling responsibilities. S. M. Miller, a prominent sociologist, confesses that his attempts to forge a "liberated" marriage made him feel both guilty and resentful. Believing in sexual equality, he shared the housework and childrearing while his wife—a physician—pursued her career. But he bitterly resented the demands on his time and energy, and admits that his wife wound up deferring her career goals to take on family tasks. He laments the fact that women—even if they have careers of their own—are considered successful only if they accommodate themselves to their husbands' careers. In short, masculine ambitions take their toll on both men and women (Miller, 1974).

We know somewhat more about how a man's self-image suffers when the traditional ticket to masculinity—income—is cancelled. In our society, masculinity is often measured by the size of the paycheck (Gould, 1974). Economic power thus is equated with sexual power. But money is a shaky foundation on which to build either a self-image or a marriage. What happens, for instance, to a man's sense of masculinity if he loses his job? What happens when his wife has her own career, or when she makes more money than he does? Some men—and women—bolster the male ego with the "fluffy little woman" stereotype. She makes more money, but has trouble balancing the checkbook. In extreme cases, loss of income even leads to temporary impotence (Gould, 1974).

How do men and women actually feel about success? In the 1960s, psychologist Matina Horner (1969) developed a dramatic theory. On the basis of tests given to undergraduates, she concluded that many women are actually afraid of success—afraid that achievement—particularly academic achievement—somehow makes them less "feminine." Horner's findings attracted popular attention and inspired a host of similar experiments. Tresemer and Hoffman (1974) discovered that many men, too, feared success. But while women seem to equate achievement with social failure, men question the career ethic itself,

(Bruce Roberts, Rapho/Photo Researchers)

and wonder if it is worth the effort. (See Chapter 9 for a discussion of Horner's study and the fear of success as a social motive.)

Other studies suggest that traditional attitudes still persist. Paludi (1979) used Horner's method of asking students to finish stories about a mythical Anne and John, students in medical school. But while Horner's imaginary students were at the top of their class, Paludi gave undergraduates several different versions. In some stories, Anne or John ranked at the top of the class; in others they ranked lower. Both men and women foretold that Anne's life would be happy if she were somewhat—but not too—successful, and only if she also had a husband and children. In other words, students worried about the effects of academic or professional success on a woman's position in society. But when it came to John, both sexes expected more. Men and women alike considered the not-too-successful John a failure (Paludi, 1979). Whether these attitudes reflect deep-seated values or just mirror current social realities, it is clear that for both men and women, success is a complex and as yet unresolved issue.

Summary

1. Social psychology is the study of how people relate to other people in groups and individually. Social psychologists study how people perceive others and what leads people to like or dislike certain people and certain groups.

2. Our first impressions of other people are formed from verbal and visual cues, which lead us to make assumptions about others. We draw inferences based on these assumptions, and modify our behavior accordingly. Sometimes these impressions are inaccurate because of insufficient information, or because we have been consciously manipulated. People who engage in manipulative behavior are often called _Machiavellian_.

3. We also mislead ourselves, through stereotyping, by rigidly categorizing people according to their appearance or background. Also, the desire to find consistent behavior patterns in the people we know can be misleading. A special example of this is the _halo_ or _devil effect:_ If we like people we tend to see everything they do positively; if we dislike them, we tend to see everything they do negatively.

4. The study of the inferences we make about the behavior of other people is called _attribution theory._ An attribution is an inference that a person makes about the actions of another—or himself— based on observing overt behavior. Attribution theory takes several circumstances into consideration, such as cause and

effect, context, distinctiveness of the information, and consensus of the information.

5. We often attribute certain behavior to others because of our own biases, and we also are inclined to make defensive attributions that help preserve our self-esteem. Moreover, people blame events on victims—accidents, rapes—as a way of distancing themselves from the likelihood of it happening to them.

6. Many factors propel us toward liking another person. Some of the major factors are: proximity, similarity of interests, complementary expectations, and rewardingness. Rewardingness refers to the fact that people tend to like those who praise or like them.

7. Rubin defined love as the junction of three important elements: caring, attachment, and intimacy.

8. Conformity is the act of yielding one's preferences or beliefs to those of a group. This sometimes leads to anticonformity, where a person wishes to do the opposite of whatever the group does. There are many factors that influence conformity: safety in numbers, a fear of rejection or isolation, identification with a strong group member.

9. Obedience to authority differs from conformity in that obedience means submitting to one person's—or a symbolic person's—orders.

10. People sometimes act in groups in a way that they would not alone. The most striking example of this kind of behavior is mob behavior. People lose their personal sense of responsibility in a group, especially in a high-anxiety situation. This is called deindividuation, because people are responding as anonymous parts of a larger group. Deindividuation produces more aggressive, hostile behavior.

11. People also take greater risks in a group than they do individually. This is because of the group pressure to conform, and the presence of strongly persuasive group members who have more information, or are more inclined to take risks.

12. Altruistic behavior is helping behavior. Many factors influence this kind of behavior: an increased sense of responsibility, empathy for the person being helped, and a clearcut case of emergency or need.

13. All groups have a leader, whether a formal one or an informal one. There are many theories as to how leaders emerge in historical instances. "The Great Man" theory holds that the most important factor in history is the "great man" who emerges regardless of the time and circumstances.

14. The personal relationship of the leader to the members of the group is most important in determining the leader's influence. Status in the community appears to be a major factor in determining who will be a leader.

15. Group decision-making is often weaker than individual decision-making. Strong pressures to conform work against the expression

of creative ideas. Caution tends to dominate group decision-making, and group members often make decisions more oriented toward the group than toward nonmembers, even if nonmembers are affected by the decision.

16. An attitude has three major components: beliefs about the object, feelings about the object, and a tendency to behave in a certain way toward the object.

17. Most attitudes derive from our personal experience and from the information we received from our parents as a child. Children not only learn through conscious means, but they also imitate their parents and peers and thus unconsciously develop attitudes. The mass media are also very influential in forming attitudes, primarily in situations where attitudes do not previously exist, and especially on people who watch a great deal of television.

18. Various factors contribute to the success of an attempt to change an attitude. If the source is credible, prestigious, and apparently well intentioned, we are more likely to allow our attitudes to be influenced by that source. "Hard-sell" approaches are rarely effective in changing attitudes. Supportive messages are more likely to influence us than nonsupportive messages, which frequently result in selective attention.

19. _Cognitive dissonance_ theory maintains that a state of unpleasant mental discord follows from the clashing of two conflicting beliefs in a person's mind. We are motivated by this discord to try to bring the two—or more—inconsistent beliefs into a consistent belief pattern. Cognitive dissonance occurs when we are faced with two incompatible beliefs, or when we find ourselves acting inconsistently with our previously held beliefs, or when our beliefs clash with our feelings.

20. Changes of behavior sometimes motivate changes of attitude. This aspect of cognitive dissonance theory is behind much of the legislation designed to integrate American society: If people can be forced to treat blacks and whites equally, they may also come to believe it.

21. One way to reduce cognitive dissonance is to add enough positive feelings to outweigh our negative feelings. Another way of reducing cognitive dissonance is to tell ourselves that the dissonant behavior is not significant, or to minimize the dissonant elements until they are no longer seriously incompatible with our previous attitudes.

22. Attitudes are least likely to change when people have built environments around themselves in which information challenging their beliefs rarely enters. Attitudes are also unlikely to change when people are deeply, psychologically committed to those beliefs. Attitudes are most likely to change when people are immersed in an environment full of ferment and intellectual activity, where beliefs and conflicting ideas are tossed around, as in a college atmosphere. Attitudes are also most likely to change

when they are challenged by an expert, trustworthy source. Fear is also an important factor in influencing attitude change; however, fear aroused out of proportion to the actual situation is ineffective in changing attitudes. Although people with low self-esteem may be more easily influenced to change an attitude, they are rarely committed to their new attitudes. Intelligent people are more likely to have their attitudes changed under the right circumstances than less intelligent people, who sometimes cling to their attitudes defensively.

Outline

Chapter 16

Issues in Social Psychology

In the last chapter, we examined the underlying theories and principles of social psychology. We saw how people's attitudes develop and how they can be changed. We touched upon how people perceive each other and the causes of their behavior. We also examined the dynamics of conformity, group interaction, and leadership.

But no examination of the theoretical bases of social psychology is complete without some practical applications of those concepts and theories. How do attitudes toward minority groups affect us? Can prejudice be reduced? How does our environment influence us and the way we relate to others in social situations? Why do human beings conflict with one another and how can conflict be reduced? In this chapter, as we move from a theoretical to a more practical concern with social problems, these are some of the questions that we will consider.

PREJUDICE AND DISCRIMINATION

Prejudice is widespread, but so is a denial of prejudice. No one—not even members of the Ku Klux Klan—likes to be called prejudiced. People are extremely skillful in rationalizing and masking their prejudices. In 1981, a man on trial for shooting at an integrated group of joggers maintained that such an act was "justifiable homicide," because mixing of the races was a "sin against God and man." It is doubtful that he would consider this remark an example of prejudice. Rather, he might call it a statement of religious belief. Although this example is extreme, it differs only in degree from how we all distort and deny our prejudices.

Although we often use the terms *prejudice* and *discrimination* interchangeably, they are, in fact, different. Prejudice is an unfair, intolerant, or unfavorable *attitude* toward another group of people. Discrimination is an

509

(©*Telegraph Sunday Magazine* by John Marmaras, Woodfin Camp & Associates)

act or a series of acts taken toward another group—or toward people from that group—that are unfair when compared with our behavior toward other groups. *Racism* is a specific instance of both prejudice and discrimination. The U. S. Commission on Civil Rights defines racism as "any attitude, action, or institutional structure which subordinates a person because of his or her color" (U.S. Commission on Civil Rights, 1969).

Prejudice and discrimination are perplexing subjects, and they are so filled with emotion that they are often hard to study. Prejudices are rarely based on experience; indeed, they flourish in its absence—for example, consider Shakespeare's anti-Semitic portrait of Shylock in *The Merchant of Venice*, written when few, if any, Jews had lived in England for centuries. Racial discrimination is even more perplexing since it exists even when it harms the person who practices it. For example, an employer who is prejudiced against blacks may hire an incompetent white worker rather than a highly qualified black one. Moreover, since World War II, a remarkable amount of mass-media attention has been focused on prejudice. Billions of dollars are spent by the U.S. government and by political action groups to help end racial discrimination in this country. But there is still racial prejudice.

Why are racial prejudices so ingrained and where do they come from? Why do they compel us so irrationally? What is the significance of stereotyping, conformity, and hostility? To answer these questions, let us first consider the roots of prejudice.

SOURCES OF PREJUDICE

.There have been many studies of the sources of prejudice, and an extraordinary number of theories have been advanced about its causes.

FRUSTRATION–AGGRESSION. Among the most popular theories are those that explain prejudice in terms of the submerged frustrations of the prejudiced group. The "scapegoat" theory is widely accepted as one of the most convincing explanations of prejudice (Allport, 1954; Hovland & Sears, 1940). **Scapegoat** is a Biblical term for a "sacrificial" creature that absorbed and exorcised the sins of society. The scapegoat theory asserts that prejudice and discrimination result from displaced aggression. Historically, for example, violence against the Jews often followed periods of economic unrest or natural catastrophe. Similarly, until recently, blacks in this country were scapegoats for the economic frustrations of lower-income Americans because these lower-income people were essentially powerless. Poor whites who feel exploited and oppressed cannot vent their anger on the proper target, and so they displace their hostility by directing it against those who are even "lower" on the social scale—in this case, blacks.

Many studies support this theory of prejudice. For example, Hovland and Sears (1940) found that falling cotton prices in the South from 1882 to 1930 were directly related to the number of lynchings of blacks that occurred there. The lower the price of cotton, the higher the likelihood was of violence against blacks.

Why are certain groups singled out as objects for displaced hostility and aggression? Berkowitz (1969) identified four factors that determine which group is selected as a scapegoat. These are:

1. *Safeness.* The target group must be weak enough to eliminate the likelihood of retaliation.
2. *Visibility.* The group must have certain characteristics that make it stand out from other groups, such as differing color, physical characteristics, or customs.
3. *Strangeness.* Humans appear to have a strong ingrained fear of what is strange to them. Children often recoil from strangers, and uneducated people especially tend to link what is strange to what is evil.
4. *A Prior Dislike for the Group.* This is important but often overlooked. People seize on what is available for their prejudices and fears. Where there is a tradition of violence against blacks, for example, those seeking a scapegoat know that such violence is permitted.

STEREOTYPES. Stereotypes are another source of prejudice. In the previous chapter we discussed how stereotypes affect our attitudes toward others. Stereotyping is not always abusive and is often unintentional. It is basically a way of simplifying our view of the world. We all do it to some extent. Most of us have a specific picture in mind when we hear phrases such as "French chef," "cover girl," "beach boy," and so forth. If a stereotype is based on actual experience, it can be a normal, adaptive, nonprejudicial way of thinking about people.

Many stereotypes, however, are not based on experience, but on hearsay, or images generated by TV dramas, or figments of our own imaginations that justify our fears and anger. Some of these prejudicial stereotypes serve more than one purpose. For example, it is useful to believe that blacks are inherently less intelligent than whites if we wish to keep them out of our schools. If, as a result, they are sent to inferior schools and get poor educations, they may indeed appear to be less intelligent, thus fulfilling our stereotype.

Stereotypes also affect how we explain a person's behavior. People's attributions tend to be consistent with their prejudices. If you believe that blacks are shiftless and lazy, your perception of a white man in a three-piece suit lolling around the park in mid-afternoon may differ greatly from your perception of a black man in the same situation (Aronson, 1980).

Where do we learn stereotypes? The overwhelming evidence is that we learn them while we are very young. Children hear their parents talk about minorities and are not allowed to play with children from minority groups. Although they may not understand why, the message is clear: These people are inferior; people like us do not mix with them. Even in families where racial prejudice is minimal, parents without meaning to may express anxiety about their children playing with minority-group children. And if—as is still true in most homes in America—a white child does not see his parents socializing with black adults, this reinforces the child's impression that whites and blacks are somehow very different; the child then tries to determine what those differences are (Worchel & Cooper, 1979).

People cling tenaciously to stereotypes even when they are shown to be

(David A. Krathwohl, Stock, Boston)

irrational. In his classic study *The Nature of Prejudice* (1954), Gordon Allport reported the following dialogue:

Mr. X: The trouble with the Jews is that they only take care of their own group.

Mr. Y: But the record of the Community Chest campaign shows that they gave more generously in proportion to their numbers to the general charities of the communities than did non-Jews.

Mr. X: That shows that they are always trying to buy favor and intrude into Christian affairs. They think of nothing but money; that is why there are so many Jewish bankers.

Mr. Y: But a recent study shows that the percentage of Jews in the banking business is negligible, far smaller than the percentage of non-Jews.

Mr. X: That's just it; they don't go in for respectable business; they are only in the movie business or run night clubs.

This is a clear-cut example of someone who does not allow the facts to intrude on his prejudicial stereotypes. A truly prejudiced person is virtually immune to any attempt to alter his or her stereotypes.

CONFORMITY. Conformity is also important in forming and sustaining prejudice. If we want to associate with people who also have clearly expressed prejudices, we are more likely to go along with their prejudices than we are to resist them. During the 1960s in the South, for example, many restaurant owners maintained that they themselves did not mind serving blacks, but that their customers would not tolerate it (Wrightsman & Deaux, 1981). Children are especially likely to conform to the attitudes of their peers, which is partly why it has often been so hard to integrate schools. Those children who are willing to go to school with black children are subject to immense peer-group pressure to conform to the hostile behavior—based on stereotypes—displayed by their friends and associates.

REDUCING PREJUDICE

In Chapter 15 we noted that people who are alike will tend to like each other. How important is racial similarity to people's liking for others? In a series of studies (Byrne & Wong, 1962; Rokeach & Mezei, 1966; Stein et al., 1965), some subjects were given a description of a person of another race whose attitudes were similar to their own, while other subjects received descriptions of a person of their own race whose attitudes were very different from their own. The results were that, in general, similarity of attitudes was more important than belonging to the same racial group in determining who was liked.

It would indeed be pleasant to believe that these findings directly bear on real contacts between people. If this were so, it would indicate—as many educators and activists believed—that simply *educating* people about the similarities between themselves and others reduces racial tensions. These studies, however, primarily apply to relatively nonintimate relationships—

working or studying together, for example. Race was far more important than similar attitudes in studies of intimate relationships such as dating or marriage.

It is also wise to remember that the subjects in these studies were presented with hypothetical people and situations, and that there was a subtle pressure to be objective and nonbiased. In real life, biases often have more importance. Silverman (1974) described various people as roommates to incoming college students. In one group, subjects were told that these choices would actually *be* their assigned roommates. In another group, the subjects were told that these were merely hypothetical roommates. Racial discrimination was far more important to the choice of *actual* roommates than in the choice of *imagined* roommates. But similarity in attitude and belief was important in both groups. Thus, although it is somewhat discouraging to see the difference between our "lip service" to racial equality and our practice of it, these studies offer some hope that people will weigh attitude similarity fairly under the right conditions.

During the late 1950s, when school desegregation was given massive attention, many people believed that school desegregation would change prejudicial attitudes. This belief has proved to be only partly true. Moreover, the attempt to educate the public with films and literature designed to explode racial myths was a dismal failure (Aronson, 1980). As we have seen, people are quite adept at ignoring what clashes with their own deep-seated beliefs.

There has, however, been some progress. It was shown, for instance, that when blacks and whites share the same goals and cooperate to reach them, prejudice lessens. The important point here is that mere *contact* between groups is not enough to lessen prejudice. The contact must be *interdependent* and *cooperative*, not competitive.

Stuart Cook (1971) and his colleagues formed small groups to cooperate

513

on management-training activities. In some of the groups, the subjects were all white; other groups included blacks. As you might expect, when the groups were successful, the subjects liked each other more, regardless of race. Even when the groups failed, so that tension and hostility were markedly higher, race did not significantly affect people's liking for each other. In other words, cooperation on the same tasks between people of equal status helped, regardless of its success or failure.

These studies show that some situations reduce prejudice more than others do. Because blacks hired in formerly segregated factories are seen by whites as competitors for jobs and status, and because most school integration has emphasized contact rather than cooperation, success in reducing racial prejudice through simple integration has been mixed. Seeing blacks working as janitors and maids does _not_ lessen prejudice; neither does an integrated school in which whites feel competitive with blacks, or one in which blacks are made to feel that their education so far has been inferior, and where they must strive to catch up.

Interracial groups organized to solve specific problems cooperatively—a student council, a working team, a study group—can, however, reduce prejudice. Unfortunately, these situations are rare in society, although studies among residents of housing projects, department store workers, and police officers all show the same thing: When racial groups work or live together in noncompetitive, nonthreatening situations, racial animosities decrease (Close et al., 1978).

THE JIGSAW APPROACH. One interesting series of studies by Elliot Aronson and his colleagues (Aronson et al., 1978) seems to point the way for future efforts at reducing racial prejudice. Each student in a class was given a different section of material to learn and report on to his or her fellow students—it was called the **jigsaw method** because the pieces fit together to form a whole. The students were left on their own, but were told that they would be tested on the material. Thus, it was to their advantage to learn from one another, to coax those who needed it, and to cooperate in assembling the "whole picture." The results were remarkable. While it took some students longer than others to realize the value of cooperation, most of the groups adapted well, and children of all races found themselves cooperating and learning from one another.

This method, however, works best with young children. It is also hard to implement such a program on any but a small scale. Still, it offers some hope for those who believe that education is the best way to change people's preconceived racial prejudices.

Environmental Psychology

In recent years, more attention has been paid to how our environment influences us and our relationships with others. Because we accept our environment as a given, we are often unaware of the effects of such factors as crowding, noise, isolation, and urban tension. **Environmental psychol-**

ogy studies how these factors contribute to the complex ways in which we relate to our world.

Environments, like people, have their own personalities, which affect us in many ways. In fact, our perceptions of various environments are often like our perceptions of people. For example, we may see some environments as "friendly" and others as "hostile."

There are two general features that influence our perceptions of physical settings. **Ambient conditions** are the physical qualities of the atmosphere: sounds, lighting, heat, humidity, and so forth. As a rule, we rarely notice ambient features unless they go awry. If the temperature is moderate, for example, we pay no attention to it. If the lighting is adequate, and if the noise level is consistent, neither intrudes on us.

Architectural features are the actual dimensions and physical make-up of the house, room, or building that we occupy. Because architectural features vary tremendously, our perceptions of them are far more complicated than those relating to ambient conditions. We tend to have strong judgments about architectural features, even if we do not know exactly why. One study showed that people seemed to rate rooms as "friendly" when chairs were arranged with no intervening barriers. "Flexibility" also contributes to a positive evaluation of a room—that is, the ease with which a room can be adapted for social uses (Mehrabian & Diamond, 1971).

(Drawing by S. Harris; © 1981 *The New Yorker Magazine*, Inc.)

ADAPTATION

Our response to an environment changes considerably as we spend some time in it. This is an example of *adaptation*, which we discussed in detail in Chapter 8. While all living things adapt to some extent, human beings are especially adaptable to their environment. For example, the residents of an industrial town live with and even ignore the odors that come from local factories, which visitors find intolerable. Similarly, the first impression of the noise at a party, where loud rock-and-roll is being played, might be that the music is unbearably loud. Yet, by the end of the party, the music might seem softer: It is not the noise level that changed, but your tolerance of it.

Times Square station of the New York City subway system. Human beings are extremely adaptable to their environment.

(Jim Anderson, Woodfin Camp & Associates)

A feature of adaptation is that people perceive new situations in terms of a familiar environment. If a resident of New York, Chicago, or any other big city visits a small suburban town, he or she is likely to find that town quiet and peaceful because of its contrast with the hurried, noisy atmosphere of a big city. If, however, a visitor to that same town had spent his or her life in a rural farm community in the Great Plains, the visitor would probably find it bustling, noisy, and crowded—also by contrast with what that person was used to (Wrightsman & Deaux, 1981).

In the past few years, social psychologists have studied how the environment affects our health and our functioning in society. According to Kiritz and Moos (1974), a competitive, hurried environment with a heavy work load, high pressure, and high rates of change seems to increase the likelihood of stress and disease. An atmosphere of support, cohesion, and affiliation, however, helps people recover from illness, feel more satisfied with life, and gain a greater sense of moral and social purpose (Kiritz & Moos, 1974). Unfortunately, stress and pressure are more common than calm and tranquility. Two of the most important aspects of any environment are the amount of space between people and population density. Let us look more closely at their effect on individuals.

PERSONAL SPACE

In New York City as many as 70,000 people live and work within a single square mile. One of New York's larger apartment complexes could house the entire population of many small towns. Sidewalks are so jammed at certain hours of the day that even walking from one place to another becomes a challenge, and traffic maneuvers such as passing, weaving, and dodging become as important to people walking on the sidewalk as to the cars on the street. Although many suburban towns were originally built to avoid this sort of crowding, they, too, have become densely populated, and it is becoming increasingly rare—especially in the older, more developed areas of the country—for people to have the kind of "elbow room" that Americans have been brought up to value and expect.

Because of increased crowding in urban and suburban areas, more attention has been paid to how human beings react to crowding and to the invasion of their "personal space." **Personal space** is a phrase coined by the anthropologist Edward T. Hall (1959). It means, quite simply, the amount of physical space between people, how they relate to this space, and how people manipulate it in their relationships with others. Research in this area indicates that substantial national, ethnic, and sex differences exist in the use of personal space.

Culture largely dictates how much personal space we require. While talking, white Americans, Englishmen, and Swedes stand farthest apart; South Americans, Pakistanis, and Arabs stand closer together. This sort of information seems trivial, but it does affect international understanding. Imagine, for example, a business conference between an American and an Arab. The American prefers to have about 3 or 4 feet between them, while the Arab is inclined to stand closer. If the American moves away, the Arab feels that the American is being cold and hostile, while the American finds the Arab, who keeps moving closer, pushy and aggressive.

Culture indicates how much personal space people require.

(Top left: Thomas Hopker, Woodfin Camp & Associates; bottom left: Sepp Seitz, Woodfin Camp & Associates; right: Jan Halaska, Photo Researchers)

In general, the more intimate we are with people, the more likely we are to sit or to stand close to them. Similarly, the more friendly people are with one another, the less they notice how close to one another they are standing or sitting. Indeed, the distance you put between yourself and others is one way of showing interest or liking, especially with someone you have just met or want to get to know. If we do not want to meet people—for instance, while studying at the library—we are inclined to view any attempt to "enter" our space as an invasion. Robert Sommer (1959) tested this by having women approach other women who were studying alone at a library table. If the experimenter sat down a few chairs away, she was ignored. But if she sat next to the subject, the subject often expressed discomfort, irritation, and even anger.

In one experiment a student posed as a policeman and interviewed other students about the contents of their wallets. As the interview progressed, the "policeman" edged closer to the students. When the "policeman" moved as close as 8 inches to a student, the student usually grew tense, uncomfortable, and suspicious.   When the distance was kept at about 2 feet, the interviews went smoothly, with no sign of discomfort from the students (Insel & Lindgren, 1978).

The circumstances in which we find ourselves are also important. For example, in a crowded room we are likely to ignore someone sitting down next to us. This aspect of personal space is seen in any city during rush hour. Even in a crowd, people have some sense of personal space and can be hostile to those who invade it. But at rush hour, transportation is so jammed that it is often impossible to preserve even a trace of this territorial sense. Thus, people who would otherwise be repelled by the closeness of strangers seem to pay no heed to their proximity during these hours. Let's look more closely at crowding, which is a particularly interesting example of the use of personal space.

517

The experience of crowding can be psychological.

(Ellen Pines Sheffield, Woodfin Camp & Associates)

CROWDING. Although it may seem unnecessary to define what we mean by "crowding," the term is used in different ways. By crowding we usually mean that we are cramped in a small space. But we can also feel crowded with plenty of space. If, for example, you go to a secluded beach to swim with your date and discover that there are five or six other people there, you may *feel* crowded even though there is no lack of physical space. In other words, the experience of being crowded can be psychological. It does not require a physically small space (Stokols et al., 1973).

THE EFFECTS OF CROWDING ON ANIMALS. Many studies have examined how animals react to crowding. Calhoun (1962) created rat colonies in which the population was far denser than normal. He found that rats developed "abnormal" traits under these conditions that had not been present before: Maternal behavior was disturbed; cannibalism and homosexuality developed. In general, the rats behaved as if their social bonds had been dissolved. Christian, Flyger, and Davis (1960) studied deaths in a herd of deer too dense for their tiny island off the Maryland coast. Although no consistent evidence of disease or malnutrition was found in the carcasses of the dead deer, their adrenal glands were greatly enlarged, apparently caused by increased stress.

Although similar reactions to high population density were observed in mice, lemmings, and hares, it is not entirely clear how these findings relate to human behavior. Human beings are far more adaptable than most other creatures. As the famed biologist Rene Dubos has said: "The readiness with which man adapts to potentially dangerous situations makes it unwise to apply directly to human life the results of experiments designed to test the acute effects of crowding on animals" (Dubos, 1970).

THE URBAN ENVIRONMENT. Although many attempts have been made to correlate urban population density with such factors as crime rate and suicide, few conclusions can be drawn from these studies. There are too many other factors involved to clearly relate crowding to crime. There is no doubt that crime and even mental illness appear to be greater in the inner city areas of highest population density. But how can we separate crowding from other socioeconomic factors?

If high density population has a negative effect on people, Milgram (1970) suggests that this is due to *sensory overload*. This means that when people are exposed to too much stimulation—too many people, too much noise, too many faces and voices vying for their attention—they can no longer cope, so they become withdrawn and isolated. As a result of this withdrawal, people pay less attention to social interactions: They tend to *deindividuate* others. As we saw in Chapter 15, *deindividuation* often leads to loss of one's sense of responsibility. It can also contribute to the coldness, hostility, and powerlessness that many people feel in cities.

Crowding seems to exaggerate a person's natural behavior (Stokols et al., 1973). That is, people who are naturally aggressive become more so in crowded urban situations. Those who are naturally passive tend to become more passive and withdrawn. One study indicates that men will respond to crowding by becoming aggressive and competitive, while women will become cooperative and interdependent (Freedman et al., 1972).

(Ray Ellis, Photo Researchers)

There are, of course, other urban problems that add to stress, such as noise and pollution. Some studies show that constant noise is as important in disturbing urban mental health as is crowding. Cohen, Glass, and Singer (1973) studied how long-term noise affected urban children. They found that reading and the ability to distinguish among sounds were noticeably poorer for children who had lived for long periods in extremely noisy places.

ISOLATION AND LONELINESS

It is a paradox that as crowding has increased in American society, so has a sense of isolation and loneliness. Zuckerman and his associates (Zuckerman et al., 1962, 1968) compared subjects under social isolation conditions, and under sensory deprivation conditions, with a nonisolated control group. Although the subjects under complete sensory deprivation suffered the most—for a discussion on the effects of sensory deprivation, see Chapter 7—the subjects in social isolation also experienced far more depression, impaired thought, and anxiety than did the control group subjects.

Stanley Schachter (1959) studied the writings of hermits and prisoners of war to pinpoint the effects of social isolation. He found that their suffering increased during the first stages of isolation, but leveled off and even declined thereafter. In part, this may be because many people undergoing severe social isolation become apathetic and withdrawn, a state of mind resembling schizophrenia. Schachter also found that isolated people spend a lot of time dreaming, thinking, and even hallucinating about other people. But isolated people who engage in physical or mental exercise suffer less than those who do nothing.

ISOLATED GROUPS. The effects of isolation have also been observed in small groups such as sailors living in underwater sea laboratories. Often, under these circumstances, hostility arises among the men, who withdraw from one another. This withdrawal is often accompanied by a territorial sense: "my bed," "my chair," "your corner." Monotony, boredom, lethargy, irritability, and even despair may develop under these circumstances. Smith and Haythorn (1972) found that the fewer the men in the underwater lab, the more pronounced this behavior became.

LONELINESS. Loneliness is very different from isolation. A person can feel lonely in a crowd. Indeed, amid a dense, urban population, thousands of people are desperately lonely. Loneliness implies an inability to break through the social and mental barriers that people erect around themselves. But loneliness often affects people the same way as social isolation does.

That loneliness is an important and distressing element in our society is seen in the growth of such services as Hot Lines, Help Lines, and clubs for single, divorced, or widowed people. One of the principal factors in the development of the "lonely society" is the loosening of traditional family bonds. In an earlier era, people often stayed near their "extended" family. Old people were considered a valuable asset to the community, just as

tribal elders are the repositories of wisdom, tradition, and experience. But with the growth of industrial society and the increased competition for good schooling, good housing, and good jobs, more people now live on their own. With the increase in the divorce rate, even the so-called nuclear family does not offer the companionship, love, and personal give-and-take that most human beings need. Now, old people are often isolated and left with no sense that their experience is valued; husbands and wives often divorce; children are separated from one or both of their parents; and frequent moves have weakened the old community ties that linked neighbor to neighbor.

Conflict

Conflict is so universal that it seems pointless to define it. Yet there are so many types of conflict and so many ways of perceiving conflict that it is useful to start with some definitions. Jones and Gerard (1967) define conflict as "a state that obtains for an individual when he is motivated to make two or more mutually incompatible responses." For Raven and Kruglanski (1970) conflict is the "tension between two or more social entities—individuals, groups, or larger organizations—which arises from incompatibility of actual or desired responses."

As you can see, these two definitions refer to two major kinds of conflict: *intrapersonal* and *interpersonal*. Intrapersonal conflict was discussed in detail in Chapter 12. Here we will focus on interpersonal conflict.

INTERPERSONAL CONFLICT

Interpersonal conflict or social conflict arises when two or more parties must divide available resources unevenly; the more one party gets, the less the other parties get (Brickman, 1974). Obviously, conflicts of this kind vary greatly from simple competition to physical struggle. Brickman suggests that there are four basic types of social conflict, which are distinguished by the amount of social control superimposed over them.

In an *unstructured conflict*, almost anything can happen. There are few

520

social controls to regulate the action. A riot, mob violence, or a barroom brawl are unstructured conflicts.

Some rules or expectations govern a *partially structured conflict:* If two people in a crowded bank see a teller opening a new window, they both might run toward it and even jostle each other to be first in line. But they would not assault each other over who got there first. Both the bank and society impose a certain structure over this kind of conflict.

In a *fully structured* (or *normative*) *conflict,* the behavior of each party is completely prescribed by the rules of society or by the situation. The resources at stake and how those resources are allocated are clearly spelled out. There are rules governing all aspects of the situation that everyone accepts. Athletic contests, games, and elections are examples of this kind of conflict.

Finally, in a *revolutionary conflict,* the socially prescribed rules are overturned or challenged. This occurs not only during social upheavals, such as the French and Russian Revolutions, but even in smaller conflicts, as when, for instance, sailors on a ship mutiny and take it over.

(Peter Southwick, Stock, Boston)

POSITIVE ELEMENTS OF CONFLICT

Most people think negatively about conflict and, indeed, it can be cruel and destructive. But it can also be beneficial. Conflict, for example, can lead to needed social change. The conflict over racial equality in the 1960s, to name one instance, certainly led to some benefits. Conflict also unites or solidifies various groups or persons involved in it. This happens during elections, when the factions behind the various primary candidates unite and work together to elect the candidate who has been nominated. Conflict and competition also provide people with the freedom to choose among ideologies, religions, or even products (Worchel & Cooper, 1978).

RESOLVING CONFLICTS

We have many ways to resolve destructive conflicts. This may not always be obvious, however, especially when the conflict is a long-standing and bitter one, as, for example, the Arab–Israeli conflict in the Middle East.

Sometimes, when opposing parties have a common goal to work toward—the election of a candidate, a ceasefire—they may lose sight of their original conflict (Sherif et al., 1958). Role reversal, when each party acts out the other party's role, also increases understanding and reduces conflict (Rapoport, 1962). Obviously, this only works in small conflicts, but it is often used in family therapy. Another method for resolving conflict involves converting the conflict into a more controlled, less destructive way of playing out the opposing positions. This is one of the bases of the Olympic Games and of other international competitions.

Unfortunately, these methods of resolving conflicts work best for fully structured conflicts. Other conflicts require different solutions. In some unstructured conflicts, the solution is to impose a structure from outside. For instance, if a fire breaks out in a public place, the panic could cause an

"What do you say we throw in the towel and say good night?"
(Drawing by Frascino, © 1981 *The New Yorker Magazine,* Inc.)

unstructured conflict during which people might be trampled trying to escape. If, however, some group or person can impose an orderly exit, then the conflict can be resolved in a less dangerous way (Kelley et al., 1965; Mintz, 1956).

Very often in conflicts, a third party has to impose some sort of structure. This may range from labor negotiators, who arbitrate a strike, to a moderate coalition leader who mediates between left- and right-wing members of a political party, to the less pleasant but noteworthy example of a military leader, who imposes authoritarian rule over an entire nation. In our time, imposing a structure is a common way of resolving conflicts.

TRUST. There are other important factors that affect a conflict and its possible resolution. One of the most elusive is *trust*. Trust is vital to all resolutions of conflicts but is hard to accurately define.

Rotter (1971) defined trust as a generalized expectation that the word, promise, or verbal or written statement of a person can be relied upon. Pruitt (1965) argues that trust is the general expectancy that a person or group will respond in a helpful rather than a harmful way. Worchel (1979) suggests that we are living in an "age of distrust," that people distrust the major institutions—government, big business, organized religions, political parties—that used to foster community cooperation. People also mistrust one another far more than they did in the past. Studies by Hochreich and Rotter (1970) and by Wrightsman and Baker (1969) have shown a sharp drop in personal trust among college students—formerly a group associated with optimistic, idealistic views about human nature.

How does trust develop? Experiments indicate that for trust to develop, one person—or group—must become more vulnerable to see if the other person—or group—will abuse that vulnerability. It is worth noting that while several tests are often needed before trust is firmly established, only *one betrayal* can completely destroy a sense of cooperation and trust between people and groups. Moreover, once *distrust* has set in, it is very hard to remove it. Distrust leads to a perception that a person—or group—is a threat, and the existence of such a threat means that something bad can always occur no matter how good present conditions are. There is, however, some evidence that trust can be partly restored if one party admits to being wrong and persuades the other that he or she is truly sorry.

CONFLICT AND THREAT. If trust is important in resolving conflicts, so are threats. Threats are, in some ways, the reverse of trust. The use of threats to resolve conflicts seems to increase as trust breaks down. How useful is a threat in resolving a conflict? Deutsch and Krauss (1960) developed an elaborate game that included a potential for threat. They found that if only one of the players could threaten, the conflict was more easily resolved than if both could. This suggests that the more widely the ability to threaten is distributed in a conflict, the more difficult the conflict is to resolve. This, of course, runs counter to the behavior of governments in conflict. It is a cliché of the American–Soviet nuclear arms race, for example, that the "balance of terror"—the threat that each nation can destroy the other— makes the resolution of international conflict more likely. It may indeed lessen the likelihood of the ultimate conflict—nuclear war. But, on a daily

(UPI)

basis it seems to make each side work harder to produce more weapons, while smaller conflicts become more frequent and are not resolved, merely stalemated.

Many variables determine if threat will be used to resolve conflict. Saving face, preserving one's public dignity, is one of the strongest elements in many conflicts where threat is used. Goffman (1959) noted that face-saving is deeply embedded in Western societies. Brown (1968) observed that threat is most often used by those who have been publicly embarrassed: Threats become the means of restoring lost dignity. The *intensity of the conflict* also determines if threat is likely to be used. Deutsch and Krauss (1960) showed that the more intense a conflict was, the more frustration it involved and, thus, the more likely it was that threat would be used to resolve that frustration. Moreover, an intense conflict seems to "raise the stakes." People want to win so much that they will threaten to win.

BARGAINING. All conflicts involve some bargaining. Even the use of a threat can be seen as a crude bargain: "If you back down, I won't punch you in the nose (or bomb your cities)." But bargaining as a strategy for reducing and resolving conflict really works only when the parties communicate peacefully. This is known as *overt bargaining:* (1) The parties in conflict have divergent interests; (2) some form of communication is possible; and (3) the parties can make provisional offers or concessions (Chertkoff & Esser, 1976). This kind of resolution is observed in labor–management negotiations, and in the forging of such international agreements as the Egyptian–Israeli peace pact.

It is a cliché that in such bargaining, the stronger your initial demands, the more likely you are to get what you want. This is seen in lawsuits in which an injured party begins by suing for an enormous damage settlement. How effective is this tactic? Chertkoff and Conley (1967) tested subjects who believed that they were either buying or selling an automobile. The subjects could discuss the price only by sending messages through intermediaries. These messages were manipulated so that the "price" was always much higher than the buyer's first offer. Yet, the buyers almost always agreed to pay more than they had originally offered. In other words, a bargainer is more likely to win concessions from an opponent if he or she starts the bid higher, rather than at a moderate, more reasonable level.

Other studies in this area show that in bargaining, people and groups who do not make strong demands, or who give in too easily to the demands of others, will be exploited. Swingle (1970) believes that this is because not using power seems to show an inability or a reluctance to use it. In either case, this allows a person to feel that he or she no longer needs to fear the opponent. Another aspect of this situation is that a powerful person or group who responds to bargaining with total cooperation and major concessions is often seen as untrustworthy. This may be because the opponent fears that this cooperation merely masks another intention— "What has he got up his sleeve?" In general, research on bargaining indicates that the best strategy involves meeting cooperation with small concessions. A failure to make any concessions usually leads to a stalemate and to a breakdown in bargaining. Making major concessions, however, is perceived as being weak or suspicious.

Anwar Sadat and Menachem Begin negotiated the Egyptian-Israeli peace pact.
(LeRoy Woodson, Woodfin Camp & Associates)

Aggression

Aggression in human beings includes all behavior that is intended to inflict physical or psychological harm on others. Intent is an important, almost a necessary element of aggression. Beck (1978) argues that human behavior cannot be considered aggressive without intent. For instance, if you are driving your car and hit someone who darts out in front of you, you have inflicted physical harm, but without intent. This is not an act of aggression. If, however, you see a woman crossing the street and refuse to put on your brakes, knowing that you will hit her, you have done something intentionally harmful—an act of aggression.

But there are other considerations that are as important as intent. Feshbach (1971) and others point out that the harm one person may inflict on another may be an end in itself, or it may be a means to an end. For instance, if a child hits another child for playing with his or her toys, that is an end in itself. If a child hits a bully who has been menacing a friend, that is an aggressive act, but it is not an end in itself; rather, it is a means of protecting a friend and expressing outrage to the bully. In the first instance, the aggression is motivated by angry feelings. In the second instance, it is more a protective act, influenced perhaps by anger, but by other feelings as well. Psychologists, thus, tend to distinguish between angry and nonangry aggression (Rule & Nesdale, 1976).

Most of us encounter angry aggression every day. Although many wars are rationalized as self-defensive acts of protection, most wars are begun as nothing more than hugely inflated acts of angry aggression. Human civilization has been almost continually punctuated by such bloody acts of aggression. War is so common that many history books date all human endeavors according to the war that was raging at the time.

Besides this constant parade of weapons and global conflicts, the crime rate is soaring. Many theorists hold that rape, for example, has nothing to

(UPI)

SHOULD YOU HOLD IT IN OR LET IT OUT?

Some influential psychotherapists believe that people who let out their pent-up anger and aggression will free themselves of inhibitions, tensions, and muscular aches and pains and enjoy deeper, healthier relationships with others. According to this view, people who are afraid to express their hostilities directly should either fantasize situations where they physically attack the object of their anger or overtly express their anger by beating a pillow. This kind of therapy encourages people to "ventilate" their emotions without guilt.

According to Leonard Berkowitz (1973), however, some behavior theorists doubt that ventilation techniques reduce internal aggression. They cite experimental evidence that shows that while people who are rewarded for acting out anger in therapy sessions do lose their inhibitions and have less anxiety, they also become more aggressive in the outside world.

The acting out of emotions verbally or physically, therefore, may not purge people of their aggression, but instead may reinforce it and ensure that people resort to it more often in the future. These psychologists recommend instead that people resolve their anger by describing their feelings to others instead of attacking them verbally or physically.

do with sex, *per se,* but is an act of aggression that expresses a male rage and a contempt for women which is encouraged by our male-dominated, male-oriented society.

Most murders involve intense anger between people who know one another. And robbery is one of the most clear-cut examples of frustration–aggression: Someone has something you want; not having it frustrates you; so you take it. These examples of aggressive behavior are all too familiar. They are in news reports daily. But there are other examples.

Many people are shocked to learn that violence in the family is also a daily occurrence. Violent assaults on spouses and children are so common that some social scientists describe the family as the "cradle of violence" (Steinmetz & Straus, 1974). In a study of some 2,000 married couples in this country, investigators found that more than 25 percent of those questioned had engaged in some form of physical violence in their married lives (Straus, 1977). Although both husbands and wives shared in this violence, husbands ranked "higher" for more harmful violence—actual beating or use of a weapon. This study also disproved the belief that family violence was more common among lower-income groups. Although upper-income groups indicated more disapproval of physical violence in the family, the actual incidence of such violence was nearly identical.

Recent reports about increases in child abuse show that aggression in the family is not restricted to husband–wife violence. According to one report, there are about 60,000 cases of child abuse a year—and this is only what is reported (Sage, 1973). Like rape, family violence—especially when it involves abuse of children—often causes so much shame and confusion to the victims that they do not report the incident (Straus, 1971).

Although the immediate results of child abuse are bad enough, its long-term psychological consequences are, perhaps, even worse. Studies indicate that abused children become violent adults. Indeed, it appears that many adults who abuse children were themselves abused when they were children. In fact, court records show that children rescued from child abuse show up far more often and far more rapidly as juvenile delinquents and as adult criminals than do other children from similar socioeconomic backgrounds (Straus, 1977).

These somewhat numbing facts suggest that aggression and violence are the norm and that they are an inevitable part of human culture. In fact, many behavioral scientists believe exactly that—that aggression in human beings is part of an instinct to kill and to destroy, a vestige of our primitive past. Other scientists, however, argue that violence is learned behavior that can be changed and controlled. Such theorists point to those human societies in which violence barely exists and to the variety of violent behavior shown by the most crime-ridden societies. As with so many aspects of psychology, there are several theories to explain the existence of violence and aggression in human society. Let us now consider some of them.

CAUSES OF AGGRESSION

The major theories of the origins and meaning of aggression fall into three categories: the psychoanalytic approach, the ethological approach—that is, the study of humans as a species of animal—and the learning-model approach.

THE PSYCHOANALYTIC APPROACH. For Freud and his followers, aggression was simply an expression of bodily needs and functions. They held that the aggressive urge, like the sexual urge, must be released, either directly or indirectly. Freud believed that one important function of society was to subdue the natural urge to aggression. Such urges may be worked off in constructive, socially acceptable ways—like jogging, boxing, or even debating—or they may be channeled into destructive, socially unacceptable ways—fights, insults, child abuse. Sometimes, the destructive side of aggression is turned back on a person, resulting in the tendency to have accidents or in suicide.

Some psychoanalysts see aggression as part of our continuing, unconscious efforts to balance the ego's rational forces with the id's irrational forces. Others link the aggressive tendency directly to the sexual urge. They believe that aggression and violence express repressed sexual needs. In a study performed by Zillman (1978), subjects were shown sexually arousing material, or violent material, or neutral material. They were then given the chance to deliver electric shocks to another subject. Those subjects who had been shown the sexually arousing material were far more likely to give the shocks than were those who had seen either the violent or the neutral material.

Many psychologists do not accept this view of aggression. As Lazarus (1974) points out, certain implications about human life follow from the belief that an aggressive drive is innate. Since an innate drive cannot be eliminated, it must be directed into socially acceptable and productive activities. Indeed, Freud argued that civilization is merely an elaborate channeling device for our sexual and aggressive energies. But humanistic psychologists, such as Maslow and Fromm, see human nature in a more

(UPI)

positive light than Freud did. They emphasize the unique and distinctively human qualities of cooperative behavior, friendship, and love.

THE ETHOLOGICAL APPROACH. Ethologists believe that aggression is largely an instinct left over from our prehistoric past, an instinct that in itself is not negative, since it serves to reduce population and to strengthen the species. The noted ethologist Konrad Lorenz popularized this theory in his book *On Aggression* (1968). In Lorenz's view, aggression only becomes a negative force when the species—our own, especially—fails to develop an appropriate instinctual guard against the use of aggression toward members of its own species.

Lorenz divided animals into those species that survived by fighting— lions, for example—and those that survived by fleeing— such as deer. They are known as the fight or flight animals. Because they could wipe out their own species, the fight animals evolved rules of behavior that ritualized aggression between members of their own species. Lions or wolves, for example, will seldom fight each other to the death. But the flight animals never had to develop this kind of behavior.

Lorenz believed that until they invented weapons, humans were among the fleers; however, clubs, spears, and guns changed all that. Thus, today, humans, alone among animals, have the means to destroy each other and lack the instinct not to. This theory has gained considerable popularity, while at the same time it has been denounced by many psychologists and social scientists as being simplistic.

The theory that aggression is an instinct is questioned by some scientists. Lazarus (1974) observed that there is no substantial research to show that people have a built-in, uncontrollable urge to fight and kill. Those who favor the innate drive theory of aggression—whether basing it on Freud's model or on the still vaguer ethological approach—maintain that aggression is a constant source of energy which, if not released, causes tension, pain, and irrational behavior. Yet, as we shall see shortly, studies show that the release of this energy through aggressive acts tends to *increase* the likelihood of further acts of aggression! If aggressive energy must be released to bring human nature into balance, why then do aggressive acts seem to lead to more aggressive acts, rather than to a more harmonious resolution of conflict and tension?

LEARNED AGGRESSIVE BEHAVIOR. Another view of aggression suggests that aggression is not a motive at all, but a form of learned behavior. We observed earlier that many social psychologists believe that frustration and displaced anger lead to racial prejudice and discrimination. The same may also be true of all aggressive and violent behavior. Frustration—especially when it is unexpected and arbitrary—seems to be strongly linked to aggressive behavior. In a study of the frustrations a group encountered doing a certain task, Worchel (1974) found that members of the group became quite aggressive when someone seemed to be deliberately thwarting the task. But they became much less aggressive when their work was impaired accidentally—for example, because a person was hard of hearing.

Many researchers, however, do not believe that frustration inevitably leads to aggression. Bandura (1973) notes that frustration leads to many kinds of behavior, such as a search for help and support, achievement strivings, withdrawal, and even escape into drugs and alcohol. Bandura suggests that frustration generates aggression in those people who have already learned aggressive attitudes as a means of coping with unpleasant situations. And frustration seems not to generate aggression in those people who have already learned to inhibit aggressive behavior.

Another theory proposes that frustration does not lead directly to aggression but rather to anger, which is then more likely to lead to aggression than is simple frustration (Berkowitz, 1965). Moreover, these feelings of anger will usually lead to aggression only if there are aggressive *cues* in the environment. For instance, if someone harasses you on the street just after you have seen a Kung-Fu film, you are more apt to respond aggressively than if you had just seen *The Sound of Music*. According to this view of human behavior, if people have weapons at hand when they are angry, they will use them sooner than if they had to search for a weapon.

According to the learning view, then, while the aggressive behavior of lower animals can be explained by innate or instinctual "urges" or "drives," aggression and violence among humans are learned according to two of the basic learning processes discussed in Chapter 5: *instrumental learning* and *observational learning*.

Instrumental learning occurs when behavior is reinforced or rewarded. In other words, if a child always gets his or her way through aggressive behavior, that behavior will be reinforced and will be more likely to recur in the future. Observational learning occurs when we observe or imitate *models*—parents, teachers, even television characters. A mother who slaps her daughter for taking a friend's toy is modeling aggressive behavior. In fact, children who are severely punished for aggressive behavior are found to be more aggressive toward others, even toward dolls. In various experiments performed by Bandura, Ross, and Ross (1963), for example, children were far more aggressive in their play after seeing adult aggression.

Of the two kinds of learning, observation has recently received the most attention as the source of aggressive behavior, and the mass media—particularly TV—has been targeted as the most significant model. In San Francisco, a 9-year-old girl was raped with a beer bottle by a group of teenagers. They were apparently reenacting a scene from the TV movie *Born Innocent*. The mother of the girl sued the TV network for $11 million in damages. She claimed that the film had inspired the attack. Similar events have taken place across the country, and there is a growing belief that violence in the mass media does indeed contribute to learning violent behavior, especially among children and teenagers.

Television is filled with violence and often glorifies it. But this by itself does not mean that observing violence on TV teaches people to behave violently. Liebert and Baron (1972) tested this connection. They showed some children excerpts from a violent television show and some others scenes from a sporting event. After the viewing, all the children were given the chance to "help" or "hurt" another child—actually nonexistent—by pushing a button. The study found that the children who had just seen the crime show were far more likely to push the "hurt" button than the children who had watched the sports event.

Obviously, these laboratory studies are not the same as behavior in the "real world." But other studies conducted in more "realistic" settings show a similar pattern. An experiment conducted at a private school in Belgium (Leyens et al., 1975), for instance, showed that boys who were exposed to a festival of violent films were far more aggressive than their schoolmates who were shown nonviolent, family-type films.

It is important to note, however, that the *context* in which the violence is observed is at least as important as the violence itself. For example, if a child sees a violent scene on television with an adult who expresses disgust at the violence, the child is less likely to respond positively to that scene. The opposite is also true: If the child sees violence in the presence of an adult enthralled by the violence, the child is being shown that this action is at least interesting, if not socially acceptable.

It is also possible that violence on television helps us not to behave aggressively, but to *unlearn* our inhibitions about aggression. As children, most of us learn that we must inhibit aggression. Studies show that repeated exposure to scenes of fictional violence can blunt the shock and anxiety of seeing real violence. Once this anxiety has been reduced, it becomes easier to engage in violent and aggressive behavior ourselves. Thus, television violence may encourage aggression by reducing our learned inhibitions about violent, aggressive behavior (Thomas & Drabman, 1977). It is also worth noting that girls are less affected than boys by television violence. This would be expected because girls undergo far more social pressure to inhibit their aggressive tendencies. But other studies have shown that in cases of justified (nonangry) aggression, women exhibit just as much aggression as men do (Frodi, Macauly, & Thome, 1977).

CAN AGGRESSION BE CONTROLLED?

A former president of the American Psychological Association recently suggested that we develop an anticruelty drug to reduce people's violent

529

tendencies. Unfortunately, such a drug would almost certainly produce more problems than solutions: How would we decide who gets it? Who would administer it? How could we keep the drug from being abused by the very people it is meant to control? As is so often the case, the simplistic response is by no means the best response. What are some of the other methods proposed to reduce violence?

REASON. Most people would probably agree with any reasonable argument against violent and aggressive behavior. This would probably have little effect on their actual behavior, however, since people rarely act out their violent and aggressive tendencies in a logical manner.

CATHARSIS. One of the oldest ideas about the control and release of aggression is that the "aggressive drive" can be reduced by expressing the aggression. Freud called this the *catharsis* of aggressive feelings. It is exactly what we mean when we say that we want to "let off steam." As we have seen, Freud presumed that we always have a reservoir of aggressive energy and that any expression of aggression would help reduce the aggressive energy that remained.

There is some evidence that when angry people are encouraged to express aggression, they do in fact become less angry and are then less aggressive. But nonangry people who are encouraged to express aggression are either unaffected by this expression or they actually become *more* aggressive (Doob & Wood, 1972). Moreover, in most of these studies, aggressive behavior decreased only if the angry subjects were allowed to express aggression toward someone they perceived as their tormentor, not if they merely expressed "random" aggression. This method also seems to work best when there are imposed limits, when the subject feels that there is an end to the expression of anger and aggression—a clear-cut break in the action, rather than an open-ended situation.

PUNISHMENT. Our society relies heavily on punishment to discourage violent behavior. How successful is it? Not very, it seems. This includes the use of punishment in both childhood and adulthood. Studies of parent–

(Susan S. Perry, Woodfin Camp & Associates)

child relationships have repeatedly shown that children who were severely punished grow up to be aggressive adults prone to violence (Aronson, 1980). In part, this may be because by punishing them, their parents are also models of aggressive behavior.

But what if people see aggression punished? This is the concept behind the ancient custom of public executions and public punishments like flogging and the stocks, but data demonstrate that this method does not stop aggressive behavior (Haney, 1979). Some children have been shown films in which an aggressive character was punished. Others were shown one where the character was rewarded for the same behavior. Then, all the children were given the chance to act aggressively under circumstances similar to those in the film. The children who saw the aggressive model being punished were less aggressive than those who saw the aggressive model being rewarded, but both groups of children were *more* aggressive than those tested who had seen *no* aggressive model at all. In other words, simply seeing an aggressive model seems to increase aggression among children, whether the model is punished or rewarded (Aronson, 1980).

REWARDING ALTERNATIVE BEHAVIOR. One hopeful tactic is to ignore aggressive behavior and reward nonaggressive behavior. Davitz (1952) used playgroups of four children. Some groups were rewarded for constructive behavior; others had been rewarded for aggressive behavior. Then, the children were deliberately frustrated, a situation that would ordinarily lead to aggression. The children who were reinforced for constructive behavior were far less frustrated and aggressive than were the children in the other group.

LONG-TERM APPROACHES. There are two other important ways to control aggression. As with the rewarding of alternative behavior, they must be present from an early age to have any real effect. They are living with nonaggressive models and learning to build empathy and to care for others. Perhaps these two principles seem obvious. Clearly, children who only see violent, quarrelsome, competitive adults will see the world as an aggressive, competitive place. But how many of us remember this when we are with children? How many of us bother to explain to children why human beings—all human beings—should be treated with dignity and respect?

Seymour Feshbach (1971) has observed that most people find it hard to inflict pain on someone unless they can *dehumanize* that person. This is why wars are filled with vicious propaganda—soldiers can kill a "Gook" far more easily than a poor peasant. In any number of studies, the evidence is clear: Children who have been taught to empathize with other people are *far* less likely to be aggressive toward others. The more empathy and understanding we have for people, the less likely we are to resort to cruel, aggressive, and violent behavior (Aronson, 1980).

Violence is widespread and deeply rooted in our culture, yet aggression and violence can be controlled—but not by our usual methods. Thus, whether we do, in fact, control them depends on how willing we are to extend ourselves, to move out of the familiar molds, to empathize with others, and to aim for higher standards than those we usually apply.

Summary

1. Prejudice is widespread. Extreme examples of racial prejudice only differ in degree from our more common biases. *Prejudice* refers to an intolerant attitude; *discrimination* refers to actual behavior; *racism* combines the two, including both attitude and behavior.

2. Prejudice flourishes in the *absence* of experience.

3. The sources of prejudice are frustration, stereotyping, and conformity.

4. *Frustration–aggression* refers to the pattern by which people displace their hatreds and frustrations about their own lives onto covenient "scapegoats." The scapegoats must be safe, visible, strange, and already disliked.

5. Stereotyping also contributes to prejudice and discrimination. Stereotyping is a simplistic form of *attribution*—the means by which we attribute attitudes and beliefs to other people's actions and behavior. Most stereotypes are learned when we are very young.

6. Conformity to group pressure also encourages prejudice. Children are especially prone to peer-group pressure in matters like race hatred. People who tend to conform also tend to harbor racial prejudice in an environment where prejudice is expected.

7. Similarity of attitude tends to reduce racial prejudice, but does not have much effect on people's intimate relations. The best way to reduce prejudice is through interdependent cooperation among racially mixed groups.

8. Environmental psychology studies the effects of such elements as crowding, noise, and social structure on our relationships to other people and to ourselves. There are two types of features that influence our perceptions of physical settings. *Ambient features* refer to such elements as heat, light, noise. *Architectural features* are the elements of the structure itself, such as shape, color, design.

9. People can *adapt* to their environment. That is, their initial responses often change after spending time in that environment.

10. *Personal space* denotes the amount of physical space between people that is needed for them to feel comfortable and unthreatened. National, ethnic, and sexual differences exist in the area of personal space. When our personal space is invaded, we tend to react with discomfort, anger, and suspicion; the more intimate we are with people, the less we care about their proximity to us.

11. Crowding can be both a psychological and a physical state. Studies show that animals become more antisocial and stressful when crowded.

12. One aspect of highly dense population is *sensory overload:* Too many faces and voices make people withdraw and become iso-

lated. This leads to *deindividuation,* by which people come to disregard other people's individual, human characteristics. Crowding tends to exaggerate people's natural tendencies toward aggression or passivity. As crowding has increased in urban society, so has *isolation.* Social isolation leads to depression, impaired thought, and anxiety. Loneliness differs from isolation—people can be lonely while in a crowd—but often produces similar effects. The structure and dynamics of the modern family are major causes of loneliness.

13. There are two major types of conflict: *intrapersonal*—conflicts within ourselves—and *interpersonal,* or social conflicts.

14. Conflict can sometimes be beneficial. It can lead to social change; it can create a new solidarity; it can provide a freedom of choice between opposing factions; it can help a group or a person assess strengths and weaknesses.

15. Giving conflicting groups a common goal sometimes reduces conflict. Role reversal, in which opponents act out conflicts, often helps in family-type confrontations. The imposition of outside control is another common way of resolving conflicts, for example, labor mediation or military dictatorship.

16. *Trust* is an important factor in reducing conflicts. For trust to develop, people must let themselves become vulnerable.

17. *Threat* appears to make conflict resolution more difficult. Threat is most likely to be used in a highly tense conflict or when one of the parties feels that he or she has been publicly embarrassed.

18. All conflict resolution includes some *bargaining. Overt bargaining* takes place when the parties in conflict have divergent interests, some form of communication, and the possibility of provisional offers or concessions.

19. Aggression includes all behavior that is meant to harm others physically or psychologically. Intent to harm is a necessary factor in aggression. Psychologists distinguish between angry and non-angry aggression.

20. Criminal aggression in the form of rape, murder, and robbery appear to be on the rise in our society. Many people believe that rape is the result of male hatred and fear of women. Studies indicate that sexually arousing material can be *more* conducive to aggression than violent material.

21. Children rescued from child abuse are far more likely to become antisocial than are children from more ordinary backgrounds. Also, adults who were abused as children often themselves resort to child abuse.

22. Freud and his followers believed that aggression is an innate urge that can take either constructive or destructive channels. According to Freud, society's role was to subordinate the natural tendency to aggression and violence. Konrad Lorenz argues that aggression in human beings is an instinct left over from our prehistoric past.

23. Most social psychologists argue that violence and aggression are learned behavior. Learned behavior is broken down into two areas: *instrumental learning* (reinforced and rewarded behavior) and *observational learning* (learning through observing role models). Children respond to adult aggression by becoming more aggressive themselves. Other contributors to aggression are *frustration, deindividuation,* and such environmental factors as *heat* and *noise.*

24. Studies indicate that children who watch media violence are more prone to aggression and hostility themselves. But *context* of viewing is also important. If children observe that TV violence gets a negative response from an adult, they are far less likely to respond to it positively themselves.

25. Studies indicate that violence and aggression can be reduced—but not through methods that are customarily used in society. In particular, *reason* and severe *punishment* are rarely successful in reducing violence. Most important in reducing aggression and violence over the long-term are the *presence of nonaggressive models* and the *teaching of empathy and caring for all human beings.*

Appendix

Measurement and Statistical Methods

Most of the experiments described in this book involve measuring one or more variables and then analyzing the data statistically. The design and scoring of all the tests we have discussed are also based on statistical methods. **Statistics** is a branch of mathematics. It provides techniques for sorting out quantitative facts and ways of drawing conclusions from them. Statistics let us organize and describe data quickly, guide the conclusions we draw, and help us make inferences.

Statistical analysis is essential to conducting an experiment or designing a test, but statistics can only handle numbers—groups of them. To use statistics, the psychologist first must measure things—count and express them in quantities.

SCALES OF MEASUREMENT

No matter what we are measuring—height, noise, intelligence, attitudes, and so on—we have to use a scale. The data we want to collect determine the scale we will use and, in turn, the scale we use helps determine the conclusions we can draw from our data.

NOMINAL SCALES. If we decide to classify a group of people by the color of their eyes, we are using a **nominal scale.** We can count how many people have blue eyes, how many have green eyes, how many have brown eyes, and so on, but we cannot say that one group has more or less eye color than another. The colors are simply different.

A nominal scale is a set of arbitrarily named or numbered categories. If we looked up how many Republican, Democratic, and Independent voters registered in a certain congressional district in the last election year, we are using a nominal scale. Since a nominal scale is more of a way of classifying than of measuring, it is the least informative kind of scale. If we want to compare our data more precisely, we will have to use a scale that tells us more.

ORDINAL SCALES. If we list horses in the order in which they finish a race, we are using an **ordinal scale.** On an ordinal scale, data are ranked from first to last according to some criterion. An ordinal scale tells the order, but nothing about the distances between what is ranked first and second or ninth and tenth. It does not tell us how much faster the winning horse ran than the horses that placed or showed. If a person ranks her preferences for various kinds of soup—pea soup first, then tomato, then onion, and so on—we know what soup she likes most and what soup she likes least, but we have no idea how much better she likes tomato than onion, if they are rated closely, or if pea soup is far more favored than either one of them.

Since we do not know the distances between the items ranked on an ordinal scale, we cannot add or subtract ordinal data. If mathematical operations are necessary, we need a still more informative scale.

INTERVAL SCALES. An **interval scale** is often compared to a ruler that has been broken off at the bottom—it only goes from, say, 5½ to 12. The intervals between 6 and 7, 7 and 8, 8 and 9, and so forth, are equal, but there is no zero. A thermometer is an interval scale—even though a certain degree registered on a Fahrenheit or centigrade thermometer specifies a certain state of cold or heat, there is no such thing as no temperature at all. One day is never twice as hot as another; it is only so many equal degrees hotter.

An interval scale tells us how many equal-sized units one thing lies above or below another thing of the same kind, but it does not tell us how many times bigger, smaller, taller, or fatter one thing is than another. An intelligence test cannot tell us that one person is three times as intelligent as another, only that he or she scored so many points above or below someone else.

RATIO SCALES. We can only say that a measurement is 2 times as long as another or 3 times as high when we use a **ratio scale,** one that has a true zero. For instance, if we measure the snowfall in a certain area over several winters, we can say that 6 times as much snow fell during a winter in which we measured a total of 12 feet as during a winter in which only 2 feet fell. This scale has a zero—there may be no snow.

Measures of Central Tendency

Usually when we measure a number of instances of anything—from the popularity of TV shows to the weights of 8-year-old boys to the number of times a man's optic nerve fires in response to electrical stimulation—we get a distribution of measurements that range from smallest to largest or lowest to highest. The measurements will usually cluster around some value near the middle. This value is the **central tendency** of the distribution of the measurements.

Suppose for example, you want to keep 10 children busy tossing rings around a bottle. You give them 3 rings to toss each turn, the game has 6 rounds, and each player scores 1 point every time he or she gets the ring around the neck of the bottle. The highest possible score is 18. The distribution of scores might end up like this: 11, 8, 13, 6, 12, 10, 16, 9, 12, 3.

What could you quickly say about the ring-tossing talent of the group? First, you could arrange the scores from lowest to highest: 3, 6, 8, 9, 10, 11, 12, 12, 13, 16. In this order, the central tendency of the distribution of scores becomes clear. Many of the scores cluster around the values between 10 and 12. There are 3 ways to describe the central tendency of a distribution. We usually refer to all three as the *average*.

THE MEAN

The arithmetical average is called the **mean**—the sum of all the scores in the group, divided by the number of scores. If you add up all the scores and divide by 10, the total number of scores in this group, you find that the mean for this group is 10.

THE MEDIAN

The **median** is the point that divides a distribution in half—50 percent of the scores fall above the median and 50 percent fall below. In the ring-tossing scores, 5 scores fall at 10 or below, 5 at 11 or above. The median is thus halfway between 10 and 11—10.5.

THE MODE

The point at which the largest number of scores occurs is called the **mode.** Here, the mode is 12. More people scored 12 than any other.

If we take many measurements of anything, we are likely to get a distribution of scores in which the mean, median, and mode are all about the same—the score that occurs most often (the mode) will also be the point that half the scores are below and half above (the median). And the same point will be the arithmetical average (the mean). This is not always true, of course, and small samples rarely come out so symmetrically. In these cases, we often have to decide which of the three measures of central tendency—the mean, median, or mode—will tell us what we want to know.

For example, a shopkeeper wants to know the general incomes of passersby so he can stock the right merchandise. He might conduct a rough survey by standing outside for a few days from 12:00 to 2:00 and asking every 10th person who walks by to check a card showing the general range of his or her income. Suppose most of the people checked the ranges between $8,000 and $10,000 a year. However, a couple of the people made a lot of money—one checked $100,000–$150,000, one checked the $200,000-or-above box. The mean for the set of income figures would be pushed higher by those 2 large figures and would not really tell the shopkeeper what he wants to know about his potential customers. In this case, he would be wiser to use the median or the mode.

Suppose instead of meeting 2 people whose incomes were so great, he noticed that people from 2 distinct income groups walked by his store—several people checked the box for $9,000–$10,000, several others checked $14,000–$15,000. The shopkeeper would find that his distribution was bimodal. It has 2 modes—$9,500 and $14,500. This might be more useful to him than the mean, which could lead him to think his customers were a unit with an average income of about $12,000.

Another way of approaching a set of scores is to arrange them into a **frequency distribution**—to select a set of intervals and count how many scores fall into each interval. A frequency distribution is useful for large groups of numbers; it puts the number of individual scores into more manageable groups.

Suppose a psychologist tests memory. She asks 50 college students to learn 18 nonsense syllables, then records how many syllables each student can recall 2 hours later. She arranges her raw scores from lowest to highest in a rank distribution:

2	6	8	10	11	14
3	7	9	10	12	14
4	7	9	10	12	15
4	7	9	10	12	16
5	7	9	10	13	17
5	7	9	11	13	
6	8	9	11	13	
6	8	9	11	13	
6	8	10	11	13	

The scores range from 2 to 17 but 50 individual scores are too cumbersome to work with. So she chooses a set of 2-point intervals and tallies the number of scores in each interval:

Interval	Tally	Frequency (f)
1–2	|	1
3–4	|||	3
5–6	⊬|	6
7–8	⊬ ||||	9
9–10	⊬ ⊬ |||	13
11–12	⊬ |||	8
13–14	⊬ ||	7
15–16	||	2
17–18	|	1

Now she can tell at a glance what the results of her experiment were: Most of the students had scores near the middle of the range, and very few

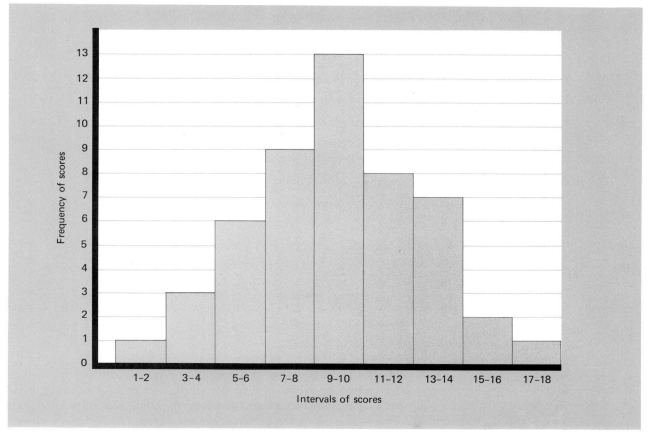

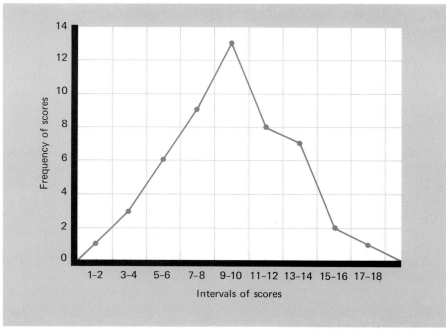

Figure A-1
A frequency histogram for a memory experiment. The bars indicate the frequency of scores within each interval.

Figure A-2
A frequency polygon drawn from data used in Figure A-1. The dots, representing the frequency of scores in each interval, are connected by straight lines.

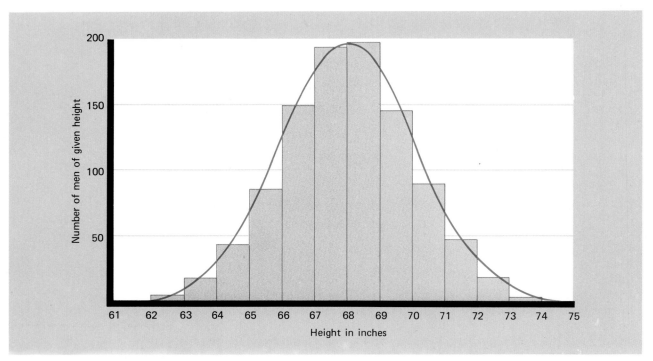

Figure A-3
A normal curve, based on measurements of the heights of 1,000 adult males.

(From A. B. Hill, *Principles of Medical Statistics*, 8th ed. London: Oxford University Press, 1966.)

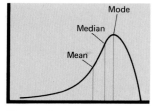

Figure A-4
A skewed distribution. Most of the scores are gathered at the high end of the distribution, causing the hump to shift to the right. Since the tail on the left is longer, we say that the curve is skewed to the left. Note that the mean, median, and mode are different.

had scores in the high or low intervals. She can see these results even better if she uses the frequency distribution to construct a bar graph—a **frequency histogram.** Marking the intervals along the horizontal axis and the frequencies along the vertical axis would give her the graph shown in Figure A–1. Another way is to construct a **frequency polygon,** a line graph. A frequency polygon drawn from the same set of data is shown in Figure A–2. Note that the figure is not a smooth curve, since the points are connected by straight lines. With many scores, however, and with small intervals, the angles would smooth out and the figure would resemble a rounded curve.

THE NORMAL CURVE

Ordinarily, if we take enough measurements of almost anything, we get a *normal distribution.* Tossing coins is a favorite example of statisticians. If you tossed 10 coins into the air 1,000 times, and recorded the heads and tails on each toss, your tabulations would reveal a normal distribution. Five heads and 5 tails would occur most often, 6 heads/4 tails and 4 heads/6 tails would be the next most frequent, and so on down to the rare all heads or all tails.

Plotting a normal distribution on a graph yields a particular kind of frequency polygon called a **normal curve.** Figure A–3 shows data on the heights of 1,000 men. Superimposed over the gray bars that reflect the actual data is an "ideal" normal curve for the same data. Note that the curve is absolutely symmetrical—the left slope parallels the right slope exactly. Moreover, the mean, median, and mode all fall on the highest point on the curve.

The normal curve is a hypothetical entity. No set of real measurements shows such a smooth gradation from one interval to the next, or so purely symmetrical a shape. But because so many things do approximate the normal curve so closely, the curve is a useful model for much that we measure.

SKEWED DISTRIBUTIONS

If a frequency distribution is asymmetrical—if most of the scores are gathered at either the high end or the low end—the frequency polygon will be *skewed*. The hump will sit to one side or the other and one of the curve's tails will be disproportionately long.

If a high school mathematics instructor, for example, gives his students a sixth-grade arithmetic test, we would expect nearly all the scores to be quite high. The frequency polygon would probably look like the one in Figure A–4. But if a sixth-grade class is asked to do advanced algebra, their scores would probably be quite low. The frequency polygon would be very similar to the one shown in Figure A–5.

Note too that the mean, median, and mode fall at different points in a skewed distribution, unlike in the normal curve, where they coincide. Usually, if you know that the mean is greater than the median of a distribution, you can predict that the frequency polygon will be skewed to the right. If the median is greater than the mean, the curve will be skewed to the left.

BIMODAL DISTRIBUTIONS

We have already mentioned a bimodal distribution in our description of the shopkeeper's survey of his customers' incomes. The frequency polygon for a bimodal distribution has two humps—one for each mode. The mean and the median may be the same, as in Figure A–6, or different, as in Figure A–7.

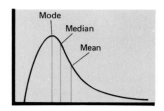

Figure A-5
In this distribution, most of the scores are gathered at the low end, so the curve is skewed to the right. The mean, median, and mode do not coincide.

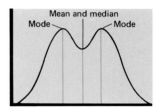

Figure A-6
A bimodal distribution in which the mean and the median are the same.

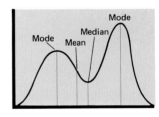

Figure A-7
In the bimodal distribution, the mean and median are different.

Measures of Variation

Sometimes it is not enough to know the distribution of a set of data and what their mean, median, and mode are. Suppose an automotive safety expert feels that too much damage occurs in tail-end accidents because automobile bumpers are not all the same height. It is not enough for him to know what the average height of an automobile bumper is. He also wants to know about the variation in bumper heights: How much higher is the highest bumper than the mean? How do the bumpers of all cars vary from the mean? Are the latest bumpers closer to the same height?

Figure A-8
Frequency polygons for two sets of measurements of automobile bumper heights. Both are normal curves and in each distribution the mean, median, and mode are 15. But the variation from the mean is different, causing the first curve to be flattened, the second much more sharply peaked.

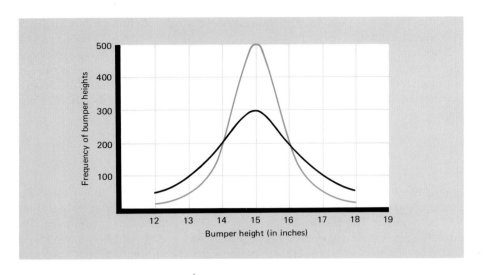

RANGE

The simplest measure of variation is the **range**—the difference between the largest and smallest measurements. Perhaps the safety expert measured the bumpers of 1,000 cars 2 years ago and found that the highest bumper was 18 inches from the ground, the lowest only 12 inches from the ground. The range was thus 6 inches—18 minus 12. This year, the highest bumper is still 18 inches high, the lowest still 12 inches from the ground. The range is still 6 inches. Moreover, he finds that the means of the 2 distributions are the same—15 inches off the ground. But look at the 2 frequency polygons in Figure A–8—there is still something he needs to know, since how the measurements cluster around the mean is drastically different. To find out how the measurements are distributed around the mean, our safety expert has to turn to a slightly more complicated measure of variation—the standard deviation.

THE STANDARD DEVIATION

The **standard deviation,** in a single number, tells us much about how the scores in any frequency distribution are dispersed around the mean. Calculating the standard deviation is one of the most useful and widely used statistical tools.

To find the standard deviation of a set of scores, we first find the mean. Then we take the first score in the distribution, subtract it from the mean, square the difference, and jot it down in a column to be added up later. We do the same for all the scores in the distribution. Then we add up the column of squared differences, divide the total by the number of scores in the distribution, and find the square root of that number. Figure A–9 shows the calculation of the standard deviation for a small distribution of scores.

In a normal distribution, however peaked or flattened the curve, about

68 percent of the scores fall between 1 standard deviation above the mean and 1 standard deviation below the mean (see Figure A–10). Another 27 percent fall between 1 standard deviation and 2 standard deviations on either side of the mean, 4 percent more between the 2nd and 3rd standard deviations on either side. More than 99 percent of the scores fall between 3 standard deviations above and 3 standard deviations below the mean. This makes the standard deviation useful for comparing two different normal distributions.

Now let us see what the standard deviation can tell our automotive safety expert about the variations from the mean in his 2 sets of data. The standard deviation for the cars he measured 2 years ago, he finds, is about 1.4. A car with a bumper height of 16.4 is 1 standard deviation above the mean of 15; one with a bumper height of 13.6 is 1 standard deviation below the mean. Since he knows that his data fall into a normal distribution, he can figure that about 68 percent of the 1,000 cars he measured

Number of scores = 10		Mean = 7
Scores	*Difference from mean*	*Difference squared*
4	7 − 4 = 3	$3^2 = 9$
5	7 − 5 = 2	$2^2 = 4$
6	7 − 6 = 1	$1^2 = 1$
6	7 − 6 = 1	$1^2 = 1$
7	7 − 7 = 0	$0^2 = 0$
7	7 − 7 = 0	$0^2 = 0$
8	7 − 8 = − 1	$-1^2 = 1$
8	7 − 8 = − 1	$-1^2 = 1$
9	7 − 9 = − 2	$-2^2 = 4$
10	7 − 10 = − 3	$-3^2 = 9$

$$\text{Sum of squares} = 30$$
$$\div$$
$$\text{Number of scores} = 10$$
$$\text{Variance} = 3$$
$$\text{Standard deviation} = \sqrt{3} = 1.73$$

Figure A-9
Step-by-step calculation of the standard deviation for a group of 10 scores with a mean of 7.

Figure A-10
A normal curve, divided to show the percentage of scores that fall within each standard deviation from the mean.

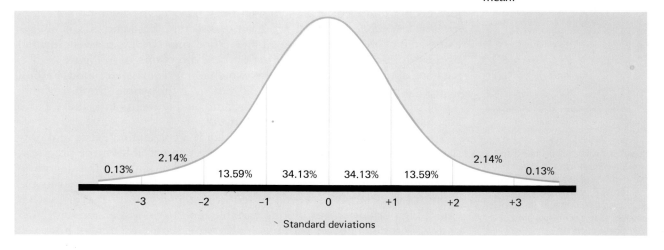

| 0.13% | 2.14% | 13.59% | 34.13% | 34.13% | 13.59% | 2.14% | 0.13% |

−3   −2   −1   0   +1   +2   +3

Standard deviations

will fall somewhere between these 2 heights: 680 cars will have bumpers between 13.6 and 16.4 inches high. For his more recent set of data, the standard deviation is just slightly less than 1. A car with a bumper height of about 14 inches is 1 standard deviation below the mean; a car with a bumper height of about 16 is 1 standard deviation above the mean. Thus, in this distribution 680 cars have bumpers between 14 and 16 inches high. This tells the safety expert that car bumpers are becoming more similar, although the range of heights is still the same (6 inches) and the mean height of bumpers is still 15.

Measures of Correlation

Measures of central tendency and measures of variation are used to describe a single set of measurements—like the children's ring-tossing scores—or to compare two or more sets of measurements—like the two sets of bumper heights. Sometimes, however, we need to know if two sets of measurements are in any way associated with one another—if they are correlated. Is smoking related to lung cancer? Is IQ related to sex? Do votes relate to income?

One fast way to determine if two variables are correlated is to draw a **scatter plot.** We assign one variable (X) to the horizontal axis of a graph, the other (Y) to the vertical axis. Then we plot a person's score on one characteristic along the horizontal axis and his or her score on the second characteristic along the vertical axis. Where the two scores intersect we draw a dot. When several scores have been plotted in this way, the pattern of dots tells if the two characteristics are in any way correlated with each other.

If the dots on a scatter plot form a straight line running between the lower left-hand corner and the upper right-hand corner, as they do in Figure A–11a, we have a perfect *positive correlation*—a high score on one of the characteristics is always associated with a high score on the other one. A straight line running between the upper left-hand corner and the lower right-hand corner, as in Figure A–11b, is the sign of a perfect *negative correlation*—a high score on one of the characteristics is always associated with a low score on the other one. If the pattern formed by the dots is cigar-shaped in either of these directions, as in Figure A–11c, we have a modest correlation—the two characteristics are related, but not highly correlated. If the dots spread out over the whole graph, forming a circle or a random pattern, as they do in Figure A–11d, there is no correlation between the two characteristics.

A scatter plot can give us a general idea if a correlation exists and how strong it is. To describe the relation between two variables more precisely, we need a **correlation coefficient**—a statistical measure of the degree to which two variables are associated. The correlation coefficient tells us the degree of association between two sets of matched scores—that is, to what extent high or low scores on one variable tend to be associated with high or low scores on another variable. It also provides an estimate of how well

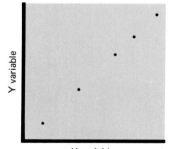

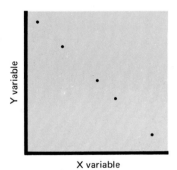

Figure A–11 a, b
Scatter plots can be used to give a rough idea of the strength and direction of correlation. Plot *a* shows a perfect positive correlation, plot *b* shows a perfect negative correlation. (cont'd)

we would be able to predict from a person's score on one characteristic how high he or she will score on another characteristic. If we know, for example, that a test of mechanical ability is highly correlated with success in engineering courses, we could predict that success on the test would also mean success as an engineering major.

Correlation coefficients can run from +1.0 to −1.0. The highest possible value (+1.0) indicates a perfect positive correlation—high scores on one variable are always and systematically related to high scores on a second variable. The lowest possible value (−1.0) means a perfect negative correlation—high scores on one variable are always and regularly related to low scores on the second variable. In life most things are far from perfect, of course, so most correlation coefficients fall somewhere between +1.0 and −1.0. A correlation below ±.20 is considered insignificant, from ±.20 to ±.40 is low, from ±.40 to ±.60 is moderate, from ±.60 to ±.80 is high, and from ±.80 to ±1.0 is very high. A correlation of zero indicates that there is no correlation between two sets of scores—no regular relation between them at all.

Correlation tells us nothing about causality. If we found a high correlation between voting preferences and income levels, for example, we still could not say that being poor made people vote Democratic or that voting for Republicans made people rich. We would still not know which came first, or if some third variable explained both income levels and voting patterns. Correlation only tells us that we have found some association between scores on two specified characteristics.

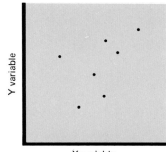

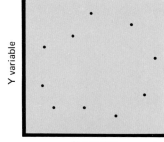

Figure A–11 c, d (cont'd)
Plot *c* shows a moderate positive correlation, but in plot *d* there is no correlation at all.

Using Statistics to Make Predictions

Behind the use of statistics is the hope that we can generalize from our results and use them to predict behavior. We hope, for example, that we can use the record of how well a group of rats run through a maze today to predict how another group of rats will do tomorrow, that we can use a person's scores on a sales aptitude test to predict how well he will sell life insurance, that we can measure the attitudes of a relatively small group of people about pollution control to indicate what the attitudes of the whole country are. But first we have to determine if our measurements are representative and if we can have confidence in them.

SAMPLING

It is often impossible, or at least impractical, to measure every single occurrence of a characteristic. No one could expect to measure the memory of every human being, or test all the rats or pigeons in the world in Skinner boxes, or record the maternal behavior of all female monkeys.

In a large population, we usually study a **sample** of cases of some reasonable, practical size and then generalize our results to the population as a whole. One way to guarantee that the results of our measurements

"Young man, I am no random sample."
(© Punch/Rothco)

are accurate for the whole population is to make sure that the sample is truly a random one.

When a neighborhood association sells chances on door prizes, then puts all the stubs into a big drum and churns it around and a blindfolded person reaches into the drum and pulls out the winning numbers, the prizewinners constitute a **random sample.** In theory, every single stub in that drum is equally likely to be picked—chance determines which numbers are selected.

A **biased sample** does not truly represent the population in question. If we want to find out if a town's garbage is being collected adequately, we could not just stand outside the best department store in town at 3:00 in the afternoon and ask everyone who happened by how many times his or her garbage had been collected that week and at what time. The people who shop at that department store in the middle of the afternoon on a work day are unlikely to represent the town's population. We would have to figure out how to make sure that all the town's neighborhoods will be presented proportionally in our sample.

Generalizations based on biased samples can lead to erroneous conclusions. If the advertising manager of a bank wanted to test a few potential campaigns designed to persuade middle-aged people with incomes over $100,000 to set up trust funds for their children, she would be unwise to base her decisions on interviews with migrant workers. The classic sampling story involves a national magazine that predicted the election of a certain candidate, who then lost the election. The magazine had based its prediction on a telephone survey. They forgot, however, that many voters did not have telephones, and many people without phones voted for the other candidate.

PROBABILITY

Errors based on inadequate sampling procedures are somebody's fault. Other kinds of errors occur randomly. In the simplest kind of experiment, a psychologist will gather a representative sample, split it randomly into two groups, and then apply some experimental manipulation to one of the groups. Afterward he will measure both groups and determine if the experimental group's score is now different from the score of the control group. But, even if there is a large difference between the scores of the two groups, the psychologist may still be wrong to attribute the difference to his manipulation. Random effects might influence his results and introduce error.

Statistics give the psychologist many ways to determine precisely if the difference between the two groups is really significant and if something other than chance produced the results, and if he or she would get the same results if he or she repeated the experiment with different subjects. These probabilities are expressed as measures of **significance.** If the psychologist computes the significance level for his or her results as .05, he knows that there are 19 chances out of 20 that the results are not due to chance. But there is still 1 chance in 20—or a .05 likelihood—that the results are due to chance. A .01 significance level would mean that there is only 1 chance in 100 that the results are due to chance.

Glossary

absolute refractory period period just after nerve cell discharge, during which the cell cannot be excited.

absolute threshold the least amount of energy that can produce a sensation 50 percent of the time.

accommodation adjustment of the eye to focus on objects at different distances.

acetylcholine a chemical that transmits nerve impulses across synapses.

achievement test test designed to measure what a person has learned.

activity substitution theory contends that the more active and productive people are in old age, the more satisfied they will be.

adaptation ability of all animals, especially humans, to adjust to their environment.

addiction strong physical need for a substance, such as some drugs.

adjustment attempts to adapt to the demands of the environment.

adolescence the developmental period between the ages of 11 and 17, marked by dramatic physiological changes and psychological preparation for and adjustment to the challenges of adulthood.

adrenal glands endocrine glands located above the kidneys that secrete epinephrine, norepinephrine, and steroids; these glands affect nerve and muscle function and the ability of the body to react to stress.

adulthood the stage of development usually beginning in the early twenties and lasting approximately 40 to 45 years in which individuals come to accept themselves and devote themselves mainly to work and family.

aerial perspective a cue to distance perception based on the relative blurriness of objects in the environment.

affective disorder severe behavior disorder characterized by inappropriate emotional responses, disordered thought, and maladaptive behavior.

affiliation motive need to be with others.

afterimage sense experience that occurs after the stimulus has ceased.

aggression hostile feelings or behavior aimed at doing harm to others.

algorithm a step-by-step method for solving problems.

altered states of consciousness (ASCs) any state of awareness that the individual or an observer would recognize as a substantial deviation from normal functioning.

altruistic behavior behavior or action on the part of an individual that is not linked to personal gain. Also called *helping behavior.*

ambient conditions the physical qualities of an environment, such as sound or heat, that affect our reaction to it.

amnesia loss of memory as a result of brain injury or psychological trauma.

amplitude the magnitude of a sound wave; primary determinant of loudness.

ampulla enlarged sac at the base of the semicircular canals in the vestibular organ of the inner ear; sense organ for equilibrium.

anal stage second stage in Freud's theory of personality development, when a child's erotic feelings center on the anus and on elimination.

androgen hormone that promotes and maintains secondary sex characteristics in males; also secreted in small amounts by females.

androgyny the presence in both sexes of male and female character traits.

anti-social personality person who suffers from a failure to internalize moral values.

anxiety feelings resembling fear, but without an identifiable source.

anxiety disorder behavior disorder characterized by chronic fear or anxiety, sometimes with physical symptoms, but not centered on a specific object.

applied psychology utilizes psychological research in concrete, practical ways to solve, or investigate, social problems.

approach-approach conflict situation in which a person is simultaneously attracted to two incompatible goals.

approach-avoidance conflict situation in which a person is simultaneously attracted to and repelled by the same goal.

aptitude test test designed to measure a person's ability to learn.

archetype in Jung's theory of personality, a thought form common to all human beings, carried in the collective unconscious.

architectural features the dimensions and makeup of a space or room and how we react to them.

association area area of the cortex responsible for integrating incoming and outgoing messages; believed to be involved in learning, memory, speech, and thinking.

attachment infantile reactions, like clinging, that gain the mother's attention.

attention focusing of awareness.

autistic thinking thinking that consists entirely of personal associations.

autokinetic illusion illusion that a stationary spot of light in a darkened room is moving.

autonomic conditioning learning to voluntarily control involuntary responses.

autonomic nervous system part of the peripheral nervous system that controls the largely involuntary functions of internal muscles and glands.

autonomy a sense of one's own abilities and powers.

aversive conditioning behavior therapy technique that aims at eliminating behavior patterns by teaching the person to associate them with pain and discomfort.

avoidance-avoidance conflict situation in which a person is simultaneosly repelled by two undesirable possibilities and cannot escape.

avoidance training teaching a learner how to prevent an unpleasant condition.

axon nerve fiber that carries impulses from one cell body to other nerve cells or to a muscle or gland.

axon terminal knob at the end of an axon; also called *synaptic knob.*

basilar membrane vibrating membrane in the cochlea of the inner ear that contains sense receptors for sound.

basket nerve ending nerve ending wrapped around the base of a hair; receptor for the pressure sense.

behavior chain a sequence in which each event acts as a cue for the next.

behavior genetics a field of psychological study concerned with determining the influence of heredity on behavior.

behavior modification attempts to change people's behavior by operant conditioning, used in therapy as well as in schools and businesses.

behaviorism school of psychology devoted to the objective study of behavior.

bimodal distribution concentration of scores at two points on a scale.

Binet-Simon scale original intelligence test designed by Binet to use with children.

binocular parallax slight difference in the position of objects as seen by one eye or the other; seen by both eyes at once, the two images come together.

binocular vision vision through both eyes at once.

biofeedback used in research on automatic conditioning to let the person measure his or her own responses.

blind spot small spot in the retina with no light-sensitive cells, where the optic nerve leaves the retina.

borderline personality disorder a personality disorder marked by an instability of mood, behavior, or emotion.

brainstem lower part of the brain, an enlargement of the spinal cord.

brightness constancy perception of brightness as the same, even though the amount of light reaching the retina changes.

Cannon-Bard theory of emotion theory that the experience of emotion occurs simultaneously with biological changes.

catatonic schizophrenia type of schizophrenia generally characterized by immobility and unresponsiveness.

categories groupings based on similarities among items.

central nervous system the brain and spinal cord.

central tendency area near the center of a frequency distribution where scores tend to congregate; measures of central tendency are the mean, median, and mode.

cerebellum area of the hindbrain that controls movement, posture, and balance.

cerebral cortex gray matter that forms the outer layer of the cerebrum.

cerebrum largest part of the brain, composed of the two cerebral hemispheres and covered by the cerebral cortex.

chemical inhibitory substance chemical at synapses that counteracts the effects of the chemical transmitters.

chemical transmitter substance chemical that carries neural impulses across synapses.

chromosome threadlike body in the cell nucleus that contains genes.

chunking grouping associated bits of material into one unit for processing by memory.

classical conditioning a type of learning in which an organism learns to transfer a response from one stimulus to a previously neutral stimulus.

client-centered therapy nondirective form of treatment for behavior disorders characterized by unconditional positive regard on the part of the therapist.

closure our inclination to perceive a complete sensation where only a partial one exists.

cochlea part of the ear containing fluid that vibrates, which in turn causes the basilar membrane to vibrate.

coding processing of material in short-term memory to fit into the categories in long-term memory.

cognition the process of acquiring, storing, retrieving, and revising knowledge.

cognitive dissonance perceived inconsistency between beliefs or knowledge or between a belief and a behavioral tendency.

cognitive map according to Tolman, a spatial representation, comparable to a road map, of routes to a goal.

cognitive psychology school of psychology devoted to the study of thought processes generally.

cognitive style a person's characteristic way of perceiving and dealing with his or her environment.

cognitive theory of emotion idea that emotion stems from one's interpretation of a physiological state occurring under specific circumstances.

cognitive theory of learning holds that the result of learning is a bonded conceptual unit that has sufficient boundary strength to resist interference from other conceptual units.

collective unconscious in Jung's theory of personality, the part of the unconscious that is inherited and common to all members of a species.

color an experience combining hue, saturation, and brightness of a visual stimulus.

color blindness partial or total inability to perceive colors.

color constancy our inclination to perceive familiar objects as retaining their color no matter what the eye sees.

common fate our tendency to perceive objects in motion together as distinct from the objects around them.

community psychology brand of psychology that attempts to prevent behavior disorders by educating members of a community about mental health and by diagnosing and treating problems early.

concept an idea that includes objects that share some characteristic.

concrete operations third stage in Piaget's theory of cognitive development (7–11 years), during which children learn to retrace their thoughts and to look at objects or problems in several different ways.

conditioned response the response an organism learns to produce when a conditioned stimulus is presented.

conditioned stimulus an originally neutral stimulus that is paired with an unconditioned stimulus and eventually produces a response when presented alone.

cones receptor cells in the retina responsible for color vision.

conflict state of tension caused by opposing demands, opportunities, or goals.

conformity behavior in accordance with prevailing standards or the standards of one's group.

conjunctive concept concept that includes only objects that have a feature in common.

conscience standards by which we judge behavior to be right or wrong.

constitutional theory personality theory that proposes a relationship between a person's body type and his or her behavior.

constructive processing the linking of new information to material already stored in long-term memory.

content validity refers to a test's having an adequate sample of the skills or knowledge that it is supposed to measure.

contingency contracting a form of operant conditioning therapy in which client and therapist set reinforcements for behavioral goals.

contingency theory proposes that for learning to occur the conditioned stimulus must tell the learner that the unconditioned stimulus is about to happen.

continuity idea that elements which "hang together" are perceived as a unit.

control group group used for comparison with the experimental group.

convergence movement of the eyes to focus light from a single source on the foveas of both eyes.

conversion disorder behavior disorder characterized by bodily symptoms, such as paralysis or blindness, with no organic cause; also called hysterical neurosis.

cornea the transparent protective coating over the front part of the eye through which light enters the eyes.

corpus callosum mass of white matter that connects the hemispheres of the cerebrum to each other and to other parts of the nervous sysem.

correlation degree of association between variables, reflecting the extent to which one changes when the other does.

correlation coefficient statistical measure of the strength of association between two variables.

countertransference a term used to denote a therapist's projecting his or her own emotions onto the patient.

creativity capacity to discover; a mixture of realistic and imaginative thinking, often resulting in novel solutions.

culture-fair test intelligence test designed to eliminate cultural bias.

dark adaptation increasing ability to see after being in the dark for a time.

daydreaming a type of autistic thinking, based on one's private thoughts and wishes.

death instincts in Freud's theory of personality, the group of instincts that lead toward destruction and death.

decibel unit of measurement for the loudness of sounds.

defense mechanism technique for avoiding anxiety or awareness of something unpleasant through self-deception.

deindividuation result of overcrowding in which people are no longer seen as individual human beings.

delta sleep the fourth and deepest stage of sleep, characterized by slow, even brain waves; decreases with age but is always the first sleep to be made up after sleep has been lost.

dendrite short nerve fiber that receives stimuli and conducts them to the cell body.

deoxyribonucleic acid (DNA) nucleic acid found in the chromosomes; controls heredity and protein synthesis.

dependent variable in an experiment, the variable that changes when the independent variable is manipulated.

depersonalization dissociative disorder in which a person suddenly feels strangely changed or different.

depression a state of sadness or futility. Neurotic depression is characterized by feelings of helplessness and worthlessness and varying degrees of inactivity. In psychotic depression, these reactions are more extreme.

desensitization behavior therapy technique designed to gradually reduce anxiety about a particular object or situation.

development psychological and physical changes in an organism over time.

developmental norms ages when an average individual is expected to reach the various milestones of development.

developmental psychology study of the psychological and physical changes that take place as a person ages.

devil effect tendency for negative ratings on some traits to result in negative ratings on other traits.

dichromat person blind to either red-green or blue-yellow.

difference threshold the difference between two stimuli that is required to produce a just noticeable difference 50 percent of the time.

discrimination distinguishing among many stimuli and responding to only one.

disengagement theory contends that old age is characterized by a decline in an individual's involvement with society.

disorganized schizophrenia disorder marked by childish behavior, delusions, and incomprehensible speech.

displacement defense mechanism involving redirection of unrealizable motives to another outlet.

dissociative disorder behavior disorder characterized by the separating of certain thoughts or experiences from the other parts of the personality.

divergent thinking Guilford's term for a type of thinking characteristic of creativity, aimed at finding several correct answers to a problem.

dominant gene a gene that takes precedence over the other gene in a pair in determining inherited characteristics.

dopamine a chemical that transmits nerve impulses across synaptic spaces.

double-bind theory proposes that, as children, schizophrenics were taught to mistrust others and to distort the expression of their own feelings.

Down's syndrome type of mental retardation resulting from extra chromosome-21 material; also called *mongolism*.

effector responding organ (muscle or gland).

ego according to Freud, the part of the personality that mediates between environmental demands, conscience, and instinctual needs; now often used as a synonym for "self."

ego ideal part of the superego, consisting of standards of what one would like to be.

eidetic image image of unusual clarity and vividness; a person with eidetic imagery is sometimes said to have a "photographic memory."

elaborative rehearsal the linking of information in short-term memory to facts and concepts already in long-term memory; also known as *constructive rehearsal*.

Electra complex equivalent in girls of the boy's Oedipus complex; persistent erotic attachment to the father and hostile feelings toward the mother.

electrical stimulation of the brain (ESB) stimulating part of the brain with electrical current to produce "counterfeit" nerve impulses.

electroconvulsive shock therapy a physical therapy where a mild electrical current is passed through the brain and into a person's nervous system for a short period, often producing convulsions and temporary coma; used to alleviate sudden and severe depression.

elevation in perception, the principle that the higher on the horizontal plane an object is, the farther away it appears; the lower the horizontal plane, the nearer it seems.

emotion a complex, conscious affective experience involving physiological changes and overt behavior.

encapsulated end organ sense receptor in the skin, consisting of a nerve ending enclosed in a shell or capsule.

encounter group therapy group emphasizing sensory experiences and interpersonal communication.

endocrine glands ductless glands that secrete hormones directly into the bloodstream.

endocrine system the internal network of glands that secrete hormones directly into the bloodstream to regulate the activity of other bodily systems.

endorphins natural painkillers produced by the body.

environmental psychology study of how environment influences human behavior.

epinephrine adrenal hormone that is released mainly in response to fear and increases heart rate; also called *adrenaline*.

episodic memory memory of specific events that have personal meaning.

escape training teaching a learner how to end an unpleasant condition once it has started.

estrogen hormone that promotes and maintains secondary sex characteristics in females.

estrus cycle female fertility cycle.

eugenics a term referring to the science of improving species through restrictive or selective breeding.

exhibitionism a character disorder in which there is a compulsion to expose one's genitals in inappropriate situations.

existential psychology school of psychology that emphasizes identity, freedom, and responsibility for one's actions.

existential therapy form of psychotherapy designed to enable people to take responsibility for their actions.

experiment controlled condition in which an independent variable is manipulated, and changes in a dependent variable are studied.

experimental group in a controlled experiment, the group subjected to a change in an independent variable.

experimental neurosis reactions produced in laboratory animals when they are subjected to certain kinds of stress or conflict.

experimenter bias problem that arises when an experimenter's values or expectations influence his or her interpretation of experimental data.

external inhibition disappearance of a conditioned response because of a change in a learner's surroundings.

extinction when a learner stops associating a conditioned stimulus with an unconditioned stimulus.

extrovert person who usually focuses on social life and the external world instead of his or her internal experience.

family therapy a therapeutic approach that sees the family as a unit and as part of the problem in an individual's treatment.

feature analysis a theory of recognition that holds that we extract the key features of an incoming stimulus and compare them with patterns of features stored in long-term memory.

fetishism an attachment to objects that symbolize another person or sex object; considered deviant only when it becomes a substitute for genital sex.

figure-ground two parts of a visual stimulus; the figure is perceived as a unit standing apart from a background.

fixed-interval schedule reinforcement of a response after a given length of time.

fixed-ratio schedule reinforcement after a specified number of correct responses.

forebrain top part of the brain, including the cerebrum, thalamus, and hypothalamus.

forgetting inability to remember learned material.

formal operations the fourth stage in Piaget's theory of cognitive development (11-15 years), characterized by development of abstract thinking.

fovea area of the retina where cones are concentrated.

fraternal twins two offspring developed from two ova fertilized at the same time; also called *dizygotic twins.*

free association in psychoanalysis, the uninhibited relation of thoughts and fantasies as they occur to the patient.

free nerve endings finely branched nerve endings in the skin that serve as receptors for pressure, pain, and temperature.

frequency in sound, the number of cycles per second; primary determinant of pitch.

frequency distribution the frequency of occurrences at various levels of a variable or variables.

frequency histogram type of bar graph showing frequency distributions.

frequency polygon figure constructed by plotting frequencies and connecting the points representing them.

frequency theory of hearing theory that pitch is determined by receptors in the ear, which fire as rapidly as the frequency of sound waves being received.

frigidity in the female, an inability to experience sexual excitation or orgasm.

frontal lobe large section of the cerebrum, containing the motor projection areas and centers for speech, problem solving, and reasoning.

frustration psychological state resulting when an obstacle prevents one from attaining a goal.

frustration-aggression hypothesis idea that aggression is the product of frustration aroused by the nonfulfillment of other motives.

functional fixedness the tendency to perceive only a limited number of uses for an object.

gamete reproductive cell (ovum or sperm).

gate-control theory of pain holds that the pain-signaling system contains a gatelike mechanism that, depending on the level of activity of the sensory fibers, may be open, partially open, or closed, thus affecting the degree to which the receptors can transmit pain messages from injured tissue to the brain.

gene DNA molecule, contained on a chromosome, that determines inheritance of traits.

genetics study of heredity.

genital stage in Freud's theory of personality development, the stage of normal adult sexual behavior.

genotype an organism's underlying genetic makeup.

gestalt pattern or whole.

Gestalt psychology school of psychology stressing patterns or wholes in perception, behavior, and so on.

Gestalt therapy form of therapy, either individual or group, that emphasizes the wholeness of one personality and attempts to reawaken people to their emotions and sensations in the here-and-now.

glucagon hormone secreted by the pancreas that regulates blood-sugar level.

glucose simple sugar; main source of body energy.

gonads reproductive glands (testes and ovaries).

group test intelligence test designed for administration to a group by one examiner.

group therapy form of psychological treatment in which the interaction of patients who meet regularly in a group helps to modify the behavior of individual members of the group.

habituation strong psychological need for a substance, without biological addiction.

halfway houses homes set up in communities that help former mental patients make the transition from institutionalization to self-support.

hallucinogenic drug drug that distorts perception, such as mescaline and LSD.

halo effect tendency for positive ratings on some traits to result in positive ratings on other traits.

hammer, anvil, stirrup the three small bones in the middle ear that, when vibrated from a received sound, hit each other in sequence and carry the vibrations into the inner ear.

hemophilia disorder that prevents the blood from clotting; a sex-linked characteristic that appears only in males.

heredity transmission of traits from parents to offspring through the genes.

heritability extent to which a characteristic is inherited, rather than produced by the environment.

hertz (Hz) unit of measurement for the frequency of waves (light, sound, and so on); cycles per second.

higher-order conditioning conditioning based on previous learning; a new conditioned stimulus is presented with the original conditioned stimulus, which now serves as an unconditioned stimulus.

hindbrain brain region containing the medulla, pons, and cerebellum.

hippocampus part of the limbic system that plays an important role in memory.

homeostasis the body's tendency to maintain physiological balance.

homosexuality an exclusive preference for sexual relations with people of the same sex.

hormone chemical secreted by the endocrine glands that produces physical or psychological changes.

hospice institution for the dying.

humanistic psychology school of psychology focusing on achieving identity through nonverbal experience and altered states of consciousness.

hunger one of the basic drives; a psychological state produced by lack of food.

hypnagogic state state between waking and sleeping that is half dream, half daydream or fantasy.

hypnosis production of a trance state, in which the hypnotized person responds readily to suggestions.

hypochondriasis an individual's consistent belief that he or she is sick, in the absence of any organic symptoms.

hypothalamus forebrain region that plays a critical role in motivation and emotional responses.

hypothesis idea that is tested experimentally.

hysterical amnesia forgetting brought on by extreme repression of an individual's personal history.

icon the visual image of objects and information received by the sensory register.

id in Freud's theory of personality, the source of instincts; the unconscious.

identical twins two offspring that develop from a single fertilized ovum; also called *monozygotic twins.*

identification unconsciously taking on the characteristics of another person.

identity a person's intellectual and emotional integration (usually during adolescence) of the various life styles, concepts, examples, and so on, which becomes his or her unique self-concept.

image recollection or reconstruction of a sense experience, often visual.

imitation consciously behaving the way another does.

impotence in the male, an inability to have or maintain an erection.

imprinting very rapid learning that occurs upon presentation of a stimulus with specific characteristics.

independent variable variable that is manipulated in an experiment, while all others are held constant.

individual differences characteristics that distinguish one person from another; they appear shortly after birth and are influenced by the combined effects of heredity, prenatal environment, and the circumstances at birth.

infantile sexuality in psychoanalytic theory, the idea that very young children have sexual drives.

information processing a research model based on computer technology currently used to study human cognitive processes, including memory and perception.

ingratiation the process of managing the impressions you make on another to increase his or her liking for you.

inhibition in classical conditioning, the process that counters the conditioned response and results in extinction.

instinct unlearned drive that leads an organism to behave in specific ways; the unlearned behavior itself.

insulin shock therapy a physical therapy consisting of intramuscular injections of insulin, which lowers the level of blood sugar, producing a brief coma; rarely used today.

intellectualization defense mechanism in which abstract thinking is used as a means of avoiding emotion.

intelligence a general term covering all intellectual abilities, defined in various ways by different investigators.

intelligence quotient (IQ) comparison of a person's chronological age with his or her mental age, as measured by an intelligence test.

intelligence test test designed to measure scholastic aptitude.

interactionism the prevailing viewpoint of personality psychologists, which states that consistencies in the individual's physical and psychological environments are responsible for consistencies in personality and behavior.

interference   decreased learning as a result of other learning.

interference theory of forgetting   the theory that we forget things because other knowledge gets in the way; there are two types of interference—proactive and retroactive inhibition.

intermittent pairing   a learning trial in which either the conditioned stimulus or the unconditioned stimulus is missing.

interneurons   neurons that connect sensory and motor neurons; also called *association neurons.*

interstimulus interval   time lapse between the presentation of a conditoned stimulus and presentation of an unconditioned stimulus.

interval scale   scale with equal differences between the points or values.

introvert   person who usually focuses on his or her own thoughts and feelings instead of the outside world.

invariance   principle of attribution theory which occurs when a cause invariably accompanies an effect and in the absence of the cause, the effect does not occur.

iodopsin   chemical substance in cones, which decomposes in response to light.

iris   colored part of the eye.

James-Lange theory of emotion   theory that physical reactions precede experienced emotions.

jigsaw method   way of reducing racial prejudice among school children by making them cooperate to master a lesson.

just noticeable difference (j.n.d.)   the smallest change or difference in stimulation that a person can detect.

kinesthesis   feedback from one's body about position or movement.

la belle indifference   effect of a somatoform disorder which makes people feel cheerful or indifferent about having a severe physical problem.

latency stage   fourth stage in Freud's theory of personality development, when the child appears to have no interest in sex.

learned helplessness   a type of conditioning in which the apathy learned in a hopeless situation is transferred to one with opportunities for improvement.

learning   the process by which experience or practice results in a relatively permanent change in behavior.

learning set   the learning of a specific approach that can be used in solving similar problems.

learning theory model of abnormal behavior   suggests that abnormal behavior, like all other behaviors, is a result of learning.

lens   transparent part of the eye that focuses light onto the retina.

lexicon   that part of long-term memory in which words are stored.

libido   according to Freud, instinctual (primarily sexual) energy.

life instincts   in Freud's theory of personality, the group of instincts that lead toward construction and integration and away from death.

light adaptation   adjustment of the eye to bright light.

limbic system   system of nerve cells including parts of the thalamus, the hypothalamus, and parts of the cerebrum; among other things, the limbic system plays a role in memory and emotion.

linear perspective   a cue to the estimation of depth and distance based on the fact that two parallel lines seem to converge at the horizon.

linguistic relativity hypothesis   Whorf's idea that thinking is patterned by the specific language one speaks.

locus of control   that which controls reinforcements in learning; can be either external or internal to a person.

long-term memory   third level in memory; a relatively permanent and highly organized storage.

manic-depressive behavior   psychosis characterized by mood swings, with extreme depression alternating with elation.

masochism   need to suffer pain.

maturation   physical development of an organism as it grows.

mean   statistical average calculated by dividing a sum of values by the number of cases.

median   a statistical average, a value below which half the cases fall.

medical model of abnormal behavior   holds that a person who behaves abnormally is physiologically or psychologically sick.

meditation   various methods of concentration, reflection, and focusing one's thoughts.

medulla   part of the hindbrain that regulates breathing, heart rate, and blood pressure.

memory   process by which learned material is retained.

memory trace   a fragile, highly perishable neural response, produced by sensory experience, which can become an actual change in the nervous system if it is repeated often enough.

metabolism   chemical conversion of food into energy in the body.

midbrain   region of the brain above the pons and cerebellum that is important in vision, hearing, and other responses.

Minnesota Multiphasic Personality Inventory (MMPI)   objective personality test originally used for psychiatric diagnosis.

mnemonics   techniques to make material easier to remember.

mode   statistical average that represents the value having the largest number of cases.

models in observational learning, the people whom we observe and learn from.

monochromat person who is totally color-blind.

monocular vision vision through one eye.

motion parallax distance cue in which our movement makes objects near us seem to move more than objects farther away.

motivation something that propels action, originating from within the person who acts.

motive a specific instance of motivation, such as hunger, thirst, achievement, and so on.

motor neurons neurons that carry messages from the central nervous system to the muscles and glands; also called *efferent neurons*.

motor projection area area of the cortex where messages to the muscles and glands originate.

multiple personality a form of dissociative neurosis involving amnesia combined with the fugue state in which an individual's personality is split into two or more distinct personalities.

myelin sheath fatty covering found on some axons.

nAch need for achievement; general motive to succeed and to gain excellence for its own sake.

narcissism a personality disorder marked by a near-total self-absorption.

naturalistic observation a research method for the systematic study of animal or human behavior in natural settings, rather than under laboratory or artificially imposed conditions.

negative reinforcement reducing or terminating a stimulus that is unpleasant for the learner.

negative transference displacement of hostility felt for a parent or other authority figure to one's therapist.

nerve bundle of nerve fibers or axons.

nervous system the brain, spinal cord, and all the nerves throughout the body.

neural impulse electrochemical discharge of a nerve cell.

neuron individual nerve cell.

neurotic disorders less severe types of abnormal behavior marked by long-lasting symptoms that have no organic causes.

nominal scale a set of categories for classifying objects.

norepinephrine adrenal hormone, released mainly in states of anger, that raises blood pressure; also acts as a transmitter of nerve impulses across synaptic spaces; also called *noradrenaline*.

norm standards against which individual scores are measured.

normal curve symmetrical, bell-shaped distribution curve that reflects the natural occurrence of many events.

NREM sleep non-rapid eye movement sleep; the first four stages of sleep, which alternate with REM sleep during the sleep cycle.

object constancy in perception, the tendency for objects to look the same despite changes in position, lighting, and other conditions.

objective test personality test that can be scored in a routine fashion, thereby eliminating bias on the part of the scorer.

observational learning a major emphasis of social learning theory that states that we are able to learn by watching other people's behavior.

obsessive-compulsive disorder behavior disorder characterized by ritualistic behavior (compulsions) and persistent unpleasant thoughts (obsessions).

occipital lobe region at back of the cortex, where visual projection areas are located.

Oedipus complex according to Freud, a boy's persistent sexual attachment to his mother and jealousy toward his father.

olfactory bulb smell center in the cerebrum.

olfactory epithelium nasal membranes containing receptor cells sensitive to odors.

operant behavior behavior designed to operate on the environment in a way that will gain something desired or avoid something unpleasant.

operant or instrumental conditioning type of learning in which desired voluntary behavior is rewarded and incorrect responses are ignored or punished.

opiates addictive drugs such as heroin and opium that dull the senses and induce a feeling of lethargic well-being.

opponent-process theory theory of color vision that holds that three sets of cones respond in an either/or fashion to each of three primary color pairs.

optic chiasma crossing point of optic nerves from the retina, near the base of the brain.

optic nerves axons of the ganglion cells in the eye that carry neural messages to the brain.

oral stage first stage in Freud's theory of personality development, in which the infant's erotic feelings center on feeding and the mouth.

ordinal scale scale indicating order or relative position of items, thus permitting ranking.

organ of Corti spiral structure in the cochlea that contains the receptor cells for hearing.

organic model of abnormal behavior the theory that abnormal behavior has a biochemical or physiological basis; particularly related to research on schizophrenia and depression.

otoliths small crystals in the vestibular organ of the inner ear that activate receptor cells to send messages about balance and head position.

oval window membrane across the opening between the middle ear and inner ear that conducts vibrations to the cochlea.

ovaries female sex glands that produce egg cells and sex hormones.

overtones partial tones that combine with a fundamental

tone to produce a compound tone; primary determinant of timbre.

ovum   female gamete, or sex cell.

pancreas   gland located near the stomach that helps in digesting proteins and also regulates blood-sugar level by secreting the hormones insulin and glucagon.

Pandemonium   a model of feature analysis that holds that certain recognition tasks are performed by "demons" at various stages of recognition.

papillae   small bumps on the tongue that contain taste receptors.

paradoxical heat   situation in which the brain registers as "hot" the simultaneous sensation of warmth and cold.

paranoid schizophrenia   common type of schizophrenia, in which the personality is dominated by hostility and delusions of persecution or grandeur.

parasympathetic division   branch of the autonomic nervous system that leads to relaxation of internal organs and muscles after stress.

pedophilia   a disorder characterized by desire for sexual relations with children.

peer group   one's associates, by whom one is treated as an equal.

penis envy   according to Freud, the female's unconscious desire to have a penis, expressed in adulthood as desire to achieve or to have a child.

perception   the process of creating meaningful patterns from jumbled sensory stimuli.

perceptual constancy   the tendency to perceive objects as stable and unchanging.

perceptual set   suggestions or preconceived ideas or expectations that can affect perception.

performance test   intelligence test that does not involve words.

peripheral nervous system   any nerves not contained in the brain or spinal cord.

personal space   the amount of physical distance between one person and another with which they feel at ease.

personal unconscious   according to Jung, one of the two levels of the unconscious; the personal unconscious contains the individual's repressed thoughts, forgotten experiences, and undeveloped ideas.

personality   a person's own characteristic pattern of behavior, emotions, motives, thoughts, and attitudes.

personality disorders   abnormal behavior marked by severe problems with a person's relations to other people.

phallic stage   third stage in Freud's theory of personality development, when the child is strongly interested in the genitals.

phenotype   an organism's measurable characteristics.

phi phenomenon   illusory movement caused by flashing lights in sequence.

phobia   intense or morbid fear of, for example, enclosed

spaces, animals, high places.

phrenology   study of head measurements, in an attempt to link head shape to intelligence and other attributes.

physical treatment   a therapeutic approach that includes such methods as electroconvulsive shock therapy, insulin shock treatment, psychosurgery, drug therapy, and physical restraint.

physiological motive   motive stemming from a bodily need (for example, thirst); also called *primary drive*.

pitch   auditory experience corresponding to frequency of sound vibrations, resulting in a higher or lower tone.

place theory of hearing   theory that different places on the basilar membrane vibrate in response to sounds of different frequencies.

pleasure principle   according to Freud, the way in which the id seeks immediate relief from discomfort.

polarization   the condition of a neuron before it fires, when positive ions are on the outside and negaitve ions are on the inside of the cell membrane.

polygenic inheritance   determination of a single trait by the interaction of several genes.

pons   hindbrain nerve center connecting the cerebellum to the cortex; helps regulate breathing and produces rapid eye movements during sleep.

positive reinforcement   following an action or response with something that is pleasant for the learner.

positive transference   development of warm feelings toward one's therapist.

post-traumatic stress disorders   a type of anxiety disorder resulting from a tragic or terrible event.

prefrontal lobotomy   an early psychosurgical technique whereby the nerves connecting the thalamus and the frontal areas of the cortex are severed; tension, anxiety, and emotional activity are decreased, but there are generally unpleasant side effects such as deterioration of intellectual ability and diminished self-control.

prejudice   an attitude composed of stereotyped beliefs, hostile feelings, and a tendency to behave in discriminatory ways.

preoperational thought   second stage in Piaget's theory of cognitive development (2-7 years), when the child develops systematic methods for representing the world internally.

pressure   a form of psychological stress in which an individual feels that he or she must live up to a particular standard of behavior or adapt to rapid change.

primacy effect   the principle that the first items in a series tend to be remembered better than later items.

primary drive   a physiologically based drive (for example, the hunger drive).

primary process thinking   in Freud's theory of personality, the process by which the id achieves immediate satisfaction of an instinct, either through conscious activity or through wish fulfillment.

primary reinforcer   reinforcer that is rewarding in itself, such as food, water, sex, and termination of pain.

proactive inhibition   process in which previous learning interferes with memory of new learning.

probability   statistical likelihood that something will occur.

projection   defense mechanism characterized by attributing one's own wishes and feelings to others.

projective test   unstructured personality test not limiting the response to be given, such as the Rorschach inkblot test and the Thematic Apperception Test (TAT).

psychoanalysis   therapeutic technique created by Freud, based on uncovering people's unconscious motives.

psychoanalytic model of abnormal behavior   a Freudian theory that behavior disorders are symbolic expressions of internal, unconscious conflicts, usually originating in infancy and childhood.

psychophysics   study of the attributes of physical stimuli and the sensations they produce.

psychosexual stages   Freud's theory of developmental stages characterized by the place where erotic feelings are centered.

psychosomatic illness   a physical disorder having an emotional origin.

psychosurgery   brain surgery designed to change behavior based on the assumption that psychological functions are localized in specific areas of the brain.

psychotherapy   a general term referring to the use of psychological techniques to treat behavior disorders and to help people deal more effectively with their environments.

punishment   an unpleasant stimulus that can inhibit an undesirable response.

pupil   small opening in the iris through which light enters the eye.

pure research   research for its own sake usually growing out of a theory or other research and rarely conducted to solve practical social problems.

radical behavior theory   a situational analysis of personality that maintains that only observable and measurable behavior is relevant in psychology.

random sample   sample chosen in such a way that each potential subject has an equal chance of being selected.

range   distance between the lowest and highest scores in a distribution.

ratio scale   scale that has a true zero.

rational therapy   a therapeutic approach based on the idea that an individual's problems have been caused by his or her misinterpretations of events and goals.

reaction formation   defense mechanism characterized by development of behavior exactly opposite to unconscious wishes.

reality principle   according to Freud, action of the ego in mediating between the demands of the environment and the demands of the id.

reality therapy   a therapeutic approach that attempts to help the individual to develop more responsible behavior.

recall   measure of retention in which a person reproduces or reconstructs learned material.

recessive gene   gene whose hereditary potential is not expressed when it is paired with a dominant gene.

recognition   measure of retention in which a person identifies learned material when presented with it.

reference group   a group with which a person identifies or compares himself or herself.

reflex   involuntary, unlearned, immediate response to a stimulus.

regression   returning to the habit patterns and desires of childhood or infancy.

rehearsal   process of repetition in short-term memory that results in materials being transferred into long-term memory; see also *rote rehearsal.*

reinforcement   strengthening a response, making it more likely to recur; in classical conditioning refers to the unconditioned stimulus.

relative refractory period   period after nerve cell discharge when the cell will not discharge again without a stronger than normal stimulus.

reliability   ability of a test to produce similar scores for an individual on separate occasions.

REM sleep   rapid eye movement sleep, characterized by saw-toothed brain wave activity, greater muscle relaxation, and a rapid movement of the eyes; REM sleep alternates with NREM sleep during the sleep cycle and is the period of sleep during which most dreams occur.

repression   defense mechanism that involves excluding uncomfortable thoughts and feelings from consciousness.

response   any behavior of an organism that can be identified and measured.

response generalization   giving a response that is slightly different from the response originally learned to the stimulus.

retention   storage of material in memory.

reticular activating system (RAS)   bundle of nerve fibers running through the hindbrain and midbrain to the hypothalamus; responsible for general arousal of the organism.

retina   layer of the eye containing receptor cells that are sensitive to light.

retinal disparity   the difference between the images cast on the two retinas when both eyes are focused on the same object.

retroactive inhibition   interference with memory of previous learning by more recent learning.

retrograde amnesia   inability to recall events that took place immediately before a critical event, even though there is no loss of earlier or later memory.

reversible figure   in perceptual organization, when the figure and ground of a pattern do not have enough contrast, or cues, to be readily perceived and distinguished.

reward   positive or negative reinforcer.

rhodopsin   chemical substance in rods, which decomposes in response to light.

ribonucleic acid (RNA)   a molecule manufactured by DNA that plays a role in protein production and possibly in memory.

risky shift   greater willingness to take decision-making risks in a group than as an individual.

rods   retinal cells responsible for night vision and not specialized to receive color.

role   expected behavior for a person occupying a certain position.

role confusion   according to Erikson, a state that may occur when an individual fails to achieve identity; the individual attempts to be all things to all people.

rooting behavior   reflex movements a newborn baby makes when its cheek is touched, including head-turning and attempts to suck.

Rorschach Test   a projective test composed of ambiguous inkblots; the way a person interprets the blots will reveal his or her unconscious thoughts.

rote rehearsal   a process of practicing information, in which the information is repeated over and over.

round window   membrane between the middle ear and inner ear that absorbs the changes in pressure when sound vibrations reach the oval window above it.

saccule   small sac at the base of the semicircular canals in the vestibular organ of the inner ear; sense organ for equilibrium.

sadism   need to inflict mental or physical pain on someone else.

scapegoat   person or group chosen as an object of displaced aggression.

scatter plot   diagram showing the association between scores on two variables.

schedule of reinforcement   program for choosing which responses to reinforce.

schemata   Piaget's term for the frameworks one uses to organize experience, which change as one develops.

schizoid personality   person who suffers from an inability to form any social relationships and lacks interest in doing so.

schizophrenia   psychosis involving withdrawal from reality, lack of emotion, and other disturbances.

scientific method   formulation and experimental testing of hypotheses about natural events and relationships.

secondary process thinking   in Freud's theory of personality, activity within the limits of objective reality.

secondary reinforcer   reinforcer whose value is learned through association with primary reinforcers.

secondary sex characteristics   sex differences, such as facial hair in men, not directly involved in reproduction.

self-actualization   the highest motive in Maslow's hierarchy; the motive to realize one's potential.

self-reinforcement   in social learning theory, the view that personal assessment such as pride or guilt can affect an individual's behavior.

self theory   personality theory of Carl Rogers, who holds that individuals are most knowledgeable about themselves and thus are best prepared to find ways of resolving their problems.

semantic memory   long-term memory, encoded in the form of words and sounds.

semicircular canals   bony structures in the inner ear, important to the sense of equilibrium.

senescence   the gradual, inevitable decline of the life processes that occurs with aging.

senile psychosis   psychotic symptoms caused by changes in the brain as a result of age.

senility   a state of advanced old age marked by lapses of memory, haziness of thought, and other signs of mental and physical deterioration.

sensation   awareness of sense stimulation.

sense organ   specialized organ receptive to sensory stimuli.

sensitivity group   group that meets over a period of time to share feelings and help members gain insight into their own emotional reactions.

sensory adaptation   changes in the responsiveness of receptors that result either in increased sensitivity (when the level of stimulation is consistently low) or reduced sensitivity (when the level of stimulation is consistently high).

sensory coding   a process that occurs during transduction in which the initially diffuse neural impulse received from a sensory receptor is coded so that when a message is received by the brain it is precise and detailed.

sensory deprivation   total or near-total removal of normal sensory stimuli.

sensory-motor stage   first stage in Piaget's theory of cognitive development (birth-2 years) when children learn to organize their perceptions and to explore and experiment with objects.

sensory nerve   bundle of afferent neurons that carries messages from the sense organs to the central nervous system.

sensory neurons   neurons that carry messages to the brain or spinal cord from internal organs or sense receptors; also called *afferent neurons.*

sensory projection area   cerebral cortex areas where messages from the sense organs register.

sensory register   first level in memory; processes information from the senses.

serotonin   a chemical that transmits neural impulses across synaptic spaces.

set   readiness to react in a certain way to a problem or situation or to perceive a situation in a certain way; as applied to altered states of consciousness, the expectations and feelings the person brings to the experience.

setting   in drug-induced experiences, the physical, social, and emotional atmosphere in which the drug is taken.

sex chromosomes X and Y chromosomes, the twenty-third chromosome pair in humans, containing genes that determine sex.

sex drive primary drive that gives rise to reproductive behavior.

sex hormones hormones, such as androgen in males and estrogen in females, that produce, maintain, and regulate sexual characteristics and behaviors.

sex-linked characteristics inherited characteristics carried by the X or Y chromosomes.

sex role learned behavior appropriate to one's sex.

shadowing distance clue which indicates distance, depth, and solidity.

shape constancy tendency to see an object as the same shape no matter what angle it is seen from.

shaping teaching complex behavior by rewarding each successive approximation to the behavior and building up to a complete response.

shock therapy electrical shocks to the brain, used in the treatment of mental illness.

short-term memory second level of memory; can retain information for a brief period of time after which it is either discarded or transferred to long-term memory.

significance probability that a statistic would not occur by chance.

similarity a principle of grouping that states that objects of a similar color, size, or shape are perceived as part of a pattern.

situationism a perspective on personality theory that holds it is the particular situation, not the internal personality variables, that determines behavior.

size constancy perception of an object as the same size regardless of the distance from which it is viewed.

skewed distribution frequency curve with the greatest concentration of scores toward one end.

Skinner box box equipped with a bar, in which an animal is placed during operant conditioning; pressing the bar releases food, which reinforces the bar-pressing behavior.

social comparison tendency to compare oneself with others, especially when one is uncertain or uneasy about one's attitudes or performance.

social facilitation effects on an individual's behavior due to the presence of other people.

social learning theory a learning theory that combines elements of traditional operant conditioning and cognitive theory, with particular emphasis placed on observational learning.

social motive learned motive associated with relationships among people, such as affiliation, achievement, and so on.

socialization process by which a child learns the behavior appropriate to his or her family and culture.

somatoform disorders mental disorders that affect the body.

somatotypes three basic physiques—endomorphic, mesomorphic, and ectomorphic—thought to influence personality.

spectrum full range of light waves of varying lengths; when refracted through a prism, these show up as colors.

sperm male gamete contained in semen.

spinal cord bundle of nerve fibers running though the spinal column, connecting the brain to the rest of the nervous system.

split-half reliability a method of determining test reliability by comparing a person's scores on odd-numbered items with his or her scores on the even-numbered items of the same test.

spontaneous recovery reappearance of an extinguished response after the passage of time, without further training.

S-R psychology school of psychology based on the stimulus-response relationship and theories of learning.

standard deviation statistical measure of variability in a group of scores or other values.

statistics use of numbers to represent data and numerical treatment of these values.

stereoscopic vision the combination of two retinal images to achieve more accuracy in depth and distance perception; possible only for animals whose eyes are set in front of their heads.

stereotypes beliefs presumed to apply to all members of a given group.

stimulus an event that produces a response.

stimulus generalization reaction to a stimulus with the same response one has learned to give to another, similar stimulus.

stress physical or psychological threat to an organism or system and the reaction to that threat.

stroboscopic motion illusory movement that results from flashing a series of still pictures in rapid succession.

structuralism school of psychology emphasizing the basic units of experiences and their combination.

sublimation defense mechanism characterized by the redirection of sexual energy (libido) into socially acceptable channels.

sucking a reflex of newborns that causes them to suck on anything that touches their faces.

superego according to Freud, the part of the psyche that represents the social and parental standards the individual has internalized (the conscience) and the ego-ideal.

superposition a relative distance cue in which one object by partly blocking a second object is perceived as being closer.

symbolic reinforcement in social learning theory, the view that reinforcement, such as attention or approval, can affect an individual's behavior, and that this reinforcement is distinct from secondary reinforcement.

sympathetic division branch of the autonomic nervous system that arouses the body in stress reactions.

synapse area composed of the axon terminal, synaptic cleft, and dendrite of the next neuron.

synaptic space the tiny space between the axon terminal of one neuron and the dendrites or cell body of another neuron.

synaptic vesicles tiny sacs on an axon terminal, which release a chemical that crosses the area between two neurons and may cause the second to fire.

synesthesia form of imagery in which a person experiences one sense in terms of another.

taste buds structures on the tongue that contain the receptor cells for taste.

template matching a model of the recognition processes that holds that incoming signals are compared or matched with templates stored in long-term memory.

temporal lobe an association area in the cerebral cortex.

testes male sex glands, which produce sperm and sex hormones.

testosterone hormone that promotes and maintains secondary sex characteristics in males; one of the androgens.

texture gradient appearance of increasing smoothness as an object is seen at greater and greater distances.

thalamus part of the forebrain that relays impulses from sense receptors, regulates electrical activity in the brain, and controls autonomic reactions.

Thematic Apperception Test (TAT) a projective test composed of ambiguous pictures; the stories a person writes about the pictures will reveal his or her unconscious thoughts and motives.

thirst state caused by a lack of water; a primary drive.

threshold level of stimulus intensity required for a neuron to fire or a receptor cell to respond.

thyroid gland endocrine gland located below the larynx that secretes thyroxin, which controls metabolism.

thyroxin hormone secreted by the thyroid gland; regulates metabolism.

timbre tone quality, produced by a sound's overtones.

token economy therapeutic technique used in some institutions, schools, and businesses to encourage changes in behavior; people are reinforced for adaptive behavior by being given tokens, which may be exchanged for privileges or something they want.

trait in genetics, any physical characteristic that can be observed; in personality, a measurable characteristic.

trait theory maintains that behavior patterns are the result of a person's traits.

transactional analysis a technique of group therapy that aims at understanding people by studying communication between two or more people.

transduction conversion of stimulus energy into a neural impulse.

transvestism abnormal behavior marked by desire to dress in the clothes of the opposite sex.

traveling wave theory of hearing a recent version of the place theory of hearing, which holds that sound waves traveling through the cochlear fluid of the ear move the different places on the basilar membrane in direct proportion to the pitch of the sound wave.

trichromat person who is able to detect all three primary colors and thus has normal color vision.

trichromatic theory theory of color vision that holds that all color perception is a combination of three basic hues.

unconditioned response the reaction that takes place whenever an unconditioned stimulus occurs.

unconditioned stimulus a stimulus that invariably causes an organism to react in a specific way.

unconscious in Freud's theory, all the ideas, thoughts, and feelings of which we are not aware.

utricle one of the two sacs in the inner ear; source of information about balance and stationary posture.

validity ability of a test to measure what it sets out to measure.

variable-interval schedule reinforcement schedule in which the first correct response after various lengths of time is reinforced.

variable-ratio schedule reinforcement schedule in which a varying number of correct responses must occur before reinforcement is presented.

variation extent of differences among scores in a sample.

verbal ability skill in using language; one of the basic abilities measured by most intelligence tests.

vestibular organ structure in the inner ear that is the sense organ for equilibrium, the vestibular sense.

vestibular sense sense of equilibrium; source of information about the position of the body in relation to gravity.

vicarious reinforcement in social learning theory, the view that seeing others rewarded or punished can encourage an individual to change his or her behavior.

visible light the small part of the spectrum of electromagnetic energy to which the human eye is sensitive.

visual acuity the ability to distinguish fine details and spatial separations.

volley principle theory that receptors in the ear respond in volley, with one group responding, then a second, then a third, and so on, so that the complete pattern of firing corresponds to the frequency of the sound wave.

voyeurism watching others engage in sexual activities or spying on nude people, when it becomes a substitute for genital sex.

words complex signs composed of letters and sounds that represent concepts, experiences, and objects.

working memory short-term memory; our attention span.

X chromosome   X-shaped sex chromosome; males have one, females two.

Y-chromosome   Y-shaped sex chromosome; found only in males.

Yerkes-Dodson law   states that the more complex the task, the lower the level of emotion that can be tolerated to do it.

zoophilia   the desire to have sex with animals.

zygote   a fertilized ovum.

References

Aaronson, D., & Scarborough, H. S. Performance theories for sentence coding: Some quantitative evidence. *Journal of Experimental Psychology: Human Perception and Performance*, 1976, *2*, 56–70.

Aaronson, D., & Scarborough, H. S. Performance theories for sentence coding: Some quantitative models. *Journal of Verbal Learning and Verbal Behavior*, 1977, *16*, 277–304.

Ainsworth, M. D. S. Infant-mother attachment. *American Psychologist*, 1979, *34*, 932–937.

Allport, G. W. *Personality: A psychological interpretation.* New York: Holt, Rinehart and Winston, 1937.

Allport, G. W. *The nature of prejudice.* New York: Anchor, 1954.

Allport, G. W. Traits revisited. *American Psychologist*, 1966, *21*, 1–10.

Allport, G. W., & Odbert, H. S. Trait-names: a psycholexical study. *Psychological Monographs*, 1936, *47* (1, Whole No. 211).

Alpern, D. M., & Agrest, S. Crime: Will he stand trial? *Newsweek*, August 29, 1977, pp. 27–28.

American Psychiatric Association. *Diagnostic and statistical manual of mental disorders* (3rd ed.) Washington, D. C.: American Psychiatric Association, 1980.

American Psychological Association. *Ethical standards of psychologists.* Washington, D. C., 1953.

American Psychological Association. Ethical standards of psychologists. *APA Monitor*, March 1977, pp. 22–23.

Amoore, J. E., Johnston, J. W., Jr., & Rubin, M. The stereochemical theory of odor. *Scientific American*, February 1964, pp. 42–49.

Anastasi, A. *Psychological testing.* New York: Macmillan, 1976.

Archer, W. *On dreams.* London: Methuen, 1935.

Arieti, S. (Ed.), *American handbook of psychiatry* (Vol. VI, chapter 36). New York: Basic Books, 1975.

Arnold, M. B. *Emotion and personality* (2 vols.). New York: Columbia University Press, 1960.

Aronfreed, J. *Conduct and consciousness: the socialization of internalized control over behavior.* New York: Academic Press, 1968.

Aronson, E. *The social animal.* San Francisco: Freeman, 1980.

Aronson, E., Cookie, S., Sikes, J., Blaney, N., & Snapp, M. *The jigsaw classroom.* Beverly Hills, Ca.: Sage, 1978.

Aronson, E., Turner, J., & Carlsmith, J. M. Communicator credibility and communication discrepancy. *Journal of Abnormal and Social Psychology*, 1963, *67*, 31–36.

Asch, S. E. Forming impressions of personality. *Journal of Abnormal and Social Psychology*, 1946, *41*, 258–290.

Asch, S. E. Effects of group pressure upon the modification and distortion of judgments. In H. Guetzkow (Ed.), *Groups, leadership, and men.* Pittsburgh: Carnegie Press, 1951.

Ashmore, R. D., & McConahay, J. B. *Psychology and America's urban dilemmas.* New York: McGraw-Hill, 1975.

Atchley, R. C. Dimensions of widowhood in later life. *Gerontologist*, 1975, *15*, 176–178.

Atchley, R. C. *The sociology of retirement.* Cambridge, Mass.: Schenkman, 1976.

Atchley, R. C. *The social forces in later life: an introduction to social gerontology.* Belmont, Ca.: Wadsworth, 1977.

Atkin, et al. Quality versus quantity in televised political ads. *Public Opinion Quarterly*, 1973, *37*, 209–224.

Atkinson, J. W., & Birch, D. *The dynamics of action.* New York: Wiley, 1970.

Atkinson, J. W., Bongort, K., & Price, L. H. Explorations using computer simulation to comprehend thematic apperceptive measurement of motivation. *Motivation & Emotion*, 1977, *1*, 1–27.

Atkinson, J. W., & Raynor, J. O. *Motivation and achievement*. Washington, D.C.: Winston, 1975.

Axelrod, J. Neurotransmitters. *Scientific American*, June 1974, pp. 58–71.

Ayllon, T., & Azrin, N. *The token economy: A motivational system for therapy and rehabilitation*. New York: Appleton-Century-Crofts, 1968.

Baddeley, A. D., & Hitch, G. Working memory. In G. H. Bower, (Ed.), *The psychology of learning and motivation* (Vol. 8). New York: Academic Press, 1974.

Bahrick, H. P., Bahrick, P. O., & Wittlinger, R. P. Those unforgettable high school days. *Psychology Today*, December 1974, pp. 50–56.

Balagura, S. *Hunger: a biopsychological analysis*. New York: Basic Books, 1973.

Baltes, P. B., & Labouvie, G. V. Adult development of intellectual performance: Description, explanation, and modification. In C. Eisdorfer & M. P. Lawton (Eds.), *The psychology of adult development and aging*. Washington, D.C.: American Psychological Association, 1973.

Baltes, P. B., & Schaie, K. W. The myth of the twilight years. *Psychology Today*, March 1974, pp. 35–40.

Baltes, P. B., & Schaie, K. W. On the plasticity of intelligence in adulthood and old age. *American Psychologist*, 1976, *31*, 720–725.

Bandura, A. Social learning through imitation. In M. R. Jones (Ed.), *Nebraska symposium on motivation*. Lincoln: University of Nebraska Press, 1962.

Bandura, A. *Aggression: A social learning analysis*. Englewood Cliffs, N. J.: Prentice-Hall, 1973.

Bandura, A. *Social learning theory*. Englewood Cliffs, N.J.: Prentice-Hall, 1977.

Bandura, A., Ross, D., & Ross, S. A. Imitation of film-mediated aggressive models. *Journal of Abnormal and Social Psychology*, 1963, *66*, 3–11.

Barr, N. I. The responsible world of reality therapy. *Psychology Today*, February 1974, pp. 64–68.

Barron, F. *Creativity and psychological health*. Princeton, N.J.: Van Nostrand, 1963.

Barron, F., Jarvik, M., & Bunnell, S., Jr. The hallucinogenic drugs. *Scientific American*, April 1964.

Bass, B. M. The substance and the shadow. *American Psychologist*, December 1974, 870–876.

Bassuk, E. L., & Gerson, S. Deinstitutionalization and mental health services. *Scientific American*, February 1978, pp. 46–53.

Bateson, G., Jackson, D. D., Haley, J., & Weakland, J. H. Toward a theory of schizophrenia. *Behavioral Science*, 1956, *1*, 251–264.

Baxter, D. W., & Olszewski, J. Congenital insensitivity to pain. *Brain*, 1960, *83*, 381.

Bayley, N. Development of mental abilities. In P. H. Mussen (Ed.), *Carmichael's manual of child psychology*. New York: Wiley, 1970.

Bazelon, D. L. Eyewitness news. *Psychology Today*, 1980, *14*, 102–106.

de Beauvoir, S. *The coming of age* (Patrick O'Brian, trans.). New York: Putnam, 1972.

Beck, R. C. *Motivation: theories and principles*. Englewood Cliffs, N.J.: Prentice-Hall, 1978.

Becker, H. S. Personal change in adult life. *Sociometry*, 1964, *27*, 40–53.

Beier, E. G. Nonverbal communication: how we send emotional messages. *Psychology Today*, October 1974, pp. 53–56.

Beier, E. G., Robinson, P., & Micheletti, G. Susanville: A community helps itself in mobilization of community resources for self-help in mental health. *Journal of Consulting and Clinical Psychology*, 1971, *36*, 142–150.

Belmont, L., & Marolla, F. A. Birth order, family size, and intelligence. *Science*, December 14, 1973, *182*(4117), 1096–1101.

Bem, S. L. Androgyny vs. the tight little lives of fluffy women and chesty men. *Psychology Today*, 1975, *9*, 59–62.

Benson, H. *The relaxation response*. New York: William Morrow, 1975.

Benson, H., Alexander, S., & Feldman, E. L. Decreased premature ventricular contractions through use of the relaxation response in patients with stable ischemic heart disease. *Lancet*, 1975, *2*, 380–382.

Benson, H., Kotch, J. B., Crassweller, K. D., & Greenwood, M. M. Historical and clinical considerations of the relaxation response. *American Scientist*, 1977, *65*, 441–445.

Benson, H., Kotch, J. B., Crassweller, K. D., & Greenwood, M. M. The relaxation response. In D. Goleman & R. Davidson (Eds.), *Consciousness: brain, states of awareness and mysticism*. New York: Harper & Row, 1979.

Benson, H., & Wallace, R. K. Decreased drug abuse with transcendental meditation—a study of 1,862 subjects. In C. J. D. Zarafonetis (Ed.), *Drug abuse proceedings of the international conference*. Philadelphia: Lea and Febiger, 1972.

Berger, R. J. The sleep and dream cycle. In A. Kales (Ed.), *Sleep: physiology and pathology*. Philadelphia: Lippincott, 1969.

Bergin, A. E. Some implications of psychotherapy research for therapeutic practice. *Journal of Abnormal Psychology*, 1966, *71*, 235–246.

Bergman, J. Are little girls being harmed by Sesame Street? In J. Stacey, S. Bereaud, & J. Daniels (Eds.), *And Jill came tumbling after: sexism in American education*. New York: Dell, 1974.

Bergman, T., Haith, M. M., & Mann, L. *Development of eye*

contact and facial scanning in infants. Paper presented at the meeting of the Society for Research in Child Development, Minneapolis, 1971.

Berkowitz, L. Some aspects of observed aggression. *Journal of Personality and Social Psychology*, 1965, 2, 359–369.

Berkowitz, L. The case for bottling up rage. *Psychology Today*, March 1972, pp. 42–46, 72.

Berkowitz, L. *Roots of aggression: a re-examination of the frustration–aggression hypothesis.* New York: Atherton, 1969.

Berlin, B., & Kay, P. *Basic color terms: their universality and evolution.* Berkeley: University of California Press, 1969.

Berne, E. Ego states in psychotherapy. *American Journal of Psychotherapy*, 1957, 11, 293–309.

Berne, E. *Games people play.* New York: Grove Press, 1964.

Berne, E. *Principles of group treatment.* New York: Grove Press, 1968.

Bernstein, I. S., & Gordon, T. P. The function of aggression in primate societies. *American Scientist*, 1974, 62, 304–311.

Berscheid, E., et al. Physical attractiveness and dating choice: a test of the matching hypothesis. *Journal of Experimental Social Psychology*, March 1971, 7(2), 173–189.

Berscheid, E., & Walster, E. Beauty and the beast. *Psychology Today*, March 1972, pp. 42–46, 72.

Bertenthal, B., & Fischer, K. *The development of self-recognition in the child.* Paper presented at the meeting of the Eastern Psychological Association, New York, 1976.

Bettelheim, B. Individual and mass behavior in extreme situations. *Journal of Abnormal and Social Psychology*, 1943, 38, 417–452.

Bettelheim, B. *The informed heart.* New York: Free Press, 1960.

Bieber, I., et al. *Homosexuality: a psychoanalytic study.* New York: Basic Books, 1962.

Birdwhistell, R. L. *Introduction to kinesics.* Louisville, Ky.: University of Louisville Press, 1952.

Birdwhistell, R. L. Toward analyzing American movement. In S. Weitz (Ed.), *Nonverbal communication: readings with commentary.* New York: Oxford University Press, 1974.

Bischoff, L. J. *Adult psychology.* New York: Harper & Row, 1976.

Blakemore, C., & Cooper, G. F. Development of the brain depends on the visual environment. *Nature*, 1970, 228, 477–478.

Block, H. H., Block, J., & Harrington, D. M. *The relationship of parental teaching strategies to ego-resiliency in preschool children.* Paper presented at the meeting of the Western Psychological Association, San Francisco, 1974.

Block, J. H. Another look at sex differentiation in the socialization behaviors of mothers and fathers. In F. Denmark & J. Sherman (Eds.), *Psychology of women: future directions of research.* New York: Psychological Dimensions, Inc., 1979.

Blodgett, H. S. The effect of the introduction of reward upon the maze performance of rats. *University of California Publications in Psychology*, 1929, 4, 117.

Blum, J. M. *Pseudoscience and mental ability: the origins and fallacies of the IQ controversy.* New York: Monthly Review Press, 1979.

Botwinick, J. *Cognitive processes in maturity and old age.* New York: Springer, 1967.

Boume, L. E., Jr., Dominowski, R. L., & Loftus, E. F. *Cognitive processes.* Englewood Cliffs, N. J.: Prentice-Hall, 1979.

Bower, E. M. *Early identification of emotionally handicapped children in school.* Springfield, Ill.: Charles C. Thomas, 1969.

Bower, G. H. A multicomponent theory of the memory trace. In K. W. Spence & J. T. Spence (Eds.), *The psychology of learning and motivation* (Vol. 1). New York: Academic Press, 1967.

Bower, G. H. How to . . . um . . . remember. *Psychology Today*, October 1973, pp. 63–70.

Bower, T. G. R. The object in the world of the infant. *Scientific American*, October 1971, pp. 20–38.

Bower, T. G. R. Repetitive processes in child development. *Scientific American*, 1976, 235(5), 38–47.

Bowers, M. *Retreat from sanity.* New York: Human Sciences Press, 1974.

Bradway, K. P. An experimental study of factors associated with Stanford-Binet IQ changes from the preschool to the junior high school. *Journal of Genetic Psychology*, 1945, 66, 107–128.

Brady, J. V., et al. Avoidance behavior and the development of gastroduodenal ulcers. *Journal of the Experimental Analysis of Behavior*, 1958, 1, 69–72.

Bramel, D. A dissonance theory approach to defensive projection. *Journal of Abnormal and Social Psychology*, 1962, 64, 121–129.

Brazelton, T. B. *Infants and mothers: differences in development.* New York: Dell, 1969.

Breland, K., & Breland, M. The misbehavior of organisms. In M. E. P. Seligman & J. L. Hager (Eds.), *Biological boundaries of learning.* Englewood Cliffs, N. J.: Prentice-Hall, 1972.

Brener, J., Kleinman, R. A., & Goesling, W. J. The effects of different exposures to augmented sensory feedback on the control of heart rate. *Psychophysiology*, 1969, 5, 510–516.

Brickman, P. (Ed.). *Social conflict.* New York: Heath, 1974.

Bridges, K. M. B. Emotional development in early infancy. *Child Development*, 1932, 3, 324–334; 340.

Broadbent, D. E. *Perception and communication.* New York: Pergamon Press, 1958.

Brock, T. C., & Balloun, J. L., Behavioral receptivity to dissonant information. *Journal of Personality and Social Psychology*, 1967, 6, 413–428.

Brody, E. B., & Brody, N. *Intelligence: nature, determinants, and consequences.* New York: Academic Press, 1976.

Brody, N. *Personality: research and theory.* New York: Academic Press, 1972.

Brody, N. Social motivation. *Annual Review of Psychology,* 1980, *31,* 143–168.

Bronfenbrenner, U. Toward an experimental ecology of human development. *American Psychologist,* 1977, *32*(7), 513–531.

Broughton, R. J. Biorhythmic variations in consciousness and psychological functions. *Canadian Psychological Review,* 1975, *16,* 217–239.

Brown, B. R. The effects of need to maintain face on interpersonal bargaining. *Journal of Experimental Social Psychology,* 1968, *4,* 107–122.

Brown, J. A. Some tests of the decay theory of immediate memory. *Quarterly Journal of Experimental Psychology,* 1958, *10,* 12–21.

Brown, P. K., & Wald, G. Visual pigments in single rods and cones of the human retina. *Science,* 1964, *144,* 45–52.

Brown, P. L., & Jenkins, H. M. Autoshaping of the pigeon's key peck. *Journal of Experimental and Analytical Behavior,* 1968, *11,* 1–8.

Brown, R. Development of the first language in the human species. *American Psychologist,* February 1973*a*, 97–106.

Brown, R. Schizophrenia, language, and reality. *American Psychologist,* May 1973*b*, 395–403.

Brown, R. W. *Social psychology.* New York: Free Press, 1965.

Brown, R. W., & Berko, J. Word association and the acquisition of grammar. *Child Development,* 1960, *31,* 1–14.

Brown, R. W., & Lenneberg, E. H. A study in language and cognition. *Journal of Abnormal Social Psychology,* 1954, *49,* 454–462.

Brown, R. W., & McNeill, D. The tip-of-the-tongue phenomenon. *Journal of Verbal Learning and Verbal Behavior,* 1966, *5,* 325–337.

Bruner, J. S. Organization of early skilled action. *Child Development,* 1973, *44,* 1–11.

Burt, C. The genetic determination of differences in intelligence: a study of monozygotic twins reared together and apart. *British Journal of Psychology,* 1966, *57,* 137–153.

Butler, R. N. The life review: an interpretation of reminiscence in the aged. *Psychiatry,* 1963, *26,* 63–76.

Byrne, D. Interpersonal attraction and attitude similarity. *Journal of Abnormal and Social Psychology,* 1961, *62,* 713–715.

Byrne, D. *An introduction to personality* (2nd ed.). Englewood Cliffs, N.J.: Prentice-Hall, 1974.

Byrne, D., & Nelson, D. Attraction as a function of attitude similarity-dissimilarity: the effect of topic importance. *Psychonomic Science,* 1964, *1,* 93–94.

Byrne, D., & Wong, T. J. Racial prejudice, interpersonal attraction, and assumed dissimilarity of attitudes. *Journal of Abnormal and Social Psychology,* 1962, *65,* 246–253.

Calhoun, J. B. Population density and social pathology. *Scientific American,* 1962, *206,* 139–148.

Cameron, P. The generation gap: time orientation. *Gerontologist,* 1972, *12,* 117–119.

Campbell, A. The American way of mating: marriage si, children only maybe. *Psychology Today,* May 1975, pp. 39–42.

Campos, J. L., Langer, A., & Krowitz, A. Cardiac responses on the visual cliff in prelocomotor human infants. *Science,* 1970, *170,* 196–197.

Cannon, W. B. The James-Lange theory of emotion: a critical examination and an alternative theory. *American Journal of Psychology,* 1927, *39,* 106–124.

Carlson, N. R. *Physiology of behavior.* Boston: Allyn and Bacon, 1977.

Carmichael, L., Hogan, H. P., & Walter, A. A. An experimental study of the effect of language on the reproduction of visually perceived forms. *Journal of Experimental Psychology,* 1932, *15,* 73–86.

Carp, F. M. (Ed.). *The retirement process.* Washington, D.C.: U.S.G.P.O., 1968 (Public Health Service Publication No. 1778).

Carpenter, G. C. Visual regard of moving and stationary faces in early infancy. *Merrill-Palmer Quarterly,* 1974, *20,* 181–194.

Carr, A. T. Compulsive neuroses: a review of the literature. *Psychological Bulletin,* 1974, *81*(5), 311–318.

Cattell, R. B. *The scientific analysis of personality.* Baltimore: Penguin, 1965.

Cermak, L. S. *Human memory: research and theory.* New York: Ronald Press, 1972.

Chance, P. Race and IQ: a family affair. *Psychology Today,* January 1975, p. 40.

Cherry, C. *On human communication: a review, a survey, and a criticism* (2nd ed.). Cambridge, Mass.: M.I.T. Press, 1966.

Cherry, E. C. Some experiments on the recognition of speech with one and two ears. *Journal of the Acoustical Society of America,* 1953, *25,* 975–979.

Chertkoff, J. M., & Conley, M. Opening offer and frequency of concession as bargaining strategies. *Journal of Personality and Social Psychology,* 1967, *7,* 181–185.

Chertkoff, J. M., & Esser, J. K. A review of experiments in explicit bargaining. *Journal of Experimental Social Psychology,* 1976, *12,* 464–486.

Chilman, C. S. Families in development at mid-stage of the family life cycle. *Family Coordinator,* 1968, *17,* 297–331.

Chomsky, N. *Aspects of the theory of syntax.* Cambridge, Mass.: M.I.T. Press, 1965.

Chorover, S. L. The pacification of the brain. *Psychology Today,* May 1974, pp. 59–70.

Christian, J. J., Glyger, V., & Davis, D. Factors in the mass mortality of a herd of sika deer. *Carvus nippon. Chesapeake Science,* 1960, *1,* 79–95.

Christie, R., & Geis, F. L. (Eds.). *Studies in Machiavellianism.*

New York: Academic Press, 1970.

Cialdini, R. B., Cacioppo, J. T., Basset, B., & Miller, J. A. Low-ball procedure for producing compliance: commitment then cost. *Journal of Personality and Social Psychology*, 1978, *36*, 463-478.

Cialdini, R. B., Vincent, J. E., Lewis, S. K., Catalan, J., Wheeler, D., & Darby, B. L. Reciprocal concessions procedure for inducing compliance: the door-in-the-face technique. *Journal of Personality and Social Psychology*, 1975, *31*, 206-215.

Clark, M., Gosnell, M., & Shapiro, D. The new war on pain. *Newsweek*, April 25, 1977, pp. 48-58.

Clark M., Gosnell, M., & Whitmore, J. The prisoners of pills. *Newsweek*, April 24, 1978, p. 77.

Clark, M., & Hager, M. Valium abuse: the yellow peril. *Newsweek*, September 24, 1979, p. 66.

Clark, R. D., & Word, L. E. Where is the apathetic bystander? Situational characteristics of the emergency. *Journal of Personality and Social Psychology*, 1974, *29*, 279-287.

Clausen, J. A. The social meaning of differential physical and sexual maturation. In S. E. Dragstin & G. H. Elder (Eds.), *Life cycle: psychological and social context*. New York: Wiley, 1975.

Clore, G. L., Bray, R. B., Atkin, S. M., & Murphy, P. Interracial attitudes and behavior at a summer camp. *Journal of Personality and Social Psychology*, 1978, *36*, 107-116.

Cohen, D. B. Repression is not the demon who conceals and hoards our forgotten dreams. *Psychology Today*, May 1974a, pp. 50-54.

Cohen, D. B. Toward a theory of dream recall. *Psychological Bulletin*, 1974, *81*, 138-154.

Cohen, D. B. Dreaming: Experimental investigation of representation and adaptive properties. In G. Schwartz & D. Shapiro (Eds.), *Consciousness and self-regulation*. New York: Plenum, 1976.

Cohen, L. B. Our developing knowledge of infant perception and cognition. *American Psychologist*, 1979, *34*, 894-899.

Cohen, R. A. Conceptual styles, culture conflict, and nonverbal tests. *American Anthropologist*, 1969, *71*, 828-856.

Cohen, S., Glass, D. C., & Singer, J. E. Apartment noise, auditory discrimination, and reading ability in children. *Journal of Experimental Social Psychology*, 1973, *9*, 407-422.

Colavita, F. B. *Interspecies differences in sensory dominance*. Paper presented at the Twelfth Annual Meeting of the Psychonomic Society, St. Louis, November 1971.

Cole, J., & Davis, J. M. Anti-anxiety drugs. In S. Arieti (Ed.), *American handbook of psychiatry* (Vol. V). New York: Basic Books, 1975.

Coleman, J. C. *Abnormal psychology and modern life* (5th ed.). Glenville, Ill.: Scott, Foresman, 1976.

Coleman, J. C. *Abnormal psychology and modern life*. Glenview, Ill.: Scott, Foresman, 1980.

Coleman, J. C., & Hammen, C. L. *Contemporary psychology and effective behavior*. Glenview, Ill.: Scott, Foresman, 1974.

Coleman, J. S. *Youth: Transition to adulthood* (Report of the President's Science Advisory Committee). Chicago: University of Chicago Press, 1974.

Collings, V. B. Human taste response as a function of locus of stimulation on the tongue and soft palate. *Perception and Psychophysics*, 1974, *16*, 169-197.

Comfort, A. *A good age*. New York: Crown, 1976.

Conger, J. J. *Adolescence and youth: psychological development in a changing world* (2nd ed.). New York: Harper & Row, 1977.

Conrad, R. Short-term memory in the deaf: a test for speech coding. *British Journal of Psychology*, 1972, *63*, 173-180.

Conway, F., & Siegelman, J. *Snapping*. New York: Dell, 1980.

Cook, S. W. Motives in a conceptual analysis of attitude-related behavior. *Nebraska Symposium on Motivation*, 1970, *18*, 179-221.

Cook, S. W. Ethical issues in the conduct of research in social relations. In P. Nejelski (Ed.), *Social research in conflict with law and ethics*. Cambridge, Mass.: Ballinger, 1976.

Coombs, C. H., Coombs, L. C., & McClelland, G. H. Preference scales for number and sex of children. *Population Studies*, 1975, *29*, 273-298.

Cooper, J. Personal responsibility and dissonance. *Journal of Personality and Social Psychology*, 1971, *18*, 354-363.

Cooper, J. Deception and role-playing: on telling the good guys from the bad guys. *American Psychologist*, 1976, *31*(8), 605-610.

Cooper, R., & Zubek, J. Effects of enriched and restricted early environments on the learning ability of bright and dull rats. *Canadian Journal of Psychology*, 1958, *12*, 159-164.

Cornsweet, T. N. *Visual perception*. New York: Academic Press, 1970.

Coser, L. *The functions of social conflict*. New York: Free Press, 1956.

Costanzo, P. R., & Woddy, E. Z. Externality as a function of obesity: persuasive style or eating—specific attribute? *Journal of Personality & Social Psychology*, 37, 2286-2296.

Cotter, L. H. Operant conditioning in a Vietnamese mental hospital. *American Journal of Psychiatry*, 1967, *124*, 23-28.

Cottrell, F., & Atchley, R. C. *Women in retirement: a preliminary report*. Oxford, Oh.: Scripps Foundation, 1969.

Cottrell, N. B., Rittle, R. H., & Wack, D. L. Presence of an audience and list type (competitional and noncompetitional as joint determinants of performance in paired-associates learning. *Journal of Personality*, 1967, *35*, 217-226.

Craig, G. J. *Human development*. Englewood Cliffs, N.J.: Prentice-Hall, 1980.

Craik, F. I. M. Human memory. *Annual Review of Psychology*, 1979, *30*, 63-102.

Craik, F. I. M., & Lockhart, R. S. Levels of processing: a framework for memory research. *Journal of Verbal Learn-*

ing and Verbal Behavior, 1972, 11, 671–684.

Crockenberg, S. B. Creativity tests: a boon or boondoggle for education? Review of Educational Research, 1980, 42, 27–44.

Cronbach, L. J. Essentials of psychological testing. New York: Harper & Row, 1970.

Csikszentmikalyi, M. Beyond boredom and anxiety. San Francisco: Jossey-Bass, 1975.

Cumming, E., & Henry, W. E. Growing old: the process of disengagement. New York: Basic Books, 1961.

Dabbs, J. M., & Leventhal, H. Effects of varying the recommendations in a fear-arousing communication. Journal of Personality and Social Psychology, 1966, 4, 525–531.

Dalal, A. S., & Barber, T. X. Yoga and hypnotism. In T. X. Barber (Ed.), LSD, marijuana, yoga and hypnosis. Chicago: Aldine, 1970.

D'Amato, M. R. Derived motives. Annual Review of Psychology, 1974, 25, 83–106.

Davis, J. H., Laughlin, P. R., & Komorita, S. S. The social psychology of small groups: cooperative and mixed-motive interaction. Annual Review of Psychology, 1976, 27, 502–516.

Davison, G. C., & Stuart, R. B. Behavior therapy and civil liberties. American Psychologist, 1975, 30, 755–763.

Davitz, J. The effects of previous training on postfrustration behavior. Journal of Abnormal and Social Psychology, 1952, 47, 309–315.

Davitz, J. R. The language of emotion. New York: Academic Press, 1969.

Davitz, J. R. A dictionary and grammar of emotion. In M. B. Arnold (Ed.), Feelings and emotions. New York: Academic Press, 1970.

Dean, S. R. Is there an ultraconscious? Canadian Psychiatric Association Journal, 1970, 15, 57–61.

de Charms, R. Review of theories of motivation: from mechanism to cognition by B. Weiner. Contemporary Psychology, 1968, 19, 4–6

de Charms, R., & Muir, M. S. Motivation: Social approaches. Annual Review of Psychology, 1978, 91–113.

Deikman, A. J. Deautomatization and the mystic experience. In R. E. Ornstein (Ed.), The nature of human consciousness. San Francisco: Freeman, 1973.

Dekker, E., Pelser, H. E., & Groen, J. Conditioning as a cause of asthmatic attacks. Journal of Psychosomatic Research, 1957, 2, 97–108.

Delgado, J. M. R. Physical control of the mind: toward a psycho-civilized society. New York: Harper & Row, 1969.

Delin, P. S. The learning to criterion of a serial list with and without mnemonic instructions. Psychosomatic Science, 1969, 16, 169–170.

Dember, W. N. The new look in motivation. American Scientist, 1965, 53, 409–427.

Dember, W. N., Earl, R. W., & Paradise, N. Response by rats to differential stimulus complexity. Journal of Comparative and Physiological Psychology, 1957, 50, 514–518.

Dement, W. C. An essay on dreams: the role of physiology in understanding their nature. In F. Barron et al. (Eds.), New directions in psychology (Vol. 2). New York: Holt, Rinehart and Winston, 1965.

Dement, W. C. Some must watch while some must sleep. San Francisco: Freeman, 1974.

Dement, W. C., Cohen, H., Ferguson, J., & Zarcone, V. A sleep researcher's odyssey: the function and clinical significance of REM sleep. In L. Madow and L. H. Snow (Eds.), The psychodynamic implications of the physiological studies on dreams. Springfield, Ill.: Charles C. Thomas, 1970.

Dement, W. C., & Wolpert, E. Relation of eye movements, body motility, and external stimuli to dream content. Journal of Experimental Psychology, 1958, 55, 543–553.

Dennis, W. Creative productivity between the ages of 20 and 80 years. Journal of Gerontology, 1966, 21, 1–8.

Dennis, W., & Dennis, M. G. The effect of cradling practices upon the onset of walking in Hopi children. Journal of Genetic Psychology, 1940, 56, 77–86.

Dent, J. Y. Dealing with the alcoholic at home. Medical World of London, 1954, 81, 245.

Deutsch, M., & Krauss, P. M. The effect of threat upon interpersonal bargaining. Journal of Abnormal and Social Psychology, 1960, 61, 181–189.

Dick-Read, G. Childbirth without fear. New York: Harper & Row, 1953.

Dickinson, A., & Mackintosh, N. J. Classical conditioning in animals. Annual Review of Psychology, 1978, 29, 587–612.

Digman, J. M. Personality factors, semantic factors, and factor analysis. Paper presented at the Society of Multivariate Experimental Psychologists, Denver, Colorado, 1977.

Di Loreto, A. O. Comparative psychotherapy: an experimental analysis. Chicago: Aldine, 1971.

Dimond, E. G. Acupuncture anaesthesia. Journal of the American Medical Association, 1971, 218, 1558.

Dobzhansky, T. Differences are not deficits. Psychology Today, December 1973, pp. 97–101.

Dollard, J., & Miller, N. E. Personality and psychotherapy. New York: McGraw-Hill, 1950.

Donahue, W., Orback, H. L., & Pollack, O. Retirement: the emerging social pattern. In C. Tibbets (Ed.), Handbook of social gerontology. Chicago: University of Chicago Press, 1960.

Doob, A. N., & Wood, L. Catharsis and aggression: the effects of annoyance and retaliation on aggressive behavior. Journal of Personality and Social Psychology, 1972, 22, 156–162.

Doty, R. W. The brain. In F. Leukel (Ed.), Issues in physiological psychology. St. Louis: Mosby, 1974.

Dubois, P. M. The hospice way of death. New York: Human Sciences Press, 1981.

Dubos, R. *Reason awake: science for man.* New York: Columbia University Press, 1970.

Dweck, C. S., & Reppucci, N. D. Learned helplessness and reinforcement responsibility in children. *Journal of Personality and Social Psychology,* 1973, 25, 109–116.

Eagly, A. H. Sex differences in influenceability. *Psychological Bulletin,* 1978, 85, 86–116.

Eisenstadt, S. N. Archetypal patterns of youth. In E. H. Erikson (Ed.), *The challenge of youth.* Garden City, N.Y.: Doubleday, 1965.

Ekman, P., & Oster, H. Facial expressions of emotion. *Annual Review of Psychology,* 1979, 30, 527–554.

Ekstrand, B. R. To sleep, perchance to dream (about why we forget). In C. P. Duncan, L. Sechvest, & A. W. Milton (Eds.), *Human memory: festchrift in honor of Benton J. Underwood.* New York: Appleton-Century-Crofts, 1972.

Elder, G. H. Parental power legitimation and its effect on the adolescent. *Sociometry,* 1963, 26, 50–65.

Elkind, D. Cognitive development in adolescence. In J. F. Adams (Ed.), *Understanding adolescence.* Boston: Allyn and Bacon, 1968.

Elkind, D. Egocentrism in adolescence. In R. E. Grinder (Ed.), *Studies in adolescence* (2nd ed.). New York: Macmillan, 1969.

Ellis, A. *Humanistic psychotherapy: the rational emotive approach.* New York: Julian Press, 1973.

Ellis, G. T., & Sekyra, F. The effect of aggressive cartoons on the behavior of first grade children. *Journal of Psychology,* 1972, 81, 37–43.

Ellsworth, P. C. From abstract ideas to concrete instances: Some guidelines for choosing natural research settings. *American Psychologist,* 1977, 32(8), 604–615.

Engen, T. The sense of smell. *Annual Review of Psychology,* 1973, 24, 187–206.

Epstein, S. The measurement of drive and conflict in humans: theory and experiment. In M. R. Jones (Ed.), *Nebraska symposium on motivation.* Lincoln: University of Nebraska Press, 1962.

Epstein, S. Explorations in personality today and tomorrow. *American Psychologist,* 1979, 34, 649–653.

Erikson, E. H. Identity and the life cycle. *Psychological Issues,* 1959, 1, 1–165.

Erikson, E. H. *Childhood and society* (2nd ed.). New York: Norton, 1963.

Erikson, E. H. *Identity: youth in crisis.* New York: Norton, 1968.

Eron, L. D., et al. Does television violence cause aggression? *American Psychologist,* 1972, 27, 253–263.

Etaugh, C. Effects of nonmaternal care on children. *American Psychologist,* 1980, 35, 309–319.

Etzioni, A. *The genetic fix.* New York: Macmillan, 1973.

Evans, R. B. Childhood parental relationships of homosexual men. *Journal of Consulting and Clinical Psychology,* 1969, 33, 129–135.

Eysenck, H. J. The effects of psychotherapy: an evaluation. *Journal of Consulting and Clinical Psychology,* 1952, 16, 319–324.

Eysenck, H. J. *The structure of human personality* (3rd ed.). London: Methuen, 1970.

Fagan, J. F., III. Infant's delayed recognition: memory and forgetting. *Journal of Experimental Child Psychology,* 1973, 16, 424–450.

Fagot, B. I. Sex differences in toddlers' behavior and parental reactions. *Developmental Psychology,* 1974, 10, 554–558.

Fantz, R. L. The origin of form perception. *Scientific American,* May 1961, pp. 450–463.

Fantz, R. L. Patterns of vision in newborn infants. *Science,* 1963, 140, 296–297.

Fantz, R. L. Visual perception from birth as shown by pattern selectivity. *Annals of the New York Academy of Sciences,* 1965, 118, 793–814.

Farb, P. *Word play.* New York: Knopf, 1974.

Fast, J. *Body language.* New York: M. Evans, 1970.

Favreau, O. E., & Corballis, M. C. Negative aftereffects in visual perception. *Scientific American,* December 1976, pp. 42–48.

Fenyvesi, C. Six months later: living with a fearful memory. *Psychology Today,* 1977, 11, 61.

Fenyvesi, C. The hostages: re-entry problems ahead. *Psychology Today,* 1980, 14, 9–10.

Feshbach, S. Dynamics and morality of violence and aggression: some psychological considerations. *American Psychologist,* 1971, 26, 281–292.

Feshbach, S. The use of behavior modification procedures: a comment on Stoltz et al. *American Psychologist,* 1976, 31, 538–541.

Festinger, L. A theory of social comparison processes. *Human Relations,* 1954, 2(2), 117–140.

Festinger, L. *A theory of cognitive dissonance.* Evanston, Ill.: Row, Peterson, 1957.

Festinger, L., Schachter, S., & Back, K. *Social pressures in informal groups: a study of human factors in housing.* New York: Harper & Row, 1950.

Figis, E. *Patriarchal attitudes.* London: Faber & Faber, 1970.

Flavell, J. H. *Cognitive development.* Englewood Cliffs, N.J.: Prentice-Hall, 1977.

Flexser, A. J., & Tulving, E. Retrieval independence in recognition and recall. *Psychological Review,* 1978, 85, 153–171.

Forward, J., Canter, R., & Kirsch, N. Role-enactment and deception methodologies. *American Psychologist,* 1976, 31(8), 595–604.

Foulkes, D. *The psychology of sleep.* New York: Scribner's, 1966.

Foulkes, D., & Fleisher, S. Mental activity in relaxed wakefulness. *Journal of Abnormal Psychology*, 1975, *84*, 66–75.

Freedman, A. M. Drugs and society. In J. O. Cole, A. M. Freedman, & A. J. Friedhoff (Eds.), *Psychopathology and psychopharmacology*. Baltimore: John Hopkins University Press, 1973.

Freedman, J. L. *Crowding and behavior*. San Francisco: Freeman, 1975.

Freedman, J. L., & Fraser, S. C. Compliance without pressure: the foot-in-the-door technique. *Journal of Personality and Social Psychology*, 1966, *4*, 195–202.

Freedman, J. L., Levy, A. S., Buchanan, R. W., & Price, J. Crowding and human aggressiveness. *Journal of Experimental Social Psychology*, 1972, *8*, 528–548.

Freedman, J. L., Sears, D. O., & Carlsmith, J. M. *Social psychology*. Englewood Cliffs, N.J.: Prentice-Hall, 1981.

Fretz, B. R., & Strang, D. J. *Preparing for graduate study in psychology: not for seniors only!* Washington, D.C.: American Psychological Association, 1980.

Freud, S. *The basic writings of Sigmund Freud* (A. A. Brill, trans. & ed.). New York: Random House, 1928.

Freud, S. *An outline of psychoanalysis*. New York: Norton, 1949.

Friedan, B. *The feminine mystique*. New York: Norton, 1963.

Friedman, E. A., & Havighurst, R. J. *The meaning of work and retirement*. Chicago: University of Chicago Press, 1954.

Friedman, M., & Rosenman, R. H. *Type A behavior and your heart*. New York: Knopf, 1974.

Frodi, A., Macaulay, J., & Thome, P. R. Are women always less aggressive than men? *Psychological Bulletin*, 1977, *84*, 634–660.

Frumkin, B., & Ainsfeld, M. Semantic and surface codes in the memory of deaf children. *Cognitive Psychology*, 1977, *9*, 475–493.

Funkenstein, D. H., King, S. H., & Drolette, M. The experimental evocation of stress. In *Symposium on stress*. Division of Medical Sciences of the National Research Council and Army Medical Services Graduate School of Walter Reed Army Medical Center. Washington, D.C.: Government Printing Office, 1953.

Gaines, J. The founder of Gestalt therapy: a sketch of Fritz Perls. *Psychology Today*, November 1974, pp. 117–118.

Gelman, Rochel. Preschool thought. *American Psychologist*, 1979, *34*, 900–905.

George, B. J. Criminal law. In D. R. Sills (Ed.), *International encyclopedia of the social sciences* (Vol. 3). New York: Macmillan, 1968.

Gerbner, G. Violence in television drama: trends and symbolic functions. In G. A. Comstock and E. A. Rubinstein (Eds.), *Television and social behavior: I. media content and control*. Washington, D.C.: Government Printing Office, 1972.

Gerbner, G., & Gross, L. *Trends in network television drama and viewer conceptions of social reality, 1967-1973: violence profile number 6*. Philadelphia: Annenberg School of Communications, University of Pennsylvania, 1974 (ERIC Document Reproduction Service No. ED 101682).

Gergen, K. J. The codification of research ethics—views of a Doubting Thomas. *American Psychologist*, 1973, *28*, 907–912.

Geschwind, N. Specializations of the human brain. *Scientific American*, 1979, *241*, 180–199.

Getzels, J. W., & Jackson, P. *Creativity and intelligence*. New York: Wiley, 1962.

Giambra, L. Daydreams: the backburner of the mind. *Psychology Today*, December 1974, pp. 66–68.

Ginsburg, H. *The myth of the deprived child*. Englewood Cliffs, N.J.: Prentice-Hall, 1972.

Gjessing, L. R. A review of the biochemistry of periodic catatonia. *Excerpta Medica, International Congress Series*, 1966 (150).

Glass, D. C. *Behavior patterns, stress and coronary disease*. New York: Wiley, 1977.

Glass, L., Holyoak, K., & Santa, J. *Cognition*. Reading, Mass.: Addison-Wesley, 1979.

Glasser, W. *Reality therapy*. New York: Harper & Row, 1965.

Gleason, H. A., Jr. *An introduction to descriptive linguistics*. New York: Holt, Rinehart & Winston, 1961.

Glenburg, A., Smith, S. M., & Green, C. Type I rehearsal: maintenance and more. *Journal of Verbal Learning and Verbal Behavior*, 1977, *16*, 339–352.

Glick, I. O., Weiss, R. S., & Parkes, C. M. *The first year of bereavement*. New York: Wiley, 1974.

Glucksberg, S., & King, L. J. Motivated forgetting mediated by implicit verbal chaining: a laboratory analog of repression. *Science*, 1967, *158*, 517–519.

Glueck, B. C., & Stoebel, C. F. Psychophysiological correlates of relaxation. In A. Sugarman & R. Tarter (Eds.), *Expanding dimensions of consciousness*. New York: Springer, 1978, pp. 99–129.

Goffman, E. *The presentation of self in everyday life*. New York: Anchor, 1959.

Goldenberg, H. *Contemporary clinical psychology*. Monterey, Ca.: Brooks/Cole, 1973.

Goldiamond, I. A diary of self-modification. *Psychology Today*, November 1973, pp. 85–102.

Goleman, D. 1,528 little geniuses and how they grew. *Psychology Today*, February 1980, pp. 28–53.

Gomes-Schwartz, B., Hadley, S. W., & Strupp, H. H. Individual psychotherapy and behavior therapy. *Annual Review of Psychology*, 1978, *29*, 435–471.

Gordon, C., Gaitz, C. M., & Scott, J. Leisure and lives: personal expressivity across the life span. In R. H. Binstock & E. Shanas (Eds.), *Handbook of aging and the social sciences*. New York: Van Nostrand Reinhold, 1977.

Gould, R. E. Measuring masculinity by the size of a paycheck.

In J. H. Pleck & J. Sawyer (Eds.), *Men and masculinity.* Englewood Cliffs, N.J.: Prentice-Hall, 1974.

Greenberg, R., & Pearlman, C. Delirium tremens and dreaming. *American Journal of Psychiatry,* 1967, *124,* 133–42.

Greer, G. *The female eunuch.* New York: McGraw-Hill, 1971.

Gregg, C., Clifton, R. K., & Haith, M. M. A possible explanation for the frequent failure to find cardiac orienting in the newborn infant. *Developmental Psychology,* 1976, *12,* 75–76.

Gregory, R. L. *Eye and brain: the psychology of seeing* (2nd ed.). New York: McGraw-Hill, 1972.

Grinker, R. R., & Spiegel, J. P. *War neurosis.* Philadelphia: Blakiston, 1945.

Grinspoon, L. Marihuana. *Scientific American,* December 1969.

Groves, P. M., & Rebec, F. V. Biochemistry and behavior: some central actions of amphetamine and antipsychotic drugs. *Annual Review of Psychology,* 1976, *27,* 91–127.

Guilford, J. P. Traits of creativity. In H. H. Anderson (Ed.), *Creativity and its cultivation.* New York: Harper & Row, 1959.

Guilford, J. P. Factorial angles to psychology. *Psychological Review,* 1961, *68,* 1–20.

Gundlach, R. H. Childhood parental relationships and the establishment of gender roles of homosexuals. *Journal of Consulting and Clinical Psychology,* 1969, *33,* 136–139.

Haan, N. Proposed model of ego functioning: coping and defense mechanisms in relation to IQ change. *Psychological Monographs,* 1963, *77* (8, Whole No. 571).

Haan, N., & Day, D. A longitudinal study of change and sameness in personality development: adolescence to later adulthood. *International Journal of Aging and Human Development,* 1974, *5,* 11–39.

Haber, R. N. Eidetic images. *Scientific American,* April 1969, pp. 36–44.

Haith, M. M., & Campos, J. J. Human infancy. *Annual Review of Psychology,* 1977, *28,* 251–293.

Hall, C. S., & Lindzey, G. *Theories of personality* (2nd ed.). New York: Wiley, 1970.

Hall, E. T. *The silent language.* Garden City, N.Y.: Doubleday, 1959.

Hamm, N. H. The politics of empiricism. *American Psychologist,* January 1974, 9–13.

Haney, C. A psychologist looks at the criminal justice system. In A. Calvin (Ed.), *Challenges and alternatives to the American criminal justice system.* Ann Arbor, Mich.: University International Press, 1979.

Hanratty, M. A. *Imitation of film-mediated aggression against live and inanimate victims.* Unpublished master's thesis, Vanderbilt University, 1969.

Hanratty, M. A., Liebert, R. M., Morris, L. W., & Fernandez,

L. E. Imitation of film-mediated aggression against live and inanimate victims. *Proceedings of the 77th Annual Convention of the American Psychological Association,* 1969, 457–458.

Hardt, J. V., & Kamuja, J. Anxiety change through electro-encephalographic alpha feedback seen only in high anxiety subjects. *Science,* 1978, *201,* 79–81.

Harlow, H. F. The formation of learning sets. *Psychological Review,* 1949, *56,* 51–65.

Harlow, H. F. Learning and satiation of responses in intrinsically motivated complex puzzle performance by monkeys. *Journal of Comparative and Physiological Psychology,* 1950, *43,* 289–294.

Harlow, H. F. The nature of love. *American Psychologist,* 1958, *13,* 673–685.

Harlow, H. F. Learning set and error factor theory. In S. Koch (Ed.), *Psychology: a study of a science.* New York: McGraw-Hill, 1959.

Harlow, H. F., & Zimmerman, R. R. Affectional responses in the infant monkey. *Science,* 1959, *130,* 421–432.

Harmatz, M. G. *Abnormal psychology.* Englewood Cliffs, N.J.: Prentice-Hall, 1978.

Härnquist, K. Relative changes in intelligence from 13 to 18. *Scandinavian Journal of Psychology,* 1968, *9,* 50–82.

Harrell, R. F., Woodyard, E., & Gates, A. I. *The effect of mother's diet on the intelligence of the offspring.* New York: Teacher's College, Columbia Bureau of Publications, 1955.

Hartley, D., Roback, H. B., & Abramowitz, S. I. Deterioration effects in encounter groups. *American Psychologist,* 1976, *31,* 247–255.

Hartman, E. L. The functions of sleep. New Haven: Yale University Press, 1973.

Hartmann, H. *Essays on ego psychology: selected problems in psychoanalytic theory.* New York: International Universities Press, 1964.

Hartmann, P., & Husband, C. The mass media and racial conflict. *Race,* 1971, *12,* 267–282.

Hassatt, J. Teaching yourself to relax. *Psychology Today,* August 1978.

Havighurst, R. J., Neugarten, B. L., & Tobin, S. S. *Disengagement and patterns of aging.* Paper presented at the meeting of the International Association of Gerontology, Copenhagen, August 1973.

Hayakawa, S. I. *Language in thought and action.* New York: Harcourt Brace Jovanovich, 1949.

Hearst, E. The classical–instrumental distinction: reflexes, voluntary behavior, and categories of associative learning. In W. K. Estes (Ed.), *Handbook of learning and cognitive processes* (Vol. 2). *Conditioning and behavior theory.* Hillsdale, N.J.: Lawrence Erlbaum, 1975.

Heath, R. G. A biochemical hypothesis on the etiology of schizophrenia. In D. D. Jackson (Ed.), *The etiology of schizophrenia.* New York: Basic Books, 1960.

Hebb, D. O. *The organization of behavior*. New York: Wiley, 1949.

Hechinger, N., & Lewin, R. Seeing without eyes. *Science*, 1981, *165*, 38–43.

Heider, E. R. Universals in color naming and memory. *Journal of Experimental Psychology*, 1972, *93*, 10–20.

Heider, E. R., & Oliver, D. C. The structure of the color space in naming and memory in two languages. *Cognitive Psychology*, 1972, *3*, 337–354.

Held, R., & Hein, A. Movement-produced stimulation in the development of visually guided behavior. *Journal of Comparative and Physiological Psychology*, 1963, *56*, 872–876.

Hendricks, J., & Hendricks, C. D. *Aging in mass society: myths and realities*. Cambridge, Mass.: Winthrop, 1977.

Henry, W. E. *The analysis of fantasy*. New York: Wiley, 1956.

Heron, W. The pathology of boredom. *Scientific American*, January 1957.

Hersher, L. (Ed.). *Four psychotherapies*. New York: Appleton-Century-Crofts, 1970.

Hess, B. *Amicability*. Unpublished doctoral dissertation, Rutgers University, 1971.

Heston, L. L. Psychiatric disorders in foster-home-reared children of schizophrenic mothers. *British Journal of Psychiatry*, 1966, *112*, 819–825.

Hilgard, E. R. Pain as a muzzle for psychology and physiology. *American Psychologist*, 1969, *24*, 103–113.

Hilgard, E. R. A neodissociation interpretation of pain reduction in hypnosis. *Psychological Reviews*, 1973, *80*, 396–411.

Hilgard, E. R. Hypnosis is no mirage. *Psychology Today*, November 1974, pp. 121–128.

Hilgard, E. R. Hypnosis. *Annual Review of Psychology*, 1975, *26*, 19–44.

Hilgard, E. R. *Divided consciousness: multiple controls in human thought and action*. New York: Wiley-Interscience, 1977.

Hilgard, E. R., & Bower, G. H. *Theories of learning* (4th ed.). Englewood Cliffs, N.J.: Prentice-Hall, 1975.

Hill, R., Foote, N., Aldous, J., Carlson, R., & McDonald, R. *Family development in three generations*. Cambridge, Mass.: Schenkman, 1970.

Hill, W. F. Activity as an autonomous drive. *Journal of Comparative and Physiological Psychology*, 1956, *49*, 15–19.

Hochreich, D. J., & Rotter, J. B. Have college students become less trusting? *Journal of Personality and Social Psychology*, 1970, *15*, 211–214.

Hodgkin, A. L., & Huxley, A. F. A quantitative description of current and its application to conduction and excitation in nerves. *Journal of Physiology*, 1952, *117*, 500–544.

Hoffer, A., & Osmond, H. The adrenochrome model and schizophrenia. *Journal of Nervous and Mental Diseases*, 1959, *128*, 18–35.

Hoffman, H. S., & DePaulo, P. Behavioral control by an imprinting stimulus. *American Scientist*, 1977, *65*, 58–66.

Hoffman, L. W. Fear of success in males and females. *Journal of Consulting and Clinical Psychology*, 1974, *42*, 353–358.

Hoffman, L. W. Changes in family roles, socialization, and sex differences. *American Psychologist*, 1977, *32*(8), 644–657.

Hoffman, L. W., & Nye, F. I. *Working mothers*. San Francisco: Jossey-Bass, 1974.

Hoffman, M. L. Personality and social development. *Annual Review of Psychology*, 1977, *28*, 295–321.

Hohmann, G. W. Some effects of spinal cord lesions on experienced emotional feelings. *Psychophysiology*, 1966, *3*, 143–156.

Holmes, D. S. Investigations of repression. *Psychological Bulletin*, October 1974, *81*, 632–653.

Holmes, D. S. Debriefing after psychological experiments: I. effectiveness of postdeception dehoaxing. *American Psychologist*, 1976a, *31*(12), 858–867.

Holmes, D. S. Debriefing after psychological experiments: II. effectiveness of postexperiment desensitizing. *American Psychologist*, 1976b, *31*(12), 868–875.

Holmes, T. H., & Rahe, R. H. The social readjustment rating scale. *Journal of Psychosomatic Research*, 1967, *11*, 213.

Honzick, M. P., Macfarlane, J. W., & Allen, L. The stability of mental test performance between two and eighteen years. *Journal of Experimental Education*, 1948, *17*, 309–324.

Hooker, E. Parental relations and male homosexuality in patient and nonpatient samples. *Journal of Consulting and Clinical Psychology*, 1969, *33*, 140–142.

Horn, J. Family therapy—a quick fix for juvenile delinquency. *Psychology Today*, March 1975, pp. 80–81.

Horn, J. L. Human abilities: a review of research and theory in the early 1970s. *Annual Review of Psychology*, 1976, *27*, 437–485.

Horn, J. L., & Donaldson, G. On the myth of the intellectual decline in adulthood. *American Psychologist*, 1976, *31*, 701–719.

Horner, M. A bright woman is caught in a double bind. *Psychology Today*, November 1969, pp. 36–38, 62.

Hovland, C. I., & Sears, R. R. Minor studies in aggression: VI. correlation of lynchings with economic indices. *Journal of Abnormal and Social Psychology*, 1940, *9*, 301–310.

Hughes, J., Smith, T. W., Kosterlitz, H. W., Fothergill, L. A., Morgan, B. A., & Morris, H. R. Identification of two related pentapeptides from the brain with potent opiate agonist activities. *Nature*, 1975, *258*, 577–579.

Hunt, E., & Love, T. How good can memory be? In A. W. Melton & E. Martin (Eds.), *Coding processes in human memory*. Washington, D.C.: Winston, 1972.

Huxley, A. *Brave new world*. New York: Harper & Row, 1939.

Inhelder, B., & Piaget, J. *The growth of logical thinking from childhood to adolescence* (A. Parson & S. Milgram, trans.). New York: Basic Books, 1958.

Insel, P. M., & Lindgren, H. C. *Too close for comfort: the psychology of crowding behavior*. Englewood Cliffs, N.J.: Prentice-Hall, 1978.

Isaacs, W., Thomas, J., & Goldiamond, I. Application of

operant conditioning to reinstate verbal behavior in psychotics. *Journal of Speech and Hearing Disabilities*, 1960, *25*, 8–12.

Iscoe, I. Community psychology and the competent community. *American Psychologist*, August 1974, 607–613.

Iverson, L. The chemistry of the brain. *Scientific American*, 1979, *241*, 134–149.

Izard, C. E. *The face of emotion.* New York: Appleton-Century-Crofts, 1971.

Jacob, R. Relaxation therapy in the treatment of hypertension: a review. *Archives of General Psychiatry*, 1977, *34*.

Janis, I. L. *Victims of groupthink: a psychological study of foreign-policy decisions and fiascos.* Boston: Houghton Mifflin, 1972.

Jenkins, C. D. Psychologic and social precursors of coronary disease. *New England Journal of Medicine*, 1971, *284*, 307–317.

Jensen, A. R. How much can we boost IQ and scholastic achievement? *Harvard Educational Review*, 1969, *39*, 1–123.

Jensen, A. R. The strange case of Dr. Jensen and Mr. Hyde. *American Psychologist*, June 1974, *29*(6), 467–468.

Jones, E. E., & Gerard, H. B. *Foundations of social psychology.* New York: Wiley, 1967.

Jones, E. E., & Nisbett, R. E. The actor and the observer: divergent perceptions of the causes of behavior. *Attribution: perceiving the causes of behavior.* Morristown, N. J.: General Learning Press, 1972.

Jones, M. C. A study of socialization patterns at the high school level. *Journal of Genetic Psychology*, 1958, *93*, 87–111.

Jones, M. C., & Bayley, N. Physical maturing among boys as related to behavior. *Journal of Educational Psychology*, 1950, *41*, 129–148.

Kagan, J. Emergent themes in human development. *American Scientist*, 1976, *64*, 186–196.

Kallman, F. J. *Heredity in health and mental disorder.* New York: Norton, 1953.

Kamin, L. J. *The science and politics of IQ.* New York: Wiley, 1974.

Kanter, R. M. Women and the structure of organizations: explorations in theory and behavior. In M. Millman & R. M. Kanter (Eds.), *Another voice.* New York: Anchor, 1975.

Kastenbaum, R. *Death, society, and human behavior.* St. Louis: Mosby, 1977.

Kastenbaum, R., & Costa, P. T., Jr. Psychological perspectives on death. *Annual Review of Psychology*, 1977, *28*, 225–249.

Kaufman, L., & Rock, I. The moon illusion. *Scientific American*, July 1962, pp. 120–130.

Keele, S. W. *Attention and human performance.* Santa Monica, Ca.: Goodyear, 1973.

Kelley, H. H. The warm–cold variable in the first impressions

of persons. *Journal of Personality*, 1950, *18*, 431–439.

Kelley, H. H. Attribution theory in social psychology. In D. Levine (Ed.), *Nebraska symposium on motivation.* Lincoln: University of Nebraska Press, 1967.

Kelley, H. H. The processes of casual attribution. *American Psychologist*, February 1973, 107–128

Kelley, H. H., et al. Collective behavior in a simulated panic situation. *Journal of Experimental Social Psychology*, 1965, *1*, 20–54.

Kelman, H. C. Process of opinion change. *Public Opinion Quarterly*, 1961, *25*, 57–78.

Kelman, H. C. Attitudes are alive and well and gainfully employed in the sphere of action. *American Psychologist*, May 1974, 310-324.

Kelman, H. C., & Lawrence, L. H. Violent man: American response to the trial of Lt. William L. Calley. *Psychology Today*, June 1972, pp. 41–45; 78–81.

Kennedy, G. C. The role of depot fat in the hypothalmic control of food intake in the rat. *Proceedings of the Royal Society*, 1953, *B140*, 578–592.

Kennedy, T. Treatment of chronic schizophrenia by behavior therapy: case reports. *Behavior Research Therapy*, 1964, *2*, 1–7.

Kennedy, W. A., & Lindner, R. S. A normative sample of intelligence and achievement of Negro elementary school children in the Southeastern United States. *Monographs of the Society for Research on Child Development*, 1963 (28).

Kennell, T. H., Trause, M. A., & Klaus, M. Evidence for a sensitive period in the human mother. In CIBA Foundation Symposium, 33 (new series), *Parent-infant interaction.* Amsterdam: Associated Scientific Publishers, 1975.

Kety, S. S. Disorders of the human brain. *Scientific American*, 1979, *241*, 202–214.

Kimble, D. P. *Psychology as a biological science.* Santa Monica, Ca.: Goodyear, 1977.

Kimmel, D. C. *Adulthood and aging.* New York: Wiley, 1974.

Kingdom, J. W. Politicians' beliefs about voters. *The American Political Scientist Review*, 1967, *61*, 137–145.

Kinsey, A. C., Pomeroy, W. B., & Martin, C. E. *Sexual behavior in the human male.* Philadelphia: Saunders, 1948.

Kintsch, W. *The representation of meaning in memory.* Hillsdale, N.J.: Lawrence Erlbaum, 1974.

Kiritz, S., & Moos, R. H. Physiological effects of social environments. *Psychosomatic Medicine*, 1974.

Klatzky, R. L. *Human memory.* San Francisco: Freeman, 1980.

Kleemeier, R. W. Intellectual changes in the senium. *Proceedings of the Social Statistics Section of the American Statistical Association.* Washington, D.C.: American Statistical Association, 1962.

Klein, G. S. The personal world through perception. In R. R. Blake & G. V. Ramsey (Eds.), *Perception: an approach to personality.* New York: Ronald Press, 1951.

Kleinhesselink, R. R., & Edwards, R. E. Seeking and avoiding belief-discrepant information as a function of its perceived refutability. *Journal of Personality and Social Psychology*, 1975, *31*, 787–790.

Kleitman, N. *Sleep and wakefulness* (rev. ed.). Chicago: University of Chicago Press, 1963.

Klineberg, O. Emotional expression in Chinese literature. *Journal of Abnormal and Social Psychology*, 1938, *33*, 517–520.

Knight, M. Child molesters try "shock" cure. *New York Times*, May 21, 1974, pp. 43, 83.

Koestler, A. *The act of creation*. New York: Macmillan, 1964.

Kohlberg, L., & Gilligan, C. The adolescent as philosopher. *Daedalus*, 1971, *100*, 1051–1086.

Korner, A. F. Individual differences at birth. Implications for early experience and later development. *American Journal of Orthopsychiatry*, 1971, *41*, 608–619.

Koulack, D., & Goodenough, D. R. Dream recall and dream recall failure: an arousal retrieval model. *Psychological Bulletin*, 1976, *83*, 975–984.

Krebs, D. Empathy and altruism. *Journal of Personality and Social Psychology*, 1975, *32*, 1134–1140.

Kübler-Ross, E. *On death and dying*. New York: Macmillan, 1969.

Kübler-Ross, E. *Death: the final stage of growth*. Englewood Cliffs, N.J.: Prentice-Hall, 1975.

Kutner, B., Wilkins, C., & Yarrow, P. Verbal attitudes and overt behavior involving racial prejudice. *Journal of Abnormal and Social Psychology*, 1952, *47*, 649–652.

Laing, R. D. *The politics of experience*. New York: Ballantine, 1967.

Lamage, F. *Painless childbirth: the Lamage method*. Chicago: Regnery, 1970.

Lamb, M. E. Paternal influences and the father's role. *American Psychologist*, 1979, *34*, 938–943.

Lambert, W. W., Solomon, R. L., & Watson, P. D. Reinforcement and extinction as factors in size estimation. *Journal of Experimental Psychology*, 1949, *39*, 637–641.

Lamm, H., & Trommsdorff, G. Group versus individual performance on tasks requiring ideational proficiency (brainstorming): a review. *European Journal of Social Psychology*, 1973, *3*, 361–388.

LaPiere, R. T. Attitudes versus actions. *Social Forces*, 1934, *13*, 230–237.

Lasch, C. *The culture of narcissism*. New York: Norton, 1979.

Lashley, K. S. In search of the engram. *Symposia of the Society for Experimental Biology*, 1950, *4*, 454–482.

Latané, B., & Darley, J. M. *The unresponsive bystander: why doesn't he help?* New York: Appleton-Century-Crofts, 1970.

Latané, B., & Rodin, J. A lady in distress: inhibiting effects of friends and strangers on bystander intervention. *Journal of Experimental Social Psychology*, 1969, *5*, 189–202.

Laughlin, H. P. *Mental mechanisms*. New York: Appleton-Century-Crofts, 1963.

Laughlin, H. P. *The ego and its defenses*. New York:

Appleton-Century-Crofts, 1970.

Lazarus, A. A. Has behavior therapy outlived its usefulness? *American Psychologist*, 1977, *32*, 550–554.

Lazarus, R. S. *Psychological stress and the coping process*. New York: McGraw-Hill, 1966.

Lazarus, R. S. *Patterns of adjustment and human effectiveness*. New York: McGraw-Hill, 1969.

Lazarus, R. S. *The riddle of man*. Englewood Cliffs, N.J.: Prentice-Hall, 1974.

Lazarus, R. S., & Erickson, C. W. Effects of failure stress upon skilled performance. *Journal of Experimental Psychology*, 1952, *43*, 100–105.

Leboyer, F. *Birth without violence*. New York: Knopf, 1975.

Leeper, R. W. A motivational theory of emotion to replace "emotion as disorganized response." *Psychological Review*, 1948, *55*, 5–21.

Lefcourt, H. M. The function of the illusions of control and freedom. *American Psychologist*, May 1973, 417–425.

Lefcourt, H. M. *Locus of control: current trends in theory and research*. Hillsdale, N.J.: Lawrence Erlbaum, 1976.

Lefkowitz, M., et al. Television violence and child aggression: a follow-up study. In G. A. Comstock & E. A. Rubinstein (Eds.), *Television and social behavior* (Vol. 3). *Television and adolescent aggression*. Washington, D. C.: U. S. Government Printing Office, 1972.

Lehman, H. C. *Age and achievement*. Princeton, N.J.: Princeton University Press, 1953.

Leonard, R. L. Self-concept and attraction for similar and dissimilar others. *Journal of Personality and Social Psychology*, 1975, *31*, 926–929.

Lesner, M. J. The effect of responsibility and choice on a partner's attractiveness following failure. *Journal of Personality*, 1965, *33*, 178–187.

Levine, F. M., & Fasnacht, G. Token rewards may lead to token learning. *American Psychologist*, November 1974, 816–820.

Levinson, B. M. Traditional Jewish cultural values and performance on the Wechsler tests. *Journal of Educational Psychology*, 1959, *50*, 177–181.

Levinson, D. J. *The seasons of a man's life*. New York: Knopf, 1978.

Levinthal, C. *The physiological approach in psychology*. Englewood Cliffs, N. J.: Prentice-Hall, 1979.

Levy, J. Human cognition and lateralization of cerebral function. *Trends in Neurosciences*, 1979, *2*, 222–225.

Lewin, K. A. *A dynamic theory of personality* (K. E. Zener & D. K. Adams, trans.). New York: McGraw-Hill, 1935.

Leyens, J. P., Camino, L., Parke, R. D., & Berkowitz, L. Effect of movie violence on aggression in a field setting as a function of group dominance and cohesion. *Journal of Personality and Social Psychology*, 1975, *32*, 346–360.

Liben, L. Operative understanding of horizontality and its relation to long-term memory. *Child Development*, 1974, *45*, 416–424.

Liddell, H. S. *Emotional hazards in animals and men*. Springfield, Ill.: Charles C. Thomas, 1956.

Lieberman, M. A. Psychological correlates of impending death: some preliminary observations. *Journal of Gerontology*, 1965, *20*, 181–190.

Lieberman, M. A. Change induction in small groups. *Annual Review of Psychology*, 1976, *27*, 217–250.

Lieberman, M. A., & Coplan, A. S. Distance from death as a variable in the study of aging. *Developmental Psychology*, 1969, *2*, 71–84.

Liebert, R. M., & Baron, R. A. Short-term effects of televised aggression on children's aggressive behavior. In J. P. Murray, E. A. Rubinstein, & G. A. Comstock (Eds.), *Television and social behavior* (Vol. 2). *Television and social learning*. Washington, D. C.: U.S. Government Printing Office, 1972.

Liebert, R. M., Poulos, R. W., & Marmor, G. S. *Developmental psychology*. Englewood Cliffs, N.J.: Prentice-Hall, 1974.

Liebert, R. M., & Schwartzberg, N. S. Effects of mass media. *Annual Review of Psychology*, Palo Alto, Ca.: Annual Reviews, 1977.

Liebeskind, J. C., & Paul, L. A. Psychological and physiological mechanisms of pain. *Annual Review of Psychology*, 1977, *28*, 41–60.

Lifton, R. L. *Thought reform and the psychology of totalism*. New York: Norton, 1961.

Lindsay, P. H., & Norman, D. A. *Human information processing* (2nd ed.). New York: Academic Press, 1977.

Lipsey, M. W. Research and relevance. *American Psychologist*, July 1974, 541–553.

Lipsitt, L. P. Babies: they're a lot smarter than they look. *Psychology Today*, December 1971, pp. 70–72, 88–89.

Llinas, R. R. The cortex of the cerebellum. *Scientific American*, January 1975, pp. 56–72.

Loftus, E. F., & Fries, J. F. Informed consent may be hazardous to health. *Science*, 1979, *204*.

Lopata, H. Z. *Widowhood in an American city*. Cambridge, Mass.: Schenkman, 1973.

Lorenz, K. Der Kumpan in der Umwelt des Vobels. *Journal of Ornithology*, 1935, *83*, 137–213, 289–413.

Lorenz, K. *On aggression*. New York: Harcourt, 1968.

Lowenthal, M. F., & Chiriboga, D. Transition to the empty nest: crisis, change, or relief. *Archives of General Psychiatry*, 1972, *26*, 8–14.

Lowenthal, M. F., Thumber, M., & Chiriboga, D., & et al. *Four stages of life*. San Francisco: Jossey-Bass, 1975.

Ludwig, A. M. Altered states of consciousness. In C. T. Tart (Ed.), *Altered states of consciousness*. New York: Wiley, 1969.

Lumsden, J. Test theory. *Annual Review of Psychology*, 1976, *27*, 251–280.

Lundin, R. W. *Personality: a behavioral analysis* (2nd ed.). New York: Macmillan, 1974.

Lykken, D. T. Guilty knowledge test: the right way to use a lie detector. *Psychology Today*, March 1975, pp. 56–60.

McBurney, D., & Collings, V. *Introduction to sensation/perception*. Englewood Cliffs, N.J.: Prentice-Hall, 1977.

McCarthy, A. Voices of their captors: when the hostages come home. *Commonweal*, 1980.

McClearn, G. E., & DeFries, J. C. *Introduction to behavioral genetics*. San Francisco: Freeman, 1973.

McClelland, D. C. Methods of measuring human motivation. In J. W. Atkinson (Ed.), *Motives in fantasy, action and society: a method of assessment and study*. New York: Van Nostrand, 1958.

McClelland, D. C. Achievement and entrepreneurship: a longitudinal study. *Journal of Personality and Social Psychology*, 1965, *1*, 389–392.

McClelland, D. C. Testing for competence rather than for "intelligence." *American Psychologist*, 1973, *28*, 1–14.

McClelland, D. C., & Atkinson, J. W. The projective expression of needs: I . The effect of different intensities of the hunger drive on perception. *Journal of Psychology*, 1948, *25*, 205–222.

McClelland, D. C., et al. *The achievement motive*. New York: Appleton-Century-Crofts, 1953.

McElheny, V. K. World biologists tighten rules on "genetic engineering" work. *New York Times*, February 28, 1975, pp. 1, 38.

McFarland, R. A. Air travel across time zones. *American Scientist*, 1975, *63*, 23–30.

McGaugh, J. L. Facilitation of memory storage processes. In F. Leukel (Ed.), *Issues in physiological psychology*. St. Louis: Mosby, 1974.

McGeer, P. L., & McGeer, E. G. Chemistry of mood and emotion. *Annual Review of Psychology*, 1980, *31*, 273–307.

McGrath, M. J., & Cohen, D. B. REM sleep facilitation of adaptive waking behavior: a review of the literature. *Psychological Bulletin*, 1978, *85*, 24–57.

McGuire, W. J. Order of presentation as a factor in "conditioning" persuasiveness. In C. I. Hovland, et al. (Eds.), *The order of presentation in persuasion*. New Haven: Yale University Press, 1957.

McGuire, W. J. Inducing resistance to persuasion. In L. Berkowitz (Ed.), *Advances in experimental social psychology* (Vol. 1). New York: Academic Press, 1964.

McKellar, P. *Imagination and thinking*. New York: Basic Books, 1957.

McMurray, G. A. Experimental study of a case of insensitivity to pain. *Archives of Neurology and Psychiatry*, 1950, *64*, 650.

Maccoby, E. E., & Jacklin, C. N. *The psychology of sex differences*. Stanford, Ca.: Stanford University Press, 1974.

MacKay, D. G. Aspects of the theory of comprehension, memory, and attention. *Quarterly Journal of Experimental Psychology*, 1973, *25*, 22–40.

MacKinnon, D. W. What makes a person creative? *Theory into Practice*, 1966, *5*, 152–156.

MacLeod, D. I. A. Visual sensitivity. *Annual Review of Psychology*, 1978, *29*, 613–645.

Maehr, M. L. Culture and achievement motivation. *American*

Psychologist, December 1974, 887–896.

Main, M. Avoidance in the service of proximity. In K. Immelmann, G. Barlow, M. Main, & L. Petrinovitch (Eds.), *Behavioral development: the biedefeld interdisciplinary project*. New York: Cambridge University Press, 1980.

Maloney, M. P., & Ward, M. P. *Mental retardation and modern society*. New York: Oxford University Press, 1979.

Mandler, G. Organization and memory. In K. W. Spence & J. T. Spence (Eds.), *The psychology of learning and motivation*. New York: Academic Press, 1967.

Mant, A. K. Definition of death. In A. Toynbee, et al. (Eds.), *Man's concern with death*. New York: McGraw-Hill, 1968.

Maratsos, M. P. Nonegocentric communication abilities in preschool children. *Child Development*, 1973, *44*, 697–700.

Marcia, J. E. Identity six years after: a follow-up study. *Journal of Youth and Adolescence*, 1976, *5*, 145–160.

Marcia, J. E., & Friedman, M. L. Ego identity status in college women. *Journal of Personality and Social Psychology*, 1970, *38*, 249–263.

Marks, W. B., Dobelle, W. H., & MacNichol, E. R. Visual pigments in single primate cones. *Science*, 1964, *143*, 1181–1183.

Marquez, G. G. *One hundred years of solitude*. New York: Avon, 1970.

Marsden, E. N. Values as determinants of friendship choice. *Connecticut College Psychological Journal*, 1966, *3*, 3–13.

Martinez-Urrutia, A. Anxiety and pain in surgical patients. *Journal of Consulting and Clinical Psychology*, 1975, *43*, 437–442.

Marx, J. L. Three mice "cloned" in Switzerland. *Science*, 1981, *211*, 375–376.

Maslow, A. H. Motivation and personality. New York: Harper & Row, 1954.

Mason, W. A., & Lott, D. F. Ethnology and comparative psychology. *Annual Review of Psychology*, 1976, *27*, 129–154.

Masserman, J. H. *Principles of dynamic psychiatry*. Philadelphia: Saunders, 1946.

Masters, W. H., & Johnson, V. E. *Human sexual inadequacy*. Boston: Little, Brown, 1970.

Matas, L., Arend, R. A., & Sroufe, L. A. Continuity of adaptation in the second year: the relationship between quality of attachment and later competence. *Child Development*, 1978, *49*, 547–556.

Matthews, A. R., Jr. *Mental disability and the criminal law*. Chicago: American Bar Foundation, 1970.

Mednick, S. A. The associative basis of creativity. *Psychological Review*, 1962, *69*(3), 220–232.

Mehabian, A., & Diamond, S. Effects of furniture arrangement, props, and personality on social interaction. *Journal of Personality and Social Psychology*, 1971, *20*, 18–30.

Meltzoff, J., & Kornreich, M. It works. *Psychology Today*, July 1971, pp. 57–61.

Melville, K. *Communes in the counter culture*. New York: Morrow, 1972.

Melzack, R., & Scott, T. H. The effects of early experience on the response to pain. *Journal of Comparative and Physiological Psychology*, 1957, *50*, 155–161.

Melzack, R., & Wall, P. D. Pain mechanisms: a new theory. *Science*, 1965, *150*, 971.

Mercer, J. R. IQ: the lethal label. *Psychology Today*, September 1972, pp. 45–97.

Meyer, R. G., & Smith, S. R. A crisis in group therapy. *American Psychologist*, 1977, *32*, 638–643.

Michael, C. R. Retinal processing of visual images. *Scientific American*, 1969, *220*, 104–112.

Milgram, S. Behavioral study of obedience. *Journal of Abnormal and Social Psychology*, 1963, *67*, 371–378.

Milgram, S. Issues in the study of obedience. *American Psychology*, 1964, *19*, 848–852.

Milgram, S. The experience of living in cities. *Science*, 1970, *167*, 1461–1468.

Milgram, S. *Obedience to authority*. New York: Harper & Row, 1974.

Miller, B. C. A multivariate developmental model of marital satisfaction. *Journal of Marriage and the Family*, 1976, *38*, 643–657.

Miller, G. A. The magical number seven, plus or minus two: some limits on our capacity for processing information. *Psychological Review*, 1956, *63*, 81–96.

Miller, S. M. The making of a confused, middle-aged husband. In J. H. Pleck & J. Sawyer (Eds.), *Men and masculinity*. Englewood Cliffs, N. J.: Prentice-Hall, 1974.

Millett, K. *Sexual politics*. New York: Doubleday, 1970.

Milner, B. Amnesia following operation on temporal lobes. In C. W. M. Whitty & P. Zangwill (Eds.), *Amnesia*. London: Butterworth, 1966.

Mintz, A. Nonadaptive group behavior. *Journal of Abnormal and Social Psychology*, 1951, *46*, 150–159.

Mintz, N. L. Effects of esthetic surroundings: II. prolonged and repeated experience in a "beautiful" and an "ugly" room. *The Journal of Psychology*, 1956, *41*, 459–466.

Mischel, W. *Personality and assessment*. New York: Wiley, 1968.

Mischel, W. Toward a cognitive social learning reconceptualization of personality. *Psychological Review*, 1973, *80*, 252–283.

Mischel, W. *Introduction to personality* (2nd ed.). New York: Holt, Rinehart & Winston, 1976.

Mischel, W. (Ed.). *The self: psychological and philosophical issues*. Totowa, N.J.: Rowman & Littlefield, 1977.

Mitchell, J. *Psychoanalysis and feminism*. New York: Pantheon, 1974.

Moray, N. Attention in dichotic listening: affective cues and the influence of instructions. *Quarterly Journal of Experimental Psychology*, 1959, *11*, 56–60.

Moriarty, T. Crime, commitment and the responsive bystander: two field experiments. *Journal of Personality and Social Psychology*, 1975, *31*, 370–376.

Moskowitz, B. A. The acquisition of language. *Scientific*

American, 1978, *239,* 92–108.

Mueller, E., & Lucas, T. A developmental analysis of peer interaction among toddlers. In M. Lewis & L. Rosenblum (Eds.), *Peer relations and friendship.* New York: Wiley, 1975.

Munsinger, H. The adopted child's IQ: a critical view. *Psychological Bulletin,* 1975, *82,* 623–659.

Murdock, B. B., Jr. The retention of individual items. *Journal of Experimental Psychology,* 1961, *62,* 618–625.

Murray, H. G., & Denny, J. P. Interaction of ability level and interpolated activity in human problem solving. *Psychological Reports,* 1969, *24,* 271–276.

Mussen, P. H., & Jones, M. C. Self-conceptions, motivations, and interpersonal attitude of late and early maturing boys. *Child Development,* 1957, *28,* 243–256.

Mussen, P. H., & Jones, M. C. The behavior-inferred motivations of late and early maturing boys. *Child Development,* 1958, *29,* 61–67.

Myers, D. G., & Lamm, H. The polarizing effect of group discussion. *American Scientist,* 1975, *63,* 297–303.

National Commission on Marihuana and Drug Abuse. *Drug use in America: problem in perspective.* Washington, D. C.: U. S. Government Printing Office, 1973a.

National Commission on Marihuana and Drug Abuse. *Drug use in America: problem in perspective. Technical papers—appendix.* Washington, D. C.: U. S. Government Printing Office, 1973b.

Nauta, W. J. H., & Feirtag, M. The organization of the brain. *Scientific American,* 1979, *241,* 88–111.

Neisser, U. *Cognitive psychology.* New York: Appleton-Century-Crofts, 1967.

Neugarten, B. L. Adult personality: toward a psychology of the life cycle. In B. L. Neugarten (Ed.), *Middle age and aging.* Chicago: University of Chicago Press, 1968.

Neugarten, B. L. The psychology of aging: an overview. APA Master lecture. Washington, D. C.: American Psychological Association, 1976.

Neugarten, B. L., & Hagestad, G. O. Age and the life course. In R. H. Binstock & E. Shanas (Eds.), *Handbook of aging and the social sciences.* New York: Van Nostrand Reinhold, 1977.

Neugarten, B. L., Havighurst, R. J., & Tobin, S. S. Personality and patterns of aging. *Gawein: Tijschrift vande Psychologiche Kring aan de Nijmessgse Universiteit Jrg.,* 1965, *13,* 249–256.

The New York Times. Days of captivity: the hostages' story. February 4, 1981.

Newcomb, T. M. Persistence and regression of changed attitudes: long-range studies. *Journal of Social Issues,* 1963, *19,* 3–14.

Nisbett, R. E., & Valins, S. *Perceiving the causes of one's own behavior.* New York: General Learning Press, 1971.

Nissen, H. W. Analysis of a complex conditioned reaction in chimpanzees. *Journal of Comparative and Physiological Psychology,* 1951, *44,* 9–16.

Norman, D. A. *Memory and attention.* New York: Wiley, 1969.

O'Carroll, M., O'Neal, E., McDonald, P., & Hori, T. Influence upon imitative aggression of a peer who also imitated. *Journal of Social Psychology,* 1976.

Offir, C. W. Field report. *Psychology Today,* October 1974, pp. 61–72.

Olds, J. Pleasure centers in the brain. *Scientific American,* October 1956, pp. 105–116.

Olds, J., & Milner, P. Positive reinforcement produced by electrical stimulation of septal area and other regions of rat brain. *Journal of Comparative and Physiological Psychology,* 1954, *47,* 419–427.

Olson, G., Olson, R., Kastin, A., & Coy, D. Endogenous opiates: through 1978. *Neuroscience and Biobehavioral Reviews,* 1979, *3,* 285–299.

Olton, D. S. Spatial memory. *Scientific American,* June 1977, pp. 82–98.

Orlofsky, J. L. Identity formation, *N* achievement, and fear of success in college men and women. *Journal of Youth and Adolescence,* 1978, *7,* 49–62.

Orlofsky, J. L., Marcia, J. E., & Lesser, I. M. Ego identity status and the intimacy versus isolation crisis of young adulthood. *Journal of Personality and Social Psychology,* February 1973, *27*(2), 211–219.

Ortar, G. Is a verbal test cross-cultural? *Scripta Hierosolymitana,* 1963, *13,* 219–235.

Oskamp, S. *Attitudes and opinions.* Englewood Cliffs, N.J.: Prentice-Hall, 1977.

Overholser, W. Forensic psychiatry. In D. R. Sills (Ed.), *International encyclopedia of the social sciences* (Vol. 12). New York: Macmillan, 1968.

Overmier, J. B., & Seligman, M. E. P. Effects of inescapable shock upon subsequent escape and avoidance learning. *Journal of Comparative and Physiological Psychology,* 1967, *63,* 23–33.

Page, E. B., & Grandon, G. M. Family configuration and mental ability. Two theories contrasted with U.S. data. *American Educational Research Journal,* 1979, *16,* 257–272.

Pahnke, W. N., & Richards, W. A. Implications of LSD and experimental mysticism. In C. T. Tart (Ed.), *Altered states of consciousness.* New York: Wiley, 1969.

Paivio, A. *Imagery and verbal processes.* New York: Holt, Rinehart and Winston, 1971.

Palmer, J. O. *The psychological assessment of children.* New York: Wiley, 1970.

Paludi, M. A. Horner revisited: How successful must Anne and John be before fear of success sets in? *Psychological Reports,* 1979, *44,* 1319–1322.

Parker, S. R. Work and leisure: theory and fact. In J. T. Haworth & M. A. Smith (Eds.), _Work and leisure_. Princeton, N.J.: Princeton Book Co., 1975.

Pattison, E. M. _The experience of dying_. Englewood Cliffs, N.J.: Prentice-Hall, 1977.

Pavlov, I. P. _Conditioned reflexes_ (G. V. Anrep, trans.). London: Oxford University Press, 1927.

Perlin, M. On behavior therapy and civil liberties. _American Psychologist_, 1976, _31_, 534–536.

Perls, F. S. _Gestalt theory verbatim_. Moab, Ut.: Real People Press, 1969.

Peterson, L. R. _Learning_. Glenview, Ill.: Scott, Foresman, 1975.

Peterson, L. R., & Peterson, M. J. Short-term retention of individual verbal items. _Journal of Experimental Psychology_, 1959, _58_, 193–198.

Pevnick, J., Jasinski, D. R., & Haertzen, C. A. Abrupt withdrawal from therapeutically administered diazepam. _Archives of General Psychiatry_, 1978, _35_, 995–998.

Pfeiffer, E., & Davis, G. C. The use of leisure time in middle age. In E. Palmore (Ed.), _Normal aging II_. Durham, N. C.: Duke University Press, 1974.

Phares, E. J. _Locus of control in personality_. Morristown, N. J.: General Learning Press, 1976.

Phares, E. J. Locus of control. In H. London & J. E. Exner, Jr. (Eds.), _Dimensions of personality_. New York: Wiley, 1978.

Phares, E. J., & Lamiell, J. T. Personality. _Annual Review of Psychology_, 1977, _28_, 113–140.

Phillips, J. L., Jr. _The origins of the intellect: Piaget's theory_. San Francisco: Freeman, 1969.

Piaget, J. _The moral development of the child_. New York: Harcout Brace, 1932.

Piaget, J. The intellectual development of the adolescent. In G. Caplan & S. Lebovici (Eds.), _Adolescence: psychosocial perspectives_. New York: Basic Books, 1969.

Piaget, J., & Szeminska, A. _The child's conception of number_ (C. Gattegno & F. M. Hodgson, trans.). New York: Humanities Press, 1952 (Original French Edition, 1941).

Pierrel, R., & Sherman, J. G. Train your pet the Barnabus way. _Brown Alumni Monthly_, February 1963, 8–14.

Pineo, P. C. Disenchantment in the later years of marriage. _Marriage and Family Living_, 1961, _23_, 3–11.

Plutchik, R. _The emotions: facts, theories, and a new model_. New York: Random House, 1962.

Poincaré, H. _The foundations of science_ (G. B. Halstead, trans.). London: Science Press, 1924.

Porter, R. W., et al. Some experimental observations on gastrointestinal ulcers in behaviorally conditioned monkeys. _Psychosomatic Medicine_, 1958, _20_, 379–394.

Posner, M. I. Short-term memory systems in human information processing. _Acta Psychologica_, 1967, _27_, 267–284.

Postman, L. Verbal learning and memory. _Annual Review of Psychology_, 1975, _26_, 291–335.

Postman, L., & Raw, L. Retention as a function of the method

of measurement. _University of California Publications in Psychology_, Berkeley, 1957, _8_, 217–270.

Prociuk, T. J., & Breen, L. J. Defensive externality and its relation to academic performance. _Journal of Personality and Social Psychology_, 1975, _31_, 549–556.

Pruitt, D. G. Definition of the situation as a determinant of international action. In H. C. Kilman (Ed.), _International behavior_. New York: Holt, Rinehart & Winston, 1965.

Pulaski, M. A. S. The rich rewards of make believe. _Psychology Today_, January 1974, pp. 68–74.

Rainwater, L. A study of personality differences between middle and lower class adolescents. _Genetic Psychology Monographs_, 1956, _54_, 3–86.

Rapoport, A. Rules for debate. In Q. Wright, W. M. Evans, & M. Deutsch (Eds.), _Preventing World War III: some proposals_. New York: Simon & Schuster, 1962.

Raven, B. H., & Kruglanski, A. Conflict and power. In Paul Swingle (Ed.), _The structure of conflict_. New York: Academic Press, 1970.

Read, P. P. _Alive_. New York: Avon, 1974.

Reed, S. F., Ernst, G. W., & Banerji, R. The role of analogy in transfer between similar problem states. _Cognitive Psychology_, 1974, _6_, 435–450.

Rees, A. H., & Palmer, F. H. Factors related to change in mental test performance. _Developmental Psychology Monographs_, 1970, _3_(2, Part 2).

Reese, H. W. Perceptual set in young children. _Child Development_, 1963, _34_, 151–159.

Reitman, J. S. Without surreptitious rehearsal, information in short-term memory decays. _Journal of Verbal Learning and Verbal Behavior_, 1974, _13_, 365–377.

Repucci, N. D., & Saunders, J. T. Social psychology of behavior modification: problems of implementation in natural settings. _American Psychologist_, September 1974, 649–660.

Rescorla, R. A. Pavlovian conditioning and its proper control procedures. _Psychological Review_, 1967, _74_, 71–80.

Rice, B. Brave new world of intelligence testing. _Psychology Today_, September 1979, pp. 27–38.

Riegel, K. F. Dialectical operations: the final period of cognitive development. _Human Development_, 1973, _16_, 346–370.

Riegel, K. F., Riegel, R. M., & Meyer, G. A study of the dropout rates of longitudinal research on aging and the prediction of death. _Journal of Personality and Social Psychology_, 1967, _5_, 342–348.

Riesen, A. H. Arrested vision. _Scientific American_, July 1950, pp. 16–19.

Ringler, N., Trause, M. A., Klaus, M., & Kennel, J. The effects of extra postpartum contact and maternal speech patterns on children's IQs, speech, and language comprehension at five. _Child Development_, 1978, _49_, 862–865.

Robitscher, J., & Williams, R. Should psychiatrists get out of the courtroom? *Psychology Today,* December 1977, p. 85.

Rodin, J. Effects of distraction on the performance of obese and normal subjects. *Journal of Comparative and Physiological Psychology,* 1973, *83,* 68–78.

Rodin, J., Slochower, J., & Fleming, B. Effects of degree of obesity, age of onset, and weight loss on responsiveness to sensory and external stimuli. *Journal of Comparative and Physiological Psychology,* 1977, *91,* 586–597.

Roe, A. *The psychology of occupations.* New York: Wiley, 1956.

Roe, A. A. Study of imagery in research scientists. *Journal of Personality,* 1951, *19,* 459–470.

Rogel, M. J. A critical evaluation of the possibility of higher primate reproductive and sexual pheromones. *Psychological Bulletin,* 1978, *85,* 810–830.

Rogers, C. R. A theory of therapy, personality, and interpersonal relationships, as developed in the client-centered framework. In S. Koch (Ed.), *Psychology: a study of a science* (Vol. 3). *Formulations of the person and the social context.* New York: McGraw-Hill, 1959.

Rogers, D. *The adult years: an introduction to aging.* Englewood Cliffs, N.J.: Prentice-Hall, 1980.

Rokeach, M., & Mezei, L. Race and shared belief as factors in social choice. *Science,* 1966, *151,* 167–172.

Rollins, B. C., & Feldman, H. Marital satisfaction over the life cycle. *Journal of Marriage and the Family,* 1970, *32,* 20–28.

Rosch, E. H. Natural categories. *Cognitive Psychology,* 1973, *4,* 328–350.

Rosenberg, M. J. An analysis of affective cognitive consistency. In M. J. Rosenberg & C. I. Hovland (Eds.), *Attitude organization and change.* New Haven: Yale University Press, 1960.

Rosenberg, S. D., & Farrell, M. P. Identity and crisis in middle-aged men. *International Journal of Aging and Human Development,* 1976, *7,* 153–170.

Rosenblood, L. K., & Goldstein, J. H. Similarity, intelligence, and affiliation. *Proceedings of the 77th Annual Convention of the American Psychological Association,* 1969, *4,* 341–342.

Rosenhan, D. L. On being sane in insane places. *Science,* 1973, *179,* 250–258.

Rosenthal, R., et al. Body talk and tone of voice: the language without words. *Psychology Today,* September 1974, pp. 64–68.

Rotter, J. B. Generalized expectancies for internal versus external control of reinforcement. *Psychological Monographs,* 1966, *80* (Whole No. 609).

Rotter, J. B. External and internal control. *Psychology Today,* 1971, *5,* 37.

Rubenstein, J., & Howes, C. The effects of peers on toddler interaction with mother and toys. *Child Development,* 1976, *46,* 597-605.

Rubin, J. A., Provenzano, F. J., & Luria, A. The eye of the beholder: parents' views on sex of newborns. *American Journal of Orthopsychiatry,* 1974, *44,* 512–519.

Rubin, Z. *Liking and loving: an invitation to social psychology.* New York: Holt, Rinehart & Winston, 1973.

Rule, B. G., & Nesdale, A. R. Emotional arousal and aggressive behavior. *Psychological Bulletin,* 1976, *83,* 851–863.

Sage, W. Violence in the children's room. *Human Behavior,* July 1973, 41–47.

Samuels, M. T. *Children's long-term memory for events.* Unpublished doctoral thesis, Cornell University, 1974.

Sanford, R. N. The effects of abstinence from food upon imaginal processes: a further experiment. *Journal of Psychology,* 1937, *3,* 145–159.

Sarason, I. G., & Sarason, B. R. *Abnormal psychology: the problem of maladaptive behavior.* Englewood, Cliffs, N.J.: Prentice-Hall, 1980.

Sarnoff, I., & Zimbardo, P. G. Anxiety, fear, and social affiliation. *Journal of Abnormal and Social Psychology,* 1961, *62,* 356–363.

Satloff, A., & Worby, C. M. The psychiatric emergency service: mirror of change. *American Journal of Psychiatry,* 1970, *126,* 11.

Sattler, J. M. *Assessment of children's intelligence.* New York: Holt, Rinehart & Winston, 1975.

Scarr, S., & Weinberg, R. A. IQ test performance of black children adopted by white families. *American Psychologist,* 1976, *31,* 726–739.

Schachter, D. L. The hypnagogic state: a critical review of the literature. *Psychological Bulletin,* 1976, *83,* 452–481.

Schachter, S. *The psychology of affiliation: experimental studies of the sources of gregariousness.* Stanford, Ca.: Stanford University Press, 1959.

Schachter, S. The assumption of identity and peripheralist and centralist controversies in motivation and emotion. In M. B. Arnold (Ed.), *Feelings and emotions.* New York: Academic Press, 1970.

Schachter, S. Some extraordinary facts about obese humans and rats. *American Psychologist,* February 1971*b,* 129–144.

Schachter, S. Eat, eat. *Psychology Today,* April 1971*a,* pp.44–47, 78–79.

Schachter, S., Goldman, R., & Gordon, A. Effects of fear, food deprivation, and obesity on eating. *Journal of Personality and Social Psychology,* 1968, *10,* 98-106.

Schachter, S., & Singer, J. E. Cognitive, social, and physiological determinants of emotional state. *Psychological Review,* 1962, *69,* 379–399.

Schaller, M. Chromatic vision in human infants: conditioned operant fixation to "hues" of varying intensity. *Bulletin of the Psychonomic Society,* 1975, *6,* 39–42.

Schein, E. H. The Chinese indoctrination program for prisoners of war: a study of attempted "brainwashing." *Psychiatry,* 1956, *19,* 149–172.

Schenkel, S., & Marcia, J. E. Attitudes toward premarital intercourse in determining ego identity status in college women. *Journal of Personality and Social Psychology,* 1972, *40,* 472–482.

Schreiber, J. *The ultimate weapon: terrorists and world order.* New York: Morrow, 1978.

Schwartz, B. *Psychology of learning and behavior.* New York: Norton, 1978.

Schwartz, G. E. TM relaxes some people and makes them feel better. *Psychology Today,* April 1974, pp. 39–44.

Sears, R. R. Sources of life satisfactions of the Terman gifted men. *American Psychologist,* 1977, 119–128.

Sears, R. R., Maccoby, E. E., & Levin, H. *Patterns of child rearing.* New York: Harper & Row, 1957.

Segal, D. J. Smoking, drinking, and your baby's health. *Mental Retardation Bulletin,* 1973–1974, *2,* 80–85.

Selfridge, O. G. Pandemonium: a paradigm for learning. In *Proceedings of a symposium on the mechanization of thought processes.* London: Her Majesty's Stationery Office, 1959.

Seligman, M. E. P. Phobias and preparedness. In M. E. P. Seligman & J. L. Hager (Eds.), *Biological boundaries of learning.* Englewood Cliffs, N.J.: Prentice-Hall, 1972.

Seligman, M. E. P. Fall into helplessness. *Psychology Today,* June 1973, pp. 43–48.

Seligman, M. E. P. *Helplessness.* San Francisco: Freeman, 1975.

Seligman, M. E. P., & Hager, J. L. *Biological boundaries of learning.* Englewood Cliffs, N.J.: Prentice-Hall, 1972.

Seligman, M. E. P., & Maier, S. F. Failure to escape traumatic shock. *Journal of Experimental Psychology,* 1967, *74,* 1–9.

Selye, H. *The stress of life.* New York: McGraw-Hill, 1976.

Shanas, E. Adjustment to retirement. In F. M. Carp (Ed.), *Retirement.* New York: Behavioral Publications, 1972.

Shephard, R. N. The mental image. *American Psychologist,* 1978, *33,* 125–137.

Sherif, M., Taub, D., & Hovland, C. I. Assimilation and contrast effects of anchoring stimuli on judgements. *Journal of Experimental Psychology,* 55, 150–155.

Shibles, W. *Death: an interdisciplinary analysis.* Whitewater, Wis.: Language Press, 1974.

Shiffrin, R. M., & Atkinson, R. C. Storage and retrieval processes in long-term memory. *Psychological Review,* 1969, *56,* 179–193.

Shiffrin, R. M., & Cook, J. R. Short-term forgetting of item and order information. *Journal of Verbal Reasoning and Verbal Behavior,* 1978, *17,* 189–218.

Sigall, H., & Aronson, E. Opinion change and the gain–loss model of interpersonal attraction. *Journal of Experimental Social Psychology,* 1967, *3,* 178–188.

Siipola, E. M. A study of some effects of preparatory set. *Psychological Monographs,* 1935, *46*(210).

Silverman, B. I. Consequences, racial discrimination, and the principle of belief congruence. *Journal of Personality and Social Psychology,* 1974, *29,* 497–508.

Simon, H. A. How big is a chunk? *Science,* February 8, 1974, pp. 482–488.

Simon, W., & Gagnon, J. H. *The sexual scene.* New Brunswick, N.J.: Transaction, Inc., 1970.

Singer, J. E., Brush, C., & Lubin, S. D. Some aspects of deindividuation: identification and conformity. *Journal of Experimental Psychology,* 1965, *1,* 356–378.

Singer, J. L. Drives, affects, and daydreams: the adaptive role of spontaneous imagery of stimulus-independent meditation. In J. Antrobus (Ed.), *Cognition and Affect: The City University of New York Symposium.* Boston: Little, Brown, 1969, pp. 131–158.

Singer, J. L. Daydreaming and the stream of thought. *American Scientist,* 1974, *41,* 417–425.

Singh, D. Preference for bar-pressing to obtain reward over freeloading in rats and children. *Journal of Comparative and Physiological Psychology,* 1970, *73,* 320–327.

Singh, D., & Query, W. T. Preference for work over "freeloading" in children. *Psychonometric Science,* 1971, *24,* 77–79.

Sinnott, E. W., Dunn, L. C., & Dobzhansky, T. F. *Principles of genetics* (5th ed.). New York: McGraw-Hill, 1958.

Skeels, H. M. Mental development of children in foster homes. *Journal of Consulting Psychology,* 1938, *2,* 33–43.

Skeels, H. M. The study of the effects of differential stimulation on mentally retarded children: a follow-up report. *American Journal of Mental Deficiencies,* 1942, *46,* 340–350.

Skeels, H. M. Adult status of children with contrasting early life experiences. *Monographs of the Society for Research in Child Development,* 1966, *31*(3), 1–65.

Skinner, B. F. Drive and reflex strength: II. *Journal of General Psychology,* 1932, *6,* 38–48.

Skinner, B. F. "Superstition" in pigeons. *Journal of Experimental Psychology,* 1948, *38,* 168–172.

Skinner, B. F. *Verbal behavior.* Englewood Cliffs, N.J.: Prentice-Hall, 1957.

Skinner, B. F. *Science and human behavior.* Riverside, N.J.: Free Press, 1965.

Skinner, B. F. *The technology of teaching.* Englewood Cliffs, N.J.: Prentice-Hall, 1968.

Slaby, R. G., Quarfoth, G. R., & McConnachie, G. A. Television violence and its sponsors. *Journal of Communication,* 1976, *26,* 88–96.

Sloane, R. B., et al. Short-term analytically oriented psychotherapy versus behavior therapy. *American Journal of Psychiatry,* 1975, *132,* 373–377.

Smith, S., & Haythorn, W. H. Effects of compatability, crowding, group size, and leadership seniority on stress, anxiety, hostility, and annoyance in isolated groups. *Journal of Personality and Social Psychology,* 1972, *22,* 67–79.

Snyder, S. H. Opiate receptors and internal opiates. *Scientific American,* 1977, *236,* 44–56.

Sommer, R. Studies in personal space. *Sociometry*, 1959, *22*, 247–260.

Sperling, G. The information available in brief visual presentations. *Psychological Monographs*, 1960, *74* (11, Whole No. 498).

Spero, M. Thoughts on computerized psychotherapy. *Psychiatry*, 1978, *41*, 279–288.

Spielberger, C. D. The effects of anxiety on complex learning and academic achievement. In C. D. Spielberger (Ed.), *Anxiety and behavior*. New York: Academic Press, 1966.

Spiesman, J. C. Autonomic monitoring of ego defense process. In N. S. Greenfield & W. C. Lewis (Eds.), *Psychoanalysis and current biological thought*. Madison: University of Wisconsin Press, 1965.

Stein, A., & Friedrich, L. K. Television content and young children's behavior. In J. P. Murray, E. A. Rubenstein, & G. A. Comstock (Eds.), *Television and social behavior* (Vol. 2). *Television and social learning*. Washington, D.C.: U.S. Government Printing Office, 1972.

Stein, D. D., Hardyck, J. A., & Smith, M. B. Race and belief: an open and shut case. *Journal of Personality and Social Psychology*, 1965, *1*, 281–289.

Steiner, J. A. A questionnaire study of risk-taking in psychiatric patients. *British Journal of Medical Psychology*, 1972, *45*, 365–374.

Steinmutz, S. K., & Straus, M. A. (Eds.). *Violence in the family*. New York: Dodd, Mead, 1974.

Stendler, C. B. Critical periods in socialization and overdependency. *Child Development*, 1952, *23*, 1–2.

Stevens, C. F. The neuron. *Scientific American*, 1979, *241*, 54–65.

Stevens, W. K. Ex-hostage says Iranians failed to "break" captives. *The New York Times*, January 23, 1981.

Stevens-Long, J. *Adult life*. Palo Alto, Ca.: Mayfield, 1979.

Stinnett, M., Carter, L. M., & Montgomery, J. E. Older persons's perceptions of their marriages. *Journal of Marriage and the Family*, 1972, *34*, 665–670.

Stock, M. B., & Smythe, P. M. Does undernutrition during infancy inhibit brain growth and subsequent intellectual development? *Archives of Disorders in Childhood*, 1963, *38*, 546–552.

Stokols, D., et al. Physical, social, and personality determinants of the perception of crowding. *Environment and Behavior*, 1973, *5*, 87–115.

Stolz, S. B., & Lott, D. F. Establishment in rats of a persistent response producing a net loss of reinforcement. *Journal of Comparative and Physiological Psychology*, 1964, *57*, 147–149.

Stolz, S. B., Wienckowski, L. A., & Brown, B. S. Behavior modification: a perspective on critical issues. *American Psychologist*, 1975, *30*, 1027–1048.

Stone, L. J., & Church, J. *Childhood and adolescence: a psychology of the growing person* (2nd ed.). New York: Random House, 1968.

Stone, R. A., & Deleo, J. Psychotherapeutic control of hypertension. *New England Journal of Medicine*, 1976, *294*, 80–84.

Straus, M. Some social antecedents of physical punishment: a linkage theory interpretation. *Journal of Marriage and the Family*, 1971, *33*, 658–663.

Straus, M. A. Normative and behavioral aspects of violence between spouses. Paper presented at the Symposium on Violence, Simon Fraser University, March 1977.

Strickland, B. R. Internal–external control of reinforcement. In T. Blass (Ed.), *Personality variables in social behavior*. Hillsdale, N.J.: Lawrence Erlbaum, 1977.

Strieb, G. F., & Schneider, C. J. *Retirement in American society: impact and progress*. Ithaca, N.Y.: Cornell University Press, 1971.

Strodtbeck, F. L., James, R. M., & Hawkins, C. Social status in jury deliberations. In E. Maccoby, T. Newcomb, & E. Hartley (Eds.), *Readings in social psychology*. New York: Holt, Rinehart & Winston, 1958.

Strongman, K. T. *The psychology of emotion*. New York: Wiley, 1978.

Strouse, J. (Ed.). *Women in analysis: dialogues on psychoanalytic views of feminity*. New York: Grossman, 1974.

Strupp, H. H. Clinical psychology, irrationalism, and the erosion of excellence. *American Psychologist*, 1976, *31*, 561–571.

Strupp, H. H., & Hadley, S. W. A tripartite model of mental health and therapeutic outcomes: with special reference to negative effects in psychotherapy. *American Psychologist*, 1977, *32*, 187–196.

Stunkard, A. J., & Fox, S. The interpretation of gastric motility and hunger. *Psychosomatic Medicine*, 1971, *33*, 123–134.

Suedfeld, P. The benefits of boredom: sensory deprivation reconsidered. *American Scientist*, January–February 1975, 60–69.

Suedfeld, P. E., & Borrie, R. A. Altering states of consciousness through sensory deprivation. In A. Sugerman & R. Tarter (Eds.), *Expanding dimensions of consciousness*. New York: Springer, 1978, 226–252.

Swingle, P. Exploitative behavior in non-zero sum games. *Journal of Personality and Social Psychology*, 1970, *16*, 121–132.

Szasz, T. Our despotic laws destroy the right to self-control. *Psychology Today*, December 1974, pp. 20–29, 127.

Tanner, J. M. The secular trend towards earlier physical maturation. *T. Soc. Geneesk.*, 1966, *44*, 524–539.

Tanner, J. M. Physical growth. In P. Mussen (Ed.), *Carmichael's manual of child psychology* (3rd ed.) (Vol. 1). New York: Wiley, 1970

Taubman, P. Conflicts in mental reports raise questions on captives. *The New York Times*, January 28, 1981.

Tavris, C. The frozen world of the familiar stranger. *Psychology Today*, June 1974, pp. 71–80.

Tavris, C., & Offir, C. *The longest war: sex differences in perspective.* New York: Harcourt, Brace, Jovanovich, 1977.

Taylor, D. W., Berry, P. C., & Block, C. H. Does group participation when using brainstorming facilitate or inhibit creative thinking? *Administrative Science Quarterly*, 1958, 2, 23–47.

Thomas, A., Chess, S., & Birch, H. G. The origin of personality. *Scientific American*, August 1970, 102–109.

Thomas, A., et al. *Behavioral individuality in early childhood.* New York: New York University Press, 1963.

Thomas, D. W., & Mayer, J. The search for the secret of fat. *Psychology Today*, September 1973, pp. 74–79.

Thomas, L. *The medusa and the snail.* Boston: G. K. Hall, 1979.

Thomas, M. H., & Drabman, R. S. Effects of television violence on expectations of others' aggression. Paper presented at the meeting of the American Psychological Association, San Francisco, August 1977.

Thomas, M. H., et al. Desensitization to portrayals of real-life aggression as a function of exposure to television violence. *Journal of Personality and Social Psychology*, 1977, 35, 450–458.

Thompson, C. Some effects of the derogatory attitude toward female sexuality. In M. R. Green (Ed.), *Interpersonal psychoanalysis: the selected papers of Clara Thompson.* New York: Basic Books, 1964.

Thompson, D. F., & Meltzer, L. Communication of emotional intent by facial expression. *Journal of Abnormal and Social Psychology*, 1964, 68, 129–135.

Thompson, R. F. *Introduction to physiological psychology.* New York: Harper & Row, 1975.

Thurstone, L. L. Primary mental abilities. *Psychometric Monographs*, 1938 (1).

Time. The trauma of captivity. December 24, 1979.

Toffler, A. *Future shock.* New York: Random House, 1970.

Tolman, E. C. Cognitive maps in rats and men. *Psychological Review*, 1948, 55, 189–208.

Tomkins, S. S., & McCarter, R. What and where are the primary affects: some evidence for a theory. *Perceptual and Motor Skills*, 1964, 18, 119–158.

Torrance, E. P. Some consequences of power differences on decision making in permanent and temporary three-man groups. In A. P. Borgatta & R. R. Bales (Eds.), *Small groups: studies in social interaction.* New York: Knopf, 1955.

Treisman, A. M. Contextual cues in selective listening. *Quarterly Journal of Experimental Psychology*, 1960, 12, 242–248.

Tresemer, D. Fear of success: popular, but unpopular. *Psychology Today*, March 1974, pp. 82–85.

Troll, L. E. The family in later life: a decade review. *Journal of Marriage and the Family*, 33, 263–290.

Tryk, H. E. Assessment in the study of creativity. In P.

McReynolds (Ed.), *Advances in psychological assessment* (Vol. 1). Palo Alto, Ca.: Science and Behavior Books, 1968.

Tryon, R. C. Genetic differences in maze-learning abilities in rats. In *39th Yearbook, Part I.* National Society for the Study of Education. Chicago: University of Chicago Press, 1940.

Tulving, E. Subjective organization and the effects of repetition in multitrial free recall learning. *Journal of Verbal Learning and Verbal Behavior*, 1966, 5, 193–197.

Tulving, E. Episodic and semantic memory. In E. Tulving & W. Donaldson (Eds.), *Organization and memory.* New York: Academic Press, 1972.

Tulving, E., & Osler, S. Effectiveness of retrieval cues in memory for words. *Journal of Experimental Psychology*, 1968, 77, 593–601.

Tulving, E., & Patkau, J. E. Concurrent effects of contextual constraint and word frequency on immediate recall and learning of verbal material. *Canadian Journal of Psychology*, 1962, 69, 344–354.

Tulving, E., & Psotka, J. Retroactive inhibition in free recall: inaccessability of information available in the memory store. *Journal of Experimental Psychology*, 1971, 87, 1–8.

Turnbull, C. M. Observations. *American Journal of Psychology*, 1961, 1, 304–308.

Ullmann, L. P., & Krasner, L. *A psychological approach to abnormal behavior* (2nd ed.). Englewood Cliffs, N.J.: Prentice-Hall, 1975.

Underwood, B. J. Interference and forgetting. *Psychological Review*, 1957, 64, 49–60.

U.S. Commission on Civil Rights. *Racism in America and how to combat it.* Washington, D.C.: U.S.G.P.O., 1969.

U.S. News & World Report. An expert's view of the hostages' ordeal. December 31, 1979.

Valenstein, E. S. *Brain control.* New York: Wiley, 1973.

Valenstein, E. S. The brain and behavior control. In *Master lectures on behavior control.* Washington, D.C.: American Psychological Association, 1977.

Valins, S. Cognitive effects of false heart-rate feedback. *Journal of Personality and Social Psychology*, 1966, 4, 400–408.

Wahba, N. A., & Bridwell, L. G. Maslow reconsidered: a review of research on the need hierarchy theory. *Organizational Behavior and Human Performance*, 1976, 15, 212–240.

Walk, R. D., & Gibson, E. J. A comparative and analytical study of visual depth perception. *Psychological Monographs*, 1961, No. 75.

Walker, P. C., & Johnson, R. F. Q. The influence of presleep suggestions on dream content: evidence and methodological problems. *Psychological Bulletin*, 1974, 81(6), 362–370.

Wallace, R. K., & Benson, H. The physiology of meditation. *Scientific American*, February 1972.

Wallach, M. A., & Kogan, N. *Modes of thinking in young*

children. New York: Holt, Rinehart & Winston, 1965.

Wallach, M. A., & Wing, C. W., Jr. *The talented student.* New York: Holt, Rinehart & Winston, 1969.

Wang, G. H. The relation between spontaneous activity and oestrous cycle in the white rat. *Comparative Psychology Monographs,* 1923, *49,* 15–19.

Warner, L. G., & De Fleur, M. L. Attitudes as an interaction concept: social constraint and social distance as intervening variables between attitudes and action. *American Sociological Review,* 1969, *34,* 153–169.

Warner, R., & Rossett, H. C. The effects of drinking on offspring. *Journal of Studies on Alcohol,* 1975, *36,* 1395–1419.

Waters, E., Wittman, J., & Sroufe, L. A. Attachment, positive affect, and competence in the peer group: two studies in construct validation. *Child Development,* 1980, *50.*

Watson, D. L., & Tharp, R. G. *Self-directed behavior: self-modification for personal adjustment.* Monterey, Ca.: Brooks/Cole, 1972.

Watson, J. B. Psychology as the behaviorist views it. *Psychological Review,* 1913, *20,* 158–177.

Watson, J. B., & Rayner, R. Conditioned emotional reactions. *Journal of Experimental Psychology,* 1920, *3,* 1–14.

Webb, W. B., & Cartwright, R. D. Sleep and dreams. *Annual Review of Psychology,* 1978, *29,* 223–252.

Weil, A. The open mind. *Psychology Today,* October 1972, pp. 51–66.

Weintraub, W., & Aronson, H. A survey of patients in classical psychoanalysis: some vital statistics. *Journal of Nervous and Mental Disorders,* 1968, *146,* 98–102.

Weisenberg, M. Pain and pain control. *Psychological Bulletin,* 1977, *84,* 1008–1044.

Weitzenhoffer, A. Hypnotism and altered states of consciousness. In A. Sugarman & R. Tarter (Eds.), *Expanding dimensions of consciousness.* New York: Springer, 1978.

Wess, J. M. Effects of coping behavior in different warning signal conditions on stress pathology in rats. *Journal of Comparative and Physiological Psychology,* 1971, *1,* 1–14.

White, R. W. *Lives in progress* (2nd ed.). New York: Holt, Rinehart & Winston, 1966.

White, R. W., & Watt, N. F. *The abnormal personality* (4th ed.). New York: Ronald Press, 1973.

Whitehead, A. N. *Dialogues of Alfred North Whitehead.* Westport, Conn.: Greenwood, 1977.

Whorf, B. L. *Language, thought, and reality.* New York: M.I.T. Press-Wiley, 1956.

Whyte, W. H. *The organization man.* New York: Simon & Schuster, 1956.

Wickelgren, W. A. *Learning and memory.* Englewood Cliffs, N.J.: Prentice-Hall, 1977.

Wickelgren, W. A. *Cognitive psychology.* Englewood Cliffs, N.J.: Prentice-Hall, 1979.

Wiesel, T. N., & Hubel, D. H. Effects of visual deprivation on morphology and physiology of cells in the cat's geniculate body. *Journal of Neurophysiology,* 1963, *26,* 978–993.

Wilks, J. Group versus individual intelligence tests in one sample of emotionally disturbed children. *Psychological Reports,* 1970, *27,* 819–822.

Willard, L. S. A comparison of Culture Fair Test scores with group and individual intelligence test scores of disadvantaged Negro Children. *Journal of Learning Disabilities,* 1968, *1,* 584–589.

Willborn, S. N. Death in America: no longer a hidden subject. *U.S. News & World Report,* November 13, 1978.

Williams, D. R., & Williams, H. Auto-maintenance in the pigeon: sustained pecking despite contingent nonreinforcement. In M. E. P. Seligman & J. L. Hager (Eds.), *Biological boundaries of learning.* Englewood Cliffs, N.J.: Prentice-Hall, 1972.

Williams, H. K. *Psychology of women: behavior in a biosocial context.* New York: Norton, 1977.

Williams, M. D. Retrieval from very long-term memory. Unpublished doctoral dissertation, University of California, San Diego, 1976.

Wilson, D. W., & Donnerstein, E. Legal and ethical aspects of nonreactive social psychological research: an excursion into the public mind. *American Psychologist,* 1976, *31,*(11), 765–773.

Winter, D. G. *The power motive.* New York: Free Press, 1973.

Winter, D. G. What makes the candidates run? *Psychology Today,* July 1976, pp. 45–49, 92.

Witkin, H. A., et al. *Psychological differentiation.* New York: Wiley, 1962.

Wolf, M., Mees, H., & Risley, T. Application of operant conditioning procedures to the behavior problems of an autistic child. *Behavior Research Therapy,* 1964, *1,* 305–312.

Wolfe, L. Why some people can't love. *Psychology Today,* June 1978, p. 55.

Wolfe, T. *Mauve gloves and madmen, clutter and vine.* New York: Farrar, Straus & Giroux, 1976.

Wolff, C. T., Friedman, S. B., Hofer, M. A., & Mason, J. W. Relationship between psychological defenses and mean urinary 17-hydroxycorticosteroid excretion rates: I. a study of parents of fatally ill children. *Psychosomatic Medicine,* 1964, *26,* 576–591.

Wolpe, J. For phobia: a hair of the hound. *Psychology Today,* June 1969, pp. 34–37.

Wolpe, J. *The practice of behavior therapy* (2nd ed.). New York: Pergamon Press, 1973.

Wolpe, J., & Rachman, S. Psychoanalytic evidence: a critique of Freud's case of little Hans. *Journal of Nervous and Mental Diseases,* 1960, *130,* 198–220.

Woodrow, K. M., et al. Pain tolerance: differences according to age, sex, and race. *Psychosomatic Medicine,* 1972, *34,* 548–556.

Woodworth, R. S. *Dynamic psychology.* New York: Columbia University Press, 1918*a.*

Woolf, V. *Second common reader.* New York: Harcourt, Brace, Jovanovich, 1957.

Worchel, P. Trust and distrust. In W. Austin & S. Worchel

(Eds.), *The social psychology of intergroup relations*. Monterey, Ca.: Brooks/Cole, 1979.

Worchel, S. The effect of those types of arbitrary thwarting on the instigation to aggression. *Journal of Personality*, 1974, *42*, 301–318.

Worchel, S., & Cooper, J. *Understanding social psychology*. Homewood, Ill.: Dossey, 1979.

Wrightsman, L., & Baker, N.J. Where have all the idealistic, imperturbable freshmen gone? *Proceedings of the 77th Annual Convention, American Psychological Association*, 1969, *4*, 290–300.

Wrightsman, L. S., & Deaux, K. *Social psychology in the 80s*. Monterey, Ca.: Brooks/Cole, 1981.

Yarney, A. D. I recognize your face but I can't remember your name: further evidence on the tip-of-the-tongue phenomenon. *Memory and Cognition*, 1973, *1*, 287–290.

Yonburg, B. *Sexual identity: sex roles and social change*. New York: Wiley, 1974.

Zajonc, R. B. Social facilitation. *Science*, 1965, *149*, 269–274.

Zajonc, R. B. *Social psychology: an experimental approach*. Belmont, Ca.: Wadsworth, 1966.

Zajonc, R. B. Attitudinal effects of mere exposure. *Journal of Personality and Social Psychology*, 1968, *8*, 1–29.

Zajonc, R. B., & Markus, G. B. Birth order and intellectual development. *Psychological Review*, 1975, *82*(1), 74–88.

Zeigarnik, B. Uber das Behalten von Erledigten und unerledigten Handlungen. *Psychologische Forschung*, 1927, *9*, 1–85.

Zelazo, P., Zelazo, N. A., & Kolb, S. "Walking" in the newborn. *Science*, April 1972, *176*, 314–315.

Zillman, D. *Hostility and aggression*. Hillsdale, N.J.: Lawrence Erlbaum, 1978.

Zimbardo, P. G. The human choice: individuation, reason, and order versus deindividuation, impulse, and chaos. In N. J. Arnold & D. Levine (Eds.), *Nebraska symposium on motivation*. Lincoln: University of Nebraska Press, 1969.

Zimbardo, P. G. The tactics and ethics of persuasion. In B. T. King & E. McGinniss (Eds.), *Attitudes, conflict and social change*. New York: Academic Press, 1972.

Zimmerman, A. M., Bruce, W. R., & Zimmerman, S. Effects of cannabinoids on sperm morphology. *Pharmacology*, 1979, *18*, 143–148.

Zubek, J. P. Review of effects of prolonged deprivation. In J. E. Rasmussen (Ed.), *Man in isolation and confinement*. Chicago: Aldine, 1973.

Zuckerman, M., Albright, R., Marks, C., & Miller, G. Stress and hallucinatory effects of perceptual isolation and confinement. *Psychological Monographs*, 1962, *76*.

Zuckerman, M., Persky, H., Link, K., & Basu, G. Experimental and subject factors determining responses to sensory deprivation, social isolation, and confinement. *Journal of Abnormal Psychology*, 1968, *73*, 183–194.

Zuckerman, M., & Wheeler, L. To dispel fantasies about the fantasy-based measure of fear of success. *Psychological Bulletin*, 1975, *82*, 932–946.

Name Index

Subject Index